Communications in Computer and Information Science 528

More information about this series at http://www.springer.com/series/7899

Constantine Stephanidis (Ed.)

HCI International 2015 – Posters' Extended Abstracts

International Conference, HCI International 2015
Los Angeles, CA, USA, August 2–7, 2015
Proceedings, Part I

 Springer

Editor
Constantine Stephanidis
University of Crete and Foundation
    for Research and Technology -
    Hellas (FORTH)
Heraklion, Crete
Greece

ISSN 1865-0929   ISSN 1865-0937 (electronic)
Communications in Computer and Information Science
ISBN 978-3-319-21379-8   ISBN 978-3-319-21380-4   (eBook)
DOI 10.1007/978-3-319-21380-4

Library of Congress Control Number: 2015943372

Springer Cham Heidelberg New York Dordrecht London

Printed on acid-free paper

Springer International Publishing AG Switzerland is part of Springer Science+Business Media
(www.springer.com)

Foreword

The 17th International Conference on Human-Computer Interaction, HCI International 2015, was held in Los Angeles, CA, USA, during 2–7 August 2015. The event incorporated the 15 conferences/thematic areas listed on the following page.

A total of 4843 individuals from academia, research institutes, industry, and governmental agencies from 73 countries submitted contributions, and 1462 papers and 246 posters have been included in the proceedings. These papers address the latest research and development efforts and highlight the human aspects of design and use of computing systems. The papers thoroughly cover the entire field of Human-Computer Interaction, addressing major advances in knowledge and effective use of computers in a variety of application areas. The volumes constituting the full 28-volume set of the conference proceedings are listed on pages VII and VIII.

I would like to thank the Program Board Chairs and the members of the Program Boards of all thematic areas and affiliated conferences for their contribution to the highest scientific quality and the overall success of the HCI International 2015 conference.

This conference could not have been possible without the continuous and unwavering support and advice of the founder, Conference General Chair Emeritus and Conference Scientific Advisor, Prof. Gavriel Salvendy. For their outstanding efforts, I would like to express my appreciation to the Communications Chair and Editor of HCI International News, Dr. Abbas Moallem, and the Student Volunteer Chair, Prof. Kim-Phuong L. Vu. Finally, for their dedicated contribution towards the smooth organization of HCI International 2015, I would like to express my gratitude to Maria Pitsoulaki and George Paparoulis, General Chair Assistants.

May 2015

Constantine Stephanidis
General Chair, HCI International 2015

HCI International 2015 Thematic Areas and Affiliated Conferences

Thematic areas:

- Human-Computer Interaction (HCI 2015)
- Human Interface and the Management of Information (HIMI 2015)

Affiliated conferences:

- 12th International Conference on Engineering Psychology and Cognitive Ergonomics (EPCE 2015)
- 9th International Conference on Universal Access in Human-Computer Interaction (UAHCI 2015)
- 7th International Conference on Virtual, Augmented and Mixed Reality (VAMR 2015)
- 7th International Conference on Cross-Cultural Design (CCD 2015)
- 7th International Conference on Social Computing and Social Media (SCSM 2015)
- 9th International Conference on Augmented Cognition (AC 2015)
- 6th International Conference on Digital Human Modeling and Applications in Health, Safety, Ergonomics and Risk Management (DHM 2015)
- 4th International Conference on Design, User Experience and Usability (DUXU 2015)
- 3rd International Conference on Distributed, Ambient and Pervasive Interactions (DAPI 2015)
- 3rd International Conference on Human Aspects of Information Security, Privacy and Trust (HAS 2015)
- 2nd International Conference on HCI in Business (HCIB 2015)
- 2nd International Conference on Learning and Collaboration Technologies (LCT 2015)
- 1st International Conference on Human Aspects of IT for the Aged Population (ITAP 2015)

Conference Proceedings Volumes Full List

HCI International 2015 Conference

The full list with the Program Board Chairs and the members of the Program Boards of all thematic areas and affiliated conferences is available online at:

http://www.hci.international/2015/

HCI International 2016

The 18th International Conference on Human-Computer Interaction, HCI International 2016, will be held jointly with the affiliated conferences in Toronto, Canada, at the Westin Harbour Castle Hotel, 17–22 July 2016. It will cover a broad spectrum of themes related to Human-Computer Interaction, including theoretical issues, methods, tools, processes, and case studies in HCI design, as well as novel interaction techniques, interfaces, and applications. The proceedings will be published by Springer. More information will be available on the conference website: http://2016.hci.international/.

General Chair
Prof. Constantine Stephanidis
University of Crete and ICS-FORTH
Heraklion, Crete, Greece
Email: general_chair@hcii2016.org

http://2016.hci.international/

Contents – Part I

Cognitive and Psychological Issues in HCI

Cross-Cultural Design

Design for Aging

Children in HCI

Product Design

Gesture, Gaze and Motion Detection, Modelling and Recognition

Reasoning, Optimisation and Machine Learning for HCI

Brain and Physiological Parameters Monitoring

Dialogue Systems

Contents – Part II

Learning Technologies

HCI in Health

Assistive Technologies and Environments

Location and Context Awareness

Urban Interaction

Automotive and Aviation

Design and User Studies

Design and Evaluation Methods, Techniques and Tools

Coding Schemes for Observational Studies of Usability in Collaborative Tangible User Interfaces

Tarfah Alrashed[1], Almaha Almalki[1], Salma Aldawood[1],
Anas Alfaris[1,2], and Areej Al-Wabil[1,3(✉)]

[1] Center for Complex Engineering Systems,
King Abdulaziz City for Science and Technology, Riyadh, Saudi Arabia
{t.alrashed,a.almalki,s.aldawood}@cces-kacst-mit.org
[2] Massachusetts Institute of Technology (MIT), Cambridge, USA
anas@mit.edu
[3] College of Computer and Information Sciences, Prince Sultan University,
Riyadh, Saudi Arabia
awabil@pscw.psu.edu.sa

Abstract. With the growing complexity in Tangible User Interfaces (TUIs) and their integration in the decision-making process, user acceptance of these TUI systems continues to be an important issue. Drawing upon recent findings in computer-mediated communication, human computer interaction, computer-supported-cooperative work, and social psychology, the present research extends the coding schemes for observational video analysis by incorporating the variables of communication and collaboration in the context of systems designed for urban planning and modeling.

Keywords: Coding scheme · TUI · HCI · User experience · Complex systems · Urban planning

1 Introduction

In this research study, we present coding schemes for structured video observations of tangible collaborative decision support systems designed for urban planning [1]. Testing the usability of collaborative TUI in the context of urban planning has not been fully addressed in the Human-Computer Interaction (HCI) design literature [2]. Therefore, applying behavioral coding in multimedia to efficiently analyze the user experience in video recordings is important. Behavioral coding of observational videos provides researchers with a lens for studying human interactions. HCI studies have examined video coding for behavioral analysis (e.g. coding schemes for non-verbal behavior of autistic users in interacting with assistive technologies, coding schemes in multimedia surveillance systems for emergency-response systems [3]).

We designed coding schemes to help in understanding the user behavior, evaluating the severity of usability issues, and identifying collaboration breakdowns and problems observed during the evaluation of collaborative TUI systems. The coding schemes were

© Springer International Publishing Switzerland 2015
C. Stephanidis (Ed.): HCII 2015 Posters, Part I, CCIS 528, pp. 3–6, 2015.
DOI: 10.1007/978-3-319-21380-4_1

developed as an adaptation of the DEVAN scheme [4] for video analysis and coding behaviors observed in usability testing of interactive systems, which take into account the specific interaction modalities in collaborative TUIs. Examples include the perception of embedding digital information in physical objects (e.g. visual, tactile and auditory perception) as well as gesture-based actions for different application domains. The coding schemes were elaborated iteratively in the context of designing an urban modeling and planning system, until a satisfactory reliability is achieved.

In an observational study we've conducted to examine the usability of a collaborative TUI system in the urban planning context [6], we considered different types of coding schemes in the process of analyzing video observations. The aim of this paper is to propose a coding scheme framework for collaborative TUIs that could be followed and applied on performance metrics in task-based usability analysis of TUIs.

2   Coding Schemes

2.1   Coding Scheme Structure

In our study, we considered three types of coding schemes for analyzing user interactions in collaborative TUI systems in the context of urban planning: actions, verbal, and non-verbal gestures. Coding schemes were applied to quantify the occurrences of these interactions between the user and the TUI system (User-to-Object), and between the users (User-to-User & User-to-Many) as shown in Fig. 1.

2.2   Codes for TUIs in Urban Planning

The codes were designed to be applied in task-based usability testing by mapping the codes to incidents and observations in time-stamped observational videos. A team of observers can apply independent coding, and agreement levels can be examined to

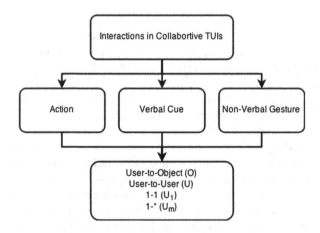

Fig. 1. Structure of the coding schemes

ensure consistent coding across observers. Trends and patterns of usability and user experience (UX) measures emerge from the quantified dataset of coded observational video recordings.

2.2.1 Actions Codes

The breakdown indication types of DEVAN were applied, such as the ACT codes for wrong actions, and the DISC codes to indicate moments in which users discontinue actions [4]. One breakdown indicator was introduced for interrupting an action during collaborative TUI-mediated interactions; the code was defined as INTER, where an action is interrupted by the system or another action.

2.2.2 Verbal Cues and Non-verbal Gestures Codes

Like in actions codes, verbal cues codes in DEVAN [4] were adapted, such as the PUZZ code for incidents in which users exhibited confusion during interaction with TUIs, and the FRUST code for frustration.

The coding schemes for verbal communication and gestures in collaborative architectural design in [5] were also adapted; they include communication control, communication technology, and design communication. An example of a communication control adaptation is the floor holding code FLO. In the context of collaborative TUI, the gesture-based cue of one user grasping a physical object of the TUI to initiate an action considers as floor holding. Another example is HAN for hand-over occurrences; the coding could indicate relinquishing the floor around the TUI or a physical hand-over of the physical object in the TUI. We introduced several breakdown indicators specific to the context of TUIs as shown in Table 1.

Table 1. Verbal and non-verbal user behavior codes

Code	Description	Definition
HESIT	Hesitation	User indicates reluctance in executing or participating in a specific task
DISAP	Disappointment	User is disappointed over a certain task or a system function
EXT	Excitement	User shows enthusiasm and eagerness
SURP	Surprise	User recognizes something suddenly and unexpectedly during interaction with the TUI
EXPL	Exploring	User tries to explore usability/functionality of digital or physical objects in the TUI of the system
BRD	Boredom	User does not indicate interest in the task he/she is performing
FRUST	Frustration	User indicates dissatisfaction over a certain task, action, or a limitation of the current system
DOUBT	Doubt	User indicates uncertainty over a specific task

3   Conclusion

In designing collaborative tangible user interfaces (TUIs) for complex systems, the usability analysis of such systems is important. Utilizing behavioral codes to rapidly analyze the user experience has been shown to be effective in testing and designing TUI systems [2, 6]. The work reported in this study contributes to the UX and usability methods' body of knowledge by introduced an aggregate coding scheme for the usability evaluation of collaborative TUI systems in the context of urban planning and design. Preliminary evidence in applying this coding scheme suggests the efficacy of these schemes in assessing the usability and UX of TUIs. Further work will examine the sensitivity of these schemes in large-scale usability evaluations of TUIs designed for city planning.

References

1. Aldawood, S., Aleissa, F., Alnasser, R., Alfaris, A., Al-Wabil, A.: Interaction design in a tangible collaborative decision support system: the city schema DSS. In: Stephanidis, C. (ed.) HCI 2014, Part II. CCIS, vol. 435, pp. 508–512. Springer, Heidelberg (2014)
2. Lasecki, W., Gordon, M., Koutra, D., Jung, M., Dow, S., Bigham, J.: Glance: rapidly coding behavioral video with the crowd. In: UIST 2014, Honolulu, HI, USA, 5–8 October 2014
3. Drain, S., Engelhardt, P.: Naturalistic observations of nonverbal children with autism: a study of intentional communicative acts in the classroom. Child Dev. Res. **2013**, 10 (2013). Article ID 296039
4. Vermeeren, A.P.O.S., den Bouwmeester, K., Aasman, J., de Ridder, H.: DEVAN: a detailed video analysis of user test data. Behav. Inf. Technol. **21**, 403–423 (2002)
5. Gabriel, G.C., Maher, M.L.: Coding and modelling communication in architectural collaborative design. Autom. Constr. **11**(2), 199–211 (2002)
6. Alrashed, T., Almalki, A., Aldawood, S., Alhindi, T., Winder, I., Noyman, A., Alfaris, A., Alwabil, A.: An observational study of usability in collaborative tangible interfaces for complex planning systems. In: 6th International Conference on Applied Human Factors and Ergonomics (AHFE 2015) and the Affiliated Conferences, AHFE (2015)

Design of Web-Based Tools to Study Blind People's Touch-Based Interaction with Smartphones

Maria Claudia Buzzi[1(✉)], Marina Buzzi[1], Barbara Leporini[2], and Amaury Trujillo[1]

[1] IIT-CNR, Via Moruzzi, Pisa, Italy
{claudia.buzzi,marina.buzzi,
amaury.trujillo}@iit.cnr.it
[2] ISTI-CNR, Via Moruzzi, Pisa, Italy
barbara.leporini@isti.cnr.it

Abstract. Nowadays touchscreen smartphones are the most common kind of mobile devices. However, gesture-based interaction is a difficult task for most visually impaired people, and even more so for blind people. This difficulty is compounded by the lack of standard gestures and the differences between the main screen reader platforms available on the market. Therefore, our goal is to investigate the differences and preferences in touch gesture performance on smartphones among visually impaired people. During our study, we implemented a web-based wireless system to facilitate the capture of participants' gestures. In this paper we present an overview of both the study and the system used.

1 Introduction

Smartphones are the most common kind of mobile devices; in the third quarter of 2014 they accounted for 66 % of the global mobile market [1]. Most smartphones use touchscreen technology, so touch-based user interfaces have become the main mobile interaction paradigm. However, touch-based interfaces are a challenge for most visually impaired people, particularly for blind users [2]. The accessibility features incorporated into smartphones to overcome issues related to visually-based touchscreen interaction are mainly based on voice interaction, such as Apple's VoiceOver or Android's TalkBack. Nevertheless, voice interaction is not always accurate, is difficult to use in noisy environments [3], and can be undesirable due to privacy or etiquette concerns [4]. Nonetheless, we feel that usable touch gestures can significantly enrich the mobile user experience of visually impaired people, despite the inherent difficulties in touch-based interaction. In a previous study by the authors on touch-based interaction in smartphones, we noted that people with different types of visual impairment performed some gestures with more or less difficulty [5]. This motivated us to further study how visually impaired people perform touch gestures. Touch gestures are characterized by a set of attributes called descriptors, which can be geometric and kinematic (e.g., number of fingers, path length, velocity, etc.), and are used by gesture recognition systems [6]. The differences in these descriptors influence the qualitative

© Springer International Publishing Switzerland 2015
C. Stephanidis (Ed.): HCII 2015 Posters, Part I, CCIS 528, pp. 7–12, 2015.
DOI: 10.1007/978-3-319-21380-4_2

aspects of the gestures, such as discoverability, ease-of-use performance, memorability, and reliability [7]. For instance, finger count, stroke count, and synchronicity have an important effect on perceived difficulty [8]. However, creating accessible computer-based interfaces across a myriad of available platforms is a complex challenge [9], particularly due to difficulties in recruiting users with disabilities for research studies [10]. For this reason, studies sometimes use sighted participants who are blindfolded or are blocked from seeing the screen [11, 12]. Furthermore, blind people may have difficulty learning touch gestures [13]. For this reason, a study with blind people suggests some guidelines to apply when performing user tests with them: not using print symbols, reducing location accuracy demand, using familiar layouts, favoring screen landmarks, and limiting time-based gestures [14].

2 Methodology

For our study, we recruited 36 participants (14 female, 22 male) from four different local centers for blind and low-vision people in Tuscany. The mean age of the participants was 45 years for females (SD = 14.3) and 50 years for males (SD = 16.8). We classified the 36 participants in four categories: severe low vision (11), blind since birth (7), blind since adolescence (6), and those who became blind in adulthood (12). Twenty-six of the participants had previously used some kind of mobile touchscreen, such as smartphones, tablets, and music players. In addition, more than half of the participants reported to have used iOS, with the rest using mostly Android.

We selected 25 gesture types, mostly from those used with Android's screen reader TalkBack, and iOS screen reader VoiceOver. The authors suggested other gestures in the set. Gesture selection was based on three main characteristics: pointer count (or finger count), stroke count, and direction. Also based on these characteristics, we classified the gestures into seven groups: swipes, letterlike shapes, taps, rotors, angled shapes, and to and fro swipes (Fig. 1). When we described the gestures to the participants, we described a given gesture by its shape or by how it is performed; we did not give a semantic to the gestures.

We experienced difficulties capturing the participants' gestures with touchscreen smartphones. We needed to capture a set of gestures performed by visually impaired participants who were on tight schedules and were spread across geographically distributed local centers. Also taking into account the project's time and budget constraints, we needed to optimize the capture sessions. Therefore, we decided to work with multiple participants at the same time, using identical Android smartphones. In addition, to facilitate data collection we developed a Web-based system aimed at capturing the user gestures (Fig. 2).

3 The Gesture Capture System

To capture a participant's gesture, we used three identical Nexus 5 smartphones with a 4.9-inch display. All of our devices had Android v4.4 as the operating system. We developed a web-based client-server architecture to capture the participant's gestures.

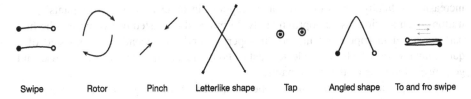

| Swipe | Rotor | Pinch | Letterlike shape | Tap | Angled shape | To and fro swipe |

Fig. 1. Reference gesture groups and examples

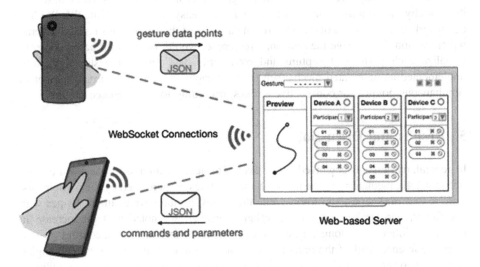

Fig. 2. Wireless client-server architecture used to capture participants' gestures

Up to three clients (smartphones) can connect simultaneously to a web server (a laptop) through a Wi-Fi local network. The connection was via WebSockets, which allowed interactive sessions between the server and the smartphones. Gesture data and capture parameters were transmitted as JSON and serialized within an SQLite database.

From the server dashboard, we could select the gesture type and start or cancel a given capture session. These commands would be sent to all the connected smartphones, so the participants could perform their gestures with minimal interruptions. We could also visualize each gesture as it was performed, using the canvas API. In addition, we integrated automated and manual mechanisms to mark a participant's gesture in case their gesture did not match the gesture type characteristics (e.g., number of fingers, strokes, direction, etc.).

4 Procedure

We arranged four different sets of capture sessions, one for every local blind association. In each location, we had one, two or three participants per session, according to their availability schedule. Additionally, we sorted the set of gesture types by increasing difficulty, according to our perception, in order to avoid participants' frustration. Each session lasted approximately 75 min and consisted of two parts. The first part consisted in capture of the gestures per se, and the second part consisted of a questionnaire in which we collected data about the profile, mobile device use and gesture preferences of the participants.

The 36 participants were asked to perform each of the 25 gestures six times, with the goal of obtaining 5400 gesture samples. For every gesture type, we initially told the participants the name of the gesture and how to perform it, and then we recorded whether they already knew or had done the gesture or not. We also asked them to rate its difficulty, using a five-point scale, from 1 (very easy) to 5 (very difficult). We had cardboard cutouts of most of the gestures in case any of the participants needed a tactile representation. To manage the session, a researcher would use the web-based server to visualize each participant capture and record the data for each gesture. We also implemented an automated mechanism to mark captures with an incorrect number of simultaneous pointers or consecutive strokes, according to the reference gesture.

5 Results and Discussion

In general, participants perceived a low level of difficulty with most of the gesture types (mean = 1.49, median = 1). The most difficult gestures, as perceived by the participants, were to and fro swipes, and rotor, while the easiest gestures were simple swipes with one finger, one stroke, and one direction. However, we noted a slight increase in perceived difficulty in longer gestures with similar descriptors. Concerning gesture shape preference, half of the participants preferred rounded gestures, six steep-angled gestures, two right-angled gestures, and ten reported having no preference. In addition, the majority of the participants also preferred gestures with one finger (22 participants), and one stroke (19 participants). Regarding differences among the visually impaired groups, we found noteworthy variations, and in one gesture, the vertical chevron, the difference in sharpness was significant.

We would like to note that despite the issues solved by our solution, we had other issues in capturing the gestures. For instance, the average age of our participants, 48 years (SD = 15.8), means younger visually impaired people are underrepresented. In addition, participants would sometimes perform a gesture outside the boundaries of the screen due to the lack of tactile edges. Other times, participants' fingernails would make contact with the display, and the gesture was not recorded as intended, especially in women with long fingernails. In the first location, an issue we had inherent to wireless capture system was multipath propagation [15]. This kind of interference occurred when the signals sent by the mobile devices to the web server, and vice versa, arrived by more than two paths or canceled each other. The construction materials used in the room where we perform the sessions caused this interference. Therefore, we relocated the equipment and participants, and in subsequent locations we did a preliminary signal strength test. Despite these issues, in the end, thanks to our capture solution we were able to make effective use of our limited time with the participants.

6 Conclusions

More research is needed regarding accessible and mobile touch-based interaction for visually impaired people, especially for those who are blind. In this paper we presented an overview of a study on gestures preferences and differences among visually impaired people. We also presented how the use of wireless and web based technologies can solve some of the problems that might arise during such studies. Given that we mainly used web technologies, similar research tools could be implemented across different mobile platforms with relative ease, compared to native solutions [16].

References

1. Rivera, J., van der Meulen, R.: Gartner Says Sales of Smartphones Grew 20 Percent in Third Quarter of 2014 Gartner. Egham, UK (2014)
2. Kane, S.K., Bigham, J.P., Wobbrock, J.O.: Slide rule: making mobile touch screens accessible to blind people using multi-touch interaction techniques. In: Proceedings of the 10th International ACM SIGACCESS Conference on Computers and Accessibility, pp. 73–80. ACM (2008)
3. Leporini, B., Buzzi, M.C., Buzzi, M.: Interacting with mobile devices via voiceover: usability and accessibility issues. In: Proceedings of 24th Australian Computer-Human Interaction Conference, pp. 339–348 (2012)
4. Kane, S.K., Jayant, C., Wobbrock, J.O., Ladner, R.E.: Freedom to roam: a study of mobile device adoption and accessibility for people with visual and motor disabilities. In: Proceedings of 11th International ACM SIGACCESS (2009)
5. Buzzi, M.C., et al.: Designing a text entry multimodal keypad for blind users of touchscreen mobile phones. In: Proceedings of the 16th international ACM SIGACCESS conference on Computers and accessibility, pp. 131–136. ACM, New York (2014)
6. Rubine, D.: Specifying gestures by example. In: Proceedings of the 18th annual conference on Computer graphics and interactive techniques, pp. 329–337. ACM (1991)
7. Ruiz, J., Y. Li, Lank, E.: User-defined motion gestures for mobile interaction. In: Proceedings of the SIGCHI Conference on Human Factors in Computing Systems. ACM, Vancouver (2011)
8. Rekik, Y., Vatavu, R.-D., Grisoni, L.: Understanding users' perceived difficulty of multi-touch gesture articulation. In: Proceedings of the 16th International Conference on Multimodal Interaction. ACM (2014)
9. Cerf, V.G.: Why is accessibility so hard? Commun. ACM 55(11), 7 (2012)
10. Sears, A., Hanson, V.: Representing users in accessibility research. In: Proceedings of the SIGCHI Conference on Human Factors in Computing Systems, pp. 2235–2238. ACM, Vancouver (2011)
11. Oh, U., Kane, S.K., Findlater,L.: Follow that sound: using sonification and corrective verbal feedback to teach touchscreen gestures. In: 15th International ACM SIGACCESS, pp. 13:1–13:8. ACM, New York (2013)
12. Sandnes, F., et al.: Making touch-based kiosks accessible to blind users through simple gestures. Univ. Access Inf. Soc. 11(4), 421–431 (2012)
13. Schmidt, M., Weber, G.: Multitouch haptic interaction. In: Stephanidis, C. (ed.) UAHCI 2009, Part II. LNCS, vol. 5615, pp. 574–582. Springer, Heidelberg (2009)

14. Kane, S.K., Wobbrock, J.O., Ladner, R.E.: Usable gestures for blind people: understanding preference and performance. In: SIGCHI Conference, pp. 413–422 (2011)
15. Bose, A., Foh, C.H.: A practical path loss model for indoor WiFi positioning enhancement. In: 6th International Conference on Information, Communications and Signal Processing, 2007. IEEE (2007)
16. Charland, A., Leroux, B.: Mobile application development: web vs. native. Commun. ACM **54**(5), 49–53 (2011)

Toward a New Design Philosophy: Politics *and* the Aesthetic of "We" Human-and-Technology in Interaction Design

Hyunkyoung Cho[(⊠)]

ASPECT, Virginia Tech, Blacksburg, USA
hkcho.vt.edu@gmail.com

Abstract. This paper suggests that the relation of politics *and* the aesthetic in interaction design depends on a situated knowledge of how to interact with each other. Its aim is to open a new way to approach interaction design philosophy in the perspective of "We" human-and-technology. As a case, interaction design with BCI stimulates a network of conceptual relations rather than merely perceptions of the visible aspects of singles works. The investigation of relations between politics *and* the aesthetic in interaction design reveals that the instrumental understanding of technology is the colonization by tolerance-tactic.

Keywords: "We" human-and-technology · Collaborative action · Interaction design with BCI · Politics and the aesthetic · Tolerance-tactic · Colonization

1 Introduction

This article suggests the relations of politics and aesthetics in the flexible, mobile, variable collaborations of computational/informational technologies open a new way of being-and-knowing of interaction design in HCI. By linking design, technology and humanity as the understandings of "We" human-and-technology in collaborative actions rooted in interdependent perspective, informational technology recomposes both human identity and technological practices as collaborative fusion between the human and technology. The new identity provoked by such technologies might be called "We" human-and-technology. In this conceptualization of "We" human-and-technology, the coded complexities of informatics technology remixes the axes and dimensions of action between politics and the aesthetic. Prior investigations of the relation of politics and the aesthetic in contemporary interactive design are stuck the binary frame of domination in which "Us" versus "Them" inforces a mutual degradation of the human and technified in thought and action.

This approach is criticized here from two perspectives. First, the real disruption of "We" human-and-technology is a reified inversion by a frame of fantasy, using the tolerance-tactic. Second, the traditional instrumental understanding of technology sees it only as an instrument for colonization, which is a limited appraisal of all that happens in technological praxes.

This study, then, traces a few intriguing, but not yet fully disclosed, relations between technology, design, and politics by exploring how new informatic arts instantiate the

© Springer International Publishing Switzerland 2015
C. Stephanidis (Ed.): HCII 2015 Posters, Part I, CCIS 528, pp. 13–18, 2015.
DOI: 10.1007/978-3-319-21380-4_3

communal, collaborative, and collective agencies of "We" human-and-technology as collective deliberations beyond the stale "I" individual-and-instrument personal domination conventionally attributed to technological rationality. It wants to slip past the binaries, inversions, and fetishism that mere toleration accepts in the colonizing and dehumanizing aspects of instrumental reason. Interaction design in HCI can find difference in domination. These differences then might advance the "friendship" of "We" "human-and-technology" mediations as a metaphor for decolonizing and rehumanizing other relationships typically flattened into the fiendishness of "I" individual-and-instrument domination. To make this transition, one must spin the art of translation another way to glimpse these aesthetic dimensions in the politics of interaction design. Hence, this analysis turns to Marx, Heidegger, and Fanon to rethink how the workings of technical rationality parallel commodification and colonization as well as those of leisure and liberation to ask how this new aesthetic sense of technology might evade dehumanizing forces.

2   The Collaborative Action of "We" Human-and- Technology

Technology reconciles the dimensions of action between politics *and* the aesthetic of interaction design. The relation of politics *and* the aesthetic has been claimed to be a mutual degradation between two opposing points of view. First is a use of aesthetics in politics: how politics has turned to the aesthetic as either a support or an ideological antagonism. Second is a use of politics in aesthetics: how the aesthetic has social and political meaning. Technology undertakes a redefinition of the aesthetic that not only challenges the representational categories into which it has been placed but also redefines the aesthetic in terms of political existence. This challenge proposes a new definition agreeing with both politics *and* the aesthetic. The investigation of relation of politics and the aesthetic is amplified by contemporary interaction design. One of significance quietness of technology based interaction design is that the collaborative action of human and technology becomes artwork itself. When interaction design artwork is constituted by collaborative action of human and technology, there is no distinction between actor and spectator, human and non-human, artist and audience.

Especially, Brain-Computer Collaborative Design expands the collaborative action into a kind of biofeedback. It suggests the brain-signal processing as a new way for collaborative action of human and computer. For example, Racing Car Game uses the design of HCI with BCI (Brain-Computer Interface). This work is constituted by the concentration between human and computer as collaborators. The brain-computer collaborative action changes the car's velocity; it can improve the attention state; when the collaboration between human and computer gets stronger, the concentration level goes higher. In Racing Car Game, brainwave is the key measure; it represents the concentration as the degree of collaborative action between human and computer. Car's velocity indicates the concentration level using electroencephalography (EEG). Racing Car Game's system is designed under BCI 2000 platform. Graphical software visualizes concentration index and hardware module controls the velocity of a racing car. BCI2000 is a general-purpose system for BCI research and development. It can also be used for data acquisition, stimulus presentation, or brain observation applications. BCI2000 consists of a Signal Acquisition module that acquires brain signals from g. USBamp or g.MOBIlab+devices. These raw signals are visualized and stored to disk, and submitted to the Signal Processing module. The Signal Processing module extracts signal features and translates them into device commands. Its commands are used by the Applications module to generate collaborative action of human and technology (Fig. 1).

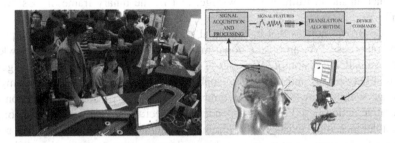

Fig. 1. Racing *Car Game* and BCI2000 Platform, Picture courtesy of Gerwin Schalk, Wadsworth Center, NY. www.bci2000org. (*Racing Car Game* developed by BioComputing Laboratory at GIST, Korea. BCI2000 has been used to replicate or extend current BCI methods in humans, and has recently been used in a number of groundbreaking BCI studies. BCI2000 has been in development since 2000 in a collaborative effort led by the Wadsworth Center. BCI2000 is available free of charge for research purposes to academic and educational institutions.)

The collaborative action through brain activities allows us a new way of interaction design as a communication without physical and visible movement between human and computer. Brain signals create a new aesthetic dimension of interaction designs constituted by the collaborative action of human and technology. Here the interaction design becomes an imagination itself. The aesthetic of brain-computer interaction design considers the collaborative action as knowledge of interaction design. It means that brain-computer collaborative design stimulates a network of conceptual relations rather than merely perceptions of the visible aspects of interaction design. At this point, the aesthetic of interaction design of "We" human-and-technology corresponds on its politics (Fig. 2).

Fig. 2. EPOC and Carrera Slot Car (EPOC is as a 14-channel wireless EEG system developed by Emotiv Systems.)

3 Tolerance-Tactic

The collaborative action of human and technology would function as one diagnostic key for the problem of the supplementary structure of the Western knowledge system rooted in logic of opposition. Instead of drawing a line intended to exclude, technology advocates inclusion, universality, and the plurality of modes of becoming. The question about the relation of politics *and* the aesthetic is then how technology could play a catalytic role for the reframing of knowledge. Especially, technology critiques relations of tolerance in the instrumental knowledge: that is, the binary frame of "Us" versus "Them".

Wendy Brown notices that instrumental knowledge promotes not the multiplicity, but the "otherness." As an upside-down image, inversion of instrumental knowledge abets the so-called division of "We" and "They." Logic of "the absolute and dangerous opposition between us and them" is a cloak veiling "the true nature of the enemy" of knowledge within knowledge [1]. In order to address the problem of inversion in a collaborative action-based context-dependent perspective, she delves into the conception of tolerance only exists in the discourse (utterance) of relationship. As a performing of discourse about relationship, tolerance symptomizes the difference. Tolerance is what distinguishes us from them. It regulates aversion in the name of magnanimity, and works as "a supplement to liberal equality." The key here is that tolerance becomes a disciplinary strategy. It functions as a tactical instrument of instrumental knowledge: Tolerance-tactic. The tactic of instrumental knowledge is idealization of tolerance, and its aim is to govern the difference itself; it is premised upon and pertains to difference; it is deployed to handle the difference that liberal equality cannot reduce, eliminate, or address.

As a conduit as well as a conduct with the difference, idealization of tolerance underscores the collaboration of human and technology in the binary frame of "Us" versus "Them." By way of tolerance-tactic, equality of we collaborators presumes sameness. And then tolerance is employed to manage difference between "Them." The interesting point is not that there are no differences between we humans and technology, but that the tolerance of instrumental knowledge converts these differences into opposites distorting essence of relationship. Tolerance fosters the power originated from mutually degraded positioning; human-subject-thought and technology-object-action, civilization-free-liberal and barbarism-unfree-nonliberal. The power means that in this instrumental knowledge, technology is reduced to a mere tool, a tolerated object in relation to tolerating subject. The live and real collaborative relationship with technology degenerates into a miscegeneation, a blasphemy.

4 Colonization

Technology reveals that the instrumental knowledge uses relations of tolerance as a tactic instrument for manipulation of our sensibility. Tolerance-tactic supports the so-called fantasy-frame: the binary of "Us" versus "Them." According to Frantz Fanon's exploration, relations of tolerance in instrumental knowledge articulate the compartmentalized colonial system. He notes, "Colonialism is the organization of a Manichaean world, of a compartmentalized world [2]." Its first and foremost principle is that "It's them or us." The instrumental perspective is "the colonized perspective": the primitive Manichae-anism of the colonizer-"Us" versus "Them." By the colonist's powers, the magical and supernatural powers, the relationship of human and technology is reduced to a permanent confrontation at the level of fantasy. Hence, in the colonial context there is no truthful behavior. And good is quite simply what hurts *us* most.

Fanon senses the significance of struggle of human agency in the midst of the agony of oppression of colonialism. And he states, "The colonized world is a world divided in two." Moreover, it uses the people against the people. The difficulty of decolonization of instrumental knowledge, deconstruction of Manichaean history of colonialism is that colonization is in the psycho-affective realm (experience), which is neither subjective nor objective, but a place of social and psychic mediation. From this view, he defines that "Colonization or decolonization: it is simply a power struggle. Colonialism is not a machine capable of thinking, a body endowed with reason." As Fanon's insight, the collaborative action of human and technology confronts the colonial condition as a process of continued agony rather than a total disappearance. It provides an opportunity to deal with "the colonized's consciousness." The analysis bases its diagnostic on psychiatric symptoms of instrumental knowledge.

In order to understand the sensibility of the colonized, the collaborative action of human and technology addresses the collective unconsciousness of the colonized, in particular, through the obsession and symbolic bliss. First of all, psychoanalytically speaking, the colonized is traumatized. The obsession is the essential mental symptom by inversion of instrumental knowledge: colonization. Fanon also emphasizes that the obsession is the most painful legacy we have encountered in the war against the colonist's power, the instrumental knowledge. According to him, "The subject finds it impossible to explain and defend a given viewpoint. An Antithetical thought process. Anything which is affirmed can be simultaneously denied with the same force." This is why obsessive personality is the fruit of the psychological warfare used in the service of colonialism.

The collaborative action of human and technology articulates that the obsession is an anxiety disorder or excessive worry of technology. The key here is that it is a product of sufferer's own mind, not one based in the actual relation (action) with the technology or its experience. The inversion of instrumental knowledge cannot avoid to conflict with the common question about the primary member: here the matter of primary member is that of the colonizing (positioning of subject and object). What the obsession teaches us is that the collaborative action of human and technology would be colonized in the general question that which is primary subject, human or technology? The defining about the primary in relationship, that is, the colonization assumes the relatively degradation: for instance, when humans become the primary subject, tech-nology is degraded as the secondary. The colonized relationship that one serves other does not admit the reciprocity. It does not allow the critical thinking to liberate from bondage the habit and custom and to examine different things. This one-way is the very violent colonization by the inversion of instrumental knowledge. Its aim would be to merely reinforce shame and fear of the colonized.

Jean-Paul Sartre writes that "Colonial violence not only aims at keeping these enslaved men at a respectful distance, it also seeks to dehumanize them. The first reaction by these oppressed people is to repress this shameful anger that is normally condemned by them and us, but that is the only refuge they have left for their humanity." The collaborative action of human and technology discerns the collective unconsciousness traversing reality and the Real.[1] The symbolic bliss works as second symptom of colonization (inversion of instrumental perspective) [3].[2] Borrowing from Freud's diagnosis, the split in relation to technology is nothing less than what is the repressed in the paradoxes of prohibition of incest; it is not possible for a computer to think on the grounds that it is ethically and morally dangerous. The repressed is the discord between the desire of prohibited and impossible relationship of we humans and technology and its guilty conscience (or hostility) [4].

Interestingly, in the repressed, the fantasy-frame of colonized world organizes the symbolic bliss. In other words, what we call reality is constituted by the Real. The Real is traumatic. In order to avoid the confronting with the Real, the fantasy-frame of the colonized world operates the symbolic bliss. The symbolic bliss is "the coming into operation of the symbolic function [5]." It converts the traumatic Real into the reality, "a horrendous discovery" into "a sort of ataraxia." The colonization of fantasy-frame is constitutive of what we call the reality. Through the exclusion of the Real by the fantasy frame, our reality becomes a model of the symbolic bliss. It implies that the collaborative action of human and technology is an attempt at decolonization. Tribulations and mental disorders by colonial war are the price we pay for our access to reality, and thus the false idea that "technology doesn't think and act with humans" means that the price for our access to "reality" is also that a colonized something (colonial violence) remains unthought.

References

1. Brown, W.: Regulating Aversion: Tolerance in the Age of Identity and Empire, p. 20. Princeton university Press, Princeton (2006)
2. Fanon, F.: The Wretched of the Earth, p. 43. Grove Press, New York (2004)
3. Zizek, S.: From virtual reality to the virtualization of reality. In: Trend, D. (ed.) Reading Digital Culture, p. 18. Blackwell Publishing, Oxford (2001)
4. Cho, H.K., Yoon, J.S.: Performative art: the politics of doubleness. Leonardo **42**(3), 282–283 (2009). The MIT Press, Cambridge
5. Lacan, J.: The Seminar of Jacques Lacan, Book II, p. 168. Cambridge University Press, Cambridge (1988)

---

[1] The reality and the Real are used in Lacanian notion.

[2] As early as 1954 Jacques Lacan points out that, "the computer is pragmatic case of symbolic bliss." See Slavoj Zizek, "From Virtual Reality to the Virtualization of Reality," in David Trend (ed.) *Reading Digital Culture* (Oxford: Blackwell Publishing, 2001), p. 18.

Method to Design Adaptable and Adaptive User Interfaces

Francesca Gullà[1]([⊠]), Lorenzo Cavalieri[1], Silvia Ceccacci[1],
Michele Germani[1], and Roberta Bevilacqua[2]

[1] Department of Industrial Engineering and Mathematical Sciences,
Università Politecnica delle Marche, Via Brecce Bianche 12, 60131
Ancona, Italy
{f.gulla,lorenzo.cavalieri,s.ceccacci,
m.germani}@univpm.it
[2] INRCA, Scientific Direction, Via Santa Margherita 5, 60124 Ancona, Italy
r.bevilacqua@inrca.it

Abstract. In order to study and develop adaptive user interfaces with the purpose to guarantee socialization, safety and environmental sustainability in a domestic day-by-day living space, a new method of holistic and adaptive user interface is proposed to support the modelling of information related to the user and the context of the interaction to generate the user profiles, subjects older than 40 years with different levels of technology affinity have been considered. The new adaptive user interfaces prototypes will be tested through different use cases in the context of smart home environments.

Keywords: User interfaces · Adaptive interfaces · User-centered design · Design for AAL

1 Introduction

Designing a multi-user adaptive interface means designing for a diversity of end-users and contexts of use, and implies making alternative design decisions at various levels of the interaction. To this end, a method for the construction of a single interface design instance is inappropriate, as it cannot accommodate for diversity of the resulting dialogue artifacts. Therefore, there is the need for a systematic process in which alternative design decisions for different parameters can be designed with appropriate dialogue patterns, along with their associated parameters (e.g. user and usage-context-attribute values). The present study provides an overview of the methods currently applied to the definition and development of Adaptive User Interfaces (AUIs). Then an approach to support the definition and design of a novel adaptive user interface able to react with the human behavior is presented, showing the results of a pilot conducting with older and disable users with a new AUI.

© Springer International Publishing Switzerland 2015
C. Stephanidis (Ed.): HCII 2015 Posters, Part I, CCIS 528, pp. 19–24, 2015.
DOI: 10.1007/978-3-319-21380-4_4

2 Research Background

The concept of a system able to adapt itself depending on requirements or criteria other than, or even at user's request, is not new. The research literature describes many approaches that can be used to design flexible user interfaces, which can be classified into two broad categories: adaptable and adaptive. Adaptable User Interfaces (AdUIs) can be defined as systems in which the activation and selection of user-computer interaction, is performed by the final user through the selection of a specific user profile from a predefined list. The Adaptability is based on the users' known characteristics and preferences; these are defined prior to their interaction session and, in any case, are assumed to remain static during the session [1]. Benyon [2] defines Adaptive Systems as systems, which can alter aspects of their structure or functionalities in order to accommodate different users' needs and their changes over time. Adaptive systems are based on the principle that the system should be capable of identifying those circumstances that necessitate adaptation, and accordingly, select and effect an appropriate course of action. The most important advantage of adaptable systems is that the users are in total control of the individual appearance and interface. Otherwise, the use of adaptive user interface seems to help to improve user interaction with systems by facilitating user performance, minimizing the need to help request, easing system.

The Adaptive User Interface research field aims to provide highly usable systems for people with different needs and characteristics in different context of use. Consequently, Adaptive User Interfaces constitute one of the major direction of Human Computer Interaction research. The AUI design is not a simple task [3] and nowadays a unified methodology wasn't modeled because many aspects are involved. Its development requires assessing the state of mind, state of psychology and level of awareness about the target user; defining a suitable adaptation behaviour [4]; assessing the adaptation timeliness [5]; defining a general method in the absence of a experimentation; assessing the usability and acceptability of a user interface without an established methodology; avoid to damage user's privacy, and give unwanted information. Therefore the AUI design is started from several fundamental choice: (1) Establish who should adapt and what should be the role of User Interface in the adaptation process, (2) Define what goals should be mainly considered in the adaptation process, (3) Define a proper set of rules to manage the adaptation, (4) Define what level of the interaction should be considered and what are the adaptation variables. (5) Define methods in the adaptation process, an inference mechanism for the user's choice. Furthermore, some studies indicate that an intermediate level of adaptivity mixed to adaptability should be consider as a good compromise, as it can help to keep users involved in the task and help them to become more skilled to perform routine and non-routine tasks [6, 7]; consequently the interface design has been implemented in order to make it adaptable and adaptive at the same time.

3 Proposed Method

In order to study and develop an adaptive and adaptable user interfaces with the purpose to guarantee socialization, safety and environments sustainability in a domestic day-by-day living space, a new method of holistic and adaptive user interface is proposed to support the modelling of information related to the user and the context of the interaction to generate singular user profiles. This implies the definition and development of holistic and adaptive user interfaces aiming to satisfy the different utilization profiles/contexts and user requirements/skills. The target of this work is the development of new methodologies for human-machine interaction and for user interfaces, according to the "design for all" paradigms [8]. The user interfaces will be adaptive, meaning that they will be easy-to-use and friendly for users, including elderly and weak people. The novel user interfaces will react with the human behaviour, and interact in accordance with the environmental conditions monitored by local sensors. The adaptation management system is based on the knowledge provided by three information models: the User Model, the Environment Model (or Domain Model) and the Interaction Model (Fig. 1).

The User Model (UM) provides the description of the user's profile pattern, according to its cognitive and physical structure, status and preferences. The user's profile pattern is outline according to the coding provided by the International Classification of Functioning, Disability and Health [9].

The Environment Model (EM) supplies the information pattern necessary to describe the environment of the human machine interaction. Such information are related to its physical characteristics (e.g. typology of interactive devices, available means of interaction, etc.) as so as to its functionalities (e.g., supported activities or tasks) and its logical characteristics (e.g., information relates to management of the system functionalities performed by the adaptive interface).

The Interaction Model (IM) is the core of whole adaptive process: this model is in charge of the user and environmental model data management. The IM have to recognize the user and store its needs and preferences. In addition it have to be able to extract human-computer interaction information, provide the correct logical and task interpretation, allow a much more suitable environmental usability and define the event activation

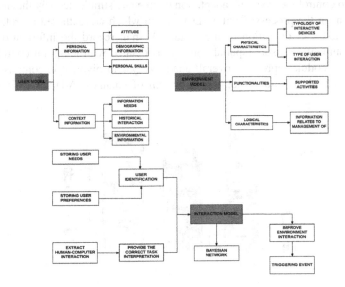

Fig. 1. The adaptation management system

schedule. Such complex adaptive systems require inference and evaluation mechanisms, which need to learn and interact with the local environment. In an adaptive mechanism there is no direct access to the whole domain reality; the system to be developed must act within a range of uncertain data: such as unreliable, missing and inaccurate data. In addition incorrect environmental data may raise inaccuracy. Probabilistic theories provide the methods to correctly deal with inaccurate data systems, resulting from lack of domain knowledge. The Bayesian approach provides a robust theory that merges together different technologies. Automatic learning is based on the idea that experience may improve the "agent" capability behaviour and future events, providing the ability to automatically update users profiles and predict users behavior [10].

4   Adaptive and Adaptable System Layout

On the basis of the model mentioned above a preliminary view of the architecture for managing the user interfaces implementation has been conceived as follows.

The system architecture is based on 3 main units, continuously communicating between each other: the database, the core engine and the user interface (Fig. 2).

A Database Management System (DBMS) is designed to achieve a large set of structured data inputs and processes the amount of data requested by numerous users; this unit is in charge to collect the data arising from the different input of the system. In particular, the information is structured in four semantic areas. User Features Profile includes the Personal Information described previously in the User Identification; User Use Profile includes the User Model Context Information: previous interaction's history, user's preferences and information needs. Log Adaptation Actions represents the collection of all adaptation actions performed by the interface. It receives the information each time that the system performs an adaptation action: this information is necessary to control the system's adaptation degree and simultaneously the user's skills improvement in the process. Context Data, upon which are gathered all relevant data for the context user definition of the system. It shall record the information derived from environmental sensors (spatial context) associated with temporal coordinates.

The core module represents overall adaptive system pivot: it is composed of two adaptive mechanisms and a monitoring system of changes. Adaptable Engine shall

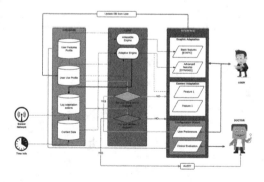

Fig. 2. Adaptive and adaptable system architecture layout

make the system adaptable according to user profile. Adaptability is based on features and preferences that are known at a first interaction, and they are assumed to remain static during a single session of interaction. This engine takes as input the collected information in the User Profile Features to adapt the graphical interface features, such as text, size and type of font. Adaptive Engine shall make the system adaptive according to the use profile. Adaptivity is based on change mechanisms which include all dynamic features, such as interaction story based preferences, information contents, icons, layout, etc. The working systems take advantages of Bayesian Network adaptation mechanism, by using software called Netica. It depends on information by User Features, User Use and Context Data database, and apply changes on the Interface level: graphical (dynamic) and contents. Change monitoring system allows to generate two alert types: User Preferences Changes takes into account the user preferences changes, in terms of both graphics and content; User Abilities Changes takes into account the interface changes (both graphical and content), store them and send an alert when they frequently change, both in a positive and negative way, going to update the User Features Profile. Finally, the interface module allows enabling system interaction and communication with user. In particular, system identifies two types of users: the consumer is the target user the adaptation support process is implemented on; the specialist doctor who represents the linking point among ICT system and health condition evaluation of the consumer. The interface structure can be synthetized into two aspects described below. Graphics can be organized basic features (static), i.e. standard features uniquely related to a disorder (colour blindness, visual disturbances, etc.). These features are related to loss of body functionalities and feasible with the aid of existing guidelines. Advanced features represent all dynamic features about adapted interface items according to specific residual function consequent to a specific disorder and they is designed on a single user. Contents represent all interface items editable according to user and actions the user acts on interface, own preferences and needs. For instance, considering a kitchen, if the user decides to enter in the oven section, the system will offer in evidence more used recipes. Finally, Configuration Wizard is a tool able to allow modify User Preferences (by user or specialist doctor) but also the Clinical Evaluation (by only specialist), a high-level questionnaire is presented in to clinical parameters configuration.

5 Conclusion and Future Works

In order to develop a novel AUI according to the "design for all" paradigm, an holistic approach is proposed. It is based on modelling information related to the user and the context of the interaction. In particular the target of this work is the development of a new methodology for human-machine interaction and for user interfaces. In accordance with the project, some areas of weakness have been highlighted; these outline the specific characteristics of the user such as sensory disturbances/perceptual, cognitive and mood disorders. A preliminary pilot is defined to evaluate the users' performance analysing on one hand, adaptability of the text elements adaptivity of interface layout and icons (size, position and contrast), on the other hand, the subjective skills in the use of technology and appropriateness of features characteristics. Subjects older than

40 years with different levels of technology affinity will be considered to generate the user profiles. All the information gathered from the pilot study will be used to define the main guidelines of the adaptation criteria interface based on disorder users. The final goal is to produce features able to automatically satisfy the different skills, abilities, needs and human preferences, and not simply finding a single solution for everyone. Future application scenarios will be the living room and the kitchen that are characterized by a large number of household appliances.

Acknowledgements. This work has been developed in the context of "D4All: Design for all" project, National Technological Cluster funded by the Italian Minister of University and Research.

References

1. Grundy, J., Hosking, J.: Developing adaptable user interfaces for component-based systems. Interact. Comput. **14**, 175–194 (2014)
2. Benyon, D.I.: System Adaptivity and the Modelling of Stereotypes. National Physical Laboratory, Division of Information Technology and Computing, Teddington (1987)
3. Yen, G.G., Acay, D.: Adaptive user interfaces in complex supervisory tasks. ISA Trans. **48**, 196–205 (2008). Oklahoma State University, School of Electrical & Computer Engineering, Stillwater, OK 74078, USA
4. Billings, C.E.: Aviation Automation: The Search for a Human-Centered Approach. Erlbaum, Mahwah (1997)
5. Horvitz, E.: Principles of mixed-initiative user interfaces (1999)
6. Bunt, A., Conati, C., McGrenere, J.: What role can adaptive support play in an adaptable system? In: 9th International Conference on Intelligent User Interfaces, Funchal, Madeira, Portugal, 13–16 January 2004
7. Zimmermann, G., Vanderheiden, G.C., Strobbe, C.: Towards deep adaptivity – a framework for the development of fully context-sensitive user interfaces. In: Stephanidis, C., Antona, M. (eds.) UAHCI 2014, Part I. LNCS, vol. 8513, pp. 299–310. Springer, Heidelberg (2014)
8. Sacco, M., Caldarola, E.G., Modoni, G., Terkaj W.: Supporting the Design of AAL through a SW Integration Framework: The D4All Project (2014)
9. International Classification of Functions, Disability and Health (ICF), World Health Organization
10. Cooper, G.F., Herskovits, E.: A bayesian method for the induction of probabilistic networks from data. Mach. Learn. **9**(4), 309–347 (1992)

Designing for Affectibility:
Principles and Guidelines

Elaine C.S. Hayashi[(✉)] and M. Cecília C. Baranauskas

Institute of Computing, University of Campinas, Campinas, São Paulo, Brazil
{hayashi, cecilia}@ic.unicamp.br

Abstract. In analogy to the concept of usability, learnability and playability, the concept of Affectibility was conceived to inform the design process – in this case with affective aspects of interaction. In this paper we present a revised set of the Principles for the Design for Affectibility, together with practical examples of use and application. The objective is to support designers in the process of creating educational systems for children, considering aspects of affect.

Keywords: Affectibility · Affect · Emotions · Design · Children interaction · Education

1 Introduction

Researches in varied areas of knowledge have been investigating the role that emotions and affect play in our lives. It has been suggested that "positive affect facilitates creative problem solving" [10]. In the field of biological sciences, studies investigated the relationship between negative affective style and weaker immune responses in an individual [21]. In the area of education, affect has been known for long to have significant importance in children's development. A crescent interest in affect is noted in the field of Human Computer Interaction, as well. However, little is known about the practical design of learning technology aiming at improved affective responses from users in their interaction with that technology.

In order to make clear what we mean by 'affect', we adopted the definition from Ortony et al. [19], who see affect as "a superordinate concept that subsumes particular valenced conditions such as emotions, moods, feelings, and preferences". Furthermore, we use the term Affectibility [9] to express the set of characteristics of a digital artifact that have the potential to elicit rather positive affective responses in the user.

Affective responses can be seen as a product from the interaction of the users with the technology, considering users' surroundings, as well as users' culture and society [5]. Note that 'interaction' implies in actions, meaning that users are active in the learning processes supported by that technology [20].

In order to better understand the learning environment, we had been working within a school community for over two years, participating in its daily activities, including classes, informal social events (e.g., gatherings during lunch breaks) and formal meetings (e.g., teachers meetings, parents meetings). This empirical knowledge was combined with theoretical studies to inform the Design Principles for Affectibility.

© Springer International Publishing Switzerland 2015
C. Stephanidis (Ed.): HCII 2015 Posters, Part I, CCIS 528, pp. 25–31, 2015.
DOI: 10.1007/978-3-319-21380-4_5

1.1 Research Process

We derived the design principles both from empirical and theoretical data. The field notes taken during a 6 months period of immersion as participant observers at an elementary school were transcribed into digital blocks of texts. We then coded [16] the blocks of texts and categorized the resulting codes. In parallel, we studied some of the major lines of thought in education and educational psychology, filtering and focusing on information related to the role of affect in education and children's development. The data obtained from the process of coding were in line with the information retrieved from the analysis of the literature on education and psychology. The combination of both empirical and theoretical data resulted in the Design Principles for Affectibility. The principles were tested [9] and now revised. The revised set of principles is presented in the next section.

   This paper is organized as follows: in Sect. 2 we present our revised set of Design Principles for Affectibility; and in Sect. 3 we discuss and conclude this paper.

2 Design Principles for Affectibility

2.1 PAf.1 Free Interpretation and Communication of Affect

Users should be able to communicate their feelings and emotions. Designers could make features available to allow users to express that. Rather than making systems that automatically recognize emotions, designers concerned with affective responses should leave to users the immensity of possible interpretations that the expression of emotional and affective responses may suggest. Boehner et al. [5] explain that affect and emotion are interpreted and produced culturally: the experience of a feeling (e.g., anger, lust) is grounded in a cultural context that makes that feeling (of anger, lust, etc.) meaningful. Socio-cultural aspects will determine the type of emotional responses that feelings might evoke (e.g. something to be proud of, ashamed of, etc. [5]). Sengers and Gaver [23] argue that multiple interpretations can be fruitful and design solutions should not promote only one single interpretation. We suggest that designers provide users with opportunities for open expression and interpretation through the system or application.

Guidelines: Avoid predetermining meanings (of signs, words, images, etc.) and let affect be freely expressed and interpreted; avoid automatic identification of affect; make available features to allow communication among users.

Examples: With the application proposed in [25] for the development of social skills in children, the player can choose the responses of the character of this adventure game. The choices for response include affective expressions. Another example of affective expression through art in learning technology is found in [12].

2.2 PAf.2 Pride in Social Values and Local Culture

Designers should consider users' social context, including their values and culture. Elements from users' culture and values should be taken into consideration and their presence should be made clear in the designed application. This can include associated values that are of interest to the learners or that are specific for their context. In order to understand what would be of interest to users, socio-technical and participatory approaches can be used by designers.

Guidelines: Be aware of what users are familiar with, what is important to them, what is part of their culture.

Examples: The digital storytelling proposed in [14] considers the Chinese cultural heritage. Kam et al. [11] were explicitly interested in the values and context from their target users. The authors first analyze village games that are traditional in the rural areas of India. Another famous and successful example of use of values and culture in design is Google Doodles[1], which often depicts people, holidays and other elements specific from certain countries.

2.3 PAf.3 Feeling of Identification and Appropriation with Personal Adjustments

Users should be able to tailor the application. An application that complies with this principle would be one that allows users to adjust the interface so that they feel emotionally more comfortable. Users should be able to add their own personal media or educational content, according to their needs or preferences. Material from learners' specific contexts composes more meaningful learning opportunities.

Guidelines: Allow users to set personal adjustments on interaction elements; provide different options for configuration and personalization; allow users to incorporate their own material to the system.

Examples: The Ely doll is a learning tool proposed in [1]. Its camera *"allows children to explore real-world phenomena by creating digital content to be brought into the play"* (p. 858). Other examples of tailoring in the design of educational technology include the customizable avatars proposed in [8]; a personalized search interface [4]; and personalized modules, which are based on the learners' previous achievements or based on their explicit choices [3].

2.4 PAf.4 Connectedness in Collaborative Educational Construction

The application should support users to work in collaboration in the construction of group learning. Notice that the participation of adults (teachers, parents, other relatives or professionals) can also be valuable in this process.

---

[1] https://www.google.com/doodles/about (Accessed March, 2015).

Guidelines: Provide mechanisms for group collaboration; allow communication and sharing.

Examples: 'Mobile Stories' is a mobile technology that empowers children to collaboratively read and create stories. Another example involves peer support, for example in the form of virtual guidance. This could be achieved via (online or offline) participation of more experienced peers, or help systems. Such guidance is also present in the system proposed in [15]. At Livemocha[2] – an online community where people support each other in the task of learning a foreign language – native speakers of a language can help other participants who are now learning that language by correcting their exercises and giving advices on their pronunciation. Participants can rate each other's contribution to the community, both as learners and "teachers".

2.5   PAf.5 Virtual Closeness and Social Awareness

Social awareness is related to the perception of the social context, e.g., perceiving the presence of others. This might provide a sense of proximity among users or promote collective activities. One of its purposes is to make it easier for people to express themselves and engage in collective interactions. Wallon [6] supports that affective exchanges are dependent on the presence of others, because emotions has a social basis. In this sense, applications should make the presence of others noted, providing feedback to the users. This feedback can also serve users to understand his/her own role within the activity, application or community.

Guidelines: Provide feedback on users' activity, presence, or feelings.

Examples: In a tabletop game for sustainability [24], trees change color and facial expression to show the levels of environmental damage during the game. The game also allows each player to know what his/her individual contribution to the game is. At Livemocha (See Footnote 2). users are aware of the online presence of other users who might help them in their language practices. They also know with how many friends they are connected. Knowing the online or offline status of other people is a common and popular element in diverse applications and it constitutes an example of the Design Principle of promoting virtual closeness with social awareness.

2.6   PAf.6 Setting the Mood with Varied Media and Modes of Interaction

According to Norman [18], "Emotions are contagious". In the game design field, it is already known how moods can be created by means of appropriate use of images and sounds. Like in movies, the narrative – coupled with camera zooms and increasing rhythm in the background music – can create strong emotional states in the viewer [22]. The design of learning technology should also profit from such resources. While the

---

[2] http://livemocha.com/ (Accessed March, 2015).

majority of applications already make use of media, such resources are not always used with the explicit purpose of obtaining determined affective responses from users.

Guidelines: Explore use of sounds, images (colors, shapes, contrasts, etc.), videos, tactile feedback, etc., to create varied emotional responses; explore the use of multiple modes of interaction (multimodal interaction: kinectic, tangible, voice response, etc.).

Examples: As an example of use of different media (images, videos, text compositions, sounds, etc.) in learning technology we can mention the interface for digital textbook proposed in [13]. Different media can also be explored during the design process with children. An example is reported in Tikkanen and Iivari [26].

3 Discussion and Conclusion

While some of the principles might not seem new, the new challenge lies in: (1) making affect and emotions explicit in the interaction design with (for and by) children; and (2) creating design processes and products that combine the Design Principles for Affectibility together with other recommendations (i.e., for usability, accessibility, etc.) with harmony, simplicity and beauty.

As Norman [17] discusses: "The new design challenge is to create true participatory designs coupled with true multi-media immersion that reveal new insights and create true novel experiences. We all participate, we all experience. We all design, we all partake. But much of this is meaningless: how do we provide richness and depth, enhanced through the active engagement of all, whether they be the originators or the recipients of the experience?" (p. 15). The combined use of the proposed design principles has the potential to contribute in this direction.

The Design Principles for Affectibility should direct educational applications towards more interactive systems, where learning activities can not only reflect real life (more meaningful), but actively be part of it, ubiquitously. Designers should not be limited by the examples from this article. Other uses may be further explored according to the available technology and creativity. For example, the expression of emotions can be manifested not only via textual formats; it might be interacted in body movements (e.g., strength or speed of movement) and in a collaborative and cultural rich way (e.g., traditional/typical group dances). In this paper we presented design principles aiming at improved affective responses from children, as a result of their interaction with learning technology. We derived the Design Principles for Affectibility from both empirical and theoretical research. We expect to have contributed with practical recommendations to explicitly account for affect in design processes. Future work includes deeper investigation of the principles usage, especially by other designers in their contexts, and assessing users' feedback.

References

1. Africano, D., Berg, S., Lindbergh, K., Lundholm, P., Nilbrink, F., Persson, A.: Designing tangible interfaces for children's collaboration. In: Proceedings of CHI EA 2004, pp. 853–868 (2004)

2. Anacleto, J.C., Villena, J.M.R., Silva, M.A.R., Fels, S.: Culturally sensitive computer support for creative co-authorship of a sex education game. In: Yang, H.S., Malaka, R., Hoshino, J., Han, J.H. (eds.) ICEC 2010. LNCS, vol. 6243, pp. 302–307. Springer, Heidelberg (2010)

3. Ananian, C.S., Ball, C.J., Stone, M.: Growing up with nell: a narrative interface for literacy. In: Proceedings of IDC 2012, pp. 228–231 (2012)

4. Azzopardi, L., Dowie, D., Marshall, K.A., Glassey, R.: MaSe: create your own mash-up search interface. In: Proceedings of SIGIR 2012 (2012)

5. Boehner, K., DePaula, R., Dourish, P., Sengers, P.: How emotion is made and measured. Int. J. Hum. Comput. Stud. **65**(4), 275–291 (2007)

6. Dantas, H.: A afetividade e a construção do sujeito na psicogenética de Wallon. Piaget, Vygotsky, Wallon, Teorias Psicogenéticas em Discussão, São Paulo, Summus Editorial (1992)

7. Erickson, T., Halverson, C., Kellogg, W.A., Laff, M., Wolf, T.: Social translucence: designing social infrastructures that make collective activity visible. Commun. ACM **45**(4), 40–44 (2002)

8. Given, L.M., Grotkowski, A., Fletcher, Q., Ruecker, S.: Customizable avatars for a health information system: an exploratory design. In: Proceedings of ASIS & T 2010, pp. 1–2 (2010)

9. Hayashi, E.C.S., Baranauskas, M.C.C.: Design principles for Affectibility. Technical report IC-13-17 (2013)

10. Isen, A., Daubman, K., Nowicki, G.: Positive affect facilitates creative problem solving. J. Pers. Soc. Psychol. **52**(6), 1122–1131 (1987)

11. Kam, M., Mathur, A., Kumar, A., Canny, J.: Designing digital games for rural children: a study of traditional village games in India. In: Proceedings of CHI 2009, pp. 31–40 (2009)

12. Kim, Y., Choi, J.: Affective interacting art. In: Yang, H.S., Malaka, R., Hoshino, J., Han, J.H. (eds.) ICEC 2010. LNCS, vol. 6243, pp. 413–415. Springer, Heidelberg (2010)

13. Kim, G., Yang, H.-R., Kang, K.-K., Kim, D.: Entertaining education: user friendly cutting interface for digital textbooks. In: Yang, H.S., Malaka, R., Hoshino, J., Han, J.H. (eds.) ICEC 2010. LNCS, vol. 6243, pp. 405–412. Springer, Heidelberg (2010)

14. Lu, F., Tian, F., Jiang, Y., Cao, X., Luo, W., Li, G., Zhang, X., Dai, G., Wang, H.: ShadowStory: creative and collaborative digital storytelling inspired by cultural heritage. In: Proceedings of CHI 2011, pp. 1919–1928 (2011)

15. McKinley, B., Lee, Y.L.: MyStoryMaker. In: Proceedings of CHI 2008, pp. 3219–3224 (2008)

16. Miles, M.B., Huberman, A.M.: Qualitative Data Analysis. Sage, Beverly Hills (1984)

17. Norman, D.: The transmedia design challenge: technology that is pleasurable and satisfying. Interactions **17**, 12–15 (2010)

18. Norman, D.: Living with Complexity. MIT Press, Cambridge (2011)

19. Ortony, A., Norman, D.A., Revelle, W.: Affect and proto-affect in effective functioning. In: Fellous, J.M., Arbib, M.A. (eds.) Who Needs Emotions? The Brain Meets the Machine, pp. 173–202. Oxford University Press, New York (2005)

20. Resnick, M.: Edutainment? No thanks I prefer playful learning. Associatzione Cicita **1**, 2–4 (2004)

21. Rosenkranz, M.A., Jackson, D.C., Dalton, K.M., Dolski, I., Ryff, C.D., Singer, B.H., Muller, D., Kalin, N.H., Davidson, R.J.: Affective style and in vivo immune response: neurobehavioral mechanisms. Proc. Natl. Acad. Sci. U.S.A. **100**, 11148–11152 (2003)

22. Scolari, C., Fraticelli, D.: Enunciando la interacción: Las reseñas y anticipos de videojuegos. VI Congreso Nacional de la Asociación Argentina de Semiótica, pp. 189–210 (2004)

23. Sengers, P., Gaver, B.: Staying open to interpretation. In: Proceedings of DIS 2006, pp. 99–108 (2006)
24. Tanenbaum, J., Antle, A.N., Seaborn, K., Tanenbaum, K., Bevans, A., Wang, S.: Futura: designing multi-touch tabletop games for sustainability. In: Proceedings of Games, Learning and Society Conference 6.0 (2010)
25. Thomas, J.M., DeRosier, M.E.: Toward effective game-based social skills tutoring for children: an evaluation of a social adventure game. In: Proceedings of FDG 2010 (2010)
26. Tikkanen, R., Iivari, N.: The role of music in the design process with children. In: Campos, P., Graham, N., Jorge, J., Nunes, N., Palanque, P., Winckler, M. (eds.) INTERACT 2011, Part III. LNCS, vol. 6948, pp. 288–305. Springer, Heidelberg (2011)

A Comparative Analysis of Usability Evaluation Methods on Their Versatility in the Face of Diversified User Input Methods

Daiju Ishikawa, Takashi Kato[✉], and Chigusa Kita

Graduate School of Informatics, Kansai University, 2-1-1 Ryozenjicho,
Takatsuki, Osaka 569-1095, Japan
tkato@kansai-u.ac.jp

Abstract. Every command consists of an action and an object, suggesting that a usability problem can occur whenever the user is unable to identify an appropriate action and/or the object associated with his/her current goal. The recent shift from mouse-based to touch-based interaction demands that any usability evaluation method be sensitive to not only object-related but also action-related usability problems. This study involved a total of 32 participants, four kinds of tasks differing in the difficulty of identifying objects and executing actions, and four qualitative methods of usability evaluation. Analyses of sets of observation data with concurrent and retrospective protocol by the same participant and interpretive protocol by a new participant indicate that while the oral instruction method seems least appropriate, the newly-devised narration method seems to have better prospects than the observation and the think aloud method for the usability evaluation of touch-based interaction.

Keywords: Usability evaluation method · Qualitative method · Touch-based interaction · Mouse-based interaction

1 Introduction

Although a variety of interactive devices and applications are now available, it remains unchanged that almost every command consists of an action and an object, causing usability problems to occur whenever the user is unable to identify an appropriate action and/or the object associated with his/her current goal. The present study was prompted by the recent shift from mouse-based to touch-based interaction, which demands re-focusing on the ease of specifying and executing required actions. In mouse-based interaction with the Web, for example, required actions are so simple (i.e., dragging and clicking) that most usability problems concern the ease of identifying appropriate objects. In touch-based interaction with the Web, however, various actions or gestures are available, some of which may not be so obvious to the user and/or may require rather precise execution. This suggests that any usability evaluation method for touch-based interaction need be sensitive to not only object-related but also action-related usability problems.

Involving a total of 32 participants, and four kinds of tasks that differed in the difficulty of identifying objects and executing actions, the present study examined the

© Springer International Publishing Switzerland 2015
C. Stephanidis (Ed.): HCII 2015 Posters, Part I, CCIS 528, pp. 32–37, 2015.
DOI: 10.1007/978-3-319-21380-4_6

effectiveness of four qualitative methods of usability evaluation. One particular focus was on the ability to not only identify both object-related and action-related user errors but also elicit verbal protocol that can help clarify the reasons or causes of such errors. Another focus was on the ability to control the cognitive load that might be placed on both participants and researchers in running evaluation studies. We believe that reducing the cognitive load is important in order to increase, both quantity- and quality-wise, spontaneous elicitation of verbal protocol.

2   The Usability Evaluation Methods Compared

Four usability evaluation methods compared were all qualitative methods that were designed to yield both observation and verbal protocol data. They were modified versions of the observation method, the think aloud protocol method [1], and the oral instruction protocol method [4], and a newly-devised, narration protocol method. There were two groups of four participants each for each of the four methods.

Except in the observation method, one group of four participants was asked to yield a particular type of verbal protocol specified by the method as they worked on assigned tasks (concurrent protocol, or CP) using a tablet device. The CP procedures of the three protocol methods are described below. One common feature was that the instruction was given at the start of the session and the experimenter basically refrained from intervening the participant's work during the session.

Having completed the tasks, while watching the video recordings of their own performance, the participants were asked to describe their interaction and recall their intentions at that time (retrospective protocol, or RP). They were told not to hesitate to repeat what might have been said in CP. The RP instruction was similar to, or probably less restrictive than, that used in other studies [2, 8].

Without performing any tasks themselves, another group of four participants attempted to describe what the person in the video was trying to accomplish and why (interpretive protocol, or IP). The participants were provided with the same tablet device, however, and were completely free to work on it as they deemed it necessary. IP is similar in its intent to the collegial protocol obtained from professionals describing recorded performance of their colleagues [3]. The videos were played for RP and IP without audios to avoid the effects of CP contents on the elicitation of RP and IP.

- Observation method with RP and IP
  The observation method was included as a method that could allow observation of more natural interaction between the user and the system, given the limitation that the usability testing in this study was conducted in an artificial, laboratory room. Participants were first asked to complete four assigned tasks without any additional requirement, such as CP, or any specific instructions on how to work on the tasks. They were later asked to provide RP for their own performance, for which IP was in turn obtained from a different participant.
- Think aloud method with CP, RP, and IP
  Participants were asked to verbalize what they were thinking as they performed the assigned tasks. Prompts to encourage verbalization when the participants remained

silent were intentionally kept less frequent than in a standard think aloud method [1] to avoid otherwise increased stress and anxiety on the part of the participants. RP and IP were obtained in the same way as above.

- Narration method with CP, RP, and IP
  The narration method involved a pair of a participant and an observer sitting next to the participant. The participant was asked to describe to the observer what he or she was thinking about the task, focusing particularly on the evaluation of the current state and the specification of the next goal or intention. The narration method, obviously not entirely new, was devised with the same intent of the question-asking protocol method [5] or more broadly the coaching method [6] as an alternative to the think aloud method. The main purpose was to alleviate the task demands placed on the participant by the requirement of monologue-type, real-time verbalization. The expectation was that participants would find it easier to talk to someone actually there rather than to engage in continuous, overt monologue [7]. It would also be easier for them to verbalize intentions and execute intended actions in sequence rather than to simultaneously verbalize their thinking and execute actions. The narrations elicited by the participants were treated as CP, and RP and IP were obtained in the same way as in the other methods.

- Oral instruction method with CP, RP, and IP
  The oral instruction method involved a pair of a participant and an operator. The participant was to give requests or instructions orally to the operator regarding what and how he or she would like the operator to perform on his/her behalf [4]. The participant was asked to provide as much clear and detailed instructions as possible and such oral instructions were treated as CP. The operator was actually a member of the research team and tried to be a "faithful" operator, who neither inferred the participant's intention nor performed anything unspecified in the instruction. The operator was to ask for clarification whenever the participant's instruction was not clear or specific enough. RP was provided by the participant and IP by a new participant in the same way as in the other methods.

3 Method

3.1 Participants

A total of 32 participants, 31 undergraduate students (14 males and 17 females) and one recent graduate (male), were recruited on the conditions that they were smartphone users but that they had no or little experience of using tablet devices. They were assigned to one of the eight conditions with four participants each.

3.2 Tasks and Equipment

Four kinds of tasks were devised that differed in the difficulty of identifying objects associated with goals and in the variety of actions available for participants to apply to goal-related objects. All tasks were performed using a tablet device (iPad 2 with iOS

7.0.3) in which Safari and Sketches were installed for the Web navigation and sketching tasks described below.

- Simple Objects/Single Action
  Using the Web browser, the participant was to find their university library regulation regarding the maximum number of books that can be loaned. The action needed was only that of tapping the target link and the sequence of links to be followed was short with each link being easily identifiable on each page.
- Complex Objects/Single Action
  Using the Web browser, the participant was to find the opening hours of one of their university cafeterias. The action needed was again only that of tapping the target link. However, the to-be-followed sequence of links was more complex and the correct links were more difficult to identify on the pages, due partly to the less straightforward mapping between the link names and the target information.
- Simple Objects/Multiple Actions
  The task was to group application icons on the home screen into one folder and vice versa. The objects for this task were application icons and the home button, which should not be difficult to identify. However, multiple and various actions were needed to complete the task.
- Complex Objects/Multiple Actions
  The tasks were to draw a map and save it in the photo library using Sketches and to close all the applications that remained open in the background. While these tasks demanded precise execution of a variety of actions, identifying target objects seemed more difficult, partly because explicit cues were not available for some parts of the tasks.

3.3 Procedure

Using the iPad 2, a group of 16 participants carried out the four tasks described above under one of the four evaluation method conditions. There were four participants in each method condition. Using the Latin square method, the order of the tasks was counterbalanced among four participants in each condition. Having completed the tasks, the participants engaged in the RP task. A different group of 16 participants performed the IP task with each participant randomly assigned a video of a particular participant in the other group. All sessions were video recorded, which captured the entire tablet and touchscreen operations along with all utterances made by the participant and the experimenter.

4   Results and Discussion

We first compiled usability problems encountered by any one of the 16 participants in any one of the four tasks. For each identified usability problem, we then checked to see whether or not CP (except in the observation method), RP, and/or IP were provided by any participant. Based on the compiled data, we constructed a problem-by-participant table to obtain an overview showing which evaluation method was relatively successful in identifying usability problems and obtaining related verbal protocol data. Although the number of individual cases in each method condition was small, some interesting patterns are still visible in the table, which we discuss in terms of the strengths and weaknesses of the four evaluation methods.

The oral instruction method, previously shown to be effective in identifying action-related as well as object-related usability problems [4], was least successful particularly in detecting usability problems related to more complex actions. One might think that such usability problems did not surface simply because all the actions were carried out by the experimenter on the participant's behalf. Further analysis based on one participant's CP, however, reveals a more interesting picture. Although the experimenter was careful not to infer the participant's intention or proceed beyond what was verbally requested, when it came to executing the requested action, he somehow did it right. That is, the oral instruction method may be less effective in detecting potential difficulty associated with execution of a correct action. This drawback may not be compensated for by additional verbal protocols such as RP and IP. Unless a given problem is initially pointed out in CP such that a correctly performed action by an experimenter is deviated from a participant's intention, it is next to impossible for the participant or a new participant to realize the presence of the problem afterwards. Another interesting observation was that the participants were more successful than those in the other method conditions in identifying correct links in the Web tasks, probably because the requirement of giving explicit instructions made them more attentive to the overall information on the page before giving a specific instruction. It seems that the oral instruction method is likely to underestimate usability problems concerning the execution aspect of complex actions and those caused by less careful but more natural interaction behavior on the part of the user.

Contrary to our expectation that RP and IP could supplement the lack of CP in the observation method, few IP data were obtained across the tasks, which was also the case in the other three methods. Evidently, interpreting someone's interaction behavior without one's own experience is much harder than expected for ordinary users. The amount of RP was not satisfactory either, implying that possible causes of usability problems basically would have to be inferred from observed, overt interaction behavior. However, our hunch is that RP could be increased with the experimenter's directive prompts pointing to not only overt but also potential usability problems. The observation method had one advantage over the other three methods such that the participants tended to proceed with the tasks further than those participants in the other methods, probably because they were able to better concentrate on the tasks in the absence of mandate verbalization and/or interaction with the experimenter. One might want to use the observation method to explore potential usability problems as far as possible within a given time and then to seek RP, using directive prompts, to clarify the reasons or causes behind those usability problems.

There were not major differences between the think aloud and the narration method with respect to the ability to identify usability problems. One notable difference, however, was in the variability of the amount of CP among the participants. The individual differences were much greater in the think aloud than in the narration method, partly because we did not prompt participants to verbalize as frequently as in a standard think aloud procedure, and partly because verbalization in the narration method was perceived more natural or less artificial than that in the think aloud method. While the observation method may need to be supplemented with RP, which could double the time and cost of usability testing, the narration method can be effective without RP and may be less susceptible to variability in verbalization among prospective participants.

Acknowledgments. This research was supported by JSPS KAKENHI Grant Number 25510018. Daiju Ishikawa is currently at Marubeni Information Systems Co., Ltd.

References

1. Carroll, J.M., Mack, R.L.: Learning to use a word processor: by doing, by thinking, and by knowing. In: Thomas, J.C., Schneider, M.L. (eds.) Human Factors in Computer Systems, pp. 13–51. Ablex, Norwood (1984)
2. Elling, S., Lentz, L., de Jong, M.: Retrospective think-aloud method: using eye movements as an extra cue for participants' verbalizations. In: CHI 2011 Proceedings of the SIGCHI Conference on Human Factors in Computing Systems, pp. 1161–1170. ACM, New York (2011)
3. Erlandsson, M., Jansson, A.: Verbal reports and domain-specific knowledge: a comparison between collegial and retrospective verbalisation. Cogn. Technol. Work **15**, 239–254 (2013)
4. Hori, M., Kihara, Y., Kato, T.: Investigation of indirect oral operation method for think aloud usability testing. In: Kurosu, M. (ed.) HCD 2011. LNCS, vol. 6776, pp. 38–46. Springer, Heidelberg (2011)
5. Kato, T.: What "question-asking protocols" can say about the user interface. Int. J. Man Mach. Stud. **25**, 659–673 (1986)
6. Mack, R.L., Robinson, J.B.: When novices elicit knowledge: question asking in designing, evaluating, and learning to use software. In: Hoffman, R.R. (ed.) The Psychology of Expertise: Cognitive Research and Empirical AI, pp. 245–268. Springer, New York (1992)
7. Olmsted-Hawala, E.L., Murphy, E.D., Hawala, S., Ashenfelter, K.T.: Think-aloud protocols: a comparison of three think-aloud protocols for use in testing data-dissemination web sites for usability. In: CHI 2010 Proceedings of the SIGCHI Conference on Human Factors in Computing Systems, pp. 2381–2390. ACM, New York (2010)
8. Van den Haak, M.J., de Jong, M.D.T., Schellens, P.J.: Retrospective vs. concurrent think-aloud protocols: testing the usability of an online library catalogue. Behav. Inf. Technol. **22**, 339–351 (2003)

Understanding IoT Through the Human Activity: Analogical Interpretation of IoT by Activity Theory

Narae Kim, Sangwon Lee[✉], and Taehyun Ha

Department of Interaction Science, Sungkyunkwan University,
Jongno, Seoul, Korea
narae0113@naver.com, upcircle@skku.edu,
ontophilla@gmail.com

Abstract. Currently Internet of Things (IoT) is one of the major issues in academia and industry. However, studies so far have tended to focus on technical aspects. The future technologies need to be developed in user perspectives because users center in connected situations based on IoT. As a part of addressing this issue, the present study proposes a conceptual model for the IoT process, which can be likened to a human activity process based on 'Activity Theory (AT)'. Focusing on how people actually work in IoT situations, we attempt to draw an analogy between IoT and AT in terms of three interaction types among input device, sensor/network, task of IoT device, standard/protocol, and output device. The proposed model provides new viewpoint and direction for future research in IoT domains.

Keywords: Internet of Things (IoT) · Activity theory (AT) · User-centric · Analogy analysis

1   Introduction

In the Internet of Things (IoT) paradigm, many of the objects that surround us will be on the network in one form or another and someday it will evolve into connecting everyday existing objects [5]. Some of the major IoT application areas such as health care and transportation already drew attention and successfully adapted them. In the future IoT era, operators will try many new initiatives and then will be focused on providing valuable services.

In academia, other researchers have been studied technical points of IoT particular in the area of technical structure and basic concept for more than a decade. IoT technologies continue to be an active area of research. Because of this aspect of IoT technologies has been studied considerably, the present study addresses the conceptual model of IoT by using the human activity but rather not to emphasize technical ways of IoT.

There are two reasons why this study utilizes Activity Theory (AT). First, for such a theory to be used to understand human work and learning, it must have a clearly worked out analysis of behavior that can support both experimental and analytical

© Springer International Publishing Switzerland 2015
C. Stephanidis (Ed.): HCII 2015 Posters, Part I, CCIS 528, pp. 38–42, 2015.
DOI: 10.1007/978-3-319-21380-4_7

methods of study. The need for this dual approach becomes apparent when we consider the problems of design in human performance, man–machine systems, human–computer interaction, and computer-based learning [3]. Second, AT has a simple but powerful hierarchy for describing activity that could be common coin for all HCI researchers [7]. For this reason, AT is used to portray the new IoT model in this paper.

The main purpose of analogy is to suggest the new way to view and characterize IoT through the human activity. The paper is organized as follows. Section 2 describes IoT. Section 3 presents example of the correspondence between AT and IoT. Section 4 suggests future research and applications.

2 The New Perspective of IoT

The core concept of IoT is that everyday objects can be equipped with identifying, sensing, networking and processing capabilities that will allow them to communicate with one another and with other devices and services over the Internet to achieve some useful objective [8]. In future, there will be intelligent applications for smarter homes and offices, smarter transportation systems, smarter hospitals, smarter enterprises and factories [2]. IoT holds the promise of improving people's lives through both automation and augmentation. The capabilities offered by the IoT can save people and organizations time and money as well as help improve decision making and outcomes in a wide range of application areas [8]. However, more researches need to be focused on an integration of human and IoT and how IoT services impact on users.

In this study, AT is used to generate the new IoT model which has the process and the outcome. In addition, many interconnected networks in IoT and AT are used to draw the new viewpoint.

To offer a better idea of how the new IoT process model can be operationalized, this study utilizes three types of interaction which use the tool during the interaction like Fig. 1. Figure 1 is the first generation of AT and it created the idea of the tool in the activity system. Three types of interaction all have IoT input and output devices as key components because IoT input and output devices are the axis of service execution in the IoT progress. Therefore, the present study demonstrates three types of interaction which have cause-and-effect relationships between IoT input and output devices.

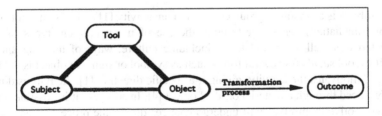

Fig. 1. Mediated relationship at the individual level in AT [6]

3   Modeling IoT with AT

Three types of interactions are the following:

(1) IoT input device ↔ Sensor/network ↔ IoT output device
(2) IoT input device ↔ Task of IoT device ↔ IoT output device
(3) IoT input device ↔ Standard/protocol ↔ IoT output device

Figure 2 is the diagram for IoT service known as Nest. This study will explain based on Fig. 2 because this is one of the processes which need tools when it interacts with others as Fig. 1. This also represents social and collective components as AT. Furthermore, it is more realistic and could be readily comprehensible. Therefore we utilize this diagram by the example of IoT progress. In Fig. 2, the IoT input device is the thermostat, sensor is the heat link, and the IoT output device would be the boiler.

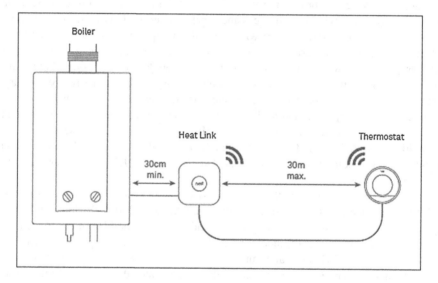

Fig. 2. The nest thermostat system

3.1   IoT Input Device ↔ Sensor/Network ↔ IoT Output Device

In AT, a subject is a person or group engaged in an activity [1] and it is an actor of AT. The tools (mediation) can occur through the use of many different types of tools, material tools as well as mental tools, including culture, ways of thinking and languages [6]. Tool stands for several forms such as symbol or sign. An object is held by a subject and motivates the activity, giving it a specific direction [1]. Activity is directed to satisfy a need through a material or ideal object [4]. In addition, it is possible that the object and motive themselves will undergo changes during the process of an activity; the object and motive will reveal themselves only in the process of doing [6]. An Outcome is a long-terms result of activity. Transforming the object into an outcome motivates the existence of the activity [6].

In IoT, the IoT input device is an agent which performs in accordance with goals and tasks. Another important elements of IoT are network and sensor as the tool in AT. Sensor and network are composed of lots of layers and those layers do many kinds of different jobs. The IoT output device refers to an object that has been modified by the subject according to required goal of activity. Execution is a result of the activity.

The IoT input device chooses the type of sensor or network depending on its cumulative experience or environment. The IoT input device also accomplishes duty by using sensor and network which make the IoT input device enable to connect other things or services. For instance, in Fig. 2, the thermostat chooses the hot link as sensor because it needs to control the boiler to keep the average room temperature also the hot link make the thermostat can connect with the boiler. To purpose of use sensor and network are to work toward a goal activity and to take a direction of activity. Finally, all the above IoT connection has some result and it is called execution. Transforming the duty into an execution motivates the existence of the doing process of IoT because IoT runs the process to achieve duty and successfully accomplished duty can appear as an execution.

3.2   IoT Input Device ↔ Task of IoT Device ↔ IoT Output Device

The division of labor informs how tasks are divided horizontally between community members as well as referring to any vertical division of power and status [1]. The division of labor refers to the explicit and implicit organization of a community as related to the transforming process of the object into the outcome [6].

The task of IoT device can be defined as a logically organized system of process to achieve the duty. The task of IoT device is conceptualized to solve tasks or problems. The task of IoT device depends on IoT input and output devices. In addition, the task of IoT device leads to the result that the IoT device can accomplish its duty and execute the service. For example, the IoT input device has to drop the temperature in Fig. 2 then 'drop the temperature' is the task of IoT device and the IoT input device runs by its own process to achieve it.

3.3   IoT Input Device ↔ Standard/Protocol ↔ IoT Output Device

Rules are guidelines and rules control activities in activity system. Rules regulate actions and interact within an activity [1]. Rules cover both explicit and implicit norms, conventions, and social relations within a community [6].

Standard and protocol in process are rules in IoT and these give guidelines how to process in IoT system. Standard and protocol also have influence on the IoT device because these rules regulate what the IoT device can and can't do. In Fig. 2, the invisible standard/protocol always controls the thermostat, the heat link and the boiler. Therefore, IoT device, sensor and network can operate properly. If there are no rules then an error could occur.

4 Discussion and Conclusion

The present paper gets the significant indication that how the IoT can be explained through the human activity. Future research needs to develop the new IoT model for the integration of human and IoT domain and the creation of new IoT services. To formulize the conceptual model for IoT process, more explicit standardization will be needed. Furthermore the new IoT perspective can be used to develop the fundamental method of the integration of human and IoT. By applying the new perspective of IoT, researchers may be able to predict properties of the future IoT and undiscovered elements.

Acknowledgments. This research was supported by the Ministry of Education, South Korea, under the Brain Korea 21 Plus Project (No. 10Z20130000013) and Basic Science Research Program (No. NRF-2014R 1A 1A2054531).

References

1. Adams, M.J., Edmond, D., Ter Hofstede, A.H.: The application of activity theory to dynamic workflow adaptation issues (2003)
2. Bandyopadhyay, D., Sen, J.: Internet of things: applications and challenges in technology and standardization. Wireless Pers. Commun. **58**(1), 49–69 (2011)
3. Bedny, G.Z., Harris, S.R.: The systemic-structural theory of activity: applications to the study of human work. Mind, cult. Act. **12**(2), 128–147 (2005)
4. Bertelsen, O.W., Bødker, S.: Activity theory. HCI Models, Theories, and Frameworks: Toward a Multidisciplinary Science, pp. 291–324 (2003)
5. Gubbi, J., Buyya, R., Marusic, S., Palaniswami, M.: Internet of Things (IoT): a vision, architectural elements, and future directions. Future Gener. Comput. Syst. **29**(7), 1645–1660 (2013)
6. Kuutti, K.: Activity theory as a potential framework for human-computer interaction research. Context and Consciousness: Activity Theory and Human-Computer Interaction, 17–44 (1996)
7. Nardi, B.A.: Context and Consciousness: Activity Theory and Human-Computer Interaction. MIT Press, Cambridge (1996)
8. Whitmore, A., Agarwal, A., Da Xu, L.: The internet of things—a survey of topics and trends. Inf. Syst. Front. **17**(2), 261–274 (2014)

A Pedagogical Approach to Usability in Serious Games

Christine Kreutzer, Madeline Marks, and Clint Bowers(⊠)

Psychology Department, University of Central Florida,
4000 Central Florida Blvd., Orlando, FL 32816, USA
{christine_kreutzer,madeline.marks}@knights.ucf.edu,
clint.bowers@ucf.edu

Abstract. Why do people learn after playing a serious game versus a game for entertainment? Serious games impart knowledge because there is a pedagogy driving the learning process. Serious games must successfully employ pedagogical methods and theories to increase the likelihood that knowledge is. The process of learning is hindered when an unusable interface demands cognitive resources that should be allocated to learning. Despite the creation of a usable system, if the player's interaction with the model is hindered, can real transfer of knowledge occur? Within the context of serious games that make use of model-based training, we suggest that a measure of pedagogical usability is warranted. The authors provide a conceptual basis for measuring pedagogical usability, specifically targeting serious games that employ modeling as the mechanism of action.

Keywords: Usability · Serious games · Pedagogy

1 Introduction

Usability has been defined as the extent to which a player is able to understand, learn, and control the functions of a system [1]. More specifically, usability focuses on the ease of use of the independent functionalities within individual components of a game (e.g. functionality of displays, player input and usefulness of in-game feedback), making it a key feature of a system [2]. Usability in serious games is of particular importance; in accordance with cognitive load theory, the process of learning is hindered when an unusable interface demands cognitive resources that should be allocated to learning [2]. Moreover, usability can influence a variety of other outcomes, such as user satisfaction [3, 4], errors [4], and attitude [5, 6].

In order for a game to be usable, developers must consider human limits in terms of memory, perception, and attention, as well as anticipate probable user errors [7]. Thus, usability should allow users to successfully execute a given task as determined by salient objectives. Despite high performance, a system is unlikely to be utilized if users are generally dissatisfied with the mechanics or interface of the system [8]. It is important to quantify how efficiently players interact with the game to both validate gameplay and further reveal insight as to the mechanics underlying serious games.

© Springer International Publishing Switzerland 2015
C. Stephanidis (Ed.): HCII 2015 Posters, Part I, CCIS 528, pp. 43–48, 2015.
DOI: 10.1007/978-3-319-21380-4_8

With this in mind, usability reflects the degree to which the system affords the user the ability to achieve objectives within a specific domain of use [9].

The last decade has seen a substantial rise in research on the emotional and affective aspects of the gaming experience. Traditional usability metrics are relevant, but must be adapted to the videogame context [10, 11]. Given the rise in interest in usability within the realm of HCI research, a variety of usability models and considerations of design principles have emerged with foci (e.g. emotion, affect, experience, pleasure, hedonic qualities) [12]. However, measures of these facets may not convey enough information about the efficacy of serious games.

2 Conceptual Basis of a New Approach Usability Evaluation

There are a variety of benefits to evaluating usability or user experience throughout the game development process [7]. Unfortunately, there are a multitude of shortcomings and challenges that inhibit the efficient and effective implementation of such evaluation. Most usability metrics are designed to evaluate traditional, task-oriented software. However, the nature of gameplay is quite different from that of traditional software [7]. Thus, this creates substantial difficulties for researchers investigating non-task-oriented software (i.e., the game industry). To overcome these difficulties, researchers have made efforts to adapt and create tools specific for the game industry. At this time, popular usability measures (e.g. efficiency) only convey how well a game is designed. These measures further fall short for the serious games designer. As such, it would be advantageous to utilize an underlying pedagogy to drive the game design process for designing serious games.

Why do people learn after playing a serious game versus a game for entertainment? Games for entertainment can be objective driven (think Call of Duty), but they are not designed to impart knowledge or skill outside of the game environment. Serious games, on the other hand, target the acquisition and transference of knowledge or skill outside the game environment. Serious games that achieve transference of knowledge do not work for the primary reason of having an eye-catching character or great theme music, rather it is the addition of an underlying pedagogy (activities that impart knowledge or skill) that is driving the learning process [13]. Therefore, serious games must successfully employ pedagogical methods and theories to increase the chance that knowledge is obtained [14]. In other words, in the field of clinical psychology, it is often said that treatment caused change; however, demonstrating cause does not explain why treatment produced change in behavior. Rather, it is a mechanism that explains how a treatment translates into events that lead to changes in behavior [15].

Given the educational nature of serious games, we suggest that usability in serious games must go above and beyond interface usability. This does not suggest that a sound underlying pedagogy will overcome all traditional UX principles; rather, despite the creation of a usable system, if the "player" does not evaluate the system as being usable can real transfer of knowledge occur? Thus, within the context of serious games that make use of model-based training, we suggest a need for a metric to assess whether a serious game integrates modeling in a user-friendly manner in serious games.

A variety of learning theories exist that have been applied to serious games [16]. Among the easiest and most effective pedagogical methods that can be implemented for serious games is behavior modeling. Modeling, as the pedagogical driver of learning and transference of knowledge, in the context described by Kazdin [15], is the mechanism of action that explains how a serious game translates into the transference of knowledge and skill. In order to effectively utilize modeling, we must first understand the history and principles of modeling.

2.1 Modeling as an Instructional Approach

Modeling has its roots in Albert Bandura's version of Social Learning Theory [16], later renamed Social Cognitive Theory [17]. Bandura explains, "Learning would be exceedingly laborious, not to mention hazardous, if people had to rely solely on the effects of their own actions to inform them what to do. Fortunately, most human behavior is learned observationally through modeling: from observing others one forms an idea of how new behaviors are performed, and on later occasions this coded information serves as a guide for action." [18, p.22] In other words, Bandura [17, 18] purported that the observer acquires an organized knowledge base, called a schema, of the modeled behavior. Later, the observer is able to drawn on the schema to execute novel behavior. With that said, it is essential to differentiate between acquisition and spontaneous performance of the observed behaviors [19].

How does modeling work? Modeling is comprised of salient behaviors to be learned, models exhibiting how to effectively execute these behaviors, opportunities for practice, feedback, and social reinforcement [18]. Specifically, Bandura [19] explains that modeling encompasses "various subsystems" [p.221]. These subsystems are: (1) attentional processes, (2) retention processes, (3) motoric reproduction processes, and (4) incentive or motivational processes.

1. *Attentional processes* explains that it is unlikely that an individual could replicate the modeled behavior, or responses, if the individual does not, "attend to, recognize, and differentiate the distinctive features of the model's responses." [19, p.222]. Serious games designers must create an environment that enables the observer, or trainees, to replicate the target behavior. The observer must be able to easily identify the model and view the demonstration of the target behavior [17, 18]. Superfluous stimuli should be kept to a minimum because it may flood the learners' attention processes, thereby misdirecting resources. In other words, the trainee is not able to devote attention to the reference stimuli being targeted for learning.
2. *Retention processes* concerns the "...long-term retention of coded modeling events." [19, p.222]. During exposure to the stimulus, the observer recodes, classifies, and reorganizes the observed elements of the target behavior into familiar and relevant representations. The translation into relevant representations allows the observer to create schemata that are more easily remembered. This is accomplished despite the lack of direct interaction with the target behavior. In other words, the observer has created a symbolic representation [19]. For these processes to occur,

serious games designers must create powerful environments that enable the observer to attend to and reproduce thru covert rehearsal [19].

3. *Motoric reproduction processes* utilizes the symbolic representation that the observer has created to guide overt performance [19]. The motoric reproduction process takes the form of rehearsal. Whether mental or physical, rehearsal is critical for retention and improved performance; however, learners may be unable to reproduce observed behaviors. The capability of the observer to reproduce the symbolic representations of the modeled behavior serves as a guide to appropriate action. Serious games designers need to provide an environment that enables the observer to rehearse the target behavior because symbolic representation alone will not result in success [19]. Thus, it is the combination of the quality of the cognitive representation and the environment that dictates whether the learner is able to reproduce the modeled behavior [20].

4. *Motivational or incentive processes* determine whether the learner will willingly exhibit the modeled behavior [21, 22]. Incentive or motivational processes can affect learning, retention, and performance. The observer creates perceptions of either positive or negative outcomes regarding the implementation of the observed behavior. Depending on the observer's conclusions regarding the outcome, the probability of the individual performing the behavior will either increase or decrease. Serious games designers need to create environments that foster motivation and self-efficacy. Bandura [22] illustrated that when the individual perceives the outcome of their behavior to produce positive incentives the observational learning promptly emerges in action.

2.2 Measuring Pedagogical Usability

The goal of a pedagogical usability metric is to evaluate the extent to which the system affords the player the opportunity to successfully complete each step of modeling. As such, each of the four subsystems of modeling as supported by theoretical and empirical work should be considered: (1) attentional processes, (2) retention processes, (3) motoric reproduction, and (4) motivational processes. Items should reflect the extent to which the model in the game was implemented into the game to accurately complete each stage of modeling.

3 Discussion

Usability testing is critical to the development of efficacious serious games. With the addition of measures that reflect underlying pedagogy, we purport that it is possible to improve the serious game design process, thereby increasing the efficacy of the learning tool. Serious games are unique in that they implement pedagogy to drive the learning process. Thus, the purpose of the present paper is to propose a theoretical basis for creating a measure of modeling in usability. The aim of the measure should be to identify the extent to which a serious game employs the pillars of modeling. We argue that games should be evaluated for the extent to which trainees have an understandable interaction with the system. More specifically, we suggest that games that utilize modeling must incorporate the four subsystems described by Bandura.

Our contribution is two-fold. First, we provide a novel notion of usability, which goes beyond traditional system usability by incorporating an evaluation of pedagogical usability. Secondly, we provide a theoretical basis for a measure that can be used at multiple points throughout the development process. The use of a measure that allows for multipoint assessment has the potential to save time and money, which is important considering the design process, is often costly. Moreover, we purport that this measure will allow designers and developers to pinpoint why a particular function does not successfully facilitate the learning process.

It is our hope to provide the serious games industry with a novel, useful, and practical measure of usability that can be utilized throughout the design process to increase the quality and efficacy of their product. By incorporating usability testing of the pedagogical approach underlying the training, the industry can ensure the production of well-designed games that have the potential to produce the anticipated learning outcomes.

References

1. Pinelle, D., Wong, N., Stach, T.: Heuristic evaluation for games: usability principles for video game design. In: Proceedings of the SIGCHI Conference on Human Factors in Computing Systems, pp. 1453–1462. ACM, April 2008
2. Olsen, T., Procci, K., Bowers, C.: Serious games usability testing: how to ensure proper usability, playability, and effectiveness. In: Marcus, A. (ed.) Design, User Experience, and Usability. Theory, Methods, Tools and Practice, pp. 625–634. Springer, Heidelberg (2011)
3. Constantine, L.L., Lockwood, L.A.: Software for Use: A Practical Guide to The Models and Methods of Usage-Centered Design. Pearson Education, Upper Saddle River (1999)
4. Nielsen, J., Phillips, V.L.: Estimating the relative usability of two interfaces: heuristic, formal, and empirical methods compared. In: Proceedings of the INTERACT 1993 and CHI 1993 Conference on Human Factors in Computing Systems, pp. 214–221. ACM May 1993
5. Preece, J.: Book Review: Developing User Interfaces: Ensuring Usability Through Product and Process by Deborah Hix and H. Rex Hartson (John Wiley and Sons, Inc., 1993). ACM SIGCHI Bulletin, 26(1), 74-75 (1994)
6. Shackel, B.: Usability-context, framework, definition, design and evaluation. Human Factors for Informatics Usability, pp. 21–37 (1991)
7. Isbister, K., Schaffer, N.: Game Usability: Advancing the Player Experience. CRC Press, Boca Raton (2008)
8. Chin, J.P., Diehl, V.A., Norman, K.L.: Development of an instrument measuring user satisfaction of the human-computer interface. In: Proceedings of the SIGCHI Conference on Human Factors in Computing Systems, pp. 213–218. ACM, May 1988
9. ISO 9241-11: Guidance on Usability, also issued by the International Organization for Standardization (1998)
10. Nacke, L., Lindley, C., Stellmach, S.: Log who's playing: psychophysiological game analysis made easy through event logging. In: Markopoulos, P., de Ruyter, B., IJsselsteijn, W.A., Rowland, D. (eds.) Fun and Games 2008. LNCS, vol. 5294, pp. 150–157. Springer, Heidelberg (2008)

11. Tychsen, A., Canossa, A.: Defining personas in games using metrics. In: Proceedings of the 2008 Conference on Future Play: Research, Play, Share, pp. 73–80. ACM, November 2008

12. Law, E.L.C., Roto, V., Hassenzahl, M., Vermeeren, A.P., Kort, J.: Understanding, scoping and defining user experience: a survey approach. In: Proceedings of the SIGCHI Conference on Human Factors in Computing Systems, pp. 719–728. ACM April 2009

13. Hassenzahl, M.: The interplay of beauty, goodness, and usability in interactive products. Hum.-Comput. Interact. **19**(4), 319–349 (2004)

14. Jordan, P.W.: Pleasure with products: human factors for body, mind and soul. In: Green, W.S., Jordan, P.W. (eds.) Human Factors in Product Design: Current Practise and Future Trends, pp. 206–217. Taylor & Francis, UK (1999)

15. Harteveld, C., Guimarães, R., Mayer, I., Bidarra, R.: Balancing pedagogy, game and reality components within a unique serious game for training levee inspection. In: Hui, K.-c., Pan, Z., Chung, RC.-k., Wang, C.C., Jin, X., Göbel, S., Li, E.C.-L. (eds.) Edutainment 2007. LNCS, vol. 4469, pp. 128–139. Springer, Heidelberg (2007)

16. Kazdin, A.E.: Mediators and mechanisms of change in psychotherapy research. Annu. Rev. Clin. Psychol. **3**, 1–27 (2007)

17. Egenfeldt-Nielsen, S.: Beyond edutainment: Exploring the educational potential of computer games (2005). Lulu.com

18. Bandura, A., Walters, R.H.: Social Learning and Personality Development. Holt Rinehart & Winston, New York (1963)

19. Bandura, A.: Social foundations of thought and behavior: A social-cognitive theory (1986)

20. Bandura, A.: Social Learning Theory. Prentice-Hall, Englewood Cliffs (1977)

21. Bandura, A.: Social-learning theory of identificatory processes. In: Goslin, D.A. (ed.) Handbook of Socialization Theory and Research, pp. 213–262. Rand McNally, Chicago (1969)

22. Bandura, A.: Influence of models' reinforcement contingencies on the acquisition of imitative responses. J. Pers. Soc. Psychol. **1**(6), 589 (1965)

Design Support Tool Using Pen Device for Simplification of Animation Design

Taiki Maruya[1(✉)], Shun'ichi Tano[1], Tomonori Hashiyama[1],
Mitsuru Iwata[1], Junko Ichino[2], and Yoichi Hyono[1]

[1] Graduate School of Information Systems,
University of Electro-Communications, 1-5-1 Chofugaoka,
Chofu, Tokyo 182-8585, Japan
maruya@media.is.uec.ac.jp,
{tano,hashiyama,miwata}@is.uec.ac.jp, hyono@cori.com
[2] Faculty of Engineering, Kagawa University, 2217-20 Hayashicho, Takamatsu,
Kagawa 761-0396, Japan
ichino@eng.kagawa-u.ac.jp

Abstract. Content using animation is widely available, and animation is often used in educational content to promote the understanding of mechanical structures and concepts. However, animations are currently created with software that requires complicated operations and programming. Such software inhibits intuitive and creative animation design. In this study, we analyze animations and determine the factors that inhibit intuitive and creative animation design. Moreover, we have developed a design support tool to make designing animations easier.

Keywords: Animation design · Pen device

1 Introduction

Animation is widely used in educational content on computers. Animated explanations of concepts and mechanical structures have become common in educational content due to the spread of e-learning. Animated explanations promote a user's understanding of concepts and mechanical structures, and abstract concepts that cannot be easily visualized by a user can be expressed by using animation. However, these animations are created with high-performance animation design software that has complicated interfaces and script language programming used for displaying the complex movements and changing attributes of animated content. For this reason, it is difficult for people who lack knowledge of and experience in animation production to create these animations, and therefore most animations are almost always created by professionals.

In addition, high-performance animation design software obstructs creative, intellectual animation design due to its complicated GUI. To compensate for the complicated GUI, there are some tools that enable the intuitive creation of animations by freehand drawing. However, these tools are not generally used due to the lack of support for the complicated movements that animated explanations require, resulting in completed animations that are of poor quality.

C. Stephanidis (Ed.): HCII 2015 Posters, Part I, CCIS 528, pp. 49–54, 2015.
DOI: 10.1007/978-3-319-21380-4_9

In this study, we have developed a design support tool to make designing animations easier and implemented a prototype of the tool.

2 Analysis of Animation

Animations were analyzed to identify the types of animation that the tool should support. We classified animation into two levels of expression: external and internal. The external level of expression was defined as animation that highlights elements of content designed to attract a user's attention and elements of decoration designed to entertain a user, such as flashing banner advertisements. The internal expression level was defined as animation that promotes a user's understanding, such as animations that illustrate mechanical structures.

Animations that belong to the internal level of expression are mainly used in four areas. The GUI animations of operation systems are used for usability improvement. PowerPoint animations are used to explain content; however, creating complicated animations in PowerPoint is difficult. Likewise, motion graphic animations and web animations are used for expressing complicated concepts. Therefore, these animations are used for explanations. However, since creating complicated explanatory animations is difficult, these animations can usually only be designed by experts. Therefore, a support tool for novice animators is require (Fig. 1).

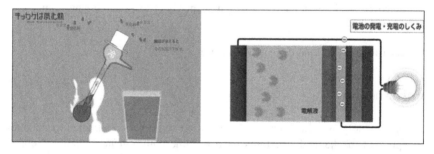

Fig. 1. Examples of animations having an internal level of expression

3 Related Work

Animation design is classified into object design and motion design processes. We investigated previous design methods and previous studies on each design process. In object design, high-performance drawing software is usually used. However, using the complicated GUI and feature-rich drawing tools found in high-performance drawing software distracts the user from visualizing the overall concept of the design. SILK [1] and DENIM [2] solve this problem by using handwriting in the GUI design and web design. In motion design, movie making software is usually used. However, complicated software operations and programming skills are necessary to use movie making software; therefore, design in accordance with intention is difficult. KOKA [3] enables the user to intuitively define motions by drawing an effect line with a pen device, which solves this problem.

Animation creating software that enables the user to design both objects and motions exists. With such software, similar problems to those found in SILK, DENIM, and KOKA occur in both processes. K-Sketch [4] solves these problems by having object design performed by handwriting and motion design defined by the stroke of a pen device.

Three problems have been pointed out by previous studies.

1. Objects must be designed before motions.
2. Quality of the finished animations remains low.
3. Supported motions are restricted.

First, in existing tools, motion can be predicted from the form and direction of the object, which inhibits free motion design. Second, using handwriting in the design process is effective; however, handwriting design tools cannot generate the regular objects and motions that are made with high-performance drawing tools. Third, it is difficult to define the timing between a large number of motions and the motions of joints. We designed our tool to solve these problems. Figure 2 shows the functions necessary for the proposed tool.

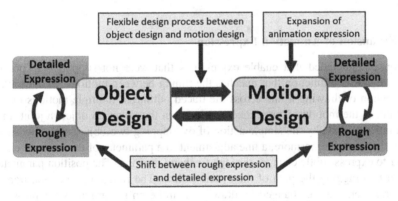

Fig. 2. Necessary functions for proposed tool

4 Tool Design

4.1 Basic Interaction

The basic definition method for motion in our tool is a real-time parameter definition based on freehand drawing input using the pen device. This is based on a recording method used by K-Sketch. First, the user chooses the kind of parameter to record from the list. Next, the user presses the "record" button and makes the system record the wait state and then the position of the stroke pen on the canvas. The position parameter defines the input of the pen stroke, and the traced outline of the motion appears on the canvas. The rotation parameter is recorded by drawing circular strokes around the center of the canvas. The scale and transparency parameters are recorded by drawing a vertical stroke on the canvas. The color parameter is recorded by drawing a stroke on the color-bar displayed on the canvas.

4.2 Flexible Design Process Between Object Design and Motion Design

Our tool comprises two screens: a motion design screen and an object design screen, and the user can create animations while transitioning between the two screens. The user can take a trial and error approach depending on the animation, making a flexible designs process in the creation of animations possible while designing both objects and motions.

4.3 Shift Between Rough Expression and Detailed Expression

Our tool can shift between rough expression such as freehand drawing and detailed expression such as that found in the design of geometric figures and fonts. This function is realized by character recognition and figure recognition algorithms. The user can progressively shift the level of detail by operating a slider in the UI. Therefore, this function provides not only design by the rough expression of freehand drawing but also results in orderly, completed animations.

4.4 Expansion of Animation Expression

Functions are included that enable expressions that were not supported in previous tools. The first is a function that matches the timing between motions. In our tool, the simple action of drawing a line across the traced outline of multiple motions matches the timing of the motions. The second is a function that gives an object a joint. In our tool, joints are made by the simple action of overlapping two objects and choosing an axis for the joint. Furthermore, a fine adjustment to a parameter of the function enables the user to express subtle changes through freehand drawing. The position parameter is changed by dragging the path of the traced outline. The rotation, scale, and transparency parameters can be changed by drawing a stroke on the graph that expresses the value of the parameter. The color parameter is changed by using an original UI that can define gradation between any two points (Fig. 3).

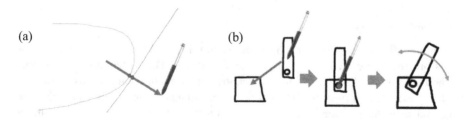

Fig. 3. (a) Example of timing matching function: match timing at red points (b) Example of joint creating function: drag objects and overlap them, and then tap axis (Color figure online).

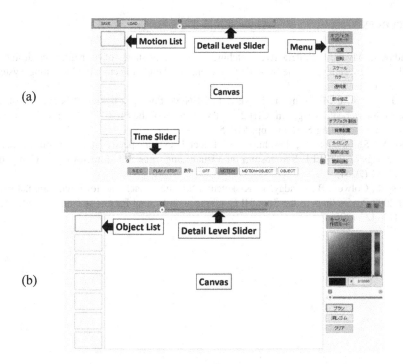

Fig. 4. (a) Motion design screen, (b) Object design screen

4.5 Prototype Tool

The prototype tool was implemented on a Windows PC. It was developed using JavaScript and worked on a web browser. The hardware used for input and output was a liquid crystalline pen tablet (Cintiq 24HD Touch) produced by Wacom. The prototype system included all of the functions described in Sect. 4 of this paper. However, character recognition and figure recognition support exist only for some characters and figures (Fig. 4).

5   Conclusion and Future Work

In this study, we have analyzed animations and pointed out problems in designing animations. Furthermore, we have developed and prototyped a design support tool for creating animations that aims to solve the problems inexperienced people have with animation production. In our future work, we will evaluate our tool and confirm the effectiveness of the proposed functions. In addition, we will improve the character recognition and figure recognition performance of our tool.

References

1. Landay, J., Myers, B.: Interactive sketching for the early stages of user interface design. In: CHI 1995 Proceedings of the SIGCHI Conference on Human Factors in Computing Systems, pp. 43–50 (1995)
2. Lin, J., Newman, M., Hong, J., Landay, J.: DENIM: finding a tighter fit between tools and practice for web site design. In: CHI 2000 Proceedings of the SIGCHI Conference on Human Factors in Computing Systems, pp. 510–517 (2000)
3. Kato, Y., Shibayama, E., Takahashi, S.: Effect lines for specifying animation effects. In: Proceedings of the IEEE Symposium on Visual Languages and Human-Centric Computing, pp. 27–34 (2004)
4. Davis, R., Colwell, B., Landay, J.: K-sketch: a 'kinetic' sketch pad for novice animators. In: CHI 2008 Proceedings of the SIGCHI Conference on Human Factors in Computing Systems, pp. 413–422 (2008)

User Experience and Other People: On User Experience Evaluation Framework for Human-Centered Design

Hiroyuki Miki[(✉)]

Oki Consulting Solutions Co., Ltd., 4-11-15, Shibaura, Minato,
Tokyo 105-0023, Japan
hmiki@cf.netyou.jp

Abstract. Recently, the word "User Experience (UX)" has been often used in usability-related areas such as web design and system design. Although it was defined in ISO 9241-210 and its importance has been growing, details of the notion and results of introduction of it have not been well clarified yet. In the previous paper, a new integrated evaluation framework of usability and UX, based on ISO 9241-11 and ACSI (American Customer Satisfaction Index) was proposed. Since the proposed framework does not consider influences to other people by the utilization but considers only interactions of a user with a product or service, it may be narrow-minded in a social age. Thus, this paper slightly extends the framework to consider influences to other people by the utilization in the related context of use.

Keywords: User experience · Usability · ISO 9241 · ISO 13407 · ISO/IEC 25010 · Evaluation framework · American customer satisfaction index

1 Introduction

Recently, the word "User Experience (UX)" has been often used in usability-related areas such as web design and system design [2, 6–11]. Although it was defined in ISO 9241-210 [6] and its importance has been growing, details of the notion and results of introduction of it have not been well clarified yet. In the previous paper [8], a new integrated evaluation framework of usability and UX, based on ISO 9241-11 [5] and ACSI (American Customer Satisfaction Index) [1] was proposed (Fig. 1).

In HCII 2014, one participant questioned that the proposed framework is so inclined to a user who interacts with a product or service that it neglects to consider negative influences to other people nearby by the utilization. For example, when a user uses a portable game machine, the framework explains only a degree of effective, efficiency, and user experience of the user. Even if the utilization annoys other people nearby, the framework does not consider it. Since we are in a highly social age with SNS and other media these days, it will be considerate to care influences to other people by the utilization in the intended context of use.

Thus, this paper slightly extends the framework to consider influences to other people by the utilization in the related context of use. In the following, firstly the

C. Stephanidis (Ed.): HCII 2015 Posters, Part I, CCIS 528, pp. 55–59, 2015.
DOI: 10.1007/978-3-319-21380-4_10

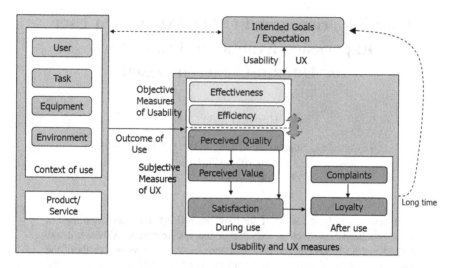

Fig. 1. Integrated evaluation framework of usability and UX at HCII 2014

previous framework is briefly explained, followed by issues to consider, revised framework, and conclusion.

2 Previous Framework

Since international standards are important in doing business worldwide, the previous framework (Fig. 1) was created based on the usability framework of ISO 9241 part11. In the creation, firstly ergonomics standards were considered followed by secondary other standards in related areas and lastly other well-known frameworks. ACSI (American Customer Satisfaction Index) was adopted to explicate satisfaction; Satisfaction in ISO 9241 part11 was replaced by the subjective measures of ACSI.

In Fig. 1, when considering usability and UX of a product or a service, tasks are conducted in a specific context of use with intended goals and expectations, and outcome of the use is measured objectively by effectiveness and efficiency and measured subjectively by perceived quality and value, satisfaction, complaints, and loyalty.

Although objective measures are still represented by effectiveness and efficiency, subjective measures are represented by UX measures derived from ACSI. Figure 1 represents both objective measures and subjective measures of UX.

While objective measures are what designers want to measure, subjective measures of UX are supposed to represent as close user's subjective evaluations as possible. Basically, there is no direct connection between effectiveness and efficiency, and the subjective measures of UX. However, if measures of effectiveness and efficiency are well designed enough to represent user's subjective evaluation of perceived quality, perceived value, and possibly other measures of UX, the connection will be tighter. When considering UX, effectiveness and efficiency need to be reevaluated by perceived quality and perceived value toward satisfaction.

With minimum changes to the usability framework of ISO 9241 part11, the integrated framework represents UX evaluation as well.

3 Issues to Consider

When considering influences to other people nearby in the Fig. 1 framework, there are at least two issues to take care of: one is how to treat other people nearby in the context of use area in the left half of the Fig. 1, and the other is how to measure the influences in the measuring part of Fig. 1, namely lower right of Fig. 1. In this section, these two issues are considered from the related international standards: ISO 9241 part11, part 210, and ISO/IEC 25010 [4]. While ISO 9241 part11 (measurement framework of usability) and part 210 (Human-centred design) are ergonomics standards, ISO/IEC 25010 is a part of software quality standards which defines system and software quality models.

3.1 Other People in "Context of Use"

As shown in the left half of Fig. 1, "context of use" consists of "user", "task", "equipment", and "environment". Since "user" appears to be most relevant to "other people" in "context of use", it is firstly investigated. There are different definitions of "user" between ISO 9241 part11 and ISO/IEC 25010. While "user" is defined as "person who interacts with the product" in ISO 9241 part11, it is defined as "individual or group that interacts with a system or benefits from a system during its utilization" in ISO/IEC 25010. Latter part of ISO/IEC 25010 definition is an evident addition to the definition of ISO 9241 part11. ISO/IEC 25010 considers "user" as not only a person who interact with a product or service but also a person who benefits from the utilization. However, other people nearby who receive negative influences do not seem to be involved.

Other than "user", since both ISO/IEC 25010 and ISO 9241 part 210 have the same definition related to a person, namely "stakeholder", it is investigated secondly. "Stakeholder" usually means those who are affected by success or failure of a task. Since other people nearby are usually irrelevant to success or failure of a task, it is also different from other people nearby.

Finally, "environment" is investigated. By definition, "environment" consists of "physical environment" and "social environment". Since other people nearby can be a part of "social environment", it will be possible to consider that "context of use" of Fig. 1 covers other people nearby.

In conclusion, there are two possibilities to consider other people nearby in "context of use" of Fig. 1. One possibility is no change of Fig. 1 that considers "environment" includes other people nearby. The other possibility is to add "Other people" to "context of use" explicitly. Not to mention, the latter choice will be more explicit. The latter choice will be also appropriate when emphasizing accessibility aspect of the framework since considering different characteristics of people is very important in considering accessibility [3].

3.2   Influences on Other People in the Intended Context of Use

In the lower right of Fig. 1, "influences on other people" might be expressed in each of effectiveness and efficiency. However, since a factor of "influences on other people" inhibits effectiveness and efficiency, it is better to be represented as an independent measure.

When adding a measure of "influences on other people" to effectiveness and efficiency, "quality in use" in ISO/IEC 25010 is informative since "quality in use" is coined after ISO 9241 part11 with reference to usability of ISO 9241 part11. While usability of ISO 9241 part11 consists of only effectiveness, efficiency, and satisfaction, "freedom from risk" and "context coverage" are added in "quality in use". "Influences on other people" are related to these two measures. In the sense that "influences on other people" requires an extension of "context coverage", it is related. In the sense that "freedom from risk" inhibits effectiveness and efficiency, it is related as well.

In conclusion, both "freedom from risk" and "context coverage" can be candidates for the extension of the Fig. 1.

4   Revised Framework

Revised framework is shown in Fig. 2. "Other people" are explicitly added to "context of use". "Freedom from risk" is rephrased as "risk mitigation" since risk free is usually unthinkable. "Context coverage" is not added since "other people" is already explicitly added to "context of use".

With respect to relations between object measures and subjective measure, results of objective measures are reevaluated in subjective measures. In this sense, no matter how objective measures are calculated, subjective measures are not affected at all if the user does not perceive "influences on other people". UX measures entirely depend on the user.

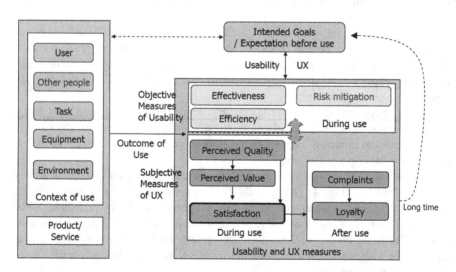

Fig. 2. Revised integrated evaluation framework of usability and UX

When "influences on other people" must be considered in the subjective part, there will be two choices. First is to replace the subjective measures part with "satisfaction" only as in ISO 9241 part11 and to measure "satisfaction" by a combined measure of the user's satisfaction and other people's satisfactions. Second is to design a product or service to make the user consider "influences on other people" or to design a product or service well to prevent "influences on other people" in order that the user does not need to care about "influences on other people".

5 Concluding Remarks

In the previous paper, an integrated evaluation framework of usability and UX was proposed. This paper proposed a revised integrated evaluation framework of usability and UX to include "influences on other people".

Since UX is a complex notion [2, 6–11], the integrated new framework is expected to be applied to and examined against real applications. Results of this paper are also expected to be considered in the creation of UX related international standards.

References

1. ACSI: The American Customer Satisfaction Index. http://www.theacsi.org/the-american-customer-satisfaction-index
2. Hartson, R., Pyla, P.S.: The UX Book: Process and Guidelines for Ensuring a Quality User Experience. Morgan Kaufmann, Amsterdam (2012)
3. ISO/IEC Guide 71: Guide for addressing accessibility in standards. ISO (2014)
4. ISO/IEC 25010: Systems and software engineering – Systems and software Quality Requirements and Evaluation (SQuaRE) – System and software quality models. ISO (2011)
5. ISO 9241-11: Ergonomic requirements for office work with visual display terminals (VDTs) – Part11: Guidance on usability. ISO (1998)
6. ISO 9241-210: Ergonomics of human-system interaction – Part 210: Human-centred design for interactive systems. ISO (2010)
7. Kurosu, M.: The conceptual model of experience engineering (XE). In: Kurosu, M. (ed.) HCII/HCI 2013, Part I. LNCS, vol. 8004, pp. 95–102. Springer, Heidelberg (2013)
8. Miki, H.: User experience evaluation framework for human-centered design. In: Yamamoto, S. (ed.) HCI 2014, Part I. LNCS, vol. 8521, pp. 602–612. Springer, Heidelberg (2014)
9. Roto, V., et al.: User Experience White Paper. http://www.allaboutux.org/uxwhitepaper (electronic version) (2011)
10. Sauro, J., Lewis, J.R.: Quantifying the User Experience. Morgan Kaufmann, Waltham (2012)
11. Tullis, T., Albert, B.: Measuring the User Experience. Morgan Kaufmann, San Francisco (2008)

Universal Usability in Mass Media via Discourse Analysis: A Case Study

Stefanie Niklander[1]([⊠]), Ricardo Soto[2,3,4], and Broderick Crawford[2,5,6]

[1] Universidad Adolfo Ibañez, Santiago, Chile
stefanie.niklander@uai.cl
[2] Pontificia Universidad Católica de Valparaíso, Valparaíso, Chile
{ricardo.soto,broderick.crawford}@ucv.cl
[3] Universidad Autónoma de Chile, Santiago, Chile
[4] Universidad Científica del Sur, Lima, Perú
[5] Universidad Central de Chile, Santiago, Chile
[6] Universidad San Sebastián, Santiago, Chile

Abstract. The Mass Media involve mechanisms that are intended to reach a wide audience by means of radio, television, newspapers, and Internet, among others. The Mass Media are also responsible for providing the suitable perception of news from different areas such as for instance politics, business, crime, or technology. However, this perception is often manipulated in order to accommodate the information according to a given criteria. This manipulation of the information is suddenly not captured by everyone causing a distortion of the real scenario. In this paper, we illustrate how the use of discourse analysis can improve understanding of such hidden information. We present a case study where this methodology is effectively used to analyze the information provided by news about a social phenomena related to the dehumanization of the female gender. Interesting results are discussed about how this useful methodology could be used to detect communication products that are not usable nor understandable for a wide audience.

Keywords: Discourse analysis · Universal usability · Mass Media

1 Introduction

The Mass Media involve mechanisms that are intended to reach a wide audience by means of a given communication form. The mechanisms via which this communication takes place may vary, for instance electronically such as radio, television, and Internet; and also in print form such as newspapers, books, and magazines. Regardless of the employed communication form, Mass Media constitute a privileged platform to distribute information. They are responsible for providing the suitable perception of news related to different areas such as politics, business, crime, technology, sports, and entertainment among others. However, this perception is often manipulated by handling the speeches, contexts, and images in order to accommodate the information according to a criteria imposed

© Springer International Publishing Switzerland 2015
C. Stephanidis (Ed.): HCII 2015 Posters, Part I, CCIS 528, pp. 60–63, 2015.
DOI: 10.1007/978-3-319-21380-4_11

for instance by the political tendency of the media, by government influences, or to force an ideology. This manipulation of the information is suddenly not captured by everyone causing a distortion of the real scenario.

In this paper, we illustrate how the use of discourse analysis can improve understanding of information provided by Mass Media in a universal usability context [3]. Discourse analysis [4] is a qualitative and interpretive methodology for analyzing social phenomena through any communication mechanism. It allows us to understand the way that social power abuse, inequality, and dominance are reproduced and enacted in the social context. We present a case study where this methodology is effectively used to gather and analyze the information that really aims at transmitting a popular Chilean newspaper with respect to a social phenomena related to the dehumanization of the female gender. Interesting results are discussed about how this useful methodology could be used to detect communication products that are not usable nor understandable for a wide audience.

2   Results and Discussion

In this paper, we employ discourse analysis as a research technique to observe how the female gender representation [1] is constructed in the chosen Mass Media. This technique allow us to analyze the language used by journalists, which take part and influence the representation of the female gender in the society. In particular, we select the "La Cuarta" newspaper as is a popular newspaper with a particular writing style. We refer to style as the personality that is introduced into the writing on the given subject. We analyze 97 news from the "La Cuarta" newspaper, from which the female gender was present on 39, those 39 appearances have been classified on three categories: female victim, woman sexual object, and fighter-professional discredited woman. From the 39 appearances, 5 correspond to the first category, 27 to woman sexual object, and 7 to fighter-professional discredited woman. Details about the three categories are given in the following:

Female Victim. This situation is caused when women are seen as victim because they suffer due to men actions. The 75 % of cases in which women are victims is produced by infidelity. We observe also that women appear in news by events of his private life which are clearly irrelevant for anyone. This lead us to conclude that the female gender is present in Mass Media only in minor issues, being unable to appear in news related to relevant topics for the country. The idea behind these messages is to relate the female gender with weak people only appearing in irrelevant news and constantly suffering because of man. In contrast, men are presented as "super-males" who control the couple relationships and have the power to deceive. Now, regarding the images related to news where the woman is constructed as a victim, all graphic elements present women as young people (not exceeding 35 years), sensual, smiling, even though all of them are living painful situations.

Woman Sexual Object. The texts where women are constructed as sexual objects abound in the "La Cuarta" newspaper. In these cases a dehumanized construction of female gender is presented. The woman exists and is displayed as a product to observe and be consumed by the male gender; its purpose on the newspaper cover, is being desired by man. Constant infantilization to which women are subject in this media is also observed. This happens when childlike qualities are attributed by diminutives. These situations take away credibility to women and to their speeches. Indeed, news sources are only of minor importance, being unable voices to act on more relevant thematics. As the news where the female is portrayed as a victim, the information where they are presented as sexual objects are also located on important parts of the newspaper cover. Again, in the images accompanying the texts, woman are always exposed with sensual and light clothing, smiling and using poses related to sex.

Fighter-Professional Discredited Woman. We observed that female gender is also represented as a fighter. In the analyzed texts, they appear to be envious of other women, reason why they constantly criticize and disqualify each other. They are built as conflicting people and capable of exposing her private life to achieve fame. Therefore, they have no limits when they attempt to get they want. The aforementioned can be seen as a new element used by the media to undermine the construction of the female gender. The woman disputes are motivated by unimportant situations, they are not clashes that produce changes in the country, they are disputes that have no laudable purpose. In these news, as in other ones, the use of double-entendre is repeated. Regarding the use of images, the same tendency occurs, that is, smiling and sensual women, and suddenly their breasts and buttocks are almost uncovered.

These results demonstrate a clear manipulation of speeches, contexts, and images in order to represent the woman as an inferior gender compared to men. As stated in [2], this can be considered dangerous in the sense that this manipulation can have a great influence on the construction of social representations of gender and the roles that each should play in society. Then, regarding this concern from an universal usability standpoint, the "La Cuarta" newspaper is not an usable nor understandable communication product for every citizen, since it generates a forced and negative representation of the female gender via manipulated and hidden messages.

3   Conclusions and Future Work

In this paper, we have employed discourse analysis for understanding the hidden messages embedded in news related to the female gender representation. The news have been gathered from a popular newspaper called "La Cuarta". We have analyzed 97 news, where the female gender was present on 39. We have detected three categories: female victim, woman sexual object, and fighter-professional discredited woman. After applying the analysis, we have observed a clear inferiority of the women representation with respect to men, where woman is always seen as a subordinated object. Based on [2], we conclude that this is dangerous since this manipulation can have an important influence on the construction of social representations in society. We have also observed a connection between discourse analysis and the universal usability concept. In fact, the "La Cuarta" newspaper is not an usable nor understandable communication product for every citizen, since it generates a forced and negative representation of the female gender via manipulated messages.

We visualize different research directions to follow, the most straightforward one is to employ the same technique to discover new social phenomena in Mass Media. Another interesting idea is to automatize the discourse analysis process to validate if a given communication product is usable and understandable for every citizen. Finally, we aim to employ the same methodology to explore analogous social behaviors on social networks.

Acknowledgements. Ricardo Soto is supported by Grant CONICYT/FONDECYT/ INICIACION/11130459 and Broderick Crawford is supported by Grant CONICYT/ FONDECYT/REGULAR/1140897

References

1. Moscovici, S.: On social representation. In: Forgas, J.P. (ed.) Social Cognition. Perpectives in Everyday Life. Academic Press, London (1981)
2. Nash, N.: Defying Male Civilization: Women in the Spanish Civil War (Women and Modern Revolution Series). Arden Press, Denver (1995)
3. Shneiderman, B.: Universal usability. Commun. ACM **43**(5), 84–91 (2000)
4. Van Dijk, T.A.: Racism and Discourse in Latin America. Lexington Books, Lanham (2009)

International and Regional Standards
for Usability and User Experience

Linghua Ran[1], Yanfang Liu[2], Wen Li[2], and Xin Zhang[1(✉)]

[1] Ergonomics Laboratory, China National Institute of Standardization,
Beijing, China
{ranlh, zhangx}@cnis.gov.cn
[2] User and Market Research Department, China Mobile Research Institute,
Beijing, China
{liuyanfang, liwen}@chinamobile.com

Abstract. This article makes an investigation on international and regional standards highly related to the usability and user experience through looking up relevant committees and sub-committees and by key words and standard-tracing on the websites of the main organizations for standardization, including ISO, ISO/IEC, IEC, ETSI, ITU, etc., and briefly introduces and analyzes the history, status and trend of development for the usability and user experience standardization.

Keywords: Standards · Standardization · Usability · User experience

1 Definition of Usability and User Experience in Standards

Since 1990s, ISO began to make standards about usability and user experience. In 1998, the definition of usability was made by ISO 9241-11:2008 [1] of ISO/TC 159/SC4 [2]. Later, the concept of user experience was first introduced in ISO standard system by ISO 9241-210:2010 [3]. The object in the definition of usability in ISO 9241-11 is very broad, while the definition in ISO/IEC, ITU and ETSI is restricted to software and ICT products. They use the term quality in use and quality of experience rather than usability.

2 Relevant International and Regional Organizations

At present, the main influential international organizations for standardization including ISO [4], ISO/IEC [5], IEC and ITU [6], and some regional organizations for standardization related to science and technology including CEN [7], ETSI [8], 3GPP [9], all began to formulate the standards of usability and user experience and established the related committee and working team (see Fig. 1).

© Springer International Publishing Switzerland 2015
C. Stephanidis (Ed.): HCII 2015 Posters, Part I, CCIS 528, pp. 64–68, 2015.
DOI: 10.1007/978-3-319-21380-4_12

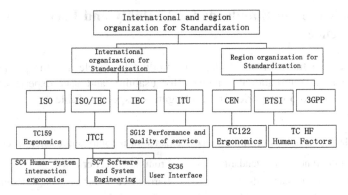

Fig. 1. International and regional organizations for standardization related to usability and user experience

3 Current International Standards for Usability and User Experience

Through looking up relevant sub-committees, key words and standard tracing in several websites of organization for standardization, we can find standards highly related to usability and user experience. These key words include human factors, ergonomics, usability, user experience, interaction, user interface, quality of experience, quality in use, accessibility, and etc. By the end of 2014, there were a total of 113 standards. Among these standards, the number of standards in ISO is highest, which accounts for 46 %. The second is ETSI, accounting for 27 %. In the perspective of its established time (see Fig. 2), the standard numbers began to increase since 2000, reached the highest from 2006 to 2011 and fell a little from 2012 to 2014.

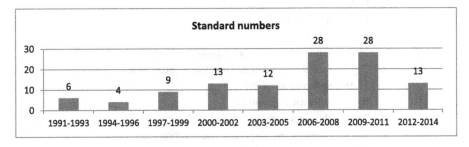

Fig. 2. Numbers and publication time for usability and user experience standards

4 Classification of Standards for Usability and User Experience

According to the function of standards in product life cycle and the perspective of objected-oriented, international standards for usability and user experience can be mainly divided into 5 categories and 6 categories respectively (Table 1).

Table 1. Categories of international standards for usability and user experience

From the function of standards	From the object-oriented
General design standards	Barrier free design or general design
Standards for specific fields or products	Software & Internet
Standards for specific module or factor	Daily necessities
Standards for the process	ICT products
Standards for the assessment	Mobile terminal
	Medical products

5 Characteristics of Standards in Different Organizations for Standardization

5.1 Standards in ISO/TC159/SC4

There are 11 working teams under the leadership of the sub-committee of SC4. The ISO 9241 standards were compiled by ISO/TC 159/SC 4. The ISO 9241 standards have had more impact. With the development of science and technology as well as human-computer interaction, these standards have been revised for several times since their release in 1992 and becoming more complete and extensive (Table 2).

Table 2. ISO 9241 standards system

Past	Title
1	Introduction
2	Job design
11	Hardware and software usability
20	Accessibility and human-system interaction
21–99	Reserved numbers
100	Software ergonomics
200	Human-system interaction processes
300	Displays and display-related hardware
400	Physical input devices-Ergonomics principles
500	Workplace ergonomics
600	Environment ergonomics

5.2 International Electrotechnical Commission (IEC)

The standards for usability and user experience made independently by IEC all possess specific industry application background and concentrate on one kind of equipment. For example, IEC 60601-1-6 standards are made for the regulation of medical electronic apparatus availability, IEC TR 61997 and IEC TR 62678 standards are made for the availability in the user interface of multimedia and system design.

5.3 ISO/IEC JTC1

ISO/IEC JTC1/SC7 and SC35 in this committee are closely related to the user experience. The Common Industry Format for usability of ISO/IEC 25060–25099 in ISO/IEC JTC1/SC35 lists many items of information about the usability of product availability. It can make a black box quantitative test, supporting human-centered design in human-computer interactive system.

5.4 International Telecommunication Union (ITU SG12)

At present, there are 13 research groups in International Telecommunication Union. With the development of 3G business, the SG12 research group works for property and quality of service (business). This group devotes to many research subjects such as terminal, multimedia and subjective evaluation, objective model and tool of multimedia quality assessment, multimedia QoS and QoE.

5.5 World Wide Web Consortium (W3C)

World Wide Web Consortium (W3C) is the most authoritative and influential technical standard organization with international neutrality. Among the Web standards published by W3C, WCAG 2.0 focuses on user experience in a broad sense. It can help domestic consumers to better use except free barrier.

5.6 European Committee for Standardization (CEN/TC122)

The European Committee for Standardization (CEN) has set up human ergonomics technical committee for standardization, which was named CEN/TC122. Now CEN/TC122 has seven working groups. Most standards made by CEN/TC122 can be directly changed into ISO standards.

5.7 European Telecommunications Standards Institute (ETSI)

The relevant standards are compiled by TC HF. TC HF will make thorough background research about human factor issues, which makes ETSI outstanding than other standard organizations and human factor businesses (Fig. 3).

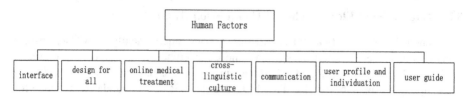

Fig. 3. Working groups in TC HF

5.8   3rd Generation Partnership Project

3GPP has made QoE index to PSS and end-to-end multimedia services. 3GPP PSS client will implement the quality assessment consistent with the definition of assessment, collect the client QoE observed value and send the observed value of the QoE transport protocol reports to the PSS server.

Acknowledgment. This work is supported by the National Key Technology R&D Program (project number: 2014BAK01B01) and China National Institute of Standardization through the "special funds for the basic R&D undertakings by welfare research institutions" (project number: 522014Y-3346).

References

1. ISO 9241-11: Ergonomic requirements for office work with visual display terminals (VDTs) - Part 11: Guidance on usability (2008)
2. http://www.iso.org/iso/home/standards_development/list_of_iso_technical_committees/iso_technical_committee.htm?commid=53372
3. ISO 9241-210: Ergonomics of human-system interaction – Part 210: Human-centred design for interactive systems (2010)
4. http://www.iso.org/iso/home/standards.htm
5. http://www.iso.org/iso/home/standards_development/who-develops-iso-standards.htm
6. http://jtc1-sc7.logti.etsmtl.ca/
7. http://www.itu.int/en/ITU-T/about/groups/Pages/sg12.aspx
8. http://www.cen.eu/Pages/default.aspx
9. http://www.etsi.org/
10. http://www.3gpp.org/

A Framework Proposal of UX Evaluation of the Contents Consistency on Multi Screens

Wangmi Seok[✉]

Faculty of Design, Okayama Prefectural University, Okayama, Japan
seok@dgn.oka-pu.ac.jp

Abstract. In the study, we attempts to define coherent experience as those where user experience is maintained in a harmonious and coherent manner in a multi-screen environment, and identify the items that offer such experience. If user experiences are provided naturally and consistently without any sense of difference, irrespective of the change of devices when user utilize the contents, loyalty to the contents will be increased automatically. In this study, specific guidelines of each screen are produced, which should be observed to provide consistent user experiences.

Keywords: Multi screen · Consistency · UX evaluation

1 Research Background and Purpose

Technology development enabled users to access same content from the various devices, and along with this trends, cognitions or usage behaviors of the contents use have changed rapidly.

Users request the efficient user experience from their perspective, which is using same contents from various devices seamlessly and using them without any additional training. User experience indicates everything internalized while using the product or services, which are feeling, memory, and satisfaction including experience. In this study, user experiences from multiscreen environment, as described above, are named as coherent experience, and are defined as [coherence of holistic experiences from the task completion, in spite of the variation of user interfaces provided by each screen, when users access contents through the screen]. In order to provide such user environment, contents producers should design user interface of each screen with a set of rules which are all encompassing although physical environment of each screen, that is sizes or operation methods, are different. If user experiences are provided naturally and consistently without any sense of difference, irrespective of the change of devices when user utilize the contents, loyalty to the contents will be increased automatically. In this study, specific guidelines of each screen are produced, which should be observed to provide consistent user experiences (Fig. 1).

© Springer International Publishing Switzerland 2015
C. Stephanidis (Ed.): HCII 2015 Posters, Part I, CCIS 528, pp. 69–73, 2015.
DOI: 10.1007/978-3-319-21380-4_13

Fig. 1. Service environment

2 Multiscreen Environment and User Experiences

Smart phone, Tablet, PC, and TV have developed from their independent area with different purpose. However environment which can access to the networks anywhere and at any time made previous independent function of each screen to be shared together. We can see or edit the photos which saved in smart phones, from TV or tablet. Recently, smart watch, another new screen, appeared and played various roles connecting to smart phones. Due to the different physical use environment, which is screen size or input-output method, same content is designed differently upon the screen.

Representative multiscreen use environment has been described in Table 1.

In the case of smart phone and tablet, which is the typical one person media, mobility function was strong, which can be used while moving, screen size was small, and direct operational methods, using fingers, were dominant. On the other hand, in the case of PC and TV, indirect operational methods were mainly applied, which use remote controls or mouse using in limited space. In the case of TV, the distance from

Table 1. Multiscreen use environment

	Mobile	Tablet PC	PC	TV
Screen size (inch)	3.5–4	7–9.7	17~	20–60
Distance (cm)	15	30	50	200
operate	Touch	Touch	Mouse, Keyboard	Remote
Main user	individual	individual	Official	Official
purpose of use	Call, Message	Call, Message, book	Job, els	Watching TV
where	Mobility	Mobility	Room	Room

users was most far, and the degree of freedom was low compared to other screens due to the environment of using remote controls.

According to Nishida Hiroko (2000), information entered through human sensory organ activates schema, which is the past knowledge response related to the information or organized experiences about past events, and then processed by the information in the schema. When users encounter a service, they utilize not only the previous related experiences, but also different kind of experiences. For example, when tablet appeared first, experiences from mobile, PC, or TV can be reminded and used. This can be interpreted as the relations with natural human cognitive ability. Users at multiscreen environment want various experiences. They are smooth connection, which is seamless contents technically, maintaining consistent task performance after switching to different screen from the previous screen with no inconveniences, and so on. As Nishida Hiroko's opinion, new information can be explained by substituting coherent experience, solving out naturally through the interpretation of the accumulation of previous experiences. While providing service of same contents on multiscreen, information amount, visual structure or shapes are not equal. This is reasonable considering physical differences among each screen. However the difference of screens which users are watching doesn't imply that contents are different or can't be used. Depending upon previous experiences of using same or similar contents from different devices, this can be used through the inference and judgment. Since such inference can be made easily on multiscreen, it is important for users to use contents from other screens without any unfamiliarity.

3   Coherent of User Experience Design

Interaction design area is expanding gradually from UI design (User Interface design) to UX design (User experience design). UI design is a touch point between people and systems or information channel between users and each system. UI design emphasizes cognitive aspects for user's convenient use. UX design is used in a broad sense implying integral user experiences of service or products including UX design. Many enterprises or researchers produce UX designs considering overall usage processes including UI design in order for users to feel valuable and meaningful experiences when they use products or service.

4   Selection of Analysis Items Measuring Coherent User Experience

Examination of the flow of user's experience of the product shows the order of cognition, access, use and disposal of the item. That is, users become to have certain experiences about the product through the whole process, from the cognition to the disposal of the product. In this study, analysis items of the measurement for these whole processes were selected to measure the coherent user experiences. This study used heuristic check list method, based on usability evaluation checklist by Jakob Nielson and evaluation checklist by Xerox, suggested analysis factors for the users experience comprehensively

Table 2. Analysis items selected from the interview

Category	Sub-Category	Coherent experience for multiscreen
Goal	Objective	Provide similar functions for each screen, and specialize it reflecting their characteristics.
	Seamlessness	Specified settings from one screen should be applied together.
Interaction method	Input method	Proper method for the characteristics of screens is available.
	Interaction rules	Although screens are different, moving direction of interface or regulations should be produced equally.
Graphic user interface	Layout	Appropriate method is available based on the characteristics of screen.
	Color	This needs to be identical or similar.
	Icon	This needs to be identical or similar.
	Font	This needs to be identical or similar.
Information architecture	Access	Appropriate method is available based on the characteristics of screen.
	Customization	This doesn't need to be provided depends on the characteristics of screens.
	Navigation	Appropriate method is available based on the characteristics of screen.
Sound user interface	Feedback	Maintaining basic consistency of each screen, and considering the usage environment (use at public space or individual use).

and formed expert group who derived appropriate elements. With the theme of 'Elements Selection for the Coherent Experience Analysis on Multiscreen Environment', focus group interview was conducted, and a discussion about maintaining the consistency with differences of the physical environment of each screen and assigning the degree of freedom was held.

Analysis items selected from the interview were summarized in Table 2.

Analysis items were classified into two large groups, which were invisible items and visible items. Invisible items imply abstract UX Goal. These items indicate the processes of users, who use the screens with a series of purpose, from downloading contents to accomplishment of the goal with contents. On the other hand, visible items are items about a touch point of interface, which is encountered when users operate contents directly from each screen, or interaction regulations which can be felt while usage.

5   Conclusions

In this study, significant user experience, which is occurred while using same contents on multiscreen, was defined as Coherent Experience, and Focus Group Interview was conducted to investigate which elements provide the coherent user experiences. For the sake of harmonized and consistent experience on multiscreen, items to meet the requirements for all screens and optional items depend on the screen environments or conditions were differentiated. User's purpose from invisible items provide similar functions, but needs to be specialized considering screen's characteristics, environments, and users' features. As for the connectivity, settings specified by one screen should be applied equally to other screens. This should be observed in contents design, and the degree of freedom of this item is low. Interaction regulations of visible items, which are direction of interface movement or regulations of operating functions from all screens, need to follow the principles, it is desirable to consider additional services of application elements, which can increase diversity effect of age or occupations. For the graphic layout, the degree of freedom of each screen is relatively high. Rather than the identity which unifies the design of all devices, providing several elements, such as point color or symbol fonts, similarly will enhance users' coherent experience in spite of different designs. As a result of YouTube analysis, information structure was a most dissimilar item by each screen. It was verified that the degree of freedom was high for designers or producers when creating the contents. In the case of sound, from the YouTube contents, independent sound feedback was not supplied by each screen. However if this service is offered, maintaining the basic consistency of each screen and considering the usage environment, public use or individual use, will make users' experience more positively. In this study, analysis items were extracted from the result of focus group interview. Therefore verification applied to the real contents has not been made. From further study, analysis item will be applied to the contents in current service, and validity verification will be made.

References

COST294-MAUSE Workshop: Meaningful Measures: Valid Useful User Experience Measurement (2008)

Hiroko, N.: An introduction to Intercultural Communication. Sogensha, Osaka (2000). ISBN 4-422-31022-4

Assessing Usability of a Post-Mission Reporting Technology

A Novel Usability Questionnaire in Practice

Mitchell J. Tindall[1](✉) and Beth F. Wheeler Atkinson[2]

[1] StraCon Services Group, LLC, Orlando, FL, USA
mitchell.tindall.ctr@navy.mil
[2] Orlando, FL Naval Air Warfare Center Training Systems Division,
Orlando, FL, USA
beth.atkinson@navy.mil

Abstract. Usability evaluation has received extensive attention in both academic and applied arenas. Despite this, there have been few formal attempts to integrate past research and best practices in an effort to develop a newly updated and adaptable approach. This poster provides an overview of the types of results yielded by a novel usability assessment approach (i.e., Experienced-based Questionnaire for Usability Assessments Targeting Elaborations [EQUATE]) when applied to a post mission reporting tool. The goal of this study was to develop software to automate performance tracking for anti-submarine aircraft, digitize performance and training information, and automate the display of post mission summaries. Although some of these technologies exist, the prototype tested during this research was the first, of which the authors are aware, to provide a single point of access for data entry, analysis and reporting. Due to the potential benefits across a variety of naval aviation platforms, the program's usability goals focused on identifying means to optimize the tool by gathering novice user feedback. Traditional methods for end-user feedback have tended to focus on user performance and satisfaction, rather than providing prescriptive inputs to identifying and rectifying issues. The results of this study provided usability input for post mission reporting, as well as identified and narrowed the heuristic dimensions used for final validation.

Keywords: Usability · Heuristic evaluation · GUIs

1 Introduction

Designing Graphic User Interfaces (GUIs) for complex applications such as those used to support naval operational and training systems is a challenging endeavor. The challenges arise from the balance between appeasing the functional needs of the

---

The views expressed herein are those of the authors and do not necessarily reflect the official position of the Department of Defense, its components, or the organizations with which the individuals are affiliated.

C. Stephanidis (Ed.): HCII 2015 Posters, Part I, CCIS 528, pp. 74–78, 2015.
DOI: 10.1007/978-3-319-21380-4_14

end-user population with ensuring the usability of the system. Despite the challenges, the goals should always be to develop systems that are accessible, easy to use, make task completion more efficient, reduce the cognitive workload on the end user, and generally satisfy the user. Even the most seasoned computer programmers cannot develop such systems without early, frequent and prolonged end-user feedback. Such feedback has traditionally been solicited through a process of usability testing. While no single definition of usability exists in the literature, it is generally defined as the quantifiable characteristics of a system that provide information to developers about the ease of use and usefulness of the system [1, 2, 5]. Literature regarding usability evaluations suggests they are necessary for developing usable interactive systems [3, 4]. While the challenges of conducting usability testing for Navy systems can be unique (e.g., domain specificity, complex systems of systems), they are not immune to the benefits of such evaluations. The following report details an initial usability evaluation of the Post Mission Assessment for Tactical Training and Trend Analysis (PMATT-TA) Increment 1 web-based application using a novel, heuristic-based measure called the Experience-based Questionnaire for Usability Assessments Targeting Elaborations (EQUATE).

1.1 PMATT-TA System Purpose and Goals

PMATT-TA Increment 1 is an online web-based application and database designed for tracking important data points from operational and training events for the maritime patrol community. The post mission data captured includes a variety of missions (e.g., mission type, communications) and contextual information (e.g., weather). The ultimate goal for capturing this data is to facilitate debriefs with aircrews to identify strengths and areas for improvement. By centrally storing post mission information, PMATT-TA also supports data calls related to trends (e.g., number of events a crew has participated in). Additionally, data increments of PMATT-TA will address a need for a digitally-based system that streamlines and automates the process of data collection, analyses, and feedback. As a result, the system benefits a range of users (e.g., aircrew, instructors, squadron, or group leaders). While the demand for PMATT-TA within the Navy is apparent, it has not yet been subject to formal usability analysis. Usability analyses must be conducted to be confident that the system achieves its goals, reduces post mission reporting time and is operable by end-users.

2 Data Collection

2.1 Recruitment

Participants ($N = 9$) evaluated the PMATT-TA Increment 1, web-based application in a laboratory setting with a desktop computer. After attaining an informed consent from qualified participants, researchers provided a brief explanation of tasks and measures as they moved through the protocol.

2.2 Measure

After completing the PMATT-TA tasks, each participant was given the EQUATE. It was developed based on an extensive review of the extant literature regarding system design and heuristic evaluation [6]. The review identified a number of items (i.e., 250) that qualified as design guidance. Through further testing eight heuristic dimensions (i.e., *Error Handling & Feedback, Graphic Design & Aesthetics, User Interaction Control, Memorability & Cognitive Facilitation, User Efficiency, Learnability, Consistency,* and *Help* were included within the EQUATE). Validation in the form of internal consistency and discriminate validity was ongoing at the time of this study but preliminary analysis has demonstrated sound psychometric properties (i.e., average internal consistency for all dimensions $< .85$).

3 Results

The quantitative analysis is intended to provide a general overview of the usability of the PMATT-TA system and a localized evaluation of the usability of system and system components across the heuristic categories previously mentioned (e.g., *Learnability, Help,* and *Consistency*).

The analysis revealed both positive and negative elements within the PMATT-TA system (see Table 1). Usability was assessed on a 5-point scale (i.e., $1 = $ *Strongly disagree*, $5 = $ *Strongly agree*, $0 = $ *Not applicable*). Items on the EQUATE are framed in both positive and negative terms (e.g., *The design provided a pleasant experience* and *There was too much clutter on the display*). Negatively framed items were reverse coded prior to analysis. Higher averages imply better usability while lower averages imply potential usability issues exist.

The average visibility across all items of the EQUATE was acceptable ($M = 3.41$, $SD = 0.24$). While this average appears to indicate the system demonstrates adequate usability from a global perspective, a more detailed evaluation of EQUATE items, dimensions, and free-responses is necessary to validate and elaborate on this assertion. Two of the heuristic categories exhibited an average score below 3.0, indicating the need for redesign, adjustment or enhancement: *Learnability* ($M = 2.89$, $SD = 0.56$) and *Help* ($M = 2.81$, $SD = 0.93$). This demonstrates that participants (i.e., usability evaluators) felt they needed more or better help to learn the system[1]. The remaining dimensions all demonstrated adequate or above adequate average scores (i.e., ≤ 3)(see Table 1 for descriptive statistics).

The opportunity for participants to articulate system issues in a free-response format was exercised extensively. The vast array of free responses required the research team to qualitatively (i.e., summarize for system developer feedback) and quantitatively (i.e., coding into respective heuristic dimensions) analyze the data provided. The

---

[1] The participants in this study lacked domain specific knowledge on how to complete a post mission report (i.e., not military participants) likely influencing their ratings of learnability. For this reason, *Learnability* for the system should be re-evaluated in future iterations of testing with end users to further evaluate this factor.

Table 1. Descriptive statistics for Evaluator responses on the EQUATE ($N = 9$)

Dimension	Range		M	SD
Graphic Design and Aesthetics	3.34	3.95	3.681	.1968
Error Handling and Feedback	3.19	4.19	3.506	.3131
User Interaction Control	3.20	4.00	3.502	.3161
Memorability and Cognitive Facilitation	2.48	4.15	3.280	.5122
User Efficiency	3.16	4.21	3.687	.4324
Learnability	2.10	3.88	2.897	.5646
Consistency	2.93	4.50	3.875	.5733
Help	1.17	3.91	2.816	.9398
Overall Usability	3.13	3.90	3.409	.2486

Note. The potential range of responses for all heuristic dimensions was 1 to 5 (i.e., 1 = *Strongly disagree*, 5 = *Strongly agree*, 0 = *Not applicable*)

quantitative analyses validated EQUATE survey items; *Learnability* and *Help* were the most frequently mentioned dimensions. In addition to validating survey responses, free-responses lent participants the opportunity to elaborate on the specifics of usability issues through severity ratings of those issues and suggesting ideas for fixing them. Specific issues were identified in subject free-responses that would not have been discovered with an analysis of only survey results.

For example, one field for inputting a unit's location was not working properly (i.e., would not accept letters, numbers or any combination of the two). Not only did this prevent participants from entering in the necessary information, it prevented them from adequately completing the overall task. Each of the nine subjects identified this as a *highly severe* issue. The information was communicated to the development team and addressed appropriately.

Aside from identifying obvious fixes, free responses embedded in the EQUATE survey allowed participants to elaborate on issues. For example, while less than half the participants reported subpar *User Efficiency* in survey items, an examination of their free-responses yielded important information for system usability. They indicated that the procedure for creating a *training event* in PMATT-TA was not sufficiently clear. They described this issue as *severe* and offered suggestions for fixing it (i.e., making the *New Event* button on the home page more conspicuous by bolding, adding color or increasing its size). Because creating a *New Event* is one of the system's main purposes, this information was vital to the system development team to enhance usability. In sum, though tedious to analyze and interpret, the opportunity for subject free-response proved essential for improving and especially fixing the PMATT-TA system.

4 Discussion

It is the goal of any armed forces to maintain a competitive advantage over the enemy by having the most advanced capabilities. Such capabilities are the result of constantly evolving hardware and software technologies. Unfortunately, developing these technologies is only one half of the equation. If they cannot be used effectively, their development has limited impact or desired effect. As a result, inexpensive, efficient, adaptable and easily analyzable systems for evaluating the usability are essential. PMATT-TA was the first system to be evaluated using a novel usability assessment method, which was developed based on an extensive review of literature and best practices. This initial analysis indicates the EQUATE provides a reasonably comprehensive, inexpensive, efficient, adaptable, and easy to analyze and interpret method for capturing end user feedback. Because of the results of this analysis, the development team benefited from the identification of critical issues prior to product development. While both the PMATT-TA and the EQUATE are still receiving research attention for validation and general improvement, preliminary analyses demonstrate the utility of each system in advancing the capability of the U.S. Navy.

Acknowledgements. This research was sponsored by the NAVAIR Section 219 and PMA-205 Air Warfare Training Development programs. We wish to thank interns who facilitated data collection and analysis, and colleagues who provided input throughout this process. The views expressed in this paper are those of the authors and do not represent the official views of the organizations with which they are affiliated.

References

1. Bowman, D.A., Gabbard, J.L., Hix, D.: A survey of usability evaluation in virtual environments: classification and comparison of methods. Presence Teleoperators Virtual Environ. **11** (4), 404–424 (2002)
2. Hix, D., Hartson, H.R.: Developing User Interfaces Ensuring Usability Through Product and Process. John Wiley, NJ (1993)
3. Shneiderman, B.: Designing User Interface Strategies for Effective Human-Computer Interaction. Addision-Wesley Reading, MA (1998)
4. Nielsen, J.: Usability Engineering. Academic Press, New York (1993)
5. Preece, J., Rogers, Y., Sharp, H., Benyon, D., Holland, S., Carey, T.: Human-Computer Interaction. Addison-Wesley Longman Ltd, London (1994)
6. Atkinson, B., Tindall, M., Igel, G.: Validated Usability Heuristics: Defining Categories and Design Guidance. Extended poster abstract submitted to HCI International (2015)

Validated Usability Heuristics: Defining Categories and Design Guidance

Beth F. Wheeler Atkinson[1(✉)], Mitchell J. Tindall[2],
and Gregory S. Igel[3]

[1] Naval Air Warfare Center Training Systems Division, Orlando, FL, USA
beth.atkinson@navy.mil
[2] StraCon Services Group, LLC, Orlando, FL, USA
mitchell.tindall.ctr@navy.mil
[3] Worldwide Embry-Riddle Aeronautical University, Daytona Beach, FL, USA
igel36c@erau.edu

Abstract. Heuristic-based usability assessment is a popular approach to assessing system usability in the field of Human-Computer Interaction (HCI) [1]. Despite the benefits of the approach (e.g., flexibility across time and platform, efficiency, utility of feedback) [1], it is also associated with sub-par reliability, validity, and comprehensiveness and requires a Human Factors (HF) expert for the analysis and interpretation of subjective feedback. While this approach has a place in the usability lifecycle of a project, tight budgets and schedule constraints can limit the variety of usability approaches that teams can implement. The purpose of the current effort is to develop a validated heuristic approach based on a review of past literature and practice and integrate this information to inform an improved system. Leveraging previous efforts as a baseline (i.e., [2]), this approach extends previous work by improving the comprehensiveness of the system by broadening the scope of past usability research and providing end-users with specific practical examples of *do's* and *don'ts* to better define broad heuristic-based categories for non-expert end-users. The logic is that broad heuristic categories have little practical meaning to end-users not familiar or educated in HF/HCI. The provision of practical examples should improve their ability to identify important usability issues while helping them communicate this information in language that is understandable to system designers. The result of this research is presented in this poster, and provides a method for the assessment of system usability that is more flexible, efficient, comprehensive and useful than past approaches.

Keywords: Usability assessment · Heuristic-based assessment · Usability heuristics · Validated approach

The views expressed herein are those of the authors and do not necessarily reflect the official position of the Department of Defense, its components, or the organizations with which the individuals are affiliated.

© Springer International Publishing Switzerland 2015
C. Stephanidis (Ed.): HCII 2015 Posters, Part I, CCIS 528, pp. 79–84, 2015.
DOI: 10.1007/978-3-319-21380-4_15

1 Introduction

Heuristic-based assessments remain a popular selection for practitioners when conducting usability testing due to the numerous benefits associated with the approach. In addition to being a relatively quick and inexpensive method, the approach is flexible across platforms, allows for utilization at various points during development, and requires a small group of experts to conduct [3], [1]. Despite these benefits, the method is associated with sub-par reliability across testers and lacks comprehensiveness in the analysis depending on implementation [1]. Additionally, reliance on human factors (HF) experts to conduct the analysis and provide feedback limits the type of design input produced by the method. As a consequence, reliance solely on heuristic-based assessment would mean a lack of end user input in the process. While this approach remains a vital tool during the usability lifecycle, resource constraints (e.g., budget, schedule, personnel access) often limit the variety of usability approaches that teams can implement.

The goal of the User Interface - Table for Evaluating & Analyzing Composite Heuristics (UI-TEACH) effort was to develop a validated heuristic approach based on a review of past literature and practice to provide an integrated system for heuristic analysis. In line with previous work [2], the method taken by the authors for the organization of the approach included defining heuristic categories and providing examples of upholding or violating the heuristics. This method takes advantage of the heuristic approach and provides qualifying information for less experienced practitioners.

This effort extended previous work in two primary ways. The first was to increase comprehensiveness. The Multiple Heuristic Evaluation Table (MHET) [2] was grounded in four paramount approaches: Nielsen's *ten usability heuristics* [4], Shneiderman's *Eight Golden Rules of Interface Design* [12], Tognazzini's *First Principles of Interaction Design* [6], and a set of principles based on Edward Tufte's visual display work [7]. The UI-TEACH expanded consideration of guidance. Specifically, the authors reviewed approximately 80 heuristic articles and identified almost 30 alterative heuristic approaches for consideration. The second difference was to conduct a content validation of the heuristics. While a qualitative analysis was the sole method underpinning the MHET, HF experts validated the heuristic categories through a card sort.

The long-term goal of this work is to leverage the UI-TEACH to develop an empirically validated heuristic-based tool to support expert-led usability assessment and generation of design guidance by end users. The concept is to rely on broad heuristics categories to organize the analysis, while providing practical examples to end-users, who likely will not be familiar or educated in HF or human computer interaction (HCI). These guidance examples should improve their capacity to identify important usability issues while helping communicate this information in a language that is understandable to system designers.

2 Heuristic Development Process

2.1 Qualitative Analysis of Literature

Revisiting the literature prior to an empirical validation allowed the authors to consider best practices, while taking advantage of progress made in other prominent usability guidance efforts. Expanded coverage supports early identification of issues and provides wider variety design guidance. Such guidance contributes to a user interface that enhances information processing and minimizes user workloads. A number of resources were identified and evaluated to ensure the UI-TEACH has included relevant, practical and comprehensive usability guidance to bolster and provide for a robust evaluation. The primary sources consulted include: *The Evaluation Checklist* [8], *Research-Based Web Design & Usability Guidelines* [3], *Audience Centered Heuristics: Older Adults* [10], *Hedonomics: The Power of Positive and Pleasurable Ergonomics* [11], *Designing the user interface: Fourth edition: Strategies for effective human-computer interaction* [12], *User Experience Interaction Guidelines* [13] and *Principles of Accessible Design* [14].

The aforementioned review of the literature provided the basis for our qualitative analysis. The analysis involved identifying overlap of conceptually related heuristics, and identification of unique aspects of approaches for consideration to expand and address gaps. The results of this analysis yielded 17 preliminary heuristic categories from a set of 250 pieces of design guidance. In order to validate the resulting heuristics and organize the design guidance, the authors' used a card sort discussed in the next section.

2.2 Card Sort

Prior to conducting a closed card sort, the research team conducted a pilot open card sort to inform the number of categories expected beyond the qualitative input. The results of this pilot were evaluated using ($N = 18$ HF majors from a southeastern university) a hierarchical cluster analysis, which revealed a division of 10 categories (Range = 5 to 17, $M = 11$, Mode = 14). A follow-up qualitative analysis of those groupings resulted in the following general descriptors of the categories: *Help, User Efficiency, User Control & Interaction, OS Properties, Data Management, Graphic Design & Aesthetics, Memorability, Cognitive Facilitation, Feedback,* and *Learnability*.

Participants ($N = 25$) for the closed card sort were recruited from a Navy command and held positions in the fields of engineering (systems, industrial, human factors), psychology (human factors, engineering, industrial/organizational), instructional systems, or student interns in related fields. They were instructed to group design guidance within the 10 categories previously mentioned. Instructions also included a caveat that up to two additional categories could be formed if a participant felt it was necessary to provide a comprehensive set of heuristics. While this varies from a traditional closed card sort, the flexibility allowed participants to identify if a group of cards did not conceptually fit within an existing category, but they felt that placing it in a *trash* group would result in a loss of critical information.

Analysis. A co-occurrence matrix was completed for each participant to identify how cards were grouped. Next, a sum of the individual co-occurrence matrices results formed a collective co-occurrence matrix as a means for developing a probability matrix. While a hierarchical cluster analysis helped inform the development of categories, the result of an orthogonal Varimax rotation confirmatory factor analysis was the predominate method for interpreting results.[1] The team established low factor loadings (i.e., < 0.05) and loading on multiple factors as criteria for card removal, which reduced ambiguity in the data. Although statisticians typically reserve factor analyses for studies with large amounts of data, Capra [14] suggests that it is possible to use a factor analysis for card sort data when there are enough cards and participants because it generates the statistical power needed for factor analysis.[2]

3   Results

Analyses resulted in the formation of 10 heuristics within the UI-TEACH approach:

- Graphic design and aesthetics: Interface display elements (e.g., color, text, graphics) and layout support a positive user experience;
- Error handling and feedback: System feedback on status and errors supports users' understanding of how to interact with the system;
- User interaction control: Mechanisms that allow the user to feel in control of actions and system preferences;
- Learnability: System design and aids support users learning how to use the system;
- Effectiveness of developmental characteristics: Characteristics of the hardware/software compatibility that affect the ability of the system to deliver the intended functionality and detect errors;
- Memorability and cognitive facilitation: System design helps ease learning and memory load (short-term and long-term memory);
- User efficiency: System design & functionality that supports completion of tasks with minimal time and effort;
- Consistency: System information & actions are consistently located and formatted throughout the interface; and
- Help: Readily accessible instructions or clarifying information that are easy to use and support task completion.

The number of heuristics is consistent with established methods (e.g., Nielsen [3]; Shneiderman [11]; Tognazzini [5]), and leverages similar descriptors for consistency. The UI-TEACH approach differs from the majority of existing methods by establishing

---

[1] Two separate analyses were conducted: hierarchical cluster analysis and factor analysis. A qualitative comparison of both approaches was completed to understand the differences and benefits of these alternate approaches. Details and results of this analysis are documented in Atkinson, Tindall, and Kaste [15].

[2] Capra [14] asserts that card sorts with a large number of cards and participants generate enough data to run a successful factor analysis. Their study contained 70 cards with 19 participants, whereas the study here contained 250 cards and 25 participants.

Table 1. Example Heuristic Category and Set of Examples Outlined in UI-TEACH Approach

Heuristic	Subset of adherence examples	Subset of violation examples
Error Handling and feedback	- Auto-save provided a backup to prevent loss of data - Brief error messages were informative	- Errors messages were delayed causing multiple errors - System feedback became overwhelming

a list of examples to provide elaboration for less experienced usability testers. Specifically, each heuristic is supported by a set of examples that demonstrate adherence to (i.e., support) or violation of a heuristic (see Table 1). Based on the results of the card sort analysis, heuristics were backed with between 67 (Graphic Design & Aesthetics) and nine (Learnability) examples.

4 Discussion

The UI-TEACH provides an alternative heuristic-based usability approach meant to simplify access to usability concepts for a range of testers while increasing the comprehensiveness of previous approaches (e.g., Atkinson et al. [2]). The authors acknowledge that the design guidance within UI-TEACH is predominately focused on graphical user interfaces and does not provide specific guidance related to multi-modal interfaces; additional examples within this area would increase the generalizability to more systems. Additionally, while the authors validated this approach through a card sort, additional validation through implementation of the method would further demonstrate how the UI-TEACH can facilitate the assessment process. One way the authors are continuing this aspect of testing is through the validation of the assessment tool that was developed in follow on phases of this overall research effort. At this time, preliminary testing of this tool – the Experience-based Questionnaire for Usability Assessments Targeting Elaborations (EQUATE) – demonstrates that end users identify a range of issues touching all heuristic categories [16].

Acknowledgements. The views expressed in this paper are those of the authors and do not represent the official views of the organizations with which they are affiliated. The NAVAIR Section 219 program sponsored this research. We wish to thank interns who facilitated data collection and analysis, and colleagues who provided input throughout this process. Gregory Igel conducted this work while under the employment of KAEGAN Corporation.

References

1. Nielsen, J.: Usability engineering. Academic Press, San Diego, CA (1993)
2. Stanton, N.A., Salmon, P.M., Walker, G.H., Baber, C., Jenkins, D.P.: Human Factors Methods: A Practical Guide for Engineering and Design. Ashgate Publishing Limited, Aldershot, England (2005)

3. Wheeler Atkinson, B.F., Bennett, T.O., Bahr, G.S., Walwanis Nelson, M.M.: Development of a multiple heuristics evaluation table (MHET) to support software development and usability analysis. In: Stephanidis, C. (ed.) HCI 2007. LNCS, vol. 4554, pp. 563–572. Springer, Heidelberg (2007)
4. Nielsen, J.: Heuristic evaluation. In: Nielsen, J., Mack, R.L. (eds.) Usability Inspection Methods, pp. 25–62. John Wiley and Sons, New York (1994)
5. Shneiderman, B.: Designing the User Interface: Strategies for Effective Human-Computer Interaction. Addison Wesley Longman, MA (1998)
6. Tognazzini, B.: First principles of interaction design (2003). http://www.asktog.com/basics/firstPrinciples.html
7. UW Computing and Communications.: Graphics and web design based on Edward Tufte's principles. http://www.washington.edu/computing/training/560/zz-tufte.html
8. Ravden, S.J., Johnson, G.I.: Evaluating Usability of Human-Computer Interfaces: A Practical Method. Halsted Press, New York (1989)
9. U.S. Government.: Research-Based Web Design and Usability Guidelines (2003). http://usability.gov/guidelines/index.html
10. AARP.: AARP Audience Centered Heuristics: Older Adults. http://www.redish.net/content/handouts/Audience-Centered_Heuristics.pdf
11. Hancock, P.A., Pepe, A.A., Murphy, L.L.: Hedonomics: The Power of Positive and Pleasurable Ergonomics. Ergonomics in Design, Winter (2005). http://www.mit.ucf.edu/Hedonomics/Hancock_Pepe_Murphy_2005.pdf
12. Shneiderman, B., Plaisant, C.: Designing the User Interface: Fourth Edition: Strategies for Effective Human-Computer Interaction. Pearson Education - Addison Wesley, University of Maryland, College Park (2005)
13. Microsoft Windows.: User Experience Interaction Guidelines for Windows 7 and Windows Vista. http://www.microsoft.com/downloads/details.aspx?displaylang=en&FamilyID=e49820cb-954d-45ae-9cb3-1b9e8ea7fe8c
14. Web Content Accessibility Guidelines 2.0 [WCAG].: Principles of Accessible Design. http://www.w3.org/TR/WCAG20/
15. Atkinson, B.F.W., Tindall, M.J., Kaste, K.P.: Data analysis for survey development: a comparison of hierarchical cluster analysis and confirmatory factor analysis. In: Poster Extended Abstract Submitted for Consideration to Human Factors and Ergonomics Society Annual Conference (2015)
16. Tindall, M.J., Atkinson, B.F.W.: Assessing usability of a post mission reporting technology: a novel usability questionnaire in practice. In: Extended Abstract submitted to the Human Computer Interaction International Annual Conference (2015)

Cognitive and Psychological Issues
in HCI

Eye Tracking Analysis of Readers' Psychological Interaction with Marketing Copy Referencing Life Values

Miao-Hsien Chuang[1(⊠)], Chin-Lung Chen[1], and Jui-Ping Ma[2]

[1] Department of Visual Communication Design,
Ming Chi University of Technology, New Taipei City, Taiwan
joyceblog@gmail.com, lung@mail.mcut.edu.tw
[2] Graduate School of Creative Industry Design,
National Taiwan University of Arts, New Taipei City 22058, Taiwan
artma2010@gmail.com

Abstract. Rather than simply reporting product information, many advertisements nowadays employ images that convey a certain life values. How do consumers respond to advertisements of this type? This study analyzed consumer responses to the advertising card of C'N'C Costume National using eye-tracking technology and a questionnaire survey. Research findings were as follows: (1) It was found that participants scanning figure and text repeatedly on the copy referencing life values more than on the copy referencing product information. This was confirmed by chi-squared testing. (2) Factor analysis identified three significant factors, namely, psychological interaction, a sense of specialness, and anticipation. (3) We discovered that females with a background in design tended to spend more time watching a male model than men of all backgrounds did. This study contributes to marketing research, demonstrating the effectiveness of conveying messages about life values to achieve more desirable advertising effects while also conveying social concern.

Keywords: Eye tracking · Advertising copy · Life values · Readers' psychological interaction

1 Introduction

Many companies still rely on celebrity endorsement and advertisements referencing dry product information to encourage consumers to choose their brand of product. Yet in today's fiercely competitive market and climate of elevated social concern, more and more brands are employing models to act out a visual narration of certain life philosophies and standards of value. The Dove Real Beauty Series focused on inner beauty rather than product details to great success. Another example is the C'N'C Costume National advertisement, which asked the users of social networking sites to share their life philosophies.

In what way do the observers respond differently to an advertisement of this type? This study first explored the literature related to value standards and consumer

© Springer International Publishing Switzerland 2015
C. Stephanidis (Ed.): HCII 2015 Posters, Part I, CCIS 528, pp. 87–92, 2015.
DOI: 10.1007/978-3-319-21380-4_16

behavior, visual flow and meaning, and the influence of gender on ways of observing advertisements. This leads us to propose the hypothesis that an advertisement focused on life values engages consumers more than those featuring only product information. We tested this hypothesis while also investigating whether the gender of viewers influences their preferences toward the gender of models.

2 Literature Review

2.1 Standard of Value and Consumer Behavior

Standard of value is a persistent preference held by people toward certain behavior, affairs, state of things, or goals. A set of value standards may be swayed by a person's personalities, life experience and socio-cultural factors, and further affects personal attitudes and behavior as a result [1, 2]. Schwartz [2] categorized value standards into the following classifications: achievement, benevolence, hedonism, conformity, power, security, self-direction, stimulation, tradition and universalism. Carman [3] asserted that value standards exert influence on one's interests, time management, and how one makes decisions and enacts one's roles in social contexts, including that of consumer. Yang [4] believed that value standards have a higher relevance with postmodern symbolic consumption. For young adults who are socially anxious or introverted, commodities that promise uniqueness or the unconventional have the most appeal. For chic, open-minded consumers, a product's beauty or cultural connotations will be more important.

2.2 Visual Flow and Meaning

Visual scanpaths can reflect the process of attention shifting within observers. Treisman and Gelade [5] compared the operation of visual attention to multiple packets that are continuously prepared by the visual system prior to the merging of information with its corresponding meaning manifesting in individual consciousness. Experiments on explicit and implicit product presentation in advertisements have established that in terms of the latter type, viewers display more frequent saccades between images and text, spend more time on them, and exhibit more positive attitudes and greater interest [6].

2.3 Advertisement Observation and the Model's Gender

There exist conflicting views among researchers on the correlation between observers' attitudes toward the advertisement and the model's gender. Some scholars purport that this relationship depends on the attributes of a product. David M. Ogilvy [7], a world-renowned advertiser, proposed that "to arouse the attention of women, babies and women must use the illustrations" and that "to arouse the attention of men, we must use the men's illustrations."

3 Methodology

The research methods employed in this study were eye tracking and a questionnaire survey. We also used SPSS to determine whether any diversities existed among the subjects with different backgrounds in terms of watching time and scanpaths, and then analyzed whether subjects showed preference toward such advertisements.

3.1 Eye Tracking Method

Independent variable: The independent variable was advertisement copy. The experiment group was shown copy conveying life values, while the control group was shown copy stressing product information.

Dependent Variable: Total Browsing Time and Scanpaths. Experimental control: identical images in the two samples and the two copies occupying similar amounts of area.

Experiment Samples: Two sets of samples were garnered from a 2008 advertising card of C'N'C Costume National (Table 1). All the models were randomly selected from Myspace Networking sites. Sample A (shown to the experimental group) kept the

Table 1. Samples from experimental group and control group

Sample A	Sample B

Source: C'N'C Costume National in SOGO Department Store, Taipei (has been modified)

white frame that circled the model's head and the original copywriting: "Make sure you trust the people you know"/Female/26 years old/New York/United States; "Love is all we need"/Male/25 years old/New York/United States. Sample B (shown to the control group) contained images of the models' heads without the white frame and the copy was changed to convey product information: No: Ad48052/Style: Female, T shirt/Color: Black/Size:L/M/S/Price: 1200; No: Ad51046/Style: Male, Jacket/Color: Black/Size: 30/32/36/Price: 2940. All the copy was in Chinese, with which all the subjects are familiar.

Experiment Equipment and Participants: This study employed Face Lab4 real-time face and fixation tracking device in conjunction with GazeTrail software analysis. The participants included 36 students in college; 18 of them had backgrounds in design, while the remaining 18 participants had backgrounds in other fields.

3.2   Questionnaire Survey

Objective: To understand how participants respond to copy conveying a message related to life values. Responses were measured on a 7-point Likert scale.

Participants: To achieve high reliability in factor analysis, this research recruited 114 participants for the questionnaire survey, half of whom had background in design.

Source of Questions: A total of 30 questions were designed drawing on the work of Huang and Chuang [8], focusing on visual narration, emotional response and theories related to aesthetical experience.

4   Results and Discussion

4.1   Eye-Tracking Analysis and Chi-square Test

This study employed data analysis using GazeTrail, classifying the types of samples into "woman copy," "woman," "man copy," "man," "left," and "right". Independent-sample t-tests found no significant difference between the factors of "observation time" and "participants' gender and background". The mean values showed that participants in the experimental group spent longer observing the advertisement referencing life values than those in the control group who were shown product-related advertisements (Table 2).

We explored the relationship between "scanning" and "type of copy" from the eye-tracking scanpath of the participants with chi-squared testing, which showed that there exists a significant relationship between the two ($X2(1) = 8.578$, Pearson chi-squared score = .003). That means participants scanning figure and text repeatedly on the copy referencing life values more than on the copy referencing product information.

Table 2. Comparison of observation times in experimental group and control group

	Woman copy	Woman	Man copy	Man	Brand	Left area	Right area
Experimental group: participants without a background in design	2.58	1.12	1.14	1.48	1.40	7.94	5.26
Experimental group: participants with a background in design	2.84	0.91	1.34	1.70	1.92	7.69	4.33
Subtotal	**2.72**	**1.01**	**1.24**	**1.59**	**1.68**	**7.80**	**4.77**
Control group: participants without a background in design	2.24	0.70	2.37	0.83	1.70	5.37	5.38
Control group: participants with a background in design	2.07	0.81	1.49	1.11	2.81	8.06	4.07
Subtotal	**2.17**	**0.75**	**1.99**	**0.95**	**2.19**	**6.55**	**4.81**

4.2 Independent Two-Way ANOVA

This study used independent sample two-way ANOVA on the participants' background and gender, and found a significant correlation between these two independent variables (p-value = .025). This study further used key result analysis and discovered that females with a background in design tended to observe male models longer than men did (p-value = .037). Meanwhile, there was no discernible difference in the watching time for women models in an advertisement.

4.3 Factor Analysis

We first conducted item analysis and tests on internal consistency and reliability related to the 30 question items. After eliminating eighteen items, we employed Varimax rotation for principal component analysis, resulting in KMO = .729 (>0.7) and good reliability. The results of the Bartlett test were also significant, deeming that factor analysis was appropriate. Furthermore, the cumulative total explained variance of the three factors reached 69.87 %. Finally, we named the three factors psychological interaction, a sense of specialness, and anticipation. The mean score given by the subjects was significantly higher than 4 (no opinion), revealing that the life values advertisement was praised by the subjects.

5   Conclusions and Suggestions

This study explored the relationship between advertising copy referencing life values and the observer's psychological interaction. The research findings were as follows: (I) The data related to eye tracking proved that copy that conveys a message about life values is likely to trigger the observer's interest. Results from factor analysis also confirmed that such advertisements motivated psychological interaction, which was in accordance with the propositions by Radach et al. [6]. (II) The data related to eye tracking also evinced that females with a background in design tended to watch men models longer than males did, which was contradictory to the claim made by David Ogilvy [7]. The results of this study make valuable contributions to the field of marketing. Future work could seek to build upon these results to increase the reliability of this methodology.

References

1. Rokeach, M.: The Nature of Human Values. Free Press, New York (1973)
2. Schwartz, S.H.: Universals in the content and structure of values: theoretical advances and empirical tests in 20 countries. Adv. Exp. Soc. Psychol. **25**(1), 1–65 (1992)
3. Carman, J.M.: Values and consumption pattern: a closed loop. Ad. Consum. Res. **5**, 403–407 (1978)
4. Yang, M.Y.: The influence of personality, value and life style on postmodernism consumer behavior: the comparison among three generations. Master's thesis, Graduate School of Management, I-Shou University, Kaohsiung City (2002)
5. Treisman, A., Gelade, G.: A feature-integration theory of attention. Cogn. Psychol. **12**(1), 97–136 (1980)
6. Radach, R., Vorstius, Ch., Radach, K., Heller, D.: Eye movements in the processing of advertisements: effects of pragmatic complexity (2001). http://congress.utu.fi/ecem11/other_applied/radach.htm
7. What is David? Ogilvy's Advertising Guidelines? http://resources.alibaba.com/topic/800252812/What_is_David_Ogilvy_s_advertising_guidelines_.htm
8. Huang, C., Chuang, M.H.: The analysis of storyness in visual composition and emotion experience. In: Symposium Conducted at the Meeting of International Association of Societies of Design Research 2009. Seoul, Korea (2009)

Questionnaire Survey on Attention of Young Adults

Junmin Du[⊠], Weiyu Sun, and Xiaofan Wang

School of Transportation Science and Engineering/Airworthiness Technologies
Research Center, Beihang University, Beijing, China
{dujm, sunwy92, 8709}@buaa.edu.cn

Abstract. Attention plays an important role in guaranteeing the safety and efficiency of task operation. People may get distracted by various internal and external causes. There are differences between individuals in their reaction to the distractions. Understanding the characteristics of attention is the basis for human-machine interface design. In this study, a questionnaire was designed, which concerned personality, environment, task, biological clock, self awareness and self control etc. 138 questionnaires were collected from young adults. Based on the questionnaires, the features of young adults' attention were described. The study results are helpful for the designer to know young people better in the attention characteristics, so as to get benefits for man-machine interface and task design.

Keywords: Attention · Distraction · Questionnaire survey · Young adults

1 Introduction

In order to obtain the satisfied result of using some products, users are expected to concentrate on interacting with the products. However, users may get distracted because of various internal and external causes. Failures of attention could be classified in terms of three categories: selective attention, focused attention and divided attention (Wickens and Hollands 1999). The origin of the selection process could be triggered by the exogenous stimuli depending on salience, or motivated by the endogenous expectations and goals (Engstrom et al. 2013). Human attention resources are limited, which can be allocated, transferred and wasted. Focused attention is affected easily by the changing situation (Wickens 1992; Berti et al. 2004). Divided attention limits describe our limited ability to time-share performance of multi-tasks, or sometimes describe our limits in integrating multiple information sources (Wickens and Hollands 1999). Human brain tends to generate some ideas spontaneously when idle attention resources occur. Researches have shown that humans drift their attention away from the current task frequently if the task is tedious or boring. Their attention would point at something that is irrelevant to the current task, such as past memories and the person concerned (Schooler et al. 2014; Baird et al. 2010; Mrazek et al. 2013).

Human characteristics are the basis for human-machine interface design. Attention is one of the important factors affecting it. A good well understanding of attention would be of help for designing the product in accordance with human characteristics.

© Springer International Publishing Switzerland 2015
C. Stephanidis (Ed.): HCII 2015 Posters, Part I, CCIS 528, pp. 93–97, 2015.
DOI: 10.1007/978-3-319-21380-4_17

This will help in creating more favorable conditions which in turn will enhance mental and physical concentration. As a result, the product to be used will become more effective.

In this research, a questionnaire was designed to find out the attention features of young adults, who were the main users for some certain products. The factors addressed include personality, environment, task feature, self awareness and self control etc. The main goal was to understand the characteristic of young adults' attention.

2 Method

2.1 Participants

150 Chinese young adults participated in the survey. Finally, a total of 138 questionnaires were collected, out of which, 43 were answered by females and 95 by males. Participants' ages were from 18 to 25, in which 5 participants were below 20 years old, 104 participants were from 21 to 23, and 29 participants were above 23. The ratio of introverted and extroverted participants was approximately 1:1, and there was no gender difference. Participants were recruited by posting advertisements at local communities.

2.2 Design

The questionnaire was comprised of 24 items in four sections: basic demographic characteristics, environment, task feature, self awareness and self control.

- Basic demographic characteristics concerned participants' ages, gender, major, personality trait (introversion or extraversion), health condition, major in university (engineering, science, arts, and management).
- Environment concerned the type of exogenous stimuli, such as light, sound, smell, space size, crowded degree, nature time.
- Task feature concerned the difficulty level of tasks (easy, medium and hard), the reason that driven people doing task (interest in, expert in, and compulsory requirement), task contents (reading mathematics, philosophy, history, law, politics, military, poem, manual instruction).
- Self awareness and self control concerned the duration for keeping attention (5–10 min, 10–20 min, 20–30 min, and above 30 min), the endogenous causes which result in distraction (mood, sleepy, interests, goal), when people became aware distraction (could not, after a while, immediately), self control on distraction (no control, after a while, immediately), the perceived difficulty when re-locate attention into task (easy, a little difficult, very difficult), the ability on ignoring distraction (high, low, very low), the self evaluation on attention control (easy, difficult, very difficult).

Most of the questions were single choice questions. A few of the questions were sorting questions. For example, the participants were asked to sort the nature time of a day (morning, noon, afternoon, evening, night) into the order as they feel easy to keep attention, with 1 being very easy and 5 being very difficult.

3 Results

3.1 Environment

Light, sound and smell affect attention through different sensory channels. More than half of the participants (female 60.5 %, male 55.8 %) believed that sound played a greater role in distraction as compared to light and smell. While 18.6 % female and 24.2 % male regarded light as the No. 1 attracted environmental factor. Also 20.9 % female and 20.0 % male considered smell was the most likely resource that lead to distraction. Although females and males had different opinions on the biggest environmental factor, there were no significant gender differences.

For the response to environmental factors, 61.6 % participants (female 69.8 %, male 56.8 %) reported that they would get distracted involuntarily even if they wanted to pay attention to the task. 35.5 % participants (female 27.9 %, male 38.9 %) said that they could completely ignore the environmental interference and continue with their tasks at hand. While 3.6 % participants (female 2.3 %, male 4.2 %) said that they would be completely distracted, unable to continue the task at hand and would pay attention to the unrelated stimulus. The data showed that most of people could be affected involuntarily by the environment. Comparing with males, females were more likely to be distracted by the environmental factors. Males had more confidence to depress the negative environmental influences than females.

The space size and population density also had an effect on attention. 58.7 % of the participants reported the spacious environment allowed them to focus more easily. The expected space size of introverts in spacious environment for a task was 1.2 times higher than that in small space. The ratio was 1.7 in extroverts. It showed that extroverts were more willing to stay in a larger place for task than introverts. Population density had a greater influence on attention than the space size. The affected range in descending order were high population density in small place (57.2 %), followed by high population density in spacious place (30.4 %), then low population density in spacious place (7.2 %), low population density in small place (5.1 %). Namely 87.6 % participants reported that crowded place (spacious or narrow) would be distracted.

The concentration time was different between genders. For the females, the easiest time to focus on a task was morning, followed by afternoon and evening. But males thought that evening was the best time to concentrate on a task, followed by morning and afternoon. Noon was considered to be the most difficult time for attention, without genders difference.

3.2 Task

Comparing personal interests, job specialization and task requirement, interest was the number one to influence attention of most people with absolute superiority (introverts 55.9 %, extroverts 42.9 %). It was followed by job specialization (introverts 25.0 %, extroverts 32.9 %) and task requirement (introverts 19.1 %, extroverts 24.3 %). There was no genders difference here.

When asking to do an obligatory task beyond interest, 76.8 % participants reported there was difficult to concentrate but it could be overcame (females 86.0 %, males 72.6 %). 10.9 % participants reported it was easy to concentrate. 12.3 % participants reported it was very difficult to concentrate, unfortunately.

For the tasks with a time limit, 72.5 % participants thought that more time lead to more difficulty in concentration, while relatively less time could make concentration easier. The rest of the participants (27.5 %) took the opposite view.

A task with moderate difficulty was most favorable for concentration. Too easy or too difficult tasks easily caused distraction. The number of people who believed difficult task was more difficult to concentrate was 1.2 times higher than those who believed easy task was more difficult to concentrate. Out of which, 67.6 % introverts supported that difficult task was more difficult to concentrate; while 58.6 % extroverts supported that easy task was more difficult to concentrate. The results also showed that the extroverts believed that they could concentrate more easily when carrying out difficult tasks.

For the reading task, the participants reported that the unfamiliar materials, compared with the materials that belonged to their major, were more difficult for them to concentrate.

3.3   Self Awareness and Self Control

81.9 % participants believed that they could keep focus for 20–30 min or more than 30 min continuously. Out of which, 53.5 % females and 30.5 % males reported for 20–30 min, 30.2 % females and 50.5 % males reported for more than 30 min. It showed that higher percentage of males had longer length of time to keep focus than females. In addition, 14.5 % participant reported that they could keep focus for 10–20 min. 3.6 % participant reported for 5–10 min. There were wide individual differences on keeping attention continuously.

For the causes that result in distractions, 34.1 % participants thought the most important one was the mood; 24.6 % participants thought it was interest on task; 21.7 % and 19.6 % participants thought it was lack of sleep and poor state of health respectively.

Most people (64.5 %) said they need time to aware their distraction state and also need other time to bring themselves to return to task. Most people felt that self awareness of distraction was easy to practice. However, it was difficult to bring oneself to return to task. For example, 34.1 % participants reported that they could self aware mind wandering immediately, and Only 1.4 % participants thought that they could not self aware. However, for the attention return to task, only 27.5 % said they could shift into task at once when they realized their mind wandering state, but as high as 8 % participants said they could not control their mind wandering.

28.3 % participants reported that they had no difficulties at all in bring themselves return to task. 67.4 % participants reported that they had certain difficulties in practicing self control to combat mind wandering although they could return to task finally.

But 4.3 % participants reported that it was very difficult for them to shift attention back to task. Meanwhile, 17.4 % participants reported that they had no difficulties in attention self control. 75.4 % participants reported they had, and 7.2 % participants reported they had great difficulties in attention self control.

4 Conclusions

The distraction could hinder the human from giving feedback to the current task, which may lead to hazardous events. On the contrary, the distraction sometimes helps to speed up the perceived time flow during boring or tedious activities, which is obvious positive for task completion. Understanding attention features would be necessary for tasks and products design.

The study results are helpful for the designer to know young people better in the attention characteristics. They could design products more suitably for people's specific features, and guide the user doing tasks in varying situations. This will make the man-machine interface more effective, make the task procedure more suitable for user, and improve the user experience as well.

Acknowledgements. This research was supported by the Aviation Science Foundation and the National Key Technology R&D Program under project: control devices ergonomics design technology and standards research (project number 2014BAK01B02).

References

Wickens, C.D., Hollands, J.G.: Engineering Psychology and Human Performance, 3rd edn, pp. 69–70. Prentice Hall, Upper Saddle River (1999)

Engstrom, J., Victor, T., Markkula, G.: Attention selection and multitasking in everyday driving: a conceptual model. In: Regan, M.A., Lee, J.D., Victor, T.W. (eds.) Driver Distraction and Inattention, pp. 27–54 (2013)

Wickens, C.D.: Engineering Psychology and Human Performance. Harper Collins, New York (1992)

Berti, S., Roeber, U., Schroger, E.: Bottom-up influences on working memory: behavioral and electrophysiological distraction varies with distractor strength. Exp. Psychol. **51**, 249–257 (2004)

Schooler, J.W., Mrazek, M.D., Franklin, M.S., Baird, B., Mooneyham, B.W., Zedelius, C., Broadway, J.M.: The middle way: finding the balance between mindfulness and mind-wandering. In: Ross, B.H. (ed.) The Psychology of Learning and Motivation, vol. 60, pp. 1–33. Academic Press, Burlington (2014)

Baird, B., Smallwood, J., Schooler, J.W.: I can shake that feeling: positive mind wandering prevents the deterioration of mood. In: Poster Presented at: Toward a Science of Consciousness, Tucson, AZ (2010)

Mrazek, M.D., Franklin, M.S., Phillips, D.T., Baird, B., Schooler, J.W.: Mindfulness training improves working memory capacity and GRE performance while reducing mind wandering. Psychol. Sci. **24**(5), 776–781 (2013)

Spatial Effect of Target Display
on Visual Search

Xiaoli Fan[1], Zhongqi Liu[1], Qianxiang Zhou[1(✉)], and Fang Xie[2]

[1] School of Biological Science and Medical Engineering,
Beihang University, Beijing 100191, China
fanfan19851414@163.com, zqxg@buaa.edu.cn
[2] General Technology Department,
China North Vehicle Research Institute, Beijing 100072, China

Abstract. The effect of spatial layout on visual performance and eye-movements characteristics was analyzed and the results would provide theoretical guidance for the ergonomics design of man-computer interface. A division method was proposed to divide the optimum visual field into nine regions based on the anatomical characteristics of human retinal and the horizon characteristics of quadrants, and corresponding software with the target displaying in different regions dynamically was completed for the experiment. Twelve subjects participated in the experiment and their reaction time and eye movement data were recorded. The significant differences and the prioritizations of different visual regions were analyzed. The results indicated that, there was significant time difference among the regions with different eccentricity, and the visual performance decreased along with the increase of eccentric distance; for the same eccentric distance, the visual performance of lower visual field was superior to the upper visual field, while the left visual field was superior to the right visual field, and the former difference was more apparent compared with the latter one. In the ergonomic study of display interface of man-computer, spatial effect of target display should be considered.

Keywords: Eye movement · Spatial effect · Visual search · Workload · Man-computer interface

1 Introduction

Vision is an important approach to gain information, from which 80 % ~ 90 % of the information external is obtained [1]. Information detection tasks form an essential part of a man-computer system, and these activities invariably involve visual search [2]. The vision working efficiency is affected by various extrinsic factors, such as the stimulus' shape and color, contrast, background color [3]. At present, there is less ergonomics research on spatial effect of target display on visual search. The space division way of visual field is only limited to previous research and has no further development [4]. RT (reaction time) and accuracy are important evaluation indicators of visual search performance, and are important reference for the analysis of vision ergonomics [5]. In order to explore the spatial effect of target display on visual search

© Springer International Publishing Switzerland 2015
C. Stephanidis (Ed.): HCII 2015 Posters, Part I, CCIS 528, pp. 98–103, 2015.
DOI: 10.1007/978-3-319-21380-4_18

more deeply, a method synthetizing performance measurement and eye movement measurement was proposed in the study. The research result will be used for the interface layout design of aeronautics and astronautics human factors engineering, which could improve the work efficiency of man-machine interaction.

The purpose of this study is to explore the characteristics of pilots' attention allocation, workload change, and cognition by eye tracking of pilots' scanning behavior and the analysis of pilots' eye movement indexes. The work will provide some valuable reference to the design of aircraft cockpit.

2 Method

2.1 Subjects

Twelve college students participated this experiment voluntarily; their ages ranged from 20 to 28. They all had reported having normal or corrected to normal visual acuity. All were right-handed.

2.2 Experiment Design

There are mainly two division ways of visual field. One is based on the anatomy characteristics of retina, and the other is based on the absolute position of visual field. The visual field is divided into four regions through the former division way, and they are fovea region(circle with radius 6°), deputy fovea zone (circle with radius from 6° to 11°), peripheral visual zone(from the circle with radius 11° to optimal vision edge), and edge visual zone (the region beyond the optimal vision) [6, 7]. For the latter division way, the visual gaze center is considered as the origin, and the visual field is divided into four mathematical quadrants from the horizontal and vertical directions [8, 9]. With the combination of the two division ways above, a new division way of visual field is proposed. Meanwhile, combining the results of pretest, the final visual field was divided into nine regions, as shown in Fig. 1.

Software was designed based on the new division way (Fig. 1). The red square with blue arrows is considered as the target stimulus, randomly appearing in one of the nine regions. When the target appears, the subjects have to press the space key immediately. Meanwhile, the target disappears, and the subjects have to press the left or right mouse

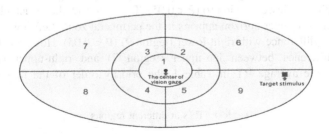

Fig. 1. Division of the visual field (Color figure online)

key according to the arrows direction. Avoiding the effect of fatigue, for each subject, the whole experiment is consisted of twelve sections, and each section has 25 trials. After each section finished, the subjects should have a rest. The RTs of correct operations are recorded by the software. RED eye tracker of iView series is used to record the eye movement data during the experiment.

3 Results and Discussion

3.1 RT Statistics and Analysis

One-way ANOVA was used to analyze the reaction time. The results showed that the difference at the nine regions was significant (F = 122.53, P < 0.05). Meanwhile, multiple comparative law was carried out, some conclusions can be obtained. Table 1 showed the average RT at different regions.

(1) Regions with different eccentricity

The RT of region 1 had significant difference with other eight regions (all in P < 0.05). Meanwhile, for the deputy fovea peripheral (region 2, 3, 4, 5) and peripheral zone (region 6, 7, 8, 9), there was significant difference between the regions in the same quadrant but with different eccentricity (P < 0.05). Table 1 showed the average reaction time at different regions and indicated that the RT of central fovea (region 1) is shortest, while the deputy fovea's (region 2, 3, 4, 5) is shorter than the peripheral zone's (region 6, 7, 8, 9).That is to say, farther the away from the visual gaze center, longer the reaction time and worse the visual search performance.

(2) Regions with the same eccentricity

In the zone of deputy fovea peripheral (region 2, 3, 4, 5), the difference of left-lower (region 4), right-lower (region 5) and left-upper (region 3) is not significant (all in P > 0.05). Right-upper (region 2) has significant difference to other three regions (left-lower, right-lower, left-upper) (all in P < 0.05) with about 20 ms average RT longer than them, which means that there is no visual advantage at the right-upper of deputy fovea peripheral. According to the average RT in Table 1, the priority order of the four regions is: left-lower (region 4) > right-lower (region 5) = left-upper (region 3) > right-upper (region 2).

In the peripheral zone (region 6, 7, 8, 9), left-upper (region 7) has significant difference with left-lower (region 8) (P < 0.05); right-upper (region 6) has significant difference with right-lower (region 9) (P < 0.05). That is to say, the visual advantage of lower horizon over upper horizon appears in the peripheral zone. Left-lower (region 8) has significant difference with right-lower (region 9) (P < 0.05). However, there is no significant difference between left-upper (region 7) and right-upper (region 6). According to the average RT in Table 1, the priority order of the four regions in

Table 1. RTs at different regions

Visual region	1	2	3	4	5	6	7	8	9
RT(ms)	513.1	656.2	630.04	613.8	627.0	696.9	688.8	657.9	672.2

peripheral zone is: left-lower > right-lower > left-upper > right-upper, which is consistent with the regions in deputy fovea peripheral.

Bumsuk Lee [12] pointed out that the left horizon was superior to the right horizon, while the lower horizon was superior to the upper horizon in the visual search. Yantao Ren [13] also gave the same conclusions, meanwhile he pointed out that the difference of upper horizon and lower horizon is larger than the difference of left horizon and right horizon, and the eccentric distance effect was very significant in visual search. In this division way of visual field, the results verified that the whole trend also conformed to these laws, and the whole the priority order is generally: 1 > 4>5 > 3>2 > 8>9 > 7>6.

3.2   The Average Fixation Duration

The eye movements of visual search are generally consisted of one planning motion and a series of correction motions. Figure 2 showed the eye movement trail of one subject when the target appeared at the 8-region, and the blue line represented the visual planning phase. When the saccades movement is lineal, the vision cannot reach the target directly but reach a position to correct the direction. There are two vision corrections before it reached the target, and the red lines represents the visual correcting phase. Larger the eccentricity is, greater deviation the saccade direction of planning motion would produce, which led to longer time of correction motions.

Figure 3 showed the eye movement contrail of one subject with the target appearing in the left and right horizons with the same eccentricity respectively. From the comparison figures, it can been seen that when the target was appearing in the left horizon,

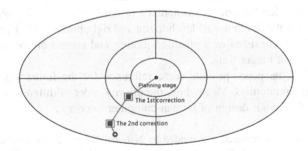

Fig. 2. Eye movement contrail of visual search (Color figure online)

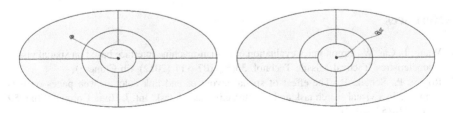

Fig. 3. Eye movement contrails in left horizon and right horizon

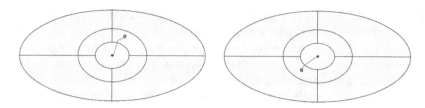

Fig. 4. Eye movement contrails in upper horizon and lower horizon

the eye movement contrail was more clear and there are less saccades in the phase of correction; while the contrail in right horizon was more messy, and there are more saccades in the phase of correction, resulting in longer RT. Meanwhile, comparing with the upper horizon, the contrail in lower horizon was clear and there are less saccades in the phase of vision correction (seen in Fig. 4).

4 Conclusion

The spatial effect of target display on visual search was researched by means of reaction time and eye-movement measurement. Based on the anatomy characteristics of retina and the absolute position characteristics of visual field, the visual field is divided into nine regions, and the following conclusions can be obtained: (1) The eccentricity effect of reaction time was very significant, and the reaction time increased following with the increase of eccentricity. Meanwhile the quadrant effect of RT was also significant: the RT of the upper horizon was longer than the lower horizon; the RT of the right horizon was longer than the left horizon; the difference of upper horizon and lower horizon is more apparent than the difference of left horizon and right horizon. (2) Eye movements of visual search are consisted of a planning motion and correction motions, and correction motions took longer time.

The results of the paper provide some reference for the future study of spatial characteristics in ergonomics. Meanwhile, the priority order of different visual regions can be used in the layout design of human-computer interface.

Acknowledgement. This research was funded by National Natural Science Fund (31170895), National Defence pre-research Fund (A0920132003), and Human Factors Engineering Key Laboratory Fund Project (HF2013-K-06).

References

1. Wang, J., Cai, W.: Ergonomics evaluation of human-machine interface based on spatial vision characteristics. Tactical Missile Technol. **33**(6), 107–111 (2012). (in Chinese)
2. Robert, P., Schaik, P.: The effect of spatial layout of and link color in web pages on performance in a visual search task and an interactive search task. Int. J. Hum. Comput. Stud. **59** (23), 327–353 (2003)

3. Maehara, G., Okubo, M., Michimata, C.: Effects of background color on detecting spot stimuli in the upper and lower visual fields. Brain Cogn. **55**(3), 558–563 (2004)
4. Wang, H.Y., Bian, T.: Experiment evaluation of fighter's interface layout based on eye tracking. Electron. Mach. Eng. **27**(6), 50–53 (2011). (in Chinese)
5. Li, Y.M., Cao, L.R.: Overview of asymmetry in visual search. Ergonomics **45**(2), 37–43 (2003). (in Chinese)
6. Lee, B., Kaneoke, Y., Kakigi, R., et al.: Human brain response to visual stimulus between lower/upper visual fields and cerebral hemispheres. Int. J. Psychophysiol. **74**(2), 81–87 (2009)
7. Previc, F.H.: Functional specialization in the lower and upper visual fields in humans: its ecological origins and neurophysiological implications. Behav. Brain Sci. **13**(3), 519–542 (1990)
8. Thomas, N.A., Elias, L.J.: Upper and lower visual field differences in perceptual asymmetries. Brain Res. **1387**, 108–115 (2011)
9. Pomplun, M.: Saccadic selectivity in complex visual search displays. Vision. Res. **46**(12), 1886–1900 (2006)

Influence of Color Combination Pattern Considered Usability to Mental Workload

Shin'ichi Fukuzumi[1(✉)], Keiko Kasamatsu[2], Yusuke Ohta[2],
Hideo Jingu[3], Nobuyuki Watanabe[3], and Yukiko Tanikawa[1]

[1] Knowledge Discovery Research Laboratories,
NEC Corporation, Minato, Japan
s-fukuzumi@aj.jp.nec.com
[2] Graduate School of System Design,
Tokyo Metropolitan University, Hachioji, Japan
[3] Research Laboratory for Affective Design Engineering,
Kanazawa Institute of Technology, Nonoichi, Japan

Abstract. About color combination using general VDT works, to clarify that feature color combination patterns considered usability are favorable color combination for human from the view point of fatigue, physiological data change during 30 min VDT works with low cognitive load were measured and subjective evaluation was carried out. In this experiment, as feature color combination patterns located on each quadrant in color combination image scale, black, blue, green and pink are used, and as fatigable color, cyan is used. As physiological data, ECG, pupil meter and GSR is measured. From the results of experiment, feature color combination patterns considered usability got higher evaluation from the view point of physiological data and subjective evaluation than a fatigable color combination. Therefore, we concluded that feature color combination patterns considered usability are no significant difference about fatigue and human can use these colors without fatigue.

Keywords: Color combination pattern · Mental workload · Usability

1 Introduction

Personal computer was spread widely with the advent of the information society, and it has become essential in a variety of fields of any industry. Information also in the context of daily life such as computer screen, of course, mobile phones and car navigation systems began to appear on the LCD (liquid crystal display) screen. Some tasks became convenient by the spread of the computer. On the other hand, the complaints on the physical symptom such as fatigue and psychological symptoms such as frustration and reduction of attention are rapidly increasing [1]. One of the causes of mental workload by VDT work, which it may have to continue watching the LCD screen. The elements of screen design have a variety such as character size, the entire layout, especially screen color combination is an essential element [2]. The element of color combination in VDT work is a factor of mental workload (MWL).

© Springer International Publishing Switzerland 2015
C. Stephanidis (Ed.): HCII 2015 Posters, Part I, CCIS 528, pp. 104–109, 2015.
DOI: 10.1007/978-3-319-21380-4_19

Our previous research [3] was reported that the difference of the background color of the screen influence the MWL, difference of color combination of central vision and peripheral vision appears at physiological and psychology responses, and MWL is low on color combination in the central region with black characters on a white background using the peripheral color of blue series. However, the actual business type screen is not necessarily only color of bluish, is used color combination that matches its operations or the customer requirements. MWL is high when these color screen are used. There are variations between the color combination, such color scheme is not suitable as a design guideline.

In this study, we have created feature color combination patterns to refer to the color combination pattern, which is provided as a design guideline. About color combination using general VDT works, to clarify that feature color combination patterns considered usability are favorable color combination for human from the view point of fatigue.

2   Method

To examine the MWL due to a difference in color combination patterns, physiological data change during 30 min VDT works with low cognitive load were measured and subjective evaluation was carried out.

2.1   Color Combination Pattern

In this experiment, as feature color combination patterns located on each quadrant in color combination image scale, black, blue, green and pink are used, and as fatigable color, cyan is used. These color combination patterns were used in our previous research [4] (Fig. 1).

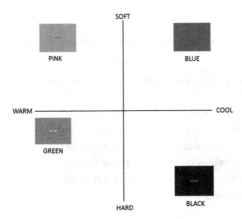

Fig. 1. The color combination patterns (Color figure online)

2.2   Measurement Indices and Evaluation Items

As physiological data, ECG, pupil meter and GSR is measured. These data are analyzed as LF/HF, change in diameter and change in potential, respectively. Two subjective evaluations are also carried out. One is VAS (Visual Analog Scale) evaluation by using a questionnaire and another is an emotional/sensitive evaluation by using 15 items and seven scales questionnaire. Table 1 shows VAS evaluation items and Table 2 shows 15 items of an emotional/sensitive evaluation.

2.3   Experimental Task

The experimental task was two-digit addition mental arithmetic task. Formula was presented in the center of the screen. This is a summation of task without the carry, is very low cognitive load. The participants performed this calculation in mental arithmetic when formula of task appeared on the screen, and enter using the numeric keypad. This task was repeated for 30 min. In order to avoid the effects of fatigue due to task, color combination conditions that can a participant attempted in a day, it was up to two conditions. Moreover, inter-color conditions were taking one hour or more break at least. Figure 2 shows an example of screen.

Table 1. Five items of VAS evaluation

5 items of VAS evaluation
Concentration
Monotony
Dazzling
Sleepy
Bored

Table 2. Fifteen items of an emotional/sensitive evaluation

Item	Item
Friendly-uncompanionable	Responsible-doubtful
Kindly-unkindly	Dependable-less dependable
Feel calm-exciting	Active-passive
Considerate-no considerate	Simple-decorative
relax-look worried	Urban-archaic
Safety-dangerous	Beautiful-ugly
Refreshing-darkish	Favorite-dislikable
Clear-jumble	

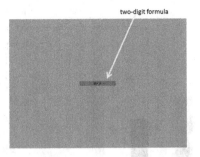

Fig. 2. An example of task screen

2.4 Participants

The participants were ten (4 male and 6 female), and average age was 22.5 ± 1.71 age. Color vision characteristics were not observed.

3   Results and Discussion

3.1 Physiological Indices

At first, the standardized data was analyzed on LF/HF. ANOVA on color combination patterns was carried. There was no significant difference between color combination patterns. Stimulus that a clear change appears in the HF is pretty strong. Therefore, it stands to reason that there is no difference on these color combination patterns that was friendly usability on this experiment. Moreover, for cyan used as a color tired easily, it had been found that it was not intended effect on the indicator in 30 min work.

Next, the result of pupil diameter shows on Fig. 3. As the result of ANOVA on color combination patterns, there was a significant difference ($p < 0.05$) on patterns. Then, multiple comparisons were carried. There were significant differences between black and pink ($p < 0.05$), and between black and cyan ($p < 0.01$). Black pattern is low

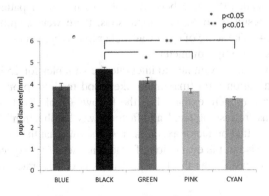

Fig. 3. The result of pupil diameter

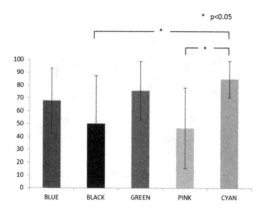

Fig. 4. Dazzling on VAS evaluation

brightness, and pupil diameter on black pattern increases. On the other hand, cyan pattern is high brightness and color contrast and pupil diameter decreases. Thus, the difference occurred between black pattern and cyan. The difference also occurred between black pattern and pink, however there was no difference on them between rest and task execution. This clarified the influence of the task execution on cyan. This was considered to be data to support that it was a color pattern that tired easily.

As the result of GSR, the standardized data was analyzed as similar with LF/HF. ANOVA on color combination patterns was carried. There was no significant difference between color combination patterns. GSR was concluded to be an effective indicator to evaluate the MWL on color pattern on our previous result. This was caused by the follows; the contrast of color combination patterns in this study was lower than the previously including cyan and it was weak as a color stimulus.

3.2   Evaluation Items

ANOVA on color combination patterns was carried for 5 items of VAS evaluation. There was a significant difference between color combination patterns on dazzling ($p < 0.05$). As the result of multiple comparisons, there were significant differences between cyan (Fig. 4). The score of cyan was higher than other patterns. This result was similar tendency as it of pupil diameter.

The factor analysis was examined to integrate the variables for 15 items. The result of cumulative contribution ratio (maximum-likelihood method, promax rotation) was 74.242 %. Three factors were extracted as the follows (Table 3); factor 1 was "gentleness", factor 2 was "refreshing feel", and factor 3 was "civilization". The factor score was calculated and plotted on factor axis. This result shows that the factor score of cyan pattern was lowest. Also in the evaluation of emotional/sensitive aspects, evaluation of cyan, which be tired easily was the lowest. This was corroborated the conventional results.

Table 3. The result of factor analysis

	factor		
	1	2	3
considerate	.866	.634	.199
kindly	.854	.556	.161
favorite	.839	.459	.233
friendly	.828	.640	.259
feel calm	.823	.582	.083
safety	.822	.587	.029
relax	.809	.511	.026
beautiful	.799	.585	.284
responsible	.754	.727	.289
clear	.676	.993	.127
simple	.624	.776	.164
refreshing	.521	.591	.164
urban	-.117	.135	.781
dependable	.564	.405	.773
active	.017	-.174	.452
cumulative contribution ratio	54.556	66.625	74.242

4 Conclusion

This study examined the influences by screen gaze task using color combination patterns which was designed by considered usability and was tired easily from the view point of physiological and emotional data.

From these results, feature color combination patterns considered usability got higher evaluation from the view point of physiological data and subjective evaluation than a fatigable color combination. Therefore, we concluded that feature color combination patterns considered usability are no significant difference about fatigue and human can use these colors without fatigue.

References

1. Tokaji, A.: A human engineering study concerning color combinations on a computer display in VDT work. Hiroshima Univ. Manag. Rev. **1**, 39–48 (2001)
2. Oikawa, T., Shinozawa, Y.: Prediction of visibility for background and character colors on the web browser. Trans. Hum. Interface Soc. **14**(2), 185–196 (2012)
3. Fukuzumi, S., Narabe, M., Kasamatsu, K., Nishimoto, N., Jingu, H., Tanikawa, Y.: Influence of peripheral screen color to physiological and psychological response of users. In: Proceedings of Life Engineering Symposium 2014 (LE 2014), pp. 321–322 (2014)
4. Yano, Y., Ohkubo, R., Tanikawa, Y., Fukuzumi, S.: A proposal of a method to describe customers' needs utilizing screen color combination patterns. Proc. Hum. Interface **2013**, 809–814 (2013)

Emotion Elicitation Using Film Clips: Effect of Age Groups on Movie Choice and Emotion Rating

Dilana Hazer[✉], Xueyao Ma, Stefanie Rukavina, Sascha Gruss, Steffen Walter, and Harald C. Traue

Medical Psychology, University of Ulm, Ulm, Germany
{dilana.hazer,xueyao.ma,stefanie.rukavina,sascha.
gruss,steffen.walter,harald.traue}@uni-ulm.de

Abstract. In affective computing an accurate emotion recognition process requires a reliable emotion elicitation method. One of the arising questions while inducing emotions for computer-based emotional applications is age group differences. In the present study, we investigate the effect of emotion elicitation on various age groups. Emotion elicitation was conducted using standardized movie clips representing five basic emotions: amusement, sadness, anger, disgust and fear. Each emotion was elicited by three different clips. The different clips are individually rated and the subjective choice of the most relevant clip is analyzed. The results show the influence of age on film-clip choice, the correlation between age and valence/arousal rating for the chosen clips and the differences in valence and arousal ratings in the different age groups.

Keywords: Emotion elicitation · Affective computing · Emotion recognition · Human-computer interaction · Film clips · Age difference

1 Introduction

Affective computing aims to numerically process and identify the emotional state of humans. In Human-Computer Interaction (HCI), a correct interpretation of emotions is indispensable to allow computers –such as "companion" systems [1] – to predict the users' needs and wishes and to appropriately adapt their behavior or respond to the current emotional states of a person. An accurate emotion recognition process requires in addition a reliable emotion elicitation method to train the classification.

For various HCI applications, how emotions can be elicited is still an essential issue in affective computing. The induction of emotions in a standardized manner can be realized with the help of specific stimuli. External stimuli can be standardized pictures, for instance from the International Affective Pictures System (IAPS) [2–4], music material [5–7] or film clips [8–10], whereas internal stimuli relate to autobiographical events of the individual subject [11] or imagination methods [12]. Further, these stimuli can be either presented in a passive viewing manner (pictures or film clips) or they can be incorporated as part of the human-computer interaction.

© Springer International Publishing Switzerland 2015
C. Stephanidis (Ed.): HCII 2015 Posters, Part I, CCIS 528, pp. 110–116, 2015.
DOI: 10.1007/978-3-319-21380-4_20

Emotional response to specific stimuli is characterized by various psychophysio-logical and behavioral patterns [13]. Their measurability also depends on the individual subjects. One of the arising questions while inducing emotions for computer-based emotional applications is the influence of specific individual variables such as gender, age or personality. Individual differences in the perception of various emotional stimuli play an essential role in the further analysis and processing of emotion recognition in affective computing studies and have been shown to have an impact on the classifi-cation accuracies [14]. Interestingly, and to the best of the authors' knowledge, stan-dardized material has not been checked for the influence of age.

In the present study, we investigate the effect of emotion elicitation using movie clips on various age groups. The choice of a specific clip as well as its rating in terms of valence and arousal is analyzed and the results are presented for three different age groups.

2 Materials and Methods

An individualized emotion setting for Human-Computer Interactions has been devel-oped to -amongst others- induce various emotional states in subjects. The emotion elicitation was conducted using standardized movie clips from Hewig et al. [8]. Compared to other elicitation methods, induction based on film clips presents some advantages being a multichannel method, dynamic rather than static and does not need imagination and suggestibility of the subjects. Five basic emotions are implemented and were induced within the setting. These include: amusement, sadness, anger, disgust and fear. Three clips of each of these basic emotions were selected and presented as one emotion presentation. After every basic emotion induction (a set of 3 clips), the sub-jects were asked to choose and rate the clip which evoked the strongest emotion. The ratings (1–9) are given for valence, arousal and for the intensity of the basic emotion itself. A total of 94 subjects participated in the experiment, recruited from the following age groups: (1) 18–35 years (n = 35; 16 men, 19 women), (2) 36–50 years (n = 31; 13 men, 18 women), and (3) 51–65 years (n = 28; 15 men, 13 women). Recruitment was performed through notices posted at the university for the 18- to 35-years-old age group and through the press for the 36- to 65-years-old age groups. All the subjects were included in the final analysis.

3 Results and Discussion

To study the effect of emotion induction on age differences, the individual feedback of the subjects regarding the film clip choice evoking the strongest emotion and the corresponding rating for valence and arousal is analyzed. In the following, the analysis results are presented showing the influence of age on film clip choice, the correlation between age and valence/arousal rating for the chosen clips and the differences in valence and arousal ratings in the different age groups.

3.1   Effect of Age on Film Clip Choice

The distributions of the clip choices for age group 1, age group 2 and age group 3 are illustrated in Figs. 1, 2 and 3, respectively. For the whole sample group (N = 94), our results show similar clip choices as suggested by Hewig et al. [8] for all 5 emotions (Fig. 4). The choice results show also that with exception to amusement in age group 1 and in age group 3, the clip choice preferences in the different groups are the same compared to the whole sample. The corresponding clip choice distribution is however different.

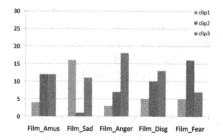

Fig. 1. Choice distribution in age group 1

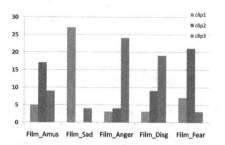

Fig. 2. Choice distribution in age group 2

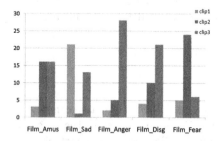

Fig. 3. Choice distribution in age group 3

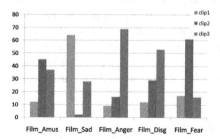

Fig. 4. Choice distribution in N = 94

Table 1 shows the Cochrans's Q test analysis regarding the significant differences among the three film clips in the total sample and in the three age groups. It shows that with exception to amusement and disgust in age group 3, the clip choice preferences in the three age groups and in the whole sample are significant.

Table 1. Cochran's Q test of film clip choices in the whole sample and in the three groups

	Amus	Sadness	Anger	Disgust	Fear
Total Cochran's Q	18.92**	61.87**	72.60**	27.09**	42.15**
Group1 Cochran's Q	9.66**	17.37**	34.69**	12.74**	19.60**
Group2 Cochran's Q	7.20*	41.10**	27.16**	12.65**	17.29**
Group3 Cochran's Q	4.57	12.50**	12.93**	3.5	7.36*

**: $P < 0.01$; *: $P < 0.05$

3.2 Correlation Between Age and Valence/Arousal Rating

Rating results for the valence and arousal of the chosen clips show also variations between the different age groups. Corresponding correlation analysis on the effect of age on the rating is presented below.

Correlation Between Age and Valence Rating: Spearman correlation analysis between age and valence rating is presented in Table 2. The results show that there are significant positive relationships between age and valence rating elicited by amusement and sadness film clips. This means that the older the person is, the higher the valence rating they give for amusement and sadness.

Table 2. Spearman correlation analysis on the influence of age on valence rating

	Amus-valence	Sad-valence	Anger-valence	Disgust-valence	Fear-valence
Age corr. coef.	0.282**	0.283*	0.044	−0.145	0.166
Sig. (2-tailed)	0.006	0.021	0.676	0.163	0.11

**: $P < 0.01$; *: $P < 0.05$ (2-tailed)

Correlation Between Age and Arousal Rating: Spearman correlation analysis between age and arousal rating is presented in Table 3. The results show that there are significant positive relationships between age and arousal rating elicited by all five emotional film clips. This means that the older the person is, the higher the arousal rating they give for all five emotions.

Table 3. Spearman correlation analysis on the influence of age on arousal rating

	Amus-arousal	Sad-arousal	Anger-arousal	Disgust-arousal	Fear-arousal
Age corr. coef.	0.237*	0.295**	0.429**	0.337**	0.240*
Sig. (2-tailed)	0.022	0.004	0	0.001	0.02

**: $P < 0.01$; *: $P < 0.05$ (2-tailed)

3.3   Influence of Age Groups on Valence and Arousal Rating

Table 4 illustrates the rating values (1–9) given for valence and arousal regarding the five emotional states of the chosen clips. The results are shown for the whole sample (N = 94) and for the three different age groups. Except the valence rating of disgust, the mean values given by group 1 are always lower, while those given by group 3 are always higher compared to the mean rating values of the whole sample.

Table 4. Mean rating values for valence and arousal of the chosen clips

	All (n = 94)		Group 1 (n = 35)		Group 2 (n = 31)		Group 3 (n = 28)	
	Mean	SD	Mean	SD	Mean	SD	Mean	SD
Amus-valence	7.56	1.141	7.26	0.78	7.61	1.334	7.89	1.227
Sad-valence	3.45	1.841	2.97	1.272	3.19	1.470	4.32	2.465
Anger-valence	2.64	2.037	2.2	1.511	2.74	1.999	3.07	2.552
Disgust-valence	2.39	1.885	2.57	1.975	2.32	1.739	2.25	1.974
Fear-valence	2.72	1.828	2.31	1.451	2.65	1.762	3.32	2.195
Amus-arousal	5.37	2.180	4.77	2.116	5.42	2.433	6.07	1.783
Sad-arousal	4.63	2.527	3.86	2.557	4.35	2.550	5.89	2.006
Anger-arousal	5.57	2.796	4.17	2.945	5.77	2.348	7.11	2.200
Disgust-arousal	5.13	2.814	4.06	2.960	5.19	2.600	6.39	2.362
Fear-arousal	5.7	2.743	4.66	3.226	5.81	2.372	6.89	1.912

All groups rated amusement with the highest mean valence. The lowest mean valence rating was given for disgust by both group 2 and group 3, while group 1 rated the lowest mean valence for anger followed by fear.

Further, all groups rated sadness with the lowest mean arousal. More differences are found in the highest mean arousal ratings, being: amusement in group 1, fear in group 2 and anger in group 3. In the whole sample N = 94, the highest arousal rating was given for fear, thus similar to the rating of group 2.

4   Conclusion

In this paper, we present the first results on the effect of emotion elicitation within various age groups. The subjective rating results of the film clips show that the choice preferences within the whole sample are similar to the original results obtained by Hewig et al. [8]. Although the distribution of the film clip choices between the different age groups is different, the film choice preferences were found to be the same. This allows adapting those clips of Hewig et al. –originally conducted on a student sample of 38 participants (21 females, 17 males; mean age 22.3 years, range 19 ± 39 years)– for all age groups for the induction of the five emotions (amusement, sadness, anger, disgust, fear).

Our correlation analysis shows significant positive relationships between age and valence rating elicited by amusement and sadness film clips and between age and arousal rating elicited by all five emotions. Also, descriptive rating analysis for the valence and arousal of the chosen clips is conducted and shows variations between the different groups.

Further statistical analysis on the correlation of arousal and valence ratings in the different age groups as well as the analysis of *emotion intensity rating* is being currently processed.

Acknowledgements. This research was supported by grants from the Transregional Collaborative Research Center SFB/TRR 62 Companion Technology for Cognitive Technical Systems funded by the German Research Foundation (DFG) and a doctoral scholarship funded by the China Scholarship Council (CSC) for Xueyao Ma.

References

1. Wendemuth, A., Biundo, S.: A companion technology for cognitive technical systems. In: Esposito, A., Esposito, A.M., Vinciarelli, A., Hoffmann, R., Müller, V.C. (eds.) COST 2102. LNCS, vol. 7403, pp. 89–103. Springer, Heidelberg (2012)
2. Lang, P., Greenwald, M., Bradley, M., Hamm, A.: Looking at pictures: affective, facial, visceral, and behavioral reactions. Psychophysiology 30(3), 261–273 (1993)
3. Bradley, M., Lang, P.: The international affective picture system (IAPS) in the study of emotion and attention. In: Coan, J.A., Allen, J.J.B. (eds.) Handbook of Emotion Elicitation and Assessment, vol. 29. Oxford University Press, Oxford (2007)
4. Frantzidis, C., Bratsas, C., Klados, M., Konstantinidis, E., Lithari, C., Vivas, A., Papadelis, C., Kaldoudi, E., Pappas, C., Bamidis, P.: On the classification of emotional biosignals evoked while viewing affective pictures: an integrated data-mining-based approach for healthcare applications. IEEE Trans. Inf. Technol. Biomed. 14(2), 309–318 (2010)
5. Daly, I., Malik, A., Hwang, F., Roesch, E., Weaver, J., Kirke, A., Williams, D., Miranda, E., Nasuto, S.J.: Neural correlates of emotional responses to music: an EEG study. Neurosci. Lett. 573, 52–57 (2014)
6. Kim, J., André, E.: Emotion recognition based on physiological changes in music listening. IEEE Trans. Pattern Anal. Mach. Intell. 30(12), 2067–2083 (2008)
7. Lundqvist, L.O., Carlsson, F., Hilmersson, P., Juslin, P.: Emotional responses to music: experience, expression, and physiology. Psychol. Music (2008)
8. Hewig, J., Hagemann, D., Seifert, J., Gollwitzer, M., Naumann, E., Bartussek, D.: A revised film set for the induction of basic emotions. Cogn. Emot. 19(7), 1095–1109 (2005)
9. Gross, J., Levenson, R.: Emotion elicitation using films. Cogn. Emot. 9(1), 87–108 (1995)
10. Kreibig, S., Wilhelm, F., Roth, W., Gross, J.: Cardiovascular, electrodermal, and respiratory response patterns to fear and sadness inducing films. Psychophysiology 44(5), 787–806 (2007)
11. Mills, C., D'Mello, S.: On the validity of the autobiographical emotional memory task for emotion induction. PLoS ONE 9(4), e95837 (2014)
12. Kothe, C., Makeig, S., Onton, J.: Emotion recognition from EEG during self-paced emotional imagery. In: Humaine Association Conference IEEE Affective Computing and Intelligent Interaction (ACII), pp. 855–858 (2013)

13. Kolodyazhniy, V., Kreibig, S., Gross, J., Roth, W., Wilhelm, F.: An affective computing approach to physiological emotion specificity: toward subject-independent and stimulus-independent classification of film-induced emotions. Psychophysiology **48**, 908–922 (2011)
14. Rukavina, S., Gruss, S., Tan, J.-W., Hrabal, D., Walter, S., Traue, H.C., Jerg-Bretzke, L.: The impact of gender and sexual hormones on automated psychobiological emotion classification. In: Kurosu, M. (ed.) HCII/HCI 2013, Part V. LNCS, vol. 8008, pp. 474–482. Springer, Heidelberg (2013)

Examining the Gender Gap in Information Assurance: A Study of Psychological Factors

Hsiao-Ying Huang[1](✉) and Masooda Bashir[2]

[1] Illinois Informatics Institute, University of Illinois at Urbana-Champaign,
Champaign, USA
hhuang65@illinois.edu
[2] Graduate School of Library and Information Science,
University of Illinois at Urbana-Champaign, Champaign, USA
mnb@illinois.edu

Abstract. The increasing cyber attacks result in an emergent need for Information Assurance professionals in the government and private sector. Young adults' psychological factors related to the career field of Information Assurance (IA) remain largely understudied despite Information Assurance Workforce (IAW) becoming a crucial issue. Gender disparity, in particular, is a concern for Information Assurance. The first of its kind, this study investigates the gender gap in the field of IA by examining psychological factors affecting young adults, including attitudes, interests, self-efficacy, and goals. Our findings on gender difference in IA from psychological perspectives provide insight for understanding gender disparity in the IA field and initiate studies to explore this issue further. The practical purpose of this study is to contribute information related to gender differences, understood with regard to psychological aspects, for IA recruitment strategies to inspire young adults, especially the underrepresented population of women, to join the IAW.

Keywords: Information assurance workforce · Gender disparity · Career choice · Vocational psychology · Cyber security education

1 Introduction

The relative lack of Information Assurance (IA) professionals in the government and private sector leaves the United States vulnerable to cyber attacks [2]. While increasing the Information Assurance Workforce (IAW) is of national priority, we know very little about what psychological factors attract young adults to this field of study. In particular, the gender disparity in IAW is a concern because women constitute only 10–15 % of the IAW [20]. Although the IAW's gender disparity is consistent with the underrepresentation of women in the Science, Technology, Engineering, and Mathematics (STEM) fields, few studies addressed the IAW's gender gap. The purpose of this study is to explore gender disparity in the IA field from a psychological perspective. In our study we focused on students that are majoring in the IA field because we believe that by understanding those who have already chosen IA as their field of study we can evolve our understanding of what psychological factors contribute to young adults'

© Springer International Publishing Switzerland 2015
C. Stephanidis (Ed.): HCII 2015 Posters, Part I, CCIS 528, pp. 117–122, 2015.
DOI: 10.1007/978-3-319-21380-4_21

decision to be in the IA field and if there are gender differences in those factors. In addition, this understanding will enable recruiting programs to develop the appropriate framework and target their efforts on the young adults that are more likely to join this workforce.

To understand young adults' career choice in the IA field, a study of motivational and cognitive processes as it relates to gender difference is necessary [9]. Questions emerge, such as, how do men and women value career goals differently, and do they believe that an IA career will contribute to achieving their career goals? To investigate these questions, we surveyed university students majoring in IA. We adopted the goal congruity theory from social psychology. Our study investigated four psychological factors: (1) students' attitudes towards an IA career, (2) students' interests in an IA career, (3) students' perception of whether an IA career fits their interests, and (4) students' personal career goals and perception of whether an IA career could fulfill those goals. The following section describes the psychological factors that were investigated in our study and how they influence different career perceptions among men and women.

2   Background

The purpose of this study is to examine gender differences among students majoring in IA by assessing four psychological factors: attitudes, interests, self-efficacy, and career goal. Previous studies have pointed out that these factors are influential when it comes to career choice among men and women. Therefore, we think it is important to investigate these four factors as a preliminary step toward understanding gender disparity in the IA field. We provide a brief illustration for each factor below.

Attitudes. Attitudes have been defined as judgments influenced by external information, past judgments of memory, and prior knowledge [1]. After processing the relevant information, new judgments are stored in one's memory and become attitudes, potentially influencing behavior [14]. Attitudes toward the idea of a career influence behaviors affecting career choice. In addition, an earlier study has revealed that genders had different attitudes toward scientific career due to social stereotypes [21]. Therefore, our first research question is:

RQ1: Are attitudes towards IA career gendered?

Interests. Interests are directly related to work performance due to their influence on individuals' educational and occupational choices, as well as efforts for goal achievement in work settings [7]. In addition, prior studies found that interest can be a strong predictor of choice of college majors and occupations [11]. Furthermore, researchers have noted the gender disparity of interest for information technology careers [15]. Thus, our second question is:

RQ2: Is there gender difference among students' interests, and is there gender difference among perceptions about whether interests match the career field of IA?

Self-efficacy. Self-efficacy in one's career refers to an individual's confidence in pursuing a career-related task [16]. Self-efficacy has been broadly used to explain the gender differences that affect career choices and career preferences [12]. Also, researchers found that self-efficacy could predict career options, occupational interests, and personal effectiveness [4]. Self-efficacy is therefore an essential factor to measure when assessing career choice. Earlier studies found gender differences related to career self-efficacy [5]. For instance, women tend to have lower expectations than men for success in their occupations [5, 12]. In terms of STEM fields, prior studies indicated that men have significantly higher degrees of self-efficacy towards computers [3, 6]. However, significant gender differences were exhibited only in the completion of complex computer tasks [3]. This finding suggests that women may have lower confidence toward personal computer skills when encountering a complicated task. Hence, our third question is as follows:

RQ3: Is there a gender difference in self-efficacy relative to IA careers?

Career Goal. Prior research has revealed that understanding one's goal is an important factor for predicting individuals' motivation and task performance [22]. According to a goal congruity perspective, goals are often stable and malleable to social roles [9]. As scholar [9] illustrate, particular social roles lead to social structures that individuals navigate in the pursuit of their goals. To understand gender differences related to career goals, we examined two types of goals–agentic goals and communal goals. An agentic goal indicates interest in pursuing status, power, achievement, and popularity. A communal goal, in contrast, refers to helping others, working with others, relational needs, and intimacy [9, 14].

Prior study found that women prefer communal goals, such as helping others and working with people, which also influences their occupational interests [18]. Furthermore, if a woman valued people-oriented or society-oriented occupations, she also favored health-related careers [13]. Also, women who considered science to be relevant to altruism tended to exhibit more interest in scientific careers [8], which corresponded to the finding that communal goal endorsement was negatively correlated to STEM interests [9]. Therefore, our fourth question is as follows:

RQ4: Relative to one's personal goal, is there a gender difference in perceptions of career goal and career fit?

Utilizing the above literature on gender differences and career choice, we proposed four research questions to examine gender differences in the IA field. As shown above, attitudes play an important role in career choice. We further examined the relationship between each factor and attitudes toward an IA career.

3 Results

Are attitudes towards IA career gendered? Our first question is whether genders exhibited different attitudes toward IA career. Results did not show significant gender differences in attitudes toward an IA career. Also, the results found that for both women and men, those with a higher interest in an IA career also had more positive attitudes toward an IA career (women: r = .42, p = .002; men: r = .66, p = .000).

Is there gender difference among students' interests and perceptions about whether there is a fit between their interests and the career field of IA? With regard to personal interest toward an IA career, women and men did not show significant difference. However, women showed a lower interest fit between personal interest and the IA field than men (t = −2.13, p = .036). We also explored the relationship between interests fit and attitudes toward an IA career. The results showed that for both women and men, those who perceived an IA career to be more fitting for their personal interests also had more positive attitudes toward an IA career (women: r = .44, p = .002; men: r = .61, p = .000).

Is there a gender difference in self-efficacy relative to IA careers? We found that women had lower self-efficacy than men (t = −4.44, p < .00) to work in the IA field, even though there was no significant gender difference in their GPA performance, which is similar to prior studies. However, self-efficacy did not show a significant correlation with attitudes toward IA for both women and men.

Relative to one's personal goal, is there a gender difference in perceptions of career goal and career fit? Finally, we examined the gender differences in personal career goal and the fit between personal goal and an IA career. Our analysis indicated that women had a higher tendency than men to consider communal goals as a personal career goal (t = 2.49, p = .015). The results did not exhibit a significant gender difference as to the fit between personal goals and an IA career. However, we found that men had higher ratings on the fit between communal goals and an IA career, and that women had higher ratings on the fit between agentic goals and an IA career. This finding indicates that men may regard an IA career as a way to fulfill communal goals; conversely, women may consider an IA career as a way to fulfill agentic goals.

To clarify the influence of career goals for an IA career, we further analyzed the relationship between career goals and attitudes toward an IA career. The results indicated that women who perceived an IA career as fitting their agentic goals had more positive attitudes towards an IA career (r = .39, p = .006). Similarly, men who thought that an IA career could fit their agentic goals also had more positive attitudes toward IA career (r = .48, p = .002). Notably, men who perceived a career in IA as fulfilling their communal goals also had more positive attitudes toward the IA field (r = .41, p < .008).

4   Discussion

Our findings suggest gender difference in three of the factors that we assessed: perception of fit between personal interests and IA career, self-efficacy, and communal goals for students majoring in the IA field. Our findings were similar to previous studies [3, 6]: although there was no gender difference relative to GPA performance, women had lower self-efficacy than men to work in the IA field. One possible explanation is that women's lower self-efficacy emerges from gender stereotypes and self-conception of technological ability rather than actual performance discrepancy [19]. However, while gender differences existed in self-efficacy, it is worth noting that self-efficacy was not correlated with attitudes toward the IA field.

Furthermore, our study provides empirical evidence that the IA field might be viewed as having a lower association with fulfilling communal goals. This may account for women having less interest in pursuing a career in IA [8, 9]. However, for men, an IA career might fulfill both their communal and agentic goals, which might further enhance their positive attitudes toward an IA career. These findings indicate two things: first, women and men may need to receive different recruiting strategies due to their preferences for career goals; second, if the IA field can be increasingly presented to young adults in terms of fulfilling communal goals, this may result in more women to the field [10].

5 Conclusion

To the best of our knowledge, this is the first study to examine the gender difference from psychological perspectives in the IA field. By examining gender differences with regard for psychological aspects, we contribute to IA recruitment strategies so that more young adults, especially women, might join the IAW. For instance, the educational programs in the IA field may consider adding more communal elements to courses and enhancing the self-efficacy of young adults, particularly women, in their mentoring and assessment strategies. Our findings enhance our understanding of gender disparity in the IA field and, hopefully, initiate future studies to further explore this issue in the IA workforce.

References

1. Albarracin, D., Johnson, B.T., Zanna, M.P. (eds.): The Handbook of Attitudes. Psychology Press, New York (2014)
2. Libicki, M., Senty, D., Pollak, J.: An examination of the cybersecurity labor market. National Security Research Division. http://www.rand.org/content/dam/rand/pubs/research_reports/RR400/RR430/RAND_RR430.pdf (2014). Accessed 07 Nov 2014
3. Busch, T.: Gender differences in self-efficacy and attitudes toward computers. J. Educ. Comput. Res. 12(2), 147–158 (1995)
4. Markman, G.D., Balkin, D.B., Baron, R.A.: Inventors and new venture formation: the effects of general self-efficacy and regretful thinking. Entrepreneurship Theor. Pract. 27(2), 149–165 (2002)
5. Wilson, F., Kickul, J., Marlino, D.: Gender, entrepreneurial self-efficacy, and entrepreneurial career intentions: Implications for entrepreneurship Education1. Entrepreneurship Theor. Pract. 31(3), 387–406 (2007)
6. Cooper, J.: The digital divide: the special case of gender. J. Comput. Assist. Learn. 22(5), 320–334 (2006)
7. Nye, C.D., Su, R., Rounds, J., Drasgow, F.: Vocational interests and performance a quantitative summary of over 60 years of research. Perspect. Psychol. Sci. 7(4), 384–403 (2012)

8. Weisgram, E.S., Bigler, R.S.: Effects of learning about gender discrimination on adolescent girls' attitudes toward and interest in science. Psychol. Women Q. **31**(3), 262–269 (2007)
9. Diekman, A.B., Clark, E.K., Johnston, A.M., Brown, E.R., Steinberg, M.: Malleability in communal goals and beliefs influences attraction to stem careers: evidence for a goal congruity perspective. J. Pers. Soc. Psychol. **101**(5), 902 (2011)
10. Diekman, A.B., Steinberg, M.: Navigating social roles in pursuit of important goals: a communal goal congruity account of STEM pursuits. Soc. Pers. Psychol. Compass **7**(7), 487–501 (2013)
11. Eccles-Parsons, J.: Expectancies, values, and academic behaviors. In: Spence, J.T. (ed.) Achievement and Achievement Motivations, pp. 75–121. Freeman, San Francisco (1983)
12. Eccles, J.S.: Understanding women's educational and occupational choices. Psychol. Women Q. **18**(4), 585–609 (1994)
13. Eccles, J.S.: Where Are All the Women? Gender Differences in Participation in Physical Science and Engineering. American Psychological Association, Washington, D.C. (2007)
14. Ajzen, I., Fishbein, M.: The influence of attitudes on behavior. In: Albarracín, D., Johnson, B.T., Zanna, M.P. (eds.) The Handbook of Attitudes, pp. 173–221. Erlbaum, Mahwah (2005)
15. Zarrett, N., Malanchuk, O., Davis-Kean, P.E., Eccles, J.: Examining the gender gap in IT by race: young adults' decisions to pursue an IT career. In: Cohoon, J.M., Aspray, W. (eds.) Women and Information Technology: Research on Underrepresentation, pp. 55–88. MIT Press, Cambridge (2006)
16. Hackett, G., Betz, N.E.: Self-efficacy and career choice and development. In: Maddux, J.E. (ed.) Self-efficacy, Adaptation, and Adjustment, pp. 249–280. Springer, Berlin (1995)
17. Hagemeyer, B., Neyer, F.J.: Assessing implicit motivational orientations in couple relationships: the partner-related agency and communion test (PACT). Psychol. Assess. **24**(1), 114 (2012)
18. Konrad, A.M., Ritchie Jr., J.E., Lieb, P., Corrigall, E.: Sex differences and similarities in job attribute preferences: a meta-analysis. Psychol. Bull. **126**(4), 593 (2000)
19. Kurtz-Costes, B., Rowley, S.J., Harris-Britt, A., Woods, T.A.: Gender stereotypes about mathematics and science and self-perceptions of ability in late childhood and early adolescence. Merrill-Palmer Q. **54**(3), 386–409 (2008)
20. LeClair, J., Shih, L., Abraham, S.: Women in STEM and cyber security fields. In: Proceedings of the 2014 Conference for Industry and Education Collaboration, Savannah, Georgia, 5–7 Feb 2014
21. Lips, H.M.: Gender and science-related attitudes as predictors of college students' academic choices. J. Vocat. Behav. **40**(1), 62–81 (1992)
22. Locke, E.A., Latham, G.P.: A Theory of Goal Setting and Task Performance. Prentice-Hall Inc, Englewood Cliffs (1990)

Development of a Research Framework to Elicit the Optimal Level of Users' Functional Intervention

Song Jung and Sangwon Lee[✉]

Sungkyunkwan University, Seoul, Korea
{pine0527,upcircle}@skku.edu

Abstract. Nowadays people live in the deluge of information. Although dissemination of information, people wander in excessive alternatives while they make decisions. This study deals with degree how well users can access and control the products or services, namely levels of users' functional intervention. To demonstrate correlation between situational confusion and levels of users' functional intervention, we examine related work such as multiple tasks, automation and cognitive load. We consider levels of users' functional intervention as a criterion to find an effective way to reduce mistakes from cognitive load. The conceptual model between levels of users' functional intervention and cognitive load is established, and then we propose an experimental design and present a method to elicit the optimal level of functional intervention that generates minimum cognitive load.

Keywords: Context complexity · Control authority · Difficulty · Cognitive load

1 Introduction

There are many mistakes on users' decision-making, but people still blame human negligence. When human interpret information via their own information processing systems, there are always vulnerabilities on decision-making because mental resources are limited. As the mobile computing environment became more complex, information surrounding the mobile ecosystem has been also complicated. However, such information enrichment does not always trigger good effects. This contextual complexity brings the diversification of optional alternatives users have, and users can control their context more specifically than they used to do before. However it does not stand for increase of accessibility. Users' confusion had increased because it is hard for them to know exactly what to control. It is necessary to provide the proper level of control authority to users performing multiple tasks. Therefore, the levels of users' functional intervention are crucial factors at stake on present overcomplicated point. We intend to provide the theoretical basis in this study. Through the following sections, we will discuss why human can commit mistakes and how to decrease such cognitive load that users can make lesser mistakes. We will take a look into the doubtable probability about the technological improvement may influence negative effects to users.

© Springer International Publishing Switzerland 2015
C. Stephanidis (Ed.): HCII 2015 Posters, Part I, CCIS 528, pp. 123–127, 2015.
DOI: 10.1007/978-3-319-21380-4_22

2 Related Work

This chapter indicates theoretical factors which influence to users' performance in the complicated context. The performance resource function is investigated as an ascertainable way to reveal effects on users' multiple tasks. Automation and users' functional intervention are examined to check whether providing partial assistance to users performing multiple tasks is useful or not. The cognitive load is also considered in order that we can estimate which factors cause excessive mental efforts and know how to reduce it.

2.1 Effects of Multiple Tasks

Users can perform more than two tasks simultaneously through their own time-sharing mechanism. When users carry out multiple tasks, they share their time with other tasks while they do the primary task. There are two factors affecting time-sharing, those are effort and difficulty. In the performance resource function [1], efforts determine the amount of mental resources those ought to be allocated, and the difficulty determines output performance from certain invested resource.

There are two types of tasks; depending on the way of tasks are operated [2]. Resource-limited task is the one that changes its performance when the invested resources increase or decrease. On the other hand, performance of data-limited task is unchanged despite change of invested resources. Resource-limited and data-limited tasks are divided in view of difficulty. If the task requires whole amount of users' resource to achieve 100 % of performance, it is resource-limited. Otherwise, if the task can be achieved by just a little bit of resource, it is data-limited. Because not every task is data-limited, performance of multiple tasks is declined by difficulty of tasks.

2.2 Automation and Users' Functional Intervention

The more tasks are multiple, the less resource is allocated for each task. Users' per-forming multiple tasks also cannot control every function organizing those tasks. Thus an adjustment of levels of the functional intervention has the same way of partial automation of system.

During multiple tasks, automation is considered as a way of supporting the main task [3]. For instance, an automated display offsets the human cognitive load by predicting task procedure and printing out associated information to users [4, 5]. Therefore, the performance of multiple tasks is able to be enhanced by applying partial automation effectively through assigning the appropriate level of functional intervention.

2.3 Cognitive Load

Cognitive load refers to cognitive demand on users' problem solving process. [6] Cognitive resource is the certain cognitive capacity of each individual. According to difficulty or familiarity of which the tasks have, requirements of cognitive load differ from task by task. If cognitive load is greater than cognitive resources, information ought to be processed goes beyond the bound of the capacity of working memory. Cognitive overload is emerged in this procedure.

There are 3 types of cognitive load. Intrinsic cognitive load is caused by difficulty and complexity of task itself. Extraneous cognitive load means unnecessary cognitive load. Germane cognitive load is mental effort to integrate newly obtained information into exist knowledge system of which users already own. Excluding extraneous cognitive load, the rest 2 kinds of cognitive load work as necessary components during problem solving. If extraneous cognitive load is reduced, users can secure extra cognitive resource. Thus, it would rather to be more reasonable to get rid of extraneous cognitive load in order to decrease total mental effort.

3   Development of a Research Framework

3.1   Research Question

We assume that required resources will be reduced as levels of users' functional intervention change. The optimal level of functional intervention can attain perfect time-sharing while users perform multiple tasks. Thus, a research framework is established as shown in Fig. 1. Levels of functional intervention are designated as independent variable to observe their effect on multiple tasks. Cognitive load, influenced by levels of functional intervention, is designated as dependent variables. Partial automation that mediates the intensity of leverage between those two variables is designated as moderating variable.

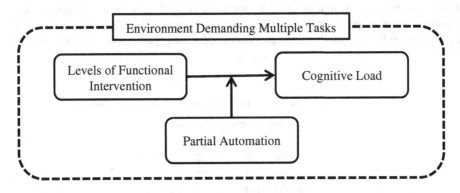

Fig. 1. Conceptual model of a research framework

Although providing a partially automated assistance is helpful for users to reduce required resources, assigning whole decisions on alternative matters to an automated system does not ensure the optimal result. For instance, when levels of functional intervention are too detailed, it causes too much cognitive load that users can not finish their tasks in time. Whereas, when the levels are too plain, users shall have difficulty to obtain what they intended.

How can we elicit the optimal level of users' functional intervention? The optimal level generates minimum cognitive load and let users operate multiple tasks smoothly. Through the following sections, an experimental design is proposed to elicit the optimal level of functional intervention that generates minimum cognitive load.

3.2   Proposal of an Experimental Design

The procedure of the experiment is shown in Fig. 2. Participants are required to perform a wayfinding task by taking a mobile map application. The task is limited to recognize one's current location and path to go. Meanwhile, participants may receive some assistance from the system or not. Factors which influence to difficulty of tasks are discussed in the next paragraph.

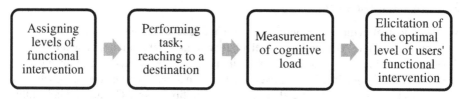

Fig. 2. Experiment procedure

Levels of functional intervention are assigned to each participant differentially as shown in Table 1. Participants are divided into six groups depending on levels of functional intervention that assigned to them. Each level consists of functional combinations to give participants partial assistants differentially. Difficulty of tasks is contingent on how many functions are automated to help participants performing their tasks.

Table 1. Levels of functional intervention and functional compositions

	GPS	Compass	Path aid
1	Off	Off	Off
2	On	Off	Off
3	On	On	Off
4	Off	Off	On
5	On	Off	On
6	On	On	On

To verify an obvious causal relationship between levels of users' functional intervention and cognitive load, exogenous variables are regulated through bringing changes only in levels of users' functional intervention. We intend to demonstrate changes of cognitive load while levels of users' functional intervention vary with the details.

Measurement of cognitive load proceeds simultaneously while participants perform their tasks. There have been many attempts to measure the cognitive load in multidirectional aspects. Indirect methods such as measuring heart rate or pupil dilation and direct methods such as measuring brain activities are possible. In spite of diversity of methods, the dual-task measurement is meant to be a better way than others in terms of its direct and suitable attribute for measuring the extraneous cognitive load [7]. Based on the measurement, the optimal level of users' functional intervention is found out when the generated cognitive load is a minimum.

4 Discussion and Conclusion

In this study, we investigated the effects of levels of users' functional intervention on cognitive load. To reveal the relation between them, we examined theoretical backgrounds and developed conceptual model based on those studies. We intended to establish the basis of the different approach to reducing cognitive load. Therefore, we anticipate that the conceptual model established in this study will be a help to planning user oriented design. Henceforth, the actual experiment will be conducted, so that the validity of established conceptual model will be obtained. It seems that this study can be expanded to contiguous areas such as automation or concise design.

Acknowledgement. This research was supported by the Ministry of Education, South Korea, under the Brain Korea 21 Plus Project (No. 10Z20130000013) and Basic Science Research Program (No. NRF-2014R 1A 1A2054531).

References

1. Wickens, C.D.: Processing Resources in Attention, Dual Task Performance, and Workload Assessment (No. EPL-81-3/ONR-81-3). Illinois University at Urbana Engineering-Psychology Research Lab (1981)
2. Norman, D.A., Bobrow, D.G.: On data-limited and resource-limited processes. Cogn. Psychol. 7(1), 44–64 (1975)
3. Wickens, C.D.: Engineering Psychology and Human Performance. Harper-Collins Publishers, New York (1992)
4. Palmer, E., Degani, A.: Electronic checklists: evaluation of two levels of automation. In: Proceedings of the Sixth Symposium on Aviation Psychology, pp. 178–183, April 1991
5. Stokes, A., Wickens, C., Kite, K.: Display technology-human factors concepts. NASA STI/Recon technical report A, vol. 91, p. 27333 (1990)
6. Sweller, J.: Cognitive load during problem solving: effects on learning. Cogn. Sci. 12(2), 257–285 (1988)
7. Brunken, R., Plass, J.L., Leutner, D.: Direct measurement of cognitive load in multimedia learning. Edu. Psychol. 38(1), 53–61 (2003)

The Effects of Life-Likeness on Persuasion and Attention-Drawing in a Mobile Digital Signage

Yu Kobayashi[(⊠)], Mao Shinoda, Dai Hasegawa, and Hiroshi Sakuta

Aoyama Gakuin University, 5-10-1 Chuo-ku Fuchinobe,
Sagamihara-shi, Kanagawa, Japan
sweep.3092@gmail.com

Abstract. In this paper, we examined the effects of life-like movements on persuasion and attention-drawing in a Mobile Digital Signage (MDS). The study employed a one-factor three-level between-participants design where we manipulated the life-likeness of movement of the MDS (life-like movement vs. simple movement vs. no-movement). We set up the three versions of the MDS at our department building for eight days in rotation, and collected the data of the number of users and the percentage of the users who answered YES at the end of the interactions. As the results of our analysis on the data of the number of users, we found that there was a main effect in the movements of MDS and the MDS with life-like movement had higher than the MDS with no movement. In addition, the analysis on the percentage of the users who answered Yes showed that there were statistically significant differences between the MDS with life-like movements and the MDS with sim ple movement, and the MDS with life-like movement and the MDS with no movement. The results indicated that the power of persuasion and attention drawing increased when the MDS performed life-like movement.

Keywords: Digital signage · Persuasive technology · Attention-drawing · Life-likeness

1 Introduction

Recently, many studies have examined interactivity in digital signage to attract audiences' attention. For example, Chen, Q. et al. proposed a digital signage that can be interact by using hand gestures of passengers instead of using input devices such as a keyboard and a touch screen [1]. And also, there was introduced a digital signage that is use of a smartphone to control the contents of digital signage [5]. But in such approaches, the digital signage cannot attract passengers' attention who do not have any interest in the contents of the digital signage in the first place because some actions are needed which from a passenger to the digital signage. Therefore, Mobile Digital Signages (MDSs) suggest a new direction of advertisement and information delivery in public spaces, introducing autonomously-controlled mobility and interactivity in digital signage. However, although it is well-known that the perception of social existence can be a key

© Springer International Publishing Switzerland 2015
C. Stephanidis (Ed.): HCII 2015 Posters, Part I, CCIS 528, pp. 128–132, 2015.
DOI: 10.1007/978-3-319-21380-4_23

factor to design persuasive computers [2], little is empirically studied on the effects of concrete strategies on persuasion by MDSs.

The present study conducted a field experiment in which we examined the effects of life-like movements on persuasion and attention-drawing in a MDS.

2   Method

In this section, we will describe our MDS system and our experiment.

2.1   System Overview

Figure 1(a) shows the outline of the MDS that offers passengers daily horoscopes. The system consists of a Kinect for Windows, a Roomba, a display (iPad), and a control PC (Surface Pro 3).

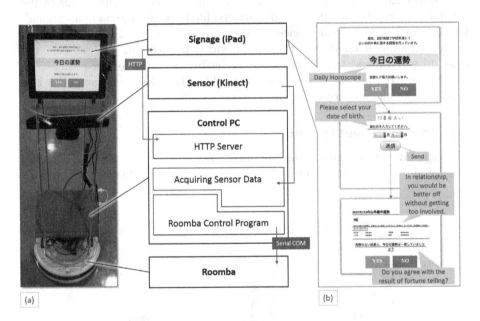

Fig. 1. System Overview (a) and Contents of the MDS (b)

And, we programmed that the MDS waits for a user to enter his/her date of birth, then it displays a result of horoscope, and at the end of the interaction it asks whether he/she will agree with the result of fortune telling presenting YES/NO buttons (Fig. 1(b)). The daily horoscope, the content of the MDS, is running on the HTTP server in the control PC, and programmed with PHP and HTML5. The iPad displays this daily horoscope as a signage by using a built-in web browser. Furthermore, the MDS is placed on the Roomba. The Roomba is controlled by a program which processes sensor data of the Kinect written in C# with .NET Framework 4.5 and Kinect for Windows SDK v1.8.

2.2   Design

The study employed a one-factor three-level between-participants design. The three conditions in which we manipulated the life-likeness of movement of the MDS, and described these conditions below.

C1: Life-like movement condition
    The MDS rotates to find passengers in every 3 s. When it found a passenger, it approaches the passenger for five seconds, and waits for the input.
C2: Simple movement condition
    The MDS repeats to move forward and back in every three seconds.
C3: No movement condition
    The MDS does not move at all.

To check our control of conditions, we took a nine item questionnaire with a five-point likert scale (1–5) where 30 participants watched video clips of the MDS in each conditions, then rated perceived life-likeness (3 items), intentionality (3 items), and human-likeness (3 items) of the MDSs. The control check study employed a one-factor three-level within-participants design. And the order of video presentation was in a counter-balanced random sequence. The results showed that there were significant differences between categories and conditions in all categories (Fig. 2).

2.3   Procedure and Hypothesis

The experiment took place at the 3rd and 5th floors of our departmenet building. First of all, to avoid the novelty effect [3,4], we put the MDSs with C1 and C3

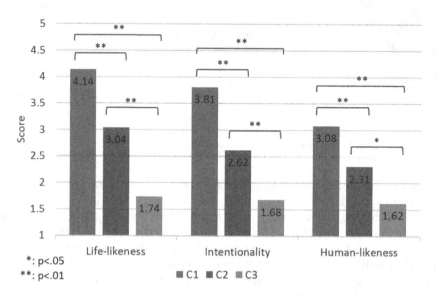

Fig. 2. The perception of MDSs in each conditions (5-point scale)

conditions for four days as the preliminary experiment. After that, we tested the three conditions for eight days for each and collected the data of the number of users and the number of the users tho answered YES at the end of the interactions.

We hypothesized that the MDS in C1 condition has more persuasive and attention-drawing effects than the MDSs in other conditions.

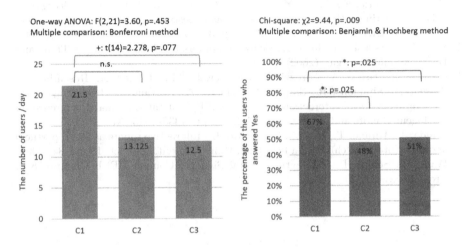

Fig. 3. The number of users per day and the percentage of the users who answered Yes

3   Results

Figure 3 shows the results of the experiment. As the results of our analysis on the data of the number of users, we found that there was a main effect in the movements of MDS ($F(2,21)=3.357$, $p=.05$) and C1 had higher than C3 (Bonferroni, $t(14)=2.278$, $p=.077$). In addition, the analysis on the percentage of the users who answered Yes showed that there were statistically significant differences between C1 (67 %) and C2 (48 %, $p=.025$), and C1 and C3 (51 %, $p=.025$).

4   Discussion and Conclusions

We examined the effects of life-likeness on persuasion and attention-drawing in a Mobile Digital Signage (MDS). The study employed three conditions (life-like movement vs. simple movement vs. no movement) in which we manipulated the life-likeness of movement of the MDS. We run the three versions of the MDS in the our department building for 8 days for each. As the results, there was a main effect found in movements of the MDS, and the MDS with life-like movement has higher than one with no movement. In addition, there was statistically significant differences of the percentae of the users who answered YES between the MDS with life-like movement and the MDS with simple movement, and between the

MDS with life-like movement and the MDS with no movement. In conclusion, the results indicated that the power of persuasion and attention drawing increased when the MDS performed life-like movement.

References

1. Chen, Q., Malric, F., Zhang, Y., Abid, M., Cordeiro, A., Petriu, E.M., Georganas, N.D.: Interacting with digital signage using hand gestures. In: Kamel, M., Campilho, A. (eds.) ICIAR 2009. LNCS, vol. 5627, pp. 347–358. Springer, Heidelberg (2009)
2. Fogg, B.: Persuasive Technology: Using Computers to Change What We Think and Do. Kaufmann, Morgan (2002)
3. Gockley, R., Bruce, A., Forlizzi, J., Michalowski, M., Mundell, A., Rosenthal, S., Sellner, B., Simmons, R., Snipes, K., Schultz, A.C., Wang, J.: Designing robots for long-term social interaction. In: 2005 IEEE/RSJ International Conference on Intelligent Robots and Systems (IROS 2005). pp. 1338–1343, August 2005
4. Kanda, T., Hirano, T., Eaton, D., Ishiguro, H.: Interactive robots as social partners and peer tutors for children: a field trial. Hum. Comput. Interact. **19**, 61–84 (2004)
5. Want, R., Schilit, B.: Interactive Digital Signage. Comput. IEEE Comput. Soc. Press **45**, 21–24 (2012)

The Influence of Different Lighting Source Positions on the Visual Comfort of Refrigerator Illumination

Linghua Ran[1], Xin Zhang[1], Hua Qin[2], Huimin Hu[1(✉)], Taijie Liu[1], and Chaoyi Zhao[1]

[1] Ergonomics Laboratory, China National Institute of Standardization, Beijing 100191, China
{ranlh, Zhangx, huhm, liutj, zhaochy}@cnis.gov.cn
[2] Department of Industrial Engineering, Beijing University of Civil Engineering and Architecture, Beijing 100044, China
qinh03@mails.tsinghua.edu.cn

Abstract. By adopting the method of user experience, this research studies the influence of the layout of the lighting source for the visual comfort of refrigerator inner illumination. There are three kinds of layout, including the lighting source on the top, at the side wall and at the back of the refrigerator, which are conducted experiments under the environment of nighttime, kitchen, living room, common market and high-end store. The result shows that with the vacancy of the refrigerator, there is few influence of the different layout of light source on the visual comfort under the same environment of external illumination. There is a significant difference on the comfort illumination level on the top light and back light under the nighttime environment. But under other outer illumination environments, there is no significant difference among these three lighting source layout.

Keywords: Lighting source positions · Refrigerator illumination · Visual comfort · User experience

1 Introduction

People get more than 80 % outer information from their vision. The internal illumination of refrigerator is the necessary visual condition for people to check goods and quickly recognize them and take them out. When choosing the appropriate illumination for the internal space of the refrigerator, we should take the visual ergonomics, visual satisfaction degree and effective use of energy into consideration.

On the aspect of internal illumination, the current research mainly focuses on the field of construction, locomotive and airplane. For example, in the construction industry, there are specific technical requirements for outdoor roadway lighting and indoor lighting. Xia [1] from Shanghai Aircraft Design and Research Institute has put forward the assessment method of civil airplane drive cabin illumination. Yao [2], from Fudan University, has made some research about the LED lighting ergonomics of the

C. Stephanidis (Ed.): HCII 2015 Posters, Part I, CCIS 528, pp. 133–137, 2015.
DOI: 10.1007/978-3-319-21380-4_24

drive cabin and its lighting. However, nowadays there is still no study on the internal lightening visual ergonomics of refrigerator in China.

2 Methods

2.1 Subjects

In all, 40 participants, comprising 21 men and 19 women were recruited, respectively. The mean ages of the participants were 40.13 (±11.14) years. All the participants have normal eyesight, natural or corrected, with no problem of color blindness or weakness. In the process of the experiment, all subjects keep good health and a good attitude.

2.2 Experimental Environment

The experiments were done in dark rooms. According to the mandatory standards GB 50034-2013 "Standard for lighting design of buildings" [3], the lighting standard value of normal supermarkets should be 300 lx and of high range market should be 500 lx. Moreover, the lighting standard values of kitchens and living rooms should be 100 lx and 100 lx–300 lx respectively. Considering that refrigerators may also be used at night without any lighting, hence the night environmental conditions should also be taken into account (Table 1).

Table 1. External environment illumination level

Experimental environment	Illuminance standard value (lx)	Experimental illuminance value (lx)
Nighttime conditions	/	5
Kitchen conditions	100 lx–150 lx	100
Living room conditions	100 lx–300 lx	170
Common supermarket environment	300 lx	300
High-end store environment	500 lx	580

2.3 Experiment Material

This research mainly focuses on three-door refrigerators. The cold storage of refrigerator has adopted the liner materials, with the size 52 cm, height 65 cm and depth 45 cm. And its inner side is vacant. There are three kinds of lighting layouts, including top lights which locate at the central top of the lumen, side lights which locate at the front side of the lumen and back lights which locate at both back sides. All these three layouts are two light bars and adopt cold and white LED point light source installing symmetrically at the relevant places (Fig. 1).

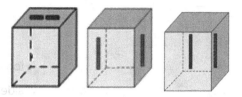

Fig. 1. Different layouts of lighting position

2.4 Experiment Procedure

Before the experiment, we introduce the whole process for the participants. During the experiment, every time when the external lighting is adjusted, the subjects will first make a visual adapt and then start to do the experiment. After the experiment, under the guidance of supervisors, subjects can adjust the inner lights to their most comfortable point. And the values are recorded by supervisors. After the experiment, we make a stationing measurement by the XYI-III shape all-digital portable illuminometer, including the illumination of the left, right and back side of the refrigerator as well as the clapboard of each layer.

3 Result and Discussion

Under the external environment of nighttime, kitchen, living room, common supermarket and high-end store, the comfortable illumination value of top, side and back light can be seen in the following Table 2.

Table 2. Comfortable illumination value of different layouts of lighting

Experimental environment	Environmental illuminance (lx)	Most Comfortable illuminance (lx)	
		Refrigerator inner with items	Empty refrigerator inner
Nighttime conditions	5	50	37
Kitchen conditions	100	69	64
Living room conditions	170	82	84
Common supermarket environment	300	123	122
High-end store environment	580	192	181

From the Table 1 and Fig. 2, we can see the value changes from 5 lx to 580 lx under the above 5 external environment. And the comfortable illumination value of the top, side and back light also increases. As a result, it reflects the objective law between the comfort level of the refrigerator and the external illumination value.

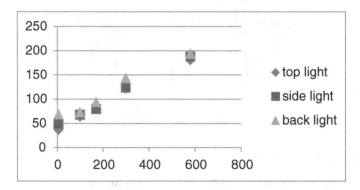

Fig. 2. Comfortable illumination value of different layouts of lighting

We make a difference analysis about the data and conclude that there is little difference under the environment of these five external conditions. In the perspective of statistics, there is no significant difference of the most comfortable illumination level of top and side lights. And only in the nighttime conditions there is a significant difference in top and back lights. No differences in other four conditions. Under these five external environments, the average comfortable illumination value of top lights is lower than that of back lights for 32 lx, 9 lx, 10 lx, 22 lx and 13 lx respectively. For the side and back lights, there is no significant difference of the side and back lights.

4   Conclusions

This research adopts the method of users' subjective experience to study the influence of different illumination layouts on the visual comfort of the inner lighting of refrigerators. The results show that there is no significant difference among these three layouts in other external illumination environment except the top and back lights in the environment of nighttime. Moreover, there is a little influence of inner lighting layout on the visual comfort. We think that the illumination value of visual comfort is equal regarding to top, side and back lights.

Next we can analyze advantages and disadvantages from the perspective of dazzling in different layouts and evenness of inner lighting in order to offer references for people who design the lighting of refrigerators.

Acknowledgment. This work is supported by China National Institute of Standardization through the "special funds for the basic R&D undertakings by welfare research institutions" (project number: 522014Y-3346) and the National Key Technology R&D Program (project number: 2014BAK01B01).

References

1. Xia, H., Zhu, Z.: Evaluation method for cockpit lighting of civil aircraft. Technol. Mark. **19** (10), 12–13 (2012)
2. Yao, Q.: Ergonomics of LED in Research on Application Civil Cockpit Lighting. Fudan University (2012)
3. GB 50034-2013: Standard for Lighting Design of Buildings (2013)

The Effect of a High-Resolution 4K Tablet on Physiological and Psychological State While Viewing Various Types of Content

Kiyomi Sakamoto[1(✉)], Seiji Sakashita[1], Kuniko Yamashita[2], and Akira Okada[2]

[1] Groupwide CTO Office, Panasonic Corporation, 3-1-1 Yagumo-nakamachi, Moriguchi City, Osaka 570-850, Japan
{sakamoto.kiyomi,sakashita.seiji}@jp.panasonic.com
[2] Department of Human Life Science, Osaka City University, 3-3-138 Sugimoto, Sumiyoshi-ku, Osaka 558-8585, Japan
{yamasita,okada}@life.osaka-cu.ac.jp

Abstract. We experimentally investigated the effects of using a high-resolution 4K tablet on physiological and psychological states while viewing various types of content. The results showed the scores for "precise–coarse," "feeling of invigoration–no feeling of invigoration" and "enjoyable–boring" when viewing 4K scenic content to be significantly higher than those for 2K scenic content. Moreover, NIRS values, an index of nervous system activity, during viewing tests of 4K scenic content, were significantly higher for 4K content than for 2K content.

Keywords: Physiological and psychological measurements · High-resolution 4K tablet · NIRS

1 Introduction

Technological progress has led to significant changes in our display-viewing environments. Higher-definition screens, with 4K TV already in production and 8K TV in prospect, and various types of viewing styles, using TVs, PCs and smartphones, make it increasingly important to consider the effects of these changes on human physical and mental health. Our belief that improvements in picture quality and presence should be accompanied by reduced viewer stress and visual fatigue prompted us to investigate the effects of using high-resolution 4K display devices on physiological and psychological state while viewing various types of video content. In a prior study [1], we conducted an investigation of the effects of using a 65-in. 4K TV on the physiological and psychological states, while viewing various types of video content, of eight participants in their 20s. The results showed the scores for "presence," "impact," "realism," "quality" and "precision" when viewing 4K scenic content to be significantly higher than those for 2K content. Significant differences were also observed between NIRS

C. Stephanidis (Ed.): HCII 2015 Posters, Part I, CCIS 528, pp. 138–143, 2015.
DOI: 10.1007/978-3-319-21380-4_25

(near infrared spectroscopic topography) values, an index of nervous system activity, while viewing tests of 4K content and of 2K content. However, further studies using various sizes and types of display will be needed to confirm whether, physiologically and psychologically, 4K viewing is superior to 2K viewing. We therefore explored and evaluated the influence of a high-resolution 4K tablet on psychological state during content viewing.

2 Methods

Subjects: Ten adults aged in their 20s participated in this experiment.

Measurements: The following items were investigated.

(1) Participants' psychological state, reported on a scale of 3 to −3 for 24 items, included "presence–no presence," "reality–no reality," "high quality–low quality," "relaxed–stressed," "comfortable–uncomfortable," and "like–dislike." These psychological items were additionally defined in the light of the results of pilot experimental interviews and those obtained in our prior study (Table 1).

(2) NIRS: Brain activity, based on total hemoglobin or oxyhemoglobin, was obtained using NIRS detectors placed on the left and right of the participant's forehead.

(3) Heart rate (HR) and heart rate variability (LF/HF; level of sympathetic nerve activity): LF/HF is defined as the ratio of the low-frequency band (LF: 0.04–0.15 Hz) to the high-frequency band (HF: 0.15–0.5 Hz) [2, 3], calculated by FFT analysis using the R-R interval based on heart rate variability obtained by electrocardiogram.

(4) Blinking rate, obtained using an electrooculogram (EOG).

(5) β/α, calculated from beta and alpha waves obtained using electroencephalogram (EEG) frequency analysis derived from the Cz reference, based on the international 10–20 method.

(6) Respiration rate (RR), calculated by monitoring a respiratory sensor unit attached to the thorax.

Apparatus:

(1) The display device was an A3-size 4K tablet (Panasonic UT-MB5015SEZ).

(2) The viewing distance was set at 1.5H (45 cm). Screen-to-eye distance was defined in relation to screen height (H). The recommended viewing distance for a 4K TV, defined as 1.5 times the display's height, was 45 cm for the A3 tablet.

(3) Test room illumination was set at 200 lx to simulate the average light level of a Japanese living room, based on JIS standardization.

Procedure: Figure 1 shows the process of the viewing test. The participants viewed four kinds of TV video content (two types of scenic material and two kinds of material with movement and action). Each set comprised 2 min of 4K and 2 min of 2K content. After viewing each program, the participants gave a subjective assessment of their psychological state, on a scale of 3 to −3. One minute of rest time was given before

Table 1. Subjective assessment items

Subjective assessment items (including 21 items)
Qualitative assessment of high resolution
"Sharp focus–no sharp focus,"
"Precision–lack of precision,"
"Precise–coarse,"
"Natural–artificial,"
"Looks like a real object–doesn't look like a real object,"
"Clear–not clear,"
"Realistic–not realistic,"
"Dynamic–static,"
"Feeling of depth–no feeling of depth"
"High quality–low quality,"
Emotional assessment of high resolution
"Presence–no presence,"
"Feeling of invigoration–no feeling of invigoration,"
"Feeling of congruity– feeling of incongruity"
"Impact–no impact,"
"Good–bad,"
"Comfortable–uncomfortable,"
"Enjoyable–boring,"
"Relaxed–stressed,"
"Like–dislike,"
"Aroused–sleepy,"
"No visual fatigue–visual fatigue"

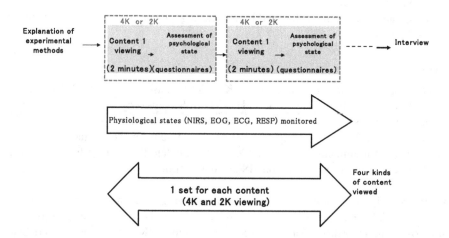

Fig. 1. The process of the viewing test using four types of content

viewing each type of content. Physiological indices were monitored while the participants underwent the viewing tests. To eliminate the order effect, the order of the content type or resolution was made unique to each participant. Moreover, the resolution of current viewing content was not informed to the participant, since it might have influenced their evaluation score.

Statistical analysis: A paired t-test was performed to statistically analyze the influence of the high-resolution 4K displays on the subjects' psychological state while viewing different types of content. The level of significance was set at $p = 0.05$.

3   Results and Discussion

The results showed that the scores for "precise–coarse," "feeling of invigoration–no feeling of invigoration" and "enjoyable–boring" when viewing 4K scenic content were significantly higher than those for 2K scenic content (Figs. 2 and 3).

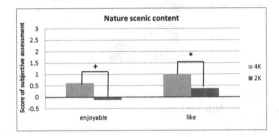

Fig. 2. Mean scores of subjective assessments at 4K and 2K when viewing nature scenes. (Eight participants). A higher score indicates a more positive evaluation. **: $p < 0.05$, +: $p < 0.1$, X-axis (subjective assessments at each resolution), Y-axis (score of subjective assessments)

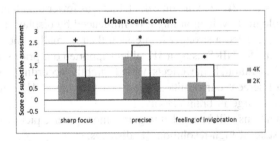

Fig. 3. Mean scores of subjective assessments at 4K and 2K when viewing urban scenes. (Eight participants). A higher score indicates a more positive evaluation. **: $p < 0.05$, +: $p < 0.1$, X-axis (subjective assessments at each resolution), Y-axis (score of subjective assessments)

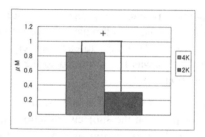

Fig. 4. NIRS (total Hb) during viewing tests for nature scenes at 4K and 2K. +: $p < 0.1$, X-axis: resolution (4K or 2K), Y-axis: NIRS (total Hb)

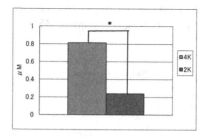

Fig. 5. NIRS (O_2Hb) when viewing tests for urban scenes at 4K and 2K. *: $p < 0.05$, X-axis: resolution (4K or 2K), Y-axis: NIRS (O_2Hb)

Moreover, NIRS (total Hb), an index of nervous system activity, during viewing tests of 4K nature scenic content, tended to be higher for 4K content than for 2K content (Fig. 4), and NIRS (O_2Hb) during viewing tests of 4K urban scenic content was significantly higher for 4K content than for 2K content (Fig. 5).

The number of psychological indices which showed a significant difference between 4K viewing and 2K viewing on a 4K tablet was fewer than that for a 65-in. 4K TV. As the psychological evaluation might be influenced by display size, it is possible that a bigger screen created a stronger impression than a smaller one.

However, the data for NIRS using a 4K tablet supported our prior study results with a 65-in. 4KTV [1]. Although the effects varied slightly according to content being viewed and type of screen, our results suggest that viewing at 4K can cause psychological elation and a surge in brain activity.

Further investigations will be needed to gain a more precise picture of the influence on psychological state of high-resolution 4K displays.

References

1. Sakamoto, K., Sakashita, S., Yamashita, K., Okada, A.: Effect of display resolution on physiological and psychological state while viewing video content. In: Proceedings of the 4th IEEE International Conference on Consumer Electronics, ICCE-Berlin, pp. 162–163, Sept 2014
2. Ishibashi, K., Kitamura, S., Kozaki, T., Yasukouchi, A.: Inhibition of heart rate variability during sleep in humans by 6700K pre-sleep light exposure. J. Physiol. Anthropol. **26**(1), 39–43 (2007)
3. Ishibashi, K., Ueda, S., Yasukouchi, A.: Effects of mental task on heart rate variability during graded head-up tilt. J. Physiol. Anthropol. **18**(6), 225–231 (1999)

Brain Mechanism Research on Visual Information Cognition of Digital Human Computer Interface

Chengqi Xue[1(✉)], Xiaoli Wu[1,2], Yafeng Niu[1], Lei Zhou[1],
Jiang Shao[1], and Zhangfan Shen[1]

[1] School of Mechanical Engineering, Southeast University,
Nanjing 211189, China
ipd_xcq@seu.edu.cn
[2] College of Mechanical and Electrical Engineering, Hohai University,
Changzhou 213022, China

Abstract. With the improvement of the degree of informatization, digital human-computer interface (hereinafter referred to as DHCI) has been gradually replacing the traditional display and control interface, which plays an essential role in the efficient and precise operation of complex informative system. In recent years, unreasonable visual information design of DHCI has been proved to be one of the main reasons that cause a lot of serious accidents, which leads to users' mistakes in cognitive understanding and decision-making periods. Complex system has a great amount of information and a complicated information structure, which is easy to result in the imbalance between visual information design and cognitive mechanism. This poster is planning to start from the brain mechanism research of visual information cognition, and carrying out visual information design research through a perspective that close to the origin attribute of human cognition, making the research on visual information analysis of the information structure and encoding method in DHCI.

Keywords: Digital human-computer interface · Cognitive brain mechanisms · Design · Visual information cognition

1 Introduction

Human brain is the most complex existence in the universe we have ever known, and the nervous system, especially the degree of the brain evolution is the main indicator that distinguishes animals' (including humans') evolution extent. The brains' mysteries are always the most challenging issues of the natural science. Visual system has received extensive attention because of its extreme importance in animal and human life, the brain mechanism of visual cognition has evolved into a relatively independent branch in neuroscience. Visual cognition has a typical "black box" property, information processing of which is difficult to directly detect. The existing methods are developed according to "sensor" and "reactor", such as eye-tracking, reaction time etc. Although behavioral studies can objectively reflect human visual cognitive process,

C. Stephanidis (Ed.): HCII 2015 Posters, Part I, CCIS 528, pp. 144–149, 2015.
DOI: 10.1007/978-3-319-21380-4_26

they are based on speculation, which cannot truly hit the brain mechanism of visual cognition.

Cerebral cortices are related to visual cognition include occipital lobe, temporal lobe and part of the frontal lobe, which constitute 25 of the 52 Brodmann areas. With another 7 visual association areas added, the surface area of these cortices sum up to around 55 % of all the neocortices. The technology of Event-Related Potentials (ERPs), applied in the high-temporal resolution analysis of the potential response in cognitive processes, will be helpful in tracking, distinguishing and comparing many important cognitive process involving perception, attention, memory, decision, etc., which are hard to probe into by traditional research. It is more close to the original attributes of human cognition compared with the method of behavioral analysis, and it has a promoting effect on the research in the field of design and cognition. Figure 1 shows the visual cognition research in ERPs.

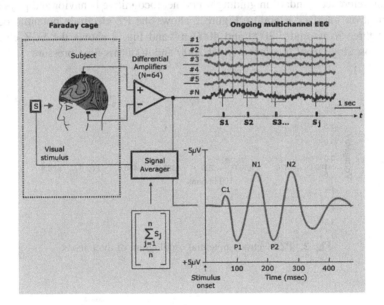

Fig. 1. Visual cognition research in ERPs

2   Method

Neuroscan SynamP2 Amplifier (Scan 4.3.1, Neurosoft Labs, Inc.) continuously records EEG (0.05–100 Hz band-pass; 500 Hz/channel sampling rate), using an electrode cap with a 64 Ag/AgCl electrode based on the extended international 10–20 system. Figure 2 shows the experiment environment in the ergonomic lab in Southeast University.

A total of 10 male and 10 female graduate students aged between 23 and 27 years (M = 25.2, SD = 2.1) who used computer almost everyday were recruited. All participants had normal or corrected vision without color blindness or color weakness.

3 Results

3.1 Study 1: Icon Memory ERP Research

In order to obtain related brain electrical components and neural basis of physiology assessment of icon elements in digital human-computer interface, the modified sample-delay matching task experimental paradigm is used under different time pressures (4000 and 2000 ms) and icon quantities (three, five and ten icons) on icon memory based on event-related potential (ERP) technology. Results demonstrate that P300 has significant volatility changes and maximum amplitude around the middle line of parietal area (PZ) and P200 has obvious volatility changes around the middle line of frontal and central area (FCZ) during icon cognition. P300 and P200 amplitudes increase as tasks become more difficult. Thus, P300 latency is positive correlated with the difficulty of the task. ERP research on icon memory characteristics will be an important reference standard in guiding users' neurocognitive behavior and physiology assessment on interface usability. Figure 2 shows the PZ electrode potential oscillogram of three icons under 2000 and 4000 ms and Fig. 3 shows the FCZ electrode potential oscillogram of five icons under 2000 and 4000 ms time pressure.

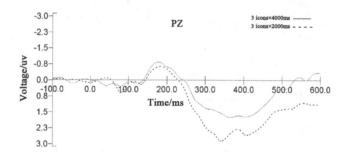

Fig. 2. PZ electrode potential oscillogram of three icons

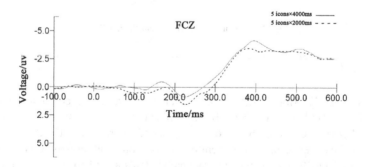

Fig. 3. FCZ electrode potential oscillogram of five icons

3.2   Study 2: Navigation Bar Visual Selective Attention ERP Research

In order to investigate the user cognitive processing of visual selective attention to icon navigation bar in the digital interface, 20 subjects were required to notice and remember the activated icons in the navigation bar selectively and judge whether or not target icon had presented in the navigation bar and if so press the button quickly. Their behavior and ERP data were collected. Experimental results demonstrate that P200 and N400 components of navigation bar selective attention exist obvious differences in amplitude and latency under different activated icon quantities. In the recognition process of target stimulus icon, accuracy rate and reaction time both exist regular changes with the activated icon quantities, and target stimulus recognition N200 component distributing in different brain areas exists obvious differences. Figure 4 shows the topographic maps of maximum amplitudes in different situations.

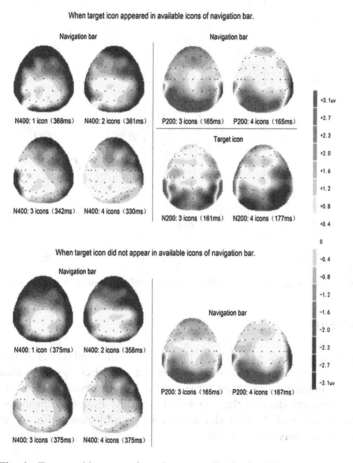

Fig. 4. Topographic maps of maximum amplitudes in different situations

3.3   Study 3: Interface Colour Matching ERP Research

By conducting interface colour matching ERP research, we can find N100 and P200 have more significant changes in colour matching and latency is around 100–200 ms. These results can be used for testing the design quality of interface and evaluated the usability of interface colour matching. Figure 5 shows the P3 electrode potential oscillogram under different colour matching situations.

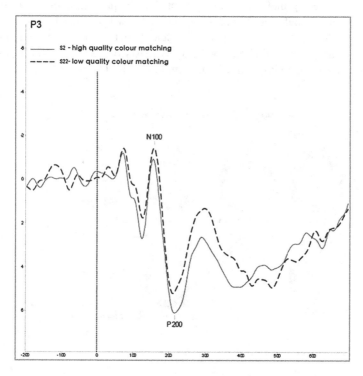

Fig. 5. P3 electrode potential oscillogram under different colour matching situations

4   Conclusion

According to brain electric experiments, the ERP evaluation indexes of digital interface elements were summarized, and interface element and EEG signal threshold values analysis was conducted. Based on these results, recommendation form of interface design was displayed. Besides, the overall and local ERP evaluation methods of digital interface were proposed. Table 1 shows the ERP physiological index and evaluation principle of digital interface elements.

Table 1. ERP physiological index and evaluation principle of digital interface elements

Interface element experiment	Experimental paradigm	ERP element	Max amplitude	Area	Evaluation principle
Icon memory	Modified sample-delayed matching task paradigm	P300	PZ P3	Parietal lobe	The higher amplitude of P300 of PZ and P3, the more difficult icon memory task
		P200	FCZ FZ	Central of frontal lobe	The later latency of P200 of FCZ and FZ, the more difficult icon memory task
Navigation bar selective attention	Serial mismatch experimental paradigm	P200	PO3	Right side of occipitoparietal	The higher amplitude of P200 of PO3, the wider selective range
		N400	FT8	Right side of frontotemporal	The earlier latency of N400 of FT8, the more interface number
Color matching	Go-Nogo	N100	P3	Left side of parietal lobe	The more positive amplitude of N100 of P3, the better interface
		P200	O_2	Right side of occipital lobe	The higher amplitude of P200 of O_2, the better interface

References

1. Girelli, M., Luck, S.J.: Are the same attentional mechanism used to detect visual search targets defined by color, orientation, and motion. Cogn. Neurosci. **9**, 238–258 (1997)
2. Kusak, G., Grune, K., Hagendorf, H., et al.: Updating of working memory in a running memory task : an event-related potential study. Int. Psychophysiol. **39**, 51–65 (2000)
3. Missonnier, P., Deiber, M.P., Gold, G., Herrmann, F.R., Millet, P.: Working memory load–related electroencephalographic parameters can differentiate progressive from stable mild cognitive impairment. Neuroscience **150**(2), 346–356 (2007)
4. Rader, S.K., Holmes, J.L., Golob, E.J.: Auditory event-related potentials during a spatial working memory task. Clin. Neurophysiol. **119**(5), 1176–1189 (2008)
5. Yi, Y., Friedman, D.: Event-related potential (ERP) measures reveal the timing of memory selection processes and proactive interference resolution in working memory. Brain Res. **1411**, 41–56 (2011)

Is Dynamic Visual Search Performance Sensitivity to the Visual Fatigue and Comfort of LED TV? A Comparative Experiment of Eight LED TVs

Yunhong Zhang[1(✉)], Na liu[2], Xin Wu[2], Jing Chang[2],
and Ruifeng Yu[2]

[1] Human Factor and Ergonomics Laboratory,
China National Institute of Standardization, Beijing, China
zhangyh@cnis.gov.cn
[2] Department of Industrial Engineering, Tsinghua University, Beijing, China
n-liul4@mails.tsinghua.edu.cn,
yurf@mail.tsinghua.edu.cn

Abstract. A comparative experiment was conducted to make clear whether dynamic visual search performance is sensitivity to the visual comfort of LED TVs by testing dynamic visual search performance and visual fatigue of eight LED TVs. 16 ordinary man from 18 to 45 years old were paid to participate in the experiment. And all subjects were arranged to doing the dynamic visual search task when velocity was 5°/s. Each participant took the same dynamic visual search tasks on the eight LED TVs in the experiment. The search time and accuracy of each participant were recorded. The results shows that there is significant difference about the accuracy and dynamic visual search time in the course of 5°/s movement velocity between different LED TVs. And there is corresponding mode of comfort, satisfaction, the subjective fatigue feeling between different LED TVs. Those results revealed that dynamic visual search performance was sensitive to visual fatigue and comfort under the situation of 5°/s movement velocity. The obtained results could be a reference for evaluating the quality of LED TVs for a specific visual search task.

Keywords: Dynamic visual search task · Visual fatigue · Comfort · LED television

1 Introduction

With the coming of the information era, the way of information communication has greatly depended on the visual display terminal (VDT). As a kind of visual display terminal, LED television is essential in our daily life. With the continuous innovation of the display industry technology, the television products are constantly upgrading, but, it is not easy to buy the suitable televisions for consumers' different goals. Generally, the consumers might watch movies, watch the games, surf the internet and do many other activities, however, these complex activities might be related to dynamic visual search performance of LED

© Springer International Publishing Switzerland 2015
C. Stephanidis (Ed.): HCII 2015 Posters, Part I, CCIS 528, pp. 150–155, 2015.
DOI: 10.1007/978-3-319-21380-4_27

TVs. Therefore, how to choose a more comfortable and efficient LED TV is important to the consumers, particularly to the ball fans and game enthusiasts, etc.

This study intends to investigate the effect of watching visual displays by dynamic visual search task paradigm and subjective survey. The study is expected to provide indicators to evaluate the efficiency of LED televisions. According to ISO international standard [1] about the user performance test methods for electronic visual displays, we adopted a dynamic visual search task paradigm [2] to evaluate the fatigue degree of LED TVs. We had tested the dynamic visual search task performance, user experience and the visual fatigue degree of 8 LED televisions, which provide the reference for the consumers, fans and gamers buying televisions. The specific evaluation indicators include the effectiveness, efficiency, comfortable and satisfaction. The visual fatigue perception scale developed by Sheedy [3] was used to evaluate the eye and mental fatigue degree.

2 Method

2.1 Participants

Sixteen ordinary users from 18 to 45 years old (8 male and 8 female, mean age = 31.56) were recruited and paid to participate in the experiment. Among them, the participants under the age of 25 were accounted for 18.8 %, 25 years old–40 years old were accounted for 68.7 %, and the participants over the age of 40 were accounted for 12.5 %. All had normal or corrected-to-normal visual acuities and healthy physical conditions, without ophthalmic diseases. They did not have any history of neurological and mental diseases. And all well-rested participants were arranged to doing the dynamic visual search tasks on eight LED television by the turn that was random in Latin square design.

2.2 Experiment Design

A within-subject factorial design was used in this experiment. The independent variable of the experiment is TV types which include eight LED TVs. In this experiment, the dynamic visual search performance, visual fatigue were measured to assess and compare which LED TV is better. The subjective questionnaire was used to investigate the visual fatigue after performing the dynamic visual search task. Participants reported their perception and evaluations by filling in a questionnaire. All the questions in the questionnaire were measured by a hundred-point scale from none to strongly serious (0 = "none" and 100 = "strongly serious").

2.3 Apparatus

Experiments were conducted in a laboratory environment which simulated home condition. It was installed in the laboratory in the Institute of Human Factors and Ergonomics lab in China National Institute of Standardization. The dynamic visual search tasks are displayed on the 8 LED TVs. We selected 8 46–48 in. (1 in. = 2.54 cm)

LED TVs as test samples from the market. The image mode of all the LED televisions sets exactly the same standard mode.

2.4   Procedures

After arriving at the laboratory, participants signed the informed consent and completed a general survey about their demographic information. The participants were asked to sit into the simulator to get ready for the test. Then we had a visual acuity and diopter measurements for the participants. After that, the participants were asked to follow their own natural state to do the dynamic visual search task when velocity was 5°/s, which is near to the velocity of ball games. Before the experiment, participants were asked to relax 10 min or more, and told the testing process and requirements. Before the experiment, the height of the table and display position were adjusted to make the participants' eyes and display center on a line. The viewing distance is about 300 cm. The experiment task is search a circular ring from dynamic circle matrix [4]. After dynamic visual searching, the participants were required to fill out the visual fatigue questionnaire. The same procedures have done on each LED TVs. Each participant spent about four hour finishing the experiment for two times.

2.5   Data Analysis

The changes value of dynamic visual search and visual fatigue were analyzed by IBM SPSS 20 Statistics software (IBM-SPSS Inc. Chicago, IL). The method of repeated-measure ANOVA analysis is applied to the response accuracy data and response time.

3   Results

3.1   The Basic Luminance Information of LED Televisions Samples

The basic luminance information of 8 LED televisions samples is as follows (Table 1).

Table 1. The basic luminance information of 8 LED televisions samples

Samples	Screen size	Physical resolution	Refresh rate	Luminance
1	47	1920 × 1080	60 Hz	$2.44E + 0.1$ cd/m^2
2	46	1920 × 1080	60 Hz	$7.94E + 0.1$ cd/m^2
3	46	1920 × 1080	60 Hz	$2.00E + 0.2$ cd/m^2
4	48	1920 × 1080	60 Hz	$1.20E + 0.2$ cd/m^2
5	47	1920 × 1080	60 Hz	$5.51E + 0.1$ cd/m^2
6	46	1920 × 1080	60 Hz	$1.01E + 0.2$ cd/m^2
7	47	1920 × 1080	60 Hz	$2.53E + 0.2$ cd/m^2
8	47	1920 × 1080	60 Hz	$2.02E + 0.2$ cd/m^2

Note: The luminance values were tested in the same place of the sane laboratory at the same light intensity running under the visual search task and the LED TVs were set up the standard mode value during the luminance determination process.

3.2 Comparison of the Visual Search Task Performance on 8 LED TVs

The visual search task performance is mainly including two aspects, one is the response accuracy data, which demonstrates the effectiveness of visual search task; the other is the average search time, reflects the efficiency of visual search task. The results show that the whole performance of samples 4 is better than others, while whole performance of samples 5 is less than others (See the Table 2).

Table 2. Comparison of visual search effectiveness and efficiency of 8 LED TVs

Samples	Visual search accuracy data	Average visual search time	Comfortable degree	Satisfaction
1	4.31	76.32	45	50
2	8.07	65.08	61	60
3	6.00	81.56	51	54
4	10.13	46.58	66	67
5	5.67	86.09	38	42
6	8.25	51.68	54	56
7	6.60	94.36	55	58
8	6.06	54.74	62	65

A repeated-measure ANOVA analysis was conducted to compare the effect of the eight types of LED TVs on participants' search effectiveness, search efficiency, comfortable degree and satisfaction.

The results shows that there is a remarkable difference between the visual search effectiveness of eight LED TVs (F = 3.532, p < 0.01). The planned comparisons revealed that the visual search effectiveness of sample 4 and 6 is remarkably higher than that of sample 1, 5 and 7 ($ps < 0.05$), and the visual search effectiveness of sample 2 is significant higher than that of sample 1 ($p < 0.05$), and the visual search effectiveness of sample 4 is significant higher than that of sample 8 ($p < 0.05$).

The results shows that there is a remarkable difference between the visual search efficiency of eight LED TVs (F = 2.212, p < 0.05). The planned comparisons revealed that the visual search efficiency of sample 4, 6 and 8 is remarkably higher than that of sample 5 and 7 ($ps < 0.05$).

The results shows that there is a remarkable difference between the comfortable degree of eight LED TVs (F = 4.050, p < 0.01). The planned comparisons revealed that the comfortable degree of sample 4 is remarkably higher than that of sample 1, 3 and 5 ($ps < 0.05$), while the comfortable degree of sample 5 is remarkably less than that of sample 2, 4, 6, 7 and 8 ($ps < 0.05$).

The results shows that there is a remarkable difference between the satisfaction of eight LED TVs (F = 3.448, p < 0.01). The planned comparisons revealed that the satisfaction of sample 4 is remarkably higher than that of sample 1, 3 and 5 ($ps < 0.05$), while the satisfaction of sample 5 is remarkably less than that of sample 2, 4, 6, 7 and 8 ($ps < 0.05$).

3.3   The Subjective Visual Fatigue Feelings After Completing Dynamic Visual Search Task on 8 LED TVs

Participants' perception about the visual fatigue after completing dynamic visual search task on 8 LED TVs was measured by nine items (see Table 3). It is demonstrated in Table 3 that there is more serious visual fatigue feelings of samples 5 on almost all items expect for dryness, while there is less visual fatigue feelings of samples 4 on almost all items except for irritation and tearing. It means the result of the subjective report is in accord with dynamic visual search.

Table 3. Comparison of the subjective visual fatigue feelings after completing dynamic visual search task on 8 LED TVs

Samples	Burning	Ache	Strain	Irritation	Tearing	Blur	Double vision	Dryness	Headache
1	21.75	25.81	28.75	31.31	17.19	33.63	30.75	27.88	18.00
2	20.63	21.38	26.13	17.44	11.44	23.31	25.19	29.06	14.94
3	26.50	25.13	30.63	26.19	16.50	29.13	27.25	32.94	20.94
4	16.44	14.50	21.88	19.75	11.06	20.56	18.13	20.44	9.69
5	28.31	31.00	36.44	27.56	18.19	38.13	31.50	28.81	21.50
6	23.88	25.81	28.06	25.25	14.94	28.88	24.88	27.13	17.94
7	21.69	28.31	26.56	26.13	13.38	26.81	25.69	23.63	17.06
8	18.75	18.81	25.63	19.44	10.88	28.44	21.94	23.94	12.38

4   Discussion and Conclusion

The study investigated the visual fatigue and comfort of LED TVs. It compared the eight LED TVs, to figure out which was better. A compare test was designed and an experiment was conducted to fulfill the study goals. The study indicated that there are significant difference between the eight LED TVs. Those results revealed that dynamic visual search performance was sensitive to visual fatigue and comfort under the situation of 5°/s movement velocity. The obtained results could be a reference for evaluating the quality of LED TVs for a specific visual search task (i.e., the safety check and the soccer game etc.).

Acknowledgement. The authors would like to gratefully acknowledge the support of the National Key Technology R&D Program of the Ministry of Science and Technology (2013BAK04B03 and 2014BAK01B03), Quality inspection industry research special funds for public welfare projects (201310095) and China National Institute of Standardization through the "special funds for the basic R&D undertakings by welfare research institutions" (552013Y-3078, 522015Y-3991).

References

1. BS EN ISO 9241-304-2008 Ergonomics of human-system interaction —part 304: user performance test methods for electronic visual displays
2. Tsanga, S.N., Chana, A.H., Yub, R.F.: Effect of display polarity and luminance contrast on visual lobe shape characteristics. Ergonomics **55**(9), 1028–1042 (2012)
3. Sheedy, J.E., Hayes, J., Engle, J.: Is all Asthenopia the same? Optom. Vis. Sci. **80**(11), 732–739 (2003)
4. DIN EN ISO 8596-2009 Ophthalmic optics - visual acuity testing - standard optotype and its presentation

Virtual, Augmented and Mixed Reality

AR and Maintenance - Visualization of Process Data and Engineering Information

Sven Buyer[✉] and Carsten Wittenberg

Robotics and Automation, Heilbronn University, Max-Planck-Str. 39, 74081
Heilbronn, Germany
{sven.buyer,carsten.wittenberg}@hs-heilbronn.de

Abstract. Nowadays the trend in the industry is to centralize production systems. For example almost autonomous power plants will be spread over the regions. In case of malfunctions the maintenance staff has to react very fast to reduce downtimes and costs. Based on a user analysis, different requirements such as fast information gathering and straightforward handling have been determined. Required documents are often spread across the company. This leads to time-intensive searching and obtaining. Modern technologies like Augmented Reality (AR) can support the staff. AR-applications have great potential for practical use, however, essential parts of today's popular desktop-based interaction concepts have to be redesigned. Computer games provide solutions for presenting complex information in a way that is easy to understand. Anforderungen an AR-Anwendungen in der Instandhaltung.

Keywords: Augmented reality · User interface · Maintenance · Mobile devices

1 Introduction

A service technician in industrial maintenance area is a self-sufficient and responsible team member of a workgroup. The basic activities are system checks, fault identification, fault analysis and problem solving. This generally requires the use of maintenance- and system documentation, process data and communication with remote specialists. An exploratory survey (n = 25 participants) gives rise that the kinds of information gathering and quick analysis of this information on site be regarded as a fundamental criterion of effective maintenance. This is confirmed by responses of the subjects on the question of the principal proceed in obtaining a contract for maintenance of a system with following points: "Use technical documents", "carry out a target-performance comparison "such as" Acquaintance with the system". A problem often turn out is a decentralized storage of required documents (see Fig. 1). This leads to time-intensive searching and obtaining the documents before it can be effectively started on the appropriate system.

Due to the above mentioned points of the document-retrieval, information seeking and the subsequent transfer of that information in real conditions, the focus of this study is on the information presentation and transfer in productive AR applications.

© Springer International Publishing Switzerland 2015
C. Stephanidis (Ed.): HCII 2015 Posters, Part I, CCIS 528, pp. 159–162, 2015.
DOI: 10.1007/978-3-319-21380-4_28

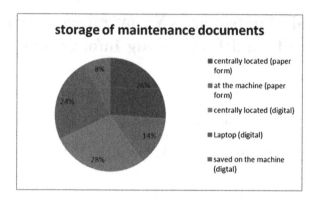

Fig. 1. Storage of maintenance documents

2   Game Design Pattern for Analysis of Digital Games

Heuristics and game design patterns for computer games are becoming more extensive and detailed. Korhonen and Koivisto [4] described heuristics which are developed in an iterative design process of a game for mobile devices. With regard to the requirements of the Augmented Reality supported maintenance it is important to provide adequate information and to integrate the menu into the gameplay. In addition there are approaches to investigate the relationship between games and application software.

Game Design Patterns on the other hand are used to describe models of game mechanics [5]. The aim is to split the game into components form which patterns can be obtained. These mechanisms are recorded and evaluated with help of a unified scheme. Collections of game design patterns allow comparison of concepts and their effects on the game play [1]. The pattern "information" deals with the flow of information within computer games and the possibilities to provide access to this information. Subcategories were dealing inter alia with tooltips, Dialogue designs or information passing. The latter deals with the intuitive transfer of information from a character or object within the game world and is an important criterion of an immersive virtual world.

An example is the use of avatars, which often provide information by changing their appearance, behavior or position in implicit form or as visible entities. Further menu options and selection function can be seen as objects of the gaming world. Thus, a context-dependent representation of these objects also represents an information transmission. It makes sense that the player knows depending on the user interface in which game context he is located on and what further options are available. This context-appropriate information is often used in strategy games to view additional actions. That means for AR there are only information or control options displayed for objects, which are in direct view.

A real transfer between the knowledge from the computer game research and the augmented reality area remains less evident in practice. Thus, research in the area of interaction design for AR applications is focused mainly on showing annotations on the display. White et al. [6] and Zhang and Sun [7] investigate the potential use of virtual hints in the form of text, diagrams or animations, as well as the spatial orientation and assignment of virtual information to real objects. Henderson and Feiner [2] are showing the overlay of three-dimensional tools as additional support for some production steps. The problem here is the occlusions of the real world and the visualization of correct spatial depth.

3 Implementation in Augmented Reality

One possible approach for an intuitive information management system in augmented reality applications is shown in Fig. 2. The user's attention in the augmented world is controlled with the help of an avatar. The reaction change of the avatar presents the user with an invalid system state and draws attention to the appropriate object. Detailed information can be found on an object associated visualization surface. For Example a digital multimeter symbolizes a bad value. Thus eliminates decoding errors manually or with help of external tools and provides relevant information at first glance.

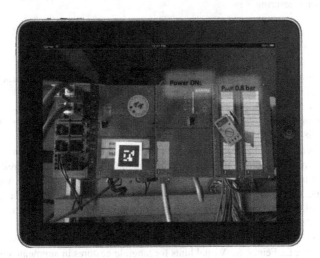

Fig. 2. Dragging the virtual multimeter as an active object

For further information the user can to drag and drop the virtual multimeter on the real PLC module (Fig. 3).

The functionality is based on the object-object scheme known from simulation- and strategy games. Selecting inherent menu items of the active object can trigger other functions such as graphical representation of measured values. As played here from a bird's perspective, usually many objects are present on the playing surface and can be applied in accordance with each other An active object (multimeter) is applied to the passive object "S7-module". Other functions such as the graphical representation of a measured value can be triggered by selecting appropriate menu items of the active object.

Fig. 3. Selecting module-item to diagnose the S7-EA-Modul the S7-EA-Modul to open module-items for measuring.

References

1. Björk, S., Holopainen, J.: Games and Design Patterns. The Game Design Reader. MIT Press, Cambridge (2006)
2. Henderson, S., Feiner, S.: Exploring the benefits of augmented reality documentation for maintenance and repair. In: IEEE Transactions on Visualization and Computer Graphics, pp. 1355–1368 (2011)
3. Kallergi, A., Verbeek, F.J.: Video games for collection exploration: games for and out of data repositories. In: Proceedings of the 14th International Academic MindTrek Conference: Envisioning Future Media Environments, pp. 143–146. New York, NY, USA (2010)
4. Korhonen, H., Koivisto, E.M.I.: Playability heuristics for mobile multi-player games. In: Proceedings of the 2nd international conference on Digital interactive media in entertainment and arts, pp. 28–35. ACM, Perth (2007)
5. Koster, R.: A Theory of Fun for Game Design. Paraglyph Press, Arizona (2005)
6. White, S., Lister, L., Feiner, S.: Visual hints for tangible gestures in augmented reality. In: 6th International Symposium on Mixed and Augmented Reality ISMAR, pp. 47–50. Nara, Japan (2007)
7. Zhang, F., Sun, H.: Dynamic labeling management in virtual and augmented environments. In: Ninth International Conference on Computer Aided Design and Computer Graphics, p. 6. Hong Kong, China (2005)

Building Virtual Roads from Computer Made Projects

Carlos Campos[1,2(✉)], João Miguel Leitão[1,3],
and António Fernando Coelho[2,3]

[1] Department of Electrical Engineering,
School of Engineering of Porto Polytechnic, Porto, Portugal
{crc,jml}@isep.ipp.pt
[2] Department of Informatics Engineering,
Engineering Faculty of Porto University, Porto, Portugal
acoelho@fe.up.pt
[3] INESC-TEC, Porto, Portugal

Abstract. Driving simulators require extensive road environments, with roads correctly modeled and similar to those found in real world. The modeling of extensive road environments, with the specific characteristics required by driving simulators, may result in a long time consuming process. This paper presents a procedural method to the modeling of large road environments. The proposed method can produce a road network design to populate an empty terrain and produce all the related road environment models. The terrain model can also be edited to produce well-constructed road environments. The road and terrain models are optimized to interactive visualization in real time, applying all the stet-of-art techniques like the level of detail selection. The proposed method allows modeling large road environments, with the realism and quality required to the realization of experimental work in driving simulators.

Keywords: Driving simulation · Immersive environments · Procedural modeling · Road environments

1 Introduction

Driving simulators come up as a very important scientific tool for the realization of immersive experimental studies in different areas, like psychology, ergonomics, and roadways engineering.

In psychology, they are used to develop research related to the driver behavior. An example is the evaluation of interference in the primary driving task, of a secondary task like the use of mobile phones, navigation systems or traffic information systems. The driving simulators are also used in ergonomics to study "In Vehicle Information Systems" that interact with the driver, like navigation systems (GPS) or mobile phones. In roadways engineering, they are used to analyze road paths in design stage, but also real roads, allowing the test with real drivers. For example, the study of factors that conducts to dangerous driving or, in traffic engineering, the study of dangerous

© Springer International Publishing Switzerland 2015
C. Stephanidis (Ed.): HCII 2015 Posters, Part I, CCIS 528, pp. 163–169, 2015.
DOI: 10.1007/978-3-319-21380-4_29

overtaking maneuvers with frontal collision probability, in roads with two lanes (one in each direction) without compromising the driver's safety.

Driving simulation experiments require the creation of extensive road environments with high level of quality, and road models prepared to visualization in real time. The creation of road models with the expected level of quality requires previous definition of the road networks and the road paths. The roads network and road path definition can be obtained through the procedurally method presented in [1]. Alternatively, the generation of models from road paths obtained by road design specialists [2], can result in a long time consuming task. After obtaining a road path it is still necessary to produce the road model and edit the surrounding environment. There are some automatic modeling tools, like the one presented in [3], which allow the efficient generation of the road models from road path definitions. These known tools can provide an important help in the road environment preparation but they are mainly focused in single roads and they cannot produce complete environments of roads networks.

This paper presents a method that allows to automatically generate models of road networks from road paths. The produced models are suitable to the implementation of immersive driving simulation experiences for scientific purposes. The work presented in this paper focuses in the generation of virtual road networks and terrain edition, as illustrate in Fig. 1.

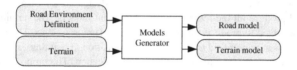

Fig. 1 Generation of geometric models

The applied road environment definition includes the specification of horizontal and vertical alignments, the 3D position of each of road path vertices, and the road surface orientation for each segment in every road [4]. The coordinates of the vertices are calculated considering the altimetry and cross-slope data of the road, producing road models similar to those found in the real world. To optimize the real time visualization, a space organization was considered and each element is hierarchically defined in different levels of detail (LOD) [5]. The model preparation also involves calculating the texture coordinates in the road triangle-strip, to produce more realistic models. The modeling process also needs to adjust the definition of the terrain in order to provide a complete well-constructed environment.

This work provides an important contribution to the procedural generation of realistic road environments aimed to virtual simulation applications.

2 Virtual Roads

The driving simulation requires visual models of road environments, usually composed from sets or strips of elementary polygons. These models can be done from the definitions of road paths, for example, by the procedural method presented in [1]. The road path represents the road trajectory over the terrain model and can be defined by a sorted list of straight segments. So, it can be fully represented by the coordinates of interconnection nodes between adjacent segments (Fig. 2).

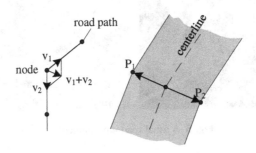

Fig. 2 Polygons vertices of the road

2.1 Road Model

The visual model of a road is obtained by stepping through the nodes of the road path and determining the polygons vertices that make up the visual model. Surfaces in graphic systems are modeled by polygonal meshes, where the triangle strip is the most common primitive. The triangle strip created along the road path fits in the data structures *TRIANGLE_STRIP* available from *OpenSceneGraph*.[1] Using vector calculus, the vertices of the polygons of the road are determined, as illustrated in Fig. 2.

As we can see in Fig. 2, the resulting vector sum of v_1 and v_2 vectors, allows determining the vertices P_1 and P_2, of the road polygons.

The cross-slope of the road is considered in the vertices polygons calculation. In road design the cross-slope is the angle (α) calculated in the curve extension. The cross-slope in curve, contributes to the increase in the security and commodity of the travel, because it allows a part of the centrifugal force to be compensated by gravity force. The z coordinate in one cross-section may vary, dependently on the altimetry and the cross-slope definition. The z coordinate of the vertex is determined from the angle α of cross-slope defined in road path design, the road width (R_w) and the altimetry Z_{road} of the road (1).

$$Z_{vertex} = Z_{road} + R_w * sen(\alpha) \tag{1}$$

---

[1] www.openscenegraph.org.

So, for each road node, the vertices of the polygons have a z coordinate considering the cross-slope. To optimize the road model visualization, the number of polygons generated in a straight line is smaller than in a curve, as also happens in other works [2]. After obtaining the polygonal model of the road, the next step is to map a texture. This process consists in the mapping 2D of texture coordinates for each vertex of the polygonal road model. The road model created is therefore more immersive and realistic, as showed in Fig. 3.

Fig. 3 Virtual road environments

To accelerate the rendering process in real time, the variation of the level of detail and spatial organization were considered. So, the created road model is spatially organized and represented by several levels of detail. For distant segments, only a rough definition of the road surface is displayed. The following levels of detail consider the visualization of the road and the horizontal signalization. The higher level of detail considers the entire road environment, with detailed objects. The level of detail selection is based on the distance to the observer.

The horizontal signalization is made by road marks, defining the lanes in each road segment. These marks may have different layouts: continuous, dashed or both, as illustrated in Fig. 4.

Fig. 4 Horizontal and vertical signalization

In order to improve the visibility detection, horizontal signalization models are hierarchical organized with the road models using different layers. The vertical signalization is placed in road environment by instantiating previously defined 3D objects (Fig. 4).

2.2   Terrain Model

The construction of roadways in the real world implies earthworks in the terrain where the road is implemented. The definition of the road environment model also considers the terrain specification. The terrain model must be modified to become in accordance with the related model of the road network.

A slope is the terrain surface which is located along the road and can be originated from an excavation or an embankment on the terrain during construction of a road, as illustrated in Figs. 3 and 5. Generally, the cut slope and embankment slopes have declivity of 1–1.5 (V/H) so that the stability of the ground is guaranteed [10]. In the proposed method, after generating the trajectory of the road, it is necessary to adjust the definition of the terrain to produce the final well-constructed visual model. For each point of the terrain, the minimum distance to the road is calculated and, according to this distance, the necessity to change the z coordinate of the point of terrain is evaluated. The z coordinate of the point of the terrain is not changed if it is positioned between the definitions of slopes, as illustrated in Fig. 5, for the point P_3.

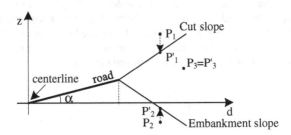

Fig. 5 Cut and embankment slope

We can also see in Fig. 5 that point P_1 is shifted down to P'_1 point, and the point P_2 is shifted up to P'_2 point. In order to optimize this process, the terrain points that are relatively far are not treated. In the edition of the terrain, the modelling information of the edited areas is registered so that, it is possible to render these areas with a different color (typically brown).

In the visualization of large terrain models, a widely used technique is to obtain more than one definition of each terrain cell through successive simplifications of its geometry [6–9]. In the visualization, the preferred representation is automatically selected, allowing to obtain optimum results [3, 5]. For large terrains, this technique, associated with the segmentation of the original model in smaller subareas, grants the best results.

3 Conclusions

The method presented in this paper allows the creation of realistic road environment models that meet the detailed standards of specification and the required performance for real time graphic systems. The presented images of road environments, were generated in the DriS[2] driving simulator using environments produced by the proposed method. The realism of the road environments was improved by the cross-slope contribution. These road environments have all the required characteristics to conduct scientific work in several fields such as psychology, ergonomics and road engineering. The resulting models allow the placement of actors and the implementation of traffic events whose effects and consequences are important to know and study [11, 12]. With this implementation, the entire environment can be obtained automatically, dramatically reducing the cost and work involved in the modeling tasks.

The generated models are optimized for visual simulation in real time and suitable for integration in driving simulators. The use of layers for the horizontal signalization, facilitates the visibility detection. The used optimization techniques allow a significant reduction of polygons in the rendering process, resulting in a fast rendering of high quality images.

In the future, large terrain visualization techniques should be further explored to maximize the quality and performance of image production in real time simulations.

Acknowledgments. The Media Arts and Technologies project (MAT), NORTE-07-01 24-FEDER-000061, is financed by the North Portugal Regional Operational Programme (ON.2 – O Novo Norte), under the National Strategic Reference Framework (NSRF), through the European Regional Development Fund (ERDF), and by national funds, through the Portuguese funding agency, Fundação para a Ciência e a Tecnologia (FCT).

References

1. Campos, C., Leitão, J., Coelho, A.: Integrated modeling of road environments for driving simulation. In: 10th International Conference on Computer Graphics Theory and Applications, Berlin (2015)
2. Bayarri, S., Fernadez, M., Perez, M.: Virtual reality for driving simulation. Commun. ACM **39**(5), 72–76 (1996)
3. Campos, C., Leitão, J., Rodrigues, C.: Modelação de Ambientes Rodoviários de Grandes Dimensões. In: 15° Encontro Português de Computação Gráfica, Portugal (2007)
4. Campos, C., Leitão, J., Coelho, A.: Geração Procedimental de Traçados Rodoviários para Simulação de Condução. In: 21° Encontro Português de Computação Gráfica, Portugal (2014)
5. Larsen, B., Christensen, N.: Real-Time Terrain Rendering Using Smooth Hardware Optimized Level of Detail. Technical University of Denmark, Lyngby (2003)
6. Garland, M., Heckbert, P.S.: Fast Polygonal Approximation of Terrains and Height Fields. School of Computer Science, Carnegie Mellon University, Pittsburgh (1995)

---

[2] Driving Simulator at Engineering Faculty, University of Porto, Portugal.

7. Heckbert, P.S., Garland, M.: Multiresolution modeling for fast rendering. In: Proceedings Graphics Interface, vol. 94, pp. 43–50 (1994)
8. Lindstrom, P., Pascucci, V.: Visualization of large terrain made easy. In: Proceedings of IEEE Visualization (2001)
9. Lindstrom, P., Hodges, L., Koller, D., Faust, N., Ribarsky, W., Turner, G.: Real-time, continuous level of detail rendering of height fields. In: Proceedings of ACM SIGGRAPH, vol. 96, pp. 109–118 (1996)
10. EP: Notebook of Road Path Standards. Estradas de Portugal (EP). ISBN-96379-6-2 (1994)
11. Thomas, G., Donikian, S.: Modelling virtual cities dedicated to behavioural animation. In: EUROGRAPHICS, vol. 19, no. 3. Blackwell Publishers, Malden (2000)
12. Leitão, J.: Agentes Autónomos Controláveis em Simuladores de Condução. Ph.D. thesis, by the Engineering Faculty of Porto University (2000)

Camouflage Assessment of Color Pattern Strategies in Different Environmental Contexts

Woon Jung Cho, Minsun Kim, Eunji Lee, Suyoung Kim,
Junghwan Han, and Kwang-Hee Han[(⊠)]

Department of Psychology, Cognitive Engineering Lab, Yonsei University,
Seoul, Korea
{chrischo, kimmin, khan}@yonsei.ac.kr,
{elee0904, thinkinghans}@gmail.com, altmrla4@naver.com

Abstract. This study examined the effectiveness of adaptive camouflage patterns according to environmental contexts. We performed visual search tasks using photo simulation to evaluate the effectiveness of camouflage strategies. Pattern combination strategies from a previous study were used. Each one of the 4 strategies (Average [A], AverageRandom [AR], Main [M], and MainRandom [MR]) were presented in 3 environmental contexts (Woodland, Rural, and Urban), and performance (Error Rate) was measured. An analysis of performance revealed the main effect of strategy and a significant interaction between strategy and the context. Strategy A appeared to be more effective than the others. The A and AR strategies were better in the Woodland context, and strategies A and M appeared to be superior to the others in the Urban and Rural contexts. This study can be the foundation for determining optimal adaptive camouflage patterns in different environmental contexts and provide a theoretical basis for future military uniforms.

Keywords: Active camouflage · Camouflage assessment · Dynamic environmental contexts · Adaptive pattern strategy

1 Introduction

Evaluating a camouflage's effectiveness is a fundamental step in determining the optimal camouflage pattern [3, 4]. Because the effectiveness of active camouflage technologies varies with the environmental contexts, continuing evaluations of the effect of pattern combination strategies, combat-contextual changes, and the camouflage's reflection are needed. Assessing camouflage strategies with a prototype is an ideal way to evaluate the camouflage's effectiveness and reflect the results on the development process of a camouflage pattern. However, it is not practically simple to evaluate a camouflage's effectiveness with a prototype in various contexts. This is the reason why researchers use the photo simulation method. Photo simulation is performed on a controlled experimental situation, which makes it possible to produce rich statistical data from different groups of observers with the same image sets. Photo simulation is used to design or evaluate a developed pattern for dynamic and various military contexts because it is implemented in digital environments [4]. In this study, we performed visual search tasks using photo

© Springer International Publishing Switzerland 2015
C. Stephanidis (Ed.): HCII 2015 Posters, Part I, CCIS 528, pp. 170–173, 2015.
DOI: 10.1007/978-3-319-21380-4_30

simulation and evaluated the effectiveness of the pattern strategies for adaptive camouflage according to environmental contexts.

2   Method

2.1   Stimuli

If dynamic environments are essential for designing adaptive patterns, controlling digital images and making patterns automatically with a computer can be efficient alternatives during the development and evaluation design processes [1]. The researchers generated camouflage patterns using an automatic patterning program [2] to evaluate the effectiveness of camouflage strategies. The stimuli included four total strategies (Average [A], Main [M], AverageRandom [AR], and MainRandom [MR]), using 2 color combination strategies (average, main) X 2 pattern arrangement strategies (arranged, random) of stimulus matrices. A total of 18 images (6 images of 3 contexts—Woodland, Rural, and Urban) were used, and each of the four strategies appeared in all 18 images.

2.2   Participants and Procedure

Thirty participants were recruited. Each of the 4 strategies (Average, Main, Average-Random, MainRandom) were presented in three environmental contexts (Woodland, Rural, Urban), and the participants were ask to evaluate the camouflage abilities. The experiment involved five practice trials to make certain that the participants understood the task. A total of 216 trials were presented to each participant in random order, and the participants were asked to detect the camouflaged targets. The targets were located in one of nine positions within each image, in random order. The participants were asked to find the camouflaged targets and click the left mouse button. Also, they were required to click the right button of the mouse when there were no camouflaged targets in the images (Fig. 1).

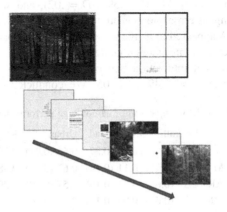

Fig. 1. Visual search task

The participants performed a total of 216 trials (environmental contexts (3)) X number of images (6) X pattern strategies (4) X target existence (3). All of the trials were randomly displayed on the monitor, and the participants received a brief rest every 36 trials. The camouflage abilities were measured by the participants' performance (error rate) on the visual search tasks (Fig. 2).

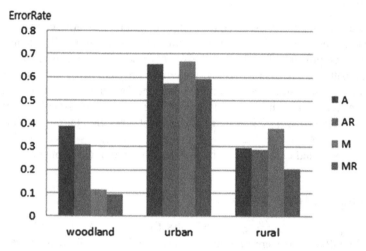

Fig. 2. Error rate

3 Results

The performance (error rate) of 4 strategies (Average, AverageRandom, Main, and MainRandom) in 3 environmental contexts (Woodland, Rural, and Urban) was analyzed with repeated measure analysis. Higher error rates were evaluated as better camouflage patterns. An analysis of performance (error rate) revealed the main effect of color pattern strategy, $F(3,93) = 15.66$, $p < .05$. Strategy A ($M = .45$, $SD = .04$) had a higher error rate than strategy M ($M = .39$, $SD = .02$), and strategy AR ($M = .39$, $SD = .03$) revealed a higher error rate than strategy MR ($M = .30$, $SD = .03$), $p < .05$. In other words, strategy A appeared to be the most effective color pattern, compared to the others, among the overall environmental context (Table 1).

There was a significant interaction between color pattern strategy and environmental contexts, $F(6,186) = 12.49$, $p < .05$. We conducted a planned contrast to

Table 1. Comparison of camouflage performance

	Overall	Woodland	Urban	Rural
Strategy A	**0.45** (0.04)	**0.39** (0.27)	**0.66** (0.21)	0.30 (0.23)
Strategy M	0.39 (0.02)	0.11 (0.14)	**0.67** (0.17)	**0.38** (0.17)
Strategy AR	0.39 (0.03)	0.31 (0.19)	0.57 (0.19)	0.29 (0.21)
Strategy MR	0.30 (0.03)	0.09 (0.15)	0.59 (0.26)	0.20 (0.21)

*Mean of Error rate (SD)

investigate which camouflage strategy was more effective in each context. The results of the planned contrast revealed that strategy A ($M = .39$, $SD = .27$) had a higher error rate (better camouflage) than the others in the Woodland context, $p < .05$. Strategies M ($M = .67$, $SD = .17$) and A ($M = .66$, $SD = .21$) had higher error rates than the others in the Urban context. Finally, strategy M ($M = .38$, $SD = .17$) had a higher error rate than the other strategies in the Rural context, $p < .05$. In other words, strategies A and AR were better in the Woodland context, and strategies A and M appeared to be superior to the others in the Urban and Rural contexts.

4 Conclusion

This study examined the effectiveness of adaptive camouflage patterns according to environmental contexts. For this purpose, we administered visual search tasks, which detect camouflaged targets using photo simulation. The findings of our camouflage analysis are below.

The result demonstrated that strategy A is least affected by the environmental contexts, so strategy A could be more likely to be applicable as Universal pattern. In addition, the camouflage effectiveness of the pattern strategy differed on the background context. In Woodland conditions, strategies A and AR were better than the other strategies. In Urban and Rural conditions, strategies M appeared to be superior to the others.

Researchers need to improve the camouflage strategies to match optimal adaptive camouflage patterns for different environmental contexts for future studies. The present study is significant for analyzing the effectiveness of camouflage patterns in varied environmental contexts. The present study can be the foundation for optimal adaptive camouflage patterns in different environmental contexts and provide a theoretical basis for future military uniforms.

Acknowledgement. This work has been supported by the Low Observable Technology Research Center program of Defense Acquisition Administration and Agency for Defense Development.

References

1. Cho, W.J., Ahn, W., Kim, M.S., Park, J., Kim, S., Han, K.-H.: Making pixel patterns automatically for camouflage – using color information from their background. In: Stephanidis, C. (ed.) Posters, Part II, HCII 2011. CCIS, vol. 174, pp. 98–101. Springer, Heidelberg (2011)
2. Cho, W.J., Seo, H.-K., Kim, H., Lee, J., Kang, D.-H., Kim, M.-K., Han, K.-H.: CamouLED: real-time generation of pixel pattern for camouflage. In: Stephanidis, C. (ed.) HCII 2013, Part II. CCIS, vol. 374, pp. 699–703. Springer, Heidelberg (2013)
3. Friskovec, M., Gabrijelcic, H., Simoncic, B.: Design and evaluation of a camouflage pattern for the Slovenian urban environment. J. Imaging Sci. Technol. **54**(2), 020507–020511 (2010)
4. Peak, J.: Guidelines for Camouflage Assessment Using Observers. NATO Research & Technology Organization Neuilly-Sur-Seine. RTO-AG-SCI-095 (2006)

Augmented Reality Central Venous Access Training Simulator

Erika Gutierrez-Puerto, Lizeth Vega-Medina, Gerardo Tibamoso,
Alvaro Uribe-Quevedo, and Byron Perez-Gutierrez[(✉)]

VR Center, Nueva Granada Military University, Bogotá, Colombia
akirekikl@gmail.com,
{lizvega,gtibamosop,alvaro.j.uribe,
byron.perez}@ieee.org

Abstract. The central venous access procedure is used for placing a catheter for venous interventions, defibrillator devices or even filters when required. The access depends on patient-related factors that may increase the procedure's difficulty. However, when performing the procedure on newborns, the level of difficulty rises considerably and any mistake may cause damages on tissues, lungs or the accessed vein, those can affect the medical condition of the patient. This work focus on the development of an augmented reality application for training pediatricians in the central venous access in newborns while allowing handling surgical tools. The system has a 3D marker tracking, that enables the user interact with models of surgical tools such as syringe, blunt guidewire, dilating device and catheter, each one of them shows up over the marker. The prototype is programmed in Unity3D with the use of AR Vuforia library and an Oculus VR with an attached webcam. The system makes a suitable tracking of the surgical instruments within a controlled lighting. To conclude, finished and suitable prototype will be tested with the help of medical students to validate their impact as simulator training in this technique.

Keywords: Augmented reality · Central venous access · Medical training simulator

1 Introduction

The central venous access (CVA) procedure is used for placing a catheter for venous interventions, defibrillator devices or even filters when required [1]. The access depends on patient-related factors that may increase the procedure's difficulty. However, when performing the procedure on newborns, the level of difficulty rises considerably because of the high vulnerability of them, and any mistake may cause serious damages on tissues, lungs or the accessed vein (those can adversely affect the medical condition of the patient), increasing risk of the life of the patient.

Training for performing this procedure is possible through adult simulation manikins that allow executing the access in a controlled environment, presenting different simulated scenarios that will be overcome by the user [2]. Even though the adult manikins share anatomical features with the newborns, the experience is not the same due to the difference in size of the workspace and anatomical structure.

© Springer International Publishing Switzerland 2015
C. Stephanidis (Ed.): HCII 2015 Posters, Part I, CCIS 528, pp. 174–179, 2015.
DOI: 10.1007/978-3-319-21380-4_31

The use of systems that involves simulation techniques into the medical field is helpful to improve medical abilities because it allows students or residents to practice procedures without time restrictions with several cases and multiple situations [3]. However, it is a challenge to combine features of physical manikins with virtual simulators through augmented reality (AR) [4–6].

This work focus on the development of an AR application for training pediatricians in the CVA procedure in newborns, while allowing handling surgical instruments such as needle, blunt guidewire, dilating device and catheter. The AR system was programmed in Unity3D [7] with Vuforia [8] and uses an Oculus VR [9] with a coupled webcam to track 3D markers, offering 3D visual cues over the newborn's 3D virtual model built from a standard newborn's anatomy and medical references. The paper is organized as follows: Sect. 2 describes the AR system architecture, system evaluation is presented in Sect. 3 and finally, conclusions and future work are presented in Sect. 4.

2 System Architecture

The CVA simulation system is composed by a live video signal of AR targets, which represents the surgical instruments related to the procedure, a virtual environment with the newborn model and a mixed view of real and virtual signals delivered to the user as Fig. 1 depicts.

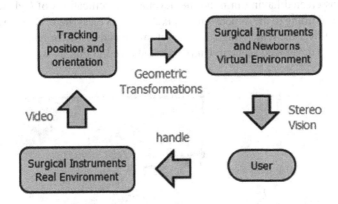

Fig. 1. CVA system architecture using AR

Initially, the user handles the AR targets and a webcam located at its head register all the movements in order to provide interaction with the surgical instruments. The computer provides the position and orientation tracking information of the targets and associates it to the surgical instruments for the required interaction with the 3D newborn model in the virtual environment. For the output, a Head Mounted Display is used to deliver stereo visual cues to the user. Figure 2 presents the set-up of the system.

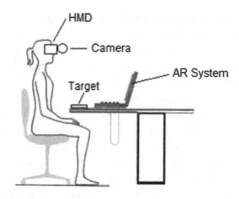

Fig. 2. AR system set-up for interaction

2.1 Development of the Virtual Environment

Unity3D software was used for the development of the virtual environment. The 3D models developed include the whole body skin, skeleton and circulatory system of a newborn, and the CVA equipment (syringe, blunt guidewire, dilating device and catheter). In order to accomplish this task, measures of each real instrument were taken. The selected tool for 3D targets tracking was Vuforia because its Cylinder tracking feature that was effective in different light and movement conditions, and suits to the syringe's shape. An image was created having in mind the developer specifications of Cylinder Target creation and according to the dimensions in pixels of the 3 ml syringe, then it was printed and positioned over the real syringe. The target image and its performance in real environment using a developed scene in Unity3D are showed in Fig. 3.

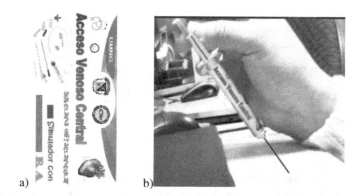

Fig. 3. (a) Cylinder target image. (b) Target registered in AR environment

To characterize the interaction between a needle and soft tissue were taken as a reference the three-stage procedure describe by Barbé [10], first the needle presses the tissue surface which is deformed, then the needle penetrates the tissue cutting it while

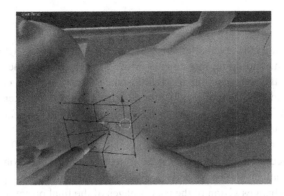

Fig. 4. Key frame animation for syringe displacement and skin deforming

the surface and frictional forces attract the skin to the surface of the needle, finally the needle is removed and the tissue again follows the direction of its movement. After the models of the patient and syringe were textured thus it proceeded to make an animation using key frames to add motion to the syringe and a Lattice as father of the patient mesh to achieve the maximum deformation (Fig. 4) eventually rendering format is chosen as video to be used in Unity3D.

The visualization part was achieved by adding two cameras one for each eye as daughters of ARCamera and selecting a plane in which project the image captured by two BackgroundCameras that are synchronized with the video received by the main camera, which are used to divide the screen. Figure 5 shows an example of two images of the system for the stereo viewing.

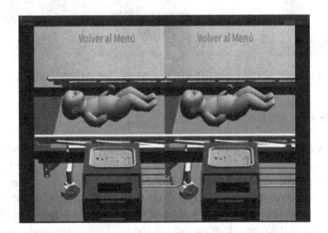

Fig. 5. Main scene binocular AR implementation

3 Application Test

For this initial stage, the evaluation of the prototype was made selecting different surgical instruments and doing movements of the marker between the camera and the total extension of the arm, maximizing this distance. Later, the user can interact with the instruments and the 3D model of the newborn moving the marker until a desired area is reached. As a visual aid for the user, the opacity of the skin can be changed in order to visualize internal organs.

The tests with the Oculus and Vuforia's prefabs, using a Microsoft LifeCam Studio webcam, were successful in recognizing the objective and its location. However, the illumination level affects the target detection, the light reflection of the paper where the marker is printed changes vision of the user. Images of the final prototype working over the user view are shown in Fig. 6.

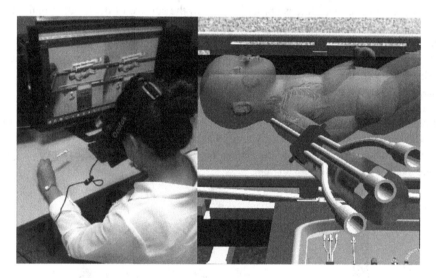

Fig. 6. AR system for CVA in newborns and its detailed view from the catheter side

4 Conclusions and Future Work

The selected AR library and the designed targets exhibited an adequate performance for an interactive use. This performance was greatly influenced by ambient light and the autofocus used on the webcam, so these features were controlled and fixed. As for the developing of the prototype using Unity3D, it was possible to integrate the components of AR with the hardware chosen. The results obtained in tests, shows that although the webcam does not provide an adequate view of the working environment as the eyes of the user due to its location over the HMD, the interaction with surgical instruments and the newborn's body permits a proper interaction. This concludes that the developed prototype can be used as a tool in a first approach to the CVA procedure.

Regarding future work, the integration of haptic feedback could improve the real-ism of the simulator letting user to feel the needle insertion. A 3DUI could be integrated to help the selection of surgical instruments as well as audio cues as in operating room are present. For the tracking of the syringe, it is proposed to use 3D tracking instead of image patterns to improve the system response. Finally, an evaluation with medical students is proposed in order to validate the impact of the simulator for training in this technique.

Acknowledgments. This project was supported by the Research Division of Nueva Granada Mil. University through grant IMP ING1776.

References

1. Walser, E.M.: Venous access ports: indications, implantation technique, follow-up, and complications. Cardiovasc. Intervent. Radiol. **35**, 751–764 (2012)
2. CAE Healthcare. http://www.bluephantom.com/category/By-Specialty_Critical-Care_Vascular-Access.aspx
3. Okuda, Y., Bryson, E.O., DeMaria, S., Jacobson, L., Quinones, J., Shen, B., Levine, A.I.: The utility of simulation in medical education: what is the evidence? Mt. Sinai J. Med.: J. Transl. Personalized Med. **76**(4), 330–343 (2009)
4. Feygin, D., Ho, C.H.: U.S. Patent No. 8,784,111 (2014)
5. Amesur, N.B., Wang, D.C., Chang, W., Weiser, D., Klatzky, R., Shukla, G., Stetten, G.D.: Peripherally inserted central catheter placement using the sonic flashlight. J. Vasc. Interv. Radiol. **20**(10), 1380–1383 (2009)
6. Larnpotang, S., Lizdas, D., Rajon, D., Luria, I., Gravenstein, N., Bisht, Y., Robinson, A.: Mixed simulators: augmented physical simulators with virtual underlays. In: IEEE Virtual Reality (VR), pp. 7–10. IEEE Press, Orlando (2013)
7. Unity 3D. http://www.unity3d.com
8. Qualcomm Vuforia Developer Portal. http://developer.vuforia.com/
9. Oculus Rift – Virtual Reality Headset for 3D Gaming. http://www.oculus.com/
10. Barbé, L., Bayle, B., De Mathelin, M., Gangi, A.: Needle insertions modeling: identifiability and limitations. Biomed. Signal Process. Control **2**(3), 191–198 (2007)

Use of Immersive Virtual Environments to Understand Human-Building Interactions and Improve Building Design

Arsalan Heydarian[1]([✉]), Evangelos Pantazis[1], David Gerber[2], and Burcin Becerik-Gerber[1]

[1] Sonny Astani Department of Civil and Environmental Engineering, University of Southern California, Los Angeles, CA 90089, USA
{heydaria, epantazi, becerik}@usc.edu
[2] School of Architecture and School of Engineering, University of Southern California, Los Angeles, CA 90089, USA
dgerber@usc.edu

Abstract. Previous research has shown occupants' behavior and interactions with building systems and components have a significant impact on the total energy consumption of buildings. Incorporating occupant requirements to the design process could result in better operations, and therefore, improve the total energy consumption of buildings. Currently, buildings are primarily designed based on several common assumptions about occupant requirements, which in many cases are incorrect and result in inefficiencies during the buildings' operation phase. With the recent improvements in the fields of virtual and augmented reality, designers now have the opportunity to accurately collect and analyze occupants' behavioral information. In this research, through the use of immersive virtual environments, the influence of different design features on end-user behavior (preferences and patterns) and performances are examined. A case study is presented, in which the authors measure the end-users' lighting preferences to better understand the impact of preferences on end-users' performances and lighting-related energy consumption.

Keywords: Immersive virtual environments · Human building interaction · Design features · Design process

1 Introduction

Building energy use accounts for roughly 41 % of the energy consumption in the United States, 37 % in the European Union, and 39 % in the United Kingdom [1, 2]. Studies have shown that occupant behavior has a significant impact on a building's overall performance and energy consumption. To better understand how human behavior and interaction affects the total energy consumption in buildings, previous research has examined occupants' interactions with building systems and components for a variety of different purposes (e.g., lighting and blinds control, temperature adjustments, noise levels and etc.). Yet, such studies have been done in actual office spaces, where many different factors and "experimental noise" could affect the studies'

© Springer International Publishing Switzerland 2015
C. Stephanidis (Ed.): HCII 2015 Posters, Part I, CCIS 528, pp. 180–184, 2015.
DOI: 10.1007/978-3-319-21380-4_32

results (e.g. difference in interior designs, outside noise levels, weather conditions). In the past two decades, the advent of virtual reality and augmented reality has provided better opportunities for researchers and practitioners to collect occupants' behavioral information. Immersive Virtual Environments (IVEs) provide a sense of presence similar to that found in physical environments, such that the user can get the feeling of the environment as if they were physically immersed in it. Such environments allow the researchers to manipulate their variables of interest while keeping design features (e.g., lighting system, interior design, etc.) constant, resulting in reduced experimental noise. Another important advantage of IVEs is that the experimenter is less salient to the participant (as participants cannot see the experimenter), facilitating behavior that is more natural.

In this research, the authors present a novel approach, where they use IVEs to collect information about end-users behavior and performance within a virtual office space to better understand how building design could be improved in order to meet occupant preferences while decreasing the buildings' energy consumption. In this paper, the authors present an experimental study that investigates the impact of preference on end-users' performance and lighting-related energy consumption in an office space through the use of IVEs.

2 Understanding End-user Behavior Through IVEs

In the past two decades, the architecture, engineering, and construction (AEC) industry has adopted new technological advancements from different fields in order to improve (cost and time) the design, construction, and operation phases of buildings. One of the adopted technologies is building information modeling (BIM) where 3D models of a building along with its geometric and semantic information can be developed and communicated among different parties. BIM has significantly improved the design process by becoming an important tool to communicate between different parties involved in a project and allowing the end-users to get a better understanding of final designs of buildings. Although BIM provides 3D models and the necessary geometric and semantic information, research has shown these models lack the spatial feeling and presence that end-users need to better understand the designed environment and provide the necessary feedback.

Various studies have shown that IVEs not only have the same advantages and capabilities as BIM models, but they also increase interactivity and immersivity for the users, providing them with a more accurate feeling of the physical environment and a sense of presence (which BIM models currently lack). To evaluate whether IVEs are adequate tools to study different design features, the authors designed an experimental study, in which they compared participants' performance, perception, and sense of presence between a physical office space and a designed office space in an IVE. By analyzing data collected from 112 participants, the authors concluded that participants perform similarly in an IVE setting as they do in the benchmarked physical environment. They also concluded that participants felt a strong sense of presence within the IVE. A detailed discussion of this study can be found in [3].

Additionally, after discovering the benefits of IVE, in their previous research, the authors used IVEs in order to explore how different design features can affect behavior. For example, the authors investigated the influence of manual and semi-automatic lighting control options in an office environment by analyzing participants' interactions in a virtual office environment. Through this study, the authors concluded that end-users are significantly more likely to use natural light if there is only a semi-automatic control system located next to their desk to open the blinds instead of having no semi-automatic control system to open the blinds or a semi-automatic control system to both open the blinds and turn the artificial lights on. A detailed discussion of this study can be found in [4].

Building off of their previous research, the authors use IVE in order to understand more about how different design features affect energy consumption and performance. More specifically, the authors aimed to better understand (1) which lighting profiles are the most preferred ones by users, (2) in which lighting profiles do users perform the best on office-related activities, and (3) how much electricity is used by implementing each lighting profile. With this data, the authors can discover which lighting profiles maximize comfort and performance and minimize building energy consumption with the end goal to incorporate this information to the design process for achieving efficient and sustainable design.

3 End-user Lighting Preferences – Experimental Study

Previous research has identified lighting as one of the major factors to affect occupants' behavior and performance in indoor environments [5]. To better evaluate the impact of different lighting settings (luminance and illuminance) and develop end-users lighting profiles, the authors collected and analyzed end-users' lighting preferences within an IVE. The parameters measured in this experiment were based on the choices the participants made to adjust the lighting levels and their corresponding performances in those lighting setting.

Prior to running the experiments, each model with different light settings (e.g. 2 blinds open and 3 light bulbs on, all blinds open with no light bulb) was simulated using simulation software (grasshopper + honeybee + ladybug), where a light map along with different lux values across the room were calculated. Once the participants selected their most preferred light setting, the corresponding simulated model (light map + lux values) was identified to better understand the participants' preferred settings' lighting-related electricity consumption.

3.1 Data Acquisition and Experimental Procedure

An office space was designed based on similar dimensions and lighting features of a physical office environment. The models with different lighting setting were designed and rendered in Revit© 2015, 3ds Max©, and Unity 3D. In order to provide a better feeling of immersion to the participants, an Oculus Rift DK2 along with a positional tracker and an Xbox controller were connected to Unity 3D.

The participants were initially placed in a dark room with all the lights turned off and all the blinds closed. They were asked to adjust the lighting levels of the room to their most preferred lighting setting in order to perform a set of office-related activities (e.g., reading, writing, watching a video). Once the participants felt comfortable with their chosen lighting level, they were asked to read a short passage and answer a few comprehension questions based on what they read. Upon completion of the provided task, they were asked to answer a set of survey questions related to how they determined their most preferred lighting setting and if there were specific features that impacted their decisions. They were also asked to fill out a survey to assess how environmentally friendly there were.

3.2   Results

40 participants were recruited for this study, in which 40 % were females and 60 % were males (average age = 26 years old). 96 % of the participants preferred to have at least one of the three blinds open and 72 % of those preferred to have all three blinds open. A sample of participants' lighting preferences profile is provided in Fig. 1 in which the participant's reading speed and comprehension (number of correctly answered questions based on the given passage) measures are shown. As shown in Fig. 1, the participant's preferred lighting setting is matched to the previously generated heat map of the lux values in the room.

4   Discussion and Future Work

The presented research in this paper anticipates and utilizes IVE as a tool to collect and incorporate human behaviors and needs during the design phase. IVEs have been adopted for practical reasons to enable more expansive and cost effective data capture and experimentation but equally as a means to develop realistic environmental settings representing a physical environment to allow for more accurate design feedback from the end-users. As part of the authors' ongoing and future work, they collect more lighting preferences data and create end-users profiles to better understand the preference types on a larger sample of the population. The authors are also in the process of collecting personality types along with lighting preferences, hypothesizing that there is a relationship between end-user personality types and their lighting preference profiles. The authors will use the collected lighting profiles as a rule set into a multi-agent system

Participant	A
Comprehension (%)	75
Reading Speed (word/s)	2.5
Preferred Light Setting	All Blinds Open 0 Light Bulb on Each Fixture
Avg. Lux Value (natural + Artificial) 	160 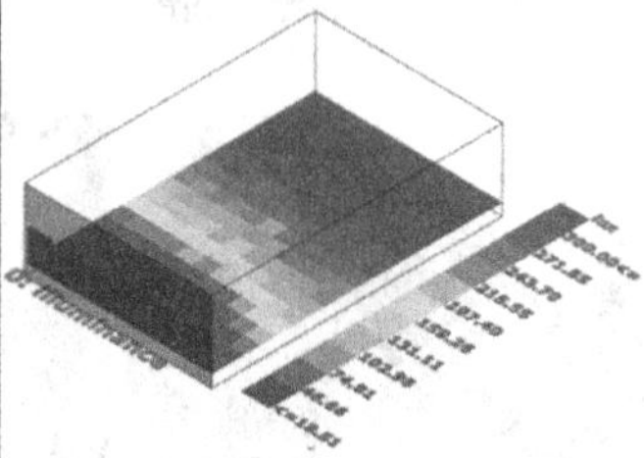

Fig. 1. Participant "A" lighting preference profile. The heat map represents the preferred lighting-setting's lux values distribute around the room and the rendered image is what the participant would see in IVE.

that will design building components with the objective to account for the end-user behavior and performance data. The authors will also explore the impact of other design features such as, wall openings and window types and sizes, on end-users' behavior.

Acknowledgments. This project is part of the National Science Foundation funding under the contract 1231001. Any discussion, procedure, results, and conclusions discussed in this paper are the authors' views and do not reflect the views of National Science Foundation. Special thanks to all the participants and people that contributed to this project, specifically Saba Khashe and Joao Carneiro for their contribution on helping with preparing and running the experiments.

References

1. EPA. National Awarness of Energy Star: (2013). http://www.energystar.gov/sites/default/uploads/about/old/files/2013%20CEE%20Report_508%20compliant.pdf
2. Pérez-Lombard, L., Ortiz, J., Pout, C.: A review on buildings energy consumption information. Energy Build. **40**, 394–398 (2008)
3. Heydarian, A., Carneiro, J.P., Gerber, D., Becerik-Gerber, B., Hayes, T., Wood, W.: Immersive virtual environments versus physical built environments: a benchmarking study for building design and user-built environment explorations. Autom. Constr. **54**, 116–126 (2015)
4. Heydarian, A., Carneiro, J.P., Gerber, D., Becerik-Gerber, B.: Immersive virtual environments, understanding the impact of design features and occupant choice upon lighting for building performance. Elsevier J. Build. Environ. **89**, 217–228 (2015)
5. Romm, J.J.: Lean and Clean Management: How to Boost Profits and Productivity By Reducing Pollution. Kodansha International, New York/Tokyo/London (1994)

A Virtual Cloth Manipulation System
for Clothing Design

Shgeru Inui[1(✉)], Yuko Mesuda[2], and Yosuke Horiba[3]

[1] International Cluster for Cutting Edge Research Institute for Fiber Engineering,
Shinshu University, 3-15-1 Tokita, Ueda, Nagano 386-8567, Japan
inui@shinshu-u.ac.jp
[2] Interdisciplinary Graduate School of Science and Technology,
Shinshu University, 3-15-1 Tokita, Ueda, Nagano 386-8567, Japan
12stll5c@shinshu-u.ac.jp
[3] Faculty of Textile Science and Technology, Shinshu University, 3-15-1 Tokita,
Ueda, Nagano 386-8567, Japan
horiba@shinshu-u.ac.jp

Abstract. We have been studied virtualization of draping which is one of a design method for clothing. It is desirable to adopt a man-machine interface in the same way as the real world for virtual draping. For this purpose, motion of hand is detected by Leap Motion as a sensor. This sensor can detect not only the motion of hand but the motion of fingers. According to the motion of hand or fingers in the real world, hand model in the virtual world is moved. Cloth is modeled with simple particles and springs, and dynamical change of cloth model form is obtained by numerical integration of motion equation. The interaction between the hand model and the cloth model is enabled, and then it is possible to grab the cloth model by the hand model in the virtual world.

Keywords: Draping · Leap motion · Cloth model · Hand model · Simulation

1 Introduction

In the processes to design clothing, paper patterns are made from a design drawing. Draping is one of the methods to make paper patterns from a design drawing. In draping method, paper patterns are made to apply cloth to a dummy and cutting unnecessary part of cloth. Though draping is a suitable method to make clothing fit to each person, it takes more time and cost than other methods. It is expected that the efficiency to design clothing is improved tremendously by virtualization of draping method. In the virtualized draping, natural man-machine interface is required.

We have been studied the virtualization of draping [1, 2]. Our method to make patterns for clothing is to map virtual cloth model on a virtual dummy model. After that, darts are made and the unnecessary part of cloth model is cut as in the real world. Another types of virtual draping systems have been studied. Cho et al. [3] made patterns to develop the surface shape of a measured dummy body. Wang et al. [4] presented a method to make patterns using contour curves and style curves. Huang et al. [5] made a wireframe model from characteristic points of human body, and made

© Springer International Publishing Switzerland 2015
C. Stephanidis (Ed.): HCII 2015 Posters, Part I, CCIS 528, pp. 185–189, 2015.
DOI: 10.1007/978-3-319-21380-4_33

patterns from the deformed wireframe. Au et al. [6] inserted planes into human body model, and then made patterns by development. Some studies are interactive. The study of Meng et al. [7] is not about draping. In this study, patterns and three-dimensional shape of clothing is correlated. When a user change the shape of the patters, the three-dimensional shape of clothing changes accordingly, and a user is able to adjust the patterns interactively. Wibowo et al. [8] studied virtual draping method with a instrument to trace the surface of a dummy in the real world. The cloth manipulation in those studies are completely different from that in the real world. The experiences in the real world is very important, and only our method can provide the same feeling in cloth manipulation as in the real world.

On the other hand, online trade becomes more and more popular than now. But it is difficult to feel the characteristics of cloth because it is impossible to touch cloth in the online trading system. When cloth handling is virtualized, it is possible to touch cloth in the virtual world. The virtual cloth is deformed according to the movement of real fingers in the virtual world. It may be possible to feel characteristics of cloth to show the appearance of the cloth deformation. We have been manipulated cloth in the virtual world by detecting the movement of hand. The purpose of this study is to manipulate virtual cloth by detecting the movement of fingers.

2   Virtual Cloth Manipulation System

2.1   Detection of the Movements of Fingers

We have been studied man-machine interface not by mouse but the method to manipulate virtual cloth naturally by hand [9–11]. Microsoft Kinect has been utilized as the sensor to detect the movement of hand. The coordinate of skeletal joints can be detected by Kinect. The coordinate of hand joint is extracted, and the coordinate is set to a node of a cloth model to manipulate the cloth model. In the real world, cloth is manipulated by the movement of fingers. Therefor, it is important to detect the movement of fingers to manipulate virtual cloth. It is not impossible to detect movement of fingers by Kinect, but it takes time to process the detection. In this study, Leap Motion sensor is utilized. With Leap Motion, it is possible to detect the movement of both fingers, and the detected movement is used as the movement of the virtual hand model.

2.2   Models

Cloth and Objects are modeled for virtualization. Cloth is modeled by particles and springs with which particles are connected. Gravity force is acted on the particles. The cloth model is simple because mechanical calculation can be processed at high speed. The coordinate of each particle is obtained from the integration of motion equation. The cloth shape can be predicted from the coordinate of each particle. The objects beside the cloth is supposed to be rigid bodies. Each object is modeled as a set of particles. Collision detection and reaction are defined between the virtual cloth and objects. For each particle of the virtual cloth and object, a radius is set and the collision is detected from the comparison between the radius and the distance of particles. When collision is detected, repulsive force acts to make the distance between particles is more than two times of the radius as reaction. The simple method is adopted for collision detection and reaction to calculate at high speed.

2.3 Processes

The coordinate of each finger joint is detected by Leap Motion. The virtual hand is also modeled as a set of particles. The detected coordinates are set to the virtual finger joints, and the fingers are moved in the virtual world according to the movement of the fingers in the real world. The virtual cloth is deformed by the interaction of the finger movements because the collision detection and reaction are defined between the virtual cloth and fingers. An explicit method, computation load of which is light, is adopted for this study to integrate motion equation of each particle. The calculation is upgraded by using GPGPU. The force acted to each particle of the cloth model can be calculated from the shape of the cloth model of the previous step. This process is suitable for parallel computation because the calculation can be processed independently for each particle.

3 Results and Discussions

The virtual cloth model is hanging with the fixed four corners in the initial state, as shown in Fig. 1. In this state, the virtual hands and fingers are moved according to the movement of the hands and fingers in the real world. The virtual cloth model can be touched to move the virtual hands and fingers in the region where the hands and fingers can contact with the cloth model, as shown in Fig. 2. When the fixations at the four corners of the cloth model are released, the cloth model falls onto the hand model and then the cloth model can be grabbed. There are some future studies as follows. Though the movement obtained by Leap Motion is more or less stable, sometimes the movement jumps. Some processes are necessary to smooth the movement. As an explicit method is adopted for high speed integration of the motion equation, sometime the calculation becomes unstable. It is necessary to stabilize the calculation so long as the

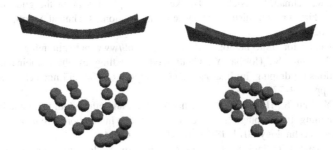

Fig. 1. The red object is the cloth model and the green object is the hand model. The cloth model is hanging with the fixed four corners. The left hand side image shows the opened hand model, and the right hand side shows the closed hand model (Color figure online).

Fig. 2. The left hand side image shows that the cloth model is pushed up by the hand model, and the right hand side image shows that the cloth model is freed and the hand model grab it.

calculation speed is not so much sacrificed. As friction is not defined, it is difficult to keep the cloth model fall into the virtual hand. Friction between virtual cloth and fingers should be defined. In the processes of draping, cloth is applied to dummy and rest part of the cloth is picked for dart. From the point of view of draping, the association between the finger movements and the deformation of cloth should be considered.

Acknowledgments. This work was partly supported by Grants-in-Aid for Scientific Research (No. 23240100, 24220012) from the Ministry of Education, Science, Sports and Culture of Japan.

References

1. Smith, T.F., Waterman, M.S.: Identification of common molecular subsequences. J. Mol. Biol. **147**, 195–197 (1981)
2. May, P., Ehrlich, H.-C., Steinke, T.: ZIB structure prediction pipeline: composing a complex biological workflow through web services. In: Nagel, W.E., Walter, W.V., Lehner, W. (eds.) Euro-Par 2006. LNCS, vol. 4128, pp. 1148–1158. Springer, Heidelberg (2006)
3. Foster, I., Kesselman, C.: The Grid: Blueprint for a New Computing Infrastructure. Morgan Kaufmann, San Francisco (1999)
4. Czajkowski, K., Fitzgerald, S., Foster, I., Kesselman, C.: Grid Information services for distributed resource sharing. In: 10th IEEE International Symposium on High Performance Distributed Computing, pp. 181–184. IEEE Press, New York (2001)
5. Foster, I., Kesselman, C., Nick, J., Tuecke, S.: The physiology of the grid: an open grid services architecture for distributed systems integration. Technical report, Global Grid Forum (2002)
6. National Center for Biotechnology Information. http://www.ncbi.nlm.nih.gov
7. Mesuda, Y., Inui, S., Horiba, Y.: Cloth model handling by the combination of some manipulations for draping. In: International Conference on Kansei Engineering and Emotion Research, pp. 769–778 (2014)
8. Mesuda, Y., Inui, S., Horiba, Y.: Combination of cut and other cloth manipulations in cloth model handling for draping. In: Proceedings of the International Symposium on Fiber Science and Technology 2014 (ISF 2014), PS7–31 (2014)
9. Cho, Y., Komatsu, T., Inui, S., Takatera, M., Shimizu, Y.: Individual pattern making using computerized draping method for clothing. Text. Res. J. **76**, 646–654 (2006)
10. Wang, J., Lu, G.D., Li, W.L., Chen, L., Sakaguti, Y.: Interactive 3D garment design with constrained contour curves and style curves. Comput. Aided Des. **41**, 614–625 (2009)

11. Huang, H.Q., Mok, P.Y., Kwok, Y.L., Au, J.S.: Block pattern generation: From parameterizing human bodies to fit feature-aligned and flattenable 3D garments. Comput. Ind. **63**, 680–691 (2012)
12. Au, C.K., Ma, Y.S.: Garment pattern definition, development and application with associative feature approach. Comput. Ind. **61**, 524–531 (2010)
13. Meng, Y., Mok, Y.P., Jin, X.: Interactive virtual try-on clothing design systems. Comput. Aided Des. **42**, 310–321 (2010)
14. Wibowo, A., Sakamoto, D., Mitani, J., Igarashi, T.: DressUp: A 3D interface for clothing design with a physical mannequin. In: Proceedings of The 6th International Conference on tangible, embedded and embodied interaction (TEI 2012), pp. 99–102 (2012)
15. Inui, S., Mesuda, Y., Horiba, Y.: Cloth handling in virtual space. In: Stephanidis, C. (ed.) HCII 2013, Part II. CCIS, vol. 374, pp. 704–707. Springer, Heidelberg (2013)
16. Mesuda, Y., Inui, S., Horiba, Y.: Virtual cloth handling. In: 5th International Congress of International Association of Societies of Design Research proceedings, pp. 5503–5510 (2013)
17. Inui, S., Mesuda, Y., Horiba, Y.: Handling of virtual cloth. Hum. Comput. Interact. Int. **2014**, 585–589 (2014)

Haptic Device Using a Soldering Test System

Manabu Ishihara[✉]

National Institute of Technology, Oyama College,
Oyama, Tochigi 323-0806, Japan
ishihara@m.ieice.org

Abstract. We learned that the present challenges are the stabilization of the wrists, representation of gravity, and the sensation of diminishing solder. The issue of wrist stabilization is difficult to improve because, with control from the haptic device, there exists an area for which stabilization is not possible. On the other hand, for the representation of gravity and sensation of diminishing solder, the representation can be changed in the software program and further experimental investigation is needed in the future.

Keywords: Virtual reality (VR) · Soldering training system · Haptic device

1 Introduction

As a result of recent advances in three dimensional (3D) video technology and stereo sound systems, virtual reality (VR) has become a familiar part of people's lives. Concurrent with these advances has been a wealth of research on touch interface technology [1], and educators have begun exploring ways to incorporate teaching tools utilizing touch properties in their curriculums [2, 3]. However, when used as teaching tools, it is important that a touch interface provide a "feel" that is as close to reality as possible. This will make replacing familiar teaching tools with digital media incorporating VR seem more attractive. For example, various learning support systems that utilize virtually reality (VR) technology [4] are being studied. Examples include a system that utilizes a stereoscopic image and writing brush display to teach the brush strokes used in calligraphy [5, 6], the utilization of a robot arm with the same calligraphy learning system [7], a system that uses a "SPIDAR" haptic device to enable remote calligraphy instruction [8], and systems that analyze the learning process involved in piano instruction [9] or in the use of virtual chopsticks [10].

The advantages of a system that uses virtual reality (VR) are that the software program can be changed to permit various types of technical training to be performed with a single device, and that the work environment can also be changed easily. Another advantage is that a network can be used to allow multiple users to train at different remote locations.

However, with a VR space connected via the Internet or other network, as a result of network latency and packet loss [11], as well as differing amounts of information, the data transmission times for various sensory operations will not necessarily be the same. An example of this phenomenon is the lag between video and sound in a network teleconference system. In an environment where latency exists, such a system cannot

© Springer International Publishing Switzerland 2015
C. Stephanidis (Ed.): HCII 2015 Posters, Part I, CCIS 528, pp. 190–195, 2015.
DOI: 10.1007/978-3-319-21380-4_34

be said to be suitable as a technical training system, and this is a problem when using a VR system.

In this study, we also created and evaluated a soldering training system.

2 Evaluation of a Soldering Test System

To facilitate the passing down of technical skills, various operations have been analyzed and the application of those analyses is being investigated. Soldering work by skilled workers and unskilled workers is also being analyzed. (1) For workers having a certain amount of experience, there is diversity of right wrist motions. (2) For beginners, various soldering iron insertion angles and motions of each wrist, and a tendency for instability are observed. (3) For skilled workers, the soldering iron insertion angle and wrist motions are stable, and soldering is completed in nearly a single operation.

On the basis of the above, the soldering iron insertion angle, wrist motion stability, and the timing with which to remove the soldering iron are suggested to be three operation characteristics. These are shown in Table 1.

2.1 Experiment Overview

In this study, we used a PHANToM Omni Device (Sensable Technologies) as our haptic device. It was attached to a control computer (CPU: Intel® Core™i5-4430 [3.00 GHz], RAM:8.00 GB, OS:64bit) running Open-Haptics™ toolkit v3.0 as the control program [12].

We began by modeling images of the surface texture for notebook and other paper types using friction experiments. When creating friction via the haptic display, it was first necessary to determine what level of friction was discernible.

We conducted both dynamic and static friction experiments, during which we measured the threshold for frictional force and points of subjective equality. Five male test subjects, approximately 20–21 years of age, participated in both experiments.

2.2 Overview of the Soldering Operation

In soldering, the substrate warming time interval and the timing with which to remove the soldering iron are entirely heat-dependent. According on the type of solder and soldering iron, various combinations exist and it would be difficult to categorize them all. Solder types include both lead solder and lead-free solder, and although lead-free solder is most widely used at present, lead solder is used in this system. Typical lead solder having a composition ratio of Sn63 %:Pb37 % is used, and the melting point for this composition ratio is 183°C. A suitable junction temperature is 60 to 70°C greater than the solder melting point, and therefore an appropriate temperature for the soldering work is assumed to be around 250°C. Accordingly, when the soldering iron is set to the appropriate temperature of 350°C, the soldering time is approximately 3 s. Setting the removal timing to within approximately 3 s prevents the soldering iron from contacting the substrate for too long, and is thought to prevent soldering defects. If the solder did not completely melt, the soldering iron should be removed once and then the soldering operation repeated. Here, a temperature-adjustable soldering iron is used and a temperature of 350°C is assumed.

Table 1. Soldering work evaluation items and their characteristic values [13]

	Theoretical value	Error range
Insertion angle of the soldering iron (degree)	45	±3
Soldering time(Second)	3	±0.5

2.3   System Overview

1. Two haptic devices are connected so that they can be operated simultaneously in the virtual space. Thus, two devices can be operated and used as the solder and soldering iron.
2. By reading in a bitmap image and determining the width and height dimensions, red–green–blue (RGB) values corresponding to coordinate points are stored in an array. When preparing a graphic image, those values are mapped to position a floor and the substrate within the 3D space.
3. A training mode and practice mode are provided for beginners and people who are unfamiliar with the system. In the training mode, soldering operations are explained one by one in stages, and while learning about the operating method, the user also gains an understanding of how to determine the solder insertion timing and the insertion angle. By controlling the haptic device so as to forcibly retract it from the substrate, the user learns the timing for removing the soldering iron. Additionally, in order to stabilize the user's wrists, control is implemented to forcibly secure the haptic device in place.

In the practice mode, pressure is constantly applied in the gravity direction to the haptic device to reproduce a gravity space and leads and lands that approximate those of actual work. This is shown in Fig. 1.

4. The viewing perspective can be changed by multiplying the model view matrix to allow movement and scaling.
5. The depth dimension can be difficult to ascertain while watching a virtual space on a screen and operating the haptic devices at hand. Therefore, the positional coordinates of the cursor (pen tip) in the screen are acquired and projected as a point onto the x-z plane.
6. As a method for acquiring the angle, the acquisition of vertical angle information of the pen tip of the haptic device itself was considered; however, vertical motion depends not only on the pen tip, but also on the arm itself, and so a suitable angle could not be obtained with this method. Therefore, we improved the accuracy by

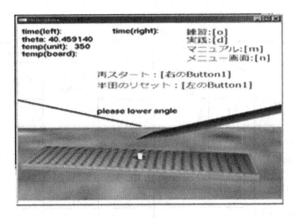

Fig. 1. Practice mode (execution screen)

reading in the angle at the location of the cursor (pen tip) in the space. A 3 × 3 matrix that specifies a cursor transform in world coordinates can be obtained, and is used to convert the angle to a Euler angle. Since the rotation is around the Z-Y-Z axes sequentially, the equation of the rotation matrix is expressed as follows.

$$
R = \begin{pmatrix} \cos\alpha\cos\beta\cos\gamma - \sin\alpha\sin\gamma & -\cos\alpha\cos\beta\cos\gamma - \sin\alpha\cos\gamma & \cos\alpha\sin\beta \\ \sin\alpha\cos\beta\cos\gamma + \cos\alpha\sin\gamma & -\sin\alpha\cos\beta\sin\gamma + \cos\alpha\cos\gamma & \sin\alpha\sin\beta \\ -\sin\beta\cos\alpha & \sin\beta\sin\gamma & \cos\beta \end{pmatrix} \quad (1)
$$

From here, the Euler angle α will be

$$
\alpha = \arctan(R[2,3]/R[1,3]), \quad (2)
$$

and so the angle can be obtained (α: angle around the z-axis). The basic posture while soldering is with arms parallel to the substrate, and so the Z axial direction in the coordinate axis in OpenGL is not considered.

7. To express the sinking feeling when solder melts, rather than being depicted as a simple cube, the substrate is depicted as a cube formed from multiple superimposed flat sheets. The sinking feeling is expressed by having the haptic device pass through a single sheet when a certain amount force is applied.

3   Evaluation

The ease of operation was evaluated. Five test subjects performed a five-level evaluation ranging from 1 (Poor) to 5 (Good). There were 7 items to be evaluated, and these and the results are shown in Table 2.

Table 2. System evaluation [units: number of people]

	5	4	3	2	1	
	Good	Slighly good	Normal	Slighly poor	Poor	Average
Operability of the system	1	3	1			4.0
Designated angle	4	1				4.8
Designated angle and timing	2	2	1			4.2
Fixation of the wrist				4	1	1.8
Procedure of the soldering	5					5
Gravitational sense		2	2	1		3.2
Sense to decrease of the solder	1	1	2	1		3.4

From the results of a survey, we learned that the present challenges are the stabilization of the wrists, representation of gravity, and the sensation of diminishing solder. The issue of wrist stabilization is difficult to improve because, with control from the haptic device, there exists an area for which stabilization is not possible. On the other hand, for the representation of gravity and sensation of diminishing solder, the representation can be changed in the software program and further experimental investigation is needed in the future.

4   Concluding Remarks

We learned that the present challenges are the stabilization of the wrists, representation of gravity, and the sensation of diminishing solder. The issue of wrist stabilization is difficult to improve because, with control from the haptic device, there exists an area for which stabilization is not possible. On the other hand, for the representation of gravity and sensation of diminishing solder, the representation can be changed in the software program and further experimental investigation is needed in the future.

Acknowledgements. This work was supported by KAKENHI Grant Number 25350369.

References

1. Ohnishi, H., Mochizuki, K.: Effect of delay of feedback force on perception of elastic force: a psychophysical approach. IEICE Trans. Commun. **E90-B**(1), 12–20 (2007)
2. Ishihara, M.: On first impression of the teaching materials which used haptic display. IEE Jpn. Trans. Fundam. Mater. **129**(7), 490–491 (2009). (in Japanese)

3. Ishihara, M.: Assessment of paper's roughnessfor haptic device. In: Proceedings of Forum Information Technology 2011, K-032, Hokkaido, Japan, September 2011. (in Japanese)
4. Hirose, M., et al. : Virtual Reality, Sangyo Tosho (1993). (in Japanese)
5. Yoshida, T., Muranaka, N., Imanishi, S.: a construction of educational application system for calligrapy master based on virtual reality. IEE Jpn. Trans. Electron. Inf. Syst. **117-C**(11), 1629–1634 (1997). (in Japanese)
6. Yoshida, T., Yamamoto, T., Imanishi, S.: A calligraphy mastering support system using virtual reality technology and its learning effects. IEE Jpn. Trans. Fundam. Mater. **123-A** (12), 1206–1216 (2003). (in Japanese)
7. Henmi, K., Yoshikawa, T.: Virtual lesson and its application to virtual calligraphy system. TVRSJ **3**(1), 13–19 (1983). (in Japanese)
8. Sakuma, M., Masamori, S., Harada, T., Hirata, Y., Satou, M.: A Remote Lesson System for Japanese Calligraphy using SPIDAR. IEICE of Japan, Technical Report, MVE 99-52, pp. 27–32, October 1999. (in Japanese)
9. Otsuka, G., Sodeyama, G., Muranaka, N., Imanishi, S.: A construction of a piano training system based on virtual reality. IEE of Jpn. Trans. Electron. Inf. Syst. **116-C**(11), 1288–1294 (1996). (in Japanese)
10. Yamaguchi, Y., Kitamura, Y., Kishino, F.: Analysis of Learning Process of Virtual Chopsticks. IEICE of Japan, Technical Report, MVE 2001-3, pp. 11–16, June 2001. (in Japanese)
11. Ishihara, M.: Empirical study regarding representing roughness with haptic devices. In: Proceedings of 2013 IEEE 2nd GCCE, pp. 471–473. Chiba, Japan, October 2013
12. Sensable OpenHaptics™ programmer's guide
13. Shihoko, K., Higa, S., Noguchi, K.: Verification of skill coaching item based on motion characteristics. In: Proceedings of FIT 2011(IPSJ and IEICE), pp. 785–786, September 2011. (in Japanese)

Learning to Juggle in an Interactive Virtual Reality Environment

Tobias Kahlert[2], Florian van de Camp[1]([⊠]), and Rainer Stiefelhagen[2]

[1] Fraunhofer IOSB, Karlsruhe, Germany
florian.vandecamp@iosb.fraunhofer.de
[2] Karlsruhe Institute of Technology (KIT), Karlsruhe, Germany
uaezk@student.kit.edu, rainer.stiefelhagen@kit.edu

Abstract. Virtual reality environments are great tools for training as they are very cheap compared to on-site training for many tasks. While the focus has mostly been on the visual experience, we present a system that combines real world interactions with the virtual visual world to train motor skills that are applicable to the real world. Body pose tracking is combined with an Oculus Rift to create such an interactive virtual environment. As an example application, we taught users to juggle using a virtual training course. A third of the users were able to immediately transfer the newly acquired skills and juggle with real balls.

1 Introduction and Related Work

Many tasks such as surgery or flying require extensive training of motor skills as the margin of error must be extremely low. Virtual reality offers a cheap way to simulate a large variety of training environments. While the focus of virtual reality systems has been on the visual presentation, we present a low cost training environment that uses the Microsoft Kinect and the Oculus Rift to create a virtual reality in which the user's real-world interactions are transferred into the virtual world. This allows the transfer of basic motor skills from the virtual world to the real world as we show in an example application that teaches users to juggle.

With recent developments in VR technology, such equipment will soon be available and affordable to the average user. Young and his team [YGAB14] compared a low-cost virtual reality system, similar to our set-up, with a high-cost virtual reality system. They showed in different experiments for three-dimensional coordination, that the low-cost system outperformed the high-cost system in nearly all cases. In a user study Santos et al. [SDP+09] compared a head-mounted display with a desktop based system for 3D navigation. They showed that users were more successful when using the desktop system, although the majority stated that the head-mounted display allowed a more natural and intuitive interaction.

Several projects exist that focus on teaching within a virtual simulation. For instance Webel et al. [WFKO13] presented a simulation, that uses the Kinect and

C. Stephanidis (Ed.): HCII 2015 Posters, Part I, CCIS 528, pp. 196–201, 2015.
DOI: 10.1007/978-3-319-21380-4_35

Oculus Rift to create a virtual world, in which the user can visit historical places like the Siena Cathedral. The nDiVE project [RWG+13] offers different tools and training programs to teach the management of supply chains. They also showed the emotional effects of experiencing death in a virtual environment [RTC+14] compared to common desktop based systems. There are also projects that focus more on training a skill than transferring knowledge. Aggarwal et al. [AGE+06] presented a virtual reality training program, that enables novice surgeons to train their skills in laparoscopic surgery at different levels of difficulty. The simulation also observes users calculating a score representing the skill level.

2   Virtual Reality and Interaction

To teach users motor skills in a virtual environment, they need to be able to interact with it. For the training effect to be useful in the real-world, the interaction in the virtual world should be as close as possible to the real world. For the task of juggling, arm movement, as well as the opening and closing of hands, are key properties of the required interaction. Figure 1 shows the setup consisting of the Occulus Rift, a Microsoft Kinect and custom made gloves. The skeleton provided by the Kinect is transformed from the Kinect's local coordinate system to the absolute coordinate system of Ogre3D, a library which we use as our graphics engine to manage and render the virtual environment. This skeleton is used to get relevant points of the user's body, like hands and head for interaction but also to render a stick figure representation of the user in the virtual world (shown in Fig. 3). The environment is shown via the Oculus Rift from a virtual camera which is attached to the position of the user's head in the virtual world. This camera is oriented according to how the user moves his head. This already allows the user to see his virtual arms as he lifts his real arms into his field of view. The hand positions provided by the Kinect are used to catch and throw virtual balls. However, an accurate representation of the hand requires a level of detail the Kinect does not offer [KE12]. Therefore the gloves, shown in Fig. 2, are used to detect the opening and closing of hands while at the same time providing basic haptic feedback. A ball is caught when it collides with the user's virtual hand while the corresponding glove detects a closed hand. A ball is thrown from a virtual hand if the user opens his real hand. The setup does not allow for a detailed model of the hand, which makes it impossible to calculate an accurate trajectory for the thrown ball. Instead, we implemented a mechanism that automatically computes a perfect trajectory from the throwing hand to the other hand. This allows users to focus on the juggle motion sequence itself.

To exploit the potential of a virtual environment, we implemented several functionalities that would not be possible in the real world. In the virtual environment, it is possible to visualize trajectories of thrown balls and highlights that help the user time and direct the throws and catches. It is also possible to slow down time which allows users to juggle in slow motion and gives them more time to react while they are still familiarizing themselves with the juggling sequence.

Fig. 1. Setup for the experiment. The virtual training environment is displayed using an Oculus Rift (A). The user is tracked by a Kinect (B). Opening and closing of hands is detected by gloves (C).

Fig. 2. Gloves for hand interaction. An analog signal is triggered if the hand is closed as the wire-mesh (b) touches the aluminum ball (a). The signal is transported via wires (c) to a microcontroller (d) which transforms it to a digital signal and forwards it to the computer (e). In addition, the aluminum ball provides haptic feedback when catching a ball.

3   Experimental Evaluation

To evaluate our virtual reality system, we performed a user study with nine persons, three women and six men, aged between 20 and 43. None of which could juggle. The goal was to teach the cascade juggling pattern as shown in Fig. 4. Users had to take a virtual training course in our setup (see Fig. 1). The virtual training environment consisted of a simple room, delimited by white lines as shown in Fig. 3. The user's avatar was positioned in the middle of the room. The progress and the current assignment were given in the form of text on the opposite wall. A computer generated voice led the user through every single exercise

Fig. 3. The images on the left show the user, while the images on the right show what the user currently sees: A view into the virtual training environment. White lines are used to define the training area. An abstract representation of the user is rendered with blue lines. Hands are drawn using 3D models indicating if the hands are opened or closed. A text in front of the user shows the current assignment (Color figure online).

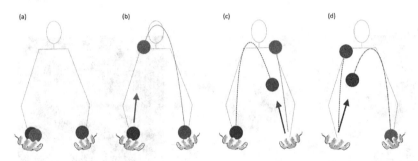

Fig. 4. The beginning of the cascade juggling patter. At the beginning hold two balls in the dominant hand and the third ball in the other hand (a). Throw one ball from the dominant hand (b). When this ball reaches it's apex, throw the ball from the other hand (c). Catch the first ball and throw the last ball, when the second ball reaches it's apex (d). To juggle, repeat step (c) and (d).

Table 1. Number of subjects able the perform n consecutive throws/catches.

n	2	3	4	5	6	7	8	9	10	11	12	13
Throws	2	2	2	1	1	0	0	0	0	0	0	1
Catches	4	2	0	2	0	0	0	0	0	0	1	0

in the course. As a first task, users had to do simple ball throwing exercises to adapt to the virtual environment. In the following stages, they were presented with tasks of increasing difficulty leading to the actual juggling sequence with one, two and finally three balls. In the final stage, all three balls had to be juggled consecutively. Every stage had to be repeated several times until a certain success rate was reached. Subsequently, real juggle balls were given to the users to try what they had learned in the virtual training for ten minutes. During that time, the number of consecutive throws and catches were counted. Finally, users were asked to fill out a questionnaire to get an insight into qualitative aspects of the virtual environment and the training course.

3.1 Results

It took 27 min to complete the virtual course on average. All users easily familiarized with the virtual environment. While the trajectory of the balls was perceived as realistic, the process of throwing and catching was not as convincing. The results for the number of consecutive throws and catches with real balls are shown in Table 1. We defined being able to juggle as throwing and catching five consecutive balls. After the training, three subjects were able to juggle despite the fact that the process of throwing was significantly simplified. In addition, all users stated that they knew how to juggle but needed more time to practice with real balls.

4 Conclusion

We presented an interactive training environment, which is able to teach motor abilities, while observing the learning progress by combining a virtual environment with the real world movements of the user. In a user study, we showed that motor skills can be conveyed from a virtual environment to the real world even if certain aspects are simplified. With these promising results, we hope to address more complex tasks in virtual courses for inaccessible or dangerous domains in the future.

References

[AGE+06] Aggarwal, R., Grantcharov, T.P., Eriksen, J.R., Blirup, D., Kristiansen, V.B., Funch-Jensen, P., Darzi, A.: An evidence-based virtual reality training program for novice laparoscopic surgeons. Ann. Surg. **244**(2), 310 (2006)

[KE12] Khoshelham, K., Elberink, S.O.: Accuracy and resolution of kinect depth data for indoor mapping applications. Sensors **12**(2), 1437–1454 (2012)

[RTC+14] Reiners, T., Teras, H., Chang, V., Wood, L.C., Gregory, S., Gibson, D., Petter, N., Teras, M.: Authentic, immersive, and emotional experience in virtual learning environments: The fear of dying as an important learning experience in a simulation (2014)

[RWG+13] Reiners, T., Wood, L.C., Gregory, S., Petter, N., Teräs, H., Gütl, C., Chang, V., Herrington, J.: nDive: the story of how logistics and supply chain management could be taught(2013)

[SDP+09] Santos, B.S., Dias, P., Pimentel, A., Baggerman, J.-W., Ferreira, C., Silva, S., Madeira, J.: Head-mounted display versus desktop for 3D navigation in virtual reality: a user study. Multimedia Tools Appl. **41**(1), 161–181 (2009)

[WFKO13] Webel, S., Franke, T., Keil, J., Olbrich, M.: Immersive experience of current and ancient reconstructed cultural attractions. In: Digital Heritage International Congress, pp. 395–398 . The Eurographics Association (2013)

[YGAB14] Young, M.K., Gaylor, G.B., Andrus, S.M., Bodenheimer, B.: A comparison of two cost-differentiated virtual reality systems for perception and action tasks. In: Proceedings of the ACM Symposium on Applied Perception, pp. 83–90. ACM (2014)

Integration of Artificial Intelligence Techniques in a Virtual Environment

Sandra Mateus[1(✉)] and John Branch[2]

[1] National University of Colombia,
Politécnico Colombiano Jaime Isaza Cadavid, Medellín, Colombia
spmateus@elpoli.edu.co
[2] National University of Colombia, Medellín, Colombia
jwbranch@unal.edu.co

Abstract. In this article, two artificial intelligence techniques such as Artificial Neural Networks and Genetic Algorithms were incorporated into a 3D working environment and turned into a game engine, which simulates a working environment in order to obtain possible warning signs to different hazards. These techniques were incorporated in the perception and reasoning of a character in the virtual environment, in order to react intelligently to given warning signs.

Keywords: Intelligent virtual environment · Artificial neural network · Genetic algorithm

1 Introduction

When a virtual environment has Artificial Intelligence incorporated, it reaches a new feature resulting in an asynchronous event distribution system which is what distinguishes it from a conventional virtual environment and hence it has high applicability [1]. According to Whiting [2], there is an interesting dilemma for animators and designers, who are constantly creating new environments with the desire to incorporate characters who are autonomous, since each environment requires a complex and time-intensive to be performed by an expert programmer, because the models are created to solve specific problems and because of its specific nature, cannot be easily reused.

Some examples of Intelligent Virtual Environments: Jia and Zhenjiang [3] developed the Platform "Paladin", which uses collaborative and neuro-evolution agents, combining the Backpropagation Networks with Evolutionary Algorithms in a 2D environment. Clement et al. [4] presented an intelligent tutoring system as an EVI for training, in order to infer the learning objectives that the student has acquired, finally trying it in a virtual lab biotecno-logy in 3D. Xi and Smith [5] create a virtual environment with game technology and intelligent agents to simulate human emergencies. Liu et al. [6] propose a framework for modeling virtual humans with a high level of autonomy, at the behavioral level and movement in a virtual environment. Gilbert and Forney [7] perfected guided by an avatar in a clothing store in a 3D virtual world of Second Life tour through virtual agents, using a robust variant of Artificial Intelligence Markup Language (AIML) and taking the challenge to the Turing test.

C. Stephanidis (Ed.): HCII 2015 Posters, Part I, CCIS 528, pp. 202–207, 2015.
DOI: 10.1007/978-3-319-21380-4_36

Based on the above, this paper shows how integrated in a 3D virtual environment, an artificial neural network and genetic algorithm in perception and reasoning of a character, for intelligent interaction with the elements of a work environment, identifying signals warning. The 3D virtual environment was created using the UDK game engine. This environment implemented init some improvements, as the technique of Path-Finding and additionally, some random obstacles were placed in order to make it more difficult path towards the goals of the character.

This paper is organized as follows: in Sect. 2, the concepts of perception and reasoning are discussed, and the 3D virtual environment created is displayed; in Sect. 3, the Artificial Neural Network implemented in the virtual environment is explained; in Sect. 4, the genetic algorithms used are presented; and Finally, the conclusions.

2 Perception and Reasoning

The Intelligent Virtual Environments must reach large capacities of complex and interactive behaviors to achieve a high level of realism [8]. This realism is based on elements that enable intelligent performance such as perception, learning, and communication through natural language and reasoning. According to the above, this paper focuses only on the perception and reasoning, cognitive and behavioral levels of a Virtual Environment.

According Marthino et al. [9], perception is considered as all events of the virtual environment are filtered according to the interests and location of the character and is based on two principles: (1) A limited perception, in which a character perceives all events, but only perceives its associated area; and (2) An inaccurate perception, in which the character perceives the virtual environment as it is, but only receives relevant events associated with it.

They also describe the reasoning as a process developed by a set of production rules which are conditions based on the model of the world, in the state of the target, the characteristic behavior and internal state information.

Given the above concepts, the character implemented in the Intelligent Virtual Environment from this work, based its reasoning on the impact of its internal target and priority of the action to perform, on the cognitive and behavioral levels.

Based on the above, a model of Intelligent Virtual Environment leaning on a game engine, which are incorporated Artificial Intelligence techniques in order to occur from a given perception with a character, a reasoning proposed proper respect to the Virtual Environment.

In this model, this can be seen as a set classifier S, which takes a set of perceptions $P_1...P_n$ and combines them to take adequate reasoning $R_1...R_n$. This reasoning to perform a certain action is supported on one of the techniques of Artificial Intelligence named in the model. So the system, decide and select an action A, according to the reasoning made (Eq. 1).

$$S(\{P_1,\ R_1\}, \{P_2,\ R_2\}, ...\{P_n,\ R_n\}) \rightarrow A \qquad (1)$$

With this model, you want to achieve the following characteristics of an Intelligent Virtual Environment described by [10]: Decisive; any action taken by the character will be reflected in an effective plan; Real Time: The character must respond in real time to the perceptions of the environment and in the same way, adequate reason to perception form received; Ordered: That follow the proper sequence in their behavior.

Perceptions were simulated in this virtual environment and their respective actions to perform, through reasoning with AI technique, are shown in Table 1.

Table 1. Perceptions and actions that the character execute in the virtual environment

Perception	Action run
Detects fire	Activate the fire alarm
Detects electrical risk	Turn off light switches
Detects wet floor	Call the cleaning staff
Workplace - do not know what to do	Use the intercom for help

In Fig. 1, shown rendering Virtual Environment, which will be the character interacting as disclosed in Table 1 and to which AI techniques are applied, explained in the following sections.

Fig. 1. Virtual environment developed with UDK

3   Intelligent Virtual Environment with Artificial Neural Network

To implement an artificial neural network in this environment, several simulations were made with some types of networks. Later, two networks were chosen: The Radial Basis Function (RBF), and Multi Layer Perceptron (MLP). After making comparisons between these two networks measurements by square error, was selected to the MLP, by the number of neurons used in the hidden layer and the error was lower, the RBF, among other features. The used algorithm is a variation of the described in [11].

A network MLP was used with a 4-10-4 configuration (4 input neurons, 10 hidden and 4 output). We also used 80 % of tickets available for training and 10 % for validation and the other 10 % for testing, to verify that the results which gives the RNA were satisfactory if reserved; this is what is defined as the process of overfitting (Training, Validation, Testing), resulting in the confusion matrix, where it is interpreted that the main diagonal are correct classifications therefore 99.2 % rated it had.

Finally, in the Fig. 2 is shown the virtual environment is shown to the RNA; in this case, is running action using the intercom for help.

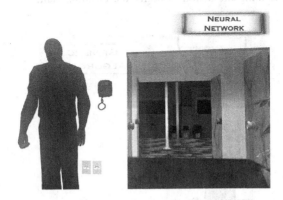

Fig. 2. Intelligent virtual environment with the MLP neural network

4   Intelligent Virtual Environment with Genetic Algorithm

Generally, in a genetic algorithm concepts of convert, adapt, and select couples are applied to generate a random selection by the combination of these couples between these mutations and generate new individuals to apply.

Stored in an array of 4 positions corresponding to the perceptions described in Table 1, the objective of this is that every time the character revised every state, all functions are executed corresponding to the genetic algorithm. After completing a cycle, i.e., whenever the character inspects a state, the results obtained by the calculus, with randomly generated in the array are evaluated.

The genetic algorithm used, which is a variation of the above in [12] is applied, in the path-finding technique. The adaptability of the individual is calculated according to Eq. 2.

$$f_i = q_i \bigg/ \sum_j q_j \qquad (2)$$

Where q_i and q_j represents the individual each other individuals. As such, the quality of the individual by the sum of the qualities of the other individuals are divided.

In the genetic algorithm, partner selection is done in reverse way round, i.e., the first individual will intersect with the last individual, the second with the penultimate and the third-last.

The tournament is where calculations are performed to select the fittest individual. Subsequently, a copy of the winners of the tournament takes place individuals and redistributing the combination and mutation operation is performed on the matrix for realization. In the latter operation, crosses between new partners resulting from the previous steps (Tournament and Copy) are performed. Finally, a crossing of genes among binary numbers, to be a new individual product of the cross, as discussed in evolutionary theory is made.

Figure 3 shows, Intelligent Virtual Environment running with Genetic Algorithm. In this case, it is running the action to notify the cleaning staff.

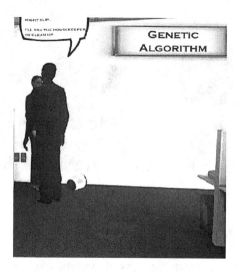

Fig. 3. Intelligent virtual environment with the genetic algorithm

5   Conclusions

In terms of software development, this paper proposes and demonstrates the use of game engines, in order to obtain a 3D Virtual Environment, balanced with a technique of Artificial Intelligence, which makes it more practical and more realistic.

Artificial Intelligence techniques have complex operations requiring extensive repetitions, which in turn affect learning in real time. It is possible to achieve real machine learning, but in many cases, this sacrifices performance. The technique selected can be very efficient, but according to given cases, from the perspective of a strategy, a given target, some techniques may perform better than others.

Neural Network from concept is understood as a technique in order to perform machine learning and you can see that in the results, there is evidence that indicates a given repetitions both fixed and random parameters learning. In the case of the Genetic

Algorithm, a high optimization is evident in solving a problem, even generating random data, can find a fairly quick solution, reducing the number of iterations; few cases where the operation is repeated, and a very isolated case where repetition is high in one case, but leaves repeated in the following.

References

1. Lozano, M.: Animación Comportamental de Personajes Inteligentes 3D basada en MINIMIN-HSP. Tesis Doctoral. Universitat de Valéncia, España (2004)
2. Whiting, J., Dinerstein, J., Egbert, K.Y., Ventura, D.: Cognitive and behavioral model ensembles for autonomous virtual characters. Comput. Intell. **26**(2), 142–159 (2010)
3. Jia, L., Zhenjiang, M.: Entertainment oriented intelligent virtual environment with agent and neural networks. In: IEEE International Workshop on Haptic Audio Visual Environments and their Applications. Ottawa, Canada (2007)
4. Clemente, J., Ramirez, J., De Antonio, A.: Applying a student modeling with non-monotonic diagnosis to intelligent virtual environment for training/instruction. Expert Syst. Appl. **41**(2), 508–520 (2014). Elsevier
5. Xi, M., Smith, S.: Simulating cooperative fire evacuation training in a virtual environment using gaming technology. In: IEEE Virtual Reality 2014, pp. 139–140. Minneapolis, Minnesota, USA: ©2014 IEEE (2014)
6. Liu, W., Zhou, L., Xing, W., Liu, X., Yuan, B.: Creating autonomous, perceptive and intelligent virtual humans in a real-time virtual environment. Tsinghua Sci. Technol. **16**(3), 233–240 (2011)
7. Gilbert, R., Forney, A.: Can avatars pass the Turing test? intelligent agent perception in a 3D virtual environment. Int. J. Hum. Comput. Stud. **73**, 30–36 (2015)
8. Cavazza, M., Lugrin, J.-L., Hartley, S., Renard, M., Nandi, A., Jacobson, J., Crooks, S.: Intelligent virtual environments for virtual reality art. Comput. Graph. **29**(6), 852–861 (2005). Elsevier
9. Martinho, C., Paiva, A., Gomes, M.: Emotions for a motion: rapid development of believable panthematic agents in intelligent virtual environments. Appl. Artif. Intell. **14**(1), 33–68 (2000)
10. Mang-Xian, Q., Hai-ming, Y.: Investigation and realization of multi-agent interaction behavior in intelligent virtual environment. In: International Conference on Cyberworlds. IEEE Computer Society (2008)
11. García, J., Carmona, E., Gallardo, L., González, M., Fernández, A., González, M.: Desarrollo de un sistema automático de discrminación del campo visual glaucomotoso basado en un clasificador neuro-fuzzy. En Revista Scielo. 77 (12) (pp. 669–676). Archivos de la Sociedad Española de Oftalmología (2002)
12. Brownlee, J.: Clever Algorithms - Nature Inspired Programming Recipes. Creative Commons, Australia (2012). ISBN 978-1-4467-8506-5

Properties of a Peripheral Head-Mounted Display (PHMD)

Denys J.C. Matthies[(✉)], Marian Haescher, Rebekka Alm,
and Bodo Urban

Fraunhofer IGD, Rostock, Germany
{denys.matthies,marian.haescher,rebekka.alm,
bodo.urban}@igd-r.fraunhofer.de

Abstract. In this paper we propose a definition for Peripheral Head-Mounted Display (PHMD) for Near Field Displays. This paper introduces a taxonomy for head-mounted displays that is based on the property of its functionality and the ability of our human eye to perceive peripheral information, instead of being technology-dependent. The aim of this paper is to help designers to understand the perception of the human eye, as well as to discuss the factors one needs to take into consideration when designing visual interfaces for PHMDs. We envision this term to help classifying devices such as Google Glass, which are often misclassified as a Head-Up Display (HUD) following NASA's definition.

Keywords: Peripheral Head-Mounted display · PHMD · Optical HMD · Display position · Peripheral perception · Google glass

1 Introduction

Nowadays, it is designers who create purposes and needs for our daily usage of computers as they also create their own language and definitions (e.g. "smartphone", which is a multisensory touchscreen mobile phone).

Before introducing another new term for Head Mounted Displays (HMD), we look into the various technologies they are based on. There are two commonly used techniques: (1) optical lens projection, which projects an image onto our eye by using a mirror-lens system and LCD, LCos, OLED or CRT technology and (2) retinal projection (RP) also called virtual retina display (VRD), which projects a picture directly onto the user's retina of the eye [4]. Because the actual built-in technology of HMDs is often unknown to the user, it is hard to classify them correctly after this scheme.

Another way to differentiate HMD's can also be determined whether the image is being displayed in either monocular (to one eye) or binocular (to both eyes) fashion. Additionally, the display can also be transparent (ST-HMD), which is usually achieved optically, with a transparent mirror-projection (OHMD), or by showing the image recorded with a video camera in front (VHMD), as shown in Fig. 1.

C. Stephanidis (Ed.): HCII 2015 Posters, Part I, CCIS 528, pp. 208–213, 2015.
DOI: 10.1007/978-3-319-21380-4_37

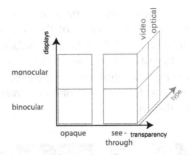

Fig. 1. Current classification based on physical and technology aspects [8]

A recently very famous HMD is Google Glass, which is denoted as a Head-Up Display (HUD) by Thad Starner [13]. Even though it sounds obvious, this definition might not adhere to the actual definition of HUD. While NASA defined this term over centuries of space flight research [11], it actually describes a display that addresses the eyes-free problem, by absolving the user from the need to angle down their head. Furthermore, it provides augmented information in the user's forward Field-of-View (FOV), which is commonly projected on a windshield. In contrast, the Head-Down Display (HDD) is located at the instrument control panel [11]. Also, a HUD is mainly used to augment additional information into reality, which is technically not feasible yet for products such as Google Glass (lens focus on the display causes a blurred environment – see Fig. 2). Since the number of HMDs is increasing and yet the classification is still not so clear for designers, it is justifiable to reclassify them. Regardless of the implemented technology, a new taxonomy that is based on the devices' functionality would be possible to classify the groups in a more precise manner. We think that a PHMD would belong to a new sub-category of HMD, which is based on their functionality, such as the smartphone is a sub-category of mobile phone.

2   Peripheral Head-Mounted Display (PHMD)

2.1   Definition

A Peripheral Head-Mounted Display (PHMD) describes a visual display (monocular or binocular) mounted to the user's head that is in the peripheral of the user's Field-of-View (FOV). Whereby the actual position of the mounting (as the display technology) is irrelevant as long as it does not cover the entire field of view. A PHMD is considered to provide an additional, always-available visual output channel, which does not limit the user performing real world tasks.

2.2   Characteristics

The most important uniqueness is that the user's FOV is not being fully covered, allowing the user to perform real world tasks without limitations, while not having the pretension to raise or create immersion, such as HMDs usually aim for. For current display technologies, while projecting image onto the eye, the screen needs to be focused by the pupil to enable a clear reading of the screen, thus the environment becomes blurred and out-of-focus. So a PHMD such as Google Glass is capable of displaying (Fig. 2) detailed information, when the pupil is focusing the display itself, as it also allows for (Fig. 2) peripheral information when the eye focuses on the real world. Still, simple information such as notifications are perceivable when focusing on the real world instead of the display.

 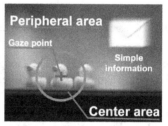

Fig. 2. Difference between detailed and peripheral information [7]

2.3 Peripheral Interaction

Since the PHMD is resting in the peripheral of the user's FOV, it has a high availability and can be quickly demanded by focusing it. Furthermore, significant changes - depending on the stimuli - of the screen content is still perceivable without focusing the display [3]. We envision this effect to be used to design peripheral information (e.g. such as visual notifications for incoming emails, approaching appointments, warnings). An efficient response to such perceived information could be accomplished in quick peripheral input described by Hausen [5] - *Peripheral Interaction*. This way, the user is not being greatly interrupted while completing real world tasks.

Notwithstanding, suitable input modalities for PHMDs that are not socially awkward remain to be discovered. Negative or positive social effects by wearing a PHMD and devoting attention on the screen while taking part in a conversation might be present, but are not proven yet. In addition, taking part in traffic while focusing on a visual input modality can lead to a considerable decrease of attention to the road.

However, compared to smartphone interaction, a quick switch to real world tasks is attainable, because there is no need for getting the device out of a pocket or bag. Furthermore, a PHMD does not need to be held by the user's hands, which offers a fully hands-free interaction. Since it is always available, it can provide peripheral visual information at any time, whereas peripheral information on smartphone in a pocket is not at all or barely perceivable (e.g. in a club/discotheque, while walking).

3   Designing Peripheral Information

Designing an optimal visual output for Head-Mounted Displays is a complex issue, since there are human factors that significantly impact users' perception [9].

3.1   Human Factors

Depth of Focus/Field: switches permanently by refocusing on objects, which is different in distances to the user. A display mounted somehow to user's eye has fixed focal distance. Focusing information such as presented on a screen leads to a change in the depth of focus. This causes blurring of information presented at other layers, which especially degrades the perception of high spatial frequency information such as text.

Eye-Movements: are actually done at a specific angle of 10°. To focus an object out of this angle, head movements are used automatically for support. However, when wearing an HMD with eye-movements that exceed this angle, since head movements do not have any effect on the interface, a drop in comfort might occur due to tired eye muscle.

Field-Of-View: describes the viewing angle of the user. The User's eye has a viewing angle of 94° from the center and 62° on the nose side [7]. The vertical angle is about 60° upwards and 75° downwards. HMDs often do not cover the whole FOV, which is also a reason for increased cybersickness.

Binocular Rivalry: describes the phenomenon, which occurs when dissimilar images are presented to the human eye [1, 2]. As the two images captured by each eye is incompatible for stereo processing, they fight for visual dominance over the other eye's side view, resulting in alternating views from the two eyes, where the non-dominant view is almost unseen. This effect often occurs when wearing a monocular HMD. In this setup, researchers [10] also observed objects that completely vanish for several seconds from user's attention.

Visual Interference: describes the phenomenon when both eyes perceive different images that are overlapping, but the brain is not able to distinguish between those. This phenomena is also known as the inability for visual separation.

Phoria: describes a muscle state of the eye, when the eyes are not focusing on a specific point. There are three different states, which can be distinguished: Esophoria, Exophoria, Orthophoria. While one eye is closed or being obstructed by a display, phoria can occur, which has the potential to cause vertigo and nausea as well [14].

Eye-Dominance: Although the user has two eyes, one eye is predominantly used. The other eye is used to make corrections and provide additional spatial information. It is recommended to wear a monocular HMD over the dominant eye [9].

3.2   Peripheral Perception

While most of these factors mentioned above become problematic when both eyes are covered with displays, a single display resting in the peripheral FOV can be considered to be unproblematic, since it does not permanently influence the perceived picture of the real world. So, when consciously focusing on the peripheral head mounted display we can perceive detailed information, as described earlier in Fig. 2. However, besides perceiving detailed information, we can also perceive information through our visual peripheral perception.

Most obvious changes are "motion", which can be perceived over the whole spectrum of the FOV. In a smaller angle, change in color is also quite well perceivable

(Fig. 3). In contrast, perceiving shapes and reading text requires very dedicated attention of the pupil. However, when being very focused on a dedicated task, rough changes in shapes are still perceivable in a peripheral way.

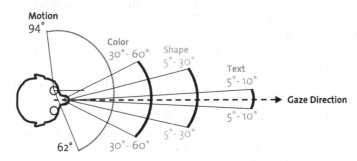

Fig. 3. differentiable areas and angels for perception of motion, color, shape & text [7]

In the field of HCI, there have also being researchers who investigated this visual "peripheral channel", such as Costanza et al. [3], who evaluated color indications in the peripheral FOV with a peripheral LED glasses in 2006.

In 2011 Ishiguro and Rekimoto [7] presented a more complex way of displaying peripheral information on a PHMD, while the switching between the detailed and peripheral view has been demonstrated to work automatically with an eye-tracker.

Recently, Hau Chua et al. [6] evaluated the display position of an OST-HMD (Google Glass) and found that notifications presented at the middle and bottom areas of our human vision is more noticeable. However, top and middle positions are less distracting and more comfortable and preferred by the users. Among all the positions, the middle right position was found to strike the best balance between noticeability, comfort, and distraction.

4   Conclusion

In this paper we presented a definition of a Peripheral Head-Mounted Display (PHMD) and discussed its uniqueness and properties. We also briefly discussed human factors designers need to understand in order to create thoughtful visual interfaces for HMDs. In summary, most HMD suffer badly of the effects of Binocular Rivalry, Depth of Field and Phoria. While a PHMD is not totally covering the FOV and also not augmenting information on real objects, it is not affected by known problems monocular HMDs usually suffer from, such as the effect of attention switching between reality and projection. Such problems have been figured out over centuries of airspace research and usually occur when trying to augment reality [12]. These potential dangers, when operating in critical situations, such as taking part in traffic, are less pronounced for PHMDs.

Acknowledgements. We would like to thank Soon Chua Hau for his valuable feedback. This research has been supported by the German Federal State of Mecklenburg-Western Pomerania and the European Social Fund under grant ESF/IV-BM-B35-0006/12.

References

1. Alais, D., Blake, R.: Grouping visual features during binocular rivalry. Vis. Res. **39**(26), 4341–4353 (1999)
2. Collins, J.F., Blackwell, L.K.: Effects of eye dominance and retinal distance on binocular rivalry. Percept. Mot. Skills **39**(2), 747–754 (1974)
3. Costanza, E., Inverso, S.A., Pavlov, E., Allen, R., Maes, P.: Eye-q: Eyeglass peripheral display for subtle intimate notifications. In: Proceedings of the 8th Conference on Human-Computer Interaction with Mobile Devices and Services. pp. 211–218. ACM (2006)
4. Genco, A., Sorce, S.: Pervasive systems and Ubiquitous Computing. Wit Press, Boston (2010)
5. Hausen, D.: peripheral interaction - exploring the design space. Ph.D. thesis, Faculty of Mathematics, Computer Science and Statistics, University of Munich (2013)
6. Hau Chua, S., Perrault, S., Matthies, D., Zhao, S.: Positioning glass: investigating display positions of monocular optical see-through head-mounted display (2015)
7. Ishiguro, Y., Rekimoto, J.: Peripheral vision annotation: noninterference information presentation method for mobile augmented reality. In: Proceedings of the 2nd Augmented Human International Conference, pp. 8–11. ACM (2011)
8. Jäckel, D.: Head-mounted displays. In: Proceedings of RTMI 2013, pp. 1–8. Ulm (2013)
9. Laramee, R.S., Ware, C.: Rivalry and interference with a head-mounted display. ACM Trans. Comput. Hum. Interact. **9**(3), 238–251 (2002)
10. Peli, E.: Optometric and perceptual issues with head-mounted displays. In: Mouroulis, P. (ed.) Visual Instrumentation: Optical Design And Engineering Principles, pp. 205–276. McGraw-Hill, New York (1999)
11. Prinzel, L., Risser, M.: Head-up displays and attention capture. NASA Technical Memorandum 213000 (2004)
12. Rash, C.E., Verona, R.W., Crowley, J.S.: Human factors and safety considerations of night-vision systems flight using thermal imaging systems. In: International Society for Optics and Photonics, Orlando, 16–20 April, pp. 142–164 (1990)
13. Starner, T.: Project glass: an extension of the self. IEEE Pervasive Comput. **12**(2), 14–16 (2013)
14. Z-Health Performance Solutions (2011). http://www.zhealth.net/articles/the-eyes-have-it

Design and Implementation of High-Resolution Sea-Lane Image Texture for Marine Virtual Environment

Hiroyo Ohishi$^{(\boxtimes)}$, Tetsuya Haneta, Tadasuke Furuya,
and Takahiro Takemoto

Tokyo University of Marine Science and Technology, Tokyo, Japan
t111011@kaiyodai.ac.jp

Abstract. In this paper, we propose the efficient approach for constructing virtual reality simulation of ship navigation that supports navigator. Therefore, we propose that simple constructing environments surrounding ships. Structures along the yard can easily displayed with one texture mapping on one NURBS (Non Uniform Rational B-spline) surface. Using this method, we take only 15 s to make one structure including cutting textures.

Keywords: NURBS surface · Virtual reality · Texture mapping · Image based rendering

1 Introduction and Related Work

There is a study based on real image in driving simulations. These many systems use a route panorama method. A width of a road and a height of driver's eyes are decided to a certain extent. The most important thing is that a distance from a car to buildings on both sides is the shortest. In most simulations, they move a virtual camera keeping a certain height. To keep positional relationship of construction in virtual reality simulation when users move around the system, we need individual stereoscopic model of each construction. In this study, we do simple modeling of stereoscopic structures using image-based rendering [1] and texture mapping on NURBS surface. We need image of constructed model from each view point.

We captured front and top image along the river with Phantom II that is multirotor and camera attached small vessel.

To use one NURBS surface and one combined texture when we generate model of building, we reduce number of textures and polygons which is needed to construct one model. It's simple and need short time and light capacity.

2 Proposed Method

As suitable for image segmentation of marine virtual environment, we improved Grow Cut [2].

© Springer International Publishing Switzerland 2015
C. Stephanidis (Ed.): HCII 2015 Posters, Part I, CCIS 528, pp. 214–219, 2015.
DOI: 10.1007/978-3-319-21380-4_38

Shown as Figs. 1 and 2, we compress input image horizontally long before labeling, and resize masking image to original size after labeling, we make calculation speed one by three hundred while maintaining the original image resolution.

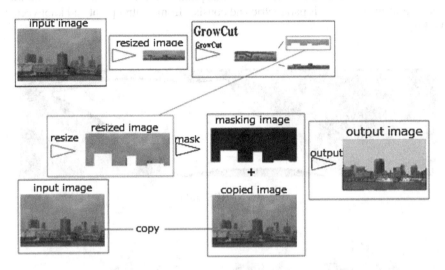

Fig. 1. Grow Cut

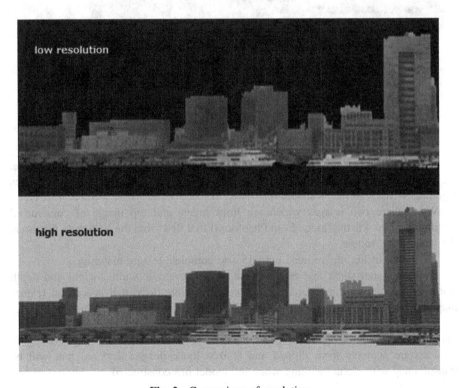

Fig. 2. Comparison of resolution

The reason we compress input image horizontally is to simplify input of restriction because buildings along the river is in a row, so we can write straight input of restriction on compressed image.

We choice NURBS surface to texture mapping. NURBS surface is easy controllable free-form surface. It is parametric and consists from control point and knot vector, like Fig. 3.

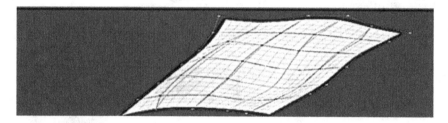

Fig. 3. NURBS surface

front image   top image

Fig. 4. Front and top image

Since NURBS surface can change any form, we can generate favorite shape. Mapping on the NURBS surface, then move control points, sticked image changes together NURBS surface's shape.

We prepare two images which are front image and top image of constructed building. Figure 4 is the image from Phantom II that flew from the bottom to the top at the "meijimaru square".

As shown in Fig. 5, we need only 15 s to complete texture mapping.

By cutting out some textures, and measure appropriate width, height and depth from texture, we acquire coordinates of control points on virtual space and texture mapping on the NURBS surface which transformed into the form of building.

We cut out front texture and top texture from two images with rectangular selection, and we combine clipped images into one texture like part of upper right of Fig. 6. This texture is made from flipped and resized those images, and red part will be transparency with alpha blending when the model has constructed.

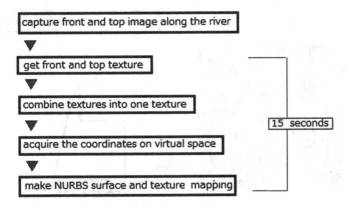

Fig. 5. Series of flow

Fig. 6. Generate model

To automatically acquire the coordinates on virtual space of control points which make NURBS surface,

NURBS surface can change its shape into structure of purpose without our help.

With the acquired coordinates of control points, the NURBS surface is pushed to shape of building, like left part of Fig. 6. We take only 15 s to generate one model including time of cutting texture images. We can see the model at the point of view on the diagonal, like lower right part of Fig. 6.

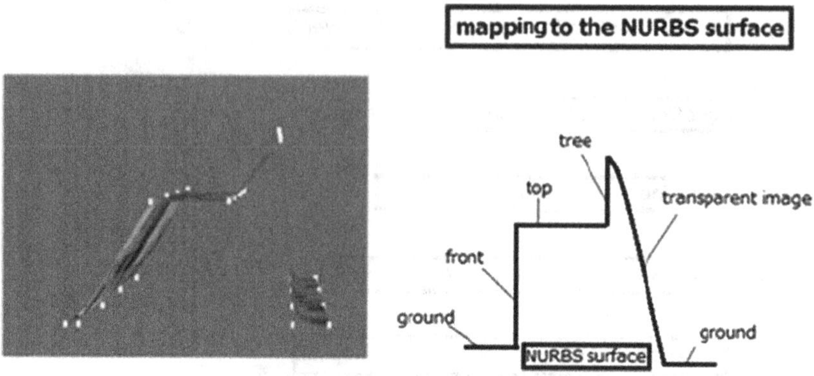

mapping to the NURBS surface

Fig. 7. Model seen from the right side

This 3-dimentional model consists of 4 × 12 control points. To push each surface to the upper, like Fig. 7, we get purpose structures.

Although image-based rendering needs multiplex textures and projection planes to generate one stereoscopic model, this method shows one model with one NURBS surface and one texture.

Figure 8 is other model which is a building along the river. Even though the shape and size of purpose model is different, it's automatically adjusted it to a certain extent.

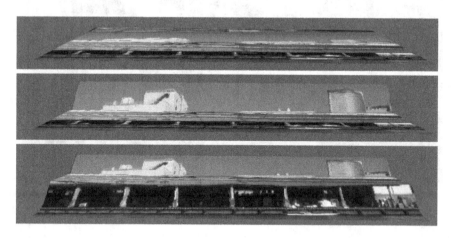

Fig. 8. Model along the river

3   Conclusions and Future Works

In this study, we proposed an efficient method of model construction of wide range virtual reality. Image segmentation is easier by using Grow Cut, and model construction is more quickly by texture mapping on NURBS surface.

Since constructed model by this method is three-dimensional, we can view it from different angles.

It is hard work to modeling a lot of structures along the bay, but using this method, it changes to easy work. All we need is one texture and one NURBS surface, so we don't have to map for one by one textures. This method saves our time, computer's memory and cost.

The generation of virtual environment on a route of ships is available not only to shipping but also in various fields. Before occurring disasters, we can consider measures to watch the environment we captured. Our originality is to generate a system utilizing both entertainment and business. In the future, we generate both sides of model, and aim to improve the quality of model with matrix transformation.

Although we cut textures manually, cutting out texture from original image will become more quickly to recognize front of buildings with Bags of Feature [3], and Deep Learning.

We generate only one model this time, but we will construct more wide area at one time with spreading and pushing out the NURBS surface.

References

1. Debevec, P.E., Taylar, C.J., Malik, J.: Modeling and rendering architecture from photographs: a hybrid geometry-and image-based approach. In: Proceedings of ACM SIGGRAPH 1996, pp. 189–198 (1996)
2. Vezhnevets, V., Konouchine, V.: GrowCut - interactive multi-label N-D image segmentation by cellular automata (2005)
3. Csurka, G., Dance, C.R., Fan, L., Willamowski, J., Bray, C.: Visual categorization with bags of keypoints. In: ECCV International Workshop on Statistical Learning in Computer Vision (2004)

Interactive Virtual Planning Tools
for Sustainable Forest Production
in Mountain Areas

Giulio Panizzoni[✉], Daniele Magliocchetti, Federico Prandi,
and Raffaele De Amicis

Fondazione GraphiTech, Via Alla Cascata 56c, 38123 Trento, Italy
{giulio.panizzoni,daniele.magliocchetti,
federico.prandi,raffaele.de.amicis}@graphitech.it

Abstract. Forest wood harvesting in mountain areas needs a deep and accurate planning to avoid possible failures and criticalities due to the complex morphology of the terrain. Steepness, difficult accessibility and on the field manual work are cost effective factors to reckon, but not always taken into account on all phases, due to the heterogeneity of competences and instruments adopted by the involved actors. Geographical information systems planning tools, demonstrated their usefulness to analyze spatial data in such conditions, but their specificity makes their adoption difficult among operators especially in a conservative industry like forestry. This document introduces an interactive web 3D planning tool based on an accurate virtual forest environment reconstruction, to support the entire wood processing chain in mountain areas, from tree marking to timber production within sawmills, accommodating the needs of all the involved actors bringing novel simulation, planning and monitoring tools at their disposal.

Keywords: Forest planning · Forest monitoring · GIS · 3D virtual globe · WebGL

1 Introduction

In the last decades, the wood market has been subject to a constant global growth in production and consumption of wood products. Projections suggest that this trend will not change before 2030 with the major production growth in Europe, Russian Federation, Eastern Europe and South America and highest consumption in Africa, Asia and the Pacific. This growth involves all the major wood sectors like wood-based panels, paper, industrial round wood and bioenergy and is caused by increasing energy resource needs combined with a rediscovery of wood in the building sector [1]. Modern timber buildings require low operating energy with performances orders of magnitude better than steel and concrete, emitting half of the solid waste, 18 % less air emissions and requiring 13 % less energy [2]. In this context, the adoption of effective planning techniques and on-the-field harvesting solutions becomes crucial to optimize production, reduce costs and respond to growing market demands. In Europe, one of the major wood producers with 45 % of forest surface [3] this becomes even more critical

© Springer International Publishing Switzerland 2015
C. Stephanidis (Ed.): HCII 2015 Posters, Part I, CCIS 528, pp. 220–225, 2015.
DOI: 10.1007/978-3-319-21380-4_39

considering that a large portion of wood resides in mountainous areas and many operations are still manual. The main goal of this study performed in the context of the European project SLOPE, is the improvement of the forest supply chain in mountain areas through the integration of a variegated set of services under the same platform, developing human machine interfaces to meet the specific user requirements of several mountain forest actors. After a first review of the state of the art of visualization interfaces for forest information systems (FIS) and an overview of the followed design process, a detail of the designed human machine interface for the final implementation is provided, describing its look and feel and technological solutions.

2 State of the Art

In forestry, the first decision support tools appeared in the 70 s as linear-programming software for the estimation of the forest areas harvesting levels [3]. Later on, with the advent of space based remote sensing, FIS evolved as extension of GIS software containing, in addition to geo-referenced data, thematic and non-formatted data with a temporal relation [4]. Being it stored in a central location or distributed as a remote service as in the current trends, georeferenced data can be classified under two main categories: imageries and vector. The former includes aerial colored and multispectral pictures [5] useful to recognize vegetation areas, roads and other visual objects. The latter including data derived from point clouds obtained through light detection and ranging (LIDAR) technology. Compared with conventional data acquisition techniques, LIDAR works at night, has very high vertical accuracy and resolution per meter and can be used to measure forest canopy heights [5] as well as count and delineate trees stand [6, 7]. In the 80 s, FIS started to be used as decision support tools, with a first application for the federal administration and industry of forest in US, demonstrating many advantages between the past technology, providing tracing maps, more clear data visualization with advanced computing calculation and data update. Further integration with enterprise-resource-planning (ERP) systems have been reported in [6] to manage operations while maintaining certification documentation and applications for fire control and road planning have been reported in [8].

In the last decade, FIS interfaces evolved from simple mapping into sophisticated systems characterized by 3D navigation, interaction and visualization. For a forest landscape planning perspective, understanding spatial patterns and temporal dynamics can take advantage from 3D visualization. Finnish researchers highlight the possibility of computer-generated images for environmental landscape planning, in particular to understand the visual impact of determined decisions in management procedures, while in [9], researchers studied its use as a deploying simulation and modelling of ecological model for environmental evolution. These applications are strengthen by [10] who illustrated the effectiveness of map exploration against map visualization. Several techniques for real-time rendering of terrain and forests have been studied in the past [11], going from planar tree billboards to more complex 3D models with lighting techniques [12] and new representation of canopy reflectance on steep terrains [13]. From the current overview, it clearly appears how FIS with advanced visualization capabilities are ideal candidates for today's forest production needs. However, until now R&D focused only on specific aspects of the wood chain like surveying, visualization or monitoring, without considering the whole process and their actors.

3 Human Computer Interface Design Process

The design process leading to the definition of the interactive interface of the virtual planning tool has started with an analysis of the actors involved inside an enhanced forest production process and their main use cases through a set of questionnaires. This workflow, developed in the context of the SLOPE project (Integrated processing and Control Systems for Sustainable Production in Farms and Forests) is summarized in Fig. 1. It differs from the classical ones introducing advanced forest surveys for digital reconstruction of a forest model used for planning and simulation, the adoption of RFID tags for trees and logs tracking and for the real-time analysis of wood quality during cutting and debranching phases. The most important actors are the following:

- Forest operator (FO): involved directly on field forest operation, like the coordinator of on-field operations or the one in charge of the digital surveys;
- Forest planner (FP): involved in the decision making processes for harvesting;

This list does not include actors like cableway and truck operators as well as forestry experts, which are mainly involved on the field and are subject to other studies more focused on mobile interfaces on rough and in-vehicle conditions. For these two main actors, four main categories of tools at their daily disposal have been recognized:

- Forest resource planning systems: featuring personnel, hardware and wood management tools through 2D maps and table interfaces;
- Forest analysis and monitoring: including built-in software to handle laser scan, ad hoc proprietary software to program UAVs flights and post-process the acquired data;
- Intelligent harvesting tools: like head processors controlling software to dynamically define cutting log length according to wood quality index computed in real-time by sensors mounted on the head;
- GIS tools: like well-known proprietary software and 3D free virtual globes;

This analysis, together with the complete scenario of Fig. 1 contributed to the definition of the following main use cases:

- 3D Forest navigation with the ability to switch datasets and maps;
- Forest data model visualization: including tree properties and terrain profiling;
- Real-time operations visualization: including harvesting and transport;
- Information hub access: with climate data, wood pricing, certifications, etc.
- Resource inspection: including staff, machineries, wood and storage area;

Fig. 1. Enhanced forest production flow

- Supply management: including plot, logs and stock storage;
- Business analytics: for income and outcome estimation;
- Wood selling: through direct selling and online auctions;

The forest operator is usually focusing on the first four points while the planner daily work, as an extension of the operator actor, performs all the above use cases. The described analysis has been used as a starting point for the definition of the interactive toolset for monitoring and planning described in the next section.

4 The Slope System

Considering the definition given by [14, 15], different parts compose a system for forest management: an input interface for data management (editing, update), an underlying database, an analytical engine for statistical and/or numerical analysis, tools for estimation and prediction to be adopted for future developments, a decision-support system and a set of visualization tools. Not all of these elements require a user interface but a forest management system should be able to wrap them under the same seamless toolset involving data acquisition and processing, decision support and 3D visualization. At the same time, particular attention should be paid to avoid redesigning an entire interface model from scratch, since novelty usually constitutes an entry barrier and a learning burden. With this principle of least astonishment in mind, and the assumption to rely on an integrated forest information model as a data source, a desktop graphical user interface layout has been designed as shown in Fig. 2.

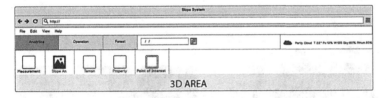

Fig. 2. Main layout

Running inside all the modern web browsers to ensure portability and with an interface which can adapt to mobile browsers, the interface has three levels of menus. The first one is a classical toolbar for saving and loading project plans, print plans, handle tools history and help. The second one includes three main buttons to switch between the three main working modes that have been identified accordingly with the use cases: planning, deployment and monitoring together with a calendar, essential for operations history and an information hub including weather conditions.

The third level includes a set of buttons specific for the selected operational mode while the 3D interactive model of the forest covers the main area. Second and third level menu buttons are medium sized in order to be easily selectable on tablets and smartphones with small screens or from operators wearing gloves. The following list provides additional details about each operation mode:

- The **planning mode**, shown in Fig. 2, provides a set of tools to retrieve geometrical and geophysical information (like slope and soil components), about the real estate to be processed. The 3D map can be viewed and inspected with the use of keyboard, mouse and touch gestures and can be enriched with specific imageries and terrain data (UAVs orthophotos and digital surface model). It allows viewing a huge amount of trees typical of forest scenario correctly georeferenced thanks to UAV data processing as well as performing terrain analysis, like distance and surface estimation or slope trend along a path.
- The **deployment mode**, shown in Fig. 3a is related to the operational phase, with tools for planning forestry operation for specific days, going from harvesting related ones like felling and processing, to more logistical or general planning ones like creating street or assigning resources and machineries. One of the most crucial functionalities on steep terrain is the optimal placement of a cable line to transport logs from the forest to the processing area. This mode enables a what-if analysis in which forestry experts can place a cable line, specifying the pillars heights and rope tension, visualize the catenary trend of the cable and inspect the covered harvesting area which depends on the height of the cable from the terrain. Additionally, this mode allows an estimate of the cable line setup costs, landing zone recognition and planning of roads to be used for logs transport to the sawmills.
- The **monitoring mode**, shown in Fig. 3b, contains all the tools to inspect information concerning forest inventory such as tree physical properties (i.e. height, diameter, and species), logs quality, parcels economical value as well as marked and tagged trees within the forest or placed on storage areas. This information can then be used for direct selling and auction of the available wood to sawmill and other customers.

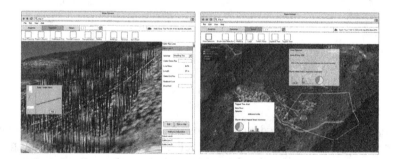

Fig. 3. Deployment (a) and monitoring (b) mode

5   Conclusions and Future Work

A user-friendly framework is essential when dealing with mapping applications, such as those in the forestry sector and the latest generation of 3D interactive applications are the ideal candidates for this task. This paper has shown a work in progress interface developed from real use case scenarios and feedbacks from field experts, as an attempt to build a new user friendly integrate system to cover the entire wood processing chain in mountainous areas. Future works will include an interface refinement, especially concerning the mobile usage, integration with the underlying forest data model and testing on the field with real experts having different levels of technological expertise. The goal is to shape the prototype around on-the-field experts' needs to build a toolset that can really be adopted in the daily business.

Acknowledgements. The work presented in this paper has received funding from the EC through the 7th Framework Programme under the Grant Agreement n. 604129 (project "SLOPE"). The authors are solely responsible for this work which does not represent the opinion of the EC. The EC is not responsible for any use that might be made of information contained in this paper.

References

1. Global demand for wood products. FAO report. (2009)
2. Evaluating the Environmental Performance of Wood Building Materials. http://www.esf. edu/ecenter/eis/woodmaterials.htm
3. Global Forest resource assessment. FAO report (2010)
4. Wing, M., Bettinger, P.: Geographic Information Systems: Applications in Natural Resource Management. Oxford University Press, Oxford (2008)
5. Lillesand, T., Kiefer, R.W.: Remote Sensing and Image Interpretation. J. Wiley & Sons Ltd, Chichester (2004)
6. Hetemäki, N.: Information Technology and The Forest Sector. IUFRO World Series, vol. 18. IUFRO, Vienna (2005)
7. Tao, W., Jian-hua, G.: Forest reconstruction using point cloud data of airborne LIDAR. In: International Conference on Management and Service Science, pp. 1–4. IEEE Press Computer Society Press, Wuhan (2009)
8. Lewis, J.L., Sheppard, R., Sutherland, K.: Computer-based visualization of forest management: A primer for resource managers, communities, and educators. J. Ecosyst. Manag. **5**(2), 5–13 (2005)
9. Zyda, M., Sheehan, J.: Modeling and Simulation: Linking Entertainment and Defense. National Research Council, Washington, DC (1997)
10. Thorndyke Perry, W., Hayes-Roth, B.: Differences in spatial knowledge acquired from maps and navigation. Cogn. psychol. **14**(4), 560–589 (1982)
11. Hoppe, H.: Smooth view-dependent level-of-detail control and its application to terrain rendering. In: Proceedings of the Conference on Visualization 1998, pp. 5–42. IEEE Computer Society Press (1998)
12. Bruneton, E., Neyret, F.: Real-time realistic rendering and lighting of forests. Comput. Graph. Forum **31**(2.1), 373–382 (2012)
13. Fan, W., Chen, J.M., Ju, W., Zhu, G.: GOST: a geometric-optical model for sloping terrains. IEEE Trans. Geosci. Remote Sens. **52**(9), 5469–5482 (2014)
14. McCloy, R.K.: Resource Management Information Systems: Process and Practices. CRC Press, Boca Raton (1995)
15. Günther, O.: Environmental information systems. Newsl. ACM SIGMOD Record **26**(1), 3–4 (1997)

Initial Evaluation of a Modern Augmented Reality Display for Deployable Embedded Training System

Lee Sciarini[✉], Jason Elfe, Tim Shilling, and Eric Martin

Naval Postgraduate School, Monterey, CA, USA
{lwsciari, jdelfe, twshilli, jemartin}@nps.edu

Abstract. When flight time is not available, flight simulators are an effective task rehearsal tool used by the military to train and maintaining aviator proficiency. Unfortunately, the physical characteristics of traditional simulator architectures prevent their use in most operational environments. Previous research has demonstrated that the embedded training (ET) simulator concept is viable but also has limitations in the display of immersive visuals (Lennerton, 2004). Recent advancements in virtual display devices and aircraft design can overcome challenges of the past and should rapidly advance the realization of ET simulators. However, the ability of technology to provide an ET solution must be supported by user acceptance and confidence that effective training transfer will occur with such a system. This effort explored the feasibility of using a modern, user worn, 3D, projection based Augmented Reality (AR) system as the visual interface for a hypothetical ET system with two fixed wing and one rotary wing aircraft. Eight Naval Aviation Subject Matter Experts (SMEs) were given a preflight questionnaire, participated in a simulated flight using the AR display, and completed a post-flight questionnaire. Results indicated that both the ET concept and the prototype AR system were highly regarded.

1 Introduction

An important outcome of training is knowledge of a process or task. Currency maintains a minimum performance level by requiring recall of the task. The value of proficiency is skillful execution of the task resulting in optimum performance. Significant resources are used to teach military aviators mission tasks and to maintain proficiency; both are becoming difficult due to the current resource constrained environment. Military currencies are evolved from resource constraints and are established to maintain an expected level of performance by repeating a previously learned task within a set period of time. Proficiency is different. Proficiency by definition implies a level of familiarity with a task resulting in confident and skillful execution despite increases in physical or mental workload. Psychological research demonstrates that task repetition followed by long or perhaps extended large currency periods is not enough to promote optimum proficiency and will result in the degradation of skills (Rose, 1989). Military deployments are notorious for creating proficiency gaps. Survey responses from fourteen F/A-18 Hornet squadrons highlighted the need for a Deployable Mission Rehearsal Trainer, revealing a large operator focus on the perishability of tactical proficiency. One

C. Stephanidis (Ed.): HCII 2015 Posters, Part I, CCIS 528, pp. 226–231, 2015.
DOI: 10.1007/978-3-319-21380-4_40

of the issues cited was the lack of training opportunities (Betts, 2008). Proficiency is achieved prior to deployment, but due to challenging operational environments, restrictions, and lack of training aids it is not possible to maintain optimum proficiency over the duration of a deployment. The Navy is increasing its standard deployment duration from six months to eight months, and during the War on Terror some deployment lengths reached ten months (Fellman, 2014). In an environment of longer deployments with fewer resources and known challenges to maintaining proficiency, the use of simulators is likely to increase.

Considerable research has focused on simulation based training as a tool to maintain proficiency because it is less dangerous and costly than actual flying. As a result, the military has made significant investments in building realistic simulators. Incremental improvements to hardware and visual display quality are frequent, but the architecture has not evolved at the same rate much resulting in designs that continue to require dedicated buildings for simulator training. Modern flight simulators are essentially Spatially Immersive Displays (SID) incorporating a replica cockpit for pilot interaction. SIDs are designed to surround the user in an immersive panoramic Field of View (FOV), with graphics generally projected by bulky fixed front or rear projection display units (Stanney and Cohn, 2008). However, SIDs do not track pilot head movement so while current simulators render dynamic views relating to aircraft movement, the visuals are static to the movements of the pilot within the aircraft (Lennnerton, 2004). Embedded simulators are an alternative to traditional simulators, capable of improving aviator proficiency while being more scalable.

The scalability of embedded simulators is ideally suited to increasing the number of platforms available for instructional training and task proficiency. Both the Army and Air Force see the value in embedded simulation, putting their own emphasis on research (Blank, 2005; PR Newswire, 2014). Previous research used chroma key display technology to validate the concept's effectiveness and user acceptance of embedded simulation (Lennerton, 2004). A follow on study demonstrated embedded simulation was capable of training Crew Resource Management (CRM) and initial low level navigation, validating its potential to support initial pilot training (Kulakowski, 2004). Both studies made initial attempts to incorporate a head tracking system designed to provide a natural viewpoint of external visuals (Kulakowski, 2004). Due to technological immaturity, the head-mounted camera concept was bulky and induced depth perception issues when looking inside the cockpit. Based on the demonstrated potential, this effort explored the feasibility of using a modern, user worn, 3D, projection based Augmented Reality (AR) system as the visual interface for a hypothetical embedded training system.

2 Methods

2.1 Participants

A total of Eight Naval Aviation Subject Matter Experts participated in this evaluation of the AR system. All participants were experienced Naval Aviators and were qualified to fly at least one of the aircraft used for this study.

2.2 Apparatus

Augmented Reality. A CastAR prototype display system developed by Technical Illusions was used with three Navy aircraft for this investigation. CastAR consists of three main components: stereoscopic enabling projection glasses, retro-reflective material, and a computer to process head movements and generate visual presentation.

Aircraft. Two fixed wing and one rotary wing aircraft were used for this study. The E/A-18G (Grolwer), E/A-6B (Prowler), and H-60S (Seahawk).

Projection Glasses. The projector glasses incorporate three technologies in order to provide the user stereoscopic views of a synthetic environment. First, two micro-projectors are located on the frame over the corresponding viewing eye project the virtual environment. Second, an IR camera located on the bridge of the glasses provides sub-millimeter head tracking accuracy with the potential of 360 degree motion when used in combination of multiple IR faducial panels. Finally, the glasses use shutter lenses which refresh at 120 Hz and provide different perspectives for each eye in order to generated and the illusion of a three dimensional picture in space.

Retro-Reflective Material. CastAR's viewing surface is provided by retro-reflective material is commonly used to provide reflective surface for safety vests and other products. This material is capable of returning 90 % of the light that hits it back in the direction it from which it arrived, the projectors in the case of the CastAR system.

Hardware and Virtual Environment. The system was controlled with a gaming-quality laptop with the Unity 3D game engine. The system also processed head movements and generated the virtual environment. A standard game controller was used to provide flight control. Only one faducial was used and placement areas were limited for each aircraft. This restricted head tracking to approximately 120 degrees for each platform. Approximate instantaneous fields of view as observed by the aviators for each of the aircraft tested are illustrated in Fig. 1.

Surveys. Pre- and post-flight surveys were used to elicit SME input concerning a range of areas including their level of experience, perspective on visual systems for embedded training and the capabilities of embedded training. The post-flight questionnaire also queried ratings of the CastAR display system. All surveys followed criteria described in the Questionnaire Construction Manual (Dyer, Matthews, Wright and Yudowitch, 1976) and the Questionnaire Construction Manual Annnex (Babbitt

Fig. 1. Representative instantaneous FOV for the EA-6B, H-60; and F-18

and Nystrom, 1989). Volunteers were also given the opportunity to provide written feedback about their experience.

2.3 Procedures

All aircraft used for this evaluation were made safe by qualified maintenance personnel. Retro-reflective material was fitted to the outside of each aircraft's canopy (Fig. 2). After the material was in place, the CastAR system was placed in the aircraft and activated. Volunteers were asked to complete a preflight survey. After the preflight, participants were seated in the aircraft and donned the CastAR glasses. The flight simulation began and participants were asked to control the virtual aircraft, look around the cockpit, and to note characteristics of the AR environment (Fig. 2). After 15 min, participants removed the glasses and disembarked the aircraft. The participants then completed a post-flight questionnaire.

Fig. 2. Retro-reflective material placed on the canopy of an E/A-18G and an aviator in an E/A-6B preparing to view the AR environment through CastAR

3 Results

Descriptive statistics were used to determine mean responses from the pre and post-flight questionnaires. Responses for all but three categories (day ship landings, night ship landings, and air combat maneuvering) were initially rated at least neutral. While not significantly different, post-flight perceptions concerning the utility of ET systems for familiarization and tactical functions were rated higher for all items with the exception of air combat maneuvering (the rating remained the same). Consideration that CastAR is an emerging technology, it was important to evaluate the system's interference with the physical components of the cockpit environment (glass displays, instruments, kneeboard, switches, breakers, and flight controls). In all cases, interference was rated at the bottom of the scale the exception of flight helmet.

4 Discussion

The initial goal of this effort was to determine the conceptual feasibility of using a system such as CastAR system as an interface for deployable ET systems in support of Naval Aviation. Overall, the system performed exceptionally well and received high ratings from the participants concerning familiarization and tactical flight tasks.

In order to achieve an understanding of how aviators view embedded training and their view the CastAR display system, SMEs were asked to provide a feasibility assessment concerning the use of embedded simulation for a variety of aviation tasks. Results revealed that on average, SMEs at least "agreed" (4 on the scale) that embedded training could be used to train emergency procedures, crew resource management (CRM), basic flight, mission rehearsal for navigation, and mission rehearsal for weapons deployment. If areas averaging greater than neutral (neither agree nor disagree) but less than agreement are included, the list of tasks expands to include day field landings, night field landings, night ship operations, search and rescue, anti-submarine warfare (ASW), low level navigation, tactical formations (TACFORM), and aerial refueling. When the post-flight SME results(after CastAR prototype use) are compared to preflight estimations, participants reported more positive estimation of an embedded system's ability to accomplish training tasks in 12 of the 18 areas with an additional 2 remaining at least equal to their initial estimation of embedded training. An examination of the two areas in which participants reported a decrease in system utility was revealed to be marginal. The results presented above suggest that the group of naval aviators queried had a generally high estimation of the potential of an embedded system to provide the environment needed to preform important familiarization and tactical flight tasks. Perhaps more importantly, SME experiences with the CastAR prototype in most cases equaled or exceeded initial estimations, suggesting that the novel approach used, with continued development, could serve as the visual display system for embedded training. Finally, one of the great litmus tests of technology is user acceptance. The favorable remarks offered by the SMEs suggest that aviators understand and would value embedded training and that a device such as CastAR has the potential for providing the visual display for such a system.

5 Conclusion

Proficiency is important to maintaining a high level of operator performance. This is especially important in aviation, where seemingly minor mistakes can have catastrophic results. In an environment of where increased deployment lengths and extended intervals between training are likely, it is important to acknowledge the potential for a decrease pilot proficiency and mission readiness. The use of embedded simulation can be an effective method of providing aviators the training they need and can use while deployed. In addition to being portable, embedded simulation with AR facilitates realistic training by combining actual equipment and a synthetic environment providing a sense of presence to the user which they would not experience otherwise. While numerous hurdles such as understanding the effects of sea state on an embedded training system or the aircraft modifications required to enable a system such as

CastAR's use as a pilot-simulation interface, the potential to provide deployable embedded training through the use of real aircraft cockpits surrounded by a virtual environment is a now firmly in the realm of the possible.

References

Babbitt, B.A., Nystrom, C.O.: Questionnaire construction manual annex. Questionnaires: Literature survey and bibliography. ESSEX CORP WESTLAKE VILLAGE CA (1989)

Betts, R.L.: Preliminary User and System Requirements for an F/A-18 Deployable Mission Rehearsal Trainer (DMRT) (Master's thesis, Naval Postgraduate School) (2008)

Blank, D.: US Army sets out embedded training goal. Jane's Defense Weekly, 02 December 2005

Dyer, R.F., Matthews, J.J., Wright, C.E., Yudowitch, K.L.: Questionnaire construction manual (No. ORA-P-77-1). OPERATIONS RESEARCH ASSOCIATES PALO ALTO CA (1976)

Fellman S.: US Navy's New Plan Aims To Lock In: 8-month Carrier Deployments. DefenseNews, 15 January 2014. http://www.defensenews.com

Kulakowski, W.W.: Exploring the Feasibility of the Virtual Environment Helicopter System (VEHELO) for Use as an Instructional Tool for Military Helicopter Pilots. (Master's thesis, Naval Postgraduate School) (2004). http://calhoun.nps.edu/public/bitstream/handle/10945/1394/04Sep_Kulakowski.pdf?sequence=1

Lennerton, M.J.: Exploring a Chromakeyed Augmented Virtual Environment for Viability as an Embedded Training System for Military Helicopters. (Master's thesis, Naval Postgraduate School) (2004). http://calhoun.nps.edu/public/handle/10945/1552

PR Newswire: Elbit Systems of America showcasing the JHMCS II and Embedded Training at Air Force Association Air Warfare Symposium and Technology Exposition: Providing Airman the Mission Advantage (2014). http://www.prnewswire.com/news-releases/elbit-systems-of-america-showcasing-the-jhmcs-ii-and-embedded-training-at-air-force-association-air-warfare-symposium-and-technology-exposition-246139861.html

Rose, A.M.: Acquisition and retention of skills. In: McMillan, G.R., Beevis, D., Salas, E., Strub, M.H., Sutton, R., Van Breda, L. (eds.) Applications of Human Performance Models to System Design, pp. 419–426. Springer, Heidelberg (1989)

Stanney, K.M., Cohn, J.V.: Virtual environments. In: Sears, A., Jacko, J.A. (eds.) The Human-Computer Interaction Handbook: Fundamentals, Evolving Technologies and Emerging Applications, pp. 621–634. Lawrence Eribaum, New York (2008)

Technical Illusions, (n.d.) from the Technical Illusions website: http://castar.com. Accessed 01 November 2014

A Virtual Reality Keyboard with Realistic Key Click Haptic Feedback

Chien-Min Wu, Chih-Wen Hsu, and Shana Smith[✉]

Department of Mechanical Engineering, National Taiwan University,
No. 1, Sec. 4, Roosevelt Rd., Taipei 10617, Taiwan (R.O.C.)
{d99522031, r00522634, ssmith}@ntu.edu.tw

Abstract. Virtual Reality (VR) technologies are increasingly used in many engineering and entertainment applications. In order to make users feel more immersed in the VR environments, many studies have focused on enhancing the sensory feedback for the users. Other than visual feedback, haptic feedback has drawn a lot of attention for increasing the realism of the VR environments. This study creates a realistic key click haptic feedback system in a 3D VR environment. The system can be used to create complex vibrations that match measured vibrations from a real keyboard. The system uses immersive 3D stereo displays to render a virtual environment and a virtual keyboard, a finger-wised data glove to track finger motions, and micro-speakers to create low-frequency 50 Hz vibrations for realistic tactile haptic feedback for each finger. When the users press a virtual key, realistic tactile feedback can be provided to the users. Since the virtual keyboard is not anchored on any physical surfaces or objects in the real world, it does not limit the VR workspace. As a result, the haptic VR keyboard can enhance human-computer interactions in an immersive VR environment.

Keywords: Virtual keyboard · Realistic tactile haptic feedback · Micro-speakers · Virtual reality · 3D

1 Introduction

Immersive VR environments now are often used for scientific research, product design, and vocational training. Most immersive VR environments use data gloves to track hand movements. However, traditional input devices such as physical keyboards are not easy to use when users have data gloves or head-mounted displays put on their bodies. In addition, physical keyboards are not easy to carry around in the immersive VR environments. As a result, different virtual keyboards have been developed to allow users to directly input data in the immersive VR environments.

Previous studies developed VR keyboards in attempts to enhance human-computer interaction in immersive VR. Study results showed that virtual keyboards without haptic feedback have higher typing error rates than virtual keyboards with haptic feedback [1]. In addition, haptic feedback has been proven to be able to improve work efficiency, work accuracy, and user pleasure [2, 3]. Therefore, virtual keyboards with haptic feedback can improve users' overall experience in immersive VR.

Du and Charbon [4] developed a VR keyboard system based on multi-level feature matching. Their virtual keyboard system did not take tactile haptic feedback into

© Springer International Publishing Switzerland 2015
C. Stephanidis (Ed.): HCII 2015 Posters, Part I, CCIS 528, pp. 232–237, 2015.
DOI: 10.1007/978-3-319-21380-4_41

consideration and thus may reduce typing accuracy. Kim and Kim [5] developed a VR keyboard which was overlaid on a real keyboard. Thus, their VR keyboard was limited by the physical keyboard, which in turn limited the workspace for some VR tasks.

Currently, many haptic feedback studies focus on mechanical tactile feedback. Mechanical tactile devices use actuators, such as linear motor, solenoid, vibration motor, piezoelectric motor, pneumatic, and speakers, to provide tactile feedback. For example, Lylykangas et al. [6] used piezoelectric actuators and different durations and delay times of the piezo vibration to provide button click sensations.

This study creates a haptic VR keyboard system to enhance human-computer interaction in immersive VR environments. The virtual keyboard system uses a pair of finger-wised data gloves. Realistic key clicking sensations are provided to each finger. The VR keyboard is not anchored on any physical objects. Therefore, the users can use the VR keyboard at any locations in the VR environments.

2 Haptic Feedback of Realistic Keystroke

2.1 Keystroke Measurement

To create realistic tactile haptic feedback, a high torque servo motor was used to stably press and release a real key of a real keyboard, a laser interferometer was used to measure the displacement and velocity of the key press. Figure 1 shows the key press device, and the measured displacement and velocity of the key.

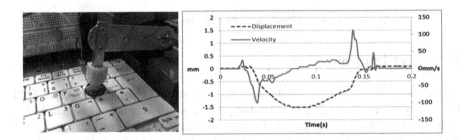

Fig. 1. The key press device and the measured displacement and velocity

Previous studies showed that the 'clicks' sensations that users feel when they press and release the key are caused by buckling and restitution forces [7]. In our research, the acceleration data of both buckling and restitution were found by calculating the first derivative of the measured velocity of the key. The results show that the buckling and restitution cause dramatic acceleration changes when users press and release of the key.

2.2 Method for Reproducing Actual Vibration Signals

In our study, actual vibration signals were reproduced by using different damped sine-wave signals to train a neural network to find the corresponding driving signals for the actuators. The neural network was used to adjust the vibrations for sensor, sensor installation, and actuator effects.

Equation (1) was used to create 300 different sine-wave signals by choosing different amplitudes (A), damping constants (α), frequencies (ω), and phases (θ). The sine-wave signals used are sufficient in training the neural network to provide realistic vibrations.

$$I(t) = Ae^{-\alpha t}(\cos(\omega t - \theta) - \sin(\omega t - \theta) \tag{1}$$

The micro-speakers were used to create vibrations that matched the measured vibrations of the key. Figure 2 shows the measured vibrations of the key and the measured vibrations of the actuator. The results show that both amplitudes of the vibrations were about ± 1.5 G, and both the center frequencies of the vibrations were about 50 Hz.

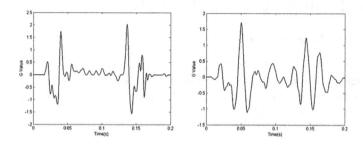

Fig. 2. The measured vibrations of the key and actuator (micro-speaker)

3 System Implementation

The system used an ASUS personal computer, a commercial program (Unity 3D), a 3D VR display device (HMD), 1 pair of P5 data gloves, and 10 micro-speakers (attached to each finger on the P5 data gloves) to create a virtual environment, display virtual objects, detect key presses, and create realistic tactile haptic feedback. Figure 3 shows an image of the testing environment.

Fig. 3. A testing environment

4 User Test

4.1 Test Mode

During the test, the participants used the HMD and P5 data gloves to receive 3D images and track their hand positions. The participants were asked to adjust a virtual object's parameters by entering values and type a string of predefined words. Three different test modes were tested. In mode 1, a physical keyboard was used. In mode 2, the virtual keyboard with a pair of P5 data gloves were used. Mode 3 was mode 2 with vibro-tactile feedback added.

4.2 User Test

During the user test, 25 participants were asked to use the three data input modes to change the dimensions of a virtual rectangular column, and type "block" in the text input field. Figure 4 shows the virtual environment. After the participants finished the three test modes, they were asked to fill out a questionnaire.

Fig. 4. Virtual environment

The user test measured the performance of our haptic VR keyboard system using a seven-point Licker scale (1 = strongly disagree, 4 = neutral, 7 = strongly agree). The mean score and the standard deviation for each test mode are shown in Table 1. Participants generally prefer to use the virtual keyboard in a fully immersive virtual environment because they did not need to take off their HMD and data gloves to enter data. Furthermore, data gloves with haptic feedback received higher responses than that without haptic feedback.

Table 1. Average score for each test mode

		Test modes		
		1	2	3
The keyboard is comfortable to use in the virtual environment	Mean	3.32	4.68	5.12
	SD	1.73	1.60	1.20
The keyboard is intuitive to use in the virtual environment	Mean	3.40	5.24	5.40
	SD	1.91	1.23	1.26
The keyboard provides real-time feedback in the virtual environment	Mean	4.72	4.64	5.04
	SD	2.03	1.29	1.21
The keyboard is convenient to use in the virtual environment	Mean	3.08	4.84	5.08
	SD	1.82	1.31	1.29
The keyboard is smooth to use in the virtual environment	Mean	3.12	4.48	4.68
	SD	1.62	1.48	1.77
I am willing to use the keyboard in the virtual environment in the future	Mean	3.96	4.96	5.44
	SD	1.70	1.27	1.19
I feel the use of the virtual keyboard is realistic in the virtual environment	Mean		4.36	5.16
	SD		1.47	1.11

5   Conclusions

This study created an interactive haptic VR keyboard system for immersive VR environments. The system can create complex vibrations that match measured vibrations from real keyboards. The results of this study show that the advantages of the haptic VR keyboard are that users can use the VR keyboard when wearing HMDs (users do not need to remove HMDs to use the VR keyboard in immersive VR environments), the VR keyboard can pop-up display at any location, as needed (users do not need to go to a specific location to use a keyboard), and the VR keyboard can be used to provide realistic key click haptic feedback. Haptic feedback can enhance users' interactions with virtual objects and allow users to control their actions more intuitively in the VR environments. As a result, the haptic virtual keyboard can be used to enhance human-computer interactions in the immersive VR environments.

References

1. Markov-Vetter, D., Moll, E., Staadt, O.: Evaluation of 3D selection tasks in parabolic flight conditions: pointing task in augmented reality user interfaces. In: The 11th ACM SIGGRAPH International Conference on Virtual-Reality Continuum and its Applications in Industry archive, pp. 287–294 (2012)
2. Koskinen, E., Kaaresoja, T., Laitinen, P.: Feel-good touch: finding the most pleasant tactile feedback for a mobile touch screen button. In: Proceedings of the 10th International Conference on Multimodal Interfaces, pp. 297–304 (2008)

3. Tzafestas, C., Birbas, K., Koumpouros, Y., Christopoulos, D.: Pilot evaluation study of a virtual paracentesis simulator for skill training and assessment: the beneficial effect of haptic display. Presence: Teleoperators Virtual Environ. **17**(2), 212–229 (2008)
4. Du, H., Charbon, E.: A virtual keyboard system based on multi-level feature matching. In: Conference on Human System Interactions, pp. 176–181 (2008)
5. Kim, S., Kim, G.J.: Using keyboards with head mounted displays. In: Proceedings of the 2004 ACM SIGGRAPH International Conference on Virtual Reality Continuum and its Applications in Industry, pp. 336–343 (2004)
6. Lylykangas, J., Surakka, V., Salminen, K., Raisamo, J., Laitinen, P., Rönning, K., Raisamo, R.: Designing tactile feedback for piezo buttons. In: Proceedings of the SIGCHI Conference on Human Factors in Computing System, pp. 3281–3284 (2011)
7. Tashiro, K., Shiokawa, Y., Maeno, T.: Realization of button click feeling by use of ultrasonic vibration and force feedback. In: EuroHaptics conference 2009 and Symposium on Haptic Interfaces for Virtual Environment and Teleoperator Systems. World Haptics 2009. Third Joint, pp. 1–6 (2009)

Control Yourself: A Mixed-Reality Natural User Interface

Elena Zhizhimontova and John Magee[✉]

Math and Computer Science Department, Clark University, 950 Main St,
Worcester, MA 01610, USA
zhizhimontova@gmail.com, jmagee@clarku.edu

Abstract. Control Yourself is a natural user interaction system with a camera and depth sensor, a processor and a display. The user's image is separated from the background of a camera's output and rendered in the program in real-time. The result is that a display shows a video of a person inside the application. The software also recognizes various types of movement such as gestures, changing positions, moving in frame and multiplayer interaction. The technology utilizes the obtained gestures and movements for GUI transformations and creation and for positioning the image or mesh of a user with the background removed. Users of the system can manipulate virtual objects and various features of the program by using gestures and movements while seeing themselves as if they were viewing a mirror with an augmented reality around them. This approach allows users to interact with software by natural movements via intuitive gestures.

Keywords: Augmented reality · Mixed reality · Control yourself · Kinect · Depth camera · Computer vision · Interactive games · Interactive games · Project-based learning

1 Introduction

When gamers discover a new video game adventure they may experience the feeling of not being a part of the game. The playing experience is typically a hardware based interface and computer screen which creates an atmosphere that tells the player that he is not in the game but outside of it. In most video games a player controls an avatar who does not look like a player. Therefore the player cannot intuitively immerse themselves into a video game as he does in real life. *Control Yourself* allows the player to get a full experience of being inside a game and to feel like a main character in the game.

Control Yourself is a Kinect-based gesture-controlled mixed-reality exercising game. The game idea is to see yourself inside the game. We developed a project where a player would have an opportunity to control the game with his or her own movements as well as to see themselves in the game as an avatar. The name "Control Yourself" gives an immediate idea of the game's concept. Figure 1 shows a screenshot of the game in action.

C. Stephanidis (Ed.): HCII 2015 Posters, Part I, CCIS 528, pp. 238–242, 2015.
DOI: 10.1007/978-3-319-21380-4_42

Fig. 1. *Control Yourself* player interacting with the environment with a live avatar mixed into the game environment (Color figure online).

The program takes the depth image provided by the Kinect, locates a person in the image, and then maps the depth image to a color image. The color image of the player is rendered into the game as it is played. The end result is that the game has a video of a cropped person inside.

After cropping the person's image the program finds the users skeleton and analyses the user's gestures. *Control Yourself* recognizes the following gestures: jump, sit (hide), stand up, punch and uppercut. A player sees him or herself in the game standing on a skateboard and moving forward. Gestures in the game work the same way that they work in real life.

The player moves on a cart while encountering obstacles and overcoming them using the gestures. *Control Yourself* keeps track of game points, crops the avatar every frame, recognizes gestures and renders the game world simultaneously. The game also has an innovative main menu and a pause menu where gestures control the options: pointing with a hand to choose an option and a clap to confirm the option (Fig. 2). Two gestures in the menu help overcome unintentional selection ("Midas Touch").

2   Development Methodology

Control Yourself was written in C# and JavaScript using Unity3D and the Kinect SDK. Various other tools were used to develop the content and control systems of the game, including Blender, iTween, SketchUp, and MonoDevelop (Fig. 3).

The program uses the Unity Kinect Wrapper to bring the Kinect SDK into the Unity Game Engine. The program takes the depth image provided by the Kinect, locates a person in the image, and then maps the depth image to a color image (Fig. 4 left). Mapping is not linear because of the parallax effect which is produced by the distance between the color camera and the depth camera

Fig. 2. Player interacting with the menu. Pointing selects an option, clap confirms.

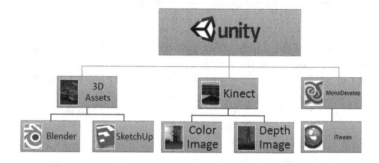

Fig. 3. Relationship of development tools used in *Control Yourself*.

Fig. 4. Left: kinect visible light camera and depth sensor are used to locate the user's image. Right: The difference in locations between the visible light camera and the depth sensor creates a parallax effect in the output. *Control Yourself* calculates the amount of this effect to remove it.

(Fig. 4 right). Consequently, the program decides how to translate the color image in order to compensate for the parallax issue dynamically in every frame. The players image is then rendered in the game and is updated in real time.

The 3D graphical assets of the game required integration with the Unity Framework (Fig. 5 right). Blender (Fig. 5 left) was used to model 3D assets or modify existing models from SketchUp. Since the game follows a rail, the animation uses iTween to designate the path that the train cart should follow.

Fig. 5. Left: blender was used to model sections of the game, in this case a tunnel with rail track. Right: Various graphical assets combined into the game scene.

3   Mixed-Reality Development as Project-Based Learning

Control Yourself begin as an undergraduate course project in a Computer Vision and Human-Computer Interaction seminar. Over 18 months, the project evolved and expanded to reach areas of game development, graphic design, and software engineering methodology [2]. The project afforded the opportunity to explore larger scale development than what is typically available in a single semester.

The project was showcased and presented at university's research day as well as the regional New England Undergraduate Computing Symposium where it won an award for best game design [3]. Dozens of people have tried *Control Yourself* and provided feedback which was incorporated into the game in an iterative development process. The enthusiasm and interest of people observing and playing the game have also been a positive impact of this project in showcasing interesting developments in computer science and recruiting diverse populations to introductory computer science courses [1].

4   Discussion

The scientific contribution of this work includes novel approaches to Natural User Interfaces (NUI). With *Control Yourself* technology, users do not need be familiar with traditional computer interfaces. Using gestures and yourself as an avatar provides users with a completely natural way of interaction with software. This technology can be incorporated not only in the gaming experience, but in a variety of activities.

A text editor could utilize our techniques with speech recognition in order to bring a natural way of interaction with a document. A user should start using the software immediately, providing gestures and observing software responses without prior knowledge in software or the current application.

Educational programs could demonstrate gestures and then ask the user to perform them as they watch themselves on the screen. Such a program could teach kids different words and corresponding movements. Another application of showing/guessing gestures can be the game "charades". The program would tell a player a word, the player would try to act it out, and online users would see the video of a person and try to guess the word.

This technology could also help people with disabilities, or those undergoing rehabilitation. For example, a program which would draw an enhanced reality world around a user, and provide useful tips about objects in the room and their usage.

Control Yourself is patented under a provisional patent with the title "Methods, apparatuses and systems for a mixed reality".

5   Conclusion

Control Yourself introduces an innovative way of human interaction with software. It encourages an intuitive and natural approach of human-computer interaction. This approach should not require any previous experience according to *Control Yourself* tenets. The software includes a vast array of potential applications including games, educational software for children of all ages as well as adults, exercising software and others.

Control Yourself currently consists of a main menu and a few levels where you can see yourself. Future work involves adding more levels, working on the quality of the cropping a person's image, additional gesture recognition, and improving the games graphics. Development of the game encountered many opportunities to overcome challenges and learn about important concepts in mixed-reality human-computer interaction.

References

1. Magee, J.J., Han, L.: Integrating a science perspective into an introductory computer science course. In: Proceedings of the 3rd IEEE Integrated STEM Education Conference (ISEC), Princeton, March 2013
2. Zhizhimontova, E.: Control Yourself - Kinect Game. Undergraduate honors thesis, Math and Computer Science Department, Clark University, Worcester (2014)
3. Zhizhimontova, E.: Control yourself - kinect game. In: The New England Undergraduate Computing Symposium (NEUCS), Boston, MA, April 2014

Cross-Cultural Design

Methodology for the Development of Interface Design Guidelines Based on Local Cultural Dimensions

Zurida Ishak[✉], Azizah Jaafar, and Norshita Mat Nayan

Institute Visual Informatic, Universiti Kebangsaan Malaysia, Bangi, Malaysia
{zuridaishak, cta4345}@gmail.com, aj@ftsm.ukm.my

Abstract. This paper will discuss the methodology for the development of interface design according to cultural dimensions of Malaysian culture. This paper will discuss previous works of cultural interface design development and the application of Malaysian cultural dimensions in interface design.

Keywords: Culture Dimensions · Interface Design · Interface Components

1 Introduction

Users from different cultures use computer interface in different ways. They have a different mental model of visual representation, navigation, interaction and layout, and have different communication patterns and expectations [1]. Reference [4] states that culture is how users of some cultures view and interpret images and specific information. When using a computer application for the first time, users will try to adapt to design components that exist on an interface. Although the user is an expert users or have regular computer use, they still need to familiarize themselves with the type of link, the meaning of icons or symbols used, menu selection, layout and how to fill data.

The cultural background of application developer also affect the design of the interface. Interface development process will encounter problems if the culture of the developer is different from the user's and developers do not carry out the study of cultural trends in advance. Developers indirectly will enter their cultural values as well as affect the functionality and aesthetic features into the interface.Otherwise, if an interface fully implement localization element will increase the efficiency and user satisfaction [3].

According to [5], website designers need to do a lot of planning, research, analysis, design, evaluation, documentation and training to understand more about the user, market and business. Therefore, web developers need to make adjustments to meet the needs of users of different cultures.

Web developers also need to follow the rules or the appropriate methodology for developing the interface according to the target culture. The following section will discuss the types of methodologies to develop cultural interface.

C. Stephanidis (Ed.): HCII 2015 Posters, Part I, CCIS 528, pp. 245–248, 2015.
DOI: 10.1007/978-3-319-21380-4_43

2   Cultural Model and Methodology

According to [1], previous cultural model are not sensitive enough to be used on other cultures because these models are too stereotype and only suitable to only one culture. These models also have disadvantages in terms of usability testing because the number of users is not exhaustive and does not represent the target culture.

Reference [1] develop a methodology for developing culture interface. There are four phases in the methodology namelyunderstand the context of use, define a cultural model for the target culture, webiste design production and evaluate the effectiveness of web communication. Local website audit and cultural marker [6] used to identify interfacecomponent. Interface components identified arevisual representations, multimedia, colour, layout, navigation, links, content & structure and language. Dimensional culture model used is the Hofstede cultural modeland Hall and Hall's.To assess the effectiveness of interface design, prototype evaluated in terms of learnability, efficiency, minimal errors, satisfaction, comprehension and desirability.

Reference [7] also build a model named 'investigative strategical model'.This model consists of four phases: Investigation, Translation, Implementation and Evaluation. To identify the cultural characteristics, ethno-methodologically techniques is used. Features of interface components are analyzed using foraging technique. For culture model, they do not put a specific model to be used by the interfacedeveloper. Then the prototype will be developed according to the information of phase 1 and phase 2. The prototype of culture interface will be evaluated in terms of preference (acceptability), usability (usage of site content and tools and also productivity (involves the development of e-commerce website).

The study focuses on the development of methodologies and guidelines for interface design. According to [7], users from the same country does not necessarily fit with Hofstede's cultural model,Especially with users of other countries. Most studies involving the development of culture interfaces using cultural dimensions of Hofstede [3, 4, 5, 8, 9, 10, 11]. Assessment tests are carried out on users coming from Western countries. Most of the interface is also designed according to the characteristics of Western society as stated in [1]. Reference [7] also states that "Computer software and the internet were predominately a North American skilled white male market. It has now become a worldwide commodity and the market has now grown to include all nations, creeds, gender and task use".

3   Malaysian Cultural Dimension and Culture Interface Model

Malaysia is a country consisting of various races, have different cultural and beliefs. An inter-cultural researchers, Dr.Asma Abdullah has expressed the cultural dimensions of Malaysian society. She has made a study of organization culture and found that Malaysian society is represented with 8 types of cultural dimensions: Harmony, Relationship, Hierarchy, Shame, High Contextual Communications, Polychronic Time, Group Orientation and Belief in God.

Therefore, this paper will discuss the methodology for the development of interface design according to cultural dimensions.To achieve the objectives of the study, the phases involved are preliminary analysis, design, development, implementation and evaluation. several key processes need to be implemented: documentation analysis, a preliminary study to strengthen the problem statement, interview for preliminary analysis, the construction of a questionnaire, a confirmation of survey question, collecting data through surveys, construction of adaptation rules, prototype development and evaluation.

In preliminary analysis, researchers have to analyze the existing interface design of intended application to see the similarities of the interface components, the preferred components and interaction of the users. These can be done by interview, questionnairs or observation. Interviews with the culture experts and interface specialists is necessary to get the latest information and trends in culture and interface design. Cultural experts interview provide information about the use of culture by other researchers and make a comparison with the use of the existing definition of Malaysian culture.

In the design phase, questionnaire of culture dimensions and interface components preferences is developed. The instrument developed is based on the description and characteristics for each dimension.The information obtained is used to propose interface components involved or equivalent to the cultural dimensions that have been identified.Then, user interface designs are grouped according to cultural dimensions and interface components.For instance,one of the interface components, metaphor, necessary to focus when designing interfaces for users who have cultural dimension of hirarchy, high contextual communication, group orientation, orientation polychronic time, and belief in God.Questions or items are divided according to the five components of the interface which are the metaphor, navigation, interaction, appearance and mental models.

After the survey questions for the cultural dimensions and also questions for interface design has been completed, the two sets of questions will go through the validation process by experts. Experts will confirm that the items or questions are appropriate to the construct described and suitableas an instruments for data collection. Experts involved are cultural experts and interfacespecialists. The survey is distributed to the target user and data collected will be used to propose an adaptation rules.

The adaptation rules and user model is developed in development phase. Interface culture prototype will also produced according to the adaptation rules. The last phase is the implementation and evaluation. In implementation phase, the prototype will be tested by the target user. They will use the non-adaptive and adaptive interface and make a comparison by answering a questionnaire and observation by the tester.

4 Conclusion

Understanding of the culture characteristics is very important in the development of application interface to be used by users from different cultures. The interface according to the specifications of culture can improve performance and user productivity. Users will feel more comfortable and satisfied with the interface according to their tastes. Culture model selection is also important to ensure that cultural identity is represented correctly. The involvement of culture experts in the development of culture interface is necessary so that an understanding of the cultural needs are parallel with interface usability requirements.

References

1. Hsieh, H.C., Holland, R., Young, M.: A theoretical model for cross-cultural web design. In: HCII, pp. 712–721 (2009)
2. Marcus, A.: Metaphor Design for User Interfaces, pp. 129–130, April 1998
3. Ford, G.: The effects of culture on performance achieved through the use of human computer interaction. In: SAICSIT 2003, pp. 218–230 (2003)
4. Sheridan, E.: Cross-CUltural web site design: Considerations for developing and strategies for validating locale appropriate on-line content. Multilingual Computing (2001)
5. Marcus A., West Gould, E.: Cultural Dimensions and Global Web User-Interface Design. Interactions, 33–46 (2000)
6. Wendy, B., Badre, A.: Culturability: The Merging of Culture and Usability. In: 4th Conference on Human Factors and the Web (1998)
7. Jainaba, J., Guven, S.S., Elke, D., Curzon, P.: Cross-Cultural Interface Design Strategy (2004)
8. Smith, A., Dunckley, L., French, T., Minocha, S., Chang, Y.: A Process Model for Developing Usable Cross-Cultural Websites. Interact. Comput. **16**, 63–91 (2004)
9. Sun, H.: Exploring Cultural Usability : A Localization Study of Mobile Text Messaging Use. In: IEEE International Professional Communication Conference, pp. 319–330 (2002)
10. Zahedi, F.M., Van Pelt, W.V., Song, J.: A Conceptual Framework for International Web Design. IEEE Trans. Prof. Commun. **44**(2), 83–103 (2001)
11. Reinecke, K., Bernstein, A.: Improving performance, perceived usability, and aesthetics with culturally adaptive user interfaces. ACM Trans. Comput. Interact. **18**(2), 1–29 (2011)

"Re:Radio", The Place Oriented Internet Radio to Enhance the Cross-Cultural Understanding in Japan

Ayaka Ito[✉] and Katsuhiko Ogawa

Graduate School of Media and Governance, Keio University, Fujisawa, Japan
{ayk,ogw}@sfc.keio.ac.jp

Abstract. The number of foreigners who visit Japan is increasing lately, however most of the services or products for foreigners are designed based on their superficial understanding and do not meet their true needs. This research's goal is to propose place oriented Internet radio called "Re:Radio", as a new media to help foreigners understand Japan at a deeper level, by providing individually customised contents. Specifically, the dialogue between a guest and personality is used as main contents. Listening to the contents at the place induces listener's self-reflection, which helps further understanding of the place. This paper introduces the concept and implementation, and the experimental results conducted in Tokyo.

Keywords: Internet radio · Personality · Dialogue · Cross-cultural understanding

1 Introduction

As transportation technology has developed in the modern world, the mobility of people has been rapidly improved and the number of foreigners who are visiting Japan is increasing [1]. Recognising diversity and building cross-cultural understanding is a crucial activity and lots of different approaches are attempted in various communicative settings. In multinational companies, cross-cultural training is introduced often as an effective occupational training tool [2]. Numerous textbooks are published to teach intercultural competence as criteria of business or academic proficiency [3]. Most universities have study abroad office for international students; offering supports via student service advisors or peer mentors when needed [4].

We have to be aware of the fact that each of the foreigners who are coming to Japan are one individual and we should not generalise them by nationality, race, and religion. However, most of the current services or products launched for foreigners in Japan are based on their superficial understandings. For example, foreigners encounter place-oriented problem such as having difficulty buying tickets at the train station, normally due to the poor usability of ticket machines only available in Japanese.

C. Stephanidis (Ed.): HCII 2015 Posters, Part I, CCIS 528, pp. 249–255, 2015.
DOI: 10.1007/978-3-319-21380-4_44

To support the better quality of living for foreigners in Japan, creating new media to provide them opportunities to understand Japan at a deeper level is meaningful. As far as the former researches and literatures are reviewed, there is almost no example of using Internet radio as a tool for building international understanding in Japan. In this research, we will propose a prototype of place-oriented Internet radio called "Re: Radio", which helps foreigners to recognise Japan from a cross-cultural perspective by providing uniquely customised contents. To achieve this, we will find the issue that improves design of the system through experimental fieldwork.

2   Concept of Re:Radio

2.1   From Mass to Personal

Conventionally, radio programs have been arranged one-way from personality to mass listeners, and interactive programs like accepting song requests or talking with listeners via phone are not dominant among radio contents. On the other hand, the aim of Re: Radio is to offer opportunities for foreigners to get the better idea of Japan by listening to individually customised contents. The important keyword is "dialogue", which enables listeners to reveal what they really think through the conversation with a personality. In order to enhance mutual understanding, it is essential for the personality to interact with listeners and try to have as constructive a discussion as possible.

2.2   Place-Oriented Dialogue

The dialogue is place-oriented, which means what they talk about or how loud they talk varies depending on which place they are at. The guest, who is later invited to be a listener of Re:Radio, have a free conversation about a certain place with the personality. Later on the personality reflects on the dialogue and creates unique radio contents specifically designed for the guest. Once the guests go back to the place where the original dialogue was had, they can listen to the edited contents again and reflect on the memory of the place. This self-reflection process allows the guest to recognise if there are any new findings or clues to the further understanding of the place.

2.3   Accumulation of Self Reflection

The contents of Re:Radio is originally customised for the individual, but since it's connected to the specific place where it was recorded, anyone who went there can listen to the contents once it's opened. By repeating this process, a pile of self-reflection is accumulated and eventually it forms a character of the place. It is drawn by many different realisations and recognitions, which is the illustration of place's dynamics. The name "Re:Radio" includes many "Re", such as reflection, recall, remember, realisation, recognition, and importantly, re-entry of the place.

3 Implementation of Re: Radio

The personality records and edits the dialogue with the guest, then creates the customised radio contents for the listener. The guest listens to the contents again, reflects and evaluates it. Evaluated contents are shared with many other listeners and accumulated self-reflections will be the foundation of new dialogues for another individual listener. By repeating this cycle, the contents of Re:Radio will be enriched (Fig. 1).

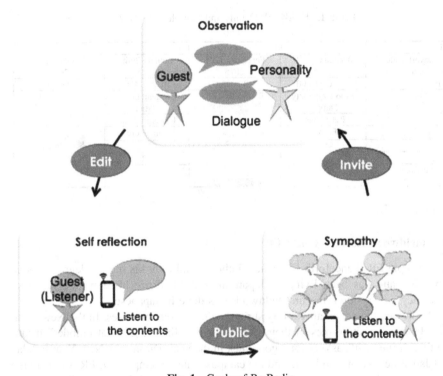

Fig. 1. Cycle of Re:Radio

4 Experiment

Lynch introduced the concept of five elements of city, which are path, edge, district, node and landmark [5]. As Re:Radio has characteristics focusing on specific places, landmark was chosen as a suitable element. We conducted fieldwork experiments twice, for two different guests using the same scheme to explore how the cycle of Re: Radio works. In the first fieldwork, guests and the personality walked around certain places and the conversation happened and was recorded. In order to reveal the architecture of effective contents design, we tried to select the guests who have various cultural backgrounds, as well as their length of the stay in Japan.

Subsequently, the personality created individually customised contents for the guests by editing recorded data, putting in background music and narration. Several points were chosen where notable conversations happened then contents were mapped on the webpage using Google Maps API. After the contents were successfully mapped in the system, we conducted the second fieldwork.

Guests and the personality walked the same route as the last time and guests listened to the contents connected to the certain landmarks. Guests filled in a questionnaire to evaluate the concept of Re:Radio and the contents afterward, asking how the contents contributed to their self-reflection about the place. First and second fieldwork details and samples' attributes are below (Table 1).

Table 1. Fieldwork Details and Samples' Attributes

Guest	FR		SG	
Fieldwork Date (L:First/R:Second)	December 12th, 2014	Februrary 12th, 2015	January 29th, 2015	February 11th, 2015
Time	14:30 - 15:00	14:00 - 15:00	10:30 - 14300	10:45 -11:30
Location	Keio University Campus		Sagamiono Station	
Status	Researcher		Undergraduate	
Nationality	France		Singapore	
Sex	Male		Male	
Age	27		22	
Route Taken				

5   Discussion

5.1   Fieldwork Result - Guest FR

Guest sample FR (henceforth FR) studied abroad and took his master degree in Keio University, and has been living in Japan since 2011. Since his Japanese language proficiency is very high, the first fieldwork was done in Japanese.

FR showed the personality a tiny shrine in the campus premises. In the New Year, many Japanese visit shrines in their vicinity. It is called "初詣 (hatsumode)" means "the first shrine visit", asking for a good luck in the year. During the New Year holiday most Japanese students go home and the campus is nearly empty, but FR was working on his master dissertation and remained on campus. FR told the personality he came this shrine and did his hatsumode here, asking for good luck for his dissertation as Japanese do, even though he is a French Christian.

Based on the conversation that happened in the first fieldwork, personality made content. The shrine was chosen as a landmark and the personality added the narration of its foundation history, with traditional Japanese music. The atmosphere of the shrine is very tranquil and instrumental healing music seemed to be suitable as background music.

5.2   Fieldwork Result - Guest SG

Guest sample SG (henceforth SG) is an undergraduate fresher of Keio University, SG arrived in Japan in September 2014. Since his language proficiency is beginner level, the fieldwork was done in his native tongue English. SG guided Sagamiono station to the personality where his university dormitory is located.

During the fieldwork SG told the personality he lost his gloves the other day and wanted to buy a new ones in Uniqlo, which is a famous Japanese fast fashion brand, at the shopping centre attached to the station. He asked the staff if there are any, however it was almost the end of the season and they were all sold out. SG tried a couple of other shops but none with good value for money was available. SG then walked into the downtown, introducing his favourite ramen shop around town. He told the personality until he gets a part time job in Japan he is very financially instable, hence for him ramen is filling and reasonably priced as a daily meal, so far. He also said there are many ramen shop in Singapore but the taste is more authentic in Japan.

The personality made two contents for sample SG based on the first fieldwork. First, the shop front of Uniqlo was chosen as a landmark, and the narration about Japanese fast fashion circumstances was inserted. As SG seems to be a ramen fan, the personality wanted him to explore Japanese ramen culture by the second content. There is a museum-type complex called "Ramen museum" about 30 min from his house, where he can try various types of ramen such as miso, shoyu and his favourite flavour tonkotsu. Visitors can purchase traditional Japanese snacks and souvenirs, and its retro atmosphere of the Showa period is something SG might want to experience. Background music that is actually used in the Ramen museum is added to the content.

5.3   Discussion

In the second fieldwork FR and SG listened to the contents and had additional conversation with the personality. FR understands a decent level of Japanese culture and knows how things work in Japan. In the fieldwork, the choice of route was totally the guest's responsibility and the reason he decided to introduce a Japanese shrine to the personality means something. Supposedly it is because FR has spent relatively long time and interacts with locals more compared to other foreigners, so he regards himself less "foreign" in this country. When FR started to listen to the content, he seemed to be a bit surprised, saying *"You actually took time to edit the conversation and put background music to make content only for me? That's great."*

This shows he was aware of the personality's effort and expresses his gratitude. Showing appreciation in return for something that was done for somebody is a shared notion amongst Japanese and FR's remark also is a clue that he fits in with Japanese culture well.

> *"It was interesting to have some additional and cultural information about the conversation. It wasn't too long, just good. Background music was also good idea and made the content more pleasant to listen to".*

On the contrary, SG has just arrived in Japan last September and everything is new and exciting to him. He seemed to be in the "honeymoon period", a typical state which studying abroad students normally get through [6]. The conversation in the first fieldwork was mostly about the difference of lifestyle, food and social systems between Singapore and Japan. These topics made the personality put in some mini stories of

Japanese fast fashion brand the growth, or an introduction of a new place of his favourite food. The personality wants to help him have new perspective and motivation of walking around a Japanese city on his own, rather than just giving a new knowledge about places.

> *"I recalled (almost) the full conversation. Immersion might be better done in famous location such as Akihabara".*

Nevertheless, we need to figure out in what context this SG's feedback was given after the second fieldwork. In the follow-up questionnaire, he gave us a clue about what the thing matters to him.

> *"Foreigners think of Japan, usually stuff like anime, shrines, memorable places. Why would anyone be specifically interested in Sagamiono? If I were a foreigner visiting the website, the first place I would click would be in order of 'well-known".*

This feedback is very symbolic. Presumably SG comprehends Re:Radio as a tool to promote "immersion" rather than the introduction of deep Japanese culture, and thought Akihabara is a suitable city in which that would be accomplished. As the contents were not originally exemplifying implications represented in the famous city such as Akihabara, we ought to clarify the reason for this is happening.

6   Conclusion and Future Studies

Why are these two guests' feedbacks so different? Is this a matter of location selection? Nonetheless both of the places where the original conversations were had are not so "touristy" hence what we may assume it is a difference of their length of stay. Unlike FR who has spent a long time in Japan, most of the tourists or studying abroad students who are new in Japan might feel as SG does. If so, the target listeners of Re:Radio will be people like SG, and original contents should be connected to so called "touristy" places, not too local ones. Although these contents are the entrance to ostensible Japanese culture at first, in the long run they should be the trigger to come to know the real culture and give listeners new a perception of Japan. In this experiment we only conducted the first two processes of Re:Radio, yet before we move onto the third process we need to illustrate the direction of the contents which is reachable by the guests and figure out the ideal place for content designing. Specifically in the third process, how we approach the listeners to produce mutual cross-cultural reflection is the key, and the proposal of the criteria to measure whether listeners could enhance their comprehension of Japanese culture will be undoubtedly important. In addition, further exploration of available system configuration is needed, using the user experience design [7].

References

1. Japanese Ministry of Justice, http://www.moj.go.jp/ENGLISH/index.html
2. Black, S., Mendenhall, M.: Cross-cultural training effectiveness: a review and a theoretical framework for future research. Acad. Manag. Rev. **15**(1), 113–136 (1990)

3. Lustig, M.W., Koester, J.: Intercultural Competence: Interpersonal Communication Across Cultures. Allyn and Bacon, Boston (2003)
4. Peterson, D.M., Briggs, P., Dreasher, L., Horner, D.D., Nelson, T.: Contributions of International Students and Programs to Campus Diversity. New Dir. Student Serv. **1999**(86), 67–77 (2002)
5. Lynch, K.: The Image of the City. MIT Press, Cambridge (1960)
6. Oudenhoven, J.: Predicting multicultural effectiveness of international students: the multicultural personality questionnaire. Int. J. Intercultural Relat. **26**(6), 679–694 (2002)
7. Buxton, B.: Sketching User Experiences. Morgan Kaufmann, San Francisco (2007)

Poke, Swipe, and Pinch:
Reinventing Adaptability Across Cultures
Using Mixed Technology

Linda Lim[✉]

Murdoch University, Murdoch, WA, Australia
email2enigma@yahoo.com

Abstract. This short paper covers the advent of Project Cul. The researcher examined the feasibility of support for the combined usage of mobile operating systems (including Omni-Touch device), markerless augmented reality, global systems for mobile communications (hybrid positioning systems), and cloud computing (public and community cloud). Since Project Cul is in its initial phase, the existing version aims to reinvent adaptability across cultures using mixed technology and anticipates creating a game-based learning simulator to ease the adjustment period of an individual upon relocating to his or her destination country, using an interaction method coined by the researcher as "poke, swipe, and pinch". Using this interaction method, users can experience Omni-Touch functionality by practicing accurate control of the hand on any surface or even in mid-air. A discussion of protocols to achieve the project aim, most similar work, how Project Cul is original, development methodology, and evaluation method are conducted.

Keywords: Omni-Touch device · Markerless augmented reality · Hybrid positioning systems · Public cloud · Community cloud

1 Introduction

The idea of Project Cul was first initiated by the author of this paper in an earlier paper [10], where two others co-authored in writing up the non-technical aspects and illustrating a conceptual framework respectively. Although the conceptual framework is necessary, it only serves as an initial brainstorming of the idea. The goal of this paper is to create a game-based learning simulator (Project Cul) to ease the adjustment period of an individual upon relocating to his or her destination country to foster cross-cultural comprehension and assimilation to the local scene of the destination country. Game-based learning [22], mobile technology [26], augmented reality [2, 3, 9], location-based services [20, 27], and cloud computing [7, 11, 13, 17] were applied to the development of Project Cul after some evaluation, and led to reinventing adaptability across cultures using mixed technology. Demographics (for example, Nationality, Country, Culture) and scenario factors (for example, Education, Employment) were derived from the evaluation of cross-cultural comprehension and assimilation. Design factors (for example, Units of Measure, Number and Currency

© Springer International Publishing Switzerland 2015
C. Stephanidis (Ed.): HCII 2015 Posters, Part I, CCIS 528, pp. 256–261, 2015.
DOI: 10.1007/978-3-319-21380-4_45

Formats) were obtained from a combination of demographics and scenario factors. The factors to be incorporated as features of the game-based learning simulator are represented by a framework (poster).

2   Discussion of Protocols to Achieve the Project Aim

Reinventing adaptability across cultures using mixed technology was called Project Cul to simplify identification. As Project Cul is in its initial stage, there were a few constraints involved. Budget is a vital factor followed by development tools (directly related to budget) and manpower with relevant technical expertise. Since Project Cul requires more technical expertise, the author has recruited new team members with different technical skill sets to continue with the next phase of Project Cul. Project funding search and project scheduling for the next phase are in progress. Project Cul followed a set of protocols involving developing system architecture, storyboarding, wireframing, prototyping, and status quo in order to achieve the project aim.

2.1   System Architecture of Project Cul

Project Cul was built using both hardware and software. Project Cul was created using an ASUS All-in-one PC series, a Third Generation iPad, and an iPhone 4S, and Microsoft Windows 8.1 was used as the operating system for the first phase. Microsoft Visual Studio 2010 was also used for coding the applications in C# or Visual Basic and XAML (for a start) for the user interface of Project Cul. More hardware and software may be added to the existing ones when the budget permits. As Project Cul aims to be platform independent, the mobile operating systems envisioned include Android, BlackBerry OS, WebOS, iOS, Symbian, Windows Phone Professional, Windows Phone Standard, and Bada [26]. Augmented Reality (AR) comprises a real-time or real-world environment which portrays the view of the physical environment where its elements are brought out to users through the use of computer-generated input like graphics (markers), sound, video or GPS data [2, 3, 9], as opposed to virtual reality bringing people into a simulated world [14]. AR can also be described as reality which has been modified with the help of a computer to improve the viewpoint of reality [2, 3, 9]. In addition to the future of AR technology, the use of markerless AR to bring reality out to users can be enhanced with the X-Ray device [26] and the Omni-Touch device [6, 8, 12, 18, 19, 21, 26]. In the area of Global Systems for Mobile Communications, the location-based systems can be categorized into network-based, handset-based, SIM-based, and hybrid [20, 27]. To obtain the location of smartphones and tablets more accurately, hybrid positioning systems (network-based and handset-based) can be used [27]. Cloud computing involves providing hardware, software, and storage services through the network or the Internet. There are four deployment models, namely; public cloud, community cloud, hybrid cloud, and private cloud [7, 11, 13, 17]. To facilitate the ease in using cloud computing services at no or low cost, public cloud (service providers via the Internet such as Amazon AWS, Microsoft, and Google, free or offered on pay per use) [7] and community cloud (shared infrastructure among many organizations from a particular community with common interests, managed internally, externally or third-party) [11] are preferred. The system architecture of Project Cul is illustrated in the poster.

2.2 Status Quo of Project Cul

The storyboarding, wireframing, and prototyping of Project Cul are conducted by the researcher. The current version of Project Cul introduces the game-based learning simulator to users by allowing them to navigate around a basic interface using the "poke, swipe, and pinch" method of user interaction. This basic interface allows users to understand the objective of this existing version of Project Cul, which is to reinvent adaptability across cultures using mixed technology, through a stipulated activity to be completed in one sitting.

3 Most Similar Work

Some searching was involved in finding the most similar work to Project Cul. Although there are several projects on game-based learning, but few projects are on simulating real-world scenarios and are platform independent. However, the most similar work to Project Cul is Virtual Heroes which provides effective and high quality training through simulations for learning, serious games, and virtual worlds on multi-platforms [1].

3.1 Virtual Heroes

The most similar work to Project Cul is Virtual Heroes [1]. ARA's Virtual Heroes Division has a remarkable, successful track record designing and releasing immersive, virtual-world-based serious games and Advanced Learning Technology (ALT) applications on multi-platforms. This organization is also uniquely competent to provide commercial-quality, immersive, 3D virtual world content for training and education. The ALT applications comprise serious games, virtual worlds, emergency management, preparedness training, modeling and simulation, virtual reality for learning, compliance training, and research and development [1].

3.2 SimCityEDU

The closest related work to Project Cul is SimCityEDU [5]. SimCityEDU is an online educational community based on the award-winning SimCityTM videogame and functions as a resource for classroom teachers who have a strong interest in utilizing digital platforms as a learning tool to drive student interest in STEM (Science, Technology, Engineering, and Mathematics) subjects [5].

4 How Project Cul Is Original

Project Cul is original as compared to Virtual Heroes [1] and SimCityEDU [5] in a few ways. Project Cul aims to reinvent adaptability across cultures using mixed technology, to be platform independent, and to be a game-based learning simulator. Virtual Heroes [1] is not entirely game-based and SimCityEDU [5] is not entirely a simulator. They are also not entirely platform independent. Project Cul enables users to simulate their destination countries using the "poke, swipe, and pinch" method of interaction while navigating around their preferred simulated environment, facilitated by the use of game-based learning [22], Omni-Touch device [6, 8, 12, 18, 19, 21, 26], markerless augmented reality [2, 3, 9], hybrid positioning systems [27], public cloud [7], and community cloud [11]. Project Cul assists users in the adjustment to their destination countries by aiming to incorporate gaming, learning, and simulation features as a bundle to foster cross-cultural comprehension and assimilation to the local scene of the destination country. Project Cul is compatible with a large display size when connected to a projector and a mobile phone, a tablet, a laptop or a desktop computer.

5 Development Methodology

The researcher chose a hybrid (Extreme [23] and Lean [25]) development methodology in reinventing adaptability across cultures using mixed technology. Project Cul needs regular improvements to system quality and user feedback on system responsiveness, so as to enhance productivity by employing system evaluation to present new user requests, in order to improve system efficiency. The Extreme [23] development methodology is selected as a result. Project Cul also requires doing away with waste, magnifying the learning process of development teams, making decisions based on facts instead of uncertain assumptions, producing results in a timely manner, encouraging and trusting development teams, providing customers with an overall experience of the system, and incorporating a synergistic work culture. The Lean [25] development methodology is also chosen for this purpose. ExLean development methodology (poster) is the name of this hybrid development methodology given by the researcher. This hybrid development methodology will continue to be used for building future versions of Project Cul.

6 Evaluation Method

Heuristic evaluation is decided upon to evaluate Project Cul because it can reveal major usability issues within a short period of time on a budget, by assessing against a set of ten usability principles called "heuristics", adding to the method severity ratings of design errors (frequency, impact, persistence), by a small group of potential users of Project Cul [15, 16, 24]. Scenario-based evaluation is chosen to evaluate Project Cul against specific user tasks or scenarios it is designated to support [28], while usability evaluation is selected to evaluate the degree of which Project Cul is simple and enjoyable to use [4].

7 Conclusion

This paper investigated reinventing adaptability across cultures using mixed technology. Game-based learning simulator framework, system architecture of Project Cul, storyboarding, wireframing, prototyping, status quo of Project Cul, ExLean development methodology, heuristic evaluation [15, 16, 24], scenario-based evaluation [28], and usability evaluation [4] were addressed. As Project Cul is still developing towards creating a game-based learning simulator to facilitate the adjustment of individuals to their destination countries, Omni-Touch device [6, 8, 12, 18, 19, 21, 26], markerless augmented reality [2, 3, 9], hybrid positioning systems [27], public cloud [7], and community cloud [11] are being incorporated, using the "poke, swipe, and pinch" method of user interaction. The current version of Project Cul constitutes a basic structure of the game-based learning simulator, where users can navigate around the simulator by "poking", "swiping", and "pinching" the interface.

References

1. Applied Research Associates, Inc. Virtual Heroes. Division of Applied Research Associates, Inc. (2014). http://www.virtualheroes.com/
2. Augmented Reality on. Augmented reality-Everything about AR. Augmented Reality on 31 March 2012. http://www.augmentedrealityon.com/
3. Chen, B.X.: If You're Not Seeing Data, You're Not Seeing. Wired, 25 August 2009. http://www.wired.com/gadgetlab/tag/augmented-reality/
4. Cockton, G.: Usability evaluation. In: Soegaard, M., Dam, R.F. (eds.) The Encyclopedia of Human-Computer Interaction, 2nd edn. The Interaction Design Foundation, Aarhus (2014). https://www.interaction-design.org/encyclopedia/usability_evaluation.html
5. Electronic Arts Inc. SimCityEDU. Electronic Arts Inc. (2014). http://www.simcity.com/en_US/simcityedu
6. Forbes. Turn Any Surface Into a Touch Screen. Forbes, 19 October 2011
7. Gens, F.: Defining Cloud Services and Cloud Computing. IDC, 23 September 2008
8. Graham-Rowe, D.: Kinect Turns Any Surface Into a Touch Screen. Technology Review, 18 October 2011
9. Graham, M., Zook, M., Boulton, A.: Augmented reality in urban places: contested content and the duplicity of code. Transactions of the Institute of British Geographers **38**(3), 464–479 (2012). doi:10.1111/j.1475-5661.2012.00539.x. http://onlinelibrary.wiley.com/doi/10.1111/j.1475-5661.2012.00539.x/abstract
10. Lim, L., Kristensen, M., Blashki, K.: The social translator: a game-based learning simulator to foster cross-cultural understanding and adaptation. IADIS Int. J. WWW/Internet IJWI **11** (1), 43–52 (2013). http://www.iadisportal.org/ijwi/
11. Mell, P., Grance, T.: The NIST Definition of Cloud Computing. National Institute of Science and Technology, September 2011. http://csrc.nist.gov/publications/nistpubs/800-145/SP800-145.pdf
12. Mitroff, S.: OmniTouch Turns Everything into a Touchscreen. PC World, 19 October 2011
13. Monaco, A.: A View Inside the Cloud. theinstitute.ieee.org (IEEE), 7 June 2012 (last update)

14. NCSA & EVL. Introducing Virtual Environments. National Center for Supercomputing Applications. University of Illinois, 27 November 1995. http://archive.ncsa.illinois.edu/Cyberia/VETopLevels/VR.Overview.html
15. Nielsen Norman Group. Heuristic Evaluation 1998–2015. http://www.nngroup.com/topic/heuristic-evaluation/
16. Nielsen Norman Group. 10 Usability Heuristics for User Interface Design by Jakob Nielsen on 1 January 1995. 1998–2015. http://www.nngroup.com/articles/ten-usability-heuristics/
17. Oestreich, K.: Converged Infrastructure. CTO Forum, 15 November 2010. Thectoforum. com
18. Smith, M.: OmniTouch projection interface makes the world your touchscreen. Engadget, 18 October 2011
19. Tarantola, A.: The OmniTouch Makes Any Surface Interactive. Gizmodo, 17 October 2011
20. Web Map Solutions. Mobile Location Apps Review. Flex Mappers, 8 January 2012. http://www.webmapsolutions.com/mobile-location-apps
21. Weir, B.: The End of Keyboards & Monitors: the OmniTouch. ABC News, 3 November 2011
22. Wikipedia. Educational Game. Wikimedia Foundation Inc., 25 February 2015. http://en.wikipedia.org/wiki/Educational_game
23. Wikipedia. Extreme Programming. Wikimedia Foundation Inc., 17 February 2015. http://en.wikipedia.org/wiki/Extreme_programming
24. Wikipedia. Heuristic Evaluation. Wikimedia Foundation Inc., 22 February 2015. http://en.wikipedia.org/wiki/Heuristic_evaluation
25. Wikipedia. Lean Software Development. Wikimedia Foundation Inc., 7 November 2014. http://en.wikipedia.org/wiki/Lean_software_development
26. Wikipedia. Mobile Technology. Wikimedia Foundation Inc., 11 October 2012. http://en.wikipedia.org/wiki/Mobile_technology
27. Wikipedia. Mobile Phone Tracking. Wikimedia Foundation Inc., 27 October 2012. http://en.wikipedia.org/wiki/GSM_localization
28. Wikipedia. Scenario (Computing). Wikimedia Foundation Inc., 27 October 2014. http://en.wikipedia.org/wiki/Scenario_%28computing%29

The Research of Chinese Pilots Operating Safety

Mei Rong[1(✉)], Min Luo[1], Yanqiu Chen[1], and Changhua Sun[2]

[1] China Academy of Civil Aviation Science and Technology, Beijing, China
{Rongmei,luomin,Chenyq}@mail.castc.org.cn
[2] Civil Aviation Administration of China, Beijing, China
ch_sun@caac.gov.cn

Abstract. In order to understand the factors that affect the operating safety of Chinese pilots more deeply, we designed the "Chinese pilots' operating safety questionnaire". In this study, a total of 2130 questionnaires were received, of which 2094 copies are valid. We conducted a statistical analysis of the closed questions, collected the various open answers, and compared the different insights of the pilots in the same question. Finally, we summarized the discoveries and potential problems in operation risk, fatigue risk, safety awareness, the pilot's health care and the application of new technology. Through this survey and research, we are more systematic and comprehensive understanding of the major factors affecting the pilots' operations safety, and get some management problems existing in civil aviation and airlines of China, such as the flight time limit prescribed to be fine enough, non-precision approach of training is not enough. The conclusion of the investigation is very important for improving the safety management of airlines and revising China civil aviation related safety policies and regulations.

Keywords: Pilots' operating safety · Non-precision approach · Fatigue risk · Safety awareness

1 Introduction

According to Reason's Swiss cheese model, the behavior of people is the last line of defense to prevent accident. However, human behavior is influenced by the environment, organization, management and other deeper factors. And solving these deeper problems is the fundamental of the accident prevention. In order to understand the feeling and the problems of the pilots about operating safety, improve the airlines' safety management and provide some suggestions for China civil aviation's regulations revised, we designed the "Chinese pilots' operating safety questionnaire" based on interviewing experts and reviewing extensive literature.

The questionnaire is divided into six parts, a total of 50 questions. The first part is the background information of pilots, mainly to understand the basic situation of persons participating in the survey, such as age, education, aircraft type, total flight hours and other information. The second part is the operation risk, mainly about the operation of non-precision approach and plateau, complex airport when an engine is

C. Stephanidis (Ed.): HCII 2015 Posters, Part I, CCIS 528, pp. 262–269, 2015.
DOI: 10.1007/978-3-319-21380-4_46

failure based on the statistical analysis of the China civil aviation incidents in the past five years. The third part is the flight time and fatigue risk, mainly about the pilot's flight time, workload, rest and subjective fatigue. The fourth part is the safety awareness, primarily to understand the safety situation awareness during flight operations and information reporting. The fifth part is mainly about the pilot's health care situation and suggestion. The sixth part is the application the new flight technology, mainly to understand the negative and positive impacts on flight operating safety by new equipment or systems.

We distribute the questionnaires to airlines' relevant responsible person in print and electronic version, and then the responsible persons randomly distribute the questionnaires to the pilots. After completion of the questionnaire, the pilots submit it to the responsible person of the airline, finally feedback to us. Airlines participating in the survey not only cover large and small airlines, but also include general aviation. Finally, we received a total of 2130 questionnaires were received, of which 2094 copies are valid, the effective rate is 98 %.

2 Statistical Analysis of the Questionnaires

We received 2094 valid questionnaires, conducted a statistical analysis of the closed questions, collect the various open answers, and compare the different insights of the pilots in the same question. Finally, we summarize the discoveries and potential problems in operation risk, time of flight and fatigue risk, safety awareness, the pilot's health care and the application of new technology. Statistical results of the main issues are as follows:

1. The characteristics of the pilot team. The pilots' age is concentrated in 25–34 years, accounting for 70.7 % of those surveyed; The pilots entering the domestic aviation school after graduated from the high school are the most, accounting for 39.0 percent of those surveyed; The vast majority of pilots' educational back ground surveyed is Bachelor degree accounted for 91.2 %.
2. Non-precision approach. As the Fig. 1 shows, most of the pilots' non-precision approach experience is less than 10 % of all the flight experience, accounting for 76percent of the surveyed pilots totally.

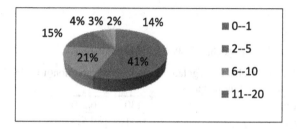

Fig. 1. The distribution of the proportion of non-precision approach in flight experience

As the Fig. 2 shows, 48.1 % of the pilots think the frequency of non-precision approach training is common。

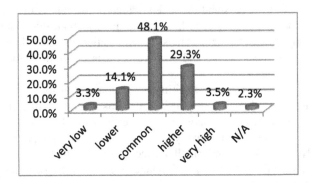

Fig. 2. The distribution of the frequency of non-precision approach training. N/A represents the number of pilots with no experience of the survey item

As the Fig. 3 shows, 36.6 % of the pilots think the effect of non-precision approach training is common.

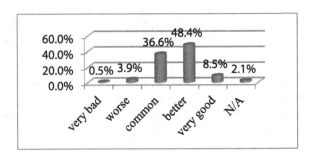

Fig. 3. The distribution of the effect of non-precision approach training

As the Table 1 shows, during non-precision approach, 6 % of the pilots admit they sometimes would violate the regulations or the operating manuals under the premise of ensuring safety.

Table 1. Possibility of violation

Whether violatethe regulations or the operating manuals	Number	Proportion(n = 2091)
Yes	130	6.2 %
No	1871	89.5 %
N/A	90	2.3 %

(1) Fatigue risk

As the Fig. 4 shows, 77.7 % of pilots think the scheduling system exists the irrationality on different degree.

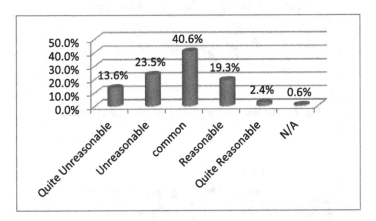

Fig. 4. The distribution of scheduling reasonability

As the Fig. 5shows, 78.6 % of the pilots' average actual sleep time per day is about 5 h < T < 8 h in the past month.

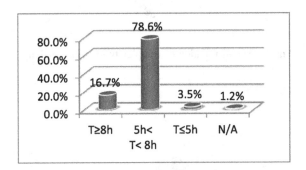

Fig. 5. The distribution of daily actual sleep time

The Fig. 6 shows that 51.1 % of pilots think their total sleep quality is just so so in the last month.

As Fig. 7 shows, 44.8 % of pilots think the complexity of mental activity of the airplane control is common. But 40.9 %of pilots think it needs more mental attention.

As the Fig. 8 shows, 64 % of the pilots have the feeling of laziness and distraction on different degree; 57.8 % of the pilots have the feeling of depression and anxiety on different degree; 53.6 % of the pilots are easy to loss temper to their colleagues, family or friends on different degree; 74.6 % of the pilots think themselves' fatigue level is above the average level.

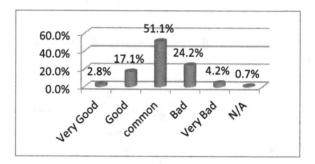

Fig. 6. The distribution of sleep quality self-evaluated

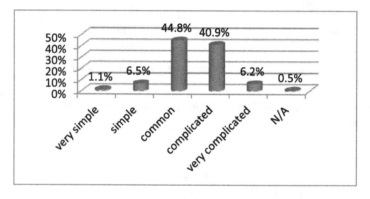

Fig. 7. The distribution of complexity of mental activity

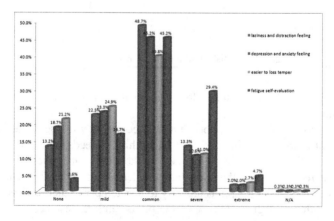

Fig. 8. The distribution of fatigue Self-evaluation

(2) Regulations Rationality and Safety Awareness

As the Table 2 shows, although 54.4 % of pilots think the regulations or operating manuals are suitable for operating, 35.1 % of pilots think there are some items notapplicable.

Table 2. Regulationsirrationality

Regulations Irrationality	Number	Proportion (n = 2073)
YES	727	35.1 %
NO	1127	54.4 %
N/A	219	10.5 %

As the Table 3 shows, if the pilot cannot get the ATC order for a long time, 36.2 % of pilots admit that he would change the aircraft flight status, and then seek the communication with ATC.

Table 3. The practices

Change status firstly and then Communicate with ATC	Number	Proportion (n = 2070)
YES	749	36.2 %
NO	1093	52.8 %
N/A	228	11.0 %

As the Table 4 shows, 11.7 % of pilots admit that he may violate the regulations or operation manuals under the premise of ensuring safety.

Table 4. Possibility of violation

Possibility of Violation	Number	Proportion (n = 2085)
YES	243	11.7 %
NO	1700	81.5 %
N/A	142	6.8 %

The most important factor that impacts the information reporting is "worry about being punished", accounted for 37.3 % as the Fig. 9 shows.

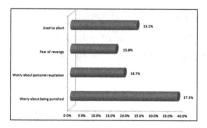

Fig. 9. The factors affect the information reporting

3   Conclusion and Recommendations

We can get the following conclusions from the questionnaire survey and give corresponding suggestion as below:

1. The pilot group of China is young, and most of them received a good education.
2. The survey results indicate that the non-precision approach happened rarely, and the rationality of the training frequency was common, and the training effect was not significant. We think it is necessary for airlines to consider in-depth study on the rationality of the non-precision approach training frequency and the training effect, and to discuss how to design or develop then on-precision approach training program, improve the rationality of the training frequency and enhance the training effect.
3. The survey results indicate that the pilot group showed a significant fatigue level. We suggest airlines and regulatory authority need to consider more about the fatigue risk on operation. It's important to develop the protection measures for individual, and methods of the fatigue risk monitoring, analysis and management for airlines.
4. The survey results indicate that the current regulations and operating manuals still have some unsuitable items, and the pilots' safety awareness needs to be improved. It's necessary to need further investigation of the applicability of regulations and operating manuals, identify the major hazards and revised timely. Also, we advised the airlines to establish reasonable rewards and punishment project, and carry out the safety culture construction to strengthen the pilots' safety awareness on obeying the rule and reporting the information.

As a first step to understand the pilots operating safety, the results obtained from the questionnaire survey are preliminary and limited. In order to gain more detailed results, we are doing more detailed investigation according to the significant problem, and combine effective interview with senior pilots in the future.

References

1. Reason, J.: Human Error. Cambridge University Press, Cambridge (1990)
2. Luo, M., Rong, M.: Hotspot of international aviation human factors. International Aviation, vol. 3 (2010)
3. Luo, M., Rong, M., Li, J., Sun, C.H., Hu, W.D.: New technologies for FRMS[C]. In: HCI International 2013 Conference (2013)
4. Wu, H.: Explore factors that would ensure the safety of non-precision approach. China Sci. Technol. 8 (2013)
5. Liu, J.: Operation and thinking of the confidential aviation safety reporting system. J. Civ. Aviat. Univ. China 4 (2009)

The Effects of Regional Culture on User Interface Experience: A Case Study of Xin'an Hangu Guan in China

Le Xi[✉], Jianxin Cheng, Junnan Ye, and Wangqun Xiao

School of Art, Design and Media, East China University of Science and Technology, M.BOX 286 NO.130, Meilong Road, Xuhui District, Shanghai 200237, China
xilutar@sina.com1, cjx.master@gmail.com2,
yejunnan971108@qq.com3, xiaoyao-1916@163.com4

Abstract. With the wide spread of mobile media around the world, the cross-cultural users could get the tourism destinations' information instant and convenient by mobile phones and other mobile terminals. However, the differences on region, culture, cognition, behavior, concepts etc. make cross-cultural users having distinctive experience of products. The effects of regional culture on user experience become more significant in tourism App's user interface (UI) design. It is a research focus at present that to solve the communication issues between the cross-cultural users and product's regional culture experience in theory and practice. In this paper, by taking the tourism App's UI design of Xin' an Hangu Guan (Chinese famous historical site of the Silk Road, world cultural heritage 2014) as an example, the methods on exploring and using regional culture when facing the experience design for cross-cultural users was discussed. At last, a method to ascend influence of regional culture by product's experience value was proposed, and expected to provide a theoretical reference for improving development of regional culture.

Keywords: Regional culture · Product experience · User interface · Product design · Cross-cultural

1 Introduction

Regional culture affects the product experience in many aspects. With the rapid development and popularization of mobile terminal, users around the world can use smart phone access to the local customs of foreign countries in any time. This convenient and efficient of information transmission effectively shortens the distance of exotic culture. However, there are still many factors that impede or interfere with the user experience in the spread of regional culture, such as concepts, behavior, cognition, and so on. These factors have significant impact on the product experience of user, especially in our design of tourism culture App product.

For the designer of interactive interface, in the face of user demand under different culture background, they both can keen perception of the user's cognitive differences, and also can deeply excavate the connotation of regional culture, and can be reasonably

© Springer International Publishing Switzerland 2015
C. Stephanidis (Ed.): HCII 2015 Posters, Part I, CCIS 528, pp. 270–275, 2015.
DOI: 10.1007/978-3-319-21380-4_47

applied to the design scheme. Around the case of interface design of tourism App about the world heritage - the Silk Road of Xin An Hangu Guan, based on the regional culture design research application system of 'Archaeology-Interpretation-Inno-vation'(AII), by the study of cross-cultural user experience, this paper put forward the main impact of regional culture on product experience, and discuss the means and methods of regional culture using in the product experience design of cross-cultural user oriented, with a view to expanding into the related areas of experience design such as visual sense, products, public environmental.

2 Research Background

The history of Xin'an Hangu Guan (Fig. 1) can be traced back to 2000 years ago. Today, it has been one of the node as a World Cultural Heritage "Silk Road", attracting more and more social attention. Xin'an Hangu Guan located in Dongguan village, Chengguan town, Xin'an, Henan province, founded in the Western Han Dynasty emperor yuan ding three year (BC 114). It is an important pass in the old course between Luoyang city and Xi'an city, but also the first pass in the Eastern starting point of the Silk Road. In 2014, as a Heritage point in the project of "The Silk Road", Xin'an pass has been successfully placed in the world Heritage lists.

Fig. 1. Panorama of Xin'an Hangu Guan

The design of tourism APP interface is a series of tourism cultural classes APP application program interface developed for the cultural transmission of the Xin'an Hangu Guan. During the process of development, we have specially studied the historic culture of Xin'an Hangu Guan and its important position and role in the Silk Road. We collect a lot of images material and cultural relic material about the Xin'an Hangu Guan, and classified them. According to the traditional operating habits of users, we optimize the App interface of operation, and make great efforts to interwork with China traditional cultural cognition.

3   Literature Review

For the development strategy and design method of cross-cultural product, a few of studies have discussed from different point of view. Du Jinling in the 'the function analysis and development trend of tourist APP based on the user experience' detailed analyzed the problems of user experience in such APP. Shen Kai in the 'The study of user experience in the cross-cultural context of interactive system" pointed that in the new era the status of cultural factors in user research should not be ignored, extracted the cultural characteristics of user requirements and four factors of culture study of user in interactive system and summarized the design process of cross-cultural interaction system. Fu Jie in the 'Revelatory of interactive design based on subconsciousness and behavioral habit' according to the personal unconscious and habits factors, discussed the characteristics of different models and how to blend them into the interactive integrated layout and detail design.

In short, the cross-cultural effectiveness of user experience is the core topic of the present study. But there are some common shortcomings and deficiencies in these studies. Firstly, the breadth of study is insufficient, for local cultural products are not designed to be comprehensive awareness and understanding. Secondly, the focus of research is more emphasis on the local culture refined, less involved in cognitive differences across cultures.

4   Method

In the HCI international 2014, we have put forward the 'AII' (Fig. 2) of the application system of study and design of regional culture. The framework has three levels, namely 'Cultural Archeology', 'Semantic Interpretation', 'Design Innovation'. In this study, we will continue to enrich and develop the application methods of 'AII' system in product experience of cross-cultural user. Meanwhile, the research method of cognition will be used in the step of 'Interpretation', further study the cognitive behavior and method of cross-cultural user, and strive to get a targeted design basis.

According to the research and application system of 'Archaeology-Interpretation-Innovation', our study is divided into three stages

Fig. 2. The regional cultural design and application system of "AII"

Step 1. We widely collect, screen and sort the cultural background information of Xin'an Hangu Guan, make a list of typical cultural features related to the Hangu Guan. After a typical representative of these features are arranged in accordance with the recognition, we select the most representative features as the image of Xin'an Hangu Guan. On the basis of these images, graphical processing and creativity is conducted.

Step 2. We conduct these outstanding characteristics of semantic interpretation and transformation, especially in the step of user cognition. Such as the interface mode of operation is set on the basis of cognitive style Chinese classical culture, and evaluate the effectiveness of its operation, to further adjust its operating form and graphics features, further adjust its mode of operation and graphic feature.

Step 3. In the stage of design and implementation, the connotation of product culture is implanted, further modifications is conducted to the related experience characteristics, at the same time, on the basis of the actual situation of tourism culture information, refine and adjust the content of the layout.

5 Results

In the study, we conducted a survey of the cultural identity markers of the Xin'an Hangu Guan, in the recyclable of 272 questionnaires, the gate tower is listed first. On the presentation of the front page, we strive to achieve customer satisfaction experience in the visual effects. In the screen language, we mainly to show the image of gate tower of Hangu Guan (Fig. 3).

In the subsequent study, we divide the interactive interface of App into three hierarchy (Fig. 4), they are icons, navigation and information. Under the three hierarchy is the background layer that is shown the main action and ways of expression of different hierarchy.

In the study of navigation hierarchy, it is mainly related to the different experience styles and cognitive style of cross-cultural user. To solve this problem, we designed two different navigation bar forms, one is in accordance with the general style of pull up and down, the menu bar enter into the home page from right to left; Another style is modeled

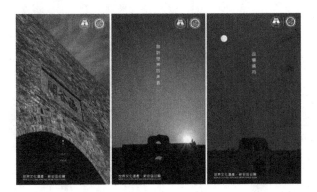

Fig. 3. The image of gate tower of UI design

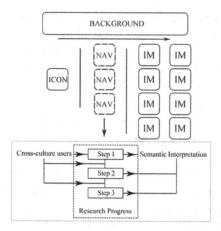

Fig. 4. The basic framework of interactive interface

Table 1. Comparison of domestic and foreign user experience

	Participants	Prefer A	Prefer B	Experience Well
Domestic users	25	10	15	19
Foreign users	25	11	14	16

on the bamboo form of ancient Chinese, entering into the home page from the bottom to top. We selected 50 users (25 users in China, 25 foreign user) who be familiar with the operating of mobile phone interface to authenticate these two style. The result of the verification is shown in Table 1. From the table, the second form of the Chinese classical style navigation bar has no significant difference in the operation and awareness of the Chinese and foreign users. It is shown that, in the operation of the graphical interface, operational obstacles caused by cultural differences is not very obvious.

Fig. 5. Two different navigation bar design comparison

On the basis of research, we have further discussed the presentation of information page and designed several sets of preliminary plan: such as sliding operation using classical Chinese patterns of auspicious clouds as style pattern, along the slip direction of auspicious clouds can enter into the next level of the interface. For another example is clicking the door of pass using the Chinese idiom meaning of 'come straight to the point', the door is opened and then shows the visual effect of Jiming Hill and Phoenix mountain located in north and south of Xin'an Hangu Guan. The final form of this scheme has not been verified by user, we will further improve in the future studies (see Fig. 5).

6 Conclusion and Discussion

The design effort of the tourism APP of Xin'an Hangu Guan is still in progress. Among them, the 'AII' system is able to help us at the cross-cultural user-oriented, more reasonable, effective convert and understand the style and features of regional culture, and allow users to understand its cultural connotations in the experience. Judging from the current situation, there are still some problems to be solved in our work, In the future study, we will further improve the 'AII' system study and design of regional culture. Based on the system, introducing the system of quantification evaluation, further achieve the understanding of the design experience.

References

1. Du, J.: Tourist class APP function analysis and development trend based on user experience. J. Changsha Railw. Univ. **15**(4), 335–336 (2014)
2. Kai, S.: The study of user experience for interactive system in a cross-cultural context, Jiangsu University, pp. 21–22
3. Hu, X.: A study of interaction design in the context of china. Publ. Commun. Sci. Technol. **2**, 155–156 (2014)
4. Ai, X., Wu, Z.: The experience economy product interaction design research thinking mode. J. Shandong Univ. Technol. (Soc. Sci.) **29**(4), 11–14 (2013)
5. Li, Y.: The research on interaction design of mobile phone based on chinese culture, Nanjing University of Science and Technology, pp. 45–48
6. Li, D.: The application of metaphor in interactive design, College of architecture and city planning of Tongji University, pp. 43–46
7. Liang, H.: Analysis of interactive design strategy from the perspective of cognitive load. J. Jilin Coll. Arts **108**(3), 22–24 (2012)
8. Fu, J.: Affordance in interaction design based on unconscious and behavior, Hunan University, pp. 18–20
9. Shao, R.: View of Luoyang from the Silk Road Starting Point, pp. 9–11. Kun Lun Press, Beijing (2008)
10. Gao, T.: Discussion on the Development of Tourism Resources in Luoyang 7, pp. 33–35 (2011)
11. Su, H.: On the Fort and Xin'an county (city), Theoretical Study on Construction of City, 14 (2012)
12. Jiangxia, C.: Zhengzhou University, The Central Plains Ancient Passes, pp. 11–17

The Study of the Cultural Values of Lighting Products Based on Intention Recognition and 3D Printing Technology

Chaoxiang Yang, Zhang Zhang[✉], Xu Yang, and Xiaohan Le

East China University of Science and Technology, Shanghai, China
darcy_yang@foxmail.com, zhangzhang@ecust.edu.cn,
670614462@qq.com, nbdxlhx@126.com

Abstract. The interaction between culture and business, culture and economy, is increasingly close under the background of the integration of the knowledge economy and the world economy. Material comforts are no longer able to meet the demand of modern products. The pursuit of products receives more attention in personal emotion, psychology and other aspects. This requires the product design should meet the cultural values of the times, and correctly interpret the values. Therefore, this paper takes lighting products as an example, firstly makes the reverse model for the product, then improves the design on the basis of three-dimensional digital model, and finally produces samples with the application of rapid prototyping 3D printing technology. Moreover, this paper uses the Kansei Engineering Theory to collect users' emotional data on product awareness and experience by questionnaires. It uses Factor analysis method and considers of product design principles, constructs cultural values and the objectives and the values for lighting design elements. The paper determines the criteria associated with perceptual weighting coefficients on the basis of users' data, and accurately designs the lighting products based on the cultural values, then forms the method of product design that upgrades the cultural values.

Keywords: Cultural values · Intention recognition · 3D printing · Lighting design

1 Introduction

Nowadays, people's thoughts, aesthetic appreciation and even values are still influenced by traditional culture. Product design with traditional elements is favored and sought after by the people. The creation of products featured with Chinese traditional culture not only can cater for people's material and spiritual needs in the advancing society, but also can provide motive force of development for product design. However, we face to a difficulty now that is how to use Chinese traditional culture for innovation and application, thus building regional design that featured with Chinese characteristics and style. Therefore, the article is aimed at the design and development of OLED lighting products featured with Chinese elements to find a design method of

© Springer International Publishing Switzerland 2015
C. Stephanidis (Ed.): HCII 2015 Posters, Part I, CCIS 528, pp. 276–283, 2015.
DOI: 10.1007/978-3-319-21380-4_48

products that meets traditional cultural orientation and sentimental demands of the consumers by utilizing kansei engineering theory and 3D printing technology.

Brief of Kansei Engineering. Kansei engineering is the product design technology presented by a Japanese scholar in the 70 s. It converts sensibility of the customers to design elements of the products and discusses feelings and needs of the customers from a psychological and perceptual point. During design process of the products, the core of kansei design is the transformation of design elements from kansei images and feelings, via which the designer can grasp the features of the products and know their relationships with the sensory images of customers and thus to check the evaluation meets his intended idea.

Brief of Design-based Cultural Level. Based on the study of design culture stated by Leong, Yang Yufu and Zheng Meiyu, referring to the existing division of design-based cultural level, and combined with the comprehension of culture itself and its contents, the article divides the culture into three levels. For the study of modeling elements and cultural level, it concludes culture-based design elements for product modeling according to the nature of cultural level. E.g., Table 1:

Table 1. Culture-based design elements for product modeling

Level	Design elements of the products
Inner "intangible" level	Has special cultural meaning and application of cultural concept
Mid "behavioral" level	Function, usage and background story of the products
Outer "tabfible" level	Shape, color, structure and surface ornamentation of the products

2 Design Method and Process of Lighting Products with Cultural Value Elements in the Framework of Kansei Engineering

Firstly, sample products shall be collected, sorted, compared and analyzed to know current design status of lighting products with cultural value elements and the main design methods, then, the main reason that caused these methods shall be analyzed.

Secondly, ten samples with typical features shall be selected out as experimental objects via discussing. Then, questionnaire survey on kansei engineering-based design of cultural value elements shall be carried out via 3D printing technology to analyze the evaluation of all sorts of products and its forming reason.

Finally, a conclusion comes out by virtue of design methods in the framework of kansei engineering: It is better to extract the morphology of cultural value elements to be applied during morphology design and application process, and this morphology does not need to keep a high similarity with that of the original cultural value elements.

3   Statistics and Correlation Analysis of Cultural Lighting Products

In total, 40 pieces of lighting products are collected for research, in which 10 pieces are left for follow-up study upon discussion by the research group. As shown in Table 2, the collected samples are sorted as follows to gather statistics of application method of cultural value elements for each sample.

There are 15 tables in total. The article can not list all of them due to its space. Statistics is carried out for the application method of cultural elements relating to every lighting product.

After all samples in Table 3 are summarized, the usage frequency of each design element during the design process of lighting products with Chinese elements can be obtained, then the occurrence rate of each design element can be calculated. Please see Table 3. After analyzing the data gained from the above tables, we can make following conclusions.

1. Culture of outer "tabfible" level is used for all lighting products with Chinese elements when designing. Comparatively, cultural value elements of inner "intangible"and mid "behavioral" level are less used and are decreasing. It can be concluded that: Cultural elements of outer "tabfible" level are necessary to the design of lighting products with Chinese elements. Cultural elements of inner "intangible" and mid "behavioral" level are on the basis of cultural elements of outer "tabfible" level, that is to say, cultural elements of outer "tabfible" level are the carrier for that of the two other levels. Besides, we can see that the design for lighting products is mainly the design for cultural elements of outer "tabfible" level. Less design for cultural elements of inner "intangible" and mid "behavioral" level is carried out, especially for the cultural elements of mid "behavioral" level.
2. For each design element, cultural morphology, structural element and cultural concept element are the most used three cultural design elements. Hence, we can know that these three cultural elements are the easiest-to-use design elements which can present the cultural value orientation easily.

Based on the above analysis, we learn the main method, status and reasons for design of OLED lighting products via application of Chinese cultural elements.

4   Kansei Image Analysis Based on Product Shape Relating to the Cultural Value Elements of Sampled Lighting Products

By applying kansei engineering theory, shape element is quite important in the designing process of lighting products, and more cultural value elements are applied relatively, which has representative and significant meanings.

Table 2. Usage method table of cultural elements for sample 2 table lamp named running under the moonlight

Sample 1: Running under the moonlight ——OLED table lamp

Application description of cultural elements: Via using the ancient carriage's shape, luminous source is combined with hood of the carriage.									
Usage of culture									
(Outer "tabfible" level)					(Mid "behavioral" level)			(Inner "intangible" level)	
Shape	Color	Material	Structure	Surface ornamentation	Function	Usage	Background story	Has cultural meaning	Apply cultural concept
Application of ancient carriage's shape							Terracotta soldiers and horses of the Qin Dynasty		Conform to traditional aesthetic appreciation

Table 3. Summary table on application of cultural elements of lamp samples

		Outer "tabfible" level						Mid "behavioral" level				Inner "intangible" level		
		Shape	Color	Material	Structure	Surface ornamentation	Total of outer "tabfible" level	Function	Usage	Background story	Total of mid "behavioral" level	Has cultural meaning	Conform to cultural concept	Total of inner "intangible" level
Design of lighting products with Chines elements	Quantity (pcs)	10	1	1	4	2	10	2	2	1	3	2	4	7
	Percentage	100&	10 %	10 %	40 %	20 %	100 %	20 %	20 %	10 %	30 %	20 %	40 %	60 %

1. *Selection and determination of kansei quotations.* For a large number of kansei adjectives, expert opinion is adopted in the article. Combined with the features of lighting products and the contents as above-mentioned, ten pieces of dimensionality are put forward to improve lighting products' designing. After comprehensive consideration is implemented, 6 pairs of relative kansei adjectives are listed in Table 4.

2. *Establish SD semantic differential table and print material lighting products via 3D technology.* If kansei quotations are combined with 10 groups of product samples, a semantic differential table of 7 steps can be established as Table 5.

3. *Statistical analysis.* After statistical analysis is carried out for the features of sampled lighting products in the above table and the corresponding kansei vocabularies, the design elements which can explain these kansei vocabularies properly can be analyzed. By using statistical method, Scoring of Features shown can be worked out in such manner. Meanwhile, by using statistical method, Scoring of Features shown in Table 6 can be worked out in such manner: 1 score shall be added for each feature of samples with high score, while 1 score shall be deducted for each feature of samples with low score.

4. *Analysis of result.* Through analyzing the above table, we can gain the research result on OLED lighting products with Chinese elements according to image cognition. It is concluded that the impacts on the sampled lighting products caused by the morphology of cultural value elements are:

Modernity: Those cultural value elements with biased abstract conceptualization and low similarity have high modernity. Innovativeness: Those lighting products with biased geometry, simple shape, biased abstract conceptualization and low similarity have high innovativeness. Interestingness: Lighting products with biased geometry and high similarity have high Interestingness. Convenience: Lighting products with biased organism, biased duplication and high similarity have high convenience, in which, those with biased duplication and high similarity with images and shapes have a greater impact on the convenience. Grade: The more biased geometry is used and the higher similarity is, the higher grade of the lighting product is, which cause a greater impact on the grade. Beauty: Lighting products with biased geometry, biased duplication and high similarity are more beautiful and have a greater effects.

The better the cultural value elements are applied to the OLED lighting products, the more cultural elements shall be abstracted rather than duplicate directly. Moreover, this does not need to keep a higher similarity with the original cultural value elements.

Table 4. Scoring table for the features of sampled lighting products

Perceptual demand	Property comparison of the product				Product shape and morphology of cultural value			
	Biased shape		Complexity of the shape		Application technique of cultural value intention		Morphology similarity relating to cultural value intention	
	Biased geometry	Biased organism	Complex shape	Simple shape	Biased abstract conceptualization	Biased duplication	High similarity	Low similarity
Modern - ancient	1	−1	0	0	3	−3	−2	2
Innovative - conservative	1	0	0	1	2	0	0	2
Interesting - monotonous	1	0	1	1	1	1	2	0
Easy to use - hard-to-use	0	2	2	1	0	2	3	0
Low-end - high-end	3	0	2	1	1	2	3	0
Beautiful - ugly	3	0	2	1	0	3	3	0

Table 5. Determination of Kansei quotations

Modern - ancient	conservative - innovative	monotonous - interesting
Hard-to-use - easy to use	low-end - high-end	ugly - beautiful

Table 6. Semantic differential table of 7 steps relating to sampled lighting products

Ancient	-3	-2	-1	0	1	2	3	Modern	Picture of samples

5 Conclusion

The practical application of the study with relation to the cultural values of lighting products based on intention recognition and 3D printing technology as that stated by this article when designing the OLED lighting products with Chinese elements is relatively a complete and feasible design procedure. All in all, we can solve three main problems as below.

1. Propose more comprehensive and reasonable cultural level classification for lighting products concerned with the study of cultural value elements.
2. Analyze modeling elements of the lighting elements and redefine cultural value-oriented modeling elements of the products when studying the OLED lighting products.
3. Investigate existing design of OLED lighting products and analyze a large amount of collected and summarized data via kansei engineering theory and 3D printing technology to gain a large amount of conclusions relating to cultural value-oriented design creativity of the lighting products, which simplify the design difficulty and dimensionality of the OLED lighting products.

References

1. Guanzhong, L.: The Culture of Design. Heilongjiang Scientific and Technical Publishers, Harbin (1996)
2. Nagamachi, M.: Kansei engineering: a new ergonomic consumer-oriented technology for product development. Int. J. Ind. Ergonomic 15(1), 3–11 (1995)
3. Borgman, A.: Discovering Design: Design Explorations and Studies, pp. 40–41. Jiangsu Fine Arts Publishing House, Nanjing (2010)
4. Nagamachi, M.: Kansei engineering as a powerful consumer-oriented technology for product development. Appl. Ergonomics 32, 289–294 (2002)
5. Wang, K.: Research on Satisfaction of Internet Products Based on Cultural Factor, Zhejiang University (2011)
6. Leong, B.D.: Culture-based knowledge towards new design thinking and practice-a dialogue. Des. Issues 19, 48–58 (2003)

Design for Aging

Strengthening Connections: Intuitive Interfaces for Life Story Work in Elder Care

Mahdi Chaker[1(✉)], Michael Cimerola[2], and Marietta Scanlon[3]

[1] Computer Engineering, Penn State University, State College, USA
mchaker@psu.edu
[2] LifeCare Senior Living, Allentown, PA, USA
mike.cimerola@gmail.com
[3] College of Engineering, Penn State University, State College, USA
mrs35@psu.edu

Abstract. This paper presents Renewed Voice, a software application designed to replace the collection methodology of using paper survey forms to conduct Life Story Work (LSW) in a resident care community. Renewed Voice integrates multiple design elements customized for older adults including an intuitive user interface, larger fonts and navigational buttons, specific color and contrast schemes, standardized page layouts, a dynamic progression and completion rate, and touch screen capability. A trial version is currently being tested at a local personal care home and memory care community.

Keywords: Software · Life story work · Survey · Resident care · Person-centered · Quality of life · Caregiver · Older adults · Intuitive · User interface · Touch screen · Personal care home · Memory care

1 Introduction

Life story work (LSW) is a term used to describe the biographical approaches utilized in health and social care settings that provide people the opportunity to discuss and record their past life events and experiences that "go beyond a routine health assessment" [1]. These recordings can be further defined as "biograph[ies], life histor[ies], [and] life stories" [1] and are compiled in a collaborative manner with residents, families, and staff. LSW collection methods can include recorded interviews, focus groups, and staff observations [1, Table 2] and usually produce a 'product' such as a "story-book, collage, notice board...biography summary, or tape recording" [1]. This 'product' has several uses, including acting as a resource to help older adults with disabilities maintain their identity rather than focus on their condition and aiding staff in learning about a new resident [1, Table 3].

LSW has the potential to improve individualized care, promote understanding of contextual behaviors of residents with dementia, reduce generational biases, facilitate transitions for residents between environments in which dependence on caregivers increases, and most importantly, foster connections between care staff, family, and residents [1].

The paper LSW survey covered topics which included family life, school careers and service, later years, religion, and hobbies. The goal was to design a life story

© Springer International Publishing Switzerland 2015
C. Stephanidis (Ed.): HCII 2015 Posters, Part I, CCIS 528, pp. 287–292, 2015.
DOI: 10.1007/978-3-319-21380-4_49

software application to meet and improve upon the challenges associated with the paper methodology.

Section 2 identifies specific challenges with pen and paper survey forms used to conduct LSW. Section 3 describes the Renewed Voice software application and its key physical and person-centered design elements that respond to the challenges of the paper survey methodology. Section 4 presents future directions and this paper concludes with Sect. 5.

2   Challenges with Current Methodology

Currently, the methodology used by a local resident care community is the completion of paper surveys to conduct LSW. Some barriers present in the pen and paper approach to LSW are accessibility, space and time constraints, and data management. The responses to these challenges will be discussed in the next section.

3   Overview of Renewed Voice

The Renewed Voice Program can be divided into two main aspects: the physical design elements of the software, and the human design elements of its motivation and impact.

3.1   Physical Design Elements

The Physical Design Elements address three main considerations: accessibility, space and time constraints, and data management.

Accessibility. Accessibility is a key factor in technology design decisions in elder care settings. The interface elements in Renewed Voice were selected to assist adults experiencing declines in cognition, vision, and motor skills associated with aging [2, pp. 137–146].

As can be seen in Figs. 1 and 2 below, the user interface consists of large buttons and fonts, specifically-chosen typefaces, and clear color contrasts between text and the background, which aid residents with tactile and sight deficiencies. Page layouts are predictable and flat, without dramatic effects, to keep information density low and the interface organized. Questions are presented to the user one at a time with clearly-defined answers to minimize the amount of text per page.

The pen and paper approach to LSW poses a challenge to users with reduced fine motor skills: if a user is unable to effectively write by hand or has illegible handwriting, the LSW process becomes difficult. Renewed Voice allows for text input through typing on a keyboard and interaction with the interface on a touch screen monitor.

A final consideration for accessibility is intuitability. Renewed Voice is designed to allow the resident to transfer their existing knowledge of paper forms to compile their life story. Clear labels and icons in navigation buttons are also included. Furthermore, the software program utilizes a design pattern of having a "next movement" as the rightmost navigation button option, and a "back movement" as the leftmost navigation button option.

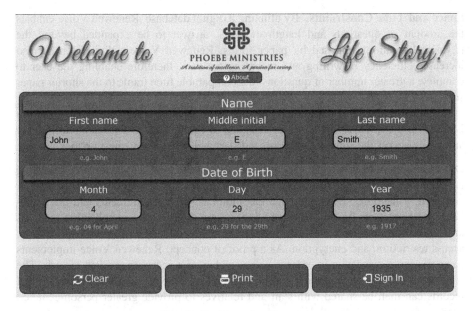

Fig. 1. Resident sign-in screen

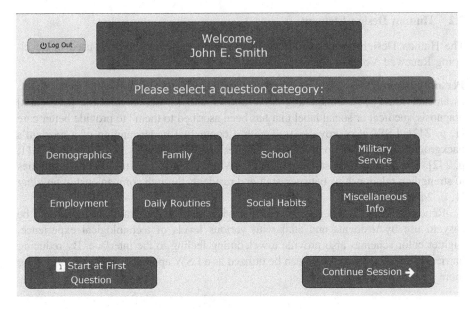

Fig. 2. Question categories screen

Space and Time Constraints. By utilizing a digital database, Renewed Voice enables the amount of questions and length of users' answer to be expanded beyond the physical limitations imposed by paper forms. Renewed Voice's digital format also increases efficiency in writing and recording answers, therefore enabling the user to complete a greater number of questions in a comparable time frame to the shorter paper surveys.

Another challenge is the limited amount of time available for care staff to perform LSW [1, p. 244]. Renewed Voice is designed to enable staff and residents to quickly and easily access the software program and start and stop on any question they choose.

Data Management. Data integrity and confidentiality are critical factors in performing LSW [1, p. 245]. Paper forms require larger spaces for storage and can be lost or damaged in handling. Digital storage has minimal space requirements and has established best practices for reliability and fault tolerance. Digital data collection methods also allow for stronger security features to be enabled, such as password protection, access restriction, and encryption. As a proof of concept, Renewed Voice implements basic password protection in order to secure and restrict access to resident records. The software is capable of generating a printable version of the resident's life story. Printed records can then be shared with staff and relatives to provide greater person-centered care.

3.2   Human Design Element

The Human Design Element addresses the person-centered approach used in developing Renewed Voice.

Person-Centered Care. Person-centered care is care that "aims to see the [resident] ... as an individual" [3]. Conducting LSW allows staff to "see beyond the [resident's] diagnosis, medical or social label that has been ascribed to them" to provide better care [1, p. 242]. LSW also provides staff with a contextual understanding of a resident's background and may help to "explain [a resident's] behaviors...in the present" [1, p. 242]. The approaches used to conduct LSW are not just activities, but opportunities to strengthen relationships between staff and residents through companionship building [1, p. 243].

Renewed Voice is designed to cover a wide range of biographical topics and be easy to use by residents and staff with various levels of technological experience. Lighter color schemes also provide a welcoming feeling to the interface. By reducing barriers to use, Renewed Voice can be utilized as a LSW approach and aid in providing more personalized care.

4   Future Work

The following sections discuss possible future additions to Renewed Voice and the impact of using the software.

4.1   Future Directions

Future developments of the software may include adding voice recordings, videos, and photos. Speech-to-text capabilities can also be incorporated, increasing accessibility for users who have difficulty entering data using a keyboard. Questions can also be accompanied by images to prompt responses.

Renewed Voice can potentially be used in multiple healthcare settings. Home use could facilitate earlier life story work and help with an individual's transition into subsequent care settings. A long-term study on the impact of using Renewed Voice in elder care would contribute to the current body of knowledge regarding LSW and inform future design choices.

4.2   Strengthening Connections

Performing LSW stimulates communication in resident care settings [1, p. 244]. Through this increased communication, staff are able to gain a better understanding of residents on an individual level [1, p. 244]. This deeper insight aids in strengthening connections between residents, family, and staff. LSW can be expanded to include input from community and faith based organizations and historical societies in an effort to provide a more detailed contextual background.

Renewed Voice aids in strengthening these connections by enabling staff to discover commonalities between residents through applying analytics to the collected life story data. Staff awareness of these previously unnoticed commonalities can highlight the need for specific beneficial social activities within the resident community.

LSW is a collaborative approach that connects residents, families, and staff through communication. However, in-person interactions between generations are decreasing for older adults [4]. Renewed Voice's interface design enables residents and staff to bridge generational gaps by reducing barriers to perform LSW.

5   Conclusions

Renewed Voice is an improvement on the pen and paper methodology for performing LSW in resident care communities. By combining physical and human design elements into an intuitable user interface, Renewed Voice promotes insightful conversations and stronger relationships between residents, family and staff.

A trial version is currently being tested at a local personal care home and memory care community.

Acknowledgements. The authors would like to thank Phoebe Ministries for implementing the Renewed Voice system in their resident care facility.

References

1. McKeown, J., et al.: Life story work in health and social care: systematic literature review. J. Adv. Nurs. **55**(2), 237–247 (2006)
2. Charness, N., Schaie, K.: Impact of Technology on Successful Aging. Springer, New York (2003)
3. Alzheimers Society: Person-centred care - Alzheimer's Society. http://www.alzheimers.org. uk/site/scripts/services_info.php?serviceID=167
4. Harley, D., et al.: Age matters. In: Proceedings of the 27th International Conference Extended Abstracts on Human Factors in Computing Systems - CHI EA 2009 (2009)

The Effect of Age on Perception and Preference of App Icon Styles

Chiwu Huang[(✉)] and Po-Ti Chen

Department of Industrial Design, National Taipei University of Technology,
1, Section 3, Zhongxiao E. Rd., Taipei 10608, Taiwan
chiwu@ntut.edu.tw

Abstract. Hand-held computer devices, such as smartphone, tablet etc., are popularly used at present. The icon styles for the apps in those devices can be generally classified into two types, namely, Aqua and Metro. How they can be perceived and preferred by people in different ages? What are the design features of these styles? This study aims to explore the relationship between icons' style and perception on different ages.

10 Aqua and 10 Metro icons with same meanings were sampled. 300 respondents, evenly distributed in genders, aged 16–65 years old, stratified in ten age groups were recruited to do the test. A 5-point Likert scale was used to evaluate the perception of icons. The study examined the perception and preference of different age groups in using app icons of Metro and Aqua style. Four distinct design features, i.e. concrete, abstract, flatness and stereoscopic were also examined. In particular, it investigated whether an icon image that is concrete and solid at the same time can be more legible and preferable by the respondent. It also analyzed whether male and female exhibit different degree of perception and preference over different styles.

It was found that the perception on Aqua icons was not significantly different among 10 age groups. In contrast, the perception of Metro icons was significantly different between two age groups: 16–30 and 31–65. All age groups prefer Aqua to Metro, especially on older groups aged beyond 31. Younger groups tend to be more comfortable with Metro than the older groups did. The study also found that perception was strongly influenced by concrete and abstract features.

Keywords: Perception · Preference · Age · Icon · App · Metro · Aqua

1 Introduction

Hand-held computer devices, such as smartphone, tablet etc., are very popular at present. The icon styles for the apps in those devices can be generally classified into two types, namely, Aqua and Metro. Each one has its own supporters. Aqua is the graphic user interface (GUI) and primary visual theme of Apple's OS X operating system. It is based around the theme of water, as its name suggests, with droplet-like elements and liberal use of translucency and reflection effects. Steve Jobs noted Aqua's

© Springer International Publishing Switzerland 2015
C. Stephanidis (Ed.): HCII 2015 Posters, Part I, CCIS 528, pp. 293–298, 2015.
DOI: 10.1007/978-3-319-21380-4_50

glossy aesthetic: "One of the design goals was when you saw it you wanted to lick it". [1] An Agua's icon always exhibits a three-dimensional looking. Metro, in contrast, adopts a rather "flat" visual design strategy compared to its counterpart. Its icons use two-dimensional symbolic shapes that are claimed to be recognized easily [2].

How they can be recognized and preferred by people in different ages? What are design features of these styles? This study aims to explore the relationship between icons' styles and recognition on different ages. This study has two hypotheses: (1) the icons' solidness and concreteness will determine the degree of recognition for an icon. (2) Age plays a role in the recognition and preference of icon's styles. Therefore this study aims to find out:

1. The effect of age groups on the perception of two app icon styles.
2. The effect of age groups on the preference of two app icon styles.
3. What features of the icon design would contribute to these effects?

2   Literature Review

According to Norman's mental models [3], ideally, the design model should be coped with user's model. An icon design should be compatible with user's expectation therefore can be understood. Peirce classified signs into three categories, icon, index and symbol [4]. The icon in this study includes these three categories. Horton [5] argued that icon itself is meaningless. Through viewers' association with past experience and memory an icon stands for something. Age-related change in cognition can be important to consider when design for older adults [6]. Therefore this study aims to test whether age has effects on the perception and preference of icon styles.

3   Methods

3.1   Test Samples

10 pairs of Aqua and Metro app icons in same function, including library, weather, camera, calendar, mail box, album, music, games, video and address book, were sampled as test objects.

3.2   Respondents

300 experienced users with hand held computer devices, e.g. smart phones, tablets etc., aged between 16–65 years old, evenly distributed in genders, stratified in ten age groups (A-J) each with a five-years interval (i.e. 16–20, 21–25, 26–30 … 61–65) were recruited online to do the evaluation. Each age group includes 30 respondents. Due to the worries about older people's unfamiliarity with online questionnaire, paper form of questionnaire was used for three age groups, 51–55, 56–60 and 61–65. Online evaluation was adopted for the rest of age groups. Convenient sampling method was used to render the sampling process.

3.3   Questionnaire

This study aims to determine the effect of ages and genders on the perception and preference of app icon styles. The ages and genders data were collected. The perception on each icons was evaluated in Likert 5-point scales, 1 = very disagree, 2 = disagree, 3 = common, 4 = agree and 5 = very agree. Questions include: (1) Does this icon remind you a "camera"? (2) Does this icon look solid? (3) Does this icon look flat? (4) Does this icon look concrete? (5) Does this icon look abstract? Finally, the respondent was asked to choose a preferable one among two icons.

3.4   Data Analysis

SPSS Statistics 20 was used to analyze the data. Descriptive statistics, Cronbach's α, Levene's test, ANOVA, Tukey's HSD and Games-Howell, correlation coefficient and independent sampling t-test were conducted.

4   Results and Discussion

The questionnaire was tested for its reliability before survey. The result showed that Cronbach's α was 0.955 (>0.7) which represents the questionnaire is highly reliable. 300 valid questionnaires were received. The result is presented in the following.

4.1   The Perception and Style Features

The average ratings of two icon styles are shown in Table 1. It is observed that the average ratings of Agua are higher than Metro on perception, solid and concrete, whereas, lower than Metro on flat and abstract. This suggests that Aqua may be easier than Metro to be perceived by the respondents. A further analysis on their correlation between recognition and variables is listed in Table 2. It is observed that both the

Table 1. Average ratings of two app icon styles (n = 300)

	Aqua	Metro
Perception	4.48	3.66
Solid	4.17	1.78
Flat	2.13	4.30
Concrete	4.31	2.24
Abstract	2.04	4.12

Table 2. Pearson coefficient between perception and design features (n = 300)

Variables	Aqua	Metro
Solid	0.806*	−0.317*
Flat	−0.587*	0.353*
Concrete	0.830*	−0.032
Abstract	−0.508*	0.513*

*p < 0.01

perception of Aqua are highly positive correlated to solid and concrete, and fairy negative correlated to flat and abstract. In contrast, the perception of Metro are fairly negative correlated to solid and concrete and fairly positive correlated to flat and abstract. That means the design feature of Aqua tend to be solid and concrete whereas Metro tend to be flat and abstract.

4.2 Age Groups on Styles

Table 3 shows the F value of perception on each Aqua and Metro icons. It is observed that only a few of icons show significant difference among age groups on Aqua. In contrast, all the icons on Metro show significant difference among age groups.

Table 3. F values of perception on Aqua and Metro icons

	A1	A2	A3	A4	A5
Aqua					
F	2.39*	.74	3.49*	1.02	1.47
	A6	A7	A8	A9	A10
Aqua					
F	.85	1.86	.58	3.06*	1.57
	M1	M2	M3	M4	M5
Metro					
F	7.87*	7.54*	4.66*	7.10*	11.32*
	M6	M7	M8	M9	M10
Metro					
F	5.46*	9.59*	11.41*	13.17*	5.57*

*p<.05

Table 4. Tukey's HSD test on the age groups

Metro icons	Age groups
M2 weather	ABC – I – DEFGHJ
M4 calendar	ABC – EI – DFGHJ
M8 game	AB – CD – EF – GHIJ
M9 video	ABC – DEFGHIJ

This means that there are very little effect on ages with Aqua. However, there are a lot of differences between age groups with Metro.

A further analysis on Tukey's HSD test (see Table 4) shows age groups can be roughly divided into two groups, ABC (16–30 years old) and DEFGHIJ (31–65 years old).

4.3   Age Groups on Preference

Figure 1 shows the frequency of preference on Metro and Aqua respectively against age groups. Although most respondents prefer Aqua to Metro, a tendency can be observed that the preference of younger generation, i.e. 16-30, shows very minor difference, at least not as dramatic as the rest of age groups. This comply with the result of Table 4. The reason may be lie in that these groups of people were brought up in a rapid computer technology development era. They tend to be familiar with all kinds of technology including GUI. However, older groups prefer Aqua to Metro. This may be due to that older people tend to be rely on their daily life experience. This is also confirm to a previous findings that icons designed with realistic image would make them easier to be recognized [7].

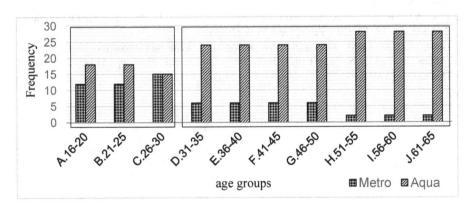

Fig. 1. Frequency of preference of age groups on Metro and Aqua

5 Conclusion

This study explored the perception of two types of icon, Aqua and Metro on different age groups of people. The following findings may be considered when design an app icon, especially when dealing with age related issues.

1. Aqua tends to be more readable and legible than Metro in average.
2. The perception may be highly positively correlated with solid and concrete characters of icon design and fairly negatively correlated with flat and abstract characters.
3. Significant difference was found between age groups on the perception of Metro icons.
4. Most respondents prefer Aqua to Metro. However younger generation (16-30) shows very little difference between two types of icon.

Acknowlededgments. Thanks for the sponsorship of the Ministry of Science and Technology, Taiwan (MOST 103-222-E-027-098).

References

1. http://en.wikipedia.org/wiki/Aqua_(user_interface)#cite_note-macworld2000-3 (browsed on 30 March 2015)
2. https://msdn.microsoft.com/en-us/library/windows/apps/hh781237.aspx (browsed on 30 March 2015)
3. Norman, D.A.: The Design of Everyday Things, pp. 189–191. Basic Books, New York (1988)
4. Fiske, J.: Introduction to Communication Studies. Yuan-Liou Publishing, Taipei (1995). Chinese edition, Interpretation by Chang, C. H.
5. Horton, W.: The Icon Book: Visual Symbols For Computer Systems and Documentation. Wiley, New York (1994)
6. Fisk, A.D., Rogers, W.A., Charness, N., Czaja, S.J., Sharit, J.: Designing for Older Adults, 2nd edn, pp. 18–19. CRC Press, New York (2009)
7. Huang, C., Tsai, C.-M.: The effect of morphological elements on the icon recognition in smart phones. In: Aykin, N. (ed.) Part 1, HCII 2007. LNCS, vol. 4559, pp. 513–522. Springer, Heidelberg (2007)

An iPad Application Prototype to Enhance Memory of Older Adults

Wonsil Jang[(⊠)]

134 Department of Graphic Design, College of Design, Iowa State University,
Ames, IA 50011, USA
swiriwon@iastate.edu

Abstract. The objective of this project is to propose a prototype of an iPad application that will satisfy the demand of old adults, whose interest is a long lasting healthy brain. Developing an application for old adults is reasonable because of rapid increase of their population. This paper focuses on a development of an iPad application within mobile UD (Universal Design) principles for older adults that will lead to further research on user testing.

Keywords: Older adults · Mobile application · iPad application · Application design · Universal design · User centered design

1 Introduction

Recently, as older adult population has rapidly increased globally, it seems relevant for older adults to increase interest of long, lasting, healthy life. According to the data, the elder population aged over 60 is expected to reach 22 % in 2050 (ESA, U.S. Department of Commerce 1995). Therefore, independent living for older adults is the expected primary goal. Such countries as U.S.A. South Korea, Japan, and Europe are in the process to make such programs that serve independent living. Moreover, extended better education allows today's old adults more experience with technology of most interactive devices, such as computers, mobile devices, and related technology (Ana et al. 2013). According to the research data, 53 % of older people in 2012 were using Internet and email and 69 % of them were using mobile phone (Ljilja et al. 2014).

The aim of this project is to make a prototype of an interactive application operable on iPad for older adults who are concerned about their memory loss. As an assistive technology, the iPad is suitable for older people to play games and communicate with their friends and family members.

2 Background

2.1 Older Adults and iPad

The computer is more familiar with older adults, than the tablet. However, many researchers said that the tablet is "more intuitive to use for people with disabilities and for senior citizens who may need graphics represented in nontraditional ways" (Walker

C. Stephanidis (Ed.): HCII 2015 Posters, Part I, CCIS 528, pp. 299–304, 2015.
DOI: 10.1007/978-3-319-21380-4_51

2011, Tina and Dietmar 2012). As an assistive device, there are not many great functioning applications that are visually supported and attractive for those who want to use it for their activities. Hence, the study focuses on the visual design based on Universal design approach.

2.2 Universal Design

UD (Universal Design) was introduced by Mace in 1988, reducing complex processes, using consistent interface, easy interaction with products, and environments for physical impairment and older adults (Kascak et al. 2014). We conduct research under UD to provide better user centered design. Project direction:

1. Easy to use navigation: Touch based devices are not familiar with old adults, so navigation is important for comfortable feeling. A home screen menu is provided as a safe point of return (Ana et al. 2013).
2. Easy to perceive: Most older adults supplement their eyesight with eyeglasses, but to help declined spatial ability (Nicole et al. 2014) and color perception, over 14pt font is provided. Also, font size can be changed in setting section for flexible usage (Keiko et al. 2001, Nicole et al. 2014).
3. Easy to touch on screen: Touch space, location, size of icons is considered for users.
4. Easy to Interact: To help easy interaction, the top center of the screen has a help icon to explain any page's function. Moreover, for a more convenient environment, recording voice and type writing function both are provided in a community menu.
5. Color set for older adults: In the design, mixing with yellow/white, blue/green, dark blue/black and purple/dark red color were avoided for clear recognition (Keiko et al. 2001).
6. Recognizable icon set: To increase affordance of elements text is provided in icons. Back button is on top of the screen as a safeguard (Ana et al. 2013).
7. Simple interface: Use few steps to the destination and a back button and home screen menu are in solid location.

2.3 Older Adults with Music

Many researchers discuss how music is helpful for older adults. One of the effects of music is reducing agitation (Witzke et al. 2008). Also they report that classical, calming, meditative and soft background music had the best effect, and playing soothing music during mealtime reduces aggressive physical and verbal behavior in older residents with dementia (Lisa et al. 2013, Chang et al. 2010). In the sound intervention, the user can listen to music that already set up in the menu.

2.4 Older Adults and Games

Although there are many challenges due to the lack of experiments for older adults, games are used for training, education, or in rehabilitation to help patients regain or keep specific abilities they may have lost. Their sight, hearing, and spatial problems and cognition impairment are barriers for investigators to develop new programs for them

(Ijsselsteijn et al. 2007, Anna et al. 2014). Simple games may provide daily activity to prevent their loss of abilities. To encourage the game activity, this application offers the function of games with a friend. Each level in a game has different functions. Right now it has only one level that is matching similar sets of pictures. Users can see a hint to learn how to play. Buttons are big enough to press; if someone needs help, they press the help button to see a written or to hear a voice instruction for convenience.

2.5   Older Adults and Communication

As time goes by, older people communicate less frequently with others and easily are isolated from society by retirement and illness. Moreover, there are many chances of distance communication, as many more people live individually than in the past. Long distance communication tools such as email and telephone calls are more common, rather than face-to-face meetings to maintain family communication and relationships. Most old adults prefer to write a letter when communicating with others; however, as people age, they tend to use a telephone than a letter because they need much effort such as spelling and grammar correction (Anna and Robin 2007). Communication section of the iPad application is a place to make one's own electric album and interact with others. Lively communication with others will help keep older adults active and have positive thinking. The community section is operated with individual's stories from their memories, using recorded voice and writing with their photos that would be a method to retain information when they lose their memories. The advantage of this section is that users do not need to go out to interact with others. They can meet each other in augmented community with recorded and written stories. Caregivers can control the community room by answering members' questions.

Figure 1: the Logo (Fig. 1) represents a person's brain. Also, it shows a smiling face with heart shaped mouth. The name of application "Lolli" implies that of a fun application like a candy they can bite. To provide an everyday life activity the name "Lolli" was created.

Lolli

Fig. 1. Logo

3   Development

3.1   Logo Development

3.2   Information Architecture

The application consists of three different menus: sound intervention, game, and communication. It requires "log in" because of interaction with others in game and communication menus (Fig. 2). Two menus: Sound intervention and Game, are for one's individual activity; however, communication menu is for interaction with others sharing stories, asking problems, giving suggestions each other. Caregivers or doctors would help to control the communication on the community room, controlling users' behaviors, mediating their conversations, and giving suggestions as a recommendation.

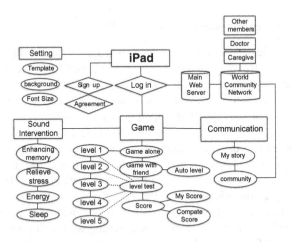

Fig. 2. Information architecture

3.3 Prototype

"Older adults can effectively navigate websites that have simplified selections per screen and flattened navigation structures" (Demiris et al. 2001, Katie et al. 2010). This prototype of application (Fig. 3) aims to provide easy and convenient interface based on UD. To avoid uncomfortable feelings on digital devices, it offers background feeling like reading an old book; a textual image similar to book paper was used for it. To avoid complicated interface, flat and rounded icons were used. Most pages have their own introduction with written and voice explanation about the page on top of the screen, named "help". In the communication menu, to make a story album requires a process of uploading pictures. Voice uploading and type writing method are used to provide various convenient functions for older adults. Home screen menu is always

Fig. 3. Prototype application design

located on the left side to help users keep their direction on the application. Back button is located in top of right side and edit menus are in left side; the menus are changed depending on the pages such as a detail page of "my story" that has menus: "new", "edit", "delete" and such as a "make story" page that has a menu of "post".

Brown tone color is used as a base color set to keep away from a complicated interface design. Big size font and icons with names are provided considering of their better concentration while playing application.

4 Conclusion

Many researchers have acknowledged that the industry for older adults will be extended; however, there are not many applications visually satisfying for older adults that understand their conditions and chronic symptoms such as color recognition and spatial problems. Technology has the potential power to enhance visual effects and provides social tools. In this sense, the three menus on the application provides significant part as it could be a portable personal activity tool with many functions. This application will have a role to help older adults as a daily tool that should lead to the next step.

The objective of this research is to make a prototype of an application. As a next step, to verify the usefulness of this application, further research of user testing is expected. In the next step, user test of recording voice function to know how effective it is and usability test to know how comfortable it is.

Acknowledgement. This author would like to thank Professor Sunghyun Kang at Iowa State University for her support for this paper.

References

Wagner, N., Hassanein, K., Head, M.: The impact of age on website usability. Comput. Hum. Behav. **37**, 270–282 (2014)

Sixty-five plus in the United States: Economics and Statistics Administration. U.S. Department of Commerce, Washington (1995)

de Barros, A.C., Leitao, R., Ribeiro, J.: Design and evaluation of a mobile user interface for older adults: navigation, interaction and visual design recommendations. Procedia Comput. Sci. **27**, 369–378 (2013)

Kascak, L.R., Rébola, C.B., Sanford, J.A.: Integrating universal design (UD) principles and mobile design guidelines to improve design of mobile health applications for older adults (2014)

Witzke, J., Rhone, R.A., Bakhaus, D., et al.: How sweet the sound: research evidence for the use of music in Alzheimer's dementia. J. Gerontol. Nurs. **34**(10), 45–52 (2008)

Gill, L.M., Englert, N.C.: A music intervention's effect on falls in a dementia unit. J. Nurse Pract. **9**, 562–567 (2013)

Tina, J., Wolfram, D.: Internet searching, tablet technology and older adults. Proc. Am. Soc. Inf. Sci. Technol. **49**(1), 1–3 (2012)

Walker, C.: Mobility in elderly assessed with iPad. Video animation tool could lead to 'activity prescriptions' [Web log post] (2011)

Barenbrock, A., Herrlich, M., Malaka, R.: Design lessons from mainstream motion-based games for exergames for older adults (2014)

Ijsselsteijn, W., Nap, H.H., de kort, Y., Poels, K.: Digital game design for elderly users (2007)

Louie, W.-Y.G., McColl, D., Nejat, G.: Playing a memory game with a socially assistive robot: a case study at a long-term care facility (2012)

Ishihara, K., Ishihara, S., Nagamachi, M., Hiramatsu, S., Osaki, H.: Age-related decline in color perception and difficulties with daily activities-measurement, questionnaire, optical and computer-graphics simulation studies. Int. J. Ind. Ergon. **28**, 153–163 (2001)

Katie, A., Siek, S.E., Ross, D.U.K., Leah, M., Haverhals, S.R.C., Meyers, J.: Colorado Care Tablet: The design of an interoperable Personal Health Application to help older adults with multimorbidity manage their medications. J. Biomed. Inf. (2010)

Demiris, G., Finkelstein, S.M., Speedie, S.M.: Considerations for the design of a Webbased clinical monitoring and educational system for elderly patients. J. Am. Med. Inf. Assoc. **8**(5), 468–472 (2001)

Applying Usability Test to Find the Interface Design Principle of HRV Device for Senior Users

Hsin-Chang Lo[1(✉)], I-Jen Sung[2], and Yu-Ting Lin[1]

[1] Department of Product Design, Ming Chuan University, Taoyuan, Taiwan
lohc@mail.mcu.edu.tw, yuting8312@gmail.com
[2] Department of Innovation Design Engineering,
National Kaohsiung First University of Science and Technology,
Kaohsiung, Taiwan
jourdan@nkfust.edu.tw

Abstract. Home use medical device industry prospers due to the ageing society. In both physiological and psychological domain, home use medical devices have received much attention in recent years. Seniors usually feel depressed or anxious because of losing health and living abilities. They can use the heart rate variability (HRV) device in analyzing their emotional response, however the interface of commercial HRV devices are not easy for them to operate. Therefore, the usability test of these devices was introduced for the senior users. Five senior user were recruited to conduct usability test of the two commercial HRV devices: ANSWatch (Taiwan Scientific Corp.) and Check-MyHeart Handheld HRV (DailyCare BioMedical Inc.) follow the typical operation task. Then the in-depth interview were conducted to find operational failure factors. All of senior users indicated that the serious failure factors are: "unable to understand English instructions" and "unable to determine the meaning of illustration". Four of them indicated that the minor ones are: "no appropriate guide"; "text is too small"; and "layout is not appropriate". Three of them indicated that "illustration surface reflection" is another problem. Therefore, we suggests that the home use HRV device interface design should consider principles such as (1) the language and icon properties, (2) step guides and text properties, (3) consistency of interface configuration, (4) color scheme to improve the operational satisfaction for the senior users.

Keywords: Usability test · Home use medical device · Heart rate variability

1 Introduction

With rapid development of technology, people's life becomes more complicated and changeful. The changes in life may easily disjoin the life of older adults to the environment, making them feel anxious. Older adults with anxiety disorders tend to have high rates of depression. Anxiety also is highly comorbid with medical illness in older populations. These comorbidities can make differential diagnosis difficult as the symptoms overlap heavily and may also lead to underdiagnosis of anxiety disorders [1].

© Springer International Publishing Switzerland 2015
C. Stephanidis (Ed.): HCII 2015 Posters, Part I, CCIS 528, pp. 305–310, 2015.
DOI: 10.1007/978-3-319-21380-4_52

Therefore, the self-emotional management product is important for the older adults. Many studies have suggested that physiological signal, such as electrocardiography (ECG), when accompanied with heart rate variability (HRV) analysis technique, can be applied in analyzing personal emotional response [2]. HRV refers to the variation of heartbeat intervals, which allows people to know how heart rate is affected by the constant coactions of sympathetic and parasympathetic influence. This technology can in term reveal information concerning autonomic flexibility, which is a key factor for estimating a person's emotional control ability. Many portable medical devices using HRV technology have been proposed, so that the users can manage their emotion easily [3, 4]. However, these devices are not designed specifically for the older population.

For the user who is not the intended target user of the product, some difficulties may arise during operation, especially when the user is older adults. Moreover, many older user maybe be afraid that their misoperation may damage the products, thus the will-ingness to use new products with complex functions is lower. The older adults often feel perplexed when facing technological products [5]. In addition, visual degeneration, which is a common problem to older adults, causes difficulties in seeing the operation interface of the products. The deteriorating finger sensitivity may cause difficulty for them to operate small buttons [6]. Some studies have proposed that usability evaluation is an useful approach to assist find operational problem when operating medical devices [7, 8], especially for the older adults [9]. In recent years, the usability evaluation has been adopted to evaluate the operational behavior of medical device interface. In this user-based evaluation procedure, the user is asked to complete the typical operating process of the device, while the researcher observes and records the mistakes made by the users or the hesitation encountered by the users. Thus, the defects in design can be identified, and the probability of misoperation can be reduced. Therefore, this study aims at the usability of home-use medical device interface, and uses HRV device as an example to propose a principle of interface design suitable for the senior users.

2   Method

2.1   Subjects

This study recruited 5 (Mean = 68.0, SD = 4.36) seniors to participate in the usability evaluation. The inclusion criteria were (1) being literate, (2) able to independent and self-living, and (3) have experience in operating home-use medical devices independ-ently (e.g. blood pressure meter, blood glucose meter, etc.) (Table 1).

Table 1. Basic data of subjects

No	Sex	Age	Experience in home-use medical devices	Presbyopia
1	Female	67	Blood pressure meter/5 years	Yes
2	Male	64	Blood pressure meter/6 years	No
3	Female	69	Blood pressure meter/2 years	Yes
4	Male	65	Blood glucose meter/10 years	Yes
5	Male	75	Blood glucose meter and Blood pressure meter/10 years	Yes

2.2   Instrumentation

The experimental devices were ANSWatch[®] (Taiwan Scientific Corp.) [3] and CheckMyHeart Handheld HRV (DailyCare BioMedical Inc.) [4] (Table 2; Fig. 1).

Table 2. Specification of experimental HRV devices

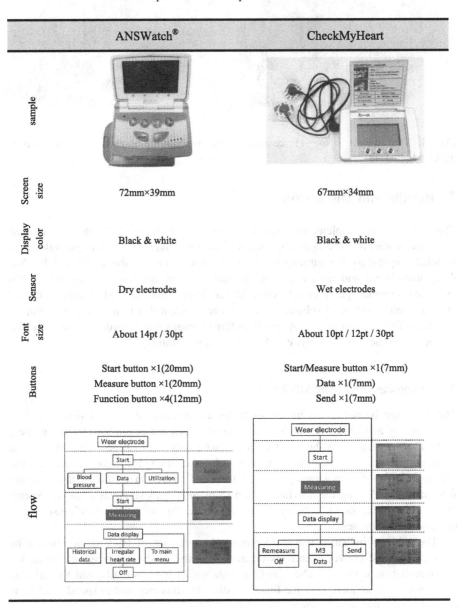

	ANSWatch[®]	CheckMyHeart
sample		
Screen size	72mm×39mm	67mm×34mm
Display color	Black & white	Black & white
Sensor	Dry electrodes	Wet electrodes
Font size	About 14pt / 30pt	About 10pt / 12pt / 30pt
Buttons	Start button ×1(20mm) Measure button ×1(20mm) Function button ×4(12mm)	Start/Measure button ×1(7mm) Data ×1(7mm) Send ×1(7mm)
flow		

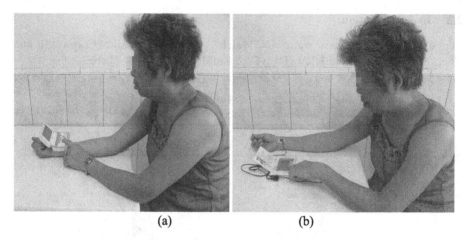

(a)   (b)

Fig. 1. The subject (No. 1) conducted the usability evaluation. (a) ANSWatch; (b) CheckMyHeart

3   Results and Discussion

The five subjects completed the usability evaluation of the two HRV devices. In their view, the problems in the operating process were most likely to occur in the followings (brackets represents the number of subjects who agreed to the item): the English description is not understood (5 subjects) and the icon meaning is unknown (5 subjects); no operation guide (4 subjects), the text is too small to read (4 subjects), poor interface configuration (4 subjects); the icons are unclear due to interface reflection (3 subjects). The opinion agreed by less than three persons was regarded as non-essential operational issue in this study, excluded from discussion.

3.1   Language and Icon Attributes

The language barrier is an important factor in product interface design. The two commercially available HRV devices used in this study are in English. It may not be a problem to general users, but for the elderly who only read Chinese had difficulty in completing the tasks as they did not understand the operating instructions. According to our interview, different languages result in users' operation mistakes, thus causing frustration [5]. Among the interface button icons of "CheckMyHeart", "M" represents "record" function, but the subjects did not associate "M" with "Memory", resulting in operational difficulties.

The subjects indicated that the icons on the interface of HRV device should be larger, and must convey meanings clearly. In terms of the meanings of icons, the interface button icons of "ANSWatch" are shown as four footballs, and the subjects could not associate them with the functions directly, thus they had to spend much time on identifying the button functions.

3.2   Step Tips and Word Level Attribute

Both the "ANSWatch" and "CheckMyHeart" do not provide step guide, but provide good auditory feedback, allowing the users to complete the tasks. However, the subjects indicated that they need appropriate tips to help them operating an unfamiliar technological (medical) product. If there were no operation guide or feedback tips in operation, they could not complete the tasks easily [5, 10].

The subjects suggested that the words in the interface should be larger, and the word meanings should be simple and clarified. The smallest font on the "Check My Heart" screen was about 10 pt, and they need to wear presbyopia glasses to read the text. Thus, "the text is too small to read" is the important factor failing their operation.

3.3   Interface Configuration Consistency

The subjects indicated that the operation interface is easy to operate when it has high consistency. The results of this study showed that "ANSWatch" uses football icons (incomprehensible) as controllers (buttons). The subjects had to spend much time on thinking about the meanings of the icons for the first operation. However, the "ANSWatch" interface has higher space consistency, meaning each football icon corresponds to an operating function, and there are acoustic and animated operation feedbacks to the subjects. Once the subjects recognized the meaning of football button, the following tasks were easy to complete. In addition, the button position and spacing were important factors influencing the subjects' operation [6]. According to the subjects' operational behavior, when they operated the commercially available HRV device with both hands, the buttons located below the screen could present their hands from covering the screen in operation. When the subjects operated buttons with their thumbs, the buttons should be separated from each other appropriately to avoid misoperation.

3.4   Interface Color Matching

The subjects indicated that the dark gray icons in the grayish background of the operation interface of "CheckMyHeart" were difficult to see. The icons were covered with bright membrane which reflects light, making it difficult for the subjects to see the button icons clearly. Therefore, the button icons should avoid using analogous colors or materials that reflect light.

4   Conclusion

This study tested the elderly on the operation of two types of home-use HRV device to analyze the product usability. The results revealed several operating problems in practical use: (1) English description is not understood, (2) icon meaning is unknown, (3) no operation guide, (4) text is too small to read, (5) poor interface configuration, (6) icons are illegible due to interface reflection. Therefore, this study suggests that the future interface design for hand-held home-use medical devices should consider (1) language barrier and icon attribute, (2) step tips and word level attribute, (3) interface configuration consistency, (4) interface color matching. The improved design to enhance the user satisfaction.

Acknowledgement. The authors appreciate Chen Ying-Hsiu and the participation of senior users. This work was sponsored under grant NSC 100-2632-H-130-001-MY2 by the National Science Council, Taiwan.

References

1. Wolitzky-Taylor, K.B., Castriotta, N., Lenze, E.J., Stanley, M.A., Craske, M.G.: Anxiety disorders in older adults: a comprehensive review. Depress. Anxiety **27**, 190–211 (2010)
2. McCraty, R., Atkinson, M., Tomasino, D., Stuppy, W.P.: Analysis of twenty-four hour heart rate variability in patients with panic disorder. Biol. Psychol. **56**, 131–150 (2001)
3. http://www.sunscientific.com/ANSWatch-Pro.html
4. http://www.dcbiomed.com/webls-en-us/Handheld-HRV.html
5. Hickman, J.M., Rogers, W.A., Fisk, A.D.: Training older adults to use new technology. J. Gerontol. Ser. B-Psychol. Sci. Soc. Sci. **62**, 77–84 (2007)
6. Dall, P.M., Kerr, A.: Frequency of the sit to stand task: An observational study of free living adults. Appl. Ergon. **41**, 58–61 (2010)
7. Demiris, G., Rantz, M., Aud, M., Marek, K., Tyrer, H., Skubic, M., Hussam, A.: Older adults attitudes towards and perceptions of smart home technologies: a pilot study. Med. Inform. Internet Med. **29**, 87–94 (2004)
8. Ehmen, H., Haesner, M., Steinke, I., Dorn, M., Gövercin, M., Steinhagen-Thiessen, E.: Comparison of four different mobile devices for measuring heart rate and ECG with respect to aspects of usability and acceptance by older people. Appl. Ergon. **43**, 582–587 (2012)
9. Lo, H.C., Tsai, C.L., Lin, K.P., Chuang, C.C., Chang, W.T.: Usability evaluation of home-use glucose meters for senior users. In: Stephanidis, C. (ed.) HCII 2014, Part II. CCIS, vol. 435, pp. 424–429. Springer, Heidelberg (2014)
10. Rubin, J., Chisnell, D., Spool, J.: Handbook of Usability Testing: How to Plan, Design, and Conduct Effective Tests, 2nd edn. Wiley, New York (2008)

Experiences of Older Patients with Multiple Chronic Conditions in the Intensive Ambulatory Care Home Telehealth Program

Rony Oosterom-Calo[1](✉), Kyle Vice[2], and Michael Breslow[3]

[1] Philips Research North America, Briarcliff Manor, USA
rony.calo@philips.com
[2] Philips Design, Andover, USA
[3] Philips HealthTech, Andover, USA

Abstract. Aim: A study was conducted to explore the experiences of older patients with chronic conditions in a home telehealth program, Philips' Intensive Ambulatory Care (IAC) at Banner Health in Phoenix AZ, which targets complex chronic patients. Methods: A purposive sampling approach was followed. The number of participants in the sample depended on data saturation. Interviews were conducted at participants' homes and audio recorded. Interviews were transcribed and the text was analyzed. An inductive approach to the analysis was adopted, whereby explanations and patterns were sought with a bottom-up approach. Specifically, first, codes were identified and created. Then, data (text) was assigned to codes. The emerging themes were captured. Results: Patients (N = 16) named benefits to being in the IAC program, including staying out of the hospital, feeling safe and having an increased peace of mind, practical and emotional support, and usefulness of the services provided within the program (e.g. pharmacological services, social work). Participants described many benefits of the program in comparison to their previous care, including reduced time to get an answer to a medical issue, increased access to doctors, better communication with medical staff, less travel time to receive care and more personal attention. Patients indicated that their experiences in the program change over time. Starting out, they experience confusion relating to new services, technologies and care professionals, which subsides over time. Many participants appreciated the support provided by professionals within the program. Most participants also accepted the technology and could easily use it, although for a minority of participants technology use and attitudes towards technology remain a challenge to adequate program engagement. Conclusion: Patients perceive many benefits to being in an intensive ambulatory home telehealth program and have in general positive experiences with it. Challenges include acclimating to telehealth and, for some patients, technology adoption and use.

Keywords: Telehealth · Experiences · Acceptance · Chronic disease management

C. Stephanidis (Ed.): HCII 2015 Posters, Part I, CCIS 528, pp. 311–316, 2015.
DOI: 10.1007/978-3-319-21380-4_53

1   Introduction

The Intensive Ambulatory Care (IAC) program at Banner Health in Arizona is a pilot program targeting complex patients with multiple chronic conditions. The program includes a multi-disciplinary care team of physicians, nurses, pharmacists, social workers, and health coaches monitoring patients at home. The program also includes the use of wireless vital sign measurement devices and a tablet computer for sharing information with patients and for video-based communication. The pilot has been ongoing since 2013 Care within IAC spans the medical as well as the psycho-social domains. The aim of the current study was to investigate the experiences of patients within the IAC program.

The experiences of patients within the home telehealth program were important to understand for three reasons. First, the IAC care delivery model is likely new to all of the included patients. Patients within the IAC program have relatively frequent contact with a multitude of care professionals who have different roles relating to patients' health management. In addition, patients within IAC are expected to pro-actively manage their health with the use of the technology set up in their homes. It was important to explore the experiences of patients with which these unique aspects in order to uncover the extent to may be perceived as helpful or unhelpful, useful, understandable and desirable and why this may be the case. Second, the program participants are older patients with multiple chronic conditions, who might have little to no experience using technologies such as those that are provided within the program. Acceptance of a new technology by the intended users (i.e., interest and willingness to use it), has been found to be imperative for successful dissemination of the technology in practice (Or and Karsh 2009). It has been found that among older adults there is a "digital divide", implying that many older adults are not likely to accept new technologies (Mitzner et al. 2010). Within a home telehealth program, it is assumed that if patients do not accept the technologies provided to them, they may reject the program altogether, which is likely to affect retention rates. In order to increase retention to the program, it is therefore imperative to understand patients' acceptance of the technologies. Finally, the program's efficacy is dependent on adequate patient engagement. Patients need to adequately utilize the program, including adequate contact with professionals and technology use. In order to optimize patient engagement in the program, it was necessary to understand patients' perspectives in relation to their engagement and uncover the reasons to why potential engagement-related issues occur.

2   Method

Sampling and Recruitment. A purposive sampling approach was used, starting with a recruitment of five patients and then adding more patients to the sample until data saturation was reached, in order to achieve maximum variation in the sample and ensure that different groups of patients are represented. Specifically, both female as well as male patients, patients who have been in the program <2 months, between 2 and 6 months, between 7 and 11 months, and >12 months, and patients living alone as well as those with a partner were recruited. IAC health coaches were asked to select participants that they thought were able to participate in interviews and ask during their visits with the patients if they were willing to participate.

Procedure. The researcher called patients that agreed to participate to set an appointment for the interview. Patients signed an informed consent when agreeing to participate in the IAC pilot. The semi-structured interviews were conducted in patients' homes by one or two researchers, were audio recorded and transcribed. A pre-defined semi-structured interview guide was used.

Analysis. Data was analyzed according to the grounded theory approach, which postulates that data collection and analysis are interrelated, and the analysis of the first interviews directs the analysis of the following interviews. An inductive approach to the analysis was adopted, whereby explanations and patterns were sought with a bottom-up approach. This approach also allows insight into data saturation. The data analysis process included the following qualitative data analysis steps: First, codes were identified and created by assigning codes to chunks of data. Then, data (text) was assigned to codes. The emerging themes were captured. Finally, codes were sorted into categories, in an iterative process. This coding process was first completed for the interview transcripts separately (open coding), then a process of axial coding was initiated, where material from the transcripts were related and compared.

3   Results

The interviews included a total of 16 participants, of which 9 were male and 7 were female (Table 1). Four participants were living alone and 12 with a partner. Participants described many benefits of the program in comparison to their previous care, and indicated that their experiences in the program change over time, as they felt confused at the beginning, but gained confidence over time.

Percieved Benefits. Patients named the following benefits to being in the IAC program, including (1) staying out of the hospital: Some of the participants remarked that they recognized that being in the program keeps them out of the hospital, due to the frequent contact with them and to monitoring their symptoms. (2) Most patients remarked that being in the program makes them feel safe and have an increased peace of mind. They indicated that the fact that they can call the telehealth center at any time, and have access to doctors if necessary, makes them feel more secure. (3) Practical and emotional support: many patients, especially those that indicated having less support structures, indicated that the home visits by the health coaches makes them feel supported. For the minority of patients that also used the social work services offered within the program, being visited at home by the social worker made them feel supported. Patients that also act as caregivers for their partners (who are more ill then they are) remarked that being in the program supports them by sharing the decision making around their partners' healthcare. Many patients remarked that the health coaches help them with practical issues. (4) Many patients remarked that the services in the program are useful to them and they appreciated them. Patients indicated their appreciation of specific services based on their own needs.

Table 1. Participant characteristics

Participant number/gender	Time in IAC program	Living alone/living with partner
1. Male	10 months	Living with partner
2. Female	10 months	Living with partner
3. Female	12 months	Living with partner
4. Male	12 months	Living with partner
5. Female	12 months	Living with partner
6. Male	12 months	Living with partner
7. Female	4 months	Living with partner
8. Male	4 months	Living with partner
9. Female	>12 months	Living with partner
10. Male	>12 months	Living with partner
11. Male	1.5 month	Living with partner
12. Female	>12 months	Living alone
13. Male	2 months	Living alone
14. Male	1 month	Living with partner
15. Female	12 months	Living alone
16. Male	~1.5 month	Living alone
N = 16 N male = 9 N female = 7	>=12 months = 9 11-6 months = 3 6-2 months = 4 <2 months = 2	Living with partner = 12 Living alone = 4

Experiences When Starting Out in the Program. Many patients remarked that starting out in the program is associated with confusion, due to the multitude of new services being offered as part of the program, which they were not used to receiving before joining the program. They explained that it took them time (most remarked that it takes about a month) to understand the different program services and how to use the telehealth devices that were set up in their homes.

Experiences Over Time. Over time, many members indicated that they became more confident in in their engagement with the professionals and technology within IAC. Many mentioned that they grew to trust the professionals and rely on them for support. Many patients knew many of the healthcare professionals from the telehealth center by name and mentioned their appreciation of the staff. However, some members still exhibited misconceptions relating to how to adequately engage in the IAC program, including incorrect use of the technology and misunderstandings of what services to expect and how to use them. Although most patients demonstrated they could use the technology, and remarked that after using it for some time they learned how to use it and do not experience many problems, some of the members displayed negative attitudes towards using the technology, especially the tablet computer.

4 Discussion

It is important to understand the experiences of patients within telehealth programs because negative experiences can lead to (1) lower adherence to the program and hence a lower program effectiveness, and (2) program drop-out. This includes their use of, and attitudes towards, the technology that is part of such a program, because most patients are older and are likely to have limited experience with such technologies. If users do not accept a technology, they may reject it and not use it. Within a telehealth program, it is crucial that patients use the technologies provided to them, in order for the program to be successful. The results of this qualitative study suggest that many older patients within a home telehealth program are willing and able to use the technologies that are offered to them. However, a minority of patients demonstrate difficulties in using the technology as well as negative attitudes towards it, even after having experience within the telehealth program.

It has been suggested that when introducing technologies to healthcare environments, it is important to keep the contact and support of the healthcare professionals (Oosterom-Calo et al. 2014; Sanders et al. 2012). This contact may be important to patients who may reject programs that include only technological aspects, and do not provide opportunities for contact and support from healthcare professionals. The results of the current study is in line with this, as the majority of the patients in the study stressed the importance of the contact with the professionals, and the trust they felt towards them, to their experiences of the program, including their feelings of peace of mind resulting from having professionals they trust watch over them and support them.

In the current study it was found that patients' experiences change over time within a telehealth program. Based on the results, it is recommended that efforts are made to help patients understand how to adequately engage in the program and support them and raise their confidence to use the technology. In addition, it is recommended that, over time, information is repeated and knowledge is reinforced.

Finally, the current qualitative work provided in-depth insight about patient experiences with the IAC program. However, it included a small and unrepresentative sample size, which does not allow making conclusions about the extent to which the observed results are representative of the entire IAC patient population.

References

Mitzner, T.L., Boron, J.B., Fausset, C.B., Adams, A.E., Charness, N., Czaja, S.J., Dijkstra, K., Fisk, A.D., Rogers, W.A., Sharit, J.: Older adults talk technology: technology usage and attitudes. Comput. Hum. Behav. **26**(6), 1710–1721 (2010)

Oosterom-Calo, R., Abma, T.A., Visse, M.A., Stut, W., te Velde, S.J., Brug, J.: An interactive-technology health behavior promotion program for heart failure patients: a pilot study of experiences and needs of patients and nurses in the hospital setting. JMIR Res. Protoc. **3**(2), e32 (2014)

Or, C.K., Karsh, B.-T.: A systematic review of patient acceptance of consumer health information technology. J. Am. Med. Inform. Assoc. **16**(4), 550–560 (2009)

Sanders, C., Rogers, A., Bowen, R., Bower, P., Hirani, S., Cartwright, M., Fitzpatrick, R., Knapp, M., Barlow, J., Hendy, J., Chrysanthaki, T., Bardsley, M., Newman, S.P.: Exploring barriers to participation and adoption of telehealth and telecare within the whole system demonstrator trial: a qualitative study. BMC Health Serv. Res. **12**(1), 220 (2012)

The Speech Recognition Ability for Different Age Groups on the Chinese Language System

Linghua Ran[1(✉)], Ling Luo[2], Xin Zhang[1], Taijie Liu[1], and Chaoyi Zhao[1]

[1] Ergonomics Laboratory, China National Institute of Standardization, Beijing 100191, China
{ranlh, Zhangx, liutj, zhaochy}@cnis.gov.cn
[2] China Standard Certification Co. Ltd., Beijing 100088, China
luoling@csc.org.cn

1 Introduction

Public address system can provide useful information for the audience, which are especially important at the railway station or the subway station. Effective public address can offer help to evacuate people at these places.

At present, most speech recognition researches are to predict and assess effects of hearing devices, to do relevant medical legal identification and evaluate the injury degree with low hearing function. In China, large public places basically broadcast through functional address system. It is very important for the public barrier free design to try to take the old people into account.

2 Experimental Method

2.1 Experiment Design

The experiment is conducted in the anechoic room of ergonomics laboratory. The audio files are the length of each sentence is about 4 s, the fade in and out time of each sentence is about 0.15 s and the interval of word front and back is 0.2 s and 0.3 s respectively.

44 subjects were divided into the old group and the young group. The young group includes 21 subjects with the average age of 25.4, and the old group includes 22 subjects with the average of 62.3.

2.2 Experimental Method

The speech recognition experiment adopts the method of subjective assessment of the public sound system [1]. The experiment is divided into two tests. The first one is the hearing level, and after that is the speech recognition test.

© Springer International Publishing Switzerland 2015
C. Stephanidis (Ed.): HCII 2015 Posters, Part I, CCIS 528, pp. 317–320, 2015.
DOI: 10.1007/978-3-319-21380-4_54

Table 1. Definition of difficulty degree

Degree of difficulty	Degree of difficulty
1	Not difficulty
2	Slightly difficult
3	Moderate difficult
4	Very difficult

The hearing level test is to measure the hearing threshold of subjects to guarantee that their hearing belongs to the normal range of their age (Table 1).

3   Experiment Results and Discussion

3.1   Hearing Level

The hearing level test showed that the hearing attenuation of Chinese young group and the old group have no significant frequency differences with the data according to the international standards of ISO 7029 [2], except in the frequency of 1000 Hz and 4000 Hz for the old group.

3.2   Speech Recognition Threshold

Under the same 50 dB environmental noise, both for the young group and for the old group, a single factor analysis was conducted and there was a significant difference between the two kinds of voices for the two age groups. It is showed in Figs. 1 and 2 that under the same noisy environment, the threshold value of male voice is lower than that of female voice in the both young and old groups. It can be seen that threshold value for the old group for the male voice is lower than to the female voice.

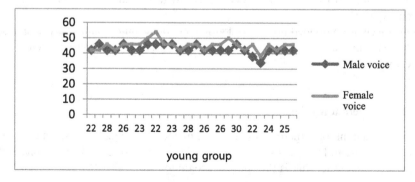

Fig. 1. The speech recognition threshold of the young group under 50 dB environmental noise

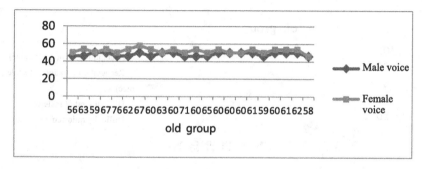

Fig. 2. The speech recognition threshold of the old group under 50 dB environmental noise

Under the same 50 dB environmental noise, the average speech recognition threshold value for the young group to the male voice is 43 dB and the signal noise ratio is −7 dB while the average value to the female voice is 45 dB and the signal noise ratio is −5 dB. The average speech recognition threshold value for the old group to the male voice is 48 dB and the signal noise ratio is −2 dB while the average value to the female voice is 52 dB and the signal noise ratio is 2 dB. So under the same noisy environment, the signal noise ratio should be at least 2 dB to make sure that more than 50 % people can identify the language correctly.

3.3 The Relationship Between Speech Recognition Score and the Signal Noise Ratio

The speech recognition score refers to the percentage of the speech signals heard and understood by subjects. The hearing loss caused by the age influences the speech recognition score, which is a function of the signal noise ration.

From the Fig. 3, it could be found that when the signal noise ratio reaches 4 dB, the accuracy of the young group to words recognition exceeds 90 % and has no obvious

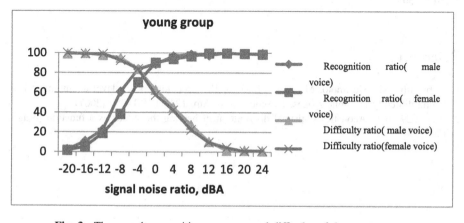

Fig. 3. The speech recognition accuracy and difficulty of the young group

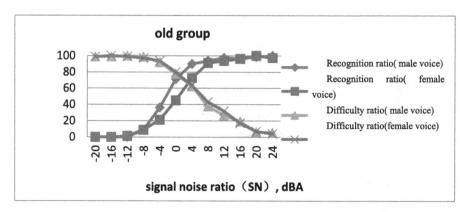

Fig. 4. The speech recognition accuracy and difficulty of the old group

change. When the signal noise ratio is under −4 dB, the difficulty of target words is over 80 % When the signal noise ratio reaches 8 dB and $F(2, 35) = 2.111$, there is no significant difference in statistics for the young group.

From the Fig. 4, it could be found that when the signal noise ratio of the old group reaches over 8 dB, their accuracy to words recognition is over 90 % and has no significant change. For the old group, when the signal noise ratio reaches 12 dB and $F(2, 37) = 2.408$, there is no significant difference in statistics.

When the environmental noise is 50 dB, in order to meet the requirements of speech recognition of the young people and to let the old people gain better hearing effects, in the sound pressure level design of audio equipment the signal noise ratio should reach 12 dB to make sure that most people can hear harmonious and beautiful sound level.

Acknowledgment. This work is supported by the National Key Technology R&D Program (project number: 2012BAK28B03-2) and China National Institute of Standardization through the "special funds for the basic R&D undertakings by welfare research institutions" (project number: 522013Y-3055).

References

1. Kobayashi, M., Morimoto, M., Sato, H., Sato, H.: Optimum speech level to minimize listening difficulty in public spaces. J. Acoust. Soc. Am. **121**(1), 251–256 (2007)
2. ISO 7029:2000: Acoustics statistical distribution of hearing thresholds as a function of age (2000)

Family Channel: Accessible Social Media for Older Adults

Christopher Romanyk[1], Pejman Salehi[1]([⊠]), Joseph Sant[1],
Lia Tsotsos[2], and Ricardo Chavez[1]

[1] School of Applied Computing,
Sheridan Institute of Technology and Advanced Learning, Oakville, Canada
{christopher.romanyk,pejman.salehi,
joe.sant,derricoc}@sheridancollege.ca
[2] Centre for Elder Research,
Sheridan Institute of Technology and Advanced Learning, Oakville, Canada
lia.tsotsos@sheridancollege.ca

Abstract. Isolation is a well-known problem amongst the elderly. This isolation might be ameliorated by engaging the elderly in social media. Unfortunately, the devices most commonly used to access social media (PCs, tablets, and phones) might not be the most appropriate for this demographic. A more appropriate device might be television. Using modern technology, it is possible to aggregate specially tagged social media posts from friends and family and narrow-cast it to other family members. Our research involves creating a television-based social media channel that is appropriate for the elderly. We present our initial work which involves developing a proof-of-concept for the Family Channel and identifying user profiles for the 65+ demographic with respect to technology use.

Keywords: Human computer interaction · Aging · Social media

1 Introduction

There is rich literature showing that visual and temporal processing abilities decline with age [1]. Concurrently, real-time sources of online information (such as social network data feeds or news sites) are sharing increasingly large amounts of information, often in small, space- and time-delimited screens or windows. As a result, the user interface currently employed by the majority of web-based real-time information services may not be suitable for older adults.

Our research has explored the ways in which older adults (65+) relate to web-based technologies, focusing specifically on how their capacity for comprehension, recall and engagement is affected by two main elements: the physical features of the device and the way in which the information is presented, in terms of type, variation, frequency, and interval. This investigation into elder-focused usability resulted in the design and implementation of the Sheridan Family Channel. Using TV, a familiar technology for this age demographic, the Family Channel delivers content by aggregating feeds from social networks and news sites and presenting them on-screen in a manner that is more

© Springer International Publishing Switzerland 2015
C. Stephanidis (Ed.): HCII 2015 Posters, Part I, CCIS 528, pp. 321–326, 2015.
DOI: 10.1007/978-3-319-21380-4_55

comfortable and accessible for older adults. Consequently, this paper further investigates the need and effectiveness of employing traditional devices, including television, for new purposes, such as web-based technologies. Additionally, this paper determines how the presentation of content critically affects usability for older adults. Through our Family Channel system, subjects were presented with simulated data feeds using a number of different interface designs. Accordingly, this paper presents the results of this controlled evaluation and offers new research ideas for enhancing usability for older adults. The rest of the paper is organized as follows. In Sect. 2 we discuss the background and motivation behind our research. Section 3 the implementation of the family channel followed by our pilot testing in Sect. 4. Finally, we conclude the paper in Sect. 5.

2 Background and Motivation

The Family Channel is a traditional television channel that displays a feed aggregated from social media. Designed with older adults in mind, this platform allows us to investigate several key issues relating to aging, HCI and real-time information systems.

Population aging is a defining characteristic of the times in which we live. In 2011, an estimated five million Canadians were 65+; that number is expected to more than double to 10.4 million by 2036. By 2051, about one in four Canadians is expected to be 65+ [2]. This demographic shift will have implications for many service delivery platforms, especially those that are technological in nature. Research has shown that the quality of life of older adults may be positively impacted by Information and Communications Technology (ICT) use [3], potentially through improved social support and psycho-social well-being [4–6]. Other research indicates that many older adults remain somewhat reluctant to adopt some new technology [7]. Blaschke and colleagues [8] identified the following barriers to technology use: age-related issues (health, mobility, and cognitive changes), characteristics of existing technologies, attitudinal issues, financial issues, and training and support issues. As of 2006 [9] 33 % of Canadians 65+ actively lived with a mobility related disability. The Family Channel as a platform was designed to be a passive interface. Currently access to social media site including Facebook or Twitter is gained through interfaces which require user actions such as scrolling or typing, this can present significant problems for persons with disabilities.

Older adults experience a number of significant changes in their lives that can also impact their level of engagement with technology, and by extension, with their peers. Retirement, changes in health or marital status or financial stresses may impact active engagement in the community and can lead to loneliness. Research has shown that loneliness can be as harmful to our health and quality of life as smoking 15 cigarettes a day [10].

Social isolation can be defined as "a state in which the individual lacks a sense of belonging socially, lacks engagement with others, has a minimal number of social contacts and they are deficient in fulfilling and quality relationships" [11]. Simon et al. [12] also suggest that intense feelings of emptiness, loneliness, abandonment, and forlornness are linked to an insufficient quality or quantity of an individual's network of social relationships. Studies of the prevalence of social isolation in community-dwelling older adults indicate that it could be as high as 43 %, [13, 14]. While connecting to social networks may alleviate loneliness and social isolation, the need to access them through the most common technologies may present a barrier. By circumventing the need to actively engage with technologies that may be difficult, unpleasant or impossible to learn, the Family Channel can still provide a way for older adults to combat loneliness and social isolation.

In the 2013–2014 Report on the Social Isolation of Seniors released by the National Seniors Council (NSC) [15], the NSC recommended that the federal government encourage a culture of social innovation by building the capacity of organizations to address isolation of older adults through social innovation. What better way to achieve this goal than to leverage one of the most ubiquitous and well-understood technologies available – the television?

3 Implementation

The Family Channel is built as a television channel optimized for delivery on set-top boxes. The Channel crawls posts generated from varied social media sites and curates them in a manner appropriate for our target audience and delivery platform. The crawling process searches social media accounts of a specific group or "Family". Posts that are tagged with specific hashtags for example #forgrandfather are captured and stored for later display (Fig. 1).

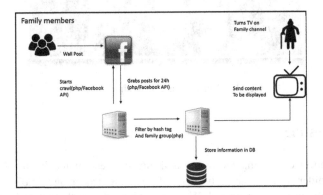

Fig. 1. The high level overview of the family channel process

Two distinct interfaces were designed. One interface closely modeled the conditions found on any number of social media websites including Facebook and Twitter. Multiple content types including, text, images, lengthy and short posts would be presented at seemingly random intervals in two separate on-screen windows and new content would generate asynchronously (Fig. 2). This would mimic the type of environment one might find on a Facebook news feed or a Twitter feed. The second interface is modeled after a more traditional medium, the television (Fig. 3).

This interface would place content in a more traditional display environment with controlled expected re-generation rates (30 s) and a singular focus (i.e. only one piece of information at a time).

Fig. 2. User interface with multiple content

Fig. 3. User interface with single content

4   Pilot Testing

As a first step in evaluating the utility and effectiveness of the Family Channel, we recruited 12 older adults between the ages of 70 and 86 (mean age 77.67; 8 females) to complete a pilot test of the Channel. We were interested in both gaining feedback about the Channel from the anticipated user group and also exploring how other factors (including cognition, dexterity, levels of technology use and perceived loneliness) might interact with perceptions about the utility of the Channel and inform improvements to the interface.

After providing informed consent (this study was approved by the Sheridan Research Ethics Board), participants completed a battery of surveys and assessments that included the following: a Participant History questionnaire (demographic information and self-reported levels of television use); the Purdue Pegboard Test (manual dexterity) [16]; the Trail Making Test (visual attention and task switching) [17];

a modified online Stroop test (measuring selective attention [18]); the UCLA Loneliness Scale (Version 3, measuring feelings of loneliness [19]); and lastly, a 'Technology Use' survey we designed that asked participants to rate how frequently they used various technology products and applications (ranging from TV, to digital cameras, various social media platforms and online sharing tools such as DropBox). Scores on this 'Technology Use' survey were totaled with higher numbers suggesting higher levels of 'tech savviness'.

Following this battery of surveys and tests, participants took time to sit and passively view the Family Channel, alternating between the two different interfaces described above. They were asked to share their feedback about the interface designs, the types of content presented and the feelings of connectedness that the Channel might inspire in them if the content were from their friends and family.

Demographically, this was a highly-educated, well-connected group of participants. They all reported using the internet for 5–10 years or more, and as a group, they were very interested in learning about (or adopting) new technologies. In general, they were relatively 'tech savvy', but we did notice a reduction in 'tech savviness' with increasing age; this coincided with an increase in loneliness scores with increasing age, as one would expect from the literature. Their feedback after viewing the interfaces shows good support for the Family Channel, with the majority of participants saying that this was an 'excellent' or 'great' idea that they could see themselves using, particularly if they were house-bound or living alone. This aligns with the original goal of the Family Channel, confirming its utility. The group was split between preferring the single or multiple-content interfaces, but some suggested that while they enjoyed the multiple content now, they would likely only want the single content in the future, or would want to be able to choose depending on how they felt. This could be because they believe family would become more important to them as they age, or, they are predicting cognitive changes in their ability to divide their attention effectively between the two rotating displays. Interestingly, we found a trend suggesting a relationship between participants' scores on the modified Stroop test and on our 'Technology Use' Survey; participants with greater difference scores on the Stroop Test (suggesting reduced selective attention skills) tended to be less 'tech savvy'. While we do not have the statistical power to make this claim definitively, it is interesting to speculate that in otherwise healthy older adults there may be a pre-clinical marker of cognitive decline, namely, rates of technology use.

5 Conclusion

The Family Channel was designed as a television-based alternative for viewing social media content from family and friends. Preliminary testing with the target group suggests that there is indeed interest in this idea, and that the single-content interface (which most closely mimics a traditional television channel) would be the most desired, particularly as the users age. Future work will more directly investigate the different parameters of the display itself (story refresh rate, font/image size, length of content, etc.) to determine the optimal settings for this demographic.

Acknowledgment. This work has been powered by the TELUS.

References

1. Richards, M., Touchon, J., Ledesert, B., Richie, K.: Cognitive decline in ageing: are AAMI and AACD distinct entities? Int. J. Geriatr. Psychiatry **14**(7), 534–540 (1999)
2. Human Resources and Skills Development Canada: Canadians in context – aging population. http://www4.hrsdc.gc.ca/.3ndic.1t.4r@-eng.jsp?iid=33. Accessed 28 Feb 2014
3. Eastman, J.K., Iyer, R.: The elderly's uses and attitudes towards the internet. J. Consum. Market. **21**(3), 208–220 (2004)
4. Adler, R.: Older Americans, broadband and the future of the net. SeniorNet (2006). www.observatory.gr/files/meletes/SeniorNetNNPaper060606.pdf
5. Czaja, S.J., Lee, C.C.: The impact of the internet on older adults. In: Charness, N., Schaie, K.W. (eds.) Impact of Technology on Successful Aging, pp. 113–133. Springer, New York (2003)
6. White, H., McConnell, E., Clipp, E., Branch, L.G., Sloane, R., Pieper, C., Box, T.L.: A randomized controlled trial of the psychosocial impact of providing internet training and access to older adults. Aging Ment. Health **6**(3), 213–221 (2002)
7. Charness, N., Boot, W.R.: Aging and information technology use: potential and barriers. Curr. Dir. Psychol. Sci. **18**(5), 253–258 (2009)
8. Blaschke, C.M., Freddolino, P.P., Mullen, E.E.: Ageing and technology: a review of the research literature. Br. J. Soc. Work **39**, 641–656 (2009)
9. Statistics Canada.: Canadian year book 2008 – limitations increase with age. http://www41.statcan.gc.ca/2008/70000/ceb70000_000-eng.htm
10. Holt-Lunstad, J., Smith, T.B., Layton, J.B.: Social relationships and mortality risk: a meta-analytic review. PLoS Med. **7**(7), e1000316 (2010). doi:10.1371/journal.pmed.1000316
11. Nicholson, N.: Social isolation in older adults: an evolutionary concept analysis. J. Adv. Nurs. **65**, 1342–1352 (2009)
12. Simon, M., Chang, E., Zhang, M., Ruan, J., Dong, X.: The prevalence of loneliness among U.S. Chinese older adults. J. Aging Health **26**, 1172–1188 (2014)
13. Nicholson, N., Molony, S., Fennie, K., Shellman, J., McCorkle, R.: Predictors of social isolation in community living older persons. Unpublished Ph.D., Yale University, New Haven, CT (2010)
14. Smith, T.F., Hirdes, J.P.: Predicting social isolation among geriatric psychiatry patients. Int. Psychogeriatr. **21**, 50–59 (2009)
15. Government of Canada: The National Seniors Council. Report on the Social Isolation of Seniors 2013–2014, Oct 2014
16. Lafeyette Instrument Company (LIC): Instructions and Normative Data For Purdue Pegboard 32020. LIC, Lafayette (1985). Purdue Pegboard
17. Strauss, E., Sherian, E.M.S., Spreen, O.: A Compendium of Neuropsychological Tests: Administration, Norms and Commentary, 3rd edn, pp. 655–677. Oxford University Press, New York (2006)
18. Chudler, E.H.: Neuroscience for kinds: colors, colors. https://faculty.washington.edu/chudler/words.html#seffect
19. Russel, D.W.: UCLA loneliness scale (version 3): reliability, validity and factor structure. J. Pers. Assess. **66**(1), 20–40 (1996)

Social Engagement in Elderly Care Homes: Towards Designing an Application to Reduce Social Loneliness

Jip ter Voort[1(✉)], Joey Radstaat[1], Marisse Douma[1], Laura Clarijs[1],
Roxanne Arnts[1], and Suleman Shahid[2]

[1] Department of Communication and Information Science,
Tilburg University, Tilburg, The Netherlands
{j.tervoort,j.a.radstaat,m.r.douma,l.e.h.clarijs,
r.arnts}@tilburguniversity.edu
[2] Tilburg Center for Cognition and Communication,
Department of Communication and Information Science,
Tilburg University, Tilburg, The Netherlands
s.shahid@uvt.nl

Abstract. This paper presents an application that is designed to reduce the loneliness of elderly and to support them in elderly care homes. The social application 'APPointment' allows users to plan social activities to undertake with fellows living within a closed community. The app was designed after conducting extensive user research and evaluation sessions with elderly. The results indicate that the target user group found the new app accessible, easy to use and most importantly quite effective in improving their social lives at the elderly care home.

Keywords: Elderly · Social loneliness · Social isolation · Application · Social engagement · Healthcare

1 Introduction

The population of elderly people, aged 65 or over, is increasing in western countries. The western world is also effected by the 'population ageing' phenomenon and as compared to the past more money is required for taking care of elderly [1]. On the contrary, most of the western countries are putting a cap on the health care and elderly care budgets. Due to budget cuts on health care programs in The Netherlands, inadequate budget is available for organizing activities for elderly, which dramatically decreases social interaction among elderly living in care homes. Besides, elderly experience the loss of loved ones and a decrease in their health, which increases social isolation even more and produces feelings of loneliness. Previous research [2] has shown that low levels of perceived social support are associated with increased depression, impaired immune functioning and reduced life expectancy. Enhancing elderly's social network appeared to be supportive in the reduction of social isolation and loneliness [3]. Most of the earlier research [4, 5] has focused on designing solutions for enabling elderly to establish connections outside an elderly care home

© Springer International Publishing Switzerland 2015
C. Stephanidis (Ed.): HCII 2015 Posters, Part I, CCIS 528, pp. 327–333, 2015.
DOI: 10.1007/978-3-319-21380-4_56

(e.g. with children or friends). Relatively less attention has been paid on designing solutions for elderly care homes, which help in strengthening social interaction among residents. The aim of this study is to design a social application for elderly living in different elderly care homes in the Netherlands in order to reduce their feelings of loneliness and improving their quality of life. The application was developed in an iterative manner. In the first phase, a number of user research sessions were conducted (both individual sessions and focus groups) at elderly care homes. After this, a number of early concepts were designed and tested with elderly. At the end a final working application was developed and tested with elderly in different elderly care homes. The rest of the paper describes this whole design process and key results.

2   User Research

A Context Inquiry (CI) was performed in order to understand users' requirement, their issues with loneliness, and their preferences on establishing social interaction with peers. The CI took place with a group of elderly in their natural context i.e. in an elderly care home after their weekly gymnastics class. The group consisted of eleven women and three men in the age of 67–83 years old. Their living situation, weekly activities, social needs and technology use were questioned in individual as well as focus group style interview sessions. Furthermore we also asked users to perform different tasks, primarily playful, on an iPad to get insights about their working knowledge of tablets and general experience with computers and technology.

Fig. 1. Focus group session

From the analysis of the interview it was concluded that the elderly are willing to meet other people of the same age and prefer interacting with people they already know. For example whenever they get a chance to meet other people e.g. during gymnastic classes they make sure that they do not miss any such opportunity as one user mentioned, "That is why we come here and work-out together, to see each other and drink a cup of coffee". They believe that better interaction with peers in an elderly care home could possibly be a solution for their social isolation. They like their activities to be planned at fixed times during the week and, if possible, to find a place in a community center. The users prefer activities like jeu de boule, socializing, bingo, having a stroll outside, grocery shopping, or visiting a museum. They think that organizing such activities with others, who experience similar feelings of loneliness, could increase social interaction. They were worried about the fact that as compared to the past the government is spending less money on improving their social lives. For example one participant mentioned it this way, "There are care centers that organize activities for people to undertake together, but you have to pay for it, and they are shutting them down! These centers should be maintained".

We also learnt that none of the elderly have a smartphone but a few elderly do use their mobile phone to get in touch with friends and children outside the elderly care homes. Generally, they use these phones for a single task i.e. dialing and receiving calls and are not very comfortable with these phones. Most of the users also mentioned that their children and grand children do visit them once in while. Most of them, especially females, would like to meet their children more often but they also understand that it is not always easy for their children. Therefore, they mentioned that improving their quality of life in the care homes is very important.

The users indicated that they are eager to learn about new technologies such as tablets and smartphones, hence using them on daily basis is considered a fun activity. They also mentioned that although they were not familiar with tablets, using a tablet does not look like a complicated job. Few users did face problems while interacting with the tablet e.g. unable to find the right button to navigate, confusing menu structures, and inability to press the buttons with right sensitivity.

3 Conceptual Design and Prototyping

The primary user requirements for the first idea of the application were deducted from user research. Based on the analysis of the CI, interviews and focus group interviews four essential parts were prominent: (1) elderly are willing to strengthen their ties with people they already know, (2) they have an interest in knowing what other people are doing (3) they like to engage in a wide range of social activities and (4) they like structure in their lives and would like these activities to be scheduled properly. With these core requirements in mind the first concept of 'APPointment' was created. This concept was refined with the aid of paper prototyping sessions and brief evaluations with elderly which yielded the final concept of 'APPointment'. This smartphone and tablet application allows users to plan new activities and join existing activities organized within one's own community in an orderly fashion with an easy to use interface that is adjusted to the elderly's needs. The application is supported by an interactive bulletin board located at a central point within the community. The mobile tablet application was designed for an iPad for the iOS platform. The interactive bulletin board is a browser-based application developed using HTML. This system was designed in such a way that it could not only be integrated within closed communities such as elderly homes or home care facilities, but could also be used to connect different elderly care homes or people living in the surrounding neighborhoods.

Fig. 2. Homescreen with eight categories

A paper prototype was designed and tested with participants who were above 75 years and most of them had participated in the user research sessions. We learnt that the contrast between pop-ups and the background should be substantial (more than the normal) for improving the reading quality. Second it was observed that a clear color scheme was needed so that people could relate colors with categories and recall them in a better way (see Fig. 1). Furthermore, these results indicate that a self-explanatory tutorial should be integrated under the help section. The 'help' option should be present in the application and should be visible on screen at all times. Based on these results a final working prototype was designed and developed. The final design included three major functional areas: (1) the home screen, (2) activity screens and (3) agenda screens. On the home screen, a category of activities can be selected (Fig. 2). These eight categories included amongst others shopping, eating, chatting and watching television. Touching one of these categories brings the user to the next screen where an overview of already planned activities can be found (Fig. 3). The user can choose to join an activity or create a new one within this category. The third screen includes an agenda overview of all the activities the user is planning to attend. An interactive bulletin board supports the system by establishing a central meeting point where users can meet and by showing upcoming activities and other relevant information like the weather.

The application is designed in such a way that the information conveyed by the interface itself is enough for the user to know what to do. While designing this app, special attention is paid on elderly's cognitive disabilities [6]. The structure of the application is very simple: a maximum two sub categories with a clear path to move back and an icon to go to the home screen. Large fonts, clear icons, big touch areas and a consistent color scheme were used throughout the application. The overall design is very minimalistic and only the most relevant information was presented at one time. To support the user in the navigation, a help button was integrated in every screen.

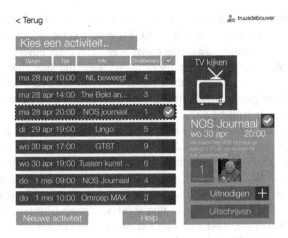

Fig. 3. Sub-screen to plan 'shopping' activities

4 Usability Evaluation

Fifteen residents of an elderly home in the age of 75–90 years old, without any severe cognitive disabilities and with very basic exposure to computers and tablets, participated in the evaluation phase. The 'APPpointment' app (both the tablet app and the interactive bulletin board) was evaluated in an elderly care home. The evaluation criteria were to (1) identify whether the usability of the application is sufficient for routine tasks, (2) do users find the app meaningful, (3) can users relate the solutions with their everyday problems of social isolation and (4) how can this app be improved both in terms of usability and new features. A task-based evaluation was conducted in which all users were asked to perform different tasks i.e. organizing new activities under different categories, joining existing activities, modifying activities and using help when stuck. Users were encouraged to think out loud during the tasks and we recorded all evaluation sessions for further analysis. Users who encountered difficulties while completing a particular task, either because of the lack of understanding or due to a usability problem, were assisted and users with a little experience with tablets were given a short tutorial.

The results indicate that the target user group found the new app accessible, efficient and most importantly quite effective in improving their social lives at the elderly care home. The results also showed that the 'APPointment' app has an understandable design with very good readability and all participants were able to understand the ecosystem of both apps. The overall concept of the app was evaluated positively and participants consider it an excellent addition to their lives especially for those times when they experience feelings of social loneliness. All participants mentioned that it was important to see what others are doing, which made it easier for them to join different activities now. They also thought that the bulletin board works as a center point and will play a major role in increasing social interaction. They also appreciated the ease with which activities could be arranged. For a future scenario, they also showed an interest in connecting the system with the outside world where other people (both familiar and may be unfamiliar) could join in for selected activities. For example one user said, "I would like to use the app, because I know people who live in the neighborhood (of the elderly care center), that way I can meet others (outside the care home) to undertake activities". The users appreciated the fact that the app brings structure to their lives and improves their social lives without overwhelming them with different unstructured possibilities. Finally users mentioned that the app would have a positive effect on their well-being.

It was often found that the lack of experience in using tablets created a number of usability issues. A few users, especially those who had not used a tablet before, were not only afraid of using the application but also overly sensitive and careful while touching the screen. We did not see any major issue with the structure of the app or with the labels but physical interaction was sometimes slow and hampered due to no prior experience. However, the user testing showed a steep learning curve once users got familiar with the application and with use of the iPad. Therefore, we believe that a proper tutorial and guided help in the beginning can not only improve the acceptability of an application but also improve the confidence level of elderly.

5   Conclusion and Future Work

This paper discussed the design of the 'APPointment' app, an application for elderly to plan and create activities to undertake with one another in an elderly care home. This study shows that elderly are worried about the issue of social loneliness, and appreciate the intention of our application to reduce loneliness and social isolation. Based on the early results, we conclude that the 'APPointment' presents a successful and accessible design for its target audience. Unlike former studies, this study integrates a social application in an existing community to strengthen social interaction among members. By taking a user centered approach during the development and thus making elderly part of the design process, valuable information was collected which led to an increased level of usability and acceptability of the final solution. The design of the application addresses the needs of the users in such a manner that even inexperienced users were able to schedule and join events. Unlike a number of previous applications, this application focused on designing the 'app ecosystem' i.e. a tablet app and a central interactive bulletin board which proved to be much more useful and user friendly in the elderly care home context. Finally the 'APPointment' app was not only appreciated by the actual users but also by the management of elderly care homes who liked the idea and showed an interest in installing such an app on a permanent basis.

A limitation of this study is that a small number of the user tests were conducted. In future we would like to run more evaluation sessions in different elderly care home in the Netherlands. Furthermore, we would like to test this application in a nursing home where elderly with more severe cognitive disabilities live. This will help us in understanding how a more specialized user group interact with this app and how can this app be improved for such groups. Based on our limited user research, we believe that elderly with more severe disabilities also face the same problem and many existing solutions designed for 'normal' elderly can be modified and customized for the special user groups. Finally, in order to get a better understanding of the effectiveness of

'APPointment', a longitudinal study should be conducted. That study would indicate whether the usability of the user interface improves over a certain amount of time, and whether the application does actually reduce social loneliness.

Acknowledgements. We would like to thank the health care organization and all our participants for providing us with useful information, which helped us tackling this growing problem among elderly in the Netherlands.

References

1. European Commission: Population ageing in Europe: facts, implications and policies (2014). http://ec.europa.eu/research/social-sciences/pdf/policy_reviews/kina26426enc.pdf. Accessed 2 April 2015
2. Winningham, R.G., Pike, N.L.: A cognitive intervention to enhance institutionalized older adults' social support networks and decrease loneliness. Aging Ment. Health **11**(6), 716–721 (2007). doi:10.1080/13607860701366228
3. Fratiglioni, L., Wang, H.X., Ericsson, K., Maytan, M., Winblad, B.: Influence of social network on occurrence of dementia: a community-based longitudinal study. Lancet **355**, 1315–1319 (2000)
4. Mikkonen, M., Va, S., Ikonen, V., Heikkila, M.O.: User and concept studies as tools in developing mobile communication services for the elderly. Pers. Ubiquit. Comput. **6**(2), 113–124 (2002)
5. Mubin, O., Shahid, S., Al Mahmud, A.: Walk 2 win: towards designing a mobile game for elderly's social engagement. In: Proceedings of the 22nd British HCI Group Annual Conference on People and Computers: Culture, Creativity, Interaction-Volume (2008)
6. Muskens, L., van Lent, R., Vijfvinkel, A., van Cann, P., Shahid, S.: Never too old to use a tablet: designing tablet applications for the cognitively and physically impaired elderly. In: Miesenberger, K., Fels, D., Archambault, D., Peňáz, P., Zagler, W. (eds.) ICCHP 2014, Part I. LNCS, vol. 8547, pp. 391–398. Springer, Heidelberg (2014)

The Gods Play Dice Together:
The Influence of Social Elements
of Gamification on Seniors' User Experience

Ingmar Wagner and Michael Minge[(✉)]

Department of Cognitive Psychology and Cognitive Ergonomics,
Berlin University of Technology,
Marchstraße 23, Sekr. MAR 3-2, 10587 Berlin, Germany
ingmar.wagner@zoho.com, michael.minge@tu-berlin.de

Abstract. Due to increasing technologization and demographic changes, more and more elderly people are facing the challenge to use internet-based services for information and communication (ICT). In order to reduce frustrating experiences with ICT, such as feelings of helplessness and fear as well as motivational barriers, gamification and serious games are a promising approach. However, we assume that, when designing gamified applications for senior citizens, social aspects play an important role. Our research question aimed at comparing subjective enjoyment and motivational effects by providing different sociable gameplay conditions.

In a laboratory experiment 18 pairs of seniors from 58–85 years of age played an online version of the dice game "Yahtzee". Each participant worked in a separate room. The pairs were assigned to one of the following social modalities: (1) isolated condition with no interaction at all, (2) shared screen-condition and playing the game against each other knowingly, or (3) shared screen-condition plus video and audio feedback between both participants. By using a set of questionnaires we measured perceived attractiveness, emotional enjoyment, and motivation during the game as well as after the experiment.

Repeated measures during the experiment show that social aspects significantly enhance positive feelings and the willingness to maintain the gaming task.

Keywords: Gamification · Serious games · Elderly people · Social interaction · Motivation · Emotion

1 Introduction

Previous research has shown that the use of game elements, such as rewards, instant feedback, progress bars, and badges in non-gaming contexts is supposed to improve learning processes, to facilitate positive experiences, and to motivate seniors' ICT usage (Bürglen et al. 2014). However, these effects strongly depend on prior experiences and individual preferences, such as knowledge about ICT and openness towards games in general. Therefore, the design of gamified applications and serious games should follow a human-centered design approach and consider needs and requirements of the specific target group (Minge et al. 2014). One goal of our research is to analyse

© Springer International Publishing Switzerland 2015
C. Stephanidis (Ed.): HCII 2015 Posters, Part I, CCIS 528, pp. 334–339, 2015.
DOI: 10.1007/978-3-319-21380-4_57

such elements in real games and their influence on enjoyment and motivation of senior citizens. In order to increase user enjoyment with technology, those elements could further be employed in the design process of interactive systems.

An important source for enjoyment and intrinsic motivation is social interaction – or "socio-pleasure" (Jordan 2000). Socializing is the crucial ingredient for Online Social Networking sites such as Twitter, Youtube, and Facebook, allowing users to interact with each other in an alternate online world in real time (Pérez and Gómez 2011). The importance of social interaction is in line with the self-determination theory (SDT) by Deci and Ryan (2000), which is based on the premise that humans are active organisms, focused on growth and innately motivated to integrate psychic elements into a connected sense of self, both individually and in terms of relatedness to larger social structures. Among competence and autonomy, related-ness is one of the central human needs in SDT.

With a closer look at games, socializing is also one of the four basic motivators for playing (Bartle 1996). Zichermann and Cunningham (2011) even assume that this is the most important motivator because "the average person is looking to socialize - not win" (Zichermann and Cunningham 2011, p. 24). Weibel et al. (2008) showed that game players generally opted for direct competition with human players, rather than with computer opponents. Playing together, either with unknown people or with close friends, has not only immediate effects on gameplay, but positively influences moti-vation in the long run (Seay et al. 2004). Player behaviour can be regulated by game instrumentality; but much more important are shared social practices (Chen 2009), which usually revolved around communication (Ducheneaut et al. 2007). As such, the option to play as a single player belonging to a team or collective, in order to work together either in "cooperative quests" or in "team-play" with and against other opponents, is an important driver for motivation and positive experiences with games.

However, when it comes to senior citizens, there have been only a few studies focusing on the influence of social elements of gaming for elderly game players. Although most people, especially younger generations have an online social network account and maintain positive opinions about their use (Pérez and Gómez 2011), generational differences begin to emerge however, with the elderly being more cautious about privacy issues and data safety (Zukowski and Brown 2007). Little is known about the motivational and emotional experiences of seniors when they play (computer) games. This was the starting point for our research question.

2 Research Question

Our study aimed at identifying the potential of sociable game elements for senior citizens: If an interactive application included sociable elements as part of the gami-fication (e.g. shared screens and/or live video and audio feeds), would the application be more enjoyable and rated more positively by seniors? If effects could be obtained, those elements could be employed as gamification elements and tested in non-gamified contexts. This could provide an effective and more enjoyable way to familiarize seniors independently with (web-based) computer systems.

3 Method

3.1 Participants

Thirty-six seniors (half of them women) from age 58 to 85 ($M = 69.9$) participated in the study. All of them were invited in pairs, but tested in separate rooms respectively. Most frequent relations were friends ($n = 14$) and married couples ($n = 10$). They knew each other for 21.7 years on average. 20 Participants were experienced with computer games and most of them ($n = 30$) with the rules of the dice game "Yahtzee", which we used as stimulus for our laboratory experiment.

3.2 Stimulus and Experimental Design

"Yahtzee" is a very popular strategy game with a clear procedure and easy rules. For our study we used an online version of "Yahtzee", which is highly usable and provides single and multiplayer game modes. The experimental manipulation consisted of three between-subjects conditions: (1) Playing the game alone in an isolated condition with no interaction at all, (2) playing the game against each other knowingly on a shared screen, and (3) playing the game on a shared screen plus video and audio feedback between both participants. The eighteen pairs were assigned randomly to one of these conditions. In each session two rounds were played. It was assumed that the perception of hedonic qualities, positive emotions, and intrinsic motivation to keep playing the game would be higher for the sociable conditions.

3.3 Dependent Variables

In order to measure immediate effects on emotions, participants filled in the 9-point valence scale of the Self-Assessment Manikin (SAM) by Lang (1980) after completing the first and the second "Yahtzee" game. Additionally, they answered the 7-point Likert-scaled single-item: "How motivated are you for a second (a third) game?" At the end of the experiment, the following questionnaires were employed to measure summary assessments: The perception of pragmatic and hedonic product qualities was captured by the AttrakDiff (Hassenzahl et al. 2008), positive and negative emotions by the use of the meCUE questionnaire (Minge and Riedel 2013), and motivation by a German version of the Intrinsic Motivation Inventory (IMI) by McAuley et al. (1989). As covariates, demographic data (i.e. age), openness towards games, and prior knowledge of "Yahtzee" were assessed.

3.4 Procedure

At the beginning, the pairs were split and each participant was led to a separate room. Each room had a PC, two monitors (one for the "Yahtzee" interface and one for the potential video and audio feedback), connection to the online game, keyboard, mouse and speakers. In case of the video and audio feedback condition, a webcam including a microphone was used. Initially, participants received a brief training for "Yahtzee", including rules and controls, so they would be able to play the game successfully. For the shared screen condition, subjects were told that they were playing against each other. For the video and audio feedback condition, the system was shown and briefly explained. If the second monitor was not used for video feedback, a static picture was presented (see Fig. 1).

Then participants were instructed to fill in the valence scale of SAM (which served as a baseline for the emotion's assessment) and to play the first round of "Yahtzee". After completing this game, participants assessed their emotional state with the SAM scale and their motivation to play a second round right away. After the second game, participants again rated their emotion and motivation for a third round. However, a third game did not take place for any participant. Finally, standardized questionnaires were completed, namely AttrakDiff, meCUE, and a German version of the IMI. Demographic data was collected at the end. An experimental session took 90 min on average. Participants were paid 10 Euro.

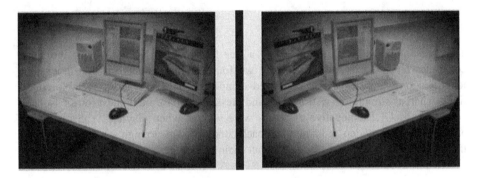

Fig. 1. The experimental setup with two separate rooms and equipment

4 Results

4.1 Repeated Measurements

Ratings of valence (SAM) and motivation (single-item) were analyzed by a MANCOVA with repeated measurements. Age, openness towards games, and prior knowledge of "Yahtzee" served as covariates. The analysis revealed a significant main effect of the different sociable conditions on motivation ($F(2, 25) = 5.381$, $p < .05$, $\eta^2_{part.} = 0.301$): The higher the degree of sociable elements, the higher is the willingness to keep playing the game. A substantial post hoc difference ($p = .03$) was found between the isolated and the shared screen condition (see Fig. 2). For valence the main effect of our experimental manipulation failed the significant level ($F(2, 25) = 0.557$, $p = .580$, $\eta^2_{part.} = 0.043$). However, mean ratings after the first round show that compared to the baseline, emotions became more positive in case of the two sociable conditions. Between the isolated and the shared screen condition this difference is significant ($p = .02$). After the second game, it is only the video and audio feedback condition, which is experienced with more positive emotions.

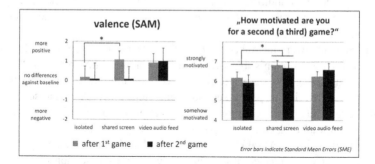

Fig. 2. Mean ratings for valence (SAM) and motivation (single-item) after the first and second game by the three sociable conditions.

4.2   Summary Assessment

The questionnaires were analyzed by a one-factorial MANCOVA with the same covariates as in Sect. 2. Descriptively we found higher ratings on the dimensions identification (AttrakDiff) and perceived competence (IMI) for both sociable conditions, whereas stimulation (AttrakDiff) and pressure (IMI) were highest for the isolated condition. MeCUE's negative emotions were highest when playing "Yahtzee" alone and lowest for the video and audio feedback condition. Due to high standard deviations the analysis did not reveal any significant main effects.

5   Discussion

The results of our experiment indicate that social game elements, such as acting together, comparing scores, and communicating with other people when playing an online game, immediately affects measures of emotions and motivation of elderly users. Interestingly the highest effect was observed for the shared screen condition which did not include a video and audio feedback. However there is evidence that direct communication could be important for a positive user experience in the long run. Reflective experiences which were measured by post experimental questionnaires were highly influenced by intra-individual differences, such as prior knowledge and openness towards games. We suppose that processes of attribution and response biases have minimized existing differences caused by the three experimental conditions. The objective of our study was not only to investigate the influences of social elements on seniors' game experiences. We also aimed at identifying the potential to motivate elder people's use of technology through social gamification elements. Our results support the assumption that socializing is an important factor for seniors' experience of interaction with technology. Therefore we will conduct further studies which aim at investigating social elements in non-gamified applications.

Acknowledgment. We would like to thank Assiel Afram and Franziska Trauzettel for their work on the studies.

References

Bartle, R.: Hearts, clubs, diamonds, spades: players who suit MUDs. J. MUD Res. **1**(1), 19 (1996)

Bürglen, J., Cymek, D., Adler, F., Grauert, J., Neef, S., Minge, M.: Insights into senior citizens' attitude towards gamification. In: HFES Europe 2014, Lisbon, Portugal (2014)

Chen, M.: Communication, coordination, and camaraderie in world of warcraft. Games Cult. **4**(1), 47–73 (2009)

Deci, E., Ryan, R.: The "what" and "why" of goal pursuits: human needs and the self-determination of behavior. Psychol. Inq. **11**(4), 227–268 (2000)

Ducheneaut, N., Moore, R.J., Nickell, E.: Virtual "third places": a case study of sociability in massively multiplayer games. J. Collaborative Comp. **16**(1/2), 129–166 (2007)

Hassenzahl, M., Burmester, M., Koller, F.: Der user experience (UX) auf der Spur: Zum Einsatz von. In: Brau, H., Diefenbach, S., Hassenzahl, M., Koller, F., Peissner, F., Röse, K. (eds.) German UPA Conference 2008, pp. 78–82 (2008). www.attrakdiff.de

Jordan, P.W.: Designing Pleasurable Products: An Introduction to the New Human Factors. Taylor & Francis, London (2000)

Lang, P.J.: Behavioral treatment and bio-behavioral assessment: computer applications. In: Sidowski, J.B., Johnson, H., Williams, T.A. (eds.) Technology in Mental Health Care Delivery Systems, pp. 119–137. Ablex, Norwood (1980)

McAuley, E., Duncan, T., Tammen, V.V.: Psychometric properties of the intrinsic motivation inventory in a competitive sport setting: a confirmatory factor analysis. Res. Q. Exerc. Sport **60**, 48–58 (1989)

Minge, M., Bürglen, J., Cymek, D.H.: Exploring the potential of gameful interaction design of ICT for the elderly. In: Stephanidis, C. (ed.) HCI 2014, Part II. CCIS, vol. 435, pp. 304–309. Springer, Heidelberg (2014)

Minge, M., Riedel, L.: meCUE – Ein modularer Fragebogen zur Erfassung des Nutzungserlebens. In: Boll, S., Maaß, S., Malaka, R. (eds.) Mensch und Computer 2013: Interaktive Vielfalt, pp. 89–98. Oldenbourg, Munich (2013). English version available: www.mecue.de

Pérez, M., Gómez, J.: Why do people use social networks? Commun. IIMA **11**(2), 41 (2011)

Seay, A., Jerome, W., Lee, K., Kraut, R.: Project massive: a study on online gaming communities. In: CHI 2004 Extended Abstracts on Human Factors in Computing Systems, Vienna, Austria, pp. 1421–1424. ACM Press, New York, 24–29 April 2004

Weibel, D., Wissmath, B., Habegger, S., Steiner, Y., Groner, R.: Playing online games against computer – vs. human-controlled components: effects on presence, flow, and enjoyment. Comput. Hum. Behav. **24**(5), 2274–2291 (2008)

Zichermann, G., Cunningham, C.: Gamification by Design: Implementing Game Mechanics in Web and Mobile Apps, 1st edn. O'Reilly Media, Newton (2011)

Zukowski, T., Brown, I.: Examining the influence of demographic factors on internet users' information privacy concerns. In: Proceedings of SAICIST 2007, pp. 197–204. Fish River Sun, Sunshine Coast, South Africa (2007)

Designing a Map-Based Application and a Conversational Agent for Addressing Memory Problems

Akihito Yoshii[1(✉)], Helena Malmivirta[2], Mika Luimula[2],
Paula Pitkäkangas[2], and Tatsuo Nakajima[1]

[1] Waseda University, Shinjuku, Japan
a_yoshii@dcl.cs.waseda.ac.jp
[2] Turku University of Applied Sciences, Turku, Finland

Abstract. Computer based recreational activities can be solution for aging. We are addressing memory related problems using a computer. We propose "Old Photos on Map" application (Vanhat Kuvat). The aim of Vanhat Kuvat is to activate one's memory by using old photos and an assistant agent to wake up the past memories and experiences of childhood surroundings and architecture as well as personal hidden stories. We describe design issues related to user interfaces and interactions.

1 Introduction

According to the Demography Report 2010 [1], population in Europe is aging dramatically. As the result of this there will be almost one person of working age for every dependent person aged under 19 or over 65 years. The situation in Finland is even more challenging. Finland will have the oldest population in Europe, measured in terms of the old-age dependency ratio [1]. Japan is in the similar situation. According to the statistics released by the government [2], the population of elderly people accounts 25 % of entire population.

In the project called Gamified Solutions in Healthcare, Finnish and Japanese research organizations are searching together new solutions for aging. Because of challenges described above we are forced to find new options for the elderly's self-care and ease the healthcare professional's work load. We have found that the use of recreational activities is useful activation method for elderly people in many ways.

One of problems caused by aging, memory related problems can affect daily life of people crucially. Researchers have suggested interventions using reminiscence activities. On the other hand, providing patients opportunities of reminiscence along with communications needs human resources; therefore, some of researchers are pursuing computer assisted interventions [11]. Life-like entities such as virtual characters (agents) can enrich communication between a user and a computer. They can incorporate with nonverbal strategies like facial expressions and gestures.

In this paper, we introduce "Old Photos on Map" application (Vanhat Kuvat) which incorporates a conversational agent, and describe a survey in terms of agent design and usability as a fundamental base of Vanhat Kuvat. The aim of Vanhat Kuvat is to activate

C. Stephanidis (Ed.): HCII 2015 Posters, Part I, CCIS 528, pp. 340–345, 2015.
DOI: 10.1007/978-3-319-21380-4_58

one's memory by using old photos for to wake up the past memories and experiences of childhood surroundings and architecture as well as personal hidden stories. This kind of memory impulses function as a link between present and future and promote the plasticity of the brain and are seen a bridge for better health and well-being. The frame of this concept is a combination of Semir Zeki's theory of neuroaesthetic [4] and John Dewey's theory of art as experience [3] and research in practice [5, 8].

2 Related Work

Several researchers [3, 4, 6, 9] have come to the conclusion that cognitive mental activity is high important for brain health. The effectiveness of using old photos to enhance brain health has examined in the research and development project Art and culture – Keys for better Brain Health [8].

In autobiographical activities like watching and sharing experiences of old photos, exploring punctum photographs allows an emotional connection to be formed with the most significant people, places and events in our lives. Subjective sense of time refers to the ability to shift to thinking about something that has happened in the past. Memory layers and visual perception are in active motion in this phase, when narratives, photographs and maps are integrated into each other. The autobiographical memory and discussions about the old photos require complicated cooperation be-tween our cognitive and emotional processes which activate different parts of the brain [7, 10].

Social interaction has also seen a significant factor in promoting brain health. A sense of belonging to the community, a sense of participation, sharing stories and experiences and, as a result of sharing, the deepening of one's own understanding and experience are regarded as important. Brain health is a lifelong, proactive process in which the brain is molded by the stimuli in the environment. The brain feels well when the environment promotes activation and involves social interaction. From the point of view of promoting brain health, it is important that the brain is occupied with new and complex tasks throughout our lives: this way, the unused reserve of our brain may also promote brain health and delay the emergence of memory disorders [8, 9].

The effectiveness of an agent for dementia patients has been examined by researchers. For example, Yasuda et al. have used a computer agent resembles a five-year-old grandchild to intervene dementia patients [11]. They have developed a conversational agent that can give 120 reminiscent questions. Using this agent, they conducted an experiment asking a patient to have a one-to-one conversation. From the result of their experiment, they have reported that most of patients had positive. One of patients said that conversations with the agent reduce hesitation or anxiety compared to real human. In addition to this experiment, they have also investigated the effectiveness of an agent with a group of patients [12].

3 System Design

This application consists of a client-side user interface (UI), server-side components and a database. Each component is described in this section.

3.1   Overview

The UI component includes a map and related buttons. The main functions are photo icons (B: showing picture), informative time period (C: filtering photos based on this criterion), search icon (A), and agent icon (D).

These UI components include an agent (E). An agent has flows of behaviors defined in JavaScript codes and stored on the server. A part of codes and data are provided by server-side components (Fig. 1).

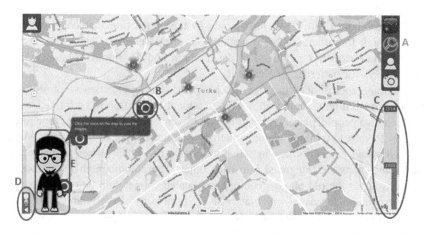

Fig. 1. System overview

3.2   Agents

In the design phase, we specified perceived personality and visual characteristics of an agent. Besides, visibility and agent interaction lead to accessibility. We formulated hypothesis that relationship between cultural differences and appearance affect the preferences of a user. Existing work suggests the effect of appearance on impression of an agent perceived by a user. Zambaka et al. have compared among agents in three different categories: humans, virtual humans and virtual nonhuman characters [13]. As a result, the persuasiveness of agents was not affected significantly by the categories. However, people tend to attracted by an agent with different gender.

An agent runs on the application has variable facial expressions and behaviors. The agent can utter words according to each location. The agent attempts to encourage patients to discuss past memories related to pictures linked to the location.

4   Survey

We have conducted a questionnaire to compare among multiple agents and interface designs with different color variations. Participants are asked to choose the most preferable ones and then we determined elements suitable for Vanhat Kuvat.

Participants are 24 Finnish people (16 males and 9 females) with ages ranging from 56–93. The age and gender were based on their self-reporting. The questionnaire was made with Webropol.[1]

Questions related to text size (Fig. 2(a)) and color scheme (Fig. 2(b)) were included to examine accessibility of user interfaces. Participants chose one of options in each question, and the combination of text size and color scheme that includes the most popular ones was adopted (Fig. 3).

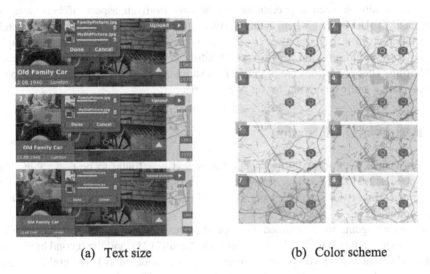

(a) Text size   (b) Color scheme

Fig. 2. Comparison of each interface element

Fig. 3. Comparison of agents

The agent questionnaire consists of multiple-choices style questions according to impression, and written style ones. We focused on three aspects in multiple-choices style questions: how much an agent is child-like, trustful and kind. The written style questions ask participant their favorite characteristics and concrete examples (i.e. existing persons or characters).

While Yasuda et al. have used a child agent in their study [11] simulating a grandchild, we are considering examining whether cultural difference in impression of child-likeness affects familiarity of an agent or not. Shedroff and Noessel describe the relationship between expectations and actions from an aspect of behaviors of characters [14]. That is, when actual services provided by an agent do not match expectation from a user, the user can be annoyed. Based on these aspects, multiple adjective were chosen: kind, trustful, child, adult, negligent, mischievous, interesting, and boring. These questions are prepared for examining cultural difference in an aspect of acceptance and expectation for an agent by people.

5   Results and Discussion

As consistence with accessibility aspect, larger text was found to be preferable. The most popular text size combination was no. 1 in Fig. 2(a) obtaining support from 19 participants. In a color scheme aspect, no. 7 (10 participants) and no. 1 (7 participants) were popular.

As for an agent, no. 5 obtained the highest points (the number of participants who have chosen the agent) in "kind" (11 points) and "adult" (21), and the second highest in "trustful" (7) and "interesting" (6). Contrary, it was considered as least "child" (2) and "negligent" (1), and second least "boring" (2) character. Therefore, the no. 5 agent can be a preferable character with positive impression.

No. 1 and 11 were respectively the first and second most "child" (21 and 18) characters. Although they are both human-like character, the ratio between head and body is different. While points of "kind" (11 and 4) and "trustful" (5 and 1) are not necessarily higher, the "negligent" (1 and 2), "mischievous" (0 and 2) and "boring" (1 and 3) points located in a range from first to third least numbers. This result suggests that a "child" character can also be candidates for an agent because of the accordance with related work regarding an agent [7, 11].

No. 3, 4, and 6 were not human characters. Especially, the no. 3 did not have a face. Points of "interesting" and "boring" for the no. 3 character were 4 and 6 respectively while the other point was 0. This result suggests that no. 3 obtains few expectations from participants while the possibility of expressions is limited.

6   Future Direction

We have described design issues of Vanhat Kuvat application along with the results of survey. Multiple categories of agents were compared regarding how much an agent is child-like, trustful and kind. Based on survey results, we are planning to experiment with these agents in a usability study.

Acknowledgments. The authors would like to thank everyone who have participated the development work, and all the test subjects who participated experiments. In addition, we would especially like to thank Ahtosalo, H., Gornicki, M., and Heinonen, T. who were conducting the survey, and Lahti, I., Gratschev, T. and Haanpää, M. who have participated software development. This work was carried out within project supported by the Finnish Funding Agency for Technology and Innovation (Tekes), City of Turku and various companies.

References

1. Demography Report 2010: Older, more numerous and diverse Europeans. European Commission, Mar 2011. http://epp.eurostat.ec.europa.eu/cache/ITY_OFFPUB/KE-ET-10-001/EN/KE-ET-10-001-EN.PDF

2. Population of elderly people, Statistics Japan. http://www.stat.go.jp/data/topics/topi721.htm. Accessed 6 Nov 2014

3. Dewey, J.: Art as Experience. Pedigree Books, New York (1934/1980)

4. Zeki, S.: Inner Vision: An Exploration of the Brain. Oxford University Press, Oxford (1999)

5. Malmivirta, H.: Art as Bridge for Personal and Professional Growth. Acta Universitatis Tamperensis, Juvenes Print, Tampere (1629)

6. Arnheim, R.: Art and Visual Perception. A Psychology of the Creative Eye (The new version). University of California Press, London (2004)

7. Halkola, U.: Mitä valokuvaterapia on? What is the therapy of the photographs? In: Halkola, U., Mannermaa, L., Koffert, T., Koulu, L. (eds.) Valokuvan terapeuttinen voima, pp. 13–22. Otava, Helsinki (2009)

8. Malmivirta, H.: Yellow cottage and a patch of potato. In: Malmivirta, H., Kivelä, S. (eds.) Art and Culture –Keys for better Brain health. Developing Service Models with a Citizen-Centred Approach. Education Materials 102, pp. 93–126. Turku University of Applied Sciences, Turku (2015)

9. Nussbaum, P.D.: Brain health: bridging neuroscience to consumer application. Generations J. Am. Soc. Aging **35**(2), 6–12 (2011)

10. Sandström, M.: Psyyke ja aivotoiminta. Neurofysiologinen näkökulma. Wsoypro, Helsinki (2010)

11. Yasuda, K., Aoe, J., Fuketa, M.: Development of an agent system for conversing with individuals with dementia. In: The 27th Annual Conference of the Japanese Society for Artificial Intelligence (2013)

12. Yasuda, K., Aoe, J., Fuketa, M.: An anime agent system for reminiscence: observation of multi-party conversation between the agent and two individuals with dementia (Japanese Paper). In: HAI Symposium (2013)

13. Zanbaka, C., Goolkasian, P. and Hodges, L.: Can a virtual cat persuade you?: the role of gender and realism in speaker persuasiveness (2006)

14. Shedroff, N. and Noessel, C.: Make It So: Interaction Design Lessons from Science Fiction, chapter 9, Rosenfeld Media, Brooklyn (2012)

Children in HCI

Examining the User Experience (UX) of Children's Interaction with Arabic Interfaces in Educational Learning Contexts

Wea'am A. Alrashed[(✉)] and Asma A. Alhussayen

King Saud University, Riyadh, Saudi Arabia
{wealrashed,aalhussayen}@KSU.EDU.SA

Abstract. A plethora of research studies have recently examined different approaches for designing playful learning interactive systems. The design challenges of offering fun, engaging and creative learning experiences for children are often coupled with complexities in objectively measuring the impact of different designs with younger populations. Consequently, the evaluation of children's experience with playful learning websites is essential for designing and improving these interactive systems to comply with the child's cognitive, physical, and perceptual abilities. This paper reports the results of an experimental study conducted on a sample of 64 children in an elementary school in Riyadh, Saudi Arabia. Its aim was to explore and analyze the user experience (UX) on Arabic educational and entertainment website de-signed for children ranging in age from 7 to 12 years. To help understand the children better and gather impression data about how they use these types of websites, observation and heuristic evaluations have been used. Observational analysis included metrics for measuring UX and usability during interaction with the web pages to understand the efficacy of these evaluation approaches in uncovering general usability issues and opportunities for design improvements. The study took place in the school's computer lab where each child interacted with the website separately from her mates. Questionnaires were designed specifically to assess the momentum emotion of the user while interacting with different sections of the website. Also, children were provided with sticky notes to freely describe their experience, perceptions, and opinions about the website. The results of our study showed that the age of the child interacting with the website has a significant impact on how she experienced the different sections in each web page. Methodological design implications for conducting UX and usability evaluations for children are discussed.

Keywords: User experience · Usability · Playful learning website · Child-computer interaction · HCI · Interaction design for children

1 Introduction

For many years now, developers have designed and launched "Playful Learning" websites for children with the intention of providing them a joyful learning experience. To provide such experience, the focus shifts from the traditional usability measures to

© Springer International Publishing Switzerland 2015
C. Stephanidis (Ed.): HCII 2015 Posters, Part I, CCIS 528, pp. 349–354, 2015.
DOI: 10.1007/978-3-319-21380-4_59

include all aspects of a good user experience. For a website to be successful and attracted to young users it must meet their growing expectations, not only by being functional but also desirable and emotionally appealing. Moreover, it is important to understand how the children, being the key users, feel and perceive these websites, especially with the recent emphasis on user-centered design.

To the best of our knowledge, there are no studies investigating the user experience of the playful learning websites designed for Saudi children in Saudi Arabia. To contribute to this research gap, we present an initial study results on users' experiences with a playful learning website. More particularly, we will describe an explorative study in which the momentary UX of children is evaluated.

Within this paper, we try to explore how the children experience playful learning websites, how their experiences influence their desire to use it in their free time and the factors affecting children's experience of playful learning websites.

A clear understanding of the previous concerns will provide guidelines inspired from the user experience to improve the design of websites dedicated to children.

2 Related Work

In recent years, the importance of the user's experience and feeling about certain systems and products has shifted the focus from the traditional usability study to UX field. This interest has risen because of the ability of UX to measure the engagement and joyful emotions effectively more than traditional usability [1]. Moreover, the user's expectations about the system and their anticipations are factors which affect their experience about the system itself [2]. Although UX is a field of study that had been researched heavily, yet a unified definition for the widely used term has not yet been reached. Effie Law et al. state three causes for the variance of UX definitions. The first of these reasons is the fact that there are many involved attributes, mostly known for being vague and constantly changing, and the decision to take in or leave out an attribute from the UX definition depends on the author's interest and background. Another reason according to Effie Law et al. is the measurability of the UX, wether to measure all the different aspects of the user's communication with a system or only one aspect of the user's communication. Finally, the diversity and complication of the theoretical framework, which supports the UX research field [11].

In our study, we employed Hassenzahl and Tractinsky's definition of UX "A consequence of a user's internal state (predispositions, expectations, needs, motivation, mood, etc.), the characteristics of the designed system (e.g. complexity, purpose, usability, functionality, etc.) and the context (or the environment) within which the interaction occurs (e.g. organizational/social setting, meaningfulness of the activity, voluntariness of use, etc.)" [14]. Their definition concentrates on the inner emotions of the user and their expectation of the designed system; as it clearly describes the factors influencing UX.

As for the evaluation of children experience, children nowadays are considered as main users of software; so the use of technology is no longer limited to adult users. Developers are attempting to design software that meets the children's abilities, interests and development needs [3]. As we all know, children do not have the knowledge and the experience that the adults have, therefore they perceive and experience the world differently. Additionally, the physical and cognitive abilities of children are different than those of the adults. Thus, their UX is measured in a different manner. Psychologist Jean Piaget divided children into different stages according to their cognitive and physical development. In the ages between seven and eleven, children are considered in the concrete operational stage [10]. In this stage, children are unable to formulate hypothesis and have difficulty understanding abstract concepts. However, they are able to classify similar items into groups, use the keyboard, control the mouse and use computer software. Also, children still admire and value software that incorporates playful activities [4]. Children have difficulty expressing their feelings and thoughts through words, but their actions and behaviors reflect their thoughts. Therefore, observers need to carefully read the behaviors and understand them within the context of concrete experiences. Also, children respond truthfully about their opinion on the software they are interacting with [5].

Evaluation methods help in enhancing the quality of the design proposed, since it's being tested by the users themselves [6]. According to Druin [5], children's roles in the design process of technology are categorized into four main roles: *user, tester, informant and design partner.* With the child's role as a user, researchers observe and gather impression data that help them understand children better. Research methods should be designed or adjusted with respect to children's abilities and needs. Regarding research that focuses on the evaluation of interactive systems numerous tools and methods have been designed such as [7].

Observational methods where the researchers are in the room with users are useful in particular with children since their behavior reflects their feelings. With this method, researchers stay with the users throughout the evaluation period to explain the software and respond to questions [5]. Several approaches are used to gather data regarding children's thoughts and feelings. Qualitative methods are capable of capturing the enjoyable and attractive parts of the software being evaluated. A more formal method is the use of quantitative surveys where questions are developed carefully so that they clear and unambiguous and answers are in a form of "Smileyometer" scale [8]. With children as users, it is important to measure the fun and enjoyment of interacting with playful learning websites as they have a significant effect on children's opinion on the website and whether they are willing to use it or not [12]. Read's study on measuring fun and usability [12] showed that usability and fun are correlated, as usability problems resulted in children having less fun with the product. Emotions last only for a short time (a few seconds), so the measurement has to be precise or retrospective [9]. Moreover, "Emocards" is a method used to assess the enjoyment and emotions of users and, based on previous work as [2] has proven to be an applicable method for conducting UX evaluation. Previous work on assessing children educational learning software included the use of heuristic evaluations for assessing the usability [13]. This study showed that heuristic evaluations were suitable for uncovering general usability issues. However, problems related to boredom and dissatisfaction were only detected through observing children as users [13].

3 Study and Method

The study took place in the school's computer lab where each child interacted with the website separately from her mates. The participating children were between the ages of 7 and 12, they were all native Arabic speakers and had experience working on desktop computers and browsing the internet. The study was conducted in 5 sessions over 2 days. Each grade level from 2nd to 6th in one separate session in order to maintain and ensure the similarity in the grade's level without mixing different grades together and avoid affecting the judgment of the children of different ages. The duration of the sessions were different with every grade level, with younger children (grades 2, 3, 4) the sessions lasted between an hour and an hour and a half as for the 5th and 6th graders the sessions lasted for half an hour to 45 min. At the start of each session, the children were briefed on the purpose of the study and the tasks to be completed. They were assured that the questions they were to answer were not exam questions and any answer that expressed their feelings was right. We also made it clear that we were not the designers of the website so that they feel comfortable expressing their thoughts on the website. The website we were evaluating had different sections including: registration and sign in section, "Skills" section, "My stories" section, "My family" section, "My diary" section, "My games" section and "My hobbies".

Each of these sections has sound effects when hovering over their icons. The children were given time to explore each section and evaluate it through smileyometer scale (see Fig. 1) before moving on to the next section. The surveys were designed specifically to assess the momentum emotion of the user while interacting with the different sections of the website and the impression of the sound effects of each section. At the end of the survey, the children chose their favorite sections and were provided with sticky notes to freely describe their experience and provide open feedback on the website.

Fig. 1. A sample of the smileyometer survey

4 Results and Conclusion

During the sessions, the children appeared excited and interested while interacting with the website. However, they were less excited with the website's registration page and were frustrated and confused since it was difficult for them to complete the registration step. Analyzing the data gathered from the surveys also indicated the registration difficulty experienced, results show that none of the younger children (ages 7–9) were able to register and only 39 % of the older children (ages 10–12) were able to complete the registration. Although none of the younger children were able to register, only 16 % of them choose the feeling "sad" in the smileyometer indicating that the majority did not realize the importance of the registration process. Although a larger percent (24 %) of the older children chose either "angry" or "sad" for not completing the registration process, it is still a small percentage (see Fig. 2). Our conclusion from this result is that the registration process is not appreciated by children at this age and should be avoided or simplified by using less complicated sign up forms. The gathered survey data also showed a variation between the two age groups in terms of the favourite website sections. The majority of the younger children (77 %) were more attracted to "My stories" section, but only (48 %) of the older children found "My stories" section interesting. (70 %) of the older children were attracted to "My hobbies" section while it only attracted (48 %) of the younger children. From this noticed variation, it is recommended to put in mind the age differences when designing such websites and allow for content variation depending on the child's age.

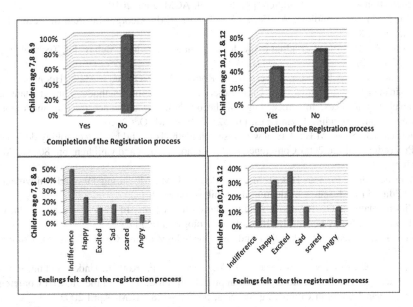

Fig. 2. The completion of the registration process and its impact on their feelings in two children's age groups.

As for the open feedback notes, the statements were categorized to either positive or negative statements. 76 % of the statements were positive, indicating a positive, enjoyable experience. However, the other 24 % of the statements expressed negative experience and the negative statements were then sub-categorized to identify the causes of the undesirable impression. Those children stated that they did not like the website and find it to be boring. Moreover, some suggested enhancements to the website; one of the recommendations was to add more games. Others felt that the colors of the webpages and some of the sound effects were annoying.

Taking these causes of dissatisfaction with the website into consideration will result in developing improved playful learning websites that deliver an exceptional user experience.

References

1. Kujala, S., Roto, V., Väänänen-Vainio-Mattila, K., Karapanos, E., Sinnelä, A.: UX curve: a method for evaluating long-term user experience. Interact. Comput. **23**(5), 473–483 (2011)
2. Roto, V., Väänänen-Vainio-Mattila, K., Law, E., Vermeeren, A.: User experience evaluation methods in product development (UXEM'09). In: Gross, T., Gulliksen, J., Kotzé, P., Oestreicher, L., Palanque, P., Prates, R.O., Winckler, M. (eds.) INTERACT 2009. LNCS, vol. 5727, pp. 981–982. Springer, Heidelberg (2009)
3. Yarosh, S., Markopoulos, P.: Design of an instrument for the evaluation of communication technologies with children. In: Proceedings of the 9th International Conference on Interaction Design and Children, pp. 266–269. ACM, June 2010
4. Bruckman, A., Bandlow, A., Forte, A.: HCI for Kids. Georgia Institute of Technology, Atlanta (2002)
5. Druin, A.: The role of children in the design of new technology. Behav. Inf. Technol. **21**(1), 1–25 (2002)
6. Vermeeren, A.P., Law, E.L.C., Roto, V., Obrist, M., Hoonhout, J., Väänänen-Vainio-Mattila, K.: User experience evaluation methods: current state and development needs. In: Proceedings of the 6th Nordic Conference on Human-Computer Interaction: Extending Boundaries, pp. 521–530. ACM, Oct 2010
7. Jensen, J.J., Skov, M.B.: A review of research methods in children's technology design. In: Proceedings of the 2005 Conference on Interaction Design and Children, pp. 80–87. ACM (June 2005)
8. Van der Sluis, F., Van Dijk, E.M.A.G., Perloy, L.M.: Measuring Fun and Enjoyment of Children in a Museum: Evaluating the Smileyometer (2012)
9. Zimmermann, P.G.: Beyond Usability–Measuring Aspects of User Experience. Doctoral dissertation, Swiss Federal Institute of Technology Zurich (2008)
10. Piaget, J.: Science of Education and the Psychology of the Child (Trans. D. Coltman). (1970)
11. Law, E.L.C., Roto, V., Hassenzahl, M., Vermeeren, A.P., Kort, J.: Understanding, scoping and defining user experience: a survey approach. In: Proceedings of the SIGCHI Conference on Human Factors in Computing Systems, pp. 719–728. ACM, April 2009
12. Sim, G., MacFarlane, S., Read, J.: All work and no play: measuring fun, usability, and learning in software for children. Comput. Educ. **46**(3), 235–248 (2006). doi:10.1016/j.compedu.2005.11.021
13. Alsumait, A., Al-Osaimi, A.: Usability heuristics evaluation for child e-learning applications. In: Proceedings of the 11th International Conference on Information Integration and Web-based Applications &Amp; Services, pp. 425–430. ACM, New York (2009). doi:10.1145/1806338.1806417
14. Hassenzahl, M., Tractinsky, N.: User experience-a research agenda. Behav. Inf. Technol. **25**(2), 91–97 (2006)

A Study of User Behavior in the Parent-Child Reading Area: A Case Study in Taipei Public Library

Jo-Han Chang[✉] and Pao-Ching Tsai

Graduate Institute of Innovation and Design,
National Taipei University of Technology, Zhongxiao E. Rd., Taipei, Taiwan
johan@ntut.edu.tw

Abstract. A library is a crucial place for children to learn. However, different environmental designs have differing effects on users. We used the Taipei Public Library (Main Library) as case to explore the environments of different reading areas and parent-child user behavior. Field survey and focus group methods were used to observe and analyze factors influencing parent-child interaction. The research results indicated that the table shape affected parent-child interaction. For example, a table in a shape of flower enabled the parent and child to work individually, whereas a round table improved parent-child interaction. Children tended to sit or stand by the bookshelf for reading. Comfortable and undisturbed reading space is the primary factor in seat selection by the users. Secondary factors included the dimensions of the table and chair set, style of the table and chairs, and illumination.

Keywords: Library · Reading environment · Focus group method

1 Introduction

Lushington and Mills (1980) reported that children's first impression on the library affects their subsequent user behavior and willingness to use the library. Thus, the spatial development of the reading area for children is crucial. The library space for children can attract children and satisfy their various reading needs. In the use of furniture, durability is necessary. Combined with lighting configurations, the space can create a safety and heart-warming (Sannwald 2007).

Wang (2007) suggested that a library should periodically evaluate the physical environments of each area in the library, including illumination, layout, traffic flow, and use rate, to promote the use of each area. The Taipei Public Library has undergone spatial planning and renovation of the Daan Main Library since 2002. In recent years, the overall spatial reform or local equipment update of child reading area is undertaken in each division library (Hung and Lin 2013). Thus, we used design intervention to explore the use of child reading area after renovation.

© Springer International Publishing Switzerland 2015
C. Stephanidis (Ed.): HCII 2015 Posters, Part I, CCIS 528, pp. 355–360, 2015.
DOI: 10.1007/978-3-319-21380-4_60

1.1   Objectives

The Main Library was used as the example of design intervention to explore the environment of different reading areas and the user behavior of children. The objectives of this study are listed as follows:

1. Observe and record the environment of different reading areas and parent-child user behavior by using a field survey method.
2. Analyze the parent-child user behavior and possible causes of such behavior by using a focus group method.

2   Literature Review

In addition to furniture such as tables, chairs, and book shelves, a comfortable reading environment is also affected by environmental factors, including indoor color and lighting. We explored the furniture and arrangement, and lighting in following sections.

2.1   Furniture and Arrangement

Furniture in the child reading area should conform to children's body size. Overly high or large furniture easily cause a sense of pressure and threat to children (Sannwald 2007). Comfortable chairs not only help maintain the balance and stability of upper limbs, but also help children concentrate (Allen et al. 1996).

Altman (1975) indicated that territorial behavior of personal space is a main approach to obtain privacy. People required different levels of privacy according to the time, location, and activity. In the reading room, different configuration of table and chairs, distance between table sets, and distance between table sets and bookshelves affected reader requirement of privacy (Tai 2009).

2.2   Lighting

Lai (2008) reported that lighting has positive attraction to children. Research has identified that children perceived that lighting and color of a library affected their willingness to access the library. Bright lighting generates a sense of safety and positive attraction in psychological aspect. Libraries can create a comfortable and cozy reading atmosphere through lighting of various levels of brightness (Sannwald 2007).

3   Methods

This study comprised two stages. The first stage was the field survey method. A non-participatory observation method was used to record the children's user behavior in different reading areas. The second stage was the focus group discussion method.

A group discussion on the observation outcome of the first stage was conducted to analyze the possible cause of the user behaviors.

3.1   Field Survey

We visited a child reading room at the first basement floor of the Main Library of the Taipei Public Library. The user behaviors (use condition and location selection) of the children and caregivers in the reading space (furniture, environmental color, lighting, and concealment were observed and recorded using photographing, video recording, and written record.

3.2   Focus Group

The focus group method was used to analyze the result of the first stage. Six graduate students studying product design or architectural design for an average of 6 years were recruited to analyze the possible causes of the different user behaviors in the various reading areas.

4   Results

4.1   First Stage: Field Survey

In this study, we divided the child reading room at the first basement floor into four areas, which were (1) staircase reading area, (2) child reading room, and (3) book reading area. The observation record and result of each reading area is provided as follows.

(1) **Staircase reading room** (Table 1).
(2) **Child reading area** (Table 2).
(3) **Book reading area** (Table 3).

Table 1. Observation record of the staircase reading area

Environment description	User behavior	
	Caregiver and a single child	Caregiver and multiple children
• Three high and two low round tables • Warm-white lighting	• Doing homework or leisure discussion is the primary task	• The caregiver sits at the position nearest to the aisle. Younger children sit in more concealed position

Table 2. Observation record of the child reading area

Environment description	User behavior	
	Caregiver and a single child	Single child
• Six flower-shaped tables and two round tables. Stair seats are set at the rear • Bookshelves are at both sides of the right and front area • Warm-white lighting	• The caregiver sits beside the child • The caregiver uses the cellphone and reads newspaper without joint reading behavior when accompanying the child	• In addition to reading, most of the children in this area do homework

Table 3. Book reading area

Environment description	User behavior		
	Caregiver and children	Single child	Multiple children
• Two round tables between the bookshelves • A sitting area is provided in front of the bookshelves. Movable chairs are available between bookshelves • Warm-white lighting	• The caregiver faces outward while the child faces inward reading	• The child tends to sit at concealed places between bookshelves • Most of the children read near the bookshelf	• When there are two children, they sit between the bookshelves in diagonal positions

4.2   Second Stage: Focus Group

The following discussion focuses on the environments and user behaviors of the four reading areas. Possible causes of such user behaviors were proposed.

(1) **Staircase reading area.**

1. The users prioritized selecting tables no. 1, 4, and 2 (Fig. 1). A possible reason was that the tables no. 1, 4, and 2 (Fig. 1) were designed conforming to users' body size and the lighting was installed above the tables.
2. The users picked the middle seats last (table no. 4 and 5, as shown in Fig. 1). A possible reason could be that activities on the seats easily disturb people on other seats and sitting on the seats was easily disturbed by others.

(2) **Child reading area.**

1. Parents and children sitting at the flower-shaped table exhibited less interaction compared with those sitting at a round table, possibly because the

Fig. 1. Floor plan of the staircase reading area

flower-shaped table separated parents and children, generating a sense of isolation.
2. Round tables were less occupied possibly because of the placement at the main traffic flow of the library. Sitting there was easily disturbed by people passing by.

(3) **Book reading area.**

1. When reading, the children tended to sit or stand by the bookshelf. This was possibly because children easily forgot where the book belonged to after finishing reading the book.
2. In addition to reading at a place near to the bookshelf, the children also read at a corner. A possibly reason was that the children were not easily disturbed by people walking by or stared at.

5 Conclusion

We used nonparticipatory observation method to record user behavior in the child reading areas. The focus group method was used to analyze the user behavior and possible causes. The research result is shown as follows:

1. The shape of the table affected parent-child interaction. For example, flower-shaped tables separated parents and children, whereas round tables improved interaction.
2. The children tended to sit or stand by the bookshelf reading. Thus, arranging seats with high degrees of freedom that children can move easily conforms to the children behavior of reading by a bookshelf directly after picking a book.
3. Comfortable and undisturbed reading space is the primary factor for a user to select a seat. Secondary factors include the dimensions of the tables and chairs, style of the tables and chairs, and lighting.

References

Allen, R.L., Bowen, J.T., Clabaugh, S., DeWitt, B.B., Francies, J., Kerstetter, J.P., Rieck, D.A.: Classroom Design Manual, 3rd edn. Academic Information Technology Services, University of Maryland, College Park (1996)

Altman, I.: The Environment and Social Behavior: Privacy, Personal Space, Territory, Crowding. Brooks/Cole Pub. Co, Monterey (1975)

Hung, S.C., Lin, J.Y.: Innovation services in Taipei public libraries. Libr. Assoc. Repub. China (Taiwan) Newsl. **21**(1), 38–44 (2013)

Lai, K.Y.: The influence of school library environment for students to read. New Horiz. Bimonthly Teach. Taipei **154**, 60–62 (2008)

Lushington, N., Mills, W.N.: Libraries Designed for Users: A Planning Handbook. Library Professional Publ, Hamden (1980)

Sannwald, W.W.: Designing libraries for customers. Libr. Adm. Manag. **21**(3), 131–138 (2007)

Tai, H.I.: Exploring the architecture design of library-the reader-book relations and construction of space. Unpublished master's thesis, National Taiwan University of Science and Technology, Taipei, Taiwan (2009)

Wang, T.Y.: The evaluation study of using and planning of elementary school libraries. Unpublished master's thesis, National Taiwan Normal University, Taipei, Taiwan (2007)

The Influence of Parenting Time on Children's Growth and Development

Jo-Han Chang and Tien-Ling Yeh[✉]

Graduate Institute of Innovation and Design,
National Taipei University of Technology, Zhongxiao E. Rd., Taipei, Taiwan
johan@ntut.edu.tw, tienling0303@gmail.com

Abstract. Double-salary families are very common nowadays in the modern society. Parents may neglect to be there with their children as their children grow up. In 2014, the Child Welfare League Foundation conducted a survey and found that almost 64 % of parents believing the biggest problem was "no time after getting off work". To avoid the lack of interaction and care in the long run, this study aimed to explore the influence of parenting time on children's growth performances. There were two parts of this study: (1) literature review. This part discussed the lifestyles of families with children based on a survey regarding time use and the important features of accompanying activities for growth performances of children aged 0–12; and (2) questionnaire analyses, exploring the influence of time parents spent with their children aged 0–12 on these children's performances. The questionnaires were issued in Oct, 2014. A total of 30 questionnaires were retrieved. The results are summarized below (ordered by after-work time):

1. Spending time with children after getting off work, during 17:30–18:30 could lead to children positive and cheerful emotions as well as good performances in auditory comprehension.
2. Spending time with children when they were reading during 20:0–21:30 helped them to pay attention to meaningful messages and information regarding the leading role of the story they were reading as well as improving their performances in language capability.
3. Spending time with children during 22:30–24:00 helped to improve their social capability and performances in peer relations.

Keywords: Companionship · Children development · Parent-child interaction

1 Introduction

According to Your life better index survey (2013) in Taiwan, about 14.76 % of employed people thought they have too much "work" time and too few "family interaction" time. Parent's guidance has long term influence on the growth of children. Leibowitze (1974) have proven that parent's parenting time has very significant correlation to the future development of the children. The main objective of this research is: To investigate the correlation between parenting time and the growth and performance of children aged 0–12.

© Springer International Publishing Switzerland 2015
C. Stephanidis (Ed.): HCII 2015 Posters, Part I, CCIS 528, pp. 361–365, 2015.
DOI: 10.1007/978-3-319-21380-4_61

2 Literature Review

2.1 The Life Form of Parenting Family

Parenting time spent by parents has great influence on the development of children (Apps and Rees 2002). In many researches, it was pointed out that parents of higher educational background, as compared to parents of lower educational background, will spend more time actively on taking care of their children (Guryan et al. 2008). Moreover, parents receiving higher education not only will invest more time in taking care of children, but also will change the distribution status of parenting time based on different development stage of children (Kalil et al. 2012).

2.2 The Relationship Between Parents-Child Interaction and Time

Landreth (2002) has proposed that through a daily companionship of 20–30 min with children for game playing, parents can build very close relationship with child, and such relationship will turn out to be very helpful to the feeling of safety, confidence and creativity of the child. According to a questionnaire survey, parents-child co-reading time is, on the average, about 11–20 min each day, then child's reading habit developed will be helpful to the enhancement of child's reading capability (Wu and Chang 2014).

2.3 Relationship Between Companionship and Child's Growth Performance

This research will study if companionship activities can generate change on important features of children, and the literature surveys are as follows:

- Sense of hearing: The interactive process is helpful to the child's listening vocabulary comprehension, more importantly, in the story and game situation, child's interactive skill and friendship with people can be built (Huang 2012).
- Sense of sight: When the baby is accompanied for reading, the level of concentration of the baby will be higher, and baby's eye will then concentrate on meaningful message and message regarding the leading role in the story (Jin 2010).
- Language development: Companionship activity can provide the baby with more complicated chances of speaking, which in turn will affect both baby's language development and reading capability (Zeng and Cheng 2011).
- Personal identity: When the baby has more frequent interaction with parents, safety attachment relationship could be easily formed between parents and the baby, and baby will not feel sorrowful easily, which in turn will promote the generation of safety attachment relationship between the baby and his peers (Li et al. 2007).
- Learning/identify: A child with good attachment relationship and parents-child interactive relationship tends to have less anxiety towards a stranger, such child tends to have better adaptive capability to the society, and better problem solving capability (Liu 2002).

3   Research Method

The research method adopted in this paper is questionnaire survey and statistical analysis. Investigating the relationship between the content of companionship and the child's growth performance, therefore, parents with children aged under 12 years old are selected for the filling of survey questionnaire. Quantity of issuance: 30 copies and duration: October, 2014.

3.1   Experimental Variables

1. Independent variable: According to American Time Use Survey, time is divided into half hour. In this research, parents' off-duty companionship time for children is studied, therefore, the research is focused on the time period from 17:00–17:30 to 24:00, and each half hour is taken as one unit.
2. Dependent variable: Child' performance, and according to the above mentioned literature, dependent variables are listed and are numbered and labeled in the order of 1–12: Vocabulary comprehension capability, friendship relationship, interpersonal interactive skill, stare at meaningful message, language capability, not being sad, low feeling of dependency, peer relationship, emotion regulation capability, problem solving capability and social capability.

3.2   Research Tool

Subjective feeling scale. Likert's five-point scale is used as measurement standard, "Very agree, agree, not sure, disagree, very disagree" are used as selection items. Based on his past companionship experience with child and observation of child's growth performance.

3.3   Statistical Analysis

1. Descriptive statistics: Basic statistics of the data.
2. Descriptive statistics and ANOVA: Whether parenting time would influence child's performance.

4   Experimental Result

4.1   Descriptive Statistics

After sorting, the average educational background is from university or college, or from university of science and technology. Ages of persons under test fall in the range of 29–49 years old, with average age of 37.9 (years old); age of child is 5.04 (years old), and the youngest age is of 0.8 month, and the eldest age is of 12 years old.

4.2 ANOVA Results

According to the results from the test of homogeneity (P > 0.05) and ANOVA, the significant items (P < 0.05) are listed in Table 2.

5 Conclusions and Discussions

5.1 Late Marriage Phenomenon

Presently, when the ages of persons under test are investigated regardless of gender, as shown in Table 1, the average age falls on 37.9, which shows that late marriage phenomenon dominates in Taiwan, meanwhile, the average educational background is above university, therefore, it is concluded that time for receiving education affects the age of marriage.

Table 1. Basic data statistics

	Count	Min.	Max.	Average	Standard deviation
Age of person	30	29.00	49.00	37.9000	5.84483
Educational background	30	2.00	5.00	4.0333	.88992
Age of child	30	.80	12.00	5.0433	3.78597

Table 2. Test result shows that parenting time will affect child's performance

Independent variables	Dependent variables	Sum of squares	Degree of freedom	Mean squares	F	Significance
17:30–18:00	Not being sad	2.917	1	2.917	4.242	.049
18:00–18:30	Vocabulary comprehension capability	2.713	1	2.713	4.428	.044
20:30–21:00	Low dependency	9.044	1	9.044	8.941	.006
21:00–21:30	Paying attention to meaningful information	1.667	1	1.667	4.811	.037
22:30–23:00	Friendship	4.408	1	4.408	6.748	.015
23:00–23:30 13	Peer relationship	3.333	1	3.333	5.773	.023

5.2 Parenting Time Will Affect Child's Performance

The result of Table 2 shows the companionship time with a child for reading, playing game and dining is on the average of about 30 min, which turns out to be helpful to a child's development.

1. In the time period of 17:30–18:30, it usually brings positive and happy mood to a child, therefore, in the sense of hearing aspect, the child tends to have better vocabulary comprehension capability.

2. In the time period of 20:30–21:30, the effectiveness of interaction with a child is most significant, at this moment, the child will notice meaningful message and the message from the leading role of a story, and the child tends to have better performance in logic of language; meanwhile, independent thinking capability of the child is trained too so that the child will not have too strong dependence on family members.

3. In later time period of 22:30–24:00, child and parents usually have difficulty to concentrate, therefore, it is recommended that the parents only chat with child or just stay quietly with the child, with this period of companionship with child, child can get along with others easily, therefore, and the child tends to have good relationship with his friends.

References

Apps, P., Rees, R.: Household production, full consumption and the costs of children. Labour Econ. **8**, 621–648 (2002)

Guryan, J., Hurst, E., Kearney, M.: Parental education and parental time with children. J. Econ. Perspect. **22**(3), 23–46 (2008)

Huang, C.Y.:. Action research on using picture books to promote interaction between children with hearing impairment. National Taipei University of Education, Taipei (2012, unpublished)

Jin, H.H.: Research eyes movement for effect of companionship on 2-3 years-old child's reading. Early Childhood Educ. **465–466**, 27–30 (2010)

Kalil, A., Ryan, R., Corey, M.: Diverging destinies: maternal education and the developmental gradient in time with children. Demography **49**, 1361–1383 (2012)

Landreth, G.L.: Play Therapy: the Art of the Relationship, 2nd edn. Brunner-Routledge, New York (2002)

Leibowitze, A.: Home investments in children. J. Polit. Econ. **82**(2), 111–131 (1974)

Li, M.Z, Dong, X.B., et al.: The self-other boundary of independent vs. interdependent self reflected in parent-child sleep arrangement. Ministry of Science and Technology, Research Project: NSC 94-2413-004-020 (2007, unpublished)

Liu, S.C.: Investigating of a secure attachment relationship and child social development. Educ. Mon. **418**, 42–45 (2002)

Zeng, S.S., Cheng, S.F.: A case study of the toy library in Chenxi Tribe. J. Taipei Municipal Univ. Educ. **2**, 35–36 (2011)

Wu, T.L., Chang, R.H.: Children's demand for environment and furniture. In: Parent-Child Reading, Conference of Ergonomics Society of Taiwan. Taichung. 28 March 2014

Your better life Index. Directorate-General of Budget, Accounting and Statistics (30 Aug 2013). Accessed 6 June 2014. http://www.dgbas.gov.tw/ct.asp?xItem=34777&ctNode=5624

A Novel 3D Wheelchair Simulation System for Training Young Children with Severe Motor Impairments

Jicheng Fu[1(✉)], Cole Garien[1], Sean Smith[1], Wenxi Zeng[1],
and Maria Jones[2]

[1] University of Central Oklahoma, Edmond, USA
{jfu,cgarien1,ssmith186,wzeng}@uco.edu
[2] University of Oklahoma Health Sciences Center, Oklahoma City, USA
maria-jones@ouhsc.edu

Abstract. Young children with severe motor impairments face a higher risk of secondary impairments in the development of social, cognitive, and motor skills, owing to the lack of independent mobility. Although power wheelchairs are typical tools for providing independent mobility, the steep learning curve, safety concerns, and high cost may prevent children aged 2–5 years from using them. We have developed a 3D wheelchair simulation system using gaming technologies for these young children to learn fundamental wheelchair driving skills in a safe, affordable, and entertaining environment. Depending on the skill level, the simulation system offers different options ranging from automatic control (i.e., the artificial intelligent (AI) module fully controls the wheelchair) to manual control (i.e., human users are fully responsible for controlling the wheelchair). Optimized AI algorithms were developed to make the simulation system easy and efficient to use. We have conducted experiments to evaluate the simulation system. The results demonstrate that the simulation system is promising to overcome the limitations associated with real wheelchairs meanwhile providing a safe, affordable, and exciting environment to train young children.

Keywords: Artificial intelligence · A* · Gaming technology · Power wheelchair · Secondary impairment · Severe motor impairment · Simulation

1 Introduction

Independent mobility has been found to be closely related to a child's social, cognitive, perceptual, and motor development [1]. Hence, children with severe motor impairments are exposed to a higher risk for the secondary impairment in the aforementioned areas [2]. Although power wheelchairs are commonly used to provide independent mobility, children aged 2–5 years may find it difficult to use the wheelchairs on a daily basis. In addition, the high price of power wheelchairs may prevent the children from having access to a wheelchair at an early age.

In contrast, wheelchair simulation systems can provide a safe and affordable environment, in which children can practice fundamental wheelchair maneuvering

© Springer International Publishing Switzerland 2015
C. Stephanidis (Ed.): HCII 2015 Posters, Part I, CCIS 528, pp. 366–371, 2015.
DOI: 10.1007/978-3-319-21380-4_62

skills at an early age. Sveistrup [3] pointed out that the wheelchair simulators can provide training in a functional, purposeful, and motivating context, which is a significant advantage over traditional training for wheelchair maneuverability. Rose et al. [4] demonstrated that the skills learned in virtual environments could be positively transferred to real environments. Holden [5] analyzed existing research results, which demonstrated experimental evidence that motor learning in a virtual environment may be superior to that of real-world practice.

In this study, we have employed the Unity 3D game engine [6] to develop a wheelchair simulation system. Users can control the wheelchair in three modes, namely, manual, automatic, and hybrid modes. The manual control mode gives a child full control over the wheelchair via a joystick. The automatic control mode, by contrast, utilizes our optimized A* algorithm to automatically maneuver the wheelchair through the environment. On average, the optimized algorithm takes half as much time to navigate than the un-optimized version due to the removal of redundant movements. The hybrid control mode allows for the control of the wheelchair to be shared by the human user and intelligence module. The optimized A* algorithm is also utilized, but in conjunction with an intent recognition algorithm so that the user and intelligence module can work together to control the wheelchair. When the user attempts to steer toward a goal, his/her intent is recognized by the intelligence module and a path is generated toward the intended goal. The intelligence module measures variances in the user's input to determine the probability of the user's intent to change goals. Once this probability reaches the intent threshold, the user's position, wheelchair orientation, and intent are used to determine the new goal. This novel strategy helps reduce frustration in young children by having the intelligence module handle fine motion control, while letting the child practice higher-level navigations.

2 Method

Figure 1 shows two screenshots of our simulation system. Figure 1a illustrates that the simulation system offers three control modes, namely, manual, automatic, and hybrid control. Figure 1b shows a training scenario in our simulation system.

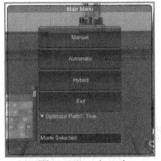

(a) Three control modes   (b) A training scenario

Fig. 1. Screenshots of the simulation system

2.1   The Optimized Path Finding

Under the automatic and hybrid control modes, the simulation system needs to find a path from the wheelchair's current position to the goal in order to assist in the smooth navigation of the wheelchair. To enable path finding, we first model the environment into a graph-like structure. Specifically, the graph structure is a grid of cells, where each cell has a position that relates to coordinates within the simulation system as shown in Fig. 2. The path considers obstacles along the way to avoid collisions. We employed the well-known A* algorithm, which is a heuristic search algorithm that is used to quickly and efficiently search through a graph structure and return the optimal path from a starting node to a goal node [7]. The heuristic function $f(n)$ used by A* is commonly defined as follows:

$$f(n) = g(n) + h(n) \qquad (1)$$

where $g(n)$ defines the distance from the node n to the starting node; and $h(n)$ is the heuristic function that defines the estimated distance from the node n to the goal node.

In reality, we have found that the path generated by A* contained many unnecessary zigzag turns. We can explain this issue by using a simple example as shown in Fig. 2. The solid circle in Fig. 2 represents the starting node; the node marked with an "X" is the goal node; and the grayed out nodes are barriers, which cannot be processed. Particularly, Fig. 2a–c show the values of $g(n)$, $h(n)$, and $f(n)$, respectively. Based on the heuristic values, a path is generated in Fig. 2c, which consists of 6 turning points. In fact, our simulation system contains a significantly larger number of cells than this simple example. As a result, the wheelchair turns very frequently and yields an unsmooth and uncomfortable driving experience.

To improve the quality of the generated paths, we have optimized the A* path finding algorithm such that it has been tailored to work more effectively and efficiently in our system. The optimized algorithm uses three markers during the optimization process, namely, the checkpoint marker, the current marker, and the next marker. The checkpoint marker is used to mark the last node found that will be included in the finalized path. The current marker is used to mark the current node that the algorithm is examining as it traverses the path. The next marker is used to mark the node that comes after the current node in the un-optimized path. This marker is important for determining whether the current node needs to be removed or not.

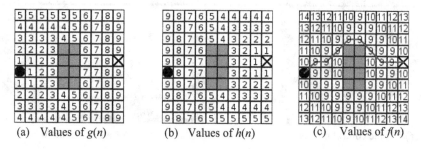

(a) Values of $g(n)$ (b) Values of $h(n)$ (c) Values of $f(n)$

Fig. 2. An example that illustrates the issues of A*

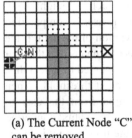 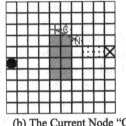 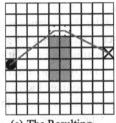

| (a) The Current Node "C" can be removed | (b) The Current Node "C" will become the checkpoint | (c) The Resulting Optimized Path |

Fig. 3. The optimized path

Initially, the algorithm starts by marking the beginning of the path with the checkpoint marker, marking the second node with the current marker, and marking the third node with the next marker (as shown in Fig. 3a). Note that the node marked with "+" represents the checkpoint marker, the node marked with "C" denotes that current marker, and the one marked with "N" is the next marker. After the nodes are marked, the algorithm checks to see if there are obstacles between the node marked with the next marker and the node marked with the checkpoint marker. If so, this means that the current node should be kept in the path and it is marked with the checkpoint marker. If there are no obstacles between the next node and checkpoint node, then the current node can be removed. Once the current node has been processed, the next node is marked as the current node and its child is marked as the next node. This process repeats until the goal is reached and the resulting path will have all redundant movements removed. Figure 3a shows an example of when the node marked with the current marker ("C") would be removed from the path. Figure 3b shows an example of when the node marked with the current marker ("C") would become marked with the checkpoint marker ("+"). Figure 3c shows the resulting path that has been run through the optimization algorithm. This optimization process is important not only because it generates a simpler path, but also because the optimized path can take less time to navigate compared to an un-optimized path.

2.2 Hybrid Control

Different from the automatic control mode, where the user specifies a goal to reach, the hybrid control mode requires our simulation system to identify the user's driving intention, i.e., where the user desires to go. This is achieved by considering inputs from the user as well as the artificial intelligence module. While the hybrid control mode still utilizes the optimized A* algorithm, we have also developed an intent recognition algorithm to identify the intended goal. As the user's input from the joystick begins to oppose that of the AI module that is guiding the wheelchair, the player's input is gathered and stored for analysis. When new input is added to the dataset, the variance of the set is calculated and stored for later use. The variance of the dataset signifies the variability or spread of the data and is used for calculating the standard deviation of the set. This statistic is important because it will allow the artificial intelligence module to filter out negligible, involuntary movements of the joystick, such as slight hand tremors. After the variance is calculated, the current input from the user is compared to the dataset to see whether the input falls within the standard deviation of the data. If the input falls within the norm, it is considered negligible. Otherwise, it means that the user may want to move to a different goal and an intent counter is incremented to reflect this. As the intent counter increases, it will eventually surpass the intent threshold. When this happens, the artificial intelligence module utilizes the input from the user to determine where the user is intending to go. To do so, the user's input is first converted into an angle that is relative to the wheelchair. For example, if the user's input is to the sharp right, the angle would be 90°. Next, a list is generated that contains an angle for each possible goal in the room. The angle is calculated between the wheelchair's orientation and the respective goal. Then, each angle in this list is compared with the input angle. The object from the list that has the closest angle to the input is identified as the new goal. After the user's intention has been recognized, the AI module will generate a new path from the wheelchair to the new goal by utilizing the optimized A* algorithm.

3   Experiments

We conducted experiments to evaluate the performance of the simulation system, specifically for the automatic and hybrid controls. The data was collected over three trial runs for each goal in each control mode.

3.1   Performance Evaluation Under the Automatic Control

To ensure the fairness of the evaluation, the starting point of the wheelchair was fixed in each experiment. We measured the time required to reach each goal using the traditional A* algorithm and our optimized A* algorithm. There were six possible goals in the training scenario, namely, tables 1–3, a sofa, a bookcase, and the window. As shown in Fig. 4a, the traditional A* generated paths that took twice as much time to traverse compared to the time required by the optimized A* algorithm.

3.2   Performance Evaluation Under the Hybrid Control

The experimental procedure was the same as that in the automatic control mode. The difference was that the user did not simply choose a goal object to navigate to, but instead, the simulation system tried to identify the driving goal first. As we are still collecting data from children with severe motor impairments, a healthy adult conducted the experiment in this study. We expect that children with severe motor impairments may have poorer performance. Figure 4b shows the experimental results, which illustrate that if the traditional A* algorithm were used, even the healthy adult would find it difficult to manipulate the simulation system. In contrast, if the optimized algorithm was used, the performance was largely improved.

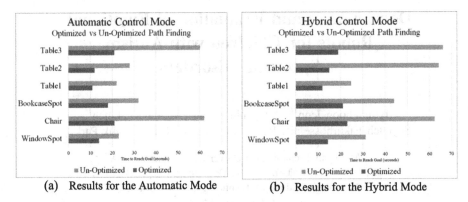

(a)   Results for the Automatic Mode   (b)   Results for the Hybrid Mode

Fig. 4. Experimental results

4   Conclusion

In this study, we presented a novel 3D wheelchair simulation system for training young children with severe motor impairments. Besides the manual control mode, we have developed optimized AI algorithms to support the automatic and hybrid control modes. The experimental results demonstrated that our system is a promising platform to provide a practical, safe, affordable, and exciting environment to train young children.

Acknowledgement. This work was supported by the Oklahoma Center for the Advancement of Science and Technology (OCAST HR12-036).

References

1. Ragonesi, C.B., Chen, X., Agrawal, S., Galloway, J.C.: Power mobility and socialization in preschool: a case study of a child with cerebral palsy. Pediatr. Phys. Ther. **22**, 322–329 (2010)
2. Kermoian, R.: Locomotor experience and psychological development in infancy. In: Pediatric Powered Mobility: Developmental Perspectives Technical Issues Clinical Approaches, pp. 7–21. RESNA, Arlington, VA (1997)
3. Sveistrup, H.: Motor rehabilitation using virtual reality. J. Neuroeng. Rehabil. **1**, 10 (2004)
4. Rose, F.D., Attree, E.A., Brooks, B.M., Parslow, D.M., Penn, P.R., Ambihaipahan, N.: Training in virtual environments: transfer to real world tasks and equivalence to real task training. Ergonomics **43**, 494–511 (2000)
5. Holden, M.K.: Virtual environments for motor rehabilitation: review. Cyberpsychol. Behav. **8**, 187–211 (2005). discussion 212-9
6. http://unity3d.com/
7. Hart, P.E., Nilsson, N.J., Raphael, B.: A formal basis for the heuristic determination of minimum cost paths. IEEE Trans. Syst. Sci. Cybern. **4**, 100–107 (1968)

Development and Evaluation of Emotional Robots for Children with Autism Spectrum Disorders

Myounghoon Jeon[1(✉)], Ruimin Zhang[1], William Lehman[1], Seyedeh Fakhrhosseini[1], Jaclyn Barnes[1], and Chung Hyuk Park[2]

[1] Michigan Technological University, Houghton, USA
{mjeon, ruiminz, welehman, sfakhrho, jaclynb}@mtu.edu
[2] New York Institute of Technology, New York, USA
chung.park@nyit.edu

Abstract. Individuals with Autism Spectrum Disorders (ASD) often have difficulty recognizing emotional cues in ordinary interaction. To address this, we are developing a social robot that teaches children with ASD to recognize emotion in the simpler and more controlled context of interaction with a robot. An emotion recognition program using the Viola-Jones algorithm for facial detection is in development. To better understand emotion expression by social robots, a study was conducted with 11 college students matching animated facial expressions and emotionally neutral sentences spoken in affective voices to various emotions. Overall, facial expressions had greater recognition accuracy and higher perceived intensity than voices. Future work will test the recognition of combined face and voices.

Keywords: Social robotics · Emotion · Autism spectrum disorders

1 Introduction

Recognizing and understanding emotional cues while interacting with other people is vital for effective communication as these cues contain information about meaning, intention, and appropriate responses. People with Autism Spectrum Disorders (ASD) often lack the ability to decipher these cues and this challenge has been identified as one of the biggest barriers to their social inclusion [1]. To help children with ASD develop richer emotional interaction, researchers have used interactive robots and shown positive results [2–8]. Robots allow for a simplified, predictable, and reliable environment where the complexity of interaction can be controlled and gradually increased [9]. Robots can also work as embedded reinforcers of learning [7] and thus, they can form rapport with children.

Our project aims to enhance the emotional communication of children with ASD using social robots. The work described here is a portion of that larger project. In order to enhance communication, we must examine how children with ASD and neurotypical children understand and interpret emotion and how the robot can encourage better emotional interaction. As a test platform, we are using an iOS-based interactive robot,

© Springer International Publishing Switzerland 2015
C. Stephanidis (Ed.): HCII 2015 Posters, Part I, CCIS 528, pp. 372–376, 2015.
DOI: 10.1007/978-3-319-21380-4_63

Romo, which is non-humanoid, but has important human expressive characteristics (eyelids, mouth, voice, etc.) [10, 11] and thus, can have emotional communication with children (Fig. 1).

Fig. 1. Romo

For successful emotional interaction, the robot needs capabilities of emotion recognition and expression. On the emotion recognition side, we are developing software to recognize emotion in facial expressions extracted from real-time video of the individual during interaction. This portion of the research is in progress. For emotional expression, we conducted an experiment with college students to determine how Romo's facial expressions and a variety of equivalent affective voice recordings are interpreted.

2 Design and Implementation of Emotion Recognition and Expression

2.1 Emotion Recognition on Romo

With emotion recognition, we can monitor a child's affective state for intervention purposes. We can also verify if the child-robot interaction successfully yields the intended goal (e.g., enhancing social interaction). While researchers have suggested a variety of emotion recognition methods, no single method has been perfectly successful [12]. Also, it should be differentiated depending on users' characteristics, tasks, and environments. We have developed a multimodal emotion recognition system (facial + voice) for drivers with Traumatic Brain Injury (TBI) [13]. For that project, we developed a facial expression recognition system using the Support-Vector Machines (SVMs) algorithm, which could detect positive, negative, and neutral states. Our second-generation facial detection system for the current project has been developed using the Viola-Jones algorithm in Objective-C. It can detect more specific affective states than our previous version, such as happiness, surprise, and anger, etc. For higher recognition accuracy and additional affective states, we are currently updating our system using the standardized database sets (e.g., Cohn-Kanade [14] and MMI data-base [15]). Future work will utilize a dataset of children's emotional expressions that we are currently creating.

2.2   Emotion Expression on Romo

After estimating a child's affective state, a robot is required to respond in an emotionally appropriate manner. For facial expression, we tested the standard expressions provided by the Romo app including curious, excited, happy, neutral, sad, scared, and sleepy (Fig. 2). For voice expression, a young male adult and a young female adult recorded emotion-independent sentences [16] ("Can I get some food?", "It's time to go.", and "What are you doing?") using affective voice types for the same seven emotion. We controlled Romo's face expression and voice expression using the Romo software development kit.

Fig. 2. Happy, curious, and sad (from left to right)

3   User Evaluation of Emotion Expression on Romo

3.1   Method and Procedure

This paper focuses on the evaluation of users' recognition of ROMO's facial and voice expressions, rather than Romo's recognition performance, which as mentioned is still in development. The study sought to understand how emotion expressed by Romo is interpreted through voice and facial cues, so that we can develop salient emotional cues that can be used in Romo and other interactive robots. Clear cues will provide a good foundation for our efforts to improve the emotional understanding of children with ASD.

Eleven college students (ages 18–22, 2 females and 9 males) participated in this experiment. No information was collected regarding participants' ASD or neurotypical status. We used a within subject design in which each participant was subject to face-only and voice-only conditions. The expression could be seen/heard multiple times by tapping the screen. There were 42 trials for voice (7 emotions, 3 different phrases, and 2 genders). For consistency, there were also 42 trials for face, each of the seven emotions repeated six times. After presentation of the stimulus, the participant was asked to choose one out of seven emotions that the stimulus conveyed and rate how strong the emotion was on a scale of 1 ("Not at all") to 7 ("Very"). The face and voice conditions were presented separately and the presentation order was alternated. Within each condition, the trials were randomized for each participant.

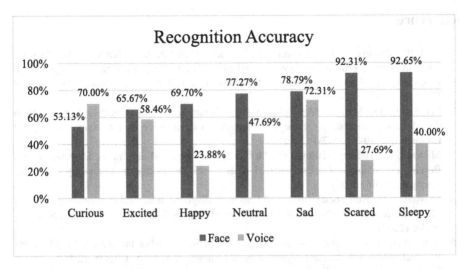

Fig. 3. Recognition accuracy for voice and face across all conditions

3.2   Results

A paired samples t-tests revealed a significant difference of recognition accuracy between faces ($M = 75.70$, $SD = 14.25$) and voices ($M = 48.57$, $SD = 19.13$), $t(6) = -2.46$, $p < .05$. For all emotions except curious, faces had higher recognition accuracy, particularly the happy, scared, and sleepy conditions (Fig. 3). There was also a trend toward more intense ratings of faces (average 5.78) compared to voices (average 4.57).

4   Discussion and Future Work

The data show that emotion conveyed by facial expression tended to be more recognizable and more intense than that in voice. However, there was no clear pattern of differences in terms of the traditional valence and arousal dimensions, which requires further research.

We plan to combine face and voice stimuli into one condition to test the strength of the combined emotion. We will utilize both matched face and voice affect and contradictory affects. The mismatched condition is expected to indicate whether faces or voices produce stronger emotional cues when combined. The emotion detection program will be expanded to recognize a wider variety of emotions and to appropriately detect children's emotional states.

Acknowledgements. This material is based upon work supported by the National Institutes of Health under grant No. 1 R01 HD082914-01.

References

1. Paul, R., Shriberg, L.D., McSweeny, J., Cicchetti, D., Klin, A., Volkmar, F.: Brief report: relations between prosodic performance and communication and socialization ratings in high functioning speakers with autism spectrum disorders. J. Autism Dev. Disord. **35**, 861–869 (2005)
2. Feil-Seifer, D., Mataric, M.: Robot-assisted therapy for children with autism spectrum disorders. In: Proceedings of the 7th International Conference on Interaction Design and Children, pp. 49–52. ACM (2008)
3. Michaud, F., Théberge-Turmel, C.: Mobile robotic toys and autism. In: Dautenhahn, K., Bond, A., Cañamero, L., Edmonds, B. (eds.) Socially Intelligent Agents, pp. 125–132. Springer, Berlin (2002)
4. Scassellati, B.: How social robots will help us to diagnose, treat, and understand autism. In: Thrun, S., Brooks, R., Durrant-Whyte, H. (eds.) Robotics Research, pp. 552–563. Springer, Berlin (2007)
5. Scassellati, B.: Affective prosody recognition for human-robot interaction. In: Microsoft Research's External Research Symposium. Redmond, WA, USA. Citeseer (2009)
6. Stanton, C.M., Kahn, P.H., Severson, R.L., Ruckert, J.H., Gill, B.T.: Robotic animals might aid in the social development of children with autism. In: 2008 3rd ACM/IEEE International Conference on Human-Robot Interaction (HRI), pp. 271–278. IEEE (2008)
7. Kim, E.S., Berkovits, L.D., Bernier, E.P., Leyzberg, D., Shic, F., Paul, R., Scassellati, B.: Social robots as embedded reinforcers of social behavior in children with autism. J. Autism Dev. Disord. **43**, 1038–1049 (2013)
8. Werry, I., Dautenhahn, K., Harwin, W.: Investigating a robot as a therapy partner for children with autism. In: Proceedings of AAATE 2001 (2001)
9. el Kaliouby, R., Picard, R., Baron-Cohen, S.: Affective computing and autism. Ann. N. Y. Acad. Sci. **1093**, 228–248 (2006)
10. DiSalvo, C.F., Gemperle, F., Forlizzi, J., Kiesler, S.: All robots are not created equal: the design and perception of humanoid robot heads. In: Proceedings of the 4th Conference on Designing Interactive Systems: Processes, Practices, Methods, and Techniques, pp. 321–326. ACM (2002)
11. Adams, A., Robinson, P.: An android head for social-emotional intervention for children with autism spectrum conditions. In: D'Mello, S., Graesser, A., Schuller, B., Martin, J.-C. (eds.) ACII 2011, Part II. LNCS, vol. 6975, pp. 183–190. Springer, Heidelberg (2011)
12. Calvo, R.A., D'Mello, S.: Affect detection: An interdisciplinary review of models, methods, and their applications. IEEE Trans. Affect. Comput. **1**, 18–37 (2010)
13. Jeon, M., Walker, B.: Emotion detection and regulation interface for drivers with traumatic brain injury. In: Proceedings of the SIGCHI Conference on Human Factors in Computing Systems (CHI11) (2011)
14. Kanade, T., Cohn, J.F., Tian, Y.: Comprehensive database for facial expression analysis. In: Proceedings. Fourth IEEE International Conference on Automatic Face and Gesture Recognition, 2000, pp. 46–53. IEEE (2011)
15. Valstar, M., Pantic, M.: Induced disgust, happiness and surprise: an addition to the MMI facial expression database. In: Proceedings of International Conference Language Resources and Evaluation, Workshop on Emotion, pp. 65–70 (2010)
16. Jeon, M., Rayan, I.A.: The effect of physical embodiment of an animal robot on affective prosody recognition. In: Jacko, J.A. (ed.) Human-Computer Interaction, Part II, HCII 2011. LNCS, vol. 6762, pp. 523–532. Springer, Heidelberg (2011)

Serious Game for the Evaluation of Cognitive Function of Kids

Donghan Kim[1] and C.J. Lim[2(✉)]

[1] Department of Electrical Engineering, Kyung Hee University, Seoul, Korea
donghani@khu.ac.kr
[2] Department of Game and Multimedia Engineering,
Korea Polytechnic University, Siheung, Korea
scjlim@gmail.com

Abstract. This paper describes the serious game contents for the evaluation of cognitive function for kids. The game contents were designed for measuring and enhancing the cognitive function of the kids (ages 5–7). We clustered the measurable cognitive functions as auditory attention, visual attention, attention shift, and impulse control. This study is based on the advisory of the Department of Psychiatry and Behavioral Science, Seoul National University College of Medicine. In impulse control task, we applied the vision based head tracking technology. This study is meaningful on the point view that we can evaluate and enhance the cognitive function of kids who are familiar with the computer environments.

Keywords: Cognitive function · Serious game · Impulse control · Visual attention · Attention shift · Auditory attention

1 Introduction

1.1 Cognitive Evaluation

Cognitive evaluation means the ability to discerning and then recognizing the object. Maintaining the cognitive evaluation skill controls the number of factors that can degrade memory or concentration in order to maintain the functionality of normal brain [1]. When the cognitive evaluation is further refined, it includes mental abilities such as knowledge, understanding, thinking skills, problem solving skills, critical thinking, creative thinking, etc. Impulse control, auditory-verbal memory, and visual-spatial memory can be enhanced through training [2–5].

1.2 Backgrounds of Cognitive Evaluation Methods

Existing cognitive evaluation has been used a problem-solving approach, which consists of 4 or 5 multiple choices with respect to each item. This is a valid approach for children over the age of 12, who are proficient in reading the letter and determining the visual information. Cognitive evaluation methods for the low age children are card selection or modeling tools, which stimulate the interest of children.

© Springer International Publishing Switzerland 2015
C. Stephanidis (Ed.): HCII 2015 Posters, Part I, CCIS 528, pp. 377–382, 2015.
DOI: 10.1007/978-3-319-21380-4_64

1.3   Significances of Serious Game for Child Cognitive Evaluation

A top priority subject to be considered for low age children is the visual-auditory material like image or sound, but not the letter. The proposed paper develops a cognitive evaluation game, which is a non-writing method and utilizes a touch gesture. It improves the usability of evaluation progress and the results.

2   Serious Game for Child Cognitive Evaluation

2.1   Operating Device

Operating device has been placed differently depending on the target age group. Since the behavior and judgment for children aged between 5 ～ 7 primarily have high randomness, the evaluation game used the NUI motion recognition camera with touch gesture and the child facing direction through facial recognition as shown in Fig. 1.

Fig. 1. Application of gesture recognition camera

The evaluation game is operated through touch interface using a touch panel display for children aged between 8 ～ 10, who are relatively outstanding in letter analysis capability. At the same time, it is planned to take advantage of voice input through the speech recognition API in the game. However, since all of the commercial speech recognition APIs are made on the basis of adult male voice, the speech recognition is not included in the final result due to low recognition rate for children's voice.

2.2   Game Flow

Once the game starts, children enter their information. The first game screen is displayed upon completion of input, and then a total of 4 games are executed in sequential order. The general progress of game is known by performing the practice exercises preferentially and each game can proceed up to a total of 6 ～ 7 steps. The game ends when all games are executed or when the game fails during play. At this time, the result of cognitive assessment data performed in the game is displayed. When the current game is either passed or failed, the next game gets started. The result of game is presented to children, but also saved as a csv file such that the available data can be transferred to the rating agency.

2.3 Game Concept

The proposed cognitive evaluation game is developed in two versions: one for children aged between $5 \sim 7$ and the other for children aged between $8 \sim 10$. The differences between two versions are the difficulty of game itself, visual preferences of children, and the differences in the concentration. The prior version is made using a primary color and a simple form of the UI as shown in Fig. 2 (Left). In contrast, greater variety of color and complex forms of the UI are used in the latter version as shown in Fig. 2 (Right).

Fig. 2. Snapshot of game evaluation screen for ages 5–7 (left) and ages 8–10 (right)

A story narrative is included in each of game such that there is no discomfort of progressing the game at the location presented in background image. In addition, the concentration of children gets elevated by naturally showing the feedback according to the game progress.

2.4 Game Engine

Unity 3D engine that can take advantage of a variety of plugin (as shown in Fig. 3) is used because we have concluded that availability on a variety of devices is important to apply the proposed gesture recognition camera and touch panel display.

 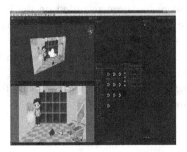

Fig. 3. Testing camera for gesture recognition and unity 3D engine

The strengths of Unity 3D engine include easy porting to another platform and linkage to a variety of gesture recognition device through the plugin package. Thus, Unity 3D engine can be effectively used.

2.5   Game Development

Unity 3D is a 3D game engine, where the proposed evaluation game should be configured in a 2D screen so that children can be easily recognized. Thus, the final visual information is needed to be configured as a 2D screen. Even though Unity supports 2D functionality, but we have determined that this is not the intention of 2D screen effect and the game contents are made using NGUI. Button and UI elements are used to configure the screen through NGUI, and then sphere collision is used for moving or manipulating object to verify the collision check as shown in Fig. 4.

 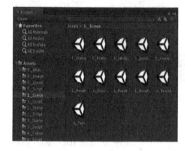

Fig. 4. Snapshot of item using sphere collision and separated scene management

Evaluation games for children aged between $5 \sim 7$ and $8 \sim 10$ are programmed differently, where each has GameManager class that controls the entire game flow including full screen UI and game progress.

Both manager and scene are set apart according to each type of game. When the game starts, it is moved to the scene in order to progress its game. Once it is completed, the results are passed to the manager such that the output data can be made as a csv file (as shown in Fig. 4). For the difficulty level, it has a linear relationship such that once a certain score has been recorded on the lower level, it automatically allows to play a higher level. However, when the condition is not satisfied, the game is terminated and output its results (as shown in Fig. 5).

In the game for children aged between $8 \sim 10$, there is a game that must process the evaluation after a certain period of time. Thus, based on this condition, it allows to select the level directly rather than using the prior data in order to enhance the easy of evaluation environment.

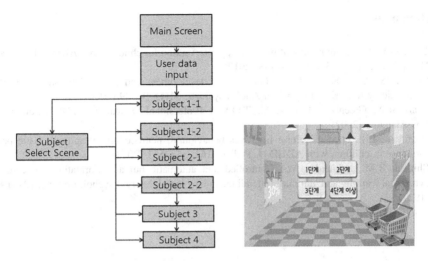

Fig. 5. Flow chart of scene progress and selecting game level

3 Conclusion

Cognitive evaluation of children in Korea is known as either the reading voucher that is run independently in a municipality or the professional domain that needs to purchase expensive evaluation/training tool separately. Flawless supply is essential in order to improve this situation, but it is not easy due to the number of expertise and unreasonable assessment method.

This paper proposed the child cognitive evaluation game to be used without restrictions of place, time, and cost. In addition, the proposed evaluation game will improve the overall children's welfare with increasing easy of expert organizations. Since the color and UI configuration, and operation methods were set differently according to the children's age, the proposed method can also be the basis for developing similar contents in future.

The proposed game is based on the children's cognitive evaluation, which evaluates the child's auditory-verbal memory and visual-spatial memory to support motivation and concentration. Developing training contents that is self-interested and improving the cognitive ability is left as a further work.

Acknowledgement. This research was supported by Technology Innovation Program of the Knowledge economy (No. 10041834, 10045351) funded by the Ministry of Knowledge Economy (MKE, Korea), the National Research Foundation of Korea Grant funded by the Korean Government (No. 2012R1A1A2043822, 2014S1A5B6035098) and the MSIP(Ministry of Science, ICT and Future Planning), Korea, under the Global IT Talent support program (NIPA-2014-ITAH0905140110020001000100100) supervised by the NIPA (National IT Industry Promotion Agency).

References

1. Choi, J.-A.: Literature review of play therapy intervention for children with ADHD. J. Korean Home Econ. Assoc. **50**(5), 125–138 (2012)
2. Shin, M.S., Cho, S., et al.: A study of the development and standardization of ADHD diagnostic system. Korean J. Child Adol. Psychiatr. **11**(1), 91–99 (2000)
3. Leark, R.A., Greenberg, L.M., et al.: T.O.V.A. Professional Manual. The TOVA Company, Los Alamitos (2007)
4. Pontifex, M.B., et al.: Exercise improves behavioural, neurocognitive, and scholastic performance in children with ADHD. J. Pediatr. **162**, 543–551 (2013)
5. Shiffrin, R.M., Schneider, W.: Controlled and automatic human information processing: perceptual learning and automatic attending, and a general theory. Psychol. Rev. **84**, 127–190 (1977)

Smart Playground: A Tangible Interactive Platform with Regular Toys for Young Kids

Duc-Minh Pham[✉], Thinh Nguyen-Vo, and Minh-Triet Tran

Faculty of Information Technology, University of Science, VNU-HCM,
Ho-chi-minh, Vietnam
{pdminh,nvpthinh}@apcs.vn, tmtriet@fit.hcmus.edu.vn

Abstract. In modern world, children need to get familiar with interactive toys to quickly improve their learning and imagination. Our approach is to add augmented information and interaction to common toys on the surface containing them, which is called Smart Playground. Popular methods use three color channels and local features to recognize objects. However, toys of children usually have various pictures with different colors drawn on many small components. Therefore depth data is useful in this case. Each toy usually have unique shape that is distinguishable from others. In this paper, we use an RGB-D sensor to collect information about both color and shape of objects. To learn the training set of toys, an approach of convolutional neural network is used to represent data (both color and depth) by high-level feature vectors. Using the combined results, the accuracy of 3D recognition is more than 90 %.

Keywords: RGB-D · 3d recognition · Deep learning · Convolutional neural network

1 Introduction

Young kids love playing with toys. Although young children in modern life have opportunities to interact and play games with mobile devices, such as tablets or smartphones, toys are still an essential part of their childhood. The problem is to integrate smart features and interactions that a kid can do with computers into regular toys. It would be necessary to make regular toys become more lively with smart interactive features so that young kids feel more excited when playing with their toys.

In this paper, we propose to develop a Smart Playground, a platform in which a regular toy becomes a tangible user interface object. When a kid puts his or her bear or doll on the surface of Smart Playground, our system recognizes which the toy is with RGB-D information captured from color and depth cameras, then displays visual effects on both that toy and other existing toys on the playground as well as plays sound effects or background music to augment the playground environment.

There are two main components in our proposed Smart Playground. The first component is a 3D toy recognition module that can recognize a regular

© Springer International Publishing Switzerland 2015
C. Stephanidis (Ed.): HCII 2015 Posters, Part I, CCIS 528, pp. 383–388, 2015.
DOI: 10.1007/978-3-319-21380-4_65

3D toy from its 3D shape and color/texture. The second component is a module to manage augmented multimedia objects linked to a given 3D toy.

The main contributions in our proposed system are as follows:

- First, we propose to transform regular toys into tangible UI objects that can be used to activate certain interactions and events on the smart playground. There is no special modification on regular toys, such as using magnetic tags or RFID chips. We employ the vision-based approach to recognize 3D object, a.k.a. regular toys, from their 3D shapes, colors, and textures.
- Second, we propose a method following the new trend in computer vision to apply deep convolutional neural network to learn higher-level features [9] from depth and color data to boost the accuracy of 3D object recognition in realtime manner.
- Third, we propose an architecture for Smart Playground to become a flexible platform that can accept more toys with augmented multimedia data. Each toy, after being trained to be recognized, is associated with a collection of multimedia data, such as video clips, audio clips, or images.

The rest of this paper has the following structure: In Sect. 2, we briefly preview the related works; the proposed method for 3D recognition with RGB-D features is presented in Sect. 3; after that, the architecture for our smart playground is introduced in Sect. 4; Sect. 5 show the experiment results and evaluations; finally, the conclusion is presented in Sect. 6.

2   Related Works

Nowadays, there are many depth sensors that open a new era for 3D research in computer vision. With depth data, not only the appearance but also the shape of objects are known. The new trend is to combine both color and depth features together for more efficient object recognition. Depth data is also a support feature for scene segmentation and classification [2]. Some approach use sparse coding to learn hierarchical feature representations from raw RGB-D data in an unsupervised way [3]. However, capturing the newest idea of deep learning, several research groups use neural networks for training RGB-D images [4–6]. Follow the new trend, we apply convolutional neural network (CNN) for our system.

3   Proposed Method for 3D Toy Recognition with RGB-D Data

To recognize a regular toy, we use both color data and depth data captured from cameras in realtime. Figure 1 illustrates the overview of our proposed method to recognize a toy with RGB-D data. The recognition process is performed on color and depth data independently, then the results are processed in the fusion module to determine the output toy ID corresponding to a regular 3D toy.

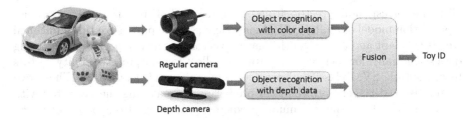

Fig. 1. Overview of our proposed method for 3D toy recognition with RGB-D data

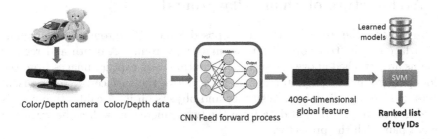

Fig. 2. Toy recognition using convolutional neural network

Instead of depending on the common approach to recognize an object from color data by using Bag-of-Words (BoW) model [1], we follow the new trend in visual object recognition to apply deep convolutional neural network (CNN) [9] to process both color data and raw 3D data into features in a high-level representation (c.f. Fig. 2). One of the most popular framework for building and testing CNN is Caffe [7]. This tool not only support an engine to calculate the parameters of CNN but also provide some available trained results from popular image data sets such as ImageNet ILSVRC2012 and MNIST. These sets have a very large number of classes and images, especially ILSVRC2012 [11]. This 1000-class data set consists of millions of images captured from various things in our real world such as animals (cat, monkey, fox), daily items (umbrella, soccer ball, balloon), means of transportation (car, canoe, boat), and natural scenes (volcano, sea, forest). Hence, the CNN trained on ILSVRC2012 contains most of features that we meet everyday in our life.

Based on the above characteristics, we propose to use the color of a specific object as input for the CNN of ILSVRC2012. The corresponding output vector of feed forward process on this CNN can be considered as a high-level global feature for the given object. For depth information, the raw 3D data need to be normalized to 2D grayscale image that describes the shape of the object before pushing to the CNN. That means, each object is now represented by two vectors of color data and depth data.

The built CNN of ILSVRC2012 consists of multiple layers that generates differently dimensional vectors. We decide to use the last feature vector of 4096 elements to represents our input data. For each type of data (color or depth), all of the corresponding vectors from our train set of 3D toys is used to construct a prediction model of multiple SVM classifiers [8]. The purpose of this additional step is to adapt and transform the feature vectors to the perspective of our using data set. Finally, for each of testing toy, we collect two output probability vectors from multiple SVM classifiers' prediction on color and depth data. These two vectors is used to generate the final prediction by matching the given toy with the class that have the maximum predicted probability from both color and depth data.

4   Architecture of Smart Playground

Figure 3 shows the overview of our proposed Smart Playground. Any regular flat surface can be transformed into a smart playground. A depth and regular cameras are attached above the surface to continuously capture images from the below playground. A projector is also hung above the surface to create visual effects and presentations on the surface and objects on it. A calibration step is performed to align captured data from the two cameras, as well as between the camera pair with the projector.

When a young kid puts a toy on the ground surface, the depth camera detects the difference in the playground surface to activate the toy recognition process. After identifying which toy is put on the surface, the server retrieves augmented multimedia objects, such as video clips, audio clips, or images linked to that toy. These multimedia objects are then performed with the projector and/or the speaker. For example, when a child puts a house model on the surface, a garden with trees and a swimming pool are projected onto the surface next to the real physical house toy. Another example is that the audio clip of Snow White story is played when a child puts a doll of Show White on the surface playground, etc.

Figure 4 illustrates the architecture to manage and process augmented multimedia objects. For each toy registered in the system, there is a specification of all augmented multimedia objects linked to that toy. The Specification Processor processes an XML- based specification of an augmented multimedia object to generate an appropriate instance of multimedia object, such as an audio clip, a video clip, a single image, an image sequence, or a 3D model, etc. The object is then performed by a corresponding presenter.

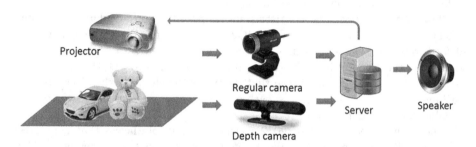

Fig. 3. Overview of smart playground

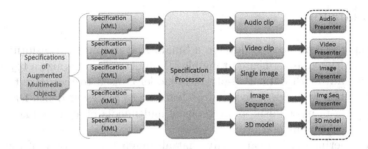

Fig. 4. Augmented multimedia object manager

5   Experiments and Implementation

In our implementation, we use PrimeSense Carmine 1.09 and Microsoft Lifecam Cinema 720p to capture depth and color data respectively.

To evaluate the accuracy of recognizing toys with RGB-D data, we first apply our proposed method on a subset of RGB-D Object Dataset[1]. My chosen data set consists of 32 classes, each class has approximately 250 images. All of the images are about daily items such as hat, ball, and camera. We use 3/4 number of images in each class for training and the remain for testing. To determine the efficiency of combining color and depth data for recognition, the recognition process is applied for only color data, then for only depth data, and finally for both of them.

On 1662 images of test set, we receive the accuracy of 88.45 % for recognition on only color data and 82.07 % for depth data. However, when we combine the predictions from both color and depth data, we reach the accuracy of 90.49 %.

Another experiments is done with our collection of color and depth data of 10 toys, each of which has the size of about 10 cm for each dimension. For each toy, we collect 50 samples from different views and different distances. All of the toys have white color and is placed on tables (Fig. 5). The accuracy is 90.63 % for color data only, 88.13 % for depth data only, and 97.12 % for combination of RGB-D.

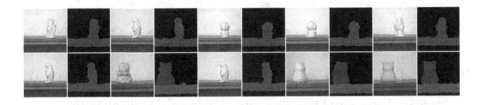

Fig. 5. Our collection with color and depth data

6   Conclusion

In this paper, we propose to develop a Smart Playground to transform regular toys into multimedia-augmented tangible UI objects. To recognize a toy, we use both color and depth data. Bag-of-words model is used to recognize toys with color data while we propose to use deep learning to represent depth feature. By using the plug-in mechanism, more types of multimedia objects and actions can also be added into our platform.

From experiments, we can verify that although the accuracy of toy recognition with only depth data is lower than that of toy recognition with color data, the fusion of results using both depth and color data provides the best accuracy. Furthermore, by using the high-level representation of depth features using convolutional neural network, we can boost the overall accuracy of the toy recognition process.

References

1. Fei-Fei, L., Fergus, R., Torralba, A.: Recognizing and Learning Object Categories. Awarded the Best Short Course Prize at ICCV (2005)
2. Gupta, S., Arbelaez, P., Malik, J.: Perceptual organization and recognition of indoor scenes from RGB-D images. In: CVPR (2013)
3. Bo, L., Ren, X., Fox, D.: Unsupervised feature learning for RGB-D based object recognition. In: Desai, J.P., Dudek, G., Khatib, O., Kumar, V. (eds.) Experimental Robotics. STAR, vol. 88, pp. 387–402. Springer, Heidelberg (2013)
4. Socher, R., Huval, B., Bhat, B., Manning, C.D., Ng, A.Y.: Convolutional-Recursive Deep Learning for 3D Object Classification. In: NIPS (2012)
5. Gupta, S., Girshick, R., Arbeláez, P., Malik, J.: Learning rich features from RGB-D images for object detection and segmentation. In: Fleet, D., Pajdla, T., Schiele, B., Tuytelaars, T. (eds.) ECCV 2014, Part VII. LNCS, vol. 8695, pp. 345–360. Springer, Heidelberg (2014)
6. Liu, L., Shao, L.: Learning discriminative representations from RGB-D video data. In: IJCAI (2013)
7. Jia, Y., Shelhamer, E., Donahue, J., Karayev, S., Long, J., Girshick, R., Guadarrama, S., Darrell, T.: Caffe: Convolutional architecture for fast feature embedding (2014)
8. Cortes, C., Vapnik, V.: Support-vector networks. Mach. Learn. 20(3), 273–297 (1995)
9. Le, Q.V., Ranzato, M.A., Monga, R., Devin, M., Corrado, G., Chen, K., Dean, J., Ng, A.Y.: Building high-level features using large scale unsupervised learning. In: ICML (2012)
10. Sun, Y., Bo, L., Fox, D.: Learning to identify new objects. In: ICRA, pp. 3165–3172 (2014)
11. ImageNet: Large Scale Visual Recognition Challenge, ILSVRC2012 (2012)

Designing Interactive Soft Toys for Children with Autism to Improve Communications Through Sensory Relaxation

Jinsil Hwaryoung Seo[✉] and Pavithra Aravindan

Soft Interaction Lab, Langford Center C411,
3137 TAMU, College Station, TX 77840, USA
{hwaryoung, pavi4nov}@tamu.edu

Abstract. Autism is a spectrum of neurodevelopmental disorders characterized by limited social skills. This paper explores a design process of interactive soft toys for children with autism that might enhance various ways of their communication. For local autism awareness events, two soft design prototypes were developed utilizing different sensory modalities (light, sound, and vibration). The researchers include the result of preliminary observation in the paper. The preliminary analysis suggests that interactive soft toys have potentials to engage children with autism through different features of the toys and evoke sensory relaxations and encourage them to talk about their experience.

Keywords: Interaction design · Soft toy · Children with autism · Touch · Sensory relaxation

1 Introduction

According to Center for disease control and prevention (CDC), It is estimated that 1 of 68 children born in the United States have some degree of Autism Spectrum Disorder (ASD) [1]. While symptoms can vary widely between individuals, autism symptoms begin to manifest in very early childhood and can be an emotional challenge for parents, causing extreme difficulties in the development of communication. Children with Autism suffer from severe communication deficits especially with social interaction and emotional control. One of the main reasons is that children with autism are very sensitive to external sensory information: light, touch, sound, etc. So it is important for them to always have some means of relaxation. Soft circuit or eTextile techniques provide great potentials for people with difficulties to explore touch-based interaction [4, 6]. To aid in day-to-day life and to develop necessary skills, some are given augmentative and alternative communication technologies (AAC). The relative popularity of these technologies has led to a proliferation of competing software. Over 250 AAC offerings within the Apple iTunes App Store© were observed with a cost range of free to $250. While these technologies have met with substantial acceptance from worried families, there appears to be a dearth of evidence to specify the overall effectiveness of these technologies [11].

© Springer International Publishing Switzerland 2015
C. Stephanidis (Ed.): HCII 2015 Posters, Part I, CCIS 528, pp. 389–393, 2015.
DOI: 10.1007/978-3-319-21380-4_66

This paper focuses on developing interactive soft toys that respond to gentle touches and hug, encouraging alternative communication through sensory relaxation. These soft toys have been presented at various local autism awareness events.

2 Background

Prior research proves that different methods of "touch" help children with autism in various ways. In clinical research, it is known that therapeutic touch is beneficial to many populations including children with autism. Escalona et al. [2] report that children with autism who have a 15 min massage session everyday for 1 month exhibited less stereotypic behavior and showed more on-task and social relatedness behavior during play observations at school, and they experienced fewer sleep problems at home. Grandin [5] presents clinical effects of 'deep touch pressure' using a 'squeeze machine'. She reports deep pressure stimulation is beneficial to calm children with autistic children. Opposed to deep touch effects, soft and slow touches haven't been fully investigated by scientists and practitioners. Recently eTextile techniques have expanded creative opportunities in terms of soft and flexible touch interfaces.

2.1 Interactive Technology for Children with Autism

Over the past 20 years, researchers have developed interactive technologies that advance our approach to autism. According to Picard, interactive technology has contributed to these fields in at least 4 ways: (a) novel sensing technology that helps us to understand children with autism better through multimodal information; (b) new techniques to infer a person's affective or cognitive state; (c) interactive system to respond to children with autism; and (d) self-monitoring technology [7].

Simple robot systems have been utilized to investigate how they have the potential to improve autistic children's communication skills [8]. It is known that children with autism tend to have low interest towards other humans. However, they prefer interacting with robots than with humans [9]. Kozima et al. developed a little toy robot, Keepon and they found that Keepon attracted the attention of and caused emotional relationship in the autistic children [8].

Recently many interactive environments and wearable projects have been developed for children with autism to help them to reduce their anxiety [10] and to learn social interactions [3].

3 Soft Toys

We have designed interactive soft toys that provide sensory relaxation and playful sensory feedback including light, sound and vibration. We aim that soft interactive toys invite children and care givers (therapists or parents) to communicate through multisensory experience. Our design focused on two friendly objects: cloud pillow and cat pillow. We used wearable electronic components such as Lilypad arduino

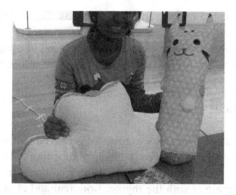

Fig. 1. Cloud pillow and cat pillow

microprocessors, Lilypad vibeboards, buzzers and LEDs as well as conductive thread and conductive yarn to create our own touch sensor (Fig. 1).

3.1 Materials/Shapes

Both pillows were created by using soft fabrics and soft circuits. White microfleece fabric was chosen for the cloud pillow. Microfleece fabric is soft, synthetic wool material often made from polyester. Fleece is warm like wool and similar in appearance, but it is much softer, lighter, and easier to wash. Microfleece is also hydrophobic, or water-repellent, making it quick to dry and warm even when wet. Microfleece is also considered to be more environmentally friendly than wool. It is wonderful to touch and is mostly geared for baby and children projects. For the cat pillow, we used organic cotton fabrics. Organic cotton is grown using methods and materials that have a low impact on the environment. Organic production systems replenish and maintain soil fertility, reduce the use of toxic and persistent pesticides and fertilizers, and build biologically diverse agriculture. We chose fabrics that are safe for children to touch and easy for parents or caregivers to maintain the quality.

Our preliminary design studies led us to design friendly shapes that invite gentle touches from children and the parents. Also friendly pillow shapes and facial expression evoked emotional connection with the soft toys and the family. A smiley face on each pillow design helped children to associate personal meanings to the object. Children picked up pillows with a face more often than without a facial expression. In addition, children loved the cat pillow than the cloud pillow and parents preferred the cloud pillow.

3.2 Interactions

When the cat pillow is picked up by a child, two vibrators embedded in the pillow actuated and created nice soft tactile feeling. When it is hugged by a child, the cat pillow starts playing a song. Blue LEDs embedded in the cloud pillow glow in a slow breathing rhythm. When a child hugs it, the glow rhythm becomes faster. Lilypad

Arduino USBs were used to utilize various interactions. To create soft, comfortable as well as playful tactile experiences, all the electronic components (LEDs, vibe board, buzzer, and registers) were securely sewn on the fabric and insulated by cotton stuffing materials. Crocheted sensors using conductive yarns were also sewn on the pillows.

4 User Experiences

From multiple local autism awareness events, we observed that some children started talking to the cat pillow while they were hugging and petting it. In addition, a few kids wanted to take it home with them. They related the vibrations from the cat as 'purring of cat'. They also sang along with the rhyme. Both (cat and cloud) pillows using soft fabrics and soft circuits invited gentle touches from children and the parents. Also friendly pillow shapes and facial expression evoked emotional connection with the soft toys and the family (Fig. 2).

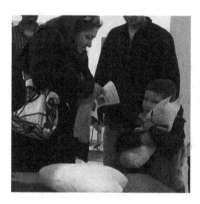

Fig. 2. A child interacting with the cat pillow

5 Conclusion

Preliminary tests and research indicate that interactive soft toys may help children with autism calm down and become relaxed. Once they feel relaxed by and engaged with the interactive soft toys, they start feeling comfortable about the situation and become open to various external stimulations. Therefore this design method is considered as a useful one that may help children with autism to talk more and connect with other people in a non-invasive but a playful way.

References

1. Centers for Disease Control and Prevention. Prevalence of Autism Spectrum Disorder Among Children Aged 8 Years — Autism and Developmental Disabilities Monitoring Network, 11 Sites, United States, 2010. Morbidity and Mortality Weekly Report. Surveillance Summaries, vol.63, no. 2 (2014)

2. Escalona, A., Field, T., Singer-Strunk, R., Cullen, C., Hartshorn, K.: Brief report: improvements in the behavior of children with autism following massage therapy. J. Autism Dev. Dis. **31**, 4 (2001)
3. Garzotto, F., Valoriani, M., Bartoli, L.: Touchless motion-based interaction for therapy of autistic children. In: Ma, M., Jain, L.C., Anderson, P. (eds.) Virtual, Augmented Reality and Serious Games for Healthcare 1, vol. 68, pp. 471–494. Springer, Heidelberg (2014)
4. Giles E, Linden, J.: Using eTextile objects for touch based interaction for visual impairment. In: International Symposium of Wearable Computing, ISWC, p 177–183 (2014)
5. Grandin, T.: Calming Effects of deep touch pressure in patients with autistic disorder, college students, and animals. J. Child Adolesc. Psychopharmacol. **2**(1), 63–72 (1992)
6. Heimdal E, Rosenqvist, T.: Textile as tangible working materials in participatory design processes: potentials and challenges. In: PDS (Participatory Design Conference), pp 215–218 (2010)
7. El Kaliouby, R., Picard, R., Baron-Cohen, S.: Affective computing and autism. Ann. N.Y. Acad. Sci. **1093**(1), 228–248 (2006)
8. Kozima, H., Michalowski, M.P., Nakagawa, C.: Keepon: A playful robot for research, therapy, and entertainment. Int. J. Soc. Robot. **1**(1), 3–18 (2009)
9. Miyamoto, E., et al.: How can robots facilitate social interaction of children with autism?: possible implications for educational environments. In: Fifth International Workshop on Epigenetic Robotics: Modeling Cognitive Development in Robotic Systems (2005)
10. Tware. T.Jacket. (2014). http://www.mytjacket.com/
11. Mirenda, P.: Autism, augmentative communication, and assistive technology what do we really know? Focus Autism Other Dev. Disabil. **16**(3), 141–151 (2001)

iCare: An Interface Design Model for Remote Communicating and Monitoring of Children Care

Tao Xu[1]($\boxtimes$) and Yun Zhou[2]

[1] School of Software and Microelectronics, Northwestern Polytechnical University,
Xi'an, China
xutao@nwpu.edu.cn

[2] Assessment of IP-based Applications, Technische Universitat Berlin and Telekom
Innovation Labs, Ernst-Reuter-Platz 7, 10587 Berlin, Germany
chouyun920@gmail.com

Abstract. School children from 6 to 12 years have characteristics of trying new things, lack of complete reasoning ability and staying in a group. It is easier for them to be in dangerous situations during this stage, which concerns parents. However, parents do not have enough time to accompany and monitor children the whole day. In this paper, we propose an interface design model for remote communicating and monitoring of children care to meet parents' requirements. After describing this model, we discuss the situation awareness and group proximity inference as implicit input in details, which is a crucial part of iCare model. Finally, we prospect prototyping and evaluation based on this model.

Keywords: Interface model · Children care · Situation awareness · Group proximity inference · Mobile computing

1 Introduction

The school children from 6 to 12 years start an independent life comparing spending all day with parents. They like trying new things and staying in a group. However, they do not yet develop a complete reasoning ability, which makes them hard to distinguish dangerous situations [3]. This concerns parents. Previous technology cannot support the monitor requirement of parents. With the development of wearable computing, the intelligent, natural, and intuitive interface turns into reality. It is interesting to instruct interface design that meets requirements of parents. This paper will first briefly introduce the needs that the school children and their parents or guardians might have. As an alternative solution, we propose a model called iCare model for interface designers. In this model, we investigate dimensions of actors, inputs, outputs and devices. As an important and innovative research point, we explore situation awareness and group proximity inference as implicit inputs. Other potential questions and features required in school children care are also involved. Finally, we discuss the future work, including prototyping and evaluation based on iCare model.

© Springer International Publishing Switzerland 2015
C. Stephanidis (Ed.): HCII 2015 Posters, Part I, CCIS 528, pp. 394–399, 2015.
DOI: 10.1007/978-3-319-21380-4_67

2   Related Work

In this section, we outline the relevant research work that helped inspire this study on monitoring school children beyond parents' view in relation with ubiquitous computing. Since ubiquitous computing covers a large number of aspects, we only address interface for children, situation awareness, and proximity interaction.

2.1   Interface for Children

We looked into the premier conferences like the ACM Conference on Human Factors in Computing Systems (CHI), Extended Abstract (CHIEA) and the ACM Conference on Interaction Design and Children (IDC) from 2009 to 2014 as the target source to explore the topics on children and related sensing technologies. The sources included different types of publications such as full papers, short papers, doctoral consortium, and demos. Besides the two conferences we mentioned, we also survey the related work from other sources. From literature reviews, we find that most prior studies mainly focus on intuitive children interface design, disabled children support, children health monitoring, etc., but without exploring how to eliminate parents' concerns and meet their monitoring requirement using wearable interface. Existing research work on children care and monitoring can be classified as two categories: activities monitoring [2] and physical information monitoring [8]. However, the topics on situation awareness and inference are rarely involved and discussed, which are essential for protecting school children and releasing parental concerns when children are in dangerous situations remotely.

2.2   Situation Awareness and Inference

Supporting parents to know situations of children remotely is an effective method to protect children from risks. Context awareness and inference has been regarded as one of the most important research points in ubiquitous computing for the past decade [4,10]. Both mobile sensors that can be taken or worn by users, and environmental sensors that are embedded in the environment, are used to perceive the context like temperature, light, noises, etc. Besides context detection, researchers also focused on applications and services using inferred information from context data. Applications using location inference and fused information from other sensors are discussed as an active topic. Compared with traditional explicit input and generated information from users like clicking and typing, the information generated from context are named as implicit information [6] and related sensor inputs are referred as implicit input [7].

2.3   Proximity Interaction

Proximity interaction has been introduced in the paper [1] in 2011 and discussed afterwards. Existing proximity interaction researches focus on device to device connectivity via proximity sensing and interaction [5]. We extend these prior work and let sensing information can be used by parents, so that monitors like parents can obtain information of partner of their children, inferred by proximity location of partners.

3   ICare Model

In this section, we will discuss characters of children from 6 to 12, and needs and concerns of their parents or guardians at first. Then we propose the model named iCare, including the dimensions of actors, input, output, and devices.

Children enter school from 6 years old generally. Between the ages of 6 and 12, child's world expands from family and is shaped and impacted also by friends, teachers, etc. They have general characteristics as follows [1]: curiosity and expanding knowledge, growing independence, developing reasoning ability, physical change, stay in group. Parents also have concerns with children during this stage and requirements of tool. During this stage, child has more willingness to be with friends or left away from parents than before. They are also lean to explore new areas outdoor and play games there. However, they are not built complete logic and reasoning mental system to avoid risks when in middle childhood. It's important to support parents to help children avoid unsafe situations and carry out self-care.

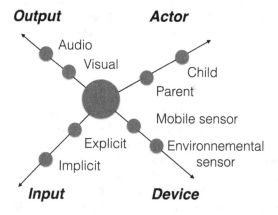

Fig. 1. Overview explanation in spider form of iCare model.

To meet requirements of parents, we propose iCare, which is the model instructing and facilitating design of friendly and intuitive interface, with the aim of supporting remote communication and monitoring for parents. The iCare model contains four dimensions: actors, input, output and devices. Figure 1 gives an overview of iCare model.

Actors. iCare model serves for two actors as users: child and parent. Based on the model, child and parent are supported with respective interfaces, including input, output and functionality. On the one hand, with regards to characteristics of children during middle childhood as we stated above, mobile and physical interface is proposed as the interface design principle based on the iCare model. Children can be supported with the ubiquitous wearable device like pendant, bracelet, etc. Physical interface provides evident physical feedback, which is perceived in a clearer way than virtual interface by children. Therefore, all interactive items are proposed with physical properties. The primitive contains <point> and the control [9] would be <point physical button>. In addition, urgent interactive items and normal interactive items are designed separately. When urgent risks happen, urgent items could be triggered directly. However, in the case of normal situation, these urgent items are more difficult to trigger than normal items. The functionality of child interface includes demanding help and communication, leveraging explicit input and implicit input that we will discuss in the sub sections of input. The functionality considering parent actor contains communication, situation awareness, gourd proximity awareness, and physical state awareness, employing only explicit input from parent's perspective. On the other hand, interface for parents can be instantiated from iCare model as virtual interface. Interaction is accessible via mobile interface with mobile devices like tablet, or via fixed interface with devices like personal computer. Merely virtual interactive items are involved for parent character. The primitive for parents leverage multitouch gestures, audio commands, mouse pointing, etc., supporting intuitive and natural input.

Input and Output. Inputs are not limited to explicit input when computing escapes from the desktop constrain. We propose explicit input and implicit input in iCare model. Explicit input refers to the inputs that are conducted explicitly by users like click, drag-n-drop, etc. Implicit input refers to the input that processed and performed from sensors, which will be discussed in the next section. The output can be conducted as visual output and audio output depending on users' requirements.

Devices. The term devices in this sub-section are defined as sensors. The child interface is equipped with diverse sensors to collect context and physical information. With regards to child actor, devices require sensors like GPS sensor obtaining geolocation for outdoor use and temperature sensor gaining temperature of environment and body for context use and physical use respectively. Sensors are classified as mobile sensors that can be equipped on body, and environmental sensors that are installed in the environment for indoor use.

4 Implicit Input

Context data that is inferred via implicit input is used to infer dangerous situations and recognize group members with permission. The general procedure of information inference is shown as in Fig. 2. Take situation awareness as example, diverse information is collected from sensors like geolocation sensor, temperature sensor, etc. Then information is sent to be fused and transformed to identify situation sequences using algorithms. Finally, dangerous situations are selected based on algorithms and represented in a notification form from interface.

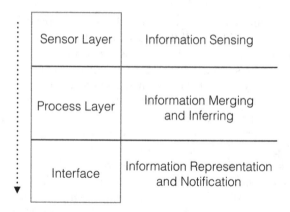

Fig. 2. Procedure of information sensing, inferring and representing.

4.1 Situation Awareness

Location is considered as one of the most important context data to know children's state. Location logging without any filtering or transforming does not help parents obtain more information about children. In addition, amounts of raw data cluster will lower user experience. Therefore, it is important to classify situations, infer situations based on locations, and notify parents in a friendly way. With regard to classification, we propose to log locations of children and define frequent areas as the familiar and safe areas. Other areas are classified as unfamiliar areas. If children enter into unfamiliar areas, a notification will send to parents as the alarm. Parents can decide this area as safe or uncertain safe. Then this additional data will be added into database for further training. The classification is based on children's location history and parents' decisions.

4.2 Group Proximity Inference

Since children in middle childhood like staying together in a group, it is interesting to let parents know location of children's partner in a dormant way. However, the information is implicit that who children's partners are. Thus, children's interface should have ability to detect other frequently surrounding children, who also worn the same devices, and to obtain permission of identification from them. Compared with active notification, the logging of locations of children's junior partner can be represented in a silent way, that is, parents can check out this information by themselves instead of receiving alarm. Group proximity detection and inference can reinforce the protection of children if children do not take devices with them or lost connection.

5 Conclusion and Future Work

In this paper, we proposed a model called iCare that is to guide for design space of interface with the aims of supporting remote monitor and care of children from 6 to 12 years. We first discussed the characteristics of children in middle childhood and requirements of parents or guardians. We then describe iCare, the model instructing the design of interface for both children and parents as users. We thirdly focus on two aspects of implicit input as part of iCare model in details: situation awareness and group proximity inference. Finally, we prospect proto-typing and evaluation in the future. In the next step, we will take consideration the details of prototyping and evaluation with the help of iCare. User-centered design (UCD) and evaluation methods will be employed in the future work. UCD can conduct to control the process of prototyping and evaluating and regards end-users involvement as the key of design.

References

1. Ballendat, T., Marquardt, N., Greenberg, S.: Proxemic interaction: designing for a proximity and orientation-aware environment. In: ACM International Conference on Interactive Tabletops and Surfaces, pp. 121–130. ACM (2010)
2. Caraban, A., Ferreira, M.J., Belim, V., Lyra, O., Karapanos, E.: Sensing And Raising Families' Awareness Of Tooth Brushing Habits, SmartHolder (2014)
3. DeBord, K.: Childhood Years, ages six through twelve. NC Cooperative Extension Service (1996)
4. Emmanouilidis, C., Koutsiamanis, R.-A., Tasidou, A.: Mobile guides: taxonomy of architectures, context awareness, technologies and applications. J. Netw. Comput. Appl. **36**(1), 103–125 (2013)
5. Gellersen, H., Fischer, C., Guinard, D., Gostner, R., Kortuem, G., Kray, C., Rukzio, E., Streng, S.: Supporting device discovery and spontaneous interaction with spa-tial references. Pers. Ubiquit. Comput. **13**(4), 255–264 (2009)
6. Krumm, J.: Ubiquitous Computing Fundamentals. CRC Press, BocaRaton (2009)
7. Schmidt, A.: Context-aware computing: context-awareness, context-aware user interfaces, and implicit interaction. In: Soegaard, M., Dam, R.F. (eds.) The Ency-clopedia of Human-Computer Interaction, 2nd edn. The Interaction Design Foun-dation, Aarhus (2013)
8. Toscos, T., Connelly, K., Rogers, Y.: Best intentions: health monitoring technology and children. In: Proceedings of the SIGCHI Conference on Human Factors in Computing Systems, pp. 1431–1440. ACM (2012)
9. Wigdor, D., Wixon, D.: Brave NUI world: Designing Natural User Interfaces for Touch and Gesture. Elsevier, Amsterdam (2011)
10. Xu, T., David, B., Chalon, R., Zhou, Y.: A context-aware middleware for ambient intelligence. In: Proceedings of the Workshop on Posters and Demos Track, p. 10. ACM (2011)

Product Design

Adaptive Depth Cue Adjustments of Interactive and Stereoscopic 3D Product Models for Design Education

Li-Chieh Chen[1(✉)], Po-Ying Chu[1], and Yun-Maw Cheng[2]

[1] Department of Industrial Design, Tatung University, Taipei, Taiwan
{lcchen, juby}@ttu.edu.tw
[2] Graduate Institute of Design Science,
Department of Computer Science and Engineering,
Tatung University, Taipei, Taiwan
kevin@ttu.edu.tw

Abstract. Recently, presenting Stereoscopic 3D (S3D) images for product design education has become an option. However, visual discomfort caused by interacting with S3D contents should be minimized. In this research, representative S3D virtual models of automobiles were constructed for experiments. These models were displayed on a 50-inch S3D TV and viewed through polarized glasses. The task was to control the rotation of an automobile and identify the design problems. Thirty students, majored in Industrial Design, were invited to participate in these experiments. The result showed that although S3D images had advantages in the task of dimension and distance estimations, the degree of visual discomfort increased significantly while the participants were interacting with the virtual product model intensively. Furthermore, adaptive adjustments of binocular depth cues, such as disparity, could reduce visual discomfort and accommodate individual differences.

Keywords: Product design education · Stereoscopic 3D virtual model · Visual depth cues

1 Introduction

Recently, some research groups had tried to use the technologies of S3D displays to present teaching materials for product design education. These examples included the systems for learning descriptive geometry through stereoscopic vision [1], and displaying the process of learning to build a handmade PC [2]. Some systems even allowed users to interact with the digital contents [3]. It was reported that stereoscopic displays did improve the performance of depth-related tasks, such as judging absolute and relative distances, finding and identifying objects, performing spatial manipulations of objects, and spatial navigating [3]. However, depth cue interactions should not be neglected [4, 5]. In fact, some of existing research did indicate that images with high frequency content associated with large disparities were the sources of eye strain [6]. In order to reduce visual discomfort, the objective of this research was to study the effects of adaptive adjustment for binocular depth cues. The details of experiment were described in the following sections.

© Springer International Publishing Switzerland 2015
C. Stephanidis (Ed.): HCII 2015 Posters, Part I, CCIS 528, pp. 403–408, 2015.
DOI: 10.1007/978-3-319-21380-4_68

2 Literature Review

Although S3D displays were found to be useful for object manipulation tasks and for finding, identifying, classifying objects or imagery [3], several content factors of S3D video could cause visual discomfort [7]. For instance, large disparity and large amount of motion are two main causes of visual discomfort while watching S3D videos [8]. In addition, the in-depth motion generally induces more visual discomfort than the planar motion [8]. To reduce the visual fatigue in viewing rotational motions, it was suggested that a control of S3D exposure was required to enhance spatial recognition and reduce visual discomfort [9]. For highly interactive systems, the interaction-induced symptoms could happen due to virtual grasping and manipulation for object transport and 3D selection [10]. While comparing the situations of cinema viewing versus video game playing using S3D TV, some research reported that video games present a strong conflict between vergence and accommodative demand. Therefore, people enjoyed cinema more than video games [11]. However, other research reported that for game playing and film viewing, system-task combinations could cause mild eyestrain and small changes in visual functions. Using a S3D system for up to 2 h was acceptable for most users, including children and adults [12]. For film viewing, age was negatively correlated with the symptom levels [13]. Furthermore, there were large individual differences in performing depth-related tasks on S3D displays [14]. To resolve the issues of visual discomfort caused by interactive manipulations of S3D contents and increase the usability of such systems, in-depth studies and exhaustive experiments are necessary.

3 Learning Materials and the Stereoscopic 3D System

3.1 Learning Materials and Digital Contents

Understanding the features of classic products and analyzing products from ergonomic aspects are the basic training in product design education. Among different categories of products, automobile is a representative product in daily life. Therefore, using automobile as a training example is widely adopted in the classroom. In the experimental S3D system, the digital contents consisted of 3D virtual models of a sport car (Fig. 1).

3.2 The Stereoscopic 3D System for Experiment

In order to create an S3D system for experiment, Visual C++ 2013 and Direct3D 11.1 were employed as the development tools. The authors modified and integrated the Direct3D stereoscopic 3D sample and Visual Studio 3D Starter Kit to construct a platform for importing 3D models in FBX format and displaying these models in either S3D or non-stereo 3D mode. The program was running on the Windows 8 operation system installed in an Acer desktop computer with a GT640 graphic card. The images, with 1920 × 1080 pixels, were displayed on a 50-inch S3D TV (120 Hz) and viewed through polarized glasses. The left-eye and right-eye images were sequentially

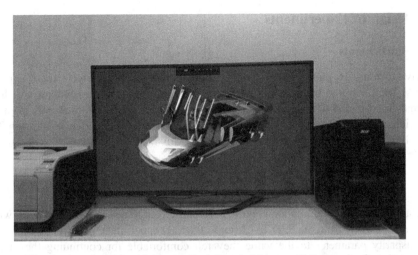

Fig. 1. A car model with images for left and right eyes (0.8 disparity factor)

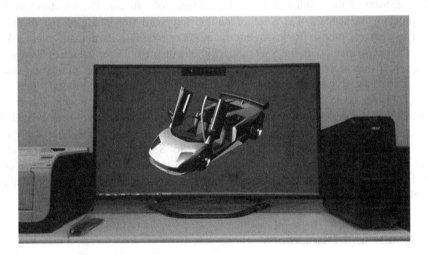

Fig. 2. A car model with a single image (0 disparity factor)

displayed at a frequency of 120 Hz. Therefore, the refresh rate of the display was 60 Hz for each eye. In addition, the experiment system allowed users to adjust the effect of disparity (from 0 to 2, with the initial value set to 1.0), by pressing the up/down arrow keys (Figs. 1 and 2). To offer minimal interactivity, the users could change the mode of model rotation. At the beginning of program execution, the 3D models rotated in 1.0 rpm with respect to the vertical axis. The user could use the left button on the computer mouse to stop or regain rotation.

4 Design of Experiments

4.1 Participants

Thirty students, 16 male and 14 female, were invited to participate in these experiments. They majored in Industrial Design and enrolled as graduate students. All had normal or corrected-to-normal vision and none reported stereopsis problems in prior experiences. They all had the basic training of drawing and the experiences of using 3D modeling software, such as Pro/E, Alias, Rhino, 3ds Max, or Maya.

4.2 Tasks and Procedures

In a laboratory with illumination control, each participant seated in front of a desk, with three meters away from the S3D TV. Prior to the S3D experiment, participants adjusted the disparity parameter to the value they felt comfortable for continuing the major tasks. The task of each participant was to control the rotation of a sport car and to identify as many design problems as possible within 6 min, i.e. 360 s. Participants seated in front of the display at a viewing distance of 240 cm. The input device for manipulating the camera was a set of remote keyboard (for changing the disparity factor values) and mouse (for changing the mode of rotation). Participants were asked to start the experiment with the S3D mode with the disparity factor value equals to one. However, if they were not comfortable, they could adjust the value. If anyone could continue to stay in the S3D mode, he/she was encouraged to spend extra 3 min, i.e. 180 s, to locate more design problems. During the experiments, they were allowed to re-adjust the disparity value whenever necessary to maintain the comfortable level. In the experiment, the number of design problems identified was considered as the major performance measure. In order to study the effects of S3D on visual comfort, total time spent in the S3D mode, degree of discomfort, and self-reported symptoms were collected. The degree of discomfort was reported on a 9-point scale, with 1 indicating slightly discomfort and 9 indicating extremely discomfort.

5 Results and Discussions

Among 30 participants, 27 participants, about 90 %, were able to use the stereoscopic 3D mode for at least 360 s (Table 1). The average time of using stereoscopic mode was 412 s, with standard deviation 78 s. The average value of the disparity factor was 1.08, with standard deviation 0.4. The average degree of visual discomfort was 2.10 on a 9-point scale. This indicated that adaptive adjustments of binocular depth cues, such as disparity, could reduce visual discomfort and accommodate individual differences. As for the self-reported symptoms, 16 participants, about 53 %, experienced eye strain, eye fatigue or dizziness. The degree of visual discomfort was related to these symptoms. Participants with low degree of visual discomfort reported few symptoms. Furthermore, there was no gender difference in the number of design problems identified, total time spent in the stereoscopic 3D mode, degree of discomfort, and self-reported symptoms.

Table 1. Measurements of experiments

Measurements	Mean	Standard deviation
Task completion time	412	78
Disparity parameter value	1.08	0.40
Degree of visual discomfort	2.10	1.09
Number of design problems identified	3.83	1.76

6 Conclusions and Recommendations for Further Work

To identify the problems and opportunities of interactive and stereoscopic 3D product models for design education, a prototype system was constructed for experiments. The result of experiment indicated that adaptive adjustments of binocular depth cues were necessary for highly interactive tasks to ensure visual comfort and depth cue integration. To develop successful applications for design education, other factors could be incorporated for experiments in the future. These factors include the interaction between perspective and stereoscopic effects, the control-display ratios of model transformations, such as rotations and translations, while interacting with the components of S3D models.

Acknowledgement. The authors would like to express our gratitude to the Ministry of Science and Technology of the Republic of China for financially supporting this research under Grant No. MOST 103-2221-E-036-019.

References

1. Guedes, K.B., Guimarães, M., Méxas, J.G.: Virtual reality using stereoscopic vision for teaching/learning of descriptive geometry. In: eLmL 2012: The Fourth International Conference on Mobile, Hybrid, and On-line Learning, pp. 24–30 (2012)
2. Mukai, A., Yamagishi, Y., Hirayama, M.J., Tsuruoka, T., Yamamoto, T.: Effects of stereoscopic 3d contents on the process of learning to build a handmade PC. Knowl. Manage. E-Learning: Int. J. **3**(3), 491–505 (2011)
3. McIntire, J.P., Havig, P.R., Geiselman, E.E.: Stereoscopic 3D displays and human performance: a comprehensive review. Displays **35**, 18–26 (2014)
4. Howard, I.P.: Interactions between visual depth cues. In: Perceiving in Depth, Other Mechanisms of Depth Perception, vol. 3. Published to Oxford Scholarship Online (2012)
5. Mikkola, M., Jumisko-Pyykko, S., Strohmeier, D., Boev, A., Gotchev, A.: Stereoscopic Depth Cues Outperform Monocular Ones on Autostereoscopic Display. IEEE J. Sel. Top. Sign. Process. **6**(6), 698–709 (2012)
6. Leroy, L., Fuchs, P., Moreau, G.: Real-time adaptive blur for reducing eye strain in stereoscopic displays. ACM Trans. Appl. Percept. **9**(2), 1–18 (2012)
7. Kim, D.W., Yoo, J.S., Seo, Y.H.: Qualitative analysis of individual and composite content factors of stereoscopic 3D video causing visual discomfort. Displays **34**, 223–240 (2013)
8. Li, J., Barkowsky, M., Le Callet, P.: Visual discomfort of stereoscopic 3D videos: Influence of 3D motion. Displays **35**, 49–57 (2014)

9. Kim, Y., Park, J.: Study on interaction-induced symptoms with respect to virtual grasping and manipulation. Int. J. Hum.-Comput. Studies **72**, 141–153 (2014)
10. Matsuura, S.: Effective Usage of Stereoscopic Visualization for the Learning of a Motional Mechanism. In: Stephanidis, C., Antona, M. (eds.) UAHCI 2013, Part III. LNCS, vol. 8011, pp. 187–194. Springer, Heidelberg (2013)
11. Read, J.C.A.: Viewer experience with stereoscopic 3D television in the home. Displays **35**, 252–260 (2014)
12. Pölönen, M., Järvenpää, T., Bilcu, B.: Stereoscopic 3D entertainment and its effect on viewing comfort: Comparison of children and adults. Appl. Ergon. **44**, 151–160 (2013)
13. Obrist, M., Wurhofer, D., Meneweger, T., Grill, T., Tscheligi, M.: Viewing experience of 3DTV: an exploration of the feeling of sickness and presence in a shopping mall. Entertainment Comput. **4**, 71–81 (2013)
14. McIntire, J.P., Havig, P.R., Harrington, L.K., Wright, S.T., Watamaniuk, S.N.J., Heft, E.L.: Clinically normal stereopsis does not ensure a performance benefit from stereoscopic 3D depth cues. 3D Research **5**, 20 (2014)

Human-Centered Product Owner:
How Human-Centered Design
Can Sharpen Scrum Methodology

Camila Kamarad Zocal Garcia[(⊠)]

Eldorado Research Institute, Campinas, Brazil
camila.garcia@eldorado.org.br

Abstract. This paper will demonstrate what the main benefits of applying Human Centered Design Techniques in a Scrum Project are, especially when they are used by the Product Owner. These techniques, like user observation, prototyping, user evaluation tests can be used in order to connect people to build the best solution and, when they are applied throughout the project sprints they can became a powerful tool to guarantees product success and outstanding results.

Keywords: Human-Centered design · Scrum · Product owner

1 Introduction

Scrum is a project management methodology that is used to address complex problems into agile development. It is focused in delivering the highest products value, by promoting effective collaboration and interaction [1]. In this scenario, it is the Product Owner responsibility to understand the client's needs and passing them to the team, in a way that guarantees the product value. The Product Owner must understand what has to be done and clearly express that in Product Backlog items. Also, the Product Owner must continuously write and prioritize requirements in order to achieve goals and missions and, what is more, she/he must ensure that all people involved at the project, clients, users, Development Team understand the Product Backlog to the level needed [1].

In order to support the Product Owner in all these tasks, Scrum defines some artifacts, Product Backlog, Sprint Backlog and Increment; however it does not specify how these should be done. There is no strict rule to be followed, but the Product Owner can decide what suits better in each project.

Taking this Scum freedom into consideration this paper will detail how a Product Owner can apply Human-Centered Design techniques in everyday activities by presenting a project in which the Product Owner followed HCD process and performed interviews, user observation, personas definition, wireframe and prototyping, heuristics analysis and usability tests throughout the project sprints and showing the results on how these techniques are a powerful tool to guarantees product success.

The mentioned project is a support system for an electrical operation center and it involves improving existent system functionality and developing some new features in

© Springer International Publishing Switzerland 2015
C. Stephanidis (Ed.): HCII 2015 Posters, Part I, CCIS 528, pp. 409–413, 2015.
DOI: 10.1007/978-3-319-21380-4_69

order to support electrical operator's decisions. The focus here is not the developed system but how a design process, specifically Human Centered design process, can be applied as a Product Owner tool. Human Centered Design was chosen because it aims at the human's needs when we are design a system or a solution and that is exactly what a Product Owner has to do, discover the problems, the needs the priorities of all people involved and affected by the product and build the best solution.

2 User Observation and Personas

Defining a Product Backlog is definitely not a simple task, especially at the beginning of a project, when the Product Owner is still getting familiar with the project context. This project, in particular, the clients and the users were different people. On the one hand, the client had his point of view, needs and ambitions regarding the product and, on the other hand, the users were the ones who really know about the process and the tasks in which the system should be included.

To solve this matter, the Product Owner has decided to take advantage of a Human-Centered Design approach: the user observation. The Product Owner used direct observation [2] so the Product Owner has deeply immersed at the user's reality, by spending some days working with them.

The user observation process was conducted in three days, inside an electrical operation center and six users were observed.

Firstly, when the user arrived at the operational center, he answered a small interview, regarding some personal information, mainly name, age, professional experience, degree. Then, the user was asked to shortly explain his daily activities and finally he started to work. The Product Owner observed the activities and took notes on what was done, how it was done, the order things were done, which systems were used to perform each tasks, how the user felt while interacting with each system.

From these observations the Product Owner could understand how an operational center works, which demands are the most important, how the operators organized themselves to handle all demands and in which context the developed product will be inserted.

As a result from the user observation process, the Product Owner built the first two artifacts that supported the Product Backlog draft. The first one was the user persona, which can be seen at Fig. 1.

This persona was used to represent the user's need to the development team and, lately, it was related to each use scenario [3].

The second artifact was a story board, built to represent all the users' activities and how the users could interact with the system. The story board can be seen at Fig. 2.

The story board was initial drafts to guide the Product Owner on define and detail the user stories. By understand the user workflow and use scenarios, the Product Owner could better understand what has to be done and transform flow and tasks in detailed user stories that became part of the Product Backlog.

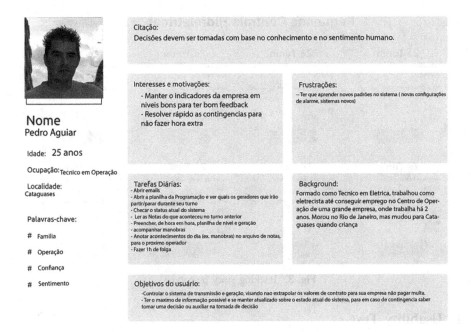

Fig. 1. User persona

Fig. 2. Story board

3 Wireframes and Prototypes

After defining the first Product Backlog version, it was time to present that to the Development Team. However, there were still some gap information about how the system must look like and how it should behave. The Development Team had the stories telling what needed to be done, but, in order to provide more detail about each Product Backlog item, the Product Owner decided to build wireframes and prototypes with the development team. An example of a story prototype can be seen at Fig. 3.

The development team worked on several paper wireframes and after many brainstorm and discussion sessions, the first prototypes were built. The team decided to use a more realistic prototype, so they developed a software prototype [3], using Axure. They were presented to users and client, to validate what was going to be built and delivered.

Pequenas Centrais Hidrelétricas

Fig. 3. Backlog story prototype

4   Usability Test

Finally, the Product Backlog was finished and the Development Team started to build the product increments. So, after each sprint interaction, the Product Owner is supposed to review the developed solution and accept or decline the software increment. As both the user and the client were a part of the design process, they were invited to take part into that review and validate the product, by participating in a usability test [3].

The usability tests consisted in defining a task regarding the product increment and observe how the users and client interact with the system. It was really important to validate whether the increment correspond to the client and users expectations. Also, it was used as an input to review the Product Backlog stories and priorities.

5   Conclusion

To conclude, Human Centered Design focuses on understand the human's need and taking that into consideration during a design process, which is exactly what the Product Owner needs in the project. In this project, in particular taking advantage of Human Centered Design techniques really helped the product success firstly because users were involved in all the process instead of only involving the client and secondly because all people involved with the project, users, clients and development team were involved from the beginning to the end of the project, taking part by telling experiences, building prototypes and solutions and validating continuously the product.

The product requirements get more easy to understand and, as a consequence, more reliable to be built. The development team gets to know for whom they are developing, by the use of personas and the prototypes give a better idea of what is going to be done.

References

1. Schwaber, K., Sutherland, J.: The Scrum Guide. The definitive Guide to Scrum (2014)
2. Ideo Toolkit: Human Centered Design. Accessed 24 November 2014
3. Maguire, M.: Methods to support human-centred design. Int. J. Hum.-Comput. Stud. **55**(4), 587–634 (2001)

Intuitive Placement of Objects in Web-Based CAD Environments

Andres Felipe Kordek[1] and Arjan Kuijper[1,2(✉)]

[1] Technische Universität Darmstadt, Darmstadt, Germany
[2] Fraunhofer IGD, Darmstadt, Germany
arjan.kuijper@igd.fraunhofer

Abstract. We develop a Computer Aided Design (CAD) editor using an open source library, with the aim to minimize the cost in the future, as compared to the development of conventional editors, and to accelerate the expansion by means of standardized languages making the development easier. We focus on snapping, a very important area in computer graphics and without a CAD application inconceivable. CAD applications offer the possibility of snappings to allow the developers an intuitive interaction with the objects in 2D or 3D space. Snapping allows by using constraints the merging of multiple objects into a new object. Two possible approaches for implementing snappings are addressed and presented. Advantages and disadvantages are discussed via a user study.

1 Introduction and Motivation

The use of current web technology has great potential for improving collaborative design and construction processes. Apart from a Web browser, no special software is needed, so that user groups with various software platforms and devices can participate in the design process immediately. With the number of untrained CAD users also the demands on the intuitive usability of the 3D application increase. In particular, the millimeter-accurate positioning of an object to the desired location in three-dimensional space is a challenge [3]. Although the desired result can be achieved using manual position information, this takes quite a bit of time. It is possible in the positioning of the objects to use so-called constraints, i.e. context-dependent rules. These are defined per object and guide the user in the ideal case quickly to the desired result. However, constraints can even interfere with the usability of the application, such as in cases where a proposed solution does not quickly lead to the desired result.

In this work two constraint-based models for object placement are implemented and compared. The focus is on the intuitive usability, which is evaluated in a user study. The first model is already in use for many years (via a command line interface) at an industrial partner. Users specify which point of an object (selected from a predefined set of options) is to be connected with what point of a neighboring object. The application then automatically calculates the desired position and orientation of the object. Instead of a command-line interface a simple list within the graphical user interface for selecting the points is

C. Stephanidis (Ed.): HCII 2015 Posters, Part I, CCIS 528, pp. 414–420, 2015.
DOI: 10.1007/978-3-319-21380-4_70

developed in this work. The second model is known from similar applications: The user moves an object with the mouse. As soon as the object goes to the proximity of another object, the application automatically suggests a positioning and orientation (so-called snapping [2,3,7]) of the object which then satisfies predetermined constraints.

The editor is a web-based application, developed as open source with standard technologies. It should serve as a tool for the design of digital factories [12] and makes components available, which can be combined to factory elements. Snapping is in CAD editors a very important tool that can built large modules with the basic components. The editor that comes in question here, provides two components: a tank and a pipe. The idea in the implementation is to expand the components with snap points and normal vectors. The snap points are the connection points of the object and the normal vectors determine the direction of the point. So it can be determined, which snap points fit together and can thus be connected using defined rules. The normals help in deciding the orientation of an object in relation to another.

The objectives of the industrial partner include the use of standard technologies, open source frameworks, and the development of a web-based CAD editor [1,9,10]. The editor is invoked by a web browser and gives the feeling of a local application. In order to ensure the requirements the following technologies are used: HTML, CSS, JSON, JavaScript, jQuery, X3D, and X3DOM [5,6,12].

2 Snapping in Computer Graphics

We present two approaches that are specially adapted to the requirements of CAD editors. It is analyzed in what way both approaches can interact with each other and what advantages and disadvantages they have. Since the early days of computer graphics new implementations are presented again and again to facilitate the user interaction. Especially with the development of CAD and graphics solutions technologies as snapping have been introduced and constantly improved. In the design of new approaches user perception is important. An example is the perception of depth in three-dimensional space, or the perception of the center of a non-symmetric element. Equally important is the user interaction that takes place with the help of a mouse and the keyboard or other input elements. A user study [7] examined the perception of asymmetric objects to a user group. This study shows the importance of considering these characteristics when creating new approaches and algorithms.

In computer graphics, the problem of aligning objects in three-dimensional space is dedicated a lot of time. Many operations must be considered and the selection of the correct control for the elements must be carefully considered. In addition, the necessary requirements must be fulfilled [3]. An approach that is considering this question, is snap-dragging [3,4]. With the help of three interactive techniques – *gravity*, *alignment*, and *transform* – the control and the design of elements is described in space. Gravity locates by means of an algorithm the point in three-dimensional space, defining the depth of a 3D scene imaged on a two-dimensional screen. The alignment-objects are lines, planes and spheres, with special properties that allow the modeling of 3D scenes. Transformations such as scaling, rotation and translation operate with the help of specific constraints on the existing alignment-Objects.

A very interesting approach, which addresses a different problem with snapping, is *Snap-and-Go* [2]. It demonstrates that it is not always desirable that an object is attracted to one or more snap points when dragged with the mouse. As a solution, the functionality of the snappings was temporarily disabled. This decision is troublesome for each user, if it is assumed that snapping is meant to facilitate usability. This property is not given in such a case. The approach *Snap-and-Go* describes how disturbing snap points are handled without disabling snapping. This allows a quick and intuitive orientation of objects and increases the usability of an editor. In the design of software projects, the user is very prominent in the foreground. He sets the destination, where the development of a product should result in. User tests are very important [7], they give insight into the perception and usability [8] of a product. Both our implementations of snappins are therefore evaluated in a user study.

3   Constraints Modeling Concepts

Constraints in computer graphics are fixed terms which describe the motion behavior and properties of an object. In this work, it is basically the behavior of objects on one another. The snapping task is to find ways that objects can be connected to each other in 3D space. To achieve this, properties must be calculated as the distance and position of objects to another. For example, features such as scaling and rotation with respect to the local and global axis system are of importance. These geometric relationships between the objects form the basis of both constraints.

Semi-Automatic Snapping: The first model illustrates and explains how snapping between objects in 3D space is performed using the context menu. The original editor has a similar process. The commands are transmitted to a command interface and then performed snapping. The idea behind the implementation using a context menu is to build a user-friendly and intuitive environment. Each element in space should have the property to trap the click events of the mouse and interpret them. Depending on given conditions, a context menu appears that lists the existing snap points elements. The following requirements are tested before the mouse event can be evaluated: (i) at least two objects must be available in 3D space; (ii) in the top bar snapping with context window must be turned on, and (iii) the snap points must be generated and displayed. Upon successful verification, a context window is shown next to the object, see Fig. 1, left. A special feature of this context window is the nature of their implementation. In case of repeated click event, the old window is deleted and a new one opened. For each item that is clicked, a new context window is generated and displayed increasing flexibility and supporting the extensibility of the snappings for future projects. Always two points can be connected. From the context window of the

Fig. 1. Example objects and computed connection. Left: Semi-automatic with context menu. Middle: Found connections in the full automatic snapping. Right: Proposed connection.

first element a starting point is selected and from the context window of another element the target point. The object with the start point is shifted to the object with the target point and positioned so that both snap points are connected. To give the user an intuitive feeling, fixed properties of each element are present. The selected item is always highlighted in yellow. As another property snappoints change color when the user goes over a point in the list item in the context menu with the mouse. When an item is selected in the context menu of the list the entry turns blue, so the user always knows which item he has selected.

Fully Automatic Snapping: In the second model the intuitive concept Snapping is implemented using the mouse.

In the development and implementation of fully automatic snappings within the Web-based CAD editor, the consideration of the right approach and the more accurate representation of the problem played a very important role. Since the CAD editor has been implemented using standardized web technologies, the decision of the development language for JavaScript was determined. The approach was taken in the field of software development using design patterns. The requirements provided by the task have lead to the implementation of the observer pattern for solving the problem.

The task is to implement the snappings with intuitive behavior. It should be ensured that the distance between the objects is considered. The first variant implements snapping with the aid of the so-called context menus. The user can call it up by clicking with the right mouse button on the element. The second implementation enables snapping out of context menus but by using the mouse only. An item is clicked with the mouse and dragged to the next element. The distance between the elements is always calculated. If two snap points are nearby, they attract and connect themselves, see Fig. 1, middle and right.

4   Results

A user evaluation was carried out test the usability of the implemented snapping methods in the CAD editor [11]. A test environment was developed for the test persons. After the test the respondents completed a questionnaire. The choice of subjects is tied to the question for which groups the CAD editor was

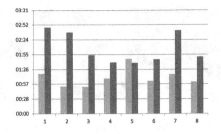

Fig. 2. Left: Testing scenarios. Right: Total timing per question person with left bar full automatic, right bar semi-automatic.

basically developed. The choice fell on eight subjects. All eight subjects come from the department of computer science and have already prior knowledge of graphic editors. The subjects are all between 27 years and 32 years old. We created a total of three test tasks for the volunteers. Each task has about the same level of difficulty. The subject had to combine several components so that the arrangement of them corresponded to the given device. Each of the three test tasks had to be performed both with the fully automatic snapping and with the semi-automatic snapping. Figure 2, left, shows the arrangement of the test environment. Top right the time is measured used for the successful completion of a task. Bottom left, the subject can choose a task and gets for each task a new image displayed that had to be assembled. When preparing the questionnaire, questions were specifically selected asking about the usability of both implementations of the snappings. The aim was to draw conclusions that are important in the decision of improvements for both methods. The respondent has five different possible answers to each question. The weighting of each possible response is 1 for strongly agree and 5 for statement is not true.

1. By using the fully automatic snappings the intuitive interaction with the components is possible ($\mu = 1.250$).
2. By using the semi-automatic snappings the intuitive interaction with the components is possible ($\mu = 2.875$).
3. I quickly learned how to use the fully automatic snapping ($\mu = 1.125$).
4. I quickly learned how to use the semi-automatic snapping ($\mu = 2.000$).
5. I get along very well with the fully automatic snapping ($\mu = 1.375$).
6. I get along very well with the semi-automatic snapping ($\mu - 2.625$).
7. In the end, I could do all tasks using the fully automatic snappings easier and faster than using the semi-automatic snappings ($\mu = 1.875$).
8. Displaying a context menu contributes to the clarity ($\mu = 2.875$).
9. Semi-automatic snapping displaying context menus is more user friendly than the fully automatic snapping out of context menus ($\mu = 3.625$).
10. With the fully automatic snapping the task needs fewer steps than the semi-automatic snapping ($\mu = 1.375$).

Concluding, the implementation of fully automated snappings was favorably to the subjects. Both Question 1, 3, 5, 7 and 10, rating the statements of the fully automatic snapping , were graded with a 1 at least 5 of 8 subjects. The statements on the semi-automatic snapping question (Question 2, 4, 6, 8 and 9), show that the majority of subjects was not in favor of it.

Figure 2 right combines the time measurements for both methods. We see that the satisfaction of the subjects with the fully automatic snapping is in line with the measured time.

5 Conclusions

In the context of this thesis, two methods were developed and presented to the objects in three-dimensional space to connect with each other, so-called snapping. Both methods are called semi-automatic and fully automatic snapping. They have different approaches and work according to certain specifications. Here, a CAD editor originated served as the setting for the implementation of both methods. Simultaneously, a user evaluation was carried out. This new insight into the usability of both Snapping obtained implementations. Thus, there was clear from the evaluation that the subjects with the fully automatic snapping basically came efficiently than the semi-automatic snapping. Several reasons were mentioned. First and foremost, however, was the ease of use and intuitive behavior in the foreground. Bottom line is that the use of fully automated Snappings contributes to the clarity and is easy to use. This in turn leads to a better usability and is thus preferable to the semi-automatic snapping.

References

1. Aderhold, A., Wilkosinska, K., Corsini, M., Jung, Y., Graf, H., Kuijper, A.: The common implementation framework as service – towards novel applications for streamlined presentation of 3d content on the web. In: Marcus, A. (ed.) DUXU 2014, Part II. LNCS, vol. 8518, pp. 3–14. Springer, Heidelberg (2014)
2. Baudisch, P., Cutrell, E., Hinckley, K., Eversole, A.: Snap-and-go: helping users align objects without the modality of traditional snapping. In: SIGCHI Conference on Human Factors in Computing Systems, pp. 301–310. ACM (2005)
3. Bier, E.A.: Snap-dragging in three dimensions. In: Proceedings of the 1990 Symposium on Interactive 3D Graphics, I3D '1990, pp. 193–204 (1990)
4. Bier, E.A., Stone, M.C.: Snap-dragging. In: Proceedings of the 13th Annual Conference on Computer Graphics and Interactive Techniques, pp. 233–240 (1986)
5. Eicke, T.N., Jung, Y., Kuijper, A.: Stable dynamic webshadows in the x3dom framework. Expert Syst. Appl. **42**(7), 3585–3609 (2015)
6. Engelke, T., Becker, M., Wuest, H., Keil, J., Kuijper, A.: MobileAR browser - a generic architecture for rapid AR-multi-level development. Expert Syst. Appl. **40**(7), 2704–2714 (2013)
7. Heo, S., Lee, Y.K., Yeom, J., Lee, G.: Design of a shape dependent snapping algorithm. In: CHI 2012 Extended Abstracts on Human Factors in Computing Systems, pp. 2207–2212 (2012)
8. Jokela, T., Iivari, N., Matero, J., Karukka, M.: The standard of user-centered design and the standard definition of usability: analyzing iso 13407 against iso 9241–11. In: Proceedings of the Latin American Conference on Human-computer Interaction, pp. 53–60 (2003)

9. Limper, M., Jung, Y., Behr, J., Sturm, T., Franke, T., Schwenk, K., Kuijper, A.: Fast, progressive loading of binary-encoded declarative-3d web content. IEEE Comput. Graph. Appl. **33**(5), 26–36 (2013)

10. Mouton, C., Parfouru, S., Jeulin, C., Dutertre, C., Goblet, J., Paviot, T., Lamouri, S., Limper, M., Stein, C., Behr, J., Jung, Y.: Enhancing the plant layout design process using X3DOM and a scalable web3d service architecture. In: The 19th International Conference on Web3D Technology, Web3D14, pp. 125–132 (2014)

11. Nazemi, K., Stab, C., Kuijper, A.: A reference model for adaptive visualization systems. In: Jacko, J.A. (ed.) Human-Computer Interaction, Part I, HCII 2011. LNCS, vol. 6761, pp. 480–489. Springer, Heidelberg (2011)

12. Stein, C., Limper, M., Kuijper, A.: Spatial data structures to accelerate the visibility determination for large model visualization on the web. In: The 19th International Conference on Web3D Technology, Web3D14, pp. 53–61 (2014)

Fashion Projection Mapping Using Basic Modeling Form

EunJu Lee[1(✉)], Yang Kyu Lim[1], Hyun Chun Jung[2],
and Jin Wan Park[3]

[1] Graduate School of Advanced Imaging Science, Chung-Ang University,
Seoul, South Korea
ejlee3271@nate.com, lim0386@gmail.com
[2] Multimedia & Film, Chung-Ang University, Seoul, South Korea
jhc06@naver.com
[3] Integrative Engineering Technology, Chung-Ang University,
Seoul, South Korea
jinpark@cau.ac.kr

Abstract. This study produced motion graphics as an application of basic modeling form design in fashion design and creates a media art work via projection mapping of the motion graphics to a torso thereby aiming at learning a sense of basic modeling form and producing a media art in fusion of fashion and media. Kandinsky (1979), in his book 'Point and Line to Plane', suggested that a variety of changes in the most basic formation of modeling can be made by changes in formation, changes in orientation and direction, structural finesse, utilization of space, inter-connected relationships in processing of corner vertices, changes and colors due to repetition, and basic modeling form theory through contrast sense of materials. This basic modeling form theory is studied to develop comprehensive thinking skills into fashion design sense by learning overall unity and harmony and the principle of Gestalt (closure, proximity, similarity) as students perform tasks that present various modeling form conditions step by step using abstract points and lines in fashion design in a process of concept, development, and fashion design application. In this study, motion graphics images are created using plane designs in basic modeling form thereby adding interactive elements to basic modeling form so that two-dimensional (2D) images are re-structured into three-dimensional (3D) works by utilizing projection mapping. A torso, which is a human model used in clothing and textiles, is set as a target of projection mapping to experience processes of conception, development, and application in basic fashion design. This study is a step prior to application of interaction technology, and software called Adobe After Effects was used to display images in the torso. This study is focused on understanding on basic modeling form, development of design sense, and stereoscopic design rather than skills required for works. Through interaction functions via upgrades, this study will be utilized in media work, show-windows in dress shops or fashion shows in future.

Keywords: Kandinsky · Digital fashion · Projection mapping · Basic design

© Springer International Publishing Switzerland 2015
C. Stephanidis (Ed.): HCII 2015 Posters, Part I, CCIS 528, pp. 421–426, 2015.
DOI: 10.1007/978-3-319-21380-4_71

1 Introduction

This study aimed to harmonize two fields: fashion design and video design that are my majors. The two fields seemed totally different subjects but there was no significant difference between them in terms of foundational subjects, and one of fashion design methods used in fashion design was applied to video design. Next, videos were applied to fashion design.

History of design starts from structuring points, lines, and surfaces. Point means beginning. It is the simplest form from which art starts. Line is made by numerous points and symbolizes time flow and history. Multiple lines create a surface. In other words, a surface is a completion of paint. All paintings are complete in a surface state. However, the meanings of point, line, and surface were disintegrated in the era of media art. In this project, the meanings of point, line, and surface using projection mapping were re-considered, and extension of new meanings of point, line, and surface were pursued.

2 Basic Design and Fashion Design

2.1 Conception

Jungmee Cho developed a basic design curriculum for fashion design education. She divided a task of step-by-step presentation of various design conditions using abstract points and lines into three phases: a conception phase at basic plane, a development phase into a costume application, and fashion design application phase in which student's own work is substituted with existing designers works. Through this task, students learn design elements and overall unity and harmony in design principles as well as the principle of Gestalt thereby aiming at increase in comprehensive thinking skill and development into fashion design sense through practical exercises.[1]

A basic plane refers to physical surface (screen) that contains work contents defined by Kandinsky (1926 to 2008) (frame space).[2] Schematic basic plain is limited by two horizontal lines and two vertical lines thereby expressing independent essence in the surrounding area by means of the division. Thus, a basic plane helps students to concentrate on modeling form without thinking effects of other conditions in the limited area. In this phase, a rectangular basic plane (15*20 cm) is used. Using points and lines, basic plane design is performed, and this is divided into sub-phases according to conditions of the number of diagrams, orientation, overlapping, shape, and texture. This phase follows the instruction from the 《Development of Contents in Fundamental Design Education for Fashion Design》 (Jungmee Cho 2010).

It was designed with the following conditional steps such as a size of point, whether or not point is located in the borderline, the number of points, overlap of points, point shape, and point texture. Fig. 1 shows typical parts of total work.

---

[1] Cho, J.: Development of Contents in Fundamental Design Education for Fashion Design, Journal of the Korean Society of Clothing and Textiles vol.34, no.8, pp.1265–1276 (2010).

[2] Kandinsky, W.: Point and Line to Plane. Yeolhwadang, Korea (2004).

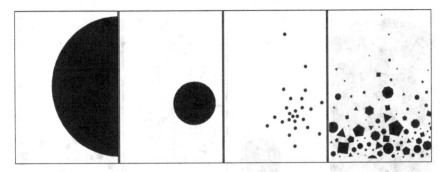

Fig. 1. Basic plane design using points

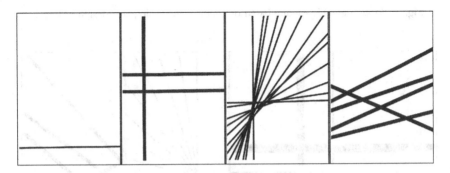

Fig. 2. Basic plane design using lines

It was designed with the following conditional steps such as thickness of line, direction of line, the number of lines, and disconnection or stop of line. Fig. 2 shows typical parts of total work.

2.2   Development

In fashion design, plane silhouette in a form of basic one-piece is used. However, in this study, motion graphic animation is produced using After Effects and Cinema4D, which are graphic software. In this phase, a rectangular basic plane (720*1280p) is used. In this phase, movements of diagrams and background music are added thereby having a rhythm even if it is based on the prior conception phase. As design elements are moved in an image, motion, weight, space in a plane can be felt realistically.

The following conditional steps such as a size of point, whether or not point is located in the borderline, the number of points, overlap of points, point shape, and point texture are arranged in time thereby changing them in the motion graphics. Fig. 3 is a captured one as a typical parts of total work.

The following conditional steps such as thickness of line, direction of line, the number of lines, and disconnection or stop of line are arranged in time thereby

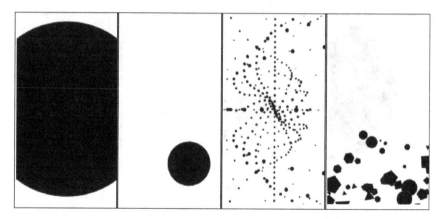

Fig. 3. Motion graphic capture based on motif of the basic plane design in Fig. 1

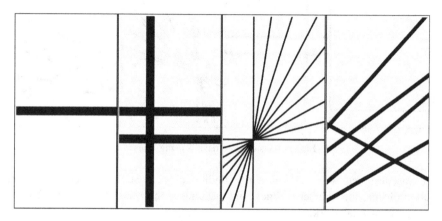

Fig. 4. Motion graphic capture based on motif of the basic plane design in Fig. 2

changing them in the motion graphic. Fig. 4 is a captured one as typical parts of total work.

2.3   Application

The fashion designs were made by drawing designs directly on picture works of existing fashion designers or mapping the designs using Adobe Photoshop. In this study, instead of the above process, a torso, which is a human model used in fashion design, is targeted for mapping using a beam projector. It is a process of development from 2D to 3D. Designs were applied to a human body which was indirectly felt via photos using projection mapping, and thus it looks more stereoscopic and realistic. This application leads to developing into media art works (Figs. 5 and 6).

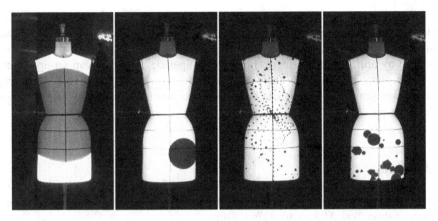

Fig. 5. Capture of projection mapping work video of the motion graphic in Fig. 3

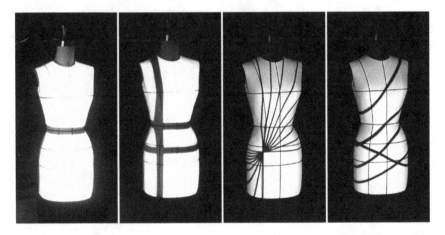

Fig. 6 Capture of projection mapping work video of the motion graphic in Fig. 4

3 Conclusions and Future Research

This study was aimed at developing fusion of three fields: fashion design, video design, and media art. The study applied fashion design using basic modeling form to new media via projection mapping to complete a work. This study was conducted with three phases: conception, development, and application. In the conception phase, various basic design principles and concepts were learnt through the basic plane design thereby providing a foundation to progress into a higher level of design process. In the development phase, designs made in the prior phase were utilized to be developed into motion graphic images thereby adding senses of motion and space. In the application process, motion graphic images were projected to a torso by utilizing projection mapping thereby re-creating 2D images into 3D works.

This study is a stage prior to interaction technique application and is focused on understanding on basic modeling form, development of design sense, and stereoscopic design rather than skills required for works. In the future, interactive works can be produced by utilizing processing techniques via upgrade. Audience can set up points, line color, shape, and sizes by themselves thereby experiencing creative and exciting design development. This study can also be utilized in show windows in dress shops or fashion shows.

References

Cho, J.: Development of contents in fundamental design education for fashion design. J. Korean Soc. Clothing Text. **34**(8), 1265–1276 (2010)
Kandinsky, W.: Point and Line to Plane. Yeolhwadang, Korea (2004)
Lee, E.: Spot Motion Torso Projection Mapping. http://vimeo.com/103978134

Creating Consistency Between Products Using Research-Driven UI Guidelines

Muzayun Mukhtar[1(✉)], Radhika Wakankar[1],
and Christopher Bertrand[2]

[1] Experience Design, CTO, Symantec Corporation, Pune, MH, India
{muzayun_muzayun, radhika_wakankar}@symantec.com
[2] Experience Design, CTO, Symantec Corporation, Mountain View, CA, USA
christopher_bertrand@symantec.com

Abstract. User Interface (UI) guidelines, used across various enterprise products or applications of a company bring consistency and cohesiveness between them. This paper discusses the user research studies carried out to arrive at a minimum threshold of visual components required to help multiple products retain the perception of consistency between interfaces. These studies help identify which elements and which combinations of these elements can help build associations. Our results showed that among various UI components, background color, header-footer and button color were the most influential, in that order. We also studied how various combinations in the background color of the content area *plus* header-footer would lead to increase or decrease in association.

Keywords: User interface guidelines · Consistency · Visual elements · Association to company · User insights · Qualitative research · Quantitative research · Brand identity · Human computer interaction · UI development

1 Introduction

When a software company develops multiple products and employs many UX teams, standard UI guidelines help balance the experience across all these products, creating an advantageous consistency. Guidelines can strengthen a company's brand and increase development efficiency, making it easy for teams to re-use and replicate company-wide patterns and color schemes. They help provide consistent design language. Users of multiple products from the company can then navigate and complete their tasks with a smaller learning curve and an easier transition between products [1].

Large companies that produce many products struggle to maintain consistency while innovatively solving for unique requirements and distinct use cases. Companies that succeed learn to balance both. Having a coherent design vision and overall consistency can also help sales teams effectively showcase products when they are selling multiple products to the IT users of fortune 500 companies. The onboarding experience for the customers using multiple products is made easier.

This cohesive experience starts with the visual language. A product graphic interface's visual language is made of collection of components or elements [2].

© Springer International Publishing Switzerland 2015
C. Stephanidis (Ed.): HCII 2015 Posters, Part I, CCIS 528, pp. 427–432, 2015.
DOI: 10.1007/978-3-319-21380-4_72

Our challenge at Symantec was to understand what critical design elements should be prioritized in adoption of company-wide guidelines, to maximize the advantages of consistent brand and design elements, while still allowing for unique individual product requirements and making guideline adoption easier for development teams.

2 Objective

Understand which aspects of visual design guidelines (such as color, button, font, navigation structure and controls) create the greatest perception of consistency across products. The goal of our research is to find out the minimum threshold that can bring about a sense of being from the same company even when multiple factors make the product user interfaces unique from each other. This paper helps identify which elements and which combinations can help build such associations.

3 Related Work and Discussion

User interface guidelines first appeared in a digital world in 1986 with the introduction of a single set of guidelines for U.S. Air Force, mostly used for mainframe technology [3]. Our secondary research indicates that a recurring goal has been on how to make guidelines more acceptable while designing & developing products.

We found efforts that stressed strategies for promoting common UI guidelines as done by Adobe researchers [4] or by Cisco researchers [5]. Efforts like research-based web design and usability guidelines [6] have data available by looking at trends in the digital communications and by aggregating available secondary research resources.

However, the user input in creating interface guidelines was hard to find. This gap in the available research made us look at more consumer focused product models like Google, who have ready access to users of all types. Google operates on the belief that users get deeply passionate about the products they work on because they 'live' these products [7]. Hence Google has a user database that they tap into all the time to get feedback on new product ideas and guidelines. In enterprise, users are harder to source and our research did not reveal similar or parallel efforts. All Google products have buttons, top-bar, consistent grid structure and search as common elements and part of their guidelines. Very often, such a design vision is difficult to permeate through the entire product families of a big company. Identifying the minimum threshold of consistent UI elements to promote brand recognition and enable cross-product learning, would help us maximize adoption of guidelines as well as the benefits of using them.

4 Research Methodology

Our research largely involves users as primary information source. In all, we conducted five user studies across U.S and India, with an external panel of usability testers (n = 450). Three studies were qualitative (n = 42) and two with quantitative (n = 408).

Table 1. List of screens showing tested UI elements and expectations

Screen	Left page	Right page	Expectations
1	Black background	White background	If seen as different, then background color is a differentiator
2	Header-footer color (guidelines specified)	Different header-footer color	If seen as different, then header-footer color is a differentiator
3	Page layout (guidelines specified)	Different page layout	If seen as different, then the page layout is important
4	UI controls (guidelines specified)	Different controls used (checkboxes, tabs etc.)	If seen as different, then UI controls being consistent are a contributing factor
5	Buttons (guidelines specified)	Different button colors	If seen as different, then buttons are a contributing factor

This research experiment was designed as a modified A/B testing where we showed participants two pages (1280 × 1024 pixels) on a screen monitor. The pages had one UI element that was different, while other UI elements were the same. For example, if we were testing for background color, the screen would have one page with white background while the other page would have black background. Other elements like header-footer color, controls used (textbox, checkboxes, tabs, tables) and button colors were all the same in both pages. Refer Table 1 for other comparisons. Elements were disguised so that they did not look identical, also the content was gibberish in order to remove bias and ensure that users could focus on visual elements. We included home pages, dashboards, and list pages, e.g., visual elements on an alerts page of one product should be consistent with the dashboard of other product.

Participants were asked to look at two screens to compare and had to answer, "Are the two screens from the same company?" with 'Yes' or 'No' (henceforth called 'Association'). If the user answers, "No, the screens are not from the same company", we assume it implies that that tested variable is important in creating association. And if 6 out of 10 users answered 'No', then we can say 'association score' created by the tested variable is 60.

For quantitative research, we carried out surveys using an online tool. To gather qualitative answers, we conducted multiple rounds of 1:1 sessions.

The user-base of enterprise products in Symantec approximates to 430,000 users (FY2013-14). Our addressable market for enterprise products is less than even our own consumer product market. In addition, users are hard to recruit because of the challenging and diligent nature of their jobs. Given such constraints we knew we could not expect to find enough of our users to complete a long complex survey in time to break down and analyze every relevant aspect of our guidelines project. Instead, we took to new innovative research tools to get a better understanding of which elements are most powerful in creating a perception of consistency.

Based on Gestalt's theories, we know that users view the screen as a consolidated perception; and it is difficult to pick one design element at a time and analyze it separately to make a judgment. With this understanding, we worked around to devise a simple technique to still arrive at the minimum common UI elements.

Based on our experience and existing literature [8], we identified five visual elements and UI components namely background color, header-footer, UI controls, page layout and button color (Fig. 1), which were weighed for this purpose. Also, there are other design elements that we could not include like typography since large product companies like ours have trademarked their own branding fonts (e.g., Symantec Sans).

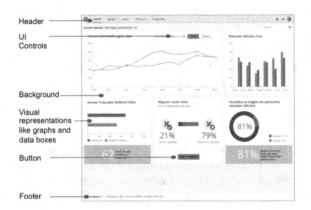

Fig. 1. A typical screen with UI components marked for reference

5   Results

The results from the qualitative study (column 2 in the Table 2 below) indicated that background color, button color and header-footer are the elements which when varied make the pages look different. For example, when we varied the button colors (one page with orange button color and other page with blue button color), most participants said that the UI pages did not belong to the same company and pointed out button color as one of the prominent reason for saying so. Therefore to bring consistency among products, button color appears to be one of the key elements to consider.

Participants said that the background color, buttons, top bar, menu layout and font color were the elements that helped them gauge similarity. Highlighted table rows, visual representations like graphs and data boxes were other items mentioned as deciding factors for the association.

Our crowd-sourced data showed that association score of background color is 52, followed by header-footer at 47 and button color at 46. Controls and page layout had approximately an association score of 30 each. Therefore, we infer that teams can use this ranking as a guide to choose factors in order to increase brand association between the product lines.

In a follow-up study (Table 3), we wanted to further understand how various combinations in the background color of the content area *plus* header-footer would lead

Table 2. Stage 1- UI screen comparisons, qualitative results, survey outcomes and observations

UI screen comparisons	Association score -1 on 1 session	Association score - survey	Observations
Black vs. white background	69	52	Background color is a differentiator
Header-footer (guidelines specified) vs. different header-footer color	54	47	Header-footer is not as clear differentiator but has higher association than others
Button color (guidelines specified) vs. page with different button color	70	46	Button color was a high deciding factor in qualitative study, emerged at third rank in survey
Page layout (guidelines specified) vs. page with different layout	15	33.5	Page layout is not a differentiating factor
UI Controls (guidelines specified) vs. page with different UI controls	15	30.5	UI controls are not a differentiating factor

Table 3. Stage 2- UI screen comparisons, qualitative results, survey outcomes and observations

UI screen Comparisons	Association score -1 on 1 session	Association score - survey	Observations
Black page vs. Black page with white header-footer	41.6	51.5	Background color is black with varying header-footer, creates a slight association
Black page vs. White page	20	39	Complete white and complete black has marginal sameness
Black page with white header-footer vs. white page	58.4	35	Background colors are different and header-footers are same, it reduces sameness
White page vs. White page with black header-footer	20	30	Background colors are white and header-footer colors are different, it reduces sameness
White page with black header-footer vs. Black page	33.3	27	Both background color and header-footer are different, there is least association

to increase or decrease in association. We picked these two, as they were top ranked as explained earlier. We found that having same background colors creates the highest association of being from the same company (85). When the background color of the pages is black and one of them has white header-footer color, it is only 51.5 association score and 48.5 drop off in recognition. Complete white and complete black screens have reduced sameness (further goes down to 39). All other combinations appear to reduce the sameness factor. Therefore, one could infer that having all white or all black background color *plus* header-footer increases sameness.

Case Study to Show Implementation. When a family of four products was evaluating the background color for their UI, they found that products when viewed together the inconsistencies became obvious especially when the end-user may be same. In this case, two had white and other two had black. The product teams required real validation from the field to arrive at decisions.

This research recommended use of same background color, and helped teams make an informed decision to align on background color before releasing a family of products with significant inconsistencies in look and feel.

6 Future Research

To make it more robust, future research can deep dive in other UI elements. We can also validate it with some more techniques like multidimensional scaling (MDS) with bigger sample size.

Acknowledgements. We would like to thank the guidelines team at Symantec to provide UI pages, product teams and users who spent time with us in these studies.

References

1. Apple iOS Human Interface Guidelines Developer Library, Design Principles (2014) (Accessed on 18-12-014 to 24-03-015) https://developer.apple.com/library/ios/documentation/UserExperience/Conceptual/MobileHIG/Principles.html
2. Curtis N.: A webinar on Reusable Components & Libraries at UIE. http://www.uie.com/brainsparks/2010/09/16/spoolcast-reusable-components-libraries-with-nathan-curtis/
3. Durability of usability guidelines, Neilson Norman Group (2005). http://www.nngroup.com/articles/durability-of-usability-guidelines/
4. Bachman, B., Valiulis, D., Aliaga, F., Treinen, M.: Four strategies for promoting common UI guidelines within Adobe In: Proceedings of the 2003 conference on Designing for user experiences, San Francisco, CA (2003)
5. Nieters, J., Grabel, D., Agrawal, V.: Tools to increase the strategic value of user experience design. In: Proceedings of the 2nd international conference on Usability and internationalization, San Jose, CA (2007)
6. Research-based web design and usability guidelines. http://guidelines.usability.gov/ Wiley, J., " Google has Designers!" (2011), http://vimeo.com/29965463
7. Schlatter, T., Levinson, D.: Visual Usability. Principles and Practices for Designing Digital Applications. Morgan Kaufmann, Massachusetts (2013)

The Teaching Method of Graphic Design in Brazil, Methodology of Brand Development and Their Market Outcomes

João Carlos Riccó Plácido da Silva[✉], Luis Carlos Paschoarelli,
and José Carlos Plácido da Silva

PPGDesign, University Estadual Paulista, Bauru, Brazil
joaocarlos_placido@hotmail.com,
{paschoarelli,placido}@faac.unesp.br

Abstract. The growth of the number of graphic designs to meet the needs of the market has reduced the development process of the same, making them incomprehensible. The use of a suitable method enables new professionals to develop more functional designs. This study lists the problems encountered on the market, using interviews in empreses, and directing the teaching of projetual method in Brazilian schools, focusing on graphic design brands. With that can identify possible improvements in this field.

Keywords: Education · Graphic marks · Projective methods

1 Introduction

The expansion of the promotional materials in the last century was greatly facilitated by both the use of digital technologies and low cost printing. In the virtual world there was an unprecedented advertising explosion that made those advertisements or newsletters massive and often poorly designed. That scenario stimulated the need for new digital interfaces that seek to be intuitive and easy to access.

With economic growth in Brazil, there is an increase in new business and the need to create brands that will be inserted in the market. Excess new brands that are not developed observing a graphic design, designed improperly and quickly cause a bad result called visual pollution. With that, a visual chaos can be observed in large cities, to which we are all subjected. The graphic designer should be professional, by concern about overexposure of information, find ways to use the current advertising media so that does not contribute even more to the problem found today. The responsibility should be delegated to design professionals, since it is they who have the knowledge necessary to analyze and organize the information in the most appropriate way, given the fact that acquire through their training concepts and tools in addition to the appropriate methodology, which aim to interfere positively in the daily lives of users, using brands and images that define and correctly disclose the institution

In the evolution of mankind, it is observed that the accumulation of capital and scientific development, as well as technological, coming from the late fifteenth century and which contributed to a significant development in the eighteenth and nineteenth

C. Stephanidis (Ed.): HCII 2015 Posters, Part I, CCIS 528, pp. 433–438, 2015.
DOI: 10.1007/978-3-319-21380-4_73

centuries, modified and accelerated the work modes then existing. The period mentioned in the craftsman turned designer and provided further specialization in certain areas of development (1).

It is observed that these developments coupled with the rate used in the production ultimately resulted in a very large gap between business and academia. This distance has been much discussed in recent years, inside and outside academia, in order to pursue actions that will bring industries and businesses to academia. The project work developed within the industry, whose main objective is profit, often dispensing steps with which the academy could collaborate assertively, for example, make its affordable and friendly products, contrary to what is observed in the market today. This meeting would provide, for example, the use of analytical methods developed at the university, or to the correct use of architectural design method as well as the ergonomic analysis of the object under development.

2 Theoretical Foundation

Historically, with the dissolution of the Bauhaus, first school of Arts and Crafts, many professionals concerned with the establishment of projects methods in design have been distributed worldwide, which facilitated the dissemination of theoretical and practical aspects developed and established by the school. The dissemination of such concepts enabled the development of critical thinking about the methods. It is worth noting that these professionals aggregated what they were studying the needs of the time to which they were living.

The concepts of the Bauhaus were not extinct with it. Later, in 1950 it opened a school of Ulm, whose pedagogical and structural bases were mirrored in the Bauhaus, there met again many professionals and new students to discuss and plan the new directions of design.

According to Wollner (2005), although the School of Ulm was created along the lines of Bauhaus, were inserted important innovations, especially with regard to the development of projective methods, known as "Ulm Methods". Reflection, analysis, synthesis, reasoning and selection have become paramount to the detriment of artistic education.

In the 1980s, in Brazil, the CNPq (National Council for Scientific and Technological Development) contributed to the spread of methods and projective techniques, based mainly on the work Experimental Methodology, Gui Bonsiepe, Petra Kellner and Holger Poessnecker. This model is still a reference to the design undergraduate education in Brazil (Linden, 2010). The first work directed to designers in Brazil, on the architectural design methodology, was Methodology Basics for Product Development, Gustavo Amarante, Bomfim, Lia Monica Rossi and Klaus-Dieter Nagel, published in 1997, which showed a consistent model product development (3).

The same design project methods are commonly used in both areas, both as graphical area for the product, since preliminary studies the design and implementation are similar. There is a possibility of some adjustments in order to improve the path followed by the designer, specifically in the case of graphic design, which uses different methods to test the developed alternatives and detect if they really are the most effective for the problem presented. In order to better understand how these methods are being used in practice, held interviews with ten professionals in the design field, in order investigate the importance of teaching design method graduation, beyond the analysis of two syllabuses course Design.

3 Materiais and Methods

For analysis of how the processes of teaching methodology in the design are understood, it was necessary to understand and establish how these students are starting their careers, how they work and how they act in the development of a particular product. Therefore, we set interviews with heads of design in order to understand how the development method is used, which references that led one method, and what are the difficulties and problems in the course of their use in order to identify how the knowledge gained university influence in their daily work. There was also checking some curricula design courses already included in the search check disciplines that discuss, or should to discuss, the topic of design methodology.

4 Procedures

4.1 Interviews

The beginning of such organization is by the questionnaire formulation. The researcher must be careful to not draw absurd questions, arbitrary, ambiguous, displaced or biased. Questions should be carried out taking into account the sequence of thought researched, i.e. they must continue the conversation, conducting the interview with some logical sense to the interviewee. For a natural narrative, often not interesting to a direct question, but to make the searched recall of his life, which makes it possible for the researcher to go instigating the memory of the interviewee (4).

From the choice of the interview in the history of life, it was also possible to select the technique of open interviews, one where there are detailed questions and more precise formulation of the sought concepts, technique that best suits exploratory purposes. This technique is used when the researcher needs to obtain the largest possible amount of information on a particular topic, garnering a better detail on the subject discussed, in addition to being used in the description of individual cases, in understanding cultural specificities for certain groups and comparison of cases (5).

The objective is therefore to interview companies in the capital of São Paulo, and also in the center of the state, home to a center of great expression of design. Because the qualitative research, a large number of respondents was not necessary. Adding to the respondents in the capital and the interior came to the total of ten people. It was decided that the interviews would always face where the researcher had control of the situation. On applied research, we opted for digital recording with the interviewee's consent and subsequently its transcription. Another method also was used the notes of key words in the statements of the respondents.

In questions developed for the interview, we tried to highlight two important points. First, try to understand how each of these professionals act methodologically in their visual identity projects, also approaching the care and difficulties through which they pass in the project development. Second, provide a "gap" so they brought some examples of identities already carried out and could then be used for further analysis

We opted for a reorganization of the issues and inclusion of others that could enter the respondent in the study of the object without doubts about which parts of the development processes were being questioned. Another caution was to permit negative responses in some of the questions, so that the respondent could clarify why the "no" indication. Using as a base the first group of questions, it was decided to add four more questions, so that the latter were a way to request the marks for later analysis. So was the new script.

The one to three questions refer to the method used, whether or not a particular method or some defined by the respondent, and that the reference used. The fourth question deals with the difficulty using the method development. In the fifth, what precautions are relevant to this type of development. In the sixth question, what is the importance of using a method. The seventh investigates what the interviewee considers as a good quality brand or to reach the desired goals. The eighth search the presentation of some brands developed by the interviewee. Already the ninth question has the sense of explanation by the respondent of the mark.

In addition to the procedures described above, it was decided to not identify respondents, saving them from worrying about the results, and so were not harmed in any way. Subsequently, the interviews were transcribed in order to make it possible to analyze the results obtained through the issues investigated. We tried to faithfully represent the reality appears therefore transcripts were made in full. This procedure therefore provided the interviewer a lot of information, which were subsequently compared with the relevant topics of each of the responses given by the interviewee.

4.2   Curriculum

Two syllabuses of institutions were selected from the same region to be analyzed, a state university and one private institution, both where researchers act as teachers in order to meet course procedures. Held a note of curricula available on the website of the institutions which were scored disciplines that approached the terms "design methodology" or "product development", both in the title, but also on the syllabus of course, since the two refer or use the teaching of architectural design direction. Attempted to identify also congruences between educational lines applied by teachers of these disciplines and create relations of these methods with students in order to draw a line of evolution based on the above subjects, and the starting point is the discipline of design methodology.

5   Results

5.1   Interviews

Regarding the first question, 90 % of respondents using specific procedures in product development, there are several means to this development. The only respondent who answered not use, proposed a more intuitive method in the search form, to further adapt it to technical and user needs. In all the interviews briefing word was present in 6 (six), in the other is expressed in another way, as the size of the company or customer trend, which in the end reveals the same analysis technique for all the points involving the product.

The nine respondents described a case involving the briefing, the Brainstorm, Rough (Raffe), the study of shape, the colors, the search for references to similar analysis and development.

The third question, which dealt with the references used for this development, all said they were based more on experience and at the crossroads of various techniques. Two of them cited the same procedure learned at university, while others were based on methods they have learned in the profession. The most mentioned terms were "own" and "several references". Some companies highlighted the not authorial method of the project, i.e. the development of several professionals working in teams to develop, they have, therefore, a single author.

Five of the respondents indicated the difficulty of finding new professionals to understand and use the methodology, not that they apply in their companies, but any method learned and used at the university. The need to resubmit these methods has been reported to enable them to adapt the method that uses each company, once considered crucial for the proper development of any product design using a suitable method.

5.2 Curriculum Frameworks

The observations resulted in a comparative table between the two Curriculum Frameworks. According to what is presented in the curriculum grid, the course of UNV 1 has a total hourly load of 2,160 presence hours with the use of 648 dedicated to the teaching of architectural design method and its applications. However there is an instability in relation to the growth disciplines, confirmed the use in the first semester, while in the second semester no discipline that covers the method, with an increasing in the 4th semester and thereafter a sharp drop was not found. These gaps can create doubt about the use or not of method in a projetual development since last semester this direction have very low hourly charge. UNV 2 has a workload of 2,400 classroom hours with the use of 510 h devoted to architectural design education. However there has been a gradual increase in the use of architectural design method, which may indicate a more interconnected use of the method in these disciplines, which can help students in understanding their application.

In the two educational institutions may be other disciplines that approach teaching and application of architectural design method, however this focus is not checked on the syllabus of discipline, implying that the teacher will determine if this direction will exist or not. Therefore we can conclude that there is a vacuum for the student's understanding of the issue.

6 Concluding Remarks

The design area has throughout its existence improved methods of product development, however, it is observed that there was not always a concern to pass through to undergraduate students. There were the survey respondents who indicated that no use of the methods, and others who pointed out its application, although we have found that the majority mistakenly. So it takes a larger and more active concern in the employment education and use of projective methods in design, providing students with the understanding of the real need to properly employ the same to obtain satisfactory final results and not contributing to greater pollution visual as we have seen today.

Another finding is that a lot of the time the new professionals in anxiety to create new brands or products end up ignoring the initial stages of the project, such as the analysis and the required initial organization. Thus, the professional just going straight to the stage of development, without even knowing if there is at least one existing, or the public that it is being addressed. It is also the Notes unaware of the manufacturing processes that will be used in the materialization of the product as well as the ergonomic analysis would provide the determination of size, weight, handles and other factors of targeted informational ergonomics generation of new brands.

The fact is that the current market needs quick solutions. However can not be excluded the natural process of development and design of pregnancy to prevent or correct possible errors or mistakes that may harm the end user. Professional design is what qualifies and knowledge required for effective concrete products that meet the needs required by the market and users. Therefore it is necessary and urgent that the education and employment of methods are strengthened and properly applied by the academy, thus becoming a constant and necessary dynamics in a revision procedure, given the significant evolution of the digital area.

References

Linden, J.C.S.V.D. et al.: A evolução dos métodos projetuais. Anais do 9P&D Design. AEND – Brasil (2010)

Wollner A., Stolarski A., Wollner, A.: e a Formação do Design Moderno no Brasil. São Paulo: Editora Cosac Naify (2005)

Norman, D.: Things that make us smart. Cambridge. Perseus Books, MA (1993)

Bomfim, G.A., Rossi, L.M., Nagel, K.-D.: Fundamentos de uma metodologia para desenvolvimento de produtos. COPPE/UFRJ, Rio de Janeiro (1977)

Bourdieu, P.: A miséria do mundo. Tradução de Mateus S. Soares. 3a edição Retropolis: Vozes, 1999. Couto, R.M.S.: Pós-Graduação de Designers Brasileiros. In: Anais do Congresso Brasileiro de Pesquisa e Desenvolvimento em Design, Brasília (2003)

Minayo, M.C.S.O.: Pesquisa Social: Teoria, Método e Criatividade. 6a edição. Petrópolis: Editoras Vozes (1996)

Analysis on Universality Evaluation Standard System of Product Design on Basis of Kansei Engineering and Virtual Reality

Wangqun Xiao[1,2], Jianxin Cheng[1(✉)], Xuejie Wang[2], Junnan Ye[1], and Le Xi[1]

[1] School of Art, Design and Media,
East China University of Science and Technology,
M.BOX 286, NO.130, Meilong Road, Xuhui District, Shanghai 200237, China
xiaoyao-1916@163.com, cjx.master@gmail.com,
yejunnan971108@qq.com, xilutar@sina.com
[2] Academy of Art and Design, Anhui University of Technology,
NO.59, East Lake Road, Ma'anshan 243002, China
402860858@qq.com

Abstract. The universality evaluation standard system of product design on basis of Kansei Engineering and virtual reality constructed in this paper will effectively solve the current practical problems of product design evaluation to the greatest degree. The reasons why people are usually at a loss when conducting product design evaluation are that, on the one hand they do not know what kind of method or means is able to achieve the goal of scientific evaluation, and on the other hand whether there is or what kind of method and model among hundreds of product design evaluation methods and models can deal with the design evaluation problem of this product.This paper aims to carry out in-depth research from the following four aspects. (1) Systemically combing the product design evaluation research results which include Kansei engineering, virtual reality, and cross-over research results of product design evaluation. (2) Scientifically summarizing the construction elements of product design universality evaluation standard system. (3) Scientifically refining construction factor and correlation factor, and extracting universality standard construction factor through researches on comparison of construction factor and correlation factor. (4) Setting priority standard through researches on the reasonable and matched priority relation of various standard construction factors, and finally constructing a product design universality evaluation standard system on basis of Kansei Engineering and virtual reality.

Keywords: Kansei engineering · Virtual reality · Product design · Evaluation standard system

1 Introduction

Product design evaluation is the complex system including two aspects, "ration" and "emotion", and multiple factors. With the further pursuit of better life of human society and the continuous enhancement of realization of science and technology,

© Springer International Publishing Switzerland 2015
C. Stephanidis (Ed.): HCII 2015 Posters, Part I, CCIS 528, pp. 439–443, 2015.
DOI: 10.1007/978-3-319-21380-4_74

the traditional product design philosophy led by "functional practice" or "technology" has converted into the modern product design philosophy led by "user experience" or "emotion". Product design evaluation has become the new concern of the current product design research, and the scientific evaluation of subjective "emotional" factors in product design evaluation is the difficulty. It is the urgent practical needs to establish a scientific and high-efficient product design evaluation system as soon as possible, so as to improve product design innovation ability and scientific level, improve the success rate of enterprise product development and shorten the development cycle, etc.

2 Analysis of Research Status

Many scholars have carried out extensive researches on product design evaluation and have achieved encouraging results. A. Mousavi et al. [1] studied the complex problem of user preferences in the practice of product design and put forward a "customer optimization path and assessment model", i.e. CORE; X. Zeng et al. [2] proposed a fuzzy multiple criteria evaluation method of "fashionable design-oriented industrial products"; Chulwoo Kim et al. [3] proposed an efficient evaluation method of user impression by using the virtual prototype to analyze products; A. Rashid et al. [4] studied an intelligent design system evaluating the product aesthetics; Carmen Llinares et al. [5] studied to use Kano model to analyze the impact of different subjective attributes on consumer purchasing decisions based on Kansei engineering theory; Mark Evans et al. [6] studied the tactile feedback model evaluation in the practice of industrial design; Hyungjun Park et al. [7] studied the design evaluation of information devices based on tangible interactive Augmented Reality Technology; Francisco Rebelo et al. [8] studied the use of virtual reality to evaluate the user experience, etc.

For emphasizing the emotional experience interaction issues of users under the new concept of and current product design, various scholars have studied the quantitative evaluation of subjective factors on "emotion" based on Kansei engineering theory [5, 6], and the use of virtual reality technology to allow users to achieve "immersive emotional interactive experience" and realize intuitive and high-efficient evaluation [3, 7, 8], etc. However, the products will show great differences due to different individual types in the product design evaluation; meanwhile, product design evaluation is accompanied by the entire cycle of products from concept, design and verification to production. Evaluation indicator and assessment methods are different at all stages, so it brings about great inconvenience and difficulties for people conducting product design evaluation. There has not been the current research involved in the issue how to make every product get the most scientific and rational design evaluation at maximum efficiency. In addition, the data acquisition picture samples in Kansei engineering will affect the quality of samples because of not strong "sense of reality", and the data collecting actual samples will cause a lot of waste of manpower and material resources; if the visual experience component in the virtual reality is not processed scientifically, it will be difficult to ensure the scientificity of product design evaluation.

Therefore, scientifically extract the common factors from products, use the high-efficient technologies, scientific theories of the quantitative evaluation in Kansei engineering and the intuitive interactive evaluation in virtual reality, to effectively integrate product design evaluation method and model, systematically build scientific and high-efficient product design universality evaluation standard system, and make a useful exploration on the researches on complex product design evaluation system.

3 Research Method

Research Method adopts the literature research method and the combination of induction and deduction method with experimental verification method. Through the collection of plenty of relevant research literature at home and abroad, understand the research perspective and research progress of each experts and scholars, grasp the development trend in this area overall and tease the relevant issues of product design evaluation system and the relevance issue of product design evaluation, Kansei engineering and virtual reality systematically and theoretically. Study the internal relation between constructing factors of product design universality evaluation standard system, use the relevant expertise and obtain product design universality evaluation standard system theory construction based on Kansei engineering theory and virtual reality technology through induction and deduction. Combined with eye tracking, EEG perception, EMG test, three-dimensional visual simulation and force feedback system experimental techniques, the author in this paper uses the combination of normative research and real evidence and selects a large number of typical cases to conduct empirical analysis, so as to verify the scientificity and high efficiency of product design universality evaluation standard system based on Kansei engineering theory and virtual reality.

4 Theory Construction of Product Design Universality Evaluation Standard System Based on Kansei Engineering Theory and Virtual Reality

4.1 Construction Element and Construction Factor of Product Design Universality Evaluation Standard System

Study construction elements of product design universality evaluation standard system centered by the product design, such as the evaluation object, the evaluation phase, evaluation indicator and evaluation method, etc., and then further deeply study the construction factors contained in various construction factors, such as performance, cost, materials, structure, shape, color and construction factors in evaluation indicator elements, product usability evaluation methods based on FAHP in evaluation method elements, product design evaluation method based on human physiological signals, product design quality gray system comprehensive evaluation and a rational multi-attribute multiplayer evaluation method in product design and other construction factors.

4.2   Relevance Factors Among Kansei Engineering Theory, Virtual Reality Technology and Product Design Evaluation

Through the theoretical researches on the application of Kansei engineering and virtual reality technologies in product design evaluation, extract the relevance factors between Kansei engineering theory and product design evaluation and the relevance factors between virtual reality technology and product design evaluation

4.3   Screening and Extracting Universality Standard Construction Factor

Conduct a comparative study of the relevance factor and the construction factor from the perspective of "quantifiable" and "emotional interactive experience", delete duplicate construction factor, condense construct and optimize the construction factor, scientifically extract the universality construction factor and establish the construction factor standard.

4.4   Theory Construction of Product Design Universality Evaluation Standard System Based on Kansei Engineering Theory and Virtual Reality

Study the hierarchical relationship and the cross relation between various construction elements; Based on the "scientificity" of Kansei engineering theory and "high efficiency" of virtual reality technology, focus on the research on the precedence relationship for reasonable match between the universality standard construction factor in construction elements and the universality standard construction factor in other construction elements, develop the precedence standards, so as to theoretically construct the product design universality evaluation standard system based on Kansei engineering theory and virtual reality technology.

5   Conclusions and Prospect

The author in this paper constructs the product design universality evaluation standard system based on Kansei engineering theory and virtual reality technology, which will effectively solve the realistic problem of current product design evaluation to the maximum: people are often at a loss during conducting the product design evaluation. On the one hand, people do not know what ways or means they can achieve the effect of the scientific evaluation; On the other hand, are there methods or models, etc. which can effectively solve design evaluation problem of the product among nearly one hundred product design evaluation methods or models. There are great differences in evaluation indicators of nearly one hundred product design evaluation methods or models, which are likely to cause thinking confusion of evaluation users and difficulty in evaluation work. Establish a set of generally applicable evaluation indicator standards and the corresponding evaluation solutions, and condense and unify the evaluation indicators, so as to make the product design evaluation become more standardized and objective, which provides theoretical support for the government establishing the scientific and standardized product design evaluation standards or specifications from the national level.

The product design universality evaluation criteria system established based on the "scientificity" of Kansei engineering and "technical advancement" of virtual reality provides scientific basis and guidance for enterprise conducting product independent innovation design, which is of important strategic significance and practical significance to enhance the product design and innovation ability, scientific level and quantitative evaluation ability in our country, improve corporate product development efficiency and reduce corporate product development risks, etc. The project research results will provide theoretical support, quantitative evaluation method and technological means for product design theory research.

References

1. Mousavi, A., Adl, P., et al.: Customer optimization route and evaluation (CORE) for product design. Int. J. Comput. Integr. Manuf. **14**(2), 236–243 (2001)
2. Zeng, X., Zhu, Y., et al.: A fuzzy multi-criteria evaluation method for designing fashion oriented industrial products. Soft. Comput. **14**, 236–243 (2010)
3. Kim, Chulwoo, Lee, Cheol, et al.: Affective Evaluation of User Impressions Using Virtual Product Prototyping. Human Factors and Ergonomics in Manufacturing & Service Industries **21**(1), 1–13 (2011)
4. Rashid, A., Mac Donald, B.J., et al.: Evaluation of the aesthetics of products and integration of the findings in a proposed intelligent design system. J. Mater. Process. Technol. **153–154**, 380–385 (2004)
5. Llinares, Carmen, Page, Alvaro F.: Kano's model in Kansei Engineering to evaluate subjective real estate consumer preferences. Int. J. Ind. Ergon. **41**, 233–246 (2011)
6. Evans, Mark, Wallace, David, et al.: An evaluation of haptic feedback modelling during industrial design practice. Des. Stud. **26**, 487–508 (2005)
7. Park, Hyungjun, Moon, Hee-Cheol: Design evaluation of information appliances using augmented reality-based tangible interaction. Comput. Ind. **64**, 854–868 (2013)
8. Rebelo, Francisco, Noriega, Paulo, et al.: Using Virtual Reality to Assess User Experience. Hum. Factors **54**(6), 964–982 (2012)

The New Product Development Research of Chinese Ming and Qing Dynasty's Furniture Based on 3-D Printing

Xuejie Wang[1(✉)], Wangqun Xiao[1,2], and Yimin Song[1]

[1] Academy of Art and Design, Anhui University of Technology,
NO.59, East Lake Road, Ma'anshan 243002, China
{402860858,929810953}@qq.com, xiaoyao-1916@163.com
[2] School of Art, Design and Media,
East China University of Science and Technology,
M.BOX 286, NO.130, Meilong Road, Xuhui District 200237, Shanghai, China

Abstract. In the protection and inheritance of the traditional cultural heritage, the use of 3-D printing technology has become a trend of globalization. As an important part of Chinese tangible culture heritage, Chinese Ming and Qing Dynasty's furniture really a rarity in the world classic furniture system. It has scientific structure, fastidious materials, elaborate fabrication, concise modelling, exquisite pattern, appropriate decoration and bears many aspects information of ancient Chinese people life style, aesthetic consciousness and value orientation. This article is starts from the typical artistic features of Chinese Ming and Qing Dynasty's furniture and using 3-D scanning technology for data acquisition to build an integrated information platform which contains pattern, texture, color, structure, modelling and so on 3-D date. Combines with design, marketing, sociology and so on to innovate and develop, finally assist new product development by using 3-D printing technology to the three dimensional real object way to show. Introduce 3-D printing technology into Chinese Ming and Qing dynasty's furniture research, ultimately reaches into the neoclassical furniture design point of view that to guide practice of neoclassical furniture research and development. This article strives to explore a new path to inherit, applied and promote Chinese traditional furniture and provide useful reference for the neoclassical furniture's new product research and development.

Keywords: 3-D printing · Product development · Chinese ming and qing dynasty's furniture

1 Introduction

In the protection and inheritance of the traditional cultural heritage, the use of 3-D printing technology has become a trend of globalization. As an important part of Chinese tangible culture heritage, Chinese Ming and Qing Dynasty's furniture really a rarity in the world classic furniture system. It has scientific structure, fastidious materials, elaborate fabrication, concise modelling, exquisite pattern, appropriate decoration and bears many aspects information of ancient Chinese people life style, aesthetic consciousness and value orientation. [1] With the arrival of 3D printing era,

C. Stephanidis (Ed.): HCII 2015 Posters, Part I, CCIS 528, pp. 444–449, 2015.
DOI: 10.1007/978-3-319-21380-4_75

the designer does not only sell simple products any more, but creation. The 3D printing cannot only be used to protect and inherit the great cultural heritage, but also endow the cultural heritage with brand new life. Facing this development opportunity, how to promote the great Chinese Ming and Qing furniture to the world and how to design the neo-classical furniture with the connotation of Chinese culture has become an important subject for the modern Chinese furniture industry.

2 Introduction of the Artistic Feature of Chinese Ming and Qing Furniture

The Chinese Ming and Qing furniture was developed based on the furniture from the Song and Yuan Dynasties, and the furniture reached its peak development in the Ming and Qing Dynasties. High-quality materials were mainly used to make the furniture, such as rosewood, nagkassar, nanmu, wenge and redwood, which had changed the long-term manufacturing method with lacquer finish. In the meantime, [2] the elegant material, natural texture and smooth gloss of the timer were also used, which generated brand new atmosphere, taste and unique aesthetic value of the furniture hard to be expressed with language. [3] Through the exquisite fine wood techniques, it has built a monument in the world furniture history. When summarizing the achievement of Ming and Qing furniture, the famous arts and crafts theorist Mr. Tian Zibing pointed it out that the reason why the Ming and Qing furniture could have high artistic achievement is because it smartly and properly used the design principles of arts and crafts. The yellow pear wood round-backed armchair shown in Fig. 1 has the classic style of Ming Dynasty, the chair circle extends from the head part downward to form the armrest, the back panel presents an "S" shape, which is decorated with small reliefs, there is an insert panel under the seat, and the "step-by-setp" plank method is used for the bottom plank. All these are classic Ming style, which has combined the pragmatic and scientific features. [4] The Qing furniture is significantly different from the Ming furniture both in style and decoration. Generally speaking, the Ming style is simple, while the Qing style is complicated; the Ming style prevails on its style, while the Qing style prevails on its decoration. Figure 2 shows a rosewood armchair with inlaid jade and flower decoration from the Qianlong Period of Qing Dynasty, which is similar to the "pillar style" wing chair. The back panel is exquisite with delicate engraving, the board engraving, is elegant below the waistband, the chair legs are stretching cabriole legs, and the foot part has the shape of lion's paws. It is of the classic Qing style, and we can see it was affected by the style of western European classic furniture.

3 The Necessity to Introduce the Research on 3D Printing Technology for the Chinese Ming and Qing Furniture

3.1 Accuracy of the Inheritance of the Chinese Ming and Qing Furniture

The inheritance of the Chinese Ming and Qing furniture should not only include the 2D images of decoration patterns, color and material, but also the overall presentation of

Fig. 1. Yellow pear wood round-backed jade armchair of Ming style

Fig. 2. Rosewood armchair with inlaid and flower decoration from the Qianlong Period of Qing Dynasty

spatial structure and the mortise and tenon joint structure. The past traditional recording method generally used the drawings, films and physical or structural model expressed with three views, and mistakes were unavoidable during the message delivery with drawings. [5] With the digital expression carrier, the message is delivered through accurate instrument and equipment, which can accurately reflect the actual object and scenario, the 3D technique representation is also used to avoid the errors during the recording process, and it can more accurately represent the structure and patterns of Chinese Ming and Qing furniture. [6] Digital product research and development is a kind of reversal design method, based on the design requirement analysis, the designer uses the 3D modeling software such as PRO/E and Rhino to import the furniture information in the 3D database, and by adding new processing information, the furniture that satisfies the requirement of era can be developed.

3.2   The Chinese Ming and Qing Furniture Has the Experiencing Characteristic of Inheritance

Based on the 3D printing technology, the design and exploration of Chinese Ming and Qing furniture has inheritance have gradually reached the frontline of the furniture design filed. With the introduction and gradual maturing and promotion of various technologies such as 3D printing, cloud computing and big data, the model of furniture design will have major change, even innovation and subversion. Then, the brand new production, business and economic forms will trigger unprecedented change in consumption model, and for the furniture designer, the 3D printing means revolutionary process in technology. [7] The development of 3D printing technology changes with each passing day, in the future, more efforts will be made to explore the new combination between the 3D printing model and the traditional culture, and more designers will provide the experiencing and participating production model to satisfy the personal and differential consumption.

4   Realization Approach for Developing New Products of Chinese Ming and Qing Furniture Based on the 3D Printing Technology

4.1   Build Systematic and Complete 3D Printing Database Related to the Chinese Ming and Qing Furniture

The establishment of 3D printing database of the Chinese Ming and Qing furniture is a complicated process. Based on the early information collection and post data processing, related developer will set the basic framework and relational structure of the database, and the development will be conducted through the API interface of Revit software platform. In this way, it can not only adequately utilize the strong 3D modeling function of Revit software, but also provide convenient and reasonable storage method for the file management on the Revit software platform. The 3D database has many similarities with the traditional 2D database, as well as some differences. Through the 3D database, we can not only obtain related 2D information mentioned above, but also various kinds of 3D digital information such as the empirical cases of Chinese Ming and Qing furniture, modeling characteristics, technology features, decoration features and the mortise and tenon joint structure, in this way to realize 3D dynamic visual browsing. The designer can export the data based on requirement to conduct reverse design. By building the 3D database of Chinese Ming and Qing furniture, it can not only help the furniture manufacturer to look up and manage the design files of traditional furniture, but also make it convenient for the designer and user to share and call related design material.

4.2   Design and Development of Neoclassical Furniture with 3D Printing Technology Based on the 3D Model Database

The 3D database of Chinese Ming and Qing furniture has provided massive 3D data information of great traditional furniture. During the research and development of neoclassical furniture, the designer can adequately utilize the 3D database and introduce a new furniture product development mode based on the 3D model, in this way to adapt to the digital design and manufacturing that have been extensively used in the furniture industry. At present, the development in the furniture industry generally uses the 2D drawings based on the 3D model, and this kind of furniture research and development model has several problems: the deepening of 2D drawing requires a lot of time, it tends to increase the error rate when the designer has to repeatedly input the data, and there is a low association between the design data and manufacturing data. Some furniture manufacturers have started to try the digital product research and development based on the 3D model. During the research and development of neoclassical furniture, because modern people are significantly different from the ancient people in life style, behavior and psychology, they also have different requirement for the furniture functions. Therefore, we should not simply replicate the great traditional furniture, but also make evolution and innovation in the category, function, style and structure of furniture, so that the modern Chinese furniture will not only have the characteristics of oriental culture, but also have the functions and aesthetics required by modern life. The designer can use 3D printing for forming treatment, and consider and optimize the design plan to satisfy the modern personalized requirement for furniture.

5   Conclusion and Prospects

The fast development of 3D printing technology can not only change the future capital and work allocation method, but also make it possible that the design and manufacturing industry won't rely on the production scale, but the creation. By introducing the 3D printing technology into the research of classic Chinese Ming and Qing furniture, the digital research method for neoclassical furniture is proposed. Finally, efforts are made to extend to the design of neoclassical furniture to guide the research and development practice of neoclassical furniture, and a new approach for the inheritance, application and promotion of traditional Chinese furniture is explored, which can provide beneficial reference to the new product research and development of neoclassical furniture. It requires the massive modern furniture designer to conduct deep exploration and research to well utilize modern 3D printing technology and effectively promote the development of outstanding traditional culture of Chinese furniture.

References

1. Hai, L., Jian, W.: Study on the Classic Chinese Furniture based on Digital Technology[J]. Furniture and Interior Decoration 1, 28–29 (2014)

2. Zhitao, Q.: Study on the Scientific Features and Value of Ming-style Furniture[D], Nanjing Forestry University (2006)
3. Zibing, T.: The Brief History of Chinese Arts & Crafts[M], Version 1, Shanghai: Oriental Press, 1, p. 300 (1985)
4. Xiaoning, Q., Junshun, Y.: Brief analysis of the application and development of chinese ming and qing furniture in modern furniture design. J. Shaanxi Univ. Sci. Technol. **26**(1), 163–165 (2008)
5. Fanwei and Guquyun: Digital Protection and Innovation of Traditional Furniture Form. Furniture Inter. Decoration **11**, 70–71 (2014)
6. Shulan, Yu., Zhihui, W.: study on the key digital technology for collaborative customization of furniture products. Manuf. Autom. **11**, 62–65 (2010)
7. Wenjia, L.: Study on the furniture design innovation based on the 3D printing of BID concept. Arts Circle **1**, 76–77 (2015)

Using Eye Tracking Technology to Evaluate New Chinese Furniture Material Design

Junnan Ye, Jianxin Cheng$^{(\boxtimes)}$, Le Xi, and Wangqun Xiao

School of Art Design and Media ECUST, M.BOX 286, NO.130 Meilong Road,
Xuhui District, Shanghai 200237, China
yejunnan971108@qq.com, cjx.master@gmail.com,
xilutar@sina.com, xiaoyao-1916@163.com

Abstract. With the rapid economic growth in China, Chinese style furniture has revived quietly and "new Chinese furniture" that accords with the demand of the time has also been generated. Not only it is an inheritance of Chinese long-standing history and culture, but also it complies with the international trend. Material is an important design element in new Chinese furniture. With our scientific and technological progress, the methods and means of design have been continuously improving and updating, and the modes of design appraisal have been emerging endlessly. However, few research is on the design appraisal of materials used in new Chinese furniture. Eye-tracking technology takes users' eye movement as the basis of measurement and appraisal, which is relatively more suitable for the inspection of the visibility, characteristic meaning and interface layout of exterior elements. Thus, it can provide product development with objective, comparable and quantitative standards of measurement.

In this research, eye-tracking technology and the method of subjective assessment are combined and desktops in new Chinese furniture are taken as an example. The eye movement features and subjective assessment results in undergraduate respondents' preference assessment of four commonly used materials for desktops (bamboo, wood, glass and metal) are recorded. It is found out through analysis and comparison that there are significance differences between professional and non-professional respondents' assessment of the materials. In the assessment of materials, as the level of subjective assessment rises, the respondents clap their eyes on the materials at a longer time more frequently, and their pupil diameter becomes larger. However, it has nothing to do with the duration of continued watching. Therefore, the time and duration of watching, and pupil diameter can be taken as effective indexes in eye movement assessment of materials of new Chinese furniture.

Keywords: Eye tracking · New Chinese Furniture · Material design · Design appraisal

1 Introduction

With the rapid development of Chinese economy, Chinese furniture is also reviving quietly and "New Chinese Furniture" which meets the requirements of the age is generated. It is the inheritance of long-standing Chinese history and culture, complying

C. Stephanidis (Ed.): HCII 2015 Posters, Part I, CCIS 528, pp. 450–455, 2015.
DOI: 10.1007/978-3-319-21380-4_76

with the international trend. New Chinese Furniture refers to furniture applying modern technology, equipment, materials and technique, meeting standardized and unitized requirements of modern furniture, reflecting characteristics of this age and adapting industrialized volume production with strong Chinese traditional cultural connotation and national features [1]. We can find that New Chinese Furniture design shall not only reflect new technology, new materials, new technique, new environment, new requirements and other features of the age but also pay attention to the research of Chinese culture, appreciation of the beauty, philosophy, style, temperament and other national features.

Material is an important design element of New Chinese Furniture. With scientific and technological progress, the design ways and means are improving and updating continuously and the ways of design evaluation is also emerging in endlessly. However, few people are researching the material design evaluation of New Chinese Furniture.

2   Eye Tracking Technology

Eye tracking technology uses sight movement of user as the measurement and evaluation basis, compares the visibility, representation implication and interface layout which are suitable for investigating the product appearance elements, which is able to provide objective, comparable and quantized measurement standard of product development.

Current eye trackers mostly applies infrared ray to catch cornea and the reflection principle of retina to record the user's eye movement track, fixation times, fixation period and other data [4]. According to research reports and materials published in recent years [5] show that eye tracker test parameters mainly include:

Eye movement frequency, Pupil size change, Average fixation standing time, Fixation point sequence, The first time to reach target interested area.

3   Experimental Method

3.1   Experimental Subject

There are 24 subjects in this experiment. All of them are graduate students, which mean they are all in marriageable age. There are 12 students of artistic design major including 6 males and 6 females; there are 12 students of non-design-related majors including 6 males and 6 females. All the subjects have normal naked eye vision or corrected visual acuity. The average age of them is 23.8 years old.

3.2   Experimental Apparatus

Experimental device is one iView X HED head-wearing eye tracker and one iMac computer with the resolution ratio of 1680*1050. Sampling frequency of eye tracker is 200 Hz. Presentation of experimental materials and data record and interpretation use

HED dedicated video analysis software BeGaze Mobile Video Analysis Software to complete. Experimental Materials

23 design works themed on New Chinese Furniture are chosen from furniture design course of senior students. After discussion and evaluation, works which are most representative for New Chinese Furniture material design are chosen. Keyshot 4.0 software is applied to render the design works. Glass, bamboo, wood and metal are endowed to the tea table in the same visual angle and four rendering effect sketches are obtained. See Fig. 1.

3.3   Experimental Procedures

The experiment is divided into two stages – eye movement experiment and evaluation experiment. The subjects do eye movement experiment and then evaluation experiment. Experiments are done separately to guarantee good sound insulation effect and uniform light condition in experimental environment.

Experimental procedures of eye movement experiment: (1) Guide the subject to sit in front of the designated table. Put on head-wearing eye tracker and make it able to catch eye data of the subject; (2) Guide the subject to stare at the smooth calibration plane of 5 independent calibration target points right ahead to complete eye calibration; (3) The experimenter explains the experimental instruction to the subject. The exercise experiment will start after the subject has grasped the experimental instruction correctly; iMac screen will display fixation point position figure with white ground. There is a black solid circle with the diameter of 20 mm in the center. The subject is asked to stare at this circle. After 5 s the formal experiment material will be presented; (5) When experimental material presents, eye tracker will record the fixation process of the subject and it will stop recording when the subject works out preferential judgment. (6) Exercise experiment is the same as the formal experimental procedures.

Procedures of subjective evaluation experiment are: (1) The experimenter explains the experimental instruction to the subject; (2) Experimental materials which are the same with eye movement experiment are presented. The subject will be given tea table evaluation form of different materials to do subjective evaluation records.

Fig. 1. Tea table top (glass, bamboo, wood, metal) effect sketch

4 Experimental Result

Look for the relationship between eye movement data and evaluation grade by analyzing the relationship between eye movement data and evaluation grade with the influence of tea tables of different top materials. Select eye movement indicators which are effective during the evaluation of eye movement analysis on New Chinese Furniture material design (Fig. 2).

We can find in this figure that subjects will have more fixation times when they have higher evaluation grade in the subjective evaluation on different table top materials. They will have less fixation times when they have lower evaluation grade. Subjective evaluation grade has the same changing principle with fixation times of subjects (Fig. 3).

We can find in this figure that subjects will have longer fixation period when they have higher evaluation grade in the subjective evaluation of different table top materials. They will have shorter fixation period when they have lower evaluation grade. Subjective evaluation grade has the same changing principle with fixation period of subjects (Fig. 4).

We can find in this figure that subjects will have shorter fixation point duration when they have higher evaluation grade in the subjective evaluation of different table top materials. They will have longer fixation point duration when they have lower evaluation grade. By analyzing fixation point distribution, we can find that fixation points of subjects will move between two tea tables of different materials when they are

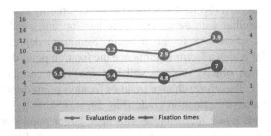

Fig. 2. Broken line chart of evaluation grade and fixation times of subjects with the influence of different materials.

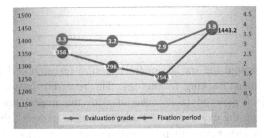

Fig. 3. Broken line chart of evaluation grade and fixation period of subjects with the influence of different materials.

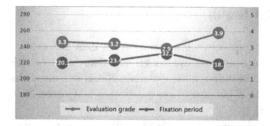

Fig. 4. Broken line chart of evaluation grade and fixation point duration of subjects with the influence of different materials.

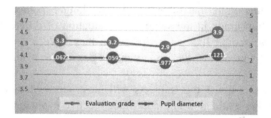

Fig. 5. Broken line chart of evaluation grade and pupil diameter of subjects with the influence of different materials.

judging their preference. At this moment subjects are comparing and making judgment. They will be more familiar with those with more fixation times and the fixation point duration will reduce when they fix on it again. Similarly, degree of familiarity of experimental material is also a factor to influence the fixation point duration of subjects. For strange observation object, subjects will stay longer at certain fixation point to observe such material. Therefore, change trend of fixation point duration is contrary to change trend of subjective evaluation grade (Fig. 5).

We can find in this figure that subjects will have larger pupil diameter when they have higher evaluation grade in the subjective evaluation of different tea table top materials. They will have smaller pupil diameter when they have lower evaluation grade. Subjective evaluation grade has the same changing principle with pupil diameter of subjects.

5   Conclusion

This article tries to design the surface material design research of New Chinese Furniture by eye movement tracking technology. The research finds out that the more fixation times subjects pay on table material with the improvement of subjective evaluation level during the evaluation of subjects on take material, the longer fixation period will be and the larger pupil diameter will be. However, fixation point duration is on the contrary. Therefore, fixation times, fixation period, fixation point duration and pupil diameter can be used as effective indicators of eye movement evaluation of New Chinese Furniture.

Certainly this article has its limitation to some extent since it only uses tea table top material design with new Chinese style as the example to research the relationship among fixation times, fixation period, fixation point duration, pupil diameter and material evaluation grade in eye movement tracking technology indicators without considering the influence of color, structure, environment, texture and other factors on eye movement indicators. Therefore, it can be further expanded in future research process.

References

Xiuchuan, H., Xu, J.: Sunlan discussion on innovative design methods of New Chinese Furniture. Trans. Beijing Inst. Technol. (Soc. Sci.) **9**(6), 28–30 (2007)

Xiangyun, Jiang: Design Materials and Processing Techniques, pp. 23–24. Beijing Institute of Technology Press, Beijing (2003)

Youzhi, Hu: Interpretation of information from eyes. China Sch. Phys. Educ. **3**, 42–43 (1999)

Sun, R.: Eye movement analysis technology and its application progress in aviation industry. J. Civil Aviat. Univ. China **21**(4), 1–5 (2009)

Xincan, Z., Hongfu, Z., Yongjun, R.: Overview of eye tracker and sight tracking technology. Comput. Eng. Appl. **42**(12), 118–120 (2006)

Research on Influence Factors of Design Education Orientation-Taking Italian Design Education as an Example

Zhang Zhang, Jianxin Cheng$^{(\boxtimes)}$, and Chaoxiang Yang

School of Art, Design, Media, East China University of Science and Technology,
200237 Shanghai, China
cjx.master@gmail.com

Abstract. Top 10 Italy design institutes proposed by "Domus" white paper were taken as original research data to study the influence of different factors on design education orientation in this work. SPSS statistic tool was employed to analyze the internal dependencies between different factors based on the factor analysis method. The results suggest that three potential common factors including the potential market scientific research factor, existing market scientific research factor and market development space of the major factor can be regarded as the main factors affecting design education orientation.

Keywords: Design education orientation · Domus · SPSS · Influence factors

1 Introduction

European and American system are the two main international design education systems currently [1]. Among them, European system, which derived from long-term social and cultural development, mainly focusing on improving problem-solving ability to conduct the market demand. On the contrary, American system was formed basing on the economic development and belonged to the business-driven mode. Although the two systems show difference, both of them are succeed in cultivating qualified designers [2].

Differing from the two education systems mentioned above, design education in China mainly followed German Bauhaus design mode founded at the beginning of last century, which obviously cannot match with the demand of society and economy development. Given this situation, design education reform in China is necessary and learning from the two systems can be the most effective approach.

Referring to the design institutes carried out under the two systems, it can be clearly noticed that variation on subject orientation eventually resulted in the significant difference on education modes and structures. As to the subject orientation, investigation on the top 50 design institutes in Europe suggested that factors including teaching languages, business partners, existing laboratory construction et al. showed great impact on design education orientation [3]. However, the effect of such factors on the subject orientation is rather difficult to evaluate, due to complex interactions between different factors. Understanding the effect of factors on the subject orientation and

© Springer International Publishing Switzerland 2015
C. Stephanidis (Ed.): HCII 2015 Posters, Part I, CCIS 528, pp. 456–459, 2015.
DOI: 10.1007/978-3-319-21380-4_77

adjusting the education structure so as to improve the discipline competitive ability is therefore a very important issue.

The purpose of this work was to study the influence factors affecting design education orientation. To realize this objective, the representative top 10 Italy design institutes proposed by "Domus" white paper were taken as survey objects for factor selection. Further, factors selected were analyzed using SPSS statistics tool based on the factor analysis method.

2 Data Sources and Research Method

2.1 Data Sources

As mentioned above, design education subject orientation can be affected by series of factors. In this work, the representative top 10 Italy design institutes proposed by "Domus" white paper published in recent two years were taken as the original data sources for factor selection.

A total of eight high-frequency vocabularies presented in the white paper were selected as main factors including five quantitative indexes and three qualitative indexes. That is, design student enrollment number for X_1, teaching language for X_2, business partners for X_3, intercollegiate partners for X_4, the number of majors for X_5, the existing laboratory construction for X_6, scientific experiment research for X_7 and design theory research for X_8. In order to achieve the quantitative analysis for the last three factors, questionnaire survey to 20 persons who are engaged in design education and have Italy design education background has been performed.

2.2 Research Method

The internal dependencies between different factors extracted from questionnaire were analyzed using SPSS statistics tool based on the factor analysis method [4]. The expression of this method is given by

$$X = AF + \varepsilon \tag{1}$$

$$A = \left(a_{ij}\right)_{pxk}, k < p \tag{2}$$

where $X = (X_1, X_2, \cdots, X_p)'$, $F = (F_1, F_2, \cdots, F_k)'$ and ε represent the factor, common factor and specific factor, respectively. A is the component matrix. As shown above, the most information of the original data can be reflected using few variables.

3 Results and Discussions

To verify the reliability of the data, factor correlation matrix has been calculated through SPSS software, and the results are listed in Table 1.

Table 1. Factor correlation matrix

	X_1	X_2	X_3	X_4	X_5	X_6	X_7	X_8
X_1	1.000	-0.139	0.545	0.457	0.711	0.468	0.309	0.399
X_2	-0.139	1.000	-0.558	-0.798	0.122	-0.465	-0.584	-0.274
X_3	0.545	-0.558	1.000	0.804	0.125	0.499	0.754	0.679
X_4	0.457	-0.798	0.804	1.000	0.089	0.515	0.835	0.646
X_5	0.711	0.122	0.125	0.089	1.000	0.006	-0.200	0.057
X_6	0.468	-0.465	0.499	0.515	0.006	1.000	0.502	0.084
X_7	0.309	-0.584	0.754	0.835	-.200	0.502	1.000	0.742
X_8	0.399	-0.274	0.679	0.646	0.057	0.084	0.742	1.000

From Table 1, it can be seen that most of the correlation coefficients are higher than 0.3 indicating that original data are suitable for factor analysis. Moreover, KMO and Barlett tests have also been carried out, the KMO value of 0.678 and lower values of Bartlett sphericity test Sig. than 0.05 also verified the realibility of the data obtained in this work.

On this basis, the variances of the data have been analyzed using SPSS to determine the numbers of common factors. The results shows that there are 3 factors with eigenvalue more than 1, and the corresponding cumulative contribution rate is 87.08 %. The number for common factors can then be confirmed to be 3. That is, there are 3 main factors show impact on design education subject orientation. Further, to understand the meaning of the 3 common factors, orthogonal rotation was performed on factor loading matrix. Three main common factors are presented in the data. The three potential common factors can be inducted by the potential market scientific research factor, existing market scientific research factor and market development space of the major factor, respectively. Among them, the potential market scientific research factor mainly includes two aspects: research on design theory and frontier technologies. The second factor represents the ability of solving practical problems on present commercial market. With regard to the third factor, it requires the sound judgement for the market developing status and trend. From the Fig. 1 below, factors accumulate into 3 clusters.

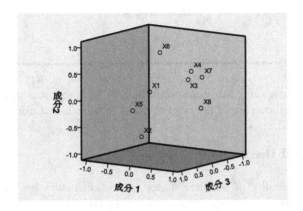

Fig. 1. Space of composition in the three dimensional figure

4   Conclusion

In this work, influence of different factors on design education orientation have been investigated. Top 10 Italy design institutes proposed by "Domus" white paper were taken as survey objects for preliminary factor selection. Further, SPSS statistics tool was empolied to analyze the internal dependencies between different factors based on the factor analysis method. Based on the results, three common factors including the potential market scientific research factor, existing market scientific research factor and market development space of the major factor can be determined. The combination effect of the 3 common factors can be used for the subject orientation on the early stage.

Acknowledgments. We thank the financial support by "the Fundamental Research Funds for the Central Universities" (No. 2222014010), the "Chen Guang" Project supported by Shanghai Municipal Education Commission and Shanghai Education Development Foundation (No. 13CG67).

References

1. Nigel, C.: Engineering Design Methods: Strategies for Product Design, 4th edn. Wiley, Chichester (2008)
2. Hertenstein, J.H., Platt, M.B., Veryzer, R.W.: The impact of industrial design effectiveness on corporate financial performance. J. Prod. Innov. Manag. 1(22), 3–21 (2005)
3. Domus book. http://digitaledition.domusweb.it/domus/books/131201domus/#/9/
4. Bruce, T.: Exploratory and Confirmatory Factor Analysis: Understanding Concepts and Applications. American Psychological Association, Washington, D.C. (2004)

Gesture, Gaze and Motion Detection, Modelling and Recognition

Input Interface Using Eye-Gaze and Blink Information

Kiyohiko Abe[1(✉)], Hironobu Sato[1], Shogo Matsuno[2], Shoichi Ohi[3],
and Minoru Ohyama[3]

[1] College of Engineering, Kanto Gakuin University,
Yokohama, Kanagawa, Japan
{abe,hsato}@kanto-gakuin.ac.jp
[2] Graduate School of Informatics and Engineering,
The University of Electro-Communications, Chofu, Tokyo, Japan
ml440004@edu.cc.uec.ac.jp
[3] School of Information Environment,
Tokyo Denki University, Inzai, Chiba, Japan
{ohi,ohyama}@mail.dendai.ac.jp

Abstract. We have developed an eye-gaze input system for people with severe physical disabilities. The system utilizes a personal computer and a home video camera to detect eye-gaze under natural light, and users can easily move the mouse cursor to any point on the screen to which they direct their gaze. We constructed this system by first confirming a large difference in the duration of voluntary (conscious) and involuntary (unconscious) blinks through a precursor experiment. Consequently, on the basis of the results obtained, we developed our eye-gaze input interface, which uses the information received from voluntary blinks. More specifically, users can decide on their input by performing voluntary blinks as substitutes for mouse clicks. In this paper, we discuss the eye-gaze and blink information input interface developed and the results of evaluations conducted.

Keywords: Eye-gaze · Eye blink · Voluntary blink · Natural light · Input interface

1 Introduction

Eye-gaze input systems have recently been proposed as novel human-machine interfaces [1] by which users can input characters or commands to personal computers. We have developed an eye-gaze input system that utilizes a personal computer and a home video camera [2]. The system estimates the user's gazing point with high accuracy, and allows the user to easily move the mouse cursor to the point at which they are gazing on the screen. The system can be used under natural light as well as artificial light sources such as fluorescent and LED lamps.

Our system incorporates an automatic detection method for the feature parameters of eye blinks. Using this method, we confirmed that there is a large difference in the duration of voluntary and involuntary blinks. In addition, we also confirmed that the

© Springer International Publishing Switzerland 2015
C. Stephanidis (Ed.): HCII 2015 Posters, Part I, CCIS 528, pp. 463–467, 2015.
DOI: 10.1007/978-3-319-21380-4_78

duration of an eye blink varies widely among individuals [3]. Methods for classifying voluntary blinks on the basis of duration have been proposed; however, they all use a fixed threshold [4, 5]. In contrast, our proposed method is calibrated using individual characteristics, which enhances its operability [3]. Through this method, we developed an eye-gaze input system that uses information from voluntary blinks. That is, users can decide on their input by performing voluntary blinks that represent mouse clicks.

2   Input Interface Using Eye-Gaze and Blink Information

2.1   Eye-Gaze and Blink Detection via Image Analysis

An eye-gaze input interface needs to detect both the location of the user's gaze and the user's selection command. Selection can be performed with an eye blink. In our system, eye-gaze and blink are detected via image analysis [2].

The system incorporates a horizontal eye-gaze detection method in which the difference in the reflectance between the iris and the sclera is used to determine the horizontal eye-gaze (Fig. 1(a)). In other words, the horizontal eye-gaze is estimated using the difference between the integral values of the light intensity on areas A and B in Fig. 1(a). We define this differential value as the horizontal eye-gaze value. The corresponding vertical eye-gaze detection method (which is also incorporated in the system) is shown in Fig. 1(b). We estimate the vertical eye-gaze by using the integral value of the light intensity on area C in Fig. 1(b). We define this integral value as the vertical eye-gaze value. By calibrating the eye-gaze input system using the relations between these eye-gaze values and the angle of sight, we can estimate the horizontal and vertical eye-gaze of the user.

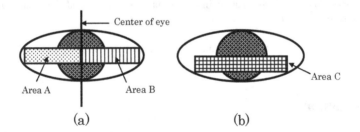

Fig. 1. Detection method for horizontal and vertical eye-gaze

In our method, the user's head movement induces large measurement errors. Therefore, the system must compensate for such movement. We compensate for the user's head movement by tracing the location of the inner corner of the eye, which we estimate from the contour of the open-eye area (eye shape). The wave pattern produced by an eye blink is estimated by measuring the pixels of the open-eye area in every frame. From this wave pattern, we measure the feature parameters of each eye blink, such as its duration and maximum amplitude.

2.2 Automatic Detection of Voluntary Blinks

Our interface detects and uses voluntary blinks [3]. It prepares to receive an input command when the user firmly closes his/her eyes, and voluntary blinks are subsequently detected by using the duration of each eye blink as a feature parameter. There are many methods for estimating the duration of an eye blink. We use the half-value width of the amplitude of an eye blink's wave pattern as its duration. There is a large difference in the duration of voluntary and involuntary blinks. Therefore, voluntary blinks can be determined from their duration. The outline of an eye blink wave pattern and its feature parameters are shown in Fig. 2. In the figure, Fp_h indicates the half-value of the maximum amplitude of the eye blink (Am) and D_h indicates the duration of the eye blink.

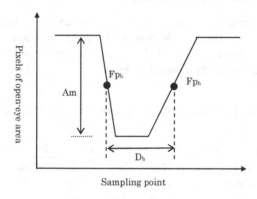

Fig. 2. Feature parameters of an eye blink

3 Evaluation Experiment

3.1 Overview of the Experiment

We evaluated our system by conducting an experiment involving eight subjects. The experimental environment comprised a home video camera (Sony HDR-HC9), and a PC (OS: Microsoft Windows 7; CPU: Intel Core i7, 2.8 GHz clock frequency). The PC was used to analyze sequential eye images captured by the video cameras. Each subject was calibrated on the system prior to the evaluation experiment. The indicators for calibration were displayed on the screen of the PC screen, as shown in Fig. 3(a). The subjects gazed at each indicator while the calibration was in progress. In addition, each subject was asked to gaze at the central indicator at the start of the calibration process, indicated by the PC emitting a beep. To calibrate the system for voluntary blink detection, the subject was asked to perform one voluntary blink. Following the calibration process, the subject selected the circle indicator (diameter: 4° as the angle of sight) on the screen of the PC by gazing, as shown in Fig. 3(b). After selecting the indicator, the subject decided on inputs via voluntary blinks. The location of the indicator randomly changed ten times per experiment.

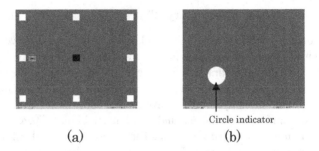

(a)   (b)

Fig. 3. Indicators for calibration and experiment

3.2 Evaluation of the Proposed Interface

Table 1 shows the results of the evaluation experiment conducted with the eight subjects. In Table 1, the indicator selection and input decision times comprise the total time taken by the subject to control the mouse cursor on the circle indicator by eye-gaze and give an input via a voluntary blink.

Table 1. Indicator selection and input decision time (ms)

Selection number	Subject							
	A	B	C	D	E	F	G	H
1	1529	1966	3260	2543	1123	4540	2792	2262
2	4196	1528	5133	1872	1623	13229	10702	6100
3	2621	1857	4040	7160	2496	1840	6006	11122
4	5413	2090	3916	7317	1295	5460	5242	5258
5	14961	2496	3291	1996	11357	11903	5272	1341
6	5709	2621	2840	2262	3494	6583	2808	1170
7	1825	1872	5023	2606	1451	5242	5492	3604
8	5476	2621	13977	6349	1170	1623	4337	30904
9	2278	2168	3713	2324	9438	3042	3088	1201
10	4586	3074	14025	3027	1373	1747	8814	6802
Average	4859.4	2229.3	5921.8	3745.6	3482.0	5520.9	5455.3	6976.4
SD	3687.0	440.7	4097.9	2127.1	3552.2	3891.6	2452.5	8519.9

The results shown in Table 1 indicate that the average time for indicator selection and input decision was 4.77 s. The results also show that all subjects were able to operate our proposed system. The average time for indicator selection and input decision in this proposed system is twice that of the eye-gaze input system developed by Hansen et al. [1]. However, their eye-gaze input system is not operated via voluntary blinks. Instead, the system decides on an input action according to eye fixations (measuring how long the eye fixates on a target such as an indicator). By contrast, our proposed interface has the advantage that it can operate general Microsoft Windows software via eye-gaze and voluntary blinks.

The results in Table 1 also show that subjects C, E, F, and G took more than ten seconds to make one selection and input. This indicates that some subjects experienced difficulty selecting the indicator by eye-gaze. We believe that these subjects failed to stably select the indicator via eye-gaze as a result of gazing point detection measurement errors caused by involuntary eye movements.

4 Conclusion

We have developed a new input interface that enables users to move a mouse cursor via eye-gaze and specify their input via voluntary blinks. The results of evaluation experiments conducted with eight subjects indicate that all subjects can operate our system. In addition, we also confirmed that the average time for indicator selection and input decision is 4.77 s. In the future, we plan to develop a more user-friendly input interface by increasing the eye-gaze detection measurement accuracy.

Acknowledgment. This work was supported by JSPS KAKENHI Grant Number 24700598.

References

1. Hansen, J.P., Torning, K., Johansen, A.S., Itoh, K., Aoki, H.: Gaze typing compared with input by head and hand. In: Proceedings of the Eye Tracking Research and Applications Symposium on Eye Tracking Research and Applications, San Antonio, Texas, USA, pp. 131–138 (2004)
2. Abe, K., Ohi, S., Ohyama, M.: Eye-gaze detection by image analysis under natural light. In: Jacko, J.A. (ed.) Human-Computer Interaction, Part II, HCII 2011. LNCS, vol. 6762, pp. 176–184. Springer, Heidelberg (2011)
3. Abe, K., Sato, H., Matsuno, S., Ohi, S., Ohyama, M.: Automatic classification of eye blink types using a frame-splitting method. In: Harris, D. (ed.) EPCE 2013, Part I. LNCS, vol. 8019, pp. 117–124. Springer, Heidelberg (2013)
4. Krolak, A., Strumillo, P.: Vision-based eye blink monitoring system for human-computer interfacing. In: Proceedings of the Human System Interaction Conference, pp. 994–998, Kracow, Poland (2008)
5. MacKenzie, I.S., Ashitani, B.: BlinkWrite: efficient text entry using eye blinks. Univ. Access Inf. Soc. **10**, 69–80 (2011)

Improvement of Robustness of Nostrils Detection by Specifying the Existable 3D Domain of Nostrils Based on Stereo Measurements of Nostrils and Pupils

Yoshinobu Ebisawa[(✉)], Kiyotaka Fukumoto, and Hiroaki Tanaka

Graduate School of Engineering, Shizuoka University, Hamamatsu, Japan
ebisawa.yoshinobu@shizuoka.ac.jp

Abstract. In the head pose detection system based on 3D positions of the pupils and nostrils which are detected using two stereo-calibrated video cameras and near-infrared light sources, the nostril detection supports the pupil detection as well as the head pose detection. However, the shadows of the nose due to the illumination of the light sources tend to cause the false detection of the nostrils. In order to improve the nostril detection, the present paper proposes a geometrical method using the 3D domain determined as the nostril existable range relative to two pupils considering the horizontal and vertical eyeball rotation. The experimental results show the improvement of the nostril detection.

Keywords: Nostril detection · Head pose detection · Pupil detection

1 Introduction

We have been developing the human head pose detection systems based on positions of the pupils and nostrils which are detected with video camera and active near-infrared illumination [1–3]. These methods do not need the learning process but shows high resolution (continuous measurement) of the position and angle of the head, compared to the various non-lighting computer vision methods; appearance template methods, detector array methods, geometric methods, and so on [4].

The light sources for illumination alternately produce so-called bright and dark pupil image (Fig. 1). From the difference images of the consecutively obtained bright and dark pupil images, two pupils of a user are easily detected because the image except the pupils are cancelled out. Once the pupils are detected, small windows are given to each pupil in the following frames and the pupils are detected within the windows. In addition, a large window for nostril detection are given below the pupils in both bright and dark pupil images. Then, small dark regions in the window are detected as nostrils. Thus the nostrils are relatively easily detected. Once the nostrils are detected, also small windows are given to each of the nostrils, which are detected within the small windows.

In [1], the 3D positions of the pupils and nostrils are detected by stereo-matching with the two optical systems, each of these systems consists of a camera-calibrated

© Springer International Publishing Switzerland 2015
C. Stephanidis (Ed.): HCII 2015 Posters, Part I, CCIS 528, pp. 468–474, 2015.
DOI: 10.1007/978-3-319-21380-4_79

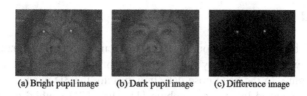

(a) Bright pupil image   (b) Dark pupil image   (c) Difference image

Fig. 1. Bright and dark pupil images obtained from camera and their difference image

video camera having a near-infrared sensitivity and the light sourced attached to each of the cameras. The average of the normal vectors of the two triangle planes passing though the two pupils and each of the two nostrils was estimated as the face direction. In [2], by assuming the mutual distances between pupils and nostrils are constant and by giving the distances in advance, the 3D positions of the pupils and the midpoint of the nostrils (internostril midpoint) are estimated by one optical system. The normal vector of the triangle plane consisting of the two pupils and the internostril midpoint and the center of gravity of the triangle are estimated as the direction and position of the head, respectively.

When the users move their head quickly, the bright and dark pupils have a positional discrepancy and the effect of the image difference method weakens. This causes the failure of the pupil detection, followed by the failure of the head pose detection. In order to improve this problem, the reference [3] proposed the image difference method with positional compensation based on head pose detection (Positionally compensated image difference based on head pose, PCID). In [3], the pose of the triangle is detected every frame based on the one-camera head pose detection method [2]. By grouping the pupils and the internostril midpoint (mutual distances are constant) as a rigid triangle that translates and rotates, the pose of the triangle in the current frame is predicted from the poses of the latest two frames using the constant translation and angular velocity model. Using the predicted pose, the 3D positions of the pupils and nostrils in the current frame are estimated. Furthermore, the 3D positions are projected onto the camera image by using the pinhole model. The projected positions mean the predicted positions of the pupils and nostrils in the current frame image. Finally, after shifting the small-area image including the pupil in the latest frame image so that the center of this pupil and the predicted pupil center in the current image accords, the images in the small-area are differentiated and then the pupil is detected.

Although we mentioned before, that the large window given below the pupils is effective for searching the nostrils, the following problem exists. In order to capture the nostrils, the optical systems are greatly inclined up and installed. Therefore, the nose is easy to make shadows beside the nose especially when a user rotates the face horizontally. The shadows tend to be misdetected as the nostrils. When the nostrils are misdetected, the PCID functions wrongly. As a result, the pupils tend to be also misdetected. Accordingly, robust nostril detection is important not only for head pose detection but also for pupil detection. In the present paper, we propose a method to increase the robustness of nostril detection.

2 Proposed Methods

Figure 2 shows the appearance of our head pose detection system. The inclination angle of the cameras was approximately 30°. Definition of the world coordinate system is shown in the figure. In the head pose detection system, the 3D positions of the pupils and nostrils are detected by stereo-matching [1]. The PCID method proposed for the one-camera method [2] is applied to the stereo camera-based method [1]. As shown in Fig. 3, referring to the positions of the two pupils, the 3D domain was determined as the range that surely includes the nostrils. The pupils move up and down (b and c) or to the left and right ($\pm a$) against the nostrils by an eyeball rotation. In addition, the nostrils rotate around the line passing through the two pupils by head tilt rotation (+60° ∼ −15°). Considering these movements, the range of the domain was determined. Furthermore, when the line connecting two pupils inclines by the user head roll rotation, the domain rotates together with the line. When at least either of the 2D nostril candidate obtained from the two cameras is misdetected, e.g., when one of the two cameras detects a true nostril while another camera detects a false nostril, the position of the nostril detected by stereo-matching tends to protrude from the 3D domain. Accordingly, using the domain can select the true nostrils from the several candidates including the false nostrils when both searching and tracking the nostrils.

For searching the nostrils, in the proposed method, the size and position of the large window were made variable. The apexes of the 3D domain (A–H in Fig. 3) were transformed from the world coordinate system to the camera image coordinate system. The smallest rectangular area including all apexes are determined in each of the camera

Fig. 2. Optical systems each including video camera, near-infrared light sources, lens, and near-infrared pass filter.

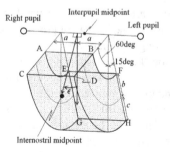

Fig. 3. Definition of nostril existable 3D domain for nostrils detection (hatched region)

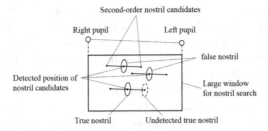

Fig. 4. Setting of second-order nostril candidates and setting of large window in image

image and is used as the large window. However, in the case that the area contained the contour of the user face, the contour images tended to induce false detection. To prevent this, the right and left of the large window were trimmed just under the right and left pupils in the image (Fig. 4). Besides, there is the case that one of the two nostrils cannot be detected, especially when the user greatly rotates the head in horizontal (yaw). To improve this problem, as shown in Fig. 4, the positions of the second-order nostril candidates were determined at both right and left sides of the detected nostril candidate. Here, the line segment connecting between each of the detected nostril candidates and its second-order candidates and the line segment connecting between both pupils was parallel. Besides, the ratio of the length of the two line segments were equaled to the ratio that had been determined in the calibration procedure where subjects were asked to turn their head to the front. All nostril candidates were stereo-matched in a round-robin, produced many 3D nostril candidates. The candidates outside the 3D domain were removed. Furthermore, the mutual distances among all the retained nostril candidates are calculated. The nostril pairs whose mutual distance was close (within ±3 mm) to the corresponding distance measured in the calibration procedure was retained as the nostril pair candidates. Finally, only one nostril pair where the angle between their mutual directional vector and the directional vector connecting the two pupils showed minimal was determined as the pair consisting of the true two nostrils (nostril confirmation method).

When also tracking the nostrils (tracking by small windows), whether the 3D nostrils are true or false was confirmed by using the above-mentioned nostril confirmation method. If they were judged to be false, the tracking process using the small windows stopped and instead the searching process using the large window started.

3 Experiments

Experiment 1: Five healthy university students participated. They were seated 70 cm from the display screen (Fig. 1). The chin of the subjects was put on a chin stand to adjust the head direction every 10° between −30° and +30° in horizontal and −20 and +20° in vertical. In each head direction, the subjects closed their eyes three times. Immediately after opening the eyes, whether the firstly detected nostrils were true or false was visually examined. In *Method 1*, the large window using the 3D domain was not utilized for searching the nostrils. Instead, a constant and appropriate size of large windows was given at a constant position below the pupils in each camera image. In *Method 2*, either the second-order nostril candidates or the nostril confirmation method using the 3D domain were not used in the searching process. Figure 5 compares the correct detection ratios (mean of 5 subjects). The proposed method showed the correct detection ratios higher than those of *Methods 1* and *2* for all of the horizontal head directions between ±40°. These results indicate the effects of the use of the large window based on the nostril existable 3D domain, the nostril confirmation process for searching, and the setting of the second-order nostril candidates. The effects appeared especially when the subjects rotate their head greatly. For the vertical directions between ±20°, the outstanding superiority of the proposed method was not seen.

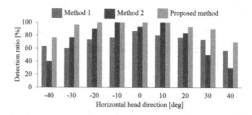

Fig. 5. Comparison of correct detection ratio when head rotates horizontally

Experiment 2: Six healthy university students participated. In *Method 3*, the nostril confirmation method using the 3D domain for the tracking process was furthermore removed from *Method 2*. The subject moved a palm up and down and covered the nose ten times for ten seconds. The head direction was 0°. The palm casted the shadow on the face. Shadows also appeared between fingers. Immediately after the nostrils perfectly appeared, whether the first detection was true nostril or false nostril was examined. Figure 6(a) and (b) show that the proposed method decreased the false detection ratio of the nostrils dramatically (43.8 % → 4.0 % in average) and increased the correct detection ratio greatly (57.3 % → 87.2 %), compared to *Method 3*, indicating that the nostril confirmation method for tracking functioned well. This is because *Method 3* tended to continue to track the false nostril (shadow) misdetected by the searching process, whereas the proposed method was able to stop the mistracking.

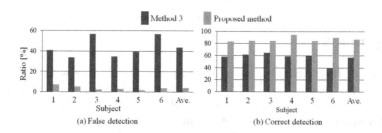

Fig. 6. Nostril detection ratios when subject covered nose by palm ten times for ten seconds

Experiment 3: Two healthy university students participated. The subject was asked to rotate his head slowly in horizontal. Figure 7 shows that the false detection and false tracking occurred (see circles A and B) in *Method 3* when the head direction angle became large, whereas the proposed method tended to prevent the mistracking.

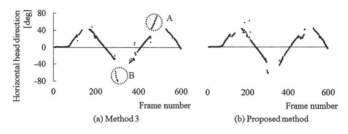

(a) Method 3   (b) Proposed method

Fig. 7. Time course of detected horizontal head direction when subject rotates head in horizontal

4 Discussion

The use of the nostril existable 3D domain functioned well in both searching and tracking nostrils processes. The proposed method is a kind of geometrical method. In the present study, we used the non-coaxial irradiation to produce the dark pupil image. This made it easy to cast the shadows on the face. However, the non-coaxial irradiation effectively produced the dark pupil image, this made it easy to detect the pupils. Since the detected pupils support the nostril detection, the occurrence of the shadows and the easiness of the pupil detection are in a trade-off relationship. Although the pupils are detected by differentiating the bright and dark pupil images in the present study, the proposed method would be useful for pupil detection using the dark pupil method by the non-coaxial irradiation.

5 Conclusions

The present paper shows that, in the head pose detection method based on 3D pupil and nostril detection by stereo-matching, the setting of the existable 3D domain of nostrils prevented the erroneous nostril detection. In the present experiments, the subjects kept opening the eyes because the nostril searching is impossible without the existence of the pupils. Dealing with blinks is the future work.

References

1. Ebisawa, Y., Nurikabe, Y.: Face pose estimation based on 3D detection of pupils and nostrils. In: Proceedings of VECIMS 2005, pp. 92–97 (2005)

2. Ebisawa, Y.: Head pose detection with one camera based on pupil and nostril detection technique. In: Proceedings of VECIMS 2008, pp. 172–177 (2008)
3. Ebisawa, Y.: Robust pupil detection by image difference with positional compensation. In: Proceedings of VECIMS 2009, pp. 143–148 (2009)
4. Murphy-Chutorian, E., Trivedi, M.M.: Head pose estimation in computer vision; a survey. IEEE Trans. Patt. Anal. Mach. Intell. **31**(4), 607–626 (2009)

Detection of Pupil and Corneal Reflection Using High-speed Camera for Gaze Detection Under Face Intense Illumination and a Solution of Glass Reflection Problem by Improving Light Source

Kiyotaka Fukumoto[✉], Yoshinobu Ebisawa, and Kohei Mochizuki

Graduate School of Engineering, Shizuoka University,
Hamamatsu 432-8561, Japan
ebisawa.yoshinobu@shizuoka.ac.jp

Abstract. In our pupil-corneal reflection-based gaze detection system, when users move the head quickly, the image difference method for detecting the pupils does not tend to function accurately. In addition, it becomes more difficult to detect the corneal reflection of the near-infrared light source as well as the pupil under face intense illumination condition because the pupils constrict and the disturbance light source, e.g. the sun, is misdetected as the corneal reflection. Moreover, when the users wear glasses, the reflections of glasses tend to be misdetected as the pupil and corneal reflection (feature points). In the present paper, we introduce a high-speed camera (2,000 fps) and propose a new detection method additionally acquiring a non-lighting image and then differentiating the image from the bright and dark images to detect the feature points even under the face intense illumination condition. In addition, a new light source for removing the glass reflections and enhancing the brightness difference between the bright and dark pupils is developed. The experimental results show that the robustness for the detection of the feature points is improved both under the face intense illumination condition and under the glasses-wearing condition.

Keywords: High-speed camera · Pupil · Corneal reflection · Intense illumination

1 Introduction

We developed the pupil-corneal reflection-based, remote, head-free gaze detection systems [1, 2], which are based on the robust pupil detection method using the two light sources and the image difference method. In these systems, an optical system for detecting the pupils consists of a video camera and a double concentric circle near-infrared LED rings (inner and outer rings) light source. The inner and outer LED rings of the light source generate the bright and dark pupil images, respectively. The pupils are detected from the difference image created by subtracting the dark pupil image from the bright pupil image. The light source also elicits the corneal reflection image. The gaze points on a PC screen are determined by the relative position between

© Springer International Publishing Switzerland 2015
C. Stephanidis (Ed.): HCII 2015 Posters, Part I, CCIS 528, pp. 475–480, 2015.
DOI: 10.1007/978-3-319-21380-4_80

the pupil and corneal reflection (feature points). However, when the users move their head, the pupil position varies between the bright and dark pupil images because of the acquisition time difference for both pupil images. Therefore, the image difference is performed after shifting the small areas including each pupil in the dark pupil image so that the corneal reflection in this dark pupil image becomes coincident with that in the bright pupil image [3]. The pupils generally become small when the illumination on the face is strong, e.g. by the sunlight. It is difficult to detect the small pupils in robust due to the similarity in image characteristics between the pupil and the glass reflections of the light source. In addition, when the users move their head quickly, this image difference method does not tend to function accurately, resulting in undetection or misdetection of the pupils. Furthermore, the corneal reflection is directly detected in the bright and dark pupil images but not in the difference image, the disturbance light source, e.g. the sun and the light source irradiating the near-infrared light. The source produces the false corneal reflection and glass reflection. To solve these problems, in the present study, we try to use a high-speed camera because the acquisition time difference is extremely short. In addition, a non-lighting image is obtained consecutively with the bright and dark pupil images, and then the corneal reflection is detected using the difference images obtained by subtracting the non-lighting image from the bright and dark pupil images. Finally, we propose a novel light source to remove the glass reflections and to increase the brightness difference between the bright and dark pupil. The experimental result show the effectiveness of the proposed methods and light source.

2   Optical System and Image Acquisition and Processing Algorithms for Detecting Pupil and Corneal Reflection

Figure 1(a) shows the optical system which consists of the high-speed camera (2,000 fps, 512 × 512 pix), the 16 mm lens, the LED light source, and the near-infrared pass filter (IR80). The camera images were able to be transmitted to the PC memory and were image-processed in the real time. The light source consisting of the near-infrared LEDs, which are arranged in a double concentric circle rings form, is attached to the camera. The inner rings (850 nm) and outer rings (940 nm) produce the bright and dark pupils, relatively, because the LEDs near the aperture of the camera brighten the pupil more than the LEDs far from the aperture and because the transmissivity of the eyeball medium for 850 nm is greater than 940 nm. The previous light source had used 5ϕ shell type of LEDs. To increase the brightness of the bright pupil, we changed from 5ϕ to 3ϕ (Fig. 1(a)) because the center of the LEDs approaches the aperture more. However, depending on glasses, the glass reflection of the outer ring showed a doughnut shape because the radius of the ring was long, whereas the glass reflection of the inner ring shows a smaller filled circle. Their shape difference caused the failure of the cancellation of the glass reflection images and retained the wrecks of the glass reflections in the difference image. To remove the wrecks, we developed the small light source having the smaller radius of outer ring (each part of the light source in Fig. 1(b)). The cancellation of the glass reflections was successful. However, since the number of LEDs decreased, the irradiation power to acquire the dark pupil image decreased.

This caused the difficulty of the pupil detection. To solve this problem, we developed the new light source that three of the above-mentioned small light sources were arranged horizontally, as shown in Fig. 1(b). The inner ring of the center small light source, which was attached to the camera, flashed in the bright pupil acquisition frame to obtain the bright pupil image. The outer rings of the three small light sources are flashed simultaneously and evenly in power in the dark pupil image acquisition frame. Here, the outer ring of the center source functioned to cancel out the glass reflection produced by the inner ring of the same source. However, the dark pupil effect due to the outer ring was weak. So, the outer rings of the right and left small light source was used to enhance the dark pupil effect.

The bright pupil image, the non-lighting image, and the dark pupil images were consecutively obtained in this order while turning the respective rings on and off as shown in Fig. 2. This figure also shows the new image processing algorithm for detecting the feature points. By subtracting (a) the non-lighting image from (b) the bright pupil image and (c) the dark pupil image, (d) the difference bright pupil image

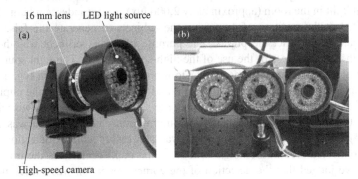

Fig. 1. (a) Optical system using high-speed camera (2,000 fps). The light source uses 3ϕ shell type of near-infrared LEDs. (b) Newly developed light source for glasses.

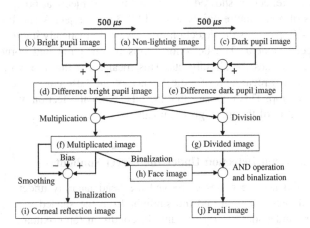

Fig. 2. Image processing algorithm using high-speed camera for detecting pupils and corneal reflections.

and (e) the difference dark pupil image were made, respectively. These subtractions theoretically remove the affections of the ambient lights and gives the bright and dark pupil images illuminated by only the light sources of the system ideally. Next, (f) the multiplicated image and (g) the divided image are produced. From these images, (i) the corneal reflection image and (j) the pupil image are obtained. The above-mentioned image processing algorithm was used in all experiments.

3 Experiments

3.1 Effectiveness of the Use of High-speed Camera for Fast Head Movement

Three university students served as subjects. They did not wear glasses and were asked to move their head laterally at a speed of approximately 20 cm/s. Their face images were captured at 60 fps and 2,000 fps. The experiments were conducted under the fluorescent light in the room (approximately 2,000 lux). An incandescent lamp (200 W) was installed at the position of 1 m from the subjects to generate the false corneal reflection and to constrict the pupils. The purpose of the experiment was the verification for the effectiveness of the use of the high-speed camera. The light source using 5ϕ shell type of LEDs, which was similar to the light source shown in Fig. 1(a), was used. We examined the detection of the pupil and corneal reflection in the pupil image (Fig. 2(i)) and the corneal reflection image (Fig. 2(j)), respectively, by visual observation. In the present study, when the maximum connected pixel area was the true pupil, we judged that the pupil detection was successful (correct detection). If the detected connected area in the neighborhood of the pupil center was the true corneal reflection, we judged that the detection of the corneal reflection was successful.

Figure 3 shows the samples of the pupil image (Fig. 2(j)) at 60 fps and 2,000 fps. The many connected pixel areas appeared in the pupil image at 60 fps. In the corresponding image at 2,000 fps, only the pupils were embossed. The detection ratios of the pupil and corneal reflection showed both 0 % for all subjects at 60 fps, whereas the detection ratios of both feature points showed 98 % for subject A and B and 58 % for subject C at 2,000 fps. Thus the detection ratios were dramatically improved by the use of the high-speed camera. The detection ratios of the pupil and corneal reflection showed the same values for all subjects. This means that the true corneal reflection tended to be detected regardless of the existence of the false corneal reflection due to the incandescent lamp. This indicates that the false corneal refection were canceled out by the differentiation of the non-lighting image.

3.2 Real Time Pupil Detection Under the Direct Sunlight

A subject who did not wear glasses moved the head laterally under the room light condition (the fluorescent light and the sunlight from the shaded windows, approximately 700 lux) and under the direct sunlight condition (approximately 40,000 lux). The distance between the pupil and the camera was approximately 80 cm. The pupil detection was performed 192 times. Figure 4(a) and (b) show the time courses of the coordinates of the right and left pupil. The ratios that both right and left pupils were detected were 99.5 % and 68.8 % under the fluorescent light and direct sunlight conditions, respectively.

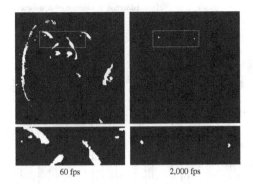

Fig. 3. Samples of the pupil image at 60 fps and 2,000 fps

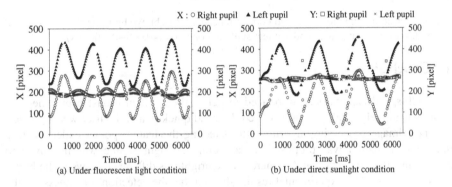

Fig. 4. Results of real time pupil detection

3.3   Effectiveness of Newly Developed Light Sources for Glasses

We compared the detection ratios of the feature points between the previous light source (Fig. 1(a)) and the newly developed light sources for glasses (Fig. 1(b)) under the direct sunlight condition (approximately 40,000–45,000 lux). Four subjects who wore glasses were asked to fixate the center of the PC screen while moving their head laterally. Figure 5(a) and (b) show the detection ratios of the pupil and corneal reflection of the right eye under the direct sunlight condition, respectively. The averaged correct detection ratios of the left and right pupils were 68.1 % and 85.0 % by the previous and newly developed light sources, respectively. Those of the left and right corneal reflections were 66.1 % and 80.1 % by the previous and newly developed light sources, respectively. Thus the detection robustness for the feature points were improved by using the newly developed light source. However, the misdetection of the corneal reflection for subject C increased compared to the previous light source. This is because the glass reflection image existed in the neighborhood of the pupil center for subject C and the image were not able to be canceled out by differentiation of the non-lighting image.

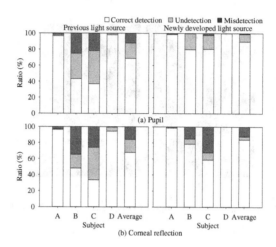

Fig. 5. Detection ratios for pupil and corneal reflection of right eye by using the previous and newly developed light source under direct sunlight condition (40,000–45,000 lux).

4   Conclusions

The high-speed camera was introduced to detect the pupil in robust even when the pupil is extremely small, the user moved the head quickly, and the user wears glasses. The new image processing algorithm for detecting the feature points under the face intense illumination was proposed. In addition, the light source was improved to remove the glass reflection and to increase the brightness difference between the bright and dark pupils. The experimental results showed that the detection robustness for the feature points was improved.

References

1. Ebisawa, Y., Fukumoto, K.: Head-free remote eye-gaze detection system based on pupil-corneal reflection method with easy calibration using two stereo-calibrated video cameras. IEEE Trans. Biomed. Eng. **60**(10), 2952–2960 (2013)
2. Ebisawa, Y., Fukumoto, K.: Head-free, remote gaze detection system based on pupil-corneal reflection method with using two video cameras -one-point and nonlinear calibrations. In: HCI International 2013, pp. 205–214 (2013)
3. Nakashima, A., Ebisawa, Y., Nurikabe, Y.: Pupil detection using light sources of different wavelengths. J. Inst. Image Inf. Telev. Eng. **60**(12), 2019–2025 (2006)

Study of Tile Menu Selection Technique Using the Relative Position of Joints for Gesture Operation

Yamato Gomi[✉] and Katsuhiko Onishi

Osaka Electro-Communication University, 1130-70 Kiyotaki, Shijonawate,
Osaka 575-0063, Japan
{mt14a004, onishi}@oecu.jp

Abstract. In this paper, we describe about our selected method by using the 3D tile menu by hand gesture motion. In the discussion of our approach,it is a mainly subject to realize the efficient selection gesture by user's arm for any position on the screen. Therefore, we designed the selection method by using relative position of the user's arm joints. The method uses user's hands, elbows and shoulder position at each arm. It recognized user's selected points by the relative position of these joints. We make the prototype system which has been implemented our method. And we examined the basic evaluation of our selection method by comparing with the conventional method. As a result of this evaluation, it is confirmed that our method allows users to perform smooth selecting operation regardless of the position.

Keywords: 3D pointing · Selection method · Gesture · Two-hand manipulation

1 Introduction

It is increasing to use natural user interface, like gesture recognition, gesture pointing operation, and so on. Especially pointing operation is much popular operation, because mobile PC, like smartphone or tablet PC, has become much popular in recent years. it has touch panel display and enable to realizing direct operation. The user can select any objects by touching on a screen and do anything what they would like to. This natural direct operation is used in some situation like on a large display environment such as projection screen or digital signage screen. There are many kinds of selection method using 3D gesture input [1–3]. But in some case, it is difficult to select object depending on the object position on a screen.

Therefore, we developed a selection method on the 3D tile menu by using hand gesture motion. The 3D tile menu is 3D GUI widget which consists of planes and selective objects. To be able to select any objects on the screen, we focus on the joint position of the user's arm. We implement our method on the 3D tile menu system. And we introduce a result of our preliminary evaluation. Figure 1 shows our prototype system.

© Springer International Publishing Switzerland 2015
C. Stephanidis (Ed.): HCII 2015 Posters, Part I, CCIS 528, pp. 481–484, 2015.
DOI: 10.1007/978-3-319-21380-4_81

Fig. 1. Our prototype system

2   3D Tile Menu

We designed a tile menu platform which is called 3D tile menu. It is consist of planes which include selective objects, such as icon. And these planes are set on depth axis in 3D environment. The user can select these objects by using 3D hand motion. Figure 2 shows manipulation methods of the 3D tile menu. Figure 2(a) shows the selecting object phase. The user can manipulate a pointer on the plane and select an object. Figure 2(b) shows the moving user's view area phase. The user can manipulate the view region by user's hand motion. The user can switch these phase by using non-dominant hand movement.

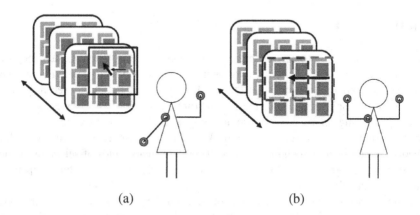

(a)	(b)

Fig. 2. 3D tile menu operation. (a) selecting object phase. (b) moving view area phase

3   Selection Method by Using the Relative Position of Joint

The selection method in 3D gesture motion is generally used overlay method. It is selected objects by expanding the user's arm to the object. However, in the large display environment, it is sometimes difficult to select the object according to the position on the screen. Because it becomes out of movable range of the arm. Therefore, we study the method based on the positional relationship between the arm joints to allow a more natural selective operation. Figure 3 shows our method summary. It uses the hand, elbow and shoulder positions. It calculated two vectors, shoulder-elbow and shoulder-hand. And it uses the angle by the two vectors to determine the selection operation. Since the orientation of the two vectors in our extended arms becomes almost same, the angle is close to 0 degree. The results were verified by preliminary experiments, the θ when fully extended arms had a value of less than 25 degree. Therefore our method uses 25 degree as the threshold of selection operation.

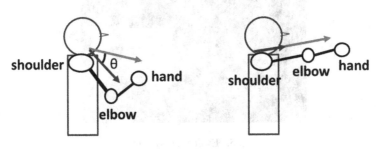

Fig. 3. Selection method overview

4   Implementation

We developed the prototype system which is implemented our method. Our system is implemented on Windows PC and measure the user's each joint position by using Kinect. Figure 4 shows an image of our system. To confirm the usability of our method, we make a comparative experiment with conventional selection method which use just user's hand position. As an experimental task, it is prepared that participant selects all objects randomly which are set 3×3 on the screen. And the task completion time is measured at each method. At first, the participants are introduced each method by performing the operation. And they practice each method in 2 min. Then, they execute each task 3 times by using all methods and the completion time is measured. The participants were intended for 5 students.

Figure 5 shows the result of it. It is confirmed that the time of our proposed method is less than that of the conventional method. And it is confirmed that the participant can select all objects easily. Through this experiment, we have found that the malfunction of the system is going as a problem. When the participant arm is fully extended, the system sometimes makes a selection that is not intended or deviates location to be selected.

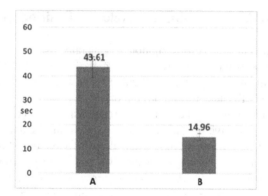

Fig. 4. Task completion time. (A) Conventional method. (B) Proposed method.

Fig. 5. Evaluation system.

5   Conclusion

In this study, we studied the tile menu selection method by using the relative position of user's arm joints. Our method uses the user's three joint position to manipulate the pointer. We implemented the method in our prototype system to confirm the usability of this method. As a result of our preliminary evaluation, we confirmed it. In the future work, it is needed to evaluate our method more precisely. And we have to study of the gestures pattern which is adequate to our method.

References

1. Vogel D.,Balakrishnan R.: Distant freehand pointing and clicking on very large,high resolution displays. In: Proceedings of UIST 2005, pp. 33–42 (2005)
2. Cheng K., Pulo K.: Direct interaction with large-scale display systems using infrared laser tracking devices. In: Proceedings of APV 2003, pp. 67–74 (2003)
3. Pfeiffer, M., Stuerzlinger, W.: 3D virtual hand pointing with EMS and vibration feedback. In: Proceedings of IEEE Symposium on 3D Use Interfaces 2015, pp. 117–120 (2015)

A Real-Time Sensing of Gait and Viewing Direction for Human Interaction in Virtual Training Applications

Gyutae Ha, Sangho Lee, Jaekwang Cha, Hojun Lee, Taewoo Kim, and Shiho Kim[(⊠)]

School of Integrated Technology, YICT, Yonsei University,
Incheon 406-840, Korea
hagyut@gmail.com, shiho@yonsei.ac.kr

Abstract. This paper presents an integrated framework for real-time sensing and synchronization of both user's moving speed with direction and viewing direction in walking-in-place experience for virtual training applications. The framework consists of two inertial measurement units (IMU) attached to each shank and a HMD made up of Android mobile device with 3-axis orientation sensor. Although there are several prior works to enable unconstrained omnidirectional walking through virtual environments, an implementation of the low cost interface solution using wearable devices is an important issue for virtual training systems. We provide a simplified technique for implementing 'Walking in Virtual Reality' without omnidirectional treadmill. In addition, this research aims to lightweight (in point of software) and portable (in point of hardware) solution to implement the Virtual Reality Walk-In-Place(VR WIP) interface for training applications.

Keywords: Virtual reality · Virtual training · Walking-in-place · Walking recognition · Wearable sensor · IMU

1 Introduction

Three-dimensional (3D) Virtual Reality (VR) technique has been widely used in many applications, including training, education and entertainment systems. However, VR applications based on Head Mount Displays (HMD) often have faced problems of navigation in the virtual environment due to the unrealistic sensing and synchronizing characteristics. Usually, conventional interaction techniques [1] depend only on the orientation of person's moving body or direction of viewing scenes. The difference in the walking and viewing direction results in an error in navigating trajectory in the virtual environment, which makes the VR system unrealistic. It is inevitable to separate viewing direction and gait direction while exploring virtual environment, especially in VR training systems because the replication of the real situation is very important. In this paper, we propose an integrated framework for solving the problem using IMU attached to each shank and built-in gyro and acceleration sensors in Android mobile devices. In addition, this research aims to provide lightweight software as well as a wearable hardware solution to implement the Virtual Reality Walk-In-Place(VR WIP) [3] interface for training applications.

© Springer International Publishing Switzerland 2015
C. Stephanidis (Ed.): HCII 2015 Posters, Part I, CCIS 528, pp. 485–490, 2015.
DOI: 10.1007/978-3-319-21380-4_82

2   Configuration of the Proposed Framework

The user interface is composed of an Android mobile device having built-in 3-axis orientation sensor and a set of IMU attached to each shank. The IMUs detect gait with walking speed and direction, while, senors in the Android mobile device take information about the viewing orientation of the user's head movement (Fig. 1).

Fig. 1. An illustration for difference between walking and viewing direction of Avatar in the VR training application.

The Android mobile device can provide 3D VR head-mounted display within a user's field of view, enabling a user to view virtual objects in the user's surroundings. Proposed system has applied to a VR training system of disaster rescue from fire in an underground subway station. Figure 2 shows the implemented configuration of the VR

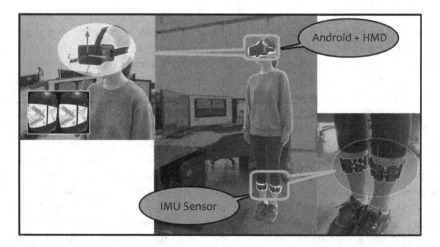

Fig. 2. Implementation of the VR training system with proposed integrated framework

training system with the proposed Integrated Framework. VR Contents are played on the Android mobile device, which also provides Bluetooth wireless interface linking to IMUs. The Avatar's motion is synchronized with user's movement, and viewing scenery is synchronized to user's viewing direction. The user needs to escape from the underground firing palace to save her/his life in a limited given time. The user needs to find the best way to escape during the training, where the exit signs among the objects in the user's view indicate the rescue route.

3   Experimental Results and Discussions

We need to recognize both the speed and direction of user's gait in order to synchronize with scene displayed in the HMD and motion of the Avatar in the virtual space. Figure 3 shows 3-axis coordinate system of IMUs attached at the shank.

Figures 4 and 5 show measured acceleration of x- and z-axis, and angular velocity of y-axis during walking-in-place actions of the user. We can find a repetitive pattern matching to the each step of gait in the measured data. Variation in y-axis acceleration

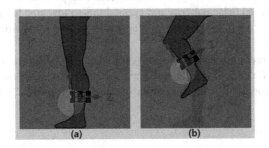

Fig. 3. Coordinate system of IMUs attached at the shank

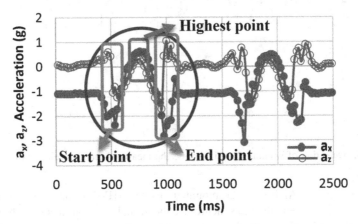

Fig. 4. Measured acceleration changes during walking-in-place. (1 g = 9.8 m/sec^2)

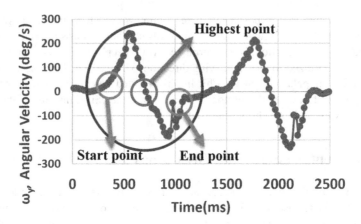

Fig. 5. Detection of walking event from the measured angular velocity of y-axis

is negligible because there is a negligible amount of movement in the y-axis direction during walking-in-place motions as shown in Fig. 3. The repetitive pattern in the measured data indicates the step-up, the highest reaching point of foot, and end point of each step. We analyzed these patterns and applied this to machine learning technique to recognize walking state [4–6]. By using learning data, our framework can detect gait speed in real-time.

The walking direction, yaw angle of the user's leg, can be detected by integration of angular velocity of x-axis. In order to obtain a better estimation of the user's orientation, we can consider tilt from the output of accelerometers [2, 7] (Fig. 6).

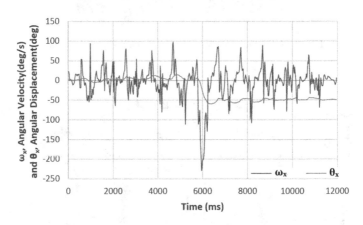

Fig. 6. Detection of walking direction using the measured angular velocity of x-axis

The sensors on Android head-mounted display (HMD) can detect a viewing direction in real-time, enabling to synchronize the virtual surroundings seen through the HMD [8]. Figure 7 shows logged moving trajectory of a Avatar with viewing direction

Fig. 7. Trajectory moving with viewing direction in the disaster rescue VR training system

in the disaster rescue VR training system. The scaling factor was used for each user to optimize the performance of the training system. These results indicate that developed algorithm and frame work can be applicable to the VR training system.

4 Conclusion

We present an integrated framework for real-time sensing and synchronization of both user's moving speed with direction and viewing direction in walking-in-place experience for virtual training applications. The proposed solution can provide a simplified technique for implementing 'Walking in Virtual Reality' without omnidirectional treadmill. Experimental results indicate that the algorithm developed for Real-time Sensing of Gait and Viewing Direction can be favorably applicable to the VR training system.

Acknowledgement. This research was supported by the MSIP(Ministry of Science, ICT and Future Planning), Korea, under the "IT Consilience Creative Program" (NIPA-2014-H0201-14-1002) supervised by the NIPA(National IT Industry Promotion Agency).

References

1. Steinicke, F., et al.: Human Walking in Virtual Environments. Springer, New York (2013)
2. Doheny, E.P., Foran, T.G., Greene, B.R.: A single gyroscope method for spatial gait analysis. In: 32nd Annual International Conference of the IEEE EMBS (2010)
3. Slater, M., Usoh, M., Steed, A.: Taking steps: the influence of a walking technique on presence in virtual reality. ACM Trans. Comput. Hum. Interact. (TOCHI) 2(3), 201–219 (1995)

4. Kim, J., Gracanin, D., Quek, F.: Sensor-fusion walking-in-place interaction technique using mobile devices. In: Virtual Reality Short Papers and Posters (VRW) 2012. IEEE (2012)
5. Mannini, A., Sabatini, A.M.: Machine learning methods for classifying human physical activity from on-body accelerometers. Sens. **10**(2), 1154–1175 (2010)
6. Jasiewicz, J.M., et al.: Gait event detection using linear accelerometers or angular velocity transducers in able-bodied and spinal-cord injured individuals. Gait Posture **24**(4), 502–509 (2006)
7. Luinge, H.J., Veltink, P.H., Baten, C.T.M.: Estimating orientation with gyroscopes and accelerometers. Technol. Health Care **7**(6), 455–459 (1999)
8. Meier, R.: Professional Android 4 Application Development. John Wiley & Sons, New York (2012)

Developing STEAM Using KINECT: A Case Study on Motion-Capture Functions

Hyung-Sook Kim[⊠] and Seong-Hee Chung

Department of Human Art and Technology, Inha University, Incheon, Korea
khsookl2@inha.ac.kr

Abstract. The purpose of this study is to develop a science & art convergence STEAM program that can be experienced through the KINECT interactive activities integration of art based on knowledge of science & technology. The program is structured based on the educational content and textbooks from the current curricula for elementary, middle-, and high-school students. Based on this, we developed the four KINECT program using the motion capture function. By using STEAM with KINECT to promote interest in science, and by providing an entertaining way to learn about science, it is possible for students to be more creative and well-rounded. It is also expected that, because the program combines art with science in a novel way, it has the potential to be widely distributed in the 2016 semester.

Keywords: STEAM · KINECT · Interactive arts · Science · Arts fusion program

1 Introduction

The 21st century is the era of the creative economy. Creative economy means an economic system that is based on the ideas, innovation and creativity. Creative economy is the most important feature of the knowledge, skills, discipline is a fusion between [3]. This flow has been recognized as important in education field, STEAM education for creative fusion talent to lead the creative economy is importantly considered. STEAM education is 'Increasing the interest and understanding of science and technology, education to develop science and technology-based fusion thinking and problem solving skills'. The STEAM education is education approach that integrates arts(A) to STEM(Science, Technology, Engineering & Mathematics) education [5]. STEM has been done to the human resources of science and technology in many developed countries, including the United States. In our country, the development of science and the arts fusion program has been attempted in a variety of ways. And gradually, not simply parallel fusion, arts-oriented programs have been developed. Art Science convergence STEAM education can develop imagination and sensibility of human to the future of science and technology talent as well as knowledge [1].

Due to the popularity of the new technologies, a variety of device that can be used in ICT-based education are being advertised. This education improves communication, cooperation, participation, openness, and sharing between learner-learner, learner-instructor, learner-content. Therefore, the ICT-based education can be a good tool for

C. Stephanidis (Ed.): HCII 2015 Posters, Part I, CCIS 528, pp. 491–495, 2015.
DOI: 10.1007/978-3-319-21380-4_83

STEAM education. In particular, gaming devices, such as KINECT has the benefit of being able to arouse the students' curiosity. KINECT is equipment that allows human gestures to be processed digitally in video. KINECT differs from other video devices as it is available to detect motion without attaching controllers to the users. KINECT is thus particularly applicable to physical activity, and creative gestures can be expanded by connecting the expressive factors from integrated artistic activities. The physical activity of these game modes attracts students' interests by applying science learning. To this end, this study joins science with art through a program called STEAM. STEAM allows users of KINECT to experience integrated and interactive art based on science, technology, and educational content. To this end, this study developed a science & art convergence STEAM program that can be experienced through the KINECT interactive activities integration of art based on knowledge of science & technology.

2 STEAM Program Development

2.1 Direction of Development

The purpose of this study is to develop a science • Art convergence program allows you to experience the scientific knowledge integrating arts activities using ICT. The contents of scientific knowledge has been configured to extend • deepen the subject, depending on grade and class periods. Program was composed interactive art game activities using Integrated arts of dance, music and art and KINECT. Through this, students were able to experience the process of scientific • technical and artistic aesthetic interaction, induced an interest in learning and divergent thinking is possible.

2.2 Method of Development

Development team of the program is organized by scientists, engineers, artists, curriculum specialists, teachers with excellent research skills and experience in the field. Development process of the program is to analyze the curriculum, and subject were extracted by each grade level and class. And ICT's professional team has developed a KINECT technology and programming based on the contents of the program.

2.3 Contents of Development

The program is structured based on the educational content and textbooks from the current curricula for elementary, middle-, and high-school students. KINECT is used in conjunction with this content to capture motion. Based on this, we developed the four KINECT program using the motion capture function. Four programs were developed for STEAM, the details for which are shown in Table 1.

Table 1. KINECT Program

Level	Theme	Program	Contents
Elementary school	Secrets of Nature	Cloud vs. Cloud	Getting into pairs and expressing the shape of a weather front when two clouds meet
			Playing a video showing rain when the shape of the weather front is formed
Middle school	Body	Adjusting to weather	Expressing behavioral changes according to the weather shown on the screen in order to understand the homeostasis of the human body and its relation to the weather
			Viewing the entire video upon completing the activity
		Fighting diabetes	A program designed to help students understand how insulin and blood-sugar levels are maintained
			Preventing hypoglycemia and diabetes by maintaining the height of the graph at a medium level using two arms
High school	Infinite Challenge	'Me' in a work of art	Expressing emotions by viewing pictures, photos, and sculptures on the screen, and mimicking their forms
			Viewing the recorded video upon completing the activity

2.4 Trial Lesson Result

Program was carried out a trial lesson at S elementary school, B middle school, I high school in Seoul. Classes took place in the science lab or classroom. Due to the lack of time, some of the resources that the students were able to experience.

After the trial lesson, the result of questionnaire provided by 'Korea Foundation for the Advancement of Science & Creativity' for students was surveyed as program satisfaction. For elementary school students, 74.1 % of students think that was fun. On the other hand, only 7.1 % of students were not responding fun in Table 2. In the case of middle and high school students was 55.8 % of the students responded that fun. And 29.9 % of students responded normally called in Table 3 (Figs. 1,2,3,4).

Table 2. Elementary students program satisfaction

	Very interesting	Interesting	Usually	No fun	Not funny at all
N	82	61	36	8	6
%	42.5 %	31.6 %	18.7 %	4.1 %	3.1 %

Table 3. Secondary students program satisfaction

	Very interesting	Interesting	Usually	No fun	Not funny at all
N	105	207	167	44	36
%	18.8 %	37.0 %	29.9 %	7.9 %	6.4 %

Fig. 1. Elementry school - cloud vs. cloud

Fig. 2. Middle school - adjusting to weather

Fig. 3. Middle school - fighting diabetes

Fig. 4. High School - 'me' in a work of art

3 Conclusion

The expected effects of this study are as follows.

First, the students were able to experience the content of scientific knowledge through interactive art activities of integration art and KINECT games by this study. This was caused an interest in science, and provide learning how new scientific knowledge. Thus, the foundation that can foster creative fusion talent.

Second, it is expected that, because the program combines art with science in a novel way, it has the potential to be widely distributed in the 2016 semester. In particular, by applying the learning of ICT technologies, such as the Kinect has expanded the range that can be used in schools and in real life.

Third, it was confirmed that the integration of the science curriculum and arts curriculum is possible. Unlike traditional learning methods was memorizing the text, the knowledge that in the short-term memory by experienced scientific knowledge in a variety of interactive activities to achieve the long-term memory as a lesson.

References

1. Joe, H.S., Kim, H., Heo, J.Y.: Understanding of fusion talent training(STEAM) through field application case. Korea Foundation for the Advancement of Science & Creativity, Issue Paper OR 2012-02-02 (2012)
2. Kim, H. S.: 2014 Fusion talent education(STEAM) program development result report. Inha University (2014)
3. Kim, J.H., Hong, S.Y.: A development of SMART teaching and learning model for ICT gifted education. J. Korean Soc. Gifted Talent. 12(2), 29–47 (2013)
4. Lim, H.S.: Smart education: Teach Smart. Human Science (2012)
5. Yakman, G.: STEAM education: an overview of creating a model of integrative education. In: Proceeding of PATT, pp. 335–358 (2008)

Depth Camera Calibration and Knife Tip Position Estimation for Liver Surgery Support System

Masanao Koeda[1(✉)], Akio Tsukushi[1], Hiroshi Noborio[1],
Katsuhiko Onishi[1], Kiminori Mizushino[2], Takahiro Kunii[3],
Kaoru Watanabe[1], Masaki Kaibori[4], Kosuke Matsui[4],
and Masanori Kwon[4]

[1] Osaka Electro-Communication University, Osaka, Japan
koeda@isc.osakac.ac.jp
[2] Embedded Wings Co. Ltd., Shijonawate, Japan
[3] Kashina System Co. Ltd., Fukuoka, Japan
[4] Kansai Medical University, Hirakata, Japan

Abstract. We have developed a liver surgery support system that uses two depth cameras and measures positional relationships between a surgical knife and a liver in real time. In this report, the overview of our system, the method for depth camera calibration, the estimation for knife tip positioning, and some experimental results are described.

1 Introduction

We have developed a new support system for liver surgery based on IT technology. In our system, the positional relationship between a surgical knife and a liver is measured in real time. The goals are that warnings such as flashing red lights or alarms indicate to the surgeons to be careful when the knife comes too close to high risk areas, and that optimal guides for knife motion are displayed in order to completely remove cancerous cells and retain a maximal healthy portion of the liver.

2 System Overview

Figure 1 shows the overview of our surgical support system. Before the operation, a 3D model of a patient's liver is generated from computed tomographic images. During the operation, the position of the knife and the patient's liver are measured by two depth cameras with different features that are mounted over the operating table. The position, orientation, deformation, and incision of the liver are calculated by GPGPU (general-purpose computing on graphics processing units) in real time by matching the measured liver shape by the depth sensor to the 3D model. Details of this process are not covered in this report. For further information, refer to [1, 2].

Our system uses two depth cameras with different features. The first is a Micron-Tracker3 (model H3-60). It is a marker tracking camera system with high precision and

C. Stephanidis (Ed.): HCII 2015 Posters, Part I, CCIS 528, pp. 496–502, 2015.
DOI: 10.1007/978-3-319-21380-4_84

it is used to measure knife positioning [3]. The detailed specifications for this sensor are listed in Table 1. The second is a KINECT for Windows v2 sensor. It has middle precision in depth measurement and wide measuring range and it used to measure the shape of a liver. These cameras have to be located at a distance and their optical axes cannot coincide. To transform these coordinate systems, calibration matrix should be created.

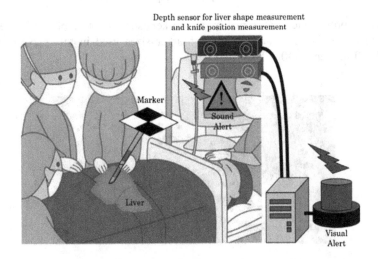

Fig. 1. System overview of our liver surgery support system

Table 1. Specification of MicronTracker3 H3-60

FOM, spherical section (radius × width × height)	240 × 200 × 160 cm
Measurement rate	16 Hz
Sensor resolution	1280 × 960 pixel
Lenses, H × V	6 mm, 50 × 38 degree
Case dimensions (W × H × D, approx.)	283 × 43 × 49 mm
Weight (approx.)	505 g
Electrical interface, data rate	IEEE1394b, 800 Mbps
Accuracy of a single marker (20,000 averaged positions at depths of 40–100 cm)	0.20 mm RMS

3 Depth Camera Calibration

To calibrate the position and orientation of these two depth cameras, we used different markers and measured their positions using each sensor. $\boldsymbol{p}_i^{\mathrm{MT}} = \left(x_i^{\mathrm{MT}} \quad y_i^{\mathrm{MT}} \quad z_i^{\mathrm{MT}} \right)^T$ and $\boldsymbol{p}_i^{\mathrm{kinect}} = \left(x_i^{\mathrm{kinect}} \quad y_i^{\mathrm{kinect}} \quad z_i^{\mathrm{kinect}} \right)^T$ are 3D coordinates of each marker which are measured by MicronTracker3 and KINECT sensor, and $i = 0, \ldots, N$ means marker identification number. Figure 2 shows the markers used for our calibration. Eight markers ($N = 8$) are used in this experiment. They are printed on adhesive printer sheets and attached to acrylic boxes. By solving the following Eq. (1), the calibration matrix $\mathbf{M}$ is calculated.

$$\mathbf{M} = \left(p_1^{\text{kinect}} \quad \cdots \quad p_N^{\text{kinect}} \right) \left(p_1^{\text{MT}} \quad \cdots \quad p_N^{\text{MT}} \right)^{-1} \tag{1}$$

To acquire a proper and precise matrix, all markers should not be placed in the same plane and n should be a large number. Marker sizes used in this experiment are H30 × W50 mm and H40 × W50 mm.

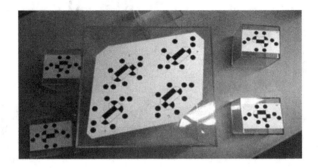

Fig. 2. Markers for depth camera calibration

4 Estimation of Knife Tip Position

It is difficult to measure the knife tip position directly and without contact during the operation because it gets covered in blood and is hidden in the incised portion of the skin or organ. Therefore, we use a marker attached to the top of the knife. Figure 3

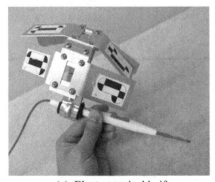

(a) Electrosurgical knife   (b) Model knife for preliminary experiments

Fig. 3. Knives with markers

shows a real electrosurgical knife (a) and a model knife with the markers that we are developing. To accurately and robustly track the knife, many markers are placed in each direction.

Before the operation, the relative vector between each marker and the tip has to be measured. To acquire a relative vector, one must set the tip of the knife to the origin point p_{table}^{MT} of the fix marker C_{table} on the flat table (Fig. 4). p_{table}^{MT} is measured by MicronTracker3. The position p_{knife}^{MT} and orientation R_{knife}^{MT} of the marker attached to the knife C_{knife} are measured in Σ_{MT} and are also measured by MicronTracker3. Σ_{MT} and Σ_{knife} are the coordinate systems of MicronTracker3 and knife, respectively. The relative vector p_{rel}^{knife} is calculated by

$$p_{rel}^{knife} = p_{table}^{MT} - p_{knife}^{MT} \tag{2}$$

in Σ_{knife}. To convert p_{rel}^{knife} to p_{rel}^{MT} in Σ_{MT},

$$p_{rel}^{MT} = R_{knife}^{MT-1} \cdot p_{rel}^{knife} \tag{3}$$

Therefore, the knife tip position p_{tip}^{MT} is calculated by

$$p_{tip}^{MT} = R_{knife}^{'MT} \cdot p_{rel}^{knife} + p_{knife}^{'MT} \tag{4}$$

where $p_{knife}^{'MT}$ and $R_{knife}^{'MT}$ mean the position and orientation of C_{knife} during the operation.

A point p^{MT} which is measured in Σ_{MT} can be converted to a point p^{kinect} in the coordination system of the KINECT Σ_{kinect} by using the calibration matrix M derived in the previous section.

$$p^{kinect} = M \cdot p^{MT} \tag{5}$$

Fig. 4. Measuring relative vectors

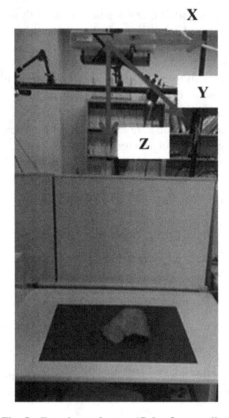

Fig. 5. Experimental setup (Color figure online)

5 Experiment and Results

By combining the above calculations, we implemented a pilot study system and conducted preliminary experiments (Figs. 5 and 6). Before we began, we used a 3D printer to make a life-size model of a liver with a red-colored material. The original data used

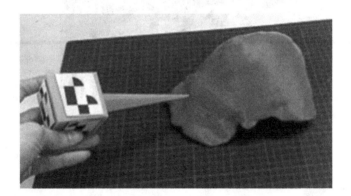

Fig. 6. Knife model with markers and liver model made using a 3D printer (Color figure online)

to create the model liver was taken from a CT (computed tomography) image from a patient. The model liver was placed on a table and two depth sensors were mounted above the table and directed downward to capture it.

This system has the ability to give visual and audio warnings. As the tip of the knife approaches to the liver, and the color of the knife tip on the monitor changes from green to red (Fig. 7) and the sound frequency increases. These experimental results showed the feasibility of our system.

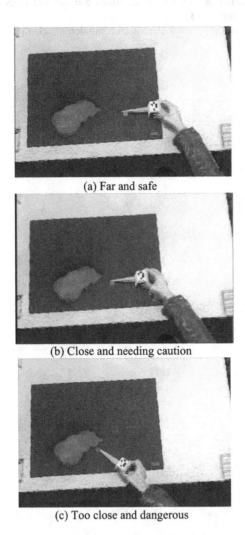

(a) Far and safe

(b) Close and needing caution

(c) Too close and dangerous

Fig. 7. Visual alert based on the distance between liver surface and the knife tip. The tip color of the model knife changes from green to red depending on the distance (Color figure online).

References

1. Noborio, H., Onishi, K., Koeda, M., Mizushino, K., Yagi, M., Kaibori, M., Kwon, M.: Motion transcription algorithm by matching corresponding depth image and Z-buffer. In: Proceedings of the 10th Anniversary Asian Conference on Computer Aided Surgery (ACCAS2014), pp. S5–3, Fukuoka, Japan, June 2014
2. Noborio, H., Onishi, K., Koeda, M., Mizushino, K., Kunii, T., Kaibori, M., Kon, M., Chen, Y.: A fast surgical algorithm operating polyhedrons using Z-Buffer in GPU. In: Proceedings of the 9th Asian Conference on Computer Aided Surgery (ACCAS 2013), pp. 110–111, Tokyo, Japan, September 2013
3. Claron Technology Inc. http://www.clarontech.com/microntracker.php

CyberTouch - Touch and Cursor Interface for VR HMD

Sangho Lee, Gyutae Ha, Jaekwang Cha, Jinhyeok Kim, Hojun Lee,
and Shiho Kim[✉]

School of Integrated Technology and Yonsei Institude of Convergence Technology,
Yonsei University, 85 Songdo-Gwahakro, Yeonsu-Gu, Incheon 406-840, Korea
{sangholee, shiho}@yonsei.ac.kr

Abstract. This paper presents a platform, named Cybertouch, for 3D Virtual Reality Head-Mounted Display (VR HMD) providing both touch and cursor interface using wearable IMU devices to enable real-time selection of operational commands together with recognition of user motions and gestures. One of the constraints of the conventional 3D HMD widely used in VR games or training systems is blocking of user's visual perception while wearing an HMD. Because the environment and input devices are invisible during the operation, there may be a limitation in an application caused by restriction of user input commands. Proposed Cybertouch provides a User Interface which is a kind of combined functions of traditional mice and touch panel devices, specialized in games or immersive virtual training applications using 3D HMD.

1 Introduction

Virtual Reality Platforms based on Low-cost 3-Dimensional Head-Mounted Displays (HMD) such as the Oculus Rift [1] are becoming popular in a variety of fields which utilize the virtual reality environments. Development of User Interface (UI) for the VR HMD platform has become one of the hottest issues both in the research and industry fields. Control input through gesture recognition have likely been to become a major method of user interface. There are many prior researches to integrate gesture recognition into a command and motion interface for the VR HMD Platforms. Andrea et al. proposed the hardware as well as the software for sensing 3D gestures to interact with head-mounted display [2]. Similarly, O. Jason et al. proposed a new intelligent text management system that actively manages the movement of text in a user's field of view by recognizing the hand gestures [3]. Moreover, Otmar et al. presented 3D interactions with a situated see-through display [4]. However, one of the biggest hurdles in the current approach is that the display device cannot visualize the users' motions on the non-see-through HMD since an entire environment beyond the device is invisible during the operation [5]. Although, various research has been done or in progress to overcome the limitation, it is still an inevitable matter to have the method to control the user interface on the non-see-through head-mounted displays. Shahram et al. proposed an initial version of multi-modal gesture interface invariant to the visibility of the display, and they constructed the scenario list to architect the gesture interface [6]. However, the conventional gesture scenarios are based on the hand

© Springer International Publishing Switzerland 2015
C. Stephanidis (Ed.): HCII 2015 Posters, Part I, CCIS 528, pp. 503–507, 2015.
DOI: 10.1007/978-3-319-21380-4_85

motions or pose without considering the functional combination of traditional touch and the cursor interface of the mouse movements [7, 8]. As far as the authors know, means to input user's intention with synchronization of movement in non-see-through HMD has not been reported yet. In this paper, we propose a user interface named Cybertouch, for 3D VR HMD providing input command interface with fully synchronized movement motions using wearable IMUs (inertial measurement units) and EMG (Electromyograph) sensors to enable real-time selection of operational commands together with recognition of user motions and gestures. A detailed concept of the proposed interface will be presented in the Sect. 2. Proposed prototype with experimental results is explained in Sect. 3, and proposed work is summarized conclusion in the Sect. 4.

2 Proposed Cybertouch Interface

We defined eight commands with a combination of gestures and motions. The major consideration when we determine the set of commands and corresponding gestures is that they should reflect the native behavior of human in order to provide experiential, affective and practical aspects of Human Computer Interaction. We use both EMG sensors and IMUs as an input device to detect hand motions and poses of fingers. There is a limitation in sensing capability to detect EMG signal related to the each finger motion by using EMG sensors attached at the forearm. By data fusion of IMU data and EMG signal, we can recognize commands by matching the combination of hand-motions and poses as shown in the Table 1. In Cybertouch, the eight essential commands consist of both basic control commands of applications and operating system. For example, Grab-Drag-Drop is a command which can be used to move an object in the game application, by the way, Grab-Drag-Drop can be used to move an icon or file for performing an OS task. Escaping is a special control command can be used to quit or exit from running environment. Table 2 shows comparison of conventional devices and proposed Cybertouch.

3 Configuration and Experimental Results

The configuration of system interface using proposed Cybertouch is illustrated in Fig. 1. The Event Listener receives the packets from IMUs or EMG devices, and it perceives the events by analyzing the packet from the wearable input devices. The detected events are dispatched to the Command Recognizer. The Command Recognizer generates input commands by comparing incoming sets of events with predefinition set of commands and gestures as shown in Table 1. The Cybertouch input commands can dispatch to OS kernel by using a message function call of the OS kernel API. The primary goal of the Cybertouch command is providing control commands of applications.

However, the command input to OS kernel makes it is possible to control the system while wearing a non-see-through HMD without using mouse or touch pannel.

Table 1. Definition of commands and corresponding hand gestures and motions

Commands	Gestures/Motions
Grab-Drag-Drop	Fist – Drag - Rest
Cursor Moving	Move
Zooming	Shrink - Expand
Rotating	Rotation
Approving (OK)	Point
Scrolling	Wave In/Out/Up/Down (Left/Right/Up/Down)
Escaping	Thumb-n-Pinky

To demonstrate the proposed Cybertouch system, we developed a VR simulator, which requires VR HMD and provides a user experience of Cybertouch commands. To configure the system, we used two IMUs with EMG sensors attached at both left and right forearms, as shown in Fig. 2.

Table 2. Comparison of conventional devices and cybertouch

Commands	Touch system	Mouse system	Cybertouch (Proposed)
Grab-drag-drop	O	O	O
Cursor moving	X	O	O
Zooming	O	X	O
Rotating	O	X	O
Approving (OK)	O	O	O
Scrolling	O	X	O
Swiping	O	X	O
Escaping	X	X	O

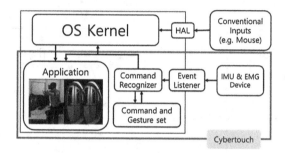

Fig. 1. A brief illustration of the proposed Cybertouch configuration

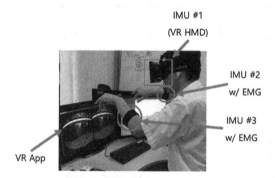

Fig. 2. Experimental setup of Cybertouch, the proposed touch and cursor interface for the VR HMD platform using IMUs and EMG sensors for gesture and motion sensing.

4 Conclusions

We have proposed a platform, named Cybertouch, for 3D Virtual Reality Head-Mounted Display (VR HMD) providing traditional input control commands of both touch and cursor interface with fully synchronized movement motions using wearable IMUs and EMG devices to enable real-time selection of operational commands together with recognition of user motions and gestures.

Proposed Cybertouch provides a User Interface which is a kind of combined functions of traditional mice and touch panel devices, specialized in games or immersive virtual training applications using 3D HMD. Our in-progress interface of Cybertouch and embedded application will be demonstrated at the conference.

Acknowledgements. This research was supported by the MSIP (Ministry of Science, ICT and Future Planning), Korea, under the "IT Consilience Creative Program" (NIPA-2014-H0201-14-1002) supervised by the NIPA (National IT Industry Promotion Agency).

References

1. Yao, R., et al.: Oculus VR Best Practices Guide. Oculus VR (2014)
2. Colaço, A., et al.: Mime: compact, low power 3D gesture sensing for interaction with head mounted displays. In: Proceedings of the 26th Annual ACM Symposium on User Interface Software and Technology. ACM (2013)
3. Orlosky, J., Kiyoshi, K., Haruo T.: Dynamic text management for see-through wearable and heads-up display systems. In: Proceedings of the 2013 International Conference on Intelligent User Interfaces. ACM (2013)
4. Hilliges, O., et al.: HoloDesk: Direct 3D interactions with a situated see-through display. In: Proceedings of the SIGCHI Conference on Human Factors in Computing Systems. ACM (2012)
5. Havig, P., John, M., Eric, G.: Virtual reality in a cave: limitations and the need for HMDs?. In: SPIE Defense, Security, and Sensing International Society for Optics and Photonics (2011)
6. Jalaliniya, S.: Towards Dynamically Switching Multimodal User Interfaces. Diss. IT University of Copenhagen (2014)
7. Nuwer, R.: Armband adds a twitch to gesture control. New Scientist **217**(2906), 21 (2013)
8. Chen, X., et al.: Multiple hand gesture recognition based on surface EMG signal. In: 2007 The 1st International Conference on Bioinformatics and Biomedical Engineering ICBBE 2007 IEEE (2007)

Human Avatar Robotic Puppeteering (HARP)

Christopher Martinez and Cameron MacDonald[✉]

University of New Haven, West Haven, USA
cmartinez@newhaven.edu, cameron.macpow@gmail.com

Abstract. The Human Avatar Robotic Puppeteering (HARP) project is focused on studying whether homologous puppeteering (controlling via mimicry) is an effective control principle for robots, given minimal user training. This project aims to develop a practical implementation at low-cost. The HARP project is a three-joint robotic crane that is capable of grasping objects. In order to control via puppeteering, the system tracks the user's hand moving in free space in real time as an avatar. This implementation relies on a Microsoft Kinect ($150) and a Leap Motion sensor ($100). This low-cost prototype is a proof-of-concept for a natural interface between user and robot, allowing gestures to be the method of communication rather than the traditional button-and-switch method. The system uses the Xbox Kinect to track the hand in reference to a known point on a table. This position is mapped using the imaging camera sensor in the Kinect, and an inverse kinematic algorithm is used to translate that position to the joint-angles for the crane. The grasping of the user's hand is sensed with the Leap Motion sensor. A key contribution to the research field is the blending of two different gesture based sensor systems to form a robust control interface.

Keywords: Robotic control · Avatar control · User interface

1 Background

The Microsoft Kinect has been used in a wide variety of experiments blending the fields of computer vision and user interaction. Gentile, Sorce, and Gentile [2] and Raheja, Chaudhary, and Singal [3] both focused on refining the sensor's hand-tracking methodology, while Gallo, Placitelli, and Ciampi [1] focused on leveraging the robust and intuitive control method to navigate medical data and images.

2 Design

The top-level architecture of the HARP prototype is a base station laptop, two sensors, a robot controller, and a robot. Each component will be described below. It is important to note that work on this project is ongoing (Figs. 1 and 2).

2.1 Gestures

Gesture recognition is performed by two sensors, which track their own respective body aspect. The Xbox Kinect tracks the hand's position, while the Leap Motion tracks

© Springer International Publishing Switzerland 2015
C. Stephanidis (Ed.): HCII 2015 Posters, Part I, CCIS 528, pp. 508–512, 2015.
DOI: 10.1007/978-3-319-21380-4_86

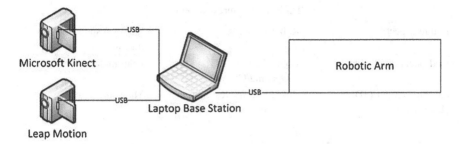

Fig. 1. Top-level diagram of HARP prototype

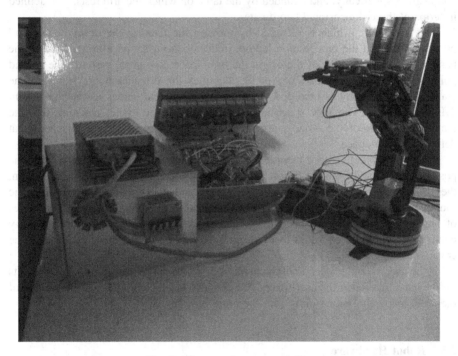

Fig. 2. Crane and crane controller

the hand's open/closed status, to serve as the basis of control input for the HARP prototype. Rather than track and mimic each individual joint of the arm, we use inverse kinematics to navigate the arm in real-time to the point in "crane-space" homologous to the hand's position in "user-space". This space-mapping method is described in later sections (Table 1).

2.2 Mapping and Kinematics

In order to map the position of the arm relative to the base station, it is first necessary to define a user-space to serve as a homologue. To do this, the base station records three

Table 1. Gestures supported

Gesture aspect	Robot response	Sensor responsible for tracking
Hand opening/Closing	Robot Claw Opening/Closing	Leap motion
Hand movement (3DOF tracked)	Robot arm moves claw in 3DOF	Microsoft kinect

calibration points, which define the hemispheric user-space. This user-space is homologous to the circle that is the maximum length of the arm of the crane rotated 360 degrees spherically, and bounded by the table on which the arm rests. It is defined in terms of three-dimensional coordinates.

The first point, which is recorded by moving the hand to the desired point and pressing a key on the base station laptop, indicates the user-space homologue of the base of the crane to serve as the origin the user-space coordinate system. The second point, recorded via a second key press, identifies the orientation or "front" of the crane. The third point is recorded via third key press and serves as the third point defining a plane. The user space is a 1:1 scaling of the crane, meaning that the maximum length of the crane's arm is exactly the radius of the hemisphere that defines the user-space.

Once the plane has been recorded, the base station enters a loop that records the position of the hand from the Kinect and the open/closed status from the Leap Motion, then translates the hand position to crane-space, and performs an inverse kinematic routine published by Scott Whitlock [4] of ContactandCoil.com. It then takes the series of angles generated by the inverse kinematics and the open/closed value and any control messages and packages them into a binary message and transmits them to the crane.

If the user's hand is outside of the hemispheric user-space, the polling routine waits for the hand to re-enter the user space. The user also has the ability to recalibrate any of the three map-calibration points with the press of a key.

2.3   Robot Hardware

The crane is an OWI-535 Robotic Arm Edge. Two versions of the on-unit circuit board are commercially available: one to interface with a detachable game-pad style controller, and the other to interface with a PC via USB. The original decision was made, partly due to budgetary and cost reasons, and partly to maintain flexibility, to build our own USB interface for the gamepad style controller. For this we prototyped an electronics package to provide the +3 V/−3 V/0 V used to rotate each joint forward, backward, and stop (respectively) We used an Arduino Lilypad 328 microcontroller as the crane controller and serial over USB interface. We have also acquired the commercial USB interface.

2.4   Robot Software

The limitations of this hardware are important to note as they greatly influence the requirements of the software. The OWI Robotic Arm Edge has no positional feedback. This means that any angle-state tracking is done via "dead reckoning". In other words the crane keeps its knowledge of its current position for each joint by taking the elapsed time since its last known position, multiplies that by the direction and rate of travel, and increments/decrements its last known position by the change in position. The controller, after performing the necessary initialization steps, loops over a message receipt subroutine, and then updates the position state variable for each angle, and then sets the motor in the appropriate forward/backward/stop state. If no message is received for a time, a timeout is detected and the controller updates the angle-state data and sets the motors in the direction of the last received position message from the base station.

All robot-side software is written in C++ using Arduino libraries as applicable and available.

3   Outcome

Work on this project is ongoing. In this instance the "dead reckoning" state tracking method has proved unreliable as there is up to a 20 % variance in the rate per second per joint. Work continues to verify that the crane responds to input from the sensors in a gesture-appropriate way, rather than providing verbatim control.

3.1   Future Work

Future work may focus on recognizing and implementing more refined gestures. It will likely also involve a new robot, as the limits of the current OWI Robotic Arm Edge solution limit exploring the idea of using photosensors to recognize gestures for controlling robots.

4   Potential Applications

There are a myriad of applications for this manner of puppeteering. As we move into a more and more automated world, some tasks will remain that require human interaction. The ability, without having to strap on any sensors, to take control of a robot will be of great use, analogous to remote desktop solutions to handle specific human-required digital interactions. This study explores just one of a host of approaches to that idea.

This technique, as it grows more and more refined, will add to or increase its presence in factory automation and remote exploration, surveillance, and rescue drones. One of the most exciting potentials is remotely controlling extreme and hazardous environment probes for deep sea, volcano, and space exploration.

References

1. Gallo, L., Placitelli, A.P., Ciampi, M.: Controller-free exploration of medical image data: Experiencing the Kinect. In: CBMS, 2011 Proceedings of the 26th IEEE International Symposium on Computer-Based Medical Systems, pp. 1–6. doi:10.1109/CBMS.2011. 5999138
2. Gentile, V., Sorce, S., Gentile, A.: continuous hand openness detection using a kinect-like device. In: 2014 Eighth International Conference on Complex Intelligent and Software Intensive Systems, pp. 553–557 (2014)
3. Raheja, J., Chaudhary, A., Singal, K.: Tracking of fingertips and centres of palm using KINECT. In: 2011 Third International Conference on Computational Intelligence Modeling & Simulation, pp. 248–252 (2011)
4. Whitlock, S.: http://www.contactandcoil.com/automation/home-automation/owi-535-robot-arm-with-usb-controller-from-c-and-net/

An "Origami" Support System by Using Finger Gesture Recognition

Koji Nishio$^{(\boxtimes)}$, Kazuto Yamamoto, and Ken-ichi Kobori

Osaka Institute of Technology, 1-79-1, Kitayama, Hirakata-City, Osaka, Japan
{koji.a.nishio,kenichi.kobori}@oit.ac.jp,
yamamoto_kazuto@is.oit.ac.jp

Abstract. We propose "Origami" simulation system using finger gesture recognition. "Origami" is a traditional and popular game using a square sheet of paper in Japan. It is built up only by folding called "Ori" operation. Thus the rule of "Origami" is very simple. However, it is difficult for children to use complicated "Ori" and it is necessary to retry "Ori" operation again and again. On the other hand, the durability of paper is limited. Therefore by using virtual paper and finger gesture recognition, there is no limitation of durability and people who play "Origami" can retry "Ori" operation until they are satisfied. Our system projects "Origami" image on the grass table and tracks fingers by using LEAP motion that is one of depth sensors. In addition, our system recognizes "Ori" gestures with finger motions and folds "Origami". Using our system, people can plays "Origami" with a feeling of folding a real paper.

Keywords: Finger-motion · Hand-gesture · Image-recognition · Paper-craft

1 Introduction

"Origami" is the art of folding paper, which has been familiar to Japanese people through the ages. It is made with a square sheet of paper by folding and unfolding. Generally, beginners operate a origami according to a operation diagram. Figure 1(a) shows an example of "Origami" shaped a war helmet "Kabuto" and Fig. 1(b) shows its procedure of folding and unfolding step-by-step.

However, most operation diagrams are not easy to recognize to beginners because they are expressed in two-dimensional as shown in Fig. 1(b) even though Origami works are three-dimensional. And also most beginners need to retry to folding and un-folding repeatedly. This makes a sheet of Origami to be broken. Therefore we propose a virtual origami system that makes to be able to play Origami in virtual space. Our system displays the image of Origami and recognizes the finger gestures of player. In addition, a player can touch and operate a image of Origami. Our system enables beginners to retry to operate origami again and again. There is no need to prepare a lot of sheets of Origami. By the way, Origami needs different operation to each hand such as holding a sheet with left hand and applying a fold line with right hand. However, the conventional system uses two-dimensional input devices such as mouse or touch panel. Then our system uses a sensor device "Leap Motion" that can tracks finger motion.

C. Stephanidis (Ed.): HCII 2015 Posters, Part I, CCIS 528, pp. 513–518, 2015.
DOI: 10.1007/978-3-319-21380-4_87

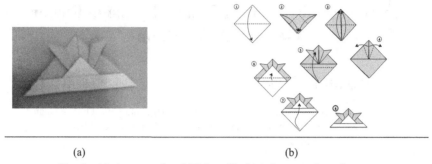

(a)   (b)

Fig. 1. (a) An example of "Origami", (b) is its procedure diagram

With this device, our system tracks player's finger motion in three dimension and recognize a hand gesture.

2 Proposed System

2.1 Components of the System

Proposed system consists of a reinforced grass plate, a mirror, a projector and a finger motion sensor as shown in Fig. 2(a). Figure 2(b) shows a view from player's eye point. A rendered image of Origami is projected as shown in Fig. 2(c) and the system watches player's finger motion in the area as shown in Fig. 2(d).

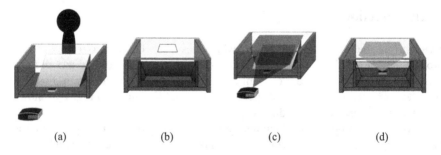

(a)   (b)   (c)   (d)

Fig. 2. Appearance of our system

2.2 Rendering of Origami Model

Our system handles one and more polygons and holds them sequentially in order from front to back. For example, Figs. 2(a) and (b) shows a list of polygons and rendered image respectively (Figs. 3 and 4).

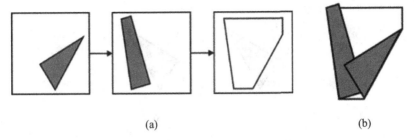

(a)   (b)

Fig. 3. List of polygons and its rendered image

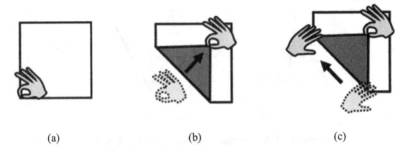

(a)   (b)   (c)

Fig. 4. Folding operation

2.3 Operations

Our system provides four types of operations, FOLD, TURNOVER, ROTATE and UNDO/REDO.

FOLD. Hold a corner of the polygon which player wants to fold and move it to the position where player wants to be. After that, move the other hand along the folding line.

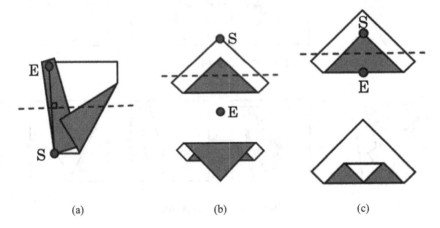

(a)   (b)   (c)

Fig. 5. Folding line and two cases of folding pattern

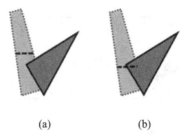

(a)   (b)

Fig. 6. Determination of overlap

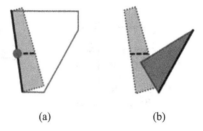

(a)   (b)

Fig. 7. Edge sharing with the folding polygon

Calculation of a folding line. Assuming that S is the holding point and E is the destination, a folding line places on a perpendicular bisector of the line SE as shown in Fig. 5.

Detection of folding polygon. Even if player picks and moves same point, there are two cases about the folding operation as shown in Fig. 5. In case of Fig. 5(b), each polygon

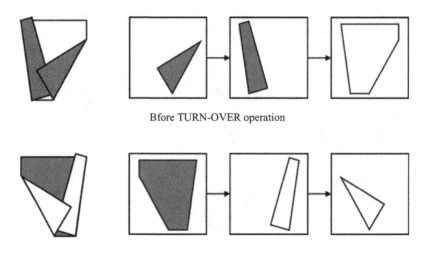

Bfore TURN-OVER operation

After TURN-OVER operation

Fig. 8. Reordering images and reordering of polygons

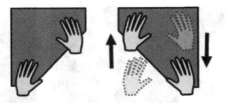

Fig. 9. ROTATE operation

across the folding line should be bent. On the other hand, in case of Fig. 5(c), some of polygons are not. Then the system judges whether bend or not. It is supposed that the polygon that has point S as its corner should be bent. If there are two or more such polygons, the one that places the front most is adopted. Polygons, which are placed in front of folding one, may also be bent as shown in Fig. 6. The dark one must not be bent in case of Fig. 6(a), and must be bent in case of Fig. 6(b). If some edge of folding polygon are shared with other polygons, those polygons must be bet too as shown in Fig. 7(a). Otherwise, the dark one sharing no edge with folding polygon does not needs to be bent as shown in Fig. 7(b).

Division and turning over. The polygon that places the front most is divided into two polygons by the folding line. One of divided polygons, picked by a player, are turned over around the folding line and places in front of the other one. After that, if a player traces the folding line, our system fixes the position of the folding line.

TURN-OVER. When a player turns over his hand picking up a corner of Origami, whole of Origami is reversed. At this time, the order of polygons in the list is reordered in reverse order as shown in Fig. 8.

ROTATE. To rotate whole of Origami, a player put his hand on the Origami image and move each hand in the opposite direction as shown in Fig. 9.

UNDO/REDO. When a player flips over his hand clockwise, the system cancels last operation. In case of anticlockwise, the system redo the operation.

3   Experiment

Using our system, some Origami work is created. Figure 10 shows one of Origami work created with our system. These experimental results show that our system works correctly and seems to be effective.

Fig. 10. Projected images on the grass-top of our system. These images show results by player's operation step by step from left top to right bottom.

4 Conclusions

We've proposed an "Origami" system by using hand gestures. To recognize those gestures, we apply one of the latest devices that can track finger motions to our system. In addition, our system projects images of "origami" on the grass top and players can operate them as real. However, the system fails to track fingers when player moves their fingers too fast. Therefore, we think that this is one of the future works.

A New Approach of Automatic Detection and Analysis of Body Language

Inass Salloum, Youssef Bou Issa[(⊠)], and Taline Boyajian

Ticket Lab Antoine University, Hadat-Baabda, Lebanon
{inass.salloum,Youssef.bouissa,
taline.boyajian}@ua.edu.lb

Abstract. In this paper we present our study concerning a new approach of automatic detection and analysis of body language in which we propose a method for extracting information related to nonverbal communication between persons. Our approach is based on the kinect sensor that processes the image and provides us many image features that we study. The final goal is to provide blind users access to information that is completely hidden.

Keywords: Body language detection · Psychological analysis · Gestures · Movements postures · Accessibility for blind users · Kinect

1 Introduction

Kinesics is the study of body language; this science provides a base to detect and analyze all postures and gestures of a person in order to reveal his psychological probable state. This science started in 1950 with Ray Birdwhistell [1]. After that, it stayed in continuous development until 1970, where a professor in psychology, Albert Mehrabian, introduced a new communication model called "The Mehrabian Model". This model divides the communication into three percentages: 7 %–10 % of the information of the communication expressed by words, 38 % goes for the tone and the way in which words are spoken and finally 55 % for the body expression: facial expressions and body postures and gestures [2]. This model shows the big role of the body in expressing emotions. Our objective is to study the possibilities to automate the analysis of the body language in order to determine the emotional and social conditions of a human being. Then we study the accessibility to this type of information that is completely hidden to blind users.

2 Background

Body language is a study that takes into consideration the combination of all body movements by examining the intentional ones as well as the completely unconscious ones; those movements can apply only in one culture or independent of all cultural barriers [8]. Most researchers now agree that words are used primarily for conveying information, while body language is used for negotiating interpersonal attitudes and, in

© Springer International Publishing Switzerland 2015
C. Stephanidis (Ed.): HCII 2015 Posters, Part I, CCIS 528, pp. 519–522, 2015.
DOI: 10.1007/978-3-319-21380-4_88

some cases, is used as a substitute for verbal messages [2]. Thus, body language is based on the behavioral patterns of nonverbal communication [8].

In this context, several systems were created to detect body postures, gestures and movements [3–5], others tried to detect facial emotions [6]. In [3] authors proposed a system to detect full body gestures of a dancer. It is based on a motion capture system consisting of 12 infrared cameras, sensors and markers on the body of the dancer; during a dance, with every motion the cameras detect the positions of the markers and their X, Y, Z coordinates in a 3 dimensional. As result, we only get the gestures and motions done by the dancer without any psychological analysis or emotional state estimation. However in [4], the authors worked on a different goal. The main idea of their study is based on body language analysis from the detection of facial expressions and hands positions and gestures. The system is composed of 2 cameras: one fixed on the face and the other on the hands. The approach consists of recording videos for the user's face and hands and then analyzing these videos by frame. During the analysis, the system will examine the set of "Facial expressions- Hands postures". It analyzes the combination of facial expressions and hands gestures. However, this system detects only the 6 universal emotions and is not in real time.

3 Our Solution

In this work, we study the possibilities to automatically generate the probable psychological state from detecting body postures and gestures by analyzing images in real time. Our Solution is divided into two parts:

1. Posture, gesture, movements detection and analysis
2. Automatic psychological analysis and Generation of the probable psychological states.

According to C. Boyes [1], we can extract the psychological state of a person by analyzing the combination of his body movements and postures.

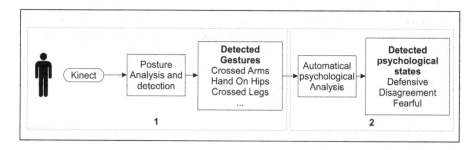

Fig. 1. Architecture of our system

3.1 Body Detection and Posture Analysis

The first part of our work concerns the identification of the most relevant gestures needed for a psychological study [1, 2]. The identification is based on the Kinect [7] that detects the positions of the body parts. We analyzed these positions in order to create a collection of automatically detected postures and gestures in real-time.

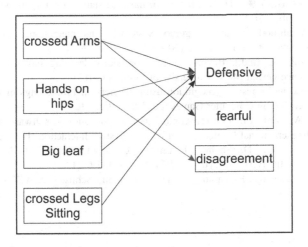

Fig. 2. Detected postures and probable psychological states

3.2 Psychological States Analysis

The second part corresponds to the real-time analysis of the combination of detected movements, and the generation of the probable psychological state of the person. In fact, each psychological state is calculated according to a specific number of gestures and series of movements made by the person. So, the probability of a person having a specific state will vary in time depending on the person's movements. Each gesture has a probability of $\frac{1}{Total\ number\ of\ relevant\ gestures}$. Then we start to calculate the probability of each state knowing that the gesture is X. As an example, the "Crossed Arms" gesture has two possible states: defensive or fearful, so the probability of each is $\frac{1}{Total\ number\ of\ possible\ states}$ in this case is $\frac{1}{2}$. So, the probability of the state Y knowing the gesture is X is calculated using the equation: $P_{YX} = P(X)*P(Y)$.

In this example $P_{(Defensive \& Crossed\ Arms)} = P_{(Fearful \& Crossed\ Arms)} = P_{(Crossed\ Arms)} * \frac{1}{2}$ At the end, we added all the probabilities of each state to find the highly probable state (see Figs. 1 and 2).

4 Conclusion

We conducted an experiment to evaluate our system. The objective of the experiment was to find if the automatic analysis corresponds to the human analysis. Therefore, 9 persons were asked to do postures and gestures in front of Kinect. At first, the probable states are calculated manually by a psychiatrist, and then generated by the system. Preliminary results show correlation between the human and the automatic analysis.

References

1. Boyes, C.: Need to know? Body Language. Collins, New York (2005)
2. Yaffe, P.: (n.d.). The 7 % rule: fact, fiction, or misunderstanding. Ubiquity, vol. 2011. ACM publication, October 2011
3. Ciglar, M.: A full-body gesture recognition system and its integration in the university of music and dramatic arts Graz, Austria (2008)
4. Shan, C., Gong, S.: (n.d.). Beyond facial expressions: learning human. Department of Computer Science Queen Mary, University of London (2013)
5. Li, Y.: Multi-scenario gesture recognition using Kinect. In: Proceedings of the 17th International Conference on Computer Games, pp. 126–130 (2012)
6. Kolakowska, A., et al.: Emotion recognition and its application in software engineering. In: 2013 The 6th International Conference on Human System Interaction (HSI). IEEE (2013)
7. Han, J., Shao, L., Xu, D., Shotton, J.: Enhanced computer vision with Microsoft Kinect sensor: a review. IEEE Trans. Cybern. **43**(5), 1318–1334 (2013)
8. Fast, J.: Body Language, Psychology, p. 183. Simon and Schuster, New York (1970)

Using Eye Tracking as Human Computer Interaction Interface

Holger Schmidt[(⊠)] and Gottfried Zimmermann

Stuttgart Media University, Stuttgart, Germany
schmidtho@hdm-stuttgart.de, gzimmermann@acm.org

Abstract. In the project *AAMS*, we have developed the e-learning platform *ALM for Ilias* as a technical basis for research in education. ALM uses eye tracking data to analyze a learner's gaze movement at runtime in order to adapt the learning content. As an extension to the actual capabilities of the platform, we plan to implement and evaluate a framework for advanced eye tracking analysis techniques. This framework will focus on two main concepts. The first concept allows for real-time analysis of a user's *text reading status* by artificial intelligence techniques, at any point in the learning process. This extends and enriches the adaptive behavior of our platform. The second concept is an interface framework for multimedia applications to connect to any eye tracking hardware that is available at runtime to be used as a user interaction input device. Since accuracy can be an issue for low-cost eye trackers, we use an object-specific *relevance factor* for the detection of selectable or related content.

Keywords: Eye tracking · e-learning platform · Adaptivity · Artificial intelligence · High-level gaze events · Real-time analysis · Human computer interaction interface · Relevance factor

1 Introduction

Over the last years, eye tracking has become a valid tool to conduct research studies of user interaction behavior. Usually, the eye tracking data is analyzed after runtime (not during runtime). As part of our research in the *Adaptable and Adaptive Multimedia Systems (AAMS)* project [1], we have developed the web-based e-learning platform *Adaptive Learning Module (ALM for Ilias)* [2] with real-time eye tracking support. The project evaluates methods of using eye tracking for adaptive system behavior [3] by analyzing gaze-in and gaze-out events on selected learning content [4].

With *ALM*, psychologists in our project conduct studies on educational research in online learning. They focus on research questions like "how can we adapt learning content to improve a learner's performance via gaze tracking" [5]. Currently, *ALM's* gaze data analysis is limited to static fixations on learning content (areas of interest) and transitions between fixations of the user's gaze movement. In order to enhance the platform's capabilities, we are developing a framework for the analysis of high-level gaze events. For example, the reading status of a learner reading a text passage could be "intensive reading", "text skimming" or "text scanning".

© Springer International Publishing Switzerland 2015
C. Stephanidis (Ed.): HCII 2015 Posters, Part I, CCIS 528, pp. 523–527, 2015.
DOI: 10.1007/978-3-319-21380-4_89

Also, we are looking into eye tracking as a user input device, for improving the user experience. The development of these features is done in an iterative manner, including proof-of-concept studies (e.g., usability tests, stability tests and performance tests).

This poster gives a brief overview of the relevant research plans in the *AAMS* project.

2 Advanced Eye Tracking Techniques

Our current e-learning platform *ALM* is limited to static gaze-in and gaze-out analysis on predefined areas of interest. Our new framework will implement advanced eye tracking techniques, with artificial intelligence components. We have developed two separate concepts to extend the platform's analysis capabilities. The first concept focuses on the automated analysis of text components. The second concept focuses on the analysis of visual multimedia content, i.e. pictures, graphics, diagrams and complex 3D models.

2.1 Text Analysis: Average Reading Speed Theory

The "intensive reading" status is our definition of a concentrated learning situation. The learning platform should support the learner in keeping this status as long as possible. The platform has to be able to detect if the reading status is changing. Thus the platform can adapt the learning content in order to help the reader to re-enter the "intensive reading" status.

The concept of the framework component for text analysis is based on the average reading speed of a user constantly reading a text. This indicator determines the theoretical status "intensive reading". Thus the framework can detect when the user's reading status changes from "intensive reading" status to a different status, i.e. "skimming" or "scanning".

In a first attempt to determine the average reading speed, we follow a pre-processing approach. The user has to read several types of text (altering text difficulty) in a continuous manner. For each text passage, the framework measures the reading time and calculates the deviation from the average reading speed as a factor (which is both specific for the text type, and for the learner).

2.2 Context Adaptation

Content adaptation is the ability of the e-learning platform to modify the presented content in dependency of the user's gaze and input actions. One research theory of the *AAMS* project is about the optimization of a user's learning process by comparing their gaze paths with pre-analyzed gaze paths of dedicated good e-learners. The aim is to maximize the learner's knowledge gain within an e-learning session [5]. For this purpose, when the learner reads text, the platform tracks their fixations on predefined areas of interest and counts them. This value is compared to threshold limits which are gleaned from reference studies to differentiate between "good" and "bad" learners (e.g. number of fixations on a specific area of interest). If the learner moves their gaze to another learning content or clicks the continue button before the threshold limit is reached, the platform will block the presentation of new text, and hold on to the current text for a predefined timeframe to force the learner to read the text again. The goals is that the learner will adjust their personal gaze behavior to that of "the optimal learner".

2.3 Text Analysis: Detection of Reading Status Change

In addition to the actual context adaptation and based on the average reading speed, the framework can detect gaze jumps (transitions) to uncommon positions on the screen in relation to the context. This detection gains its improvement from two techniques. First, the actual text needs to be classified in reading difficulties, along the lines of the reference texts for the average reading speed detection (see 2.1). This allows for a more accurate analysis of the gaze data since it takes the difficulty level of the text into account.

Second, the framework has to modify a virtual map that classifies each sector of the screen in relation to the actual fixation. I.e., from the viewpoint of the actual fixation every text passages before this fixation becomes classified as red. Only a small passage of text behind the fixation is classified as green (green indicates the passage of continuous reading). A buffer zone around the green zone is classified as orange due to possible spikes. This has to be calculated in real-time to benefit from it. With this virtual map, the framework can predict whether the upcoming reading position (next fixation) is a result of "intensive reading" or a jump or status change. Thus we are able to detect interruptions of continuous (intensive) reading. In addition, the framework is able to detect different reading statuses; hence, the framework needs to be extended to support several reading patterns like, "text skimming" [6] and "text scanning".

2.4 Relevance Factor Adaptation

The reference application for the "relevance factor" concept is a 3D multimedia application which shows a car engine as full dismountable 3D model. The aim of the 3D model is to make the learner understand the individual components of an engine and how they work together. An engine has to be dismounted in a certain order, e.g., the cylinder head cannot be dismounted before the valve cover is removed. The framework needs to know the dismounting order of the components at every point in the process; we call this "the plot". With this knowledge, we can improve the user's experience of using eye tracking as an input mechanism by having their gaze "snap in" to those multimedia objects that are most relevant at the current time. This concept can be applied to arbitrary multimedia applications.

Therefore, every part of the dismountable engine has a "relevance factor" attached to it, which indicates the probability of this particular part to be dismounted next. Globally viewed, the relevance factor for every object is null. As the application drives through the plot, the framework decides about the relevance factor of every object in real-time. The more relevant an object is in relation to the plot, the higher the relevance factor of this object becomes. The eye tracking framework analyses the list of relevance factors and selects the highest values as "active objects". With an eye tracker connected, the framework can link these selected objects to the user's gaze. This results in an automated selection of highly relevant objects as soon as the user's gaze is within the objects nearby region.

2.5   Using the Framework as Input Device

In 3D environments, it is difficult to exactly determine small areas of interest for gaze tracking, especially in case of the z-axis (depth of the screen) without the information of the user's depth focus. The "relevance factor" can be used to compensate for this problem. With the "relevance factor" concept, we can use eye tracking as an input device for selecting explicit content objects in a 3D environment.

3   Conclusion

We have introduced two new concepts as an extension to our *Adaptive Learning Module (ALM)* platform. The first concept is about the analysis of text reading statuses. We will employ artificial intelligence techniques as an extension to the currently implemented static local real-time analysis of gaze fixation and transition counting. The second concept uses relevance factors for objects in a story-driven multimedia environment. A prototype will allow eye tracking to be used as an additional user interface input device, with explicit content dependency, especially for 3D environments. We will implement these concepts as a prototype to conduct usability studies with students, stability tests and performance tests to proof both concepts.

As a second use case, the "text reading status" concept can be applied in certain multimedia applications with text objects. We could analyze text based tutorials (which are essential for the usability of the related multimedia application) in the same way we analyze the text components in the e-learning environment. Also, the "relevance factor" concept can be used in an e-learning environment to analyze picture content or diagrams in relation to text components. For this purpose, the text component stands for the plot, thus driving the relevance factors of the individual graphic objects to guide the user's gaze to the most relevant graphical components.

With both concepts, we aim to improve the user's experience in a wide range of learning and multimedia applications, and develop and validate new functionalities for our e-learning platform.

References

1. Science Campus Tübingen, campus website, April 2015. http://www.wissenschaftscampus-tuebingen.de/-www/-en/index.html
2. Ilias 4 Open-Source Framework, project website, April 2015. http://www.ilias.de/docu/-goto.php?target=cat_582&client_id=docu

3. Schmidt, H., Wassermann, B., Zimmermann, G.: An adaptive and adaptable learning platform with real-time eye-tracking support: lessons learned. In: Trahasch, S., Plötzner, R., Schneider, G., Gayer, C., Sassiat, D., Wöhrle, N (eds.), Tagungsband DeLFI 2014, pp. 241–252. Köllen Druck & Verlag GmbH, Bonn (2014)
4. Wassermann, B., Hardt, A., Zimmermann, G.: Generic Gaze Interaction events for web browsers: using the eye tracker as input device. In: WWW 2012 Workshop: Emerging Web Technologies, Facing the Future of Education (2012)
5. Schubert, C., Scheiter, K., Schüler, A.: Viewing behavior during multimedia learning: can eye tracking measures predict learning success? In: 7th European Conference on Eye Movement Research. Lund, Sweden, August 2013
6. Geoffrey, B.D., Payne, S.J.: How much do we understand when skim reading? In: CHI 2006 Extended Abstracts on Human Factors in Computing Systems (CHI EA 2006), pp. 730–735. ACM, New York (2008). doi:10.1145/1125451.1125598

A Shoe Mounted System for Parkinsonian Gait Detection and Real-Time Feedback

Arash Tadayon[1(✉)], Jonathan Zia[1], Lekha Anantuni[1],
Troy McDaniel[1], Narayanan Krishnamurthi[2],
and Sethuraman Panchanathan[1]

[1] Center for Cognitive Ubiquitous Computing,
Arizona State University, Tempe, AZ, USA
{arash.tadayon,jonathan.zia,lekha.anantuni,
troy.mcdaniel,panch}@asu.edu
[2] College of Nursing and Health Innovation,
Arizona State University, Phoenix, AZ, USA
narayanan.krishnamurthi@asu.edu

Abstract. Conditions like Parkinson's disease (PD) remain largely a mystery in the way that they affect individuals even under today's modern medical practices. One of the main secondary effects associated with PD can be seen in issues with the individual's gait and is referred to as Freezing of Gait (FoG). The symptom often responds poorly and sometimes paradoxically to treatment with dopaminergic medication that is traditionally used to treat the other symptoms of PD. However, a linkage found that FoG, during walking, results when the sequence effect is superimposed on a reduced step length. Prior research has focused on the development of technologies that use audio or visual feedback to help the individual adjust their gait. These systems may not be deployable in real-world environments since people rely on sight and sound for navigation. This research proposes the development of a system to measure step length in real-time and to provide haptic feedback to offset the progression of FoG episodes.

Keywords: Adaptive interfaces · Anticipatory interfaces · Mobile HCI · Context-dependent system

1 Introduction

Conditions like Parkinson's disease (PD) remain largely a mystery in the way that they affect individuals even under today's modern medical practices. According to the Parkinson's Disease Foundation, an estimated 7–10 million people worldwide are living with PD [1]. Within the United States, approximately 60,000 people are diagnosed with the disease each year and have a combined direct and in-direct cost of $25 billion per year. Parkinson's disease is a neurodegenerative brain disorder that usually progresses over a long duration (often around 20 years) within an individual. While the disease itself is not fatal, the Center for Disease Control rated complications from the disease as the 14th top cause of death in the U.S. [2]. Because of these staggering

C. Stephanidis (Ed.): HCII 2015 Posters, Part I, CCIS 528, pp. 528–533, 2015.
DOI: 10.1007/978-3-319-21380-4_90

numbers, there has been a national push toward conducting fruitful research on PD. There are now multiple treatment methods to offset the symptoms of the disease—i.e., medication and an invasive procedure known as deep brain stimulation (DBS).

The symptoms of PD can be categorized into three main groups: primary motor symptoms, secondary motor symptoms and non-motor symptoms. Primary motor symptoms include tremor, bradykinesia, rigidity, and postural instability, which often have secondary motor symptoms. One of the main secondary effects associated with PD can be seen in issues with the individual's gait and is referred to as Freezing of Gait (FoG). It is an episodic phenomenon that is unexplained by rigidity or bradykinesia, and is more common in advanced PD. The episodes occur more frequently during high pressure or timed tasks such as walking down a narrow hallway or crossing a street in a given amount of time, and can have a large impact on an individual's quality of life since independence is diminished. The episodes are generally characterized by the individual feeling that they are unable to move or that their feet are "glued to the floor," and can often result in a fall. Because this secondary symptom is still not well understood, there does not exist effective treatment options to address it. The symptom often responds poorly and sometimes paradoxically to treatment with dopaminergic medication that is traditionally used to treat other symptoms of PD. However, a linkage found that FOG, during walking, results when the sequence effect is superimposed on a reduced step length [3].

Because of the dangers of this symptom, much research has been done in this area to offset the episodes and to prevent them from occurring as frequently. However, the majority of this research has focused on the development of technologies that use audio or visual feedback to help the individual adjust their gait. These systems may not be deployable in real-world environments since people rely on sight and sound for navigation. This research proposes the development of a system to measure step length in real-time and to provide haptic feedback to an individual to offset the progression of FOG episodes. Specifically, we are looking to extend the existing model for normal human gait to detect the abnormal cycles in Parkinsonian gait. This will involve the development of new, adaptable algorithms that can accommodate variations that are based on human-centric characteristics. Secondly, this research looks to develop a ubiquitous system that can monitor day-to-day activities and provide real-time feedback to the user to predict and offset FoG episodes.

2   Related Work

Immediately before the onset of a FOG episode, one of the main physiological events that is observed is a profound and incremental decrease in stride length [3, 4]. Thus, many researchers have attempted to identify these physiological events and to warn the individual before the actual FOG episode occurs. Prior work has found that if the user is mentally aware of the shortening of stride lengths, then they can adjust their gait accordingly. Current approaches have looked at different ways of notifying the user that their stride length has become increasingly small including through visual feedback [5] and audio feedback [6]. These devices provide cues (audio or visual) to guide the user in their step rhythm and cadence, and to make them aware of the need to take longer steps. With these cues, the user can change their behavior pattern and often avoid the FOG episode. However, the main limitation of these approaches is that they rely on technology that would be very difficult for users to wear and use on a day-to-day basis. These technologies obstruct either the user's vision or hearing, which can be dangerous in a navigation situation. Another limitation is that the algorithms that were developed for these devices rely on making slight modifications to the models used for the normal gait cycle, and therefore, do not necessarily accurately represent Parkinsonian gait.

3 Proposed Approach

The proposed approach has two main objectives:

1. Create a new model for Parkinsonian gait that models the cycles better than the traditional approach of modifying a normal gait model.
2. Develop a minimally intrusive device that can be worn by an individual during daily activities.

3.1 A New Model for Parkinsonian Gait

We begin by developing an accurate model to represent Parkinsonian gait characteristics. This is a challenging problem in that Parkinsonian cycles, immediately before and during a FOG event, do not follow regular gait cycles, and thus distinct features and events will need to be identified within this new model. Traditional detection of heel-strike and toe-off events that occur in normal gait should be avoided because these characteristics are often degraded beyond recognition in patients with PD. We therefore consider analysis on the frequency domain as the main method of step detection, and use pressure shifts between the toe and heel as a validation method, rather than detection, to develop a model for start and stop events. We will apply this model to an assistive device that the user can wear everyday with minimal intrusion.

3.2 A Minimally Intrusive Device

To achieve the goal of developing a device that can be used in everyday environments, the device needs to be relatively small and should be easily embeddable into clothing that the user already wears. Furthermore, it should not be significantly heavy since it will be adding weight to each of the user's feet, and fatigue while walking can be a major concern. We propose the development of a device that can be worn on the user's sock and can be easily hidden using pockets over the sock. The batteries for the device will be worn over the shank to decrease the amount of weight carried by the foot since these are the heaviest pieces.

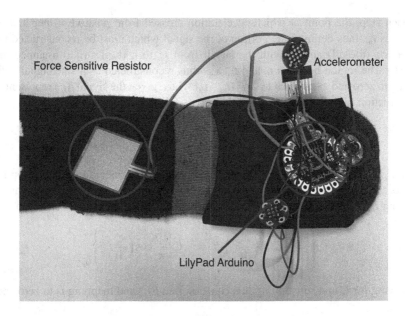

Fig. 1. Components of wearable system

4 Implementation

A wearable system has been built that consists of two small devices that can be worn over each of the user's socks (Fig. 1). The devices consist only of a LilyPad Arduino 328, a LilyPad accelerometer, an XBee module, and a force sensitive resistor. Processing is currently being done offline; however, in future iterations, these devices will integrate with the user's smartphone as a user interface and as a means for actuation. The device was built using the Arduino LilyPad board for easy embedding into the sock. The accelerometer is worn above the toe since this was the location that was found to have the least angular displacement during toe-off events, and reduced the distortion of the signal during those events. The pressure sensor is worn under the heel and is used as a method of validating steps taken by the user. The pressure data relies on a threshold value that will be person-centric and easily adjustable depending on the user. The device streams data for both acceleration and pressure that is annotated with timestamps to a computer for storage. Once the gait data is collected, it is processed to first identify which events were steps and then to determine the length of each of those steps.

To reconstruct the signal to counter the distortion caused by toe-off acceleration, the following method was implemented. It was assumed that only the toe-off portion of the signal was significantly distorted, so the toe-off portion of the signal was reconstructed based on the rest of the signal. The signal was approximated as a sinusoid with one crossing of the time axis between toe-off and heel-strike (one full step). Given that the acceleration and velocity of the foot at toe-off and heel-strike are known to be zero, the area under the acceleration curve over the course of one step is also known to be zero.

For each step, the point at which acceleration crossed from positive to negative was labeled as t_m, thus defining the portion of the signal which must be reconstructed to be between t_0 (toe-off) and t_m with the signal from t_m to t_f (heel strike) assumed to be accurate. The region between t_0 and t_m was thus reconstructed as a sine signal with t_0 mapped to zero and t_m mapped to $\Delta t = (t_m - t_0)$. Thus, given the signal $f(t')$ represents the reconstruction of the signal, it can be defined as follows:

$$f(t') = C sin\left(\frac{\pi}{\Delta t}t'\right), t'[0, \Delta t]$$

where C is the amplitude. Given that the area under the acceleration for one step must be zero, the magnitude of the area under the curve from t_0 to t_m must be equivalent to that from t_m to t_f. Thus, letting A represent the area under the curve from t_m to t_f,

$$-A = \int_{t_0}^{t_m} C sin\left(\frac{\pi}{\Delta t}t'\right)dt' = -C\left[\frac{\Delta t}{\pi}cos\left(\frac{\pi}{\Delta t}t'\right)\right]_{t_0}^{t_m}$$

Solving for C and substituting this equation into $f(t')$ and mapping t_0 to zero and t_m to Δt,

$$f(t') = \frac{A\pi sin\left(\frac{\pi}{\Delta t}t'\right)}{2\Delta t}, t'[0, \Delta t]$$

To implement this, the area under the curve from t_m to t_f for each step was calculated and substituted for A, and $f(t)$ was calculated to replace the signal from t_0 to t_m for each step, evaluating the function for $t' = t - t_0$ to correctly map the values.

5 Early Evaluation

Two major components have been assessed: the accuracy of detecting when a step has been taken and the accuracy in step length calculation for that step. These components were assessed for an individual with regular gait so that a baseline could be determined for the validity of distance calculation using a single accelerometer. Ten trails were conducted where a user walked 8 steps forward, turned around, and then walked 8 steps back. Each step was manually measured and logged for distance. Step length was measured using the distance between heel-strike events on a single foot. As shown in Fig. 2, the pressure values validated the starting and stopping points for each step. The acceleration curve follows what we would expect to see for normal gait and allows us to visually identify where the heel-strike and toe-off events are occurring as well as adequately showing the mid-swing. The system was able to accurately detect every step event within the data, however, was limited in accuracy with respect to the distance calculated. This was due to the posture of the foot during mid swing that we do not account for with a single accelerometer approach. We will be modifying our proposed system to use an IMU to solve for this issue in accuracy since we will be able to get angular acceleration from the foot and shank.

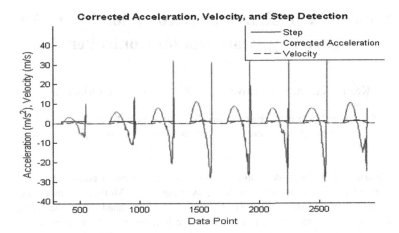

Fig. 2. Corrected acceleration, velocity and step detection graph

6 Conclusion and Future Work

Although much more evaluation needs to be done, preliminary results have shown that this system does have promise for being able to detect asynchronous steps. Future work will augment the single-accelerometer approach to include an IMU to more accurately determine angular acceleration of the foot and thus make the distance calculation much more accurate. We will test the effectiveness of site-specific haptic stimulation as well once step length is more accurately determined since recent research has shown its effectiveness [7]. We hope that this system will become an effective tool for the anticipation and prevention of FOG episodes.

References

1. National Institute of Neurological Disorders and Stroke. http://www.ninds.nih.gov/disorders/parkinsons_disease
2. Parkinson's Disease Foundation. http://www.pdf.org/en/symptoms_secondary
3. Chee, R., Murphy, A., Danoudis, M., Georgiou-Karistianis, N., Iansek, R.: Gait freezing in Parkinson's disease and the stride length sequence effect interaction. Brain **132**, 2151–2160 (2009)
4. Nieuwboer, A., Chavret, F., Willems, A., Desloovere, K.: Does freezing in Parkinson's disease change limb coordination? kinematic analysis. J. Neurol. **254**, 1268–1277 (2007)
5. Nieuwboer, A.: Cueing for freezing of gait in patients with Parkinson's disease: a rehabilitation perspective. Mov. Disord. **23**, S475–S481 (2008)
6. Bächlin, M., Plotnik, M., Roggen, D., Maidan, I., Hausdorff, J.M., Giladi, N., Troster, G.: Wearable assistant for Parkinson's disease patients with the freezing of gait symptom. Inf. Technol. Biomed. **14**, 436–446 (2010)
7. Rabin, E., Chen, J., Muratori, L., Difrancisco-donoghue, J., Werner, W.G.: Haptic feedback from manual contact improves balance control in people with Parkinson's disease. Gait Posture **38**, 373–379 (2013)

Handwritten Character Recognition in the Air by Using Leap Motion Controller

Kazuki Tsuchida, Hidetoshi Miyao^(✉), and Minoru Maruyama

Computer Science and Engineering, Shinshu University, Nagano, Japan
{miyao,maruyama}@cs.shinshu-u.ac.jp

Abstract. In order to develop a system which can precisely and quickly recognize handwritten characters in the air by using a Leap Motion Controller, we propose the following method: (1) A user has to register handwritten characters as template patterns before use. Each pattern is represented by a sequence of motion vectors calculated by using adjacent sampling data. (2) In the recognition phase, an input pattern is represented in the same method as above. The input pattern is compared with each of the registered template patterns by using DP matching and we can obtain a distance (degree of similarity) between them. Our system outputs the character class corresponding to the pattern with a minimum distance as a recognition result. In our experiments for recognition of 46 Japanese hiragana characters and 26 alphabets, a high average recognition rate of 86.7 % and a short average processing time of 196 ms were obtained.

Keywords: Character recognition · Leap motion · DP matching

1 Introduction

When a user enters character information to a computer, in general, he/she uses a computer keyboard and a mouse. However, if he/she wears a head-mounted display or his/her hands are too dirty, he/she could not use the devices. Even in such cases, users may want to enter character information. For example, they may want to search the Web while they are cooking and their hands are too dirty to touch a keyboard. Therefore, the purpose of our study is to develop a system which can recognize handwritten characters in the air by using a hand motion-sensing device.

In related works, personal authentication systems using hand or pen gestures in the air have been developed [1, 2]. On the other hand, a recognition method of handwritten alphabet characters in the air by Leap Motion controller has been proposed [3]. In this method, many people registered variety shapes of alphabet characters beforehand and they are used as template patterns in the character recognition phase. When a word is handwritten, the system allows users not to denote pen down (start) and pen up (end) points of writing a character. However, the system has the following drawbacks:

- In order to get a high recognition rate for many kinds of user input, many template patterns are needed.
- Since a character segmentation process is needed, the search area of character recognition phase is expanded.

© Springer International Publishing Switzerland 2015
C. Stephanidis (Ed.): HCII 2015 Posters, Part I, CCIS 528, pp. 534–538, 2015.
DOI: 10.1007/978-3-319-21380-4_91

Therefore, it is more likely to decrease recognition rates and slow down response time. To solve these problems, our system adopts the following ways:

- We assume that our system is used personally and the user has to register handwritten characters as template patterns before use.
- We introduce gestures which can indicate start /end points of writing a character.

Moreover, in addition to recognizing alphabet characters, we try to deal with recognizing Japanese hiragana characters whose shapes are more complex than those of alphabets.

2 Entering Characters and Their Representation

In order to get information of handwritten characters in the air, we use Leap Motion controller [4] which is a hand motion-sensing device. It can detect 3D positions of human hands and 10 fingers with up to 0.01 mm accuracy. Its sensor field is a roughly hemispherical area above the device, whose diameter is about 0.6 m. Using the device, an input character pattern is sampled every 75 ms and it is recorded by time series data which consists of the center positions of a palm of a user's hand at the sampling points. The palm position is represented by the x and y coordinates, in other words, we ignore z coordinate (depth direction) since characters is mainly handwritten on the x-y plane.

To segment each handwritten character, the first data is captured when the user flexes his/her thumb and the data acquisition process is completed when his/her palm stays in the air for 225 ms. Finally, the input pattern is represented by a sequence of motion vectors calculated by using adjacent data.

In the registration phase, handwritten characters represented by the above method are registered as template patterns. On the other hand, in the recognition phase, an input pattern is also captured and represented in the same method as shown in Fig. 1.

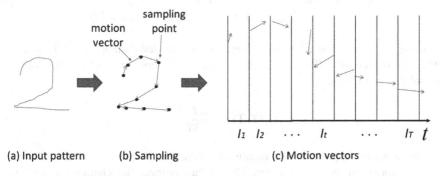

(a) Input pattern   (b) Sampling   (c) Motion vectors

Fig. 1. Input pattern and its motion vectors

3 Character Recognition Using DP Matching

A user has to register handwritten characters as template patterns before use. After that, an input pattern written by the same user is compared with each of the template patterns and the most similar pattern is found in the recognition phase. In this comparison process, we use dynamic programming matching (DP matching) since it can properly calculate the similarity between patterns even when the numbers of motion vectors for both the patterns do not coincide with each other.

Next, we explain a matching method between one of the template patterns and an input pattern. For template pattern c and the input pattern, time series motion vectors of them are represented by $J_1^c, \cdots, J_\tau^c, \cdots, J_T^c$ and $I_1, \cdots, I_t, \cdots, I_T$, respectively. If the tth motion vector of the input pattern coincides with the τth motion vector of the template pattern c, the local cost of DP matching is calculated by the following equation:

$$d_c(t, \tau) = \left\| J_\tau^c - I_t \right\|^2. \tag{1}$$

The accumulated distance $g_c(t, \tau)$ is calculated as follows:
Initial value:

$$g_c(t, 1) = \begin{cases} 3d_c(t, 1), (t = 1) \\ g_c(t - 1, 1) + 3d_c(t, 1), (t > 1) \end{cases} \tag{2}$$

$$g_c(t, 2) = min \begin{cases} g_c(t - 2, 1) + d_c(t - 1, 2) + 2d_c(t, 2) \\ g_c(t - 1, 1) + 2d_c(t, 2) \\ g_c(t, 1) + 2d_c(t, 2) \end{cases} \tag{3}$$

Recurrence formula $(\tau \geq 3)$:

$$g_c(t, \tau) = min \begin{cases} g_c(t - 2, \tau - 1) + d_c(t - 1, \tau) + 2d_c(t, \tau) \\ g_c(t - 1, \tau - 1) + 2d_c(t, \tau) \\ g_c(t - 1, \tau - 2) + d_c(t, \tau - 1) + 2d_c(t, \tau) \end{cases} \tag{4}$$

Using the above formulas, the minimum accumulated distance $g_c(T, T)$ is calculated. To reduce the effect of difference number of motion vectors, this value is normalized as follows:

$$G_c(T, T) = \frac{g_c(T, T)}{3T}. \tag{5}$$

For all template patterns, the minimum accumulated distances are calculated and they are sorted in ascending order. The system outputs the character class corresponding to the pattern with the minimum distance as a recognition result. Moreover, the character classes for the 2nd, 3rd, 4th and 5th minimum distance are also output as recognition candidates.

4   Experimental Results

Our system was developed by Microsoft Visual Studio C#. Figure 2 shows the screenshot of the system when one of the Japanese hiragana characters is entered. The left large window displays trajectory pattern of the handwritten character and the middle large window shows the corresponding recognition result. The four small windows on the right represent the 2nd, 3rd, 4th, and 5th candidates.

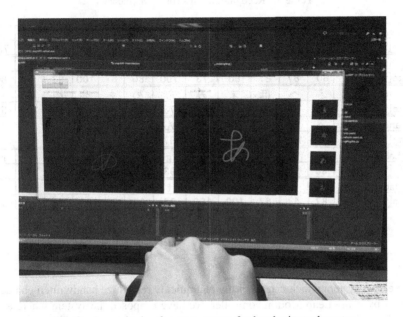

Fig. 2. An example of system output for handwritten character

In our experiment, 5 test users registered 46 Japanese hiragana characters and 26 lower-case letters of the alphabet as template patterns and they also wrote each character three times as test patterns. Table 1 shows the recognition rates for the test patterns. In total, a high average recognition rate of 86.7 % were obtained. However, some conflictions occurred for several patterns. The error-prone types are described below the table. Since each character is represented by one stroke even if the character consists of 2 or more strokes, it is difficult to distinguish patterns which differs only in the connection part of strokes. For this reason, the input patterns "e and t" tend to be misrecognized each other.

Next, we will discuss about the processing time. The average processing time from a user finishes writing a character till the recognition result is displayed, was 196 ms by using a PC (CPU: Intel Core-i7-4796, 3.60 GHz and Memory: 32.0 GB). Therefore, the system can operate in real time.

Finally, to evaluate the usability of the system, we heard opinions of the test users. The obtained opinions are as follows:

- Response time is fast.
- Since the system can register shape and writing order of input characters personally, the recognition rate tends to be high. However, the registration process is tedious task.
- Thumb gets tired as many characters are entered.
- It is difficult to get the timing of the start point of character input.

Table 1. Recognition rates for each character

Japanese	あ	い	う	え	お	か	き	く	け	こ	さ	し	す
rate[%]	100	87	67	87	100	100	100	93	87	60	67	87	73
Japanese	せ	そ	た	ち	つ	て	と	な	に	ぬ	ね	の	は
rate[%]	93	80	87	87	80	73	100	80	87	100	93	73	80
Japanese	ひ	ふ	へ	ほ	ま	み	む	め	も	や	ゆ	よ	ら
rate[%]	93	100	93	100	80	93	73	87	100	87	93	100	53
Japanese	り	る	れ	ろ	わ	を	ん						
rate[%]	93	100	100	93	100	93	87						
Alphabet	a	b	c	d	e	f	g	h	i	j	k	l	m
rate[%]	80	60	93	87	60	73	93	93	93	93	100	93	73
Alphabet	n	o	p	q	r	s	t	u	v	w	x	y	z
rate[%]	87	87	47	67	100	100	73	87	93	93	93	87	93

Types of conflict : "う, ら", "こ, て, z", "さ, せ", "a, q", "b, p", "e, t"

5 Conclusion

To develop a system which can precisely and quickly recognize handwritten characters in the air by using Leap Motion controller, we have proposed the system where a user can register characters as template patterns in advance, the input characters are segmented properly by pre-defined gestures, and they are recognized by DP matching method. In our experiments, for 46 Japanese hiragana characters and 26 alphabets, a high average recognition rate of 86.7 % and a short average processing time of 196 ms were obtained. Therefore, it should be suitable for practical use. However, we have to improve the system according to the test users' opinions.

References

1. Kratz, S., Aumi, T.: AirAuth: evaluating in-air hand gestures for authentication. In: MobileHCI 2014 (2014)
2. Bashir, M., Scharfenberg, G., Kempf, J.: Person authentication by handwriting in air using a biometric smart pen device. In: BIOSIG 2011, pp. 219–226 (2011)
3. Vikram, S., Li, L., Russell, S.: Handwriting and gestures in the air, recognizing on the fly. In: CHI 2013 Extended Abstracts (2013)
4. Leap Motion. https://www.leapmotion.com/. Accessed 25 March 2015

Comfort Analysis in EVA Reachable Envelope Based on Human-Spacesuit Integrated Biomechanical Modeling

Xiaodong Wang, Chunhui Wang[(⊠)], Zheng Wang, and Hao Li

National Key Laboratory of Human Factors Engineering,
China Astronaut Research and Training Center, Beijing 100094, China
{sjtuwxd,chunhui_89,wzhteana}@163.com

Abstract. We proposed a biomechanical framework for modeling human-spacesuit arm interaction while carrying out EVAs. In the model, there is detailed definition of spacesuit joint rotations, included spacesuit joint stiffness model and a delicate human arm musculoskeletal model in the Anybody Modeling System. The framework is able to predict human joint torque, muscle forces and joint reactions in various positions and postures while wearing spacesuit. Based on the predicted maximum muscle force, we made an evaluation of the comfort scale in various positions in the reach envelope. The predicted most comfortable area was compared to measured most comfortable area for model prediction validation.

Keywords: EVA, spacesuit · Reach envelope · Comfort · Biomechanical modeling

1 Background

Humans have explored the space for decades since Gagarin's first spacewalk and Armstrong's first step on the moon. During the exploration, many missions are conducted through EVAs, such as space station construction and maintenance, scientific experiments and sample collection. As astronauts are faced with extreme environment in space, appropriate protection is necessary by wearing spacesuit. However, the heavy and pressured spacesuit design also restricts the mobility of astronaut, making astronaut working within a smaller envelope and conquering additional resistance to keep posture [1, 2]. Till now, most studies adopt the experimental method of kinematic measure for determining EVA reach envelope and most comfortable area. Only few studies tried using model-based methods to handle work envelope issues. A kinematic model using D-H parameters in robotics and Monte Carlo method is introduced by researchers in ACC (China Astronaut Research and Training Center) to predict EVA work envelope [3]. And the comfort is first evaluated by Schmidt using dynamic modeling method and relative joint torque criterion [4].

Biomechanical modeling method offers a quantified solution to ergonomic assessment of human joint and muscle workload by calculating joint torques and muscle activation [5]. Since there are few studies on comfort analysis in EVA reach

C. Stephanidis (Ed.): HCII 2015 Posters, Part I, CCIS 528, pp. 539–545, 2015.
DOI: 10.1007/978-3-319-21380-4_92

envelope using biomechanical modeling method, we propose a human-spacesuit integrated modeling method for handling this issue. The predicted reach envelope and its comfort are compared with former experimental results for validation.

2 Method

2.1 Kinematic Model of Spacesuit Arm

Typical kinematic model of spacesuit includes seven joints, which are very similar to the joint definition of human arm, except that the joints in spacesuit arm are in certain serial order and position while some human joints sequence is just defined that way. The joints in the model correspond to certain bearing or soft joint in spacesuit arm. Segments contain spacesuit arm mass, center of mass, moment of inertia and other properties are connected by these joints, as is shown in Fig. 1.

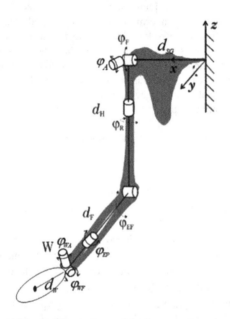

Fig. 1 Kinematic model of spacesuit arm

2.2 Joint Stiffness Measurement and Modeling

Soft-designed joint has a tendency of bounding to its neutral position when it is bent, that is the reason why astronaut in spacesuit has difficulty keeping a non-neutral posture for two long. The tendency is described as joint stiffness which usually works as resistance. Many technique solutions were proposed to measure the joint stiffness, such as RSST (Robotic Space Suit Tester), 'fisher-scale' method and so on. In our study, we used self-motored isokinetic test method to measure spacesuit joint stiffness, which was a working mode in BTE Primus Rehabilitation System and its working theory is the same as 'fish-scale' method except that it bends spacesuit joint automatically.

The measured stiffness shows hysteresis characteristics, which follows different trajectory for flexion and extension, as in shown in Fig. 2. We proposed using neural network optimized Preisach hysteresis model to describe the stiffness that is related to both the current joint angle and angle histories. Because angle histories were not available for comfort analysis, we adopted a simplified three-order polynomial regression to model hysteresis. The stiffness model defined the dynamic property of spacesuit joint.

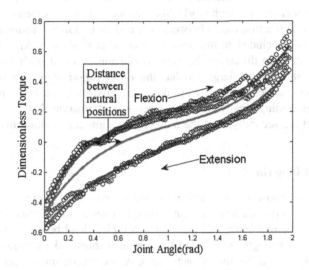

Fig. 2 Hysteresis of elbow joint stiffness

2.3 Human Musculoskeletal System Modeling

We modeled the human arm musculoskeletal system in AnyBody using available bone, joint, muscle and joint reaction definitions [6]. These definitions were based on hundreds of anthropometric and anatomic researches of human musculoskeletal system. We utilized Hill type three-element muscle model to describe the feature that muscle capability changes with muscle length and contracting velocity. As human musculoskeletal system is a redundant system that is believed to contract muscles in an optimal way, we chose the criterion that minimizes that maximum muscle activation as the optimization goal for the inverse dynamic analysis. Considering that the muscle with the maximum activation is most inclined to be fatigued, the criterion postpones muscle fatigue at most. Finally, the inverse dynamic analysis solved all the muscle forces and joint reactions using optimization methods.

2.4 Human Spacesuit Arm Integration

We implemented human spacesuit arm integration using the methods widely used in interface modeling between human and exoskeleton [7]. The integration can be divided into two parts: kinematic and dynamic integration.

In kinematic integration, human hand and spacesuit glove were connected by fixed soft joint which constrains six degrees of freedoms. Human and spacesuit elbow position were also constrained to make sure that human elbow and spacesuit elbow center stay close. Soft joint was included because it allows minimal error which simulates the contact between spacesuit and human skin. By kinematic integration, spacesuit arm moves consistently with human arm.

Astronaut moves spacesuit arm with his own arm by reaction forces between each other, and this is what dynamic integration does. Virtual muscles were introduced to form the reaction element, which works like reaction forces. This method was recently used for predicting reaction forces between foot and ground in gait analysis [8]. Virtual muscles were also included in the inverse dynamic analysis as unknown forces like other muscles. A main difference between virtual muscles and other muscles is that their force capabilities are large so that the optimization algorithm handles them inferior to other muscles. Generally speaking, the algorithm can be divided into two steps for understanding: firstly, find the reaction combination that will produce the minimal activation; secondly, find the muscle activation combination that is minimal.

2.5 Comfort Criteria

In our study, we chose muscle activation and relative joint torque as our comfort criteria. It has been proved that endurance time inclines as muscle load declines. And endurance time changes little after arriving at a typical load between ten and twenty percent of muscle strength, which can be seen as a threshold for comfort. And this percent definition is exactly muscle activation. As maximum muscle activation is the bottleneck and it determines comfort, we chose it as our criterion.

2.6 Reach Envelope and Comfort Prediction

Based on the integrated biomechanical model, we traversed all the arm postures according to the kinematic model of spacesuit arm and its joint RoM. In the simulation, average parameters of subjects such as muscle strength scale, height, weight, upper arm and lower arm length were adopted. The joints included in traverse included φ_F, φ_A, φ_R and φ_{EF} as these joints determine the position of hand while other joints only change hand orientation and position little. The resolution is set to 10° for all the joint angles. A total of over 10000 postures were evaluated using the integrated model, returning the hand position, maximum muscle activation and joint torques of shoulder, elbow and wrist joint. With these data, we determined which space was reachable and then determined the minimal muscle activation index and minimal composite index based on relative joint torque. Reach envelope was then modified by collision detection and elimination between suit glove and spacesuit trunk. Minimal index in a space was chosen because there are several postures for a given space or even give point, among these astronauts will choose the most comfortable one automatically. Finally, comfort was evaluated with the minimal criterion index.

3 Experiment

3.1 Subjects

Nine subjects participated in the reach envelope and comfort evaluation experiment with height of 172±7 cm and weight of 70±12 kg

3.2 Data Collection

Reflective markers were placed on spacesuit glove for hand position capture with NDI Optotrak when subjects moved horizontally and vertically layer by layer in the reachable area. Reach envelope was then determined with the captured positions.

When assessing comfort, subjects were firstly required to give three heights that were comfortable: lowest, medium and highest. For every height, a horizontal supporting bar was placed at a comfortable distance from subjects to relieve the effect of gravity. Subjects were required to move his hand along the bar, finding the most comfortable left and right boundaries.

4 Result and Validation

4.1 Comfort Analysis Using Different Criteria

Two different criteria were proposed for comfort assessment, one based on maximum muscle activation and the other based on relative joint torque of the total arm. We compared the result on the horizontal plane where $z = 212$ mm, as is shown in the following picture. The region in the middle of every figure is the predicted reach envelope. The area with the smaller index is more comfortable compared to those with larger index. It is shown that the comfortable areas using the two different criteria are very close, except that their scales are different.

4.2 Most Comfortable Area Validation

In the experiment, subjects were required to find the most comfortable area on the lowest, medium and highest horizontal plane. After taking an average of the measured areas, we determined the plane where z axis is respectively −82 mm, 34 mm and 200 mm as the lowest, medium and highest horizontal plane. We showed the measured most comfortable area in the comfort contour map predicted using max muscle activation criterion as follows. The measured most comfortable area (white area) was within the predicted most comfortable area which validated the model.

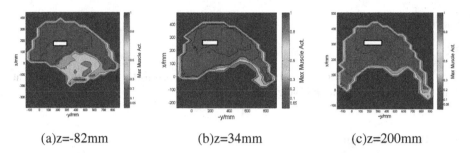

(a)z=-82mm   (b)z=34mm   (c)z=200mm

Fig. 3 Predicted comfort scale and measured most comfortable area

5 Discussion

Considering that fatigue is usually produced in muscle with maximum activation, max muscle activation criterion is a reasonable physiological comfort scale. Based on the max muscle activation criterion, we compared the predicted comfort contour map and the measured most comfortable area for model validation. The measured most comfortable area is within the predicted most comfortable area. But it is not in the center; instead it is near to the body and goes left. This is reasonable considering that subjects evaluated the comfort not only according to the muscle feeling, but also according to contact feeling of pressure between spacesuit and human arm, which is related to the reaction element used in dynamic integration. The model prediction is closely related to anthropometric parameters in human model, which may differ a little from subjects. Besides, we adopted the regression polynomial of flexion and abduction for the elbow and shoulder respectively in the simulation. However, when subjects moved left and right searching for the most comfortable area, the stiffness trajectory would approach the medium regression as is shown in Fig. 3. So the neutral position where stiffness was zero and usually most comfortable would have a bias of about 12°. All these factors contribute to the offset of the most comfortable area.

6 Conclusion

Human-spacesuit integrated biomechanical modeling is an effective tool for determining reach envelope and comfort in it. Generally speaking, the contributions of our work to ergonomic assessment of spacesuit are summarized as following: firstly, we proposed and realized a complete biomechanical modeling framework for human-spacesuit integration; Secondly, we proposed predicting comfort scale in the reachable envelope using quantified method based on predicted muscle activations instead of subjective ratings alone. The comfort-scale assessment in the reach envelope is just a case illustration of the applicability of human-spacesuit arm integration model in an inverse biomechanical framework. The model can be used for modeling realistic operational tasks when motion data is collected, making work envelope analysis of astronauts in EVAs related to operation. In future, the model is supposed to include detailed surface definition of spacesuit and human skin for more delicate simulation.

Acknowledgments. This work was supported by National Basic Research Program of China (NO. 2011CB711000), and advanced space medico-engineering research project of China (No: 2011SY5405002).

References

1. Newman, D., Schmidt, P., Rahn, D.: Modeling the extravehicular mobility unit (EMU) space suit: physiological implications for extravehicular activity (EVA). SAE Technical paper (2000)
2. Ross, A.: Z-1 prototype space suit testing summary. In: 43rd International Conference on Environmental Systems (2013)
3. Si, H., Liao, Q., Zhang, W.: Monte Carlo based predictive method for determining work envelope of spacesuit in EVA operation. Mechatron. Autom. Contr. Syst. **237**, 583–590 (2014)
4. Schmidt, P. B.: An investigation of space suit mobility with applications to EVA operations. Massachusetts Institute of Technology (2001)
5. Chaffin, D.B.: The evolving role of biomechanics in prevention of overexertion injuries. Ergonomics **52**(1), 3–14 (2009)
6. Damsgaard, M., Rasmussen, J., Christensen, S.T., et al.: Analysis of musculoskeletal systems in the anybody modeling system. Simul. Model. Pract. Theory **14**(8), 1100–1111 (2006)
7. Cho, K., Kim, Y., Yi, D., et al.: Analysis and evaluation of a combined human–exoskeleton model under two different constraints condition. In: Proceedings of the International Summit on Human Simulation (2012)
8. Jung, Y., Jung, M., Lee, K., et al.: Ground reaction force estimation using an insole-type pressure mat and joint kinematics during walking. J. Biomech. **47**(11), 2693–2699 (2014)

Interaction Design for Navigating Virtual Spaces–An Example by Using Kinect

Yen-Liang Wu[✉]

Digital Media Design, Asia University, Taichung, Taiwan
aw@aisa.edu.tw

Abstract. In the physical space, we use our feet to navigate different views of space and turn our head to look up and down to observe the ground and ceiling. Therefore, the objective of the study is to establish a 3D motion sensing spatial navigation system and investigate 3D interaction designs for navigating virtual spaces. The interaction design for the navigation system were divided three parts: (a.) walking by foot to move forward, (b.) turning the shoulder to rotate direction, (c.) tilting head up and down to look up and down. In the usability test, all the subjects can utilize the interactions to navigate the virtual space. A set of preliminary motion sensing design principles for 3D navigation have also been identified in the study.

Keywords: 3D navigation · Kinect · Virtual space · Motion-sensing design

1 Introduction

Virtual reality (VR) systems allow users to travel within a virtual space. These virtual travels could be adjusted for distance and provide various traveling modes of different speeds such as walking, driving, and flying [1]. VR technology also provides architects with a media for the general public to experience their design spaces in advance. In the past, however, those who wish to navigate virtual spaces would have to use keyboards, mouse, gamepad, joystick and other input devices. Younger demographics who grew up with video games may be familiar with these input devices, but people with little experience in using them might find them difficult to use [5]. In the past, more intuitive mechanical, optical, magnetic and 3D tracking and positioning technologies have been applied in interactive 3D navigation. However, these devices are expensive and difficult to setup [1], so most of these projects remained in the lab and were unable to achieve the commercial popularity enjoyed by game consoles such as Nintendo Wii equipped with the WiiMote motion sensing technology. Although Wii has initiated the development of motion sensing technologies and encouraged Sony and Microsoft to develop their own motion sensing devices in the form of Move and Kinect, there are still differences between these devices. For example, users of Kinect would not require any controller unlike those using WiiMote or Move. Kinect users simply use their entire body as the interactive input. Hence, Kinect has provided users with a more natural method of interacting with virtual spaces, opening more possibilities [4].

Despite these achievements, we navigate in the real space by using our legs to walk and change our directions, and turn our heads to move our eyes to focus on different

C. Stephanidis (Ed.): HCII 2015 Posters, Part I, CCIS 528, pp. 546–551, 2015.
DOI: 10.1007/978-3-319-21380-4_93

areas that we want to see [3]. Is it possible to use Kinect as a motion sensing input device and allow users to navigate virtual spaces as though they are in the real space? Therefore, this study aims to establish a 3D motion sensing spatial navigation system and investigate motion sensing designs for navigating virtual spaces.

2 Related Work

There are several research projects [5–7] to explore the interaction design by using motion-sensing device Kinect. Roupé et al. [5] has investigated virtual space navigational issues using Kinect. Their interaction design for the navigation system utilized body forward and backward to control the movement of camera and utilized the shoulders to turn left and right. They also utilized the gestures to operate the model changing.

The another project by Dam et al. [6] proposed several navigation and selection techniques for navigating the virtual spaces and to test which techniques is easier to operator for user. Their interaction designs for navigation are: (a.) Virtual Foot DPad-calculated the distance from one of the feet to the torso. When the distance reached the certain number, the movement will be triggered. (b.) Dail DPads-utilized the virtual hand to touch the virtual control pad like the game pad on the screen. The user utilized the hands to navigate the virtual space. (c.) Virtual circle-based on the concept of controlling a joystick, the system recorded the initial stand position of the user. When the user stood forward, the movement forward of camera will be occurred. The project also utilized the shoulders turn to control the movement direction.

However, real world navigation behavior that involves tilting the head up and down could not be used in their system. It would not be easier to navigate the ceiling. Hence, the spatial navigation system we have developed in this study achieved an improvement over this inadequacy.

3 Methodology and Steps

3.1 Interaction Analysis and Design

The motion sensing and navigation system designed for this research is based on the fact that people would navigate real space by walking and look at different areas by turning their heads and moving their eyes in order to observe surroundings. Hence, the motion sensing and navigation system we developed has been designed according to the movements of our limbs and bodies as we navigate the real world. Motion was divided into 3 navigational mechanisms of (a.) Moving of the legs Fig. 1-a; (b.) turning left and right Fig. 1-b; (c.) moving the head and visual focus up and down Fig. 1-c. Kinect could be used to track the location and rotational angle of 20 physical points on the user, including the head, shoulders, hands, and feet. Hence, we would use the same principle, tracking changes of these locations to manipulate (dolly in, pan right/left, and tilt up/down) the cameras in virtual space.

Fig. 1. The interaction design for navigation (a): walking movement, (b): turning shoulders to control direction, (c): moving the head to focus up and down

3.2 Implementation

The interactive design of the spatial navigation system described above utilized the game engine Unity3D as a development tool and based on the example Unity 3D project created by RF Solutions [8]. Kinect SDK 1.8 for Windows was used to establish a link between Kinect and the computer. The motion sensing navigation system was established that allows the user to walk on the spot to control the Avatar's movements (based on speed of the feet moving, while the speed was high, the Avatar will move faster), turn user's shoulders left and right to change the direction of the Avatar (detected which z value of left and right shoulder is bigger), and tilt user's heads up and down to tilt the camera at the back of the Avatar to tilt up and down (detected the rotation of head).

3.3 Usability Testing

Tests in this study were mainly motion sensing trials that involved different virtual space navigational tasks. The think aloud testing method of cognitive experiments (Ericsson and Simon, 1993) was utilized in order to understand the cognitive stages of the subject when using this system, confirm that the motion sensing design could be intuitively learned and operated without any prior instruction or directions, and identify any minor design details that need to be improved or adjusted.

   Subjects: 4 persons that have no prior experience of using Kinect motion sensing
   Display: 80 inch projector screen
   VR interaction and navigational trials:
   Task 1. Walk in a straight line – the subjects were requested to walk in a straight to collide all of the red balls. While the Avatar collided the ball, the ball will be destroyed Fig. 2. This trial tests for problems in movements.

Fig. 2. Walk in a straight line to collide the red balls (Color figure online)

Fig. 3. Turn left and right to collide the blue balls (Color figure online)

Task 2. Turn left and right – the subjects were requested to walk and turn their shoulders to turn the direction and to collide all blue balls which were arrange to some corners Fig. 3. This trial tests for problems during turning.

Task 3. Look up and down – the subjects were requested to look up and down their focus on the all yellow balls which were arranged between the ground and ceiling. They must utilize the yellow cross to collide the yellow balls and to destroy them Fig. 4. The subjects were tested to see if they could see these balls easily in order to test for problems when tilting the head up and down.

4 Discussion

In the usability test, all the subjects can utilize the interactions to navigate the virtual space. We try to summary the some findings from the usability test. They can easily move straight forward by walking on the spot and rotate direction by turning their

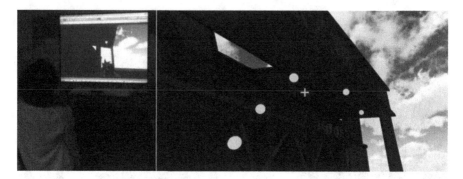

Fig. 4. Look up and down by utilizing yellow cross to collide the yellow balls (Color figure online)

shoulders. But they felt the movement speed too slow while navigating in the virtual space. On the contrary, they would feel tired if they walked faster. From the test of look up and down, they can easy to look up and down in a small vertical angle of view. But we find all of users have the difficult to look up the yellow balls if the elevation angle is high for the subjects. They should struggle to tilt their spines up for colliding the objective ball. The interaction designs for navigating in the virtual space also have an insufficiency in movement forward only. The users cannot move backward. They should turn their direction 180° degrees to move back.

5 Conclusion

A preliminary virtual spatial navigation system has been developed in this study that allows the user to use Kinect motion sensing to walk, turn, and look up and down. A set of preliminary motion sensing design principles have also been identified in this study during actual testing by the users. For example, (1.)Walking on the spot to control movement of the body, with the speed of the steps taken being used to determine the walking speed in the virtual space. (2.) Turning the shoulder left or right to control the movement direction in the virtual space. (3.) Tilting the head up and down to tilt the visual focus in the VR space. These three basic design principles for virtual spatial navigation would also be closer to actual navigational behaviors in the real world.

References

1. Bowman, D.A., Kruijff, E., Laviola, J.J., Poupyrev, I.: 3D User Interfaces-Theory and Practice. Addison-Wesley Professional, Redwood city (2004)
2. Ericsson, K.A., Simon, H.A.: Protocol analysis: verbal reports as data. The MIT Press, revised edition (1993)
3. Corbusier, L.: Towards a New Architecture. Dover Publications, New York (1985)
4. Loguidice, B., Loguidice, C.: My Xbox: Xbox 360, Kinect and Xbox LIVE, Que Publishing (2012)

5. Roupé, M., Bosch-Sijtsema, P., Johansson, M.: Interactive navigation interface for Virtual Reality using the human body. Comput. Environ. Urban Syst. **43**, 42–50 (2014)
6. Dam, P.F., Braz, P., Raposo, A.B.: A study of navigation and selection techniques in virtual environments using microsoft kinect®. In: 15th International Conference on Human-Computer Interaction – HCI International 2013. Las Vegas, NV, USA, July 2013
7. Boulos, M.K.N., Blanchard, B., Walker, J.M.C., Tripathy, R.G.-O.A.: Web GIS in practice X: a microsoft kinect natural user interface for google earth navigation. Int. J. Health Geogr., **10**(1) (2011)
8. RF Solutions, Kinect with MS-SDK. https://www.assetstore.unity3d.com/en/#!/content/7747

Natural User Interface for Board Games Using Lenticular Display and Leap Motion

Kazuhisa Yanaka[✉] and Daichi Ishiguro

Kanagawa Institute of Technology, 1030 Shimo-Ogino, Atsugi-Shi,
Kanagawa, Japan
yanaka@ic.kanagawa-it.ac.jp,
blackstone94113@gmail.com

Abstract. Various board games, including chess, are now played on PCs, but they differ from actual board games because a mouse is typically used to move the pieces. Moving a piece by pinching it with one's fingers, as in actual board games, is desirable to increase a player's sense of reality. That the pieces look as if they were floating in the air is desirable so that the players can pinch them easily. Thus, we used an autostereoscopic display in which a lenticular lens is used to cover the liquid crystal display of a PC. As a result, each piece of the board game looks as if it were popping out of the 3D display screen, without the need for the player to wear special glasses. In addition, we use a Leap Motion Controller, a motion-capture device that is particularly suitable for capturing the position and movement of fingers so that a computer can recognize where in the 3D space the fingers are and whether the fingers are pinching a piece or not. Therefore, the user can operate the piece easily and intuitively.

Keywords: Natural user interface · Board game · Lenticular display · Leap motion controller

1 Introduction

Board games, such as chess, have been popular since ancient times. Various board games are now played on PCs, but these games considerably differ from actual board games in the sense that an artificial input device such as a mouse is typically used to move the pieces. Moving a piece by pinching it with fingers, as in actual board games, is an ideal interface to increase the sense of reality of the player. A desirable feature is that the pieces look as if they were floating in the air so that the players can pinch them easily. Thus, we build a new human interface that consists of a Windows PC, an autostereoscopic 3D display, and a leap motion controller [1]; the third device is a 3D motion-capture apparatus specialized for human fingers. A chess player can operate a virtual piece that looks as if it were floating in the air by a gesture of pinch-ing and moving it by hand directly. The configuration of our system is shown in Fig. 1.

© Springer International Publishing Switzerland 2015
C. Stephanidis (Ed.): HCII 2015 Posters, Part I, CCIS 528, pp. 552–557, 2015.
DOI: 10.1007/978-3-319-21380-4_94

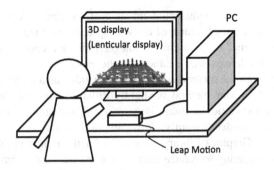

Fig. 1. System configuration

2 3D Display

Using 3D displays is highly effective to improve the usability of 3D games because binocular parallax provides an important clue to obtain depth information.

Stereoscopic image display methods [2] are roughly classified into two. One is the method in which a user wears stereo glasses such as polarized or liquid-crystal shutter glasses. The other is the autostereoscopic method in which a user can see stereo images without needing to wear special glasses. Although the latter method has a limitation in that the image tends to be indistinct when the amount of popping out becomes large, its advantage is that it does not require special glasses. Among various autostereoscopic methods, the lenticular display is adopted in the present study because it displays bright and high-quality 3D images. The simplest lenticular method can be produced by placing a lenticular sheet, which consists of an array of minute semi-cylindrical lenses, on a liquid crystal display (LCD), as shown in Fig. 2(a). How-ever, a moiré pattern is visible. If the lenticular sheet is slightly slanted to the LCD, as shown in Fig. 2(b), the moiré becomes less visible. This condition is known as the slanted lenticular method [3]. In this study, we use a ready-made 24-inch 3D display (Newsight Japan NSJ-MVLL24AD3, 1920 × 1080 pixels) with a built-in slanted lenticular lens.

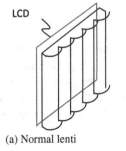

(a) Normal lenti

(b) Slanted lenticular display

Fig. 2. Lenticular displays

Until several years ago, substantial initial cost to manufacture a custom-made lenticular lens was necessary because of the widespread belief that the ratio of the lens pitch and pixel pitch had to be a simple integer ratio. However, using inexpensive ready-made lenticular lenses was enabled by the emergence of the fractional view method [4, 5]. Although the method adopted in this study can also be classified into the fractional view method, our method is slightly different from the original fractional view method in that the lenticular image is synthesized from a finite number (e.g., eight or sixteen) of images rendered from various camera positions.

We use an Open Graphics Library (OpenGL) for the rendering. OpenGL has the function of double buffering to reduce flicker. In our system, this function is used for real-time rendering of multiple-view lenticular images, as shown in Fig. 3. A len-ticular image is synthesized from the images read from the back buffer because the images are composed of pixels. Our method is fast because a time-consuming process such as ray tracing is unnecessary. The obtained lenticular image is displayed on the LCD.

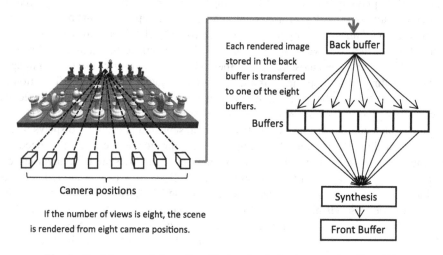

Fig. 3. Real-time rendering of multi-view lenticular image using OpenGL

3   Acquisition of Position and Shape of Hand

In addition, the PC has to know where in the 3D space the fingers are and whether the fingers are pinching a displayed piece or not. We use a Leap Motion Controller, a motion-capture device particularly suitable for capturing the position and motion of hands and fingers. Unlike using a mouse, no hand contact or touching is necessary because the 3D position data of the fingers are calculated from two images captured with two monochromatic infrared cameras.

3.1 Display of Hand Position and Grip Decision

Microsoft Visual C ++ and Leap Motion SDK 2.0 were used to develop our appli-cation program. Displaying the current position of the player's hand in a way is nec-essary so that the player can pick up the intended piece among many pieces. In this system, the location of the palm is acquired as the return value of a member function "palmPosition()" of the Hand class. Whether the fingers are grasping a piece or not is determined by acquiring the return value of a member function "pinchStrength()" of the Hand class. The return value expresses the degree of the opening and closing motion of the thumb and index finger.

When a hand is above the board, the square directly below it becomes red, as shown in Fig. 4(a). When the hand is closed to pick up a piece, the square becomes green and the squares of the possible destinations of the piece become blue, as shown in Fig. 4(b). Possible destinations differ depending on the type of piece. However, the actual destination of the piece is not limited to the colored squares so that the player can easily correct any wrong move. Therefore, the user can easily operate the piece.

(a) When the hand is open   (b) When the hand is closed

Fig. 4. Coloring of the square directly under the palm

3.2 Processing When a Piece Is Placed on the Board

3.2.1 Adjustment of the Position of the Piece

If the piece is placed away from the center of the square, the player will have difficulty recognizing the square on which the piece is located. Therefore, the piece is auto-matically moved to the center of the square.

3.2.2 Processing When a Piece is Moved to a Square on Which Another Piece is Placed

If the color (black or white) of the piece moved to the square differs from that of the piece that has been placed on the square, the enemy's piece is moved outside of the board, as shown in Fig. 5(a). If the color of the piece moved to the square is the same as that of the piece that has been placed on the square, the piece moved is automatically returned to the former position, as shown in Fig. 5(b), because such a move is not allowed in chess.

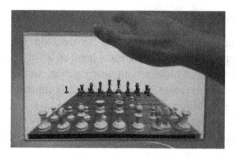
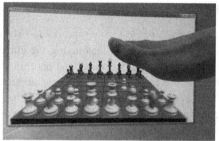

(a) When opponent's piece is taken.   (b) Friend's piece cannot be taken.

Fig. 5. When a piece is moved to an occupied place

4 Experimental Results and Discussions

The devices used in the experiment are listed in Table 1.

Table 1. Devices used in the experiment

	Name of device	Developer
CPU	Intel Core i7-3770 Processor	Intel
GPU	GeForce GF-GTX750Ti-EL2GHD	NVIDIA
3D display (lenticular)	NSJ-MVLL24AD3	Newsight Japan
Motion capture device	Leap Motion	Leap Motion

Our experimental system worked as designed. Since the board and pieces were au-tostereoscopic and each piece could be picked and moved with fingers, a high sense of presence was achieved although no force feedback existed. When an external GPU was used, a practically sufficient frame rate was obtained even when the resolution of the image was 720 × 1280, as shown in Table 2.

Table 2. Average frame rate (frames per second)

Resolution	HD Graphics 4000		GeForce GTX 750 Ti	
	8 views	16 views	8 views	16 views
720 × 1280	10.3	6.5	21.6	14.4
360 × 640	27.7	17.3	38.5	30.0

At present, precisely matching the position of a virtual piece displayed on 3D space and the position of the actual human hand is difficult for several reasons. First, the amount of popping out is not large enough because the 3D image is blurred when the popping out becomes large. Therefore, increasing the space where the virtual space and the real space overlap is difficult. Second, the position of the virtual piece changes slightly in the 3D space when the player's viewpoint moves. The probable reason is that the 3D image consists of a finite number of rays emitted from a finite number of LCD pixels, in addition to the problem that the calibration is difficult. Therefore, a 3D display system with a slightly higher density of ray is required. In particular, the vertical displacement seems large because this system does not provide vertical parallax up to now. This problem can be solved if integral imaging, which has not only horizontal but also vertical parallax, is adopted in the future.

5 Conclusion

We have developed a new NUI for digital board games, such as chess, in which a lenticular display and a motion-capture device are combined. To view pieces that have been created with 3DCG and look as if they were floating in the air, players need not wear special stereo glasses because a lenticular display, which is a kind of autostereoscopic display, is used instead. In our system, the position information of the player's fingers is obtained by the 3D motion-capture device called Leap Motion Controller. Whether the fingers are grasping a piece or not is also detected by the device. Therefore, players can move pieces naturally and intuitively with their fingers in the 3D space although no force feedback exists in this system. Therefore, a realistic operation that feels close to that of an analog board game has been achieved.

In the future, when the amount of popping out becomes large and the alignment between the 3D display and motion-capture device becomes more accurate, more natural and intuitive operations of pieces will be possible, and the completeness of the game will increase. The results of this study are considered to be applicable to other board games such as Shogi, Go, and Othello.

Acknowledgments. This study was supported by the Japan Society for the Promotion of Science, KAKENHI Grant No. 25330244.

References

1. Leap Motion Official Site. https://www.leapmotion.com/
2. Holliman, N.S., Dodgson, N.A., Favalora, G.E., Pockett, L.: Three-dimensional displays: a review and applications analysis. IEEE Trans. Broadcast. **57**(2), 362–371 (2011)
3. Berkel, C.V., Clarke, J.: Characterization and optimization of 3D-LCD module de-sign. Proc. SPIE **3012**, 179–187 (1997)
4. Ishii, M.: Fractional view 3D display. In: Proceedings of 3D Image Conference 2004, pp. 65–68 (2004) (in Japanese)
5. Ishii, M.: Spatial Image by Fractional View Display, ITE Technical Report vol. 30, no. 58, pp. 33–38 (2006) (in Japanese)

A Mouse-Like Hands-Free Gesture Technique for Two-Dimensional Pointing

Yusaku Yokouchi and Hiroshi Hosobe$^{(\boxtimes)}$

Faculty of Computer and Information Sciences, Hosei University,
3-7-2 Kajino-cho, Koganei-shi, Tokyo 184-8584, Japan
hosobe@acm.org

Abstract. The use of motion sensing for input devices is becoming increasingly popular. In particular, hands-free gesture input is promising for such devices. We propose a mouse-like hands-free gesture technique for two-dimensional pointing. It is characterized as follows: (1) a user horizontally moves his/her hand to position a cursor shown on a vertical screen; (2) the user activates cursor movement by opening his/her hand, and deactivates it by clenching; (3) the user performs target selection by "clicking" in the air with his/her index finger; (4) the user is assisted in quick but precise cursor movement by automatic acceleration. We present results of a user study that experimentally compared the mouse-like technique with a tablet-like one.

1 Introduction

The use of motion sensing for input devices such as the Nintendo Wii remote and Microsoft Kinect is becoming increasingly popular. In particular, hands-free gesture input is promising for such devices. Research efforts have often been devoted to ray casting and its variants [5] that are pointing techniques based on the sensed directions of users' hands or fingers. However, a different approach can also be taken for pointing by using the sensed positions of users' hands or fingers, that is, mapping the sensed positions to two-dimensional (2D) or three-dimensional (3D) coordinates in virtual spaces [4]. Along this line, previous research on 3D pointing [3] compared a tablet-like absolute positioning-based technique with a mouse-like relative one, and experimentally showed that the tablet-like one was better.

We propose a mouse-like hands-free gesture technique for 2D pointing. It is characterized as follows:

1. A user horizontally moves his/her hand to position a cursor shown on a vertical screen (Fig. 1(a));
2. The user activates cursor movement by opening his/her hand, and deactivates it by clenching;
3. The user performs target selection by "clicking" in the air with his/her index finger (Fig. 1(b));

© Springer International Publishing Switzerland 2015
C. Stephanidis (Ed.): HCII 2015 Posters, Part I, CCIS 528, pp. 558–563, 2015.
DOI: 10.1007/978-3-319-21380-4_95

4. The user is assisted in quick but precise cursor movement by automatic acceleration.

We performed a user study to experimentally compare the mouse-like technique with a tablet-like one. We studied eight subjects who performed target selection tasks. A two-way ANOVA on the experimental results indicated a significant difference between the two techniques. Six out of the eight subjects answered that the mouse-like technique was easier to use.

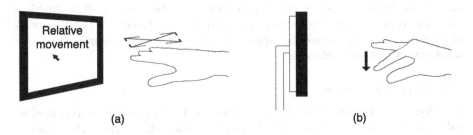

(a)   (b)

Fig. 1. Mouse-like pointing technique.

2   Proposed Technique

This section proposes a mouse-like hands-free gesture technique for 2D pointing.

2.1   Cursor Movement

Most of hands-free gesture techniques for 2D pointing can be grouped into two categories: ones based on the sensed directions of users' hands or fingers; the others based on the sensed positions of hands or fingers. The latter category can be further grouped into two approaches: the tablet-like approach that uses absolute positioning of hands or fingers; the mouse-like one that adopts relative positioning of hands or fingers.

We propose a mouse-like pointing technique. Our technique is unique in that it utilizes the horizontal movement of a user's hand to obtain a cursor position on a vertical screen as shown in Fig. 1(a). More specifically, if the user moves his/her hand toward the screen, the cursor moves upward on the screen; if the user moves his/her hand toward the user, the cursor moves downward on the screen; if the user moves his/her hand to the left or to the right, the cursor moves in the same direction. We can expect that, compared to the vertical movement, the horizontal movement of the user's hand reduces his/her fatigue. Although the movement of the hand and the corresponding movement of the cursor are not parallel, this situation is common to existing 2D pointing devices such as mice and touchpads.

Since our pointing technique is based on the mouse-like approach, the cursor moves on the screen only while it is activated. For this purpose, we let the user make the following hand gestures: to activate the movement of the cursor, the user opens his/her hand; to deactivate it, the user clenches.

In addition, we incorporate a cursor acceleration method that is common to existing 2D pointing devices to assist users in quick but precise cursor movement. In the case of mice, cursor acceleration uses a nonlinear mapping from the velocity of a mouse to the velocity of the cursor. More specifically, if the user moves the mouse slowly, the cursor moves slowly on the screen; if the user moves the mouse more quickly, the cursor moves much more quickly. This enables the user to do almost stress-free cursor movement on a large screen while enabling the user to do careful cursor movement if necessary. Since our pointing technique is based on the mouse-like approach, we can naturally incorporate cursor acceleration into our technique.

2.2 Target Selection

We adopt a hand gesture again to let the user select a target on the screen. Specifically, the user selects the target by "clicking" in the air with his/her index finger as shown in Fig. 1(b). Since the user moves only his/her index finger without needing to move his/her hand, we can expect that this operation has almost no negative effect on the cursor movement operation. Also, we can incorporate other operations in the same way by using other fingers than the index finger.

3   Implementation

We implemented the proposed technique by using the Leap Motion controller [4]. The controller uses infrared LEDs and cameras to recognize hand gestures that a user performs above it. We implemented the necessary program as a Windows Presentation Foundation application in the C# language of Microsoft Visual Studio 2013. The program consists of 850 lines of code.

We used the position of the user's middle finger as the position of the user's hand. To identify whether the user opens or clenches his/her hand, we used Leap Motion's "confidence" data. To identify whether the user "clicks" with his/her index finger, we used its relative height compared to the average height of his/her ring and little fingers.

We implemented mouse acceleration by simulating that of Windows XP [1]. Specifically, if the distance of the movement of the user's hand per frame is less than 0.44 mm, the movement of the cursor is 12.0 pixels/mm; if the hand movement is between 0.44 and 1.25 mm, the cursor movement is 18.1 pixels/mm; if the hand movement is between 1.26 and 3.86 mm, the cursor movement is 27.5 pixels/mm; if the hand movement is more than 3.86 mm, the cursor movement is 56.8 pixels/mm.

4   Experiments

This section describes the experiments that we conducted to evaluate the performance of the proposed mouse-like technique.

4.1 Method

We experimentally compared the proposed mouse-like technique with a tablet-like one. The tablet-like technique directly maps the absolute position of a user's hand to coordinates on a screen (Fig. 2(a)), and enables the user to perform target selection by "tapping" in the air (Fig. 2(b)).

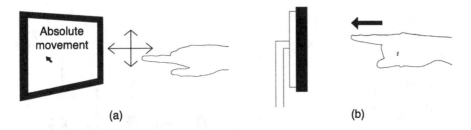

(a)   (b)

Fig. 2. Tablet-like pointing technique.

We designed a task to evaluate the performance of users' pointing by using the mouse-like and the tablet-like technique. In this task, a user selects targets that repeatedly appear at random positions on the screen. The position of a new target is always at most 1000-pixel distant from the previous one. The size of the target is 74×100 pixels that are almost equal to the size of a standard icon on Windows with a 1920×1080-resolution screen. We designed this task in a similar way to that for a predictive cursor movement technique [2]. However, the behavior of targets in our task is more random than that for the predictive cursor movement technique.

We studied eight subjects who performed the target selection task. All the subjects were male and right-handed, and their average age was 21.8 years. Half of them used the mouse-like and the tablet-like technique in this order, and the others used these techniques in the reverse order. They had a five-minute practice and a five-minute rest before and after the task respectively. A subject repeated the task 100 times for each technique, that is, 200 times in total. The needed time of an experiment for a subject was approximately 30 min. We used a 1920×1080-resolution LCD display. We recorded the time for each task, the number of misclicks, and the position of each target. After the experiment of each subject, we made an inquiry with five-grade assessment about the usability and the fatigability of the two techniques.

4.2 Results

We compared the two techniques by analyzing the data that we obtained from the experiments. To simplify the analysis, we classified target distances into ten levels. The two-way ANOVA on the two techniques and the target distances indicated significant differences between the two techniques ($F(1, 1580) = 3.900$,

$p < 0.001$) and between the target distances ($F(9, 1580) = 7.006$, $p < 0.01$). However, no interaction occurred between the two techniques and the target distances. Figure 3 plots relations between target distances and pointing times. The bars indicate the average times of all the subjects, and the error bars indicate the standard deviations. The mouse-like technique resulted in smaller standard deviations than the tablet-like one for most of the target distances.

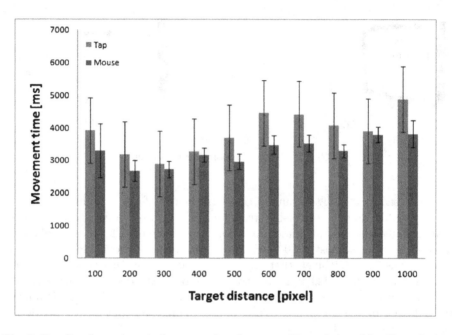

Fig. 3. Results of experiments for comparing the mouse-like and the tablet-like pointing technique.

Both techniques resulted in the average error rates of approximately 40 %. By contrast, the average error rate for the same task using a mouse was approximately 4 %. This indicates that the hand gesture techniques were less stable than mouse-based operations. The total numbers of misclicks were 774 for the mouse-like technique and 862 for the tablet-like one.

In the inquiries after the experiments, six out of the eight subjects answered that the mouse-like technique was easier to use. Four out of the eight subjects answered that the tablet-like technique had caused more fatigue than the mouse-like one. Also, we received comments that they had experienced difficulty in selecting targets located near sides of the screen. Both techniques obtained only a few high evaluations, which indicated that subjects had felt stress in hands-free gesture pointing.

5 Conclusions and Future Work

We proposed a mouse-like hands-free gesture technique for 2D pointing. It uses the horizontal movement of a user's hand, and adopts hand gestures to enable relative cursor movement and target selection. We experimentally evaluated the performance of the proposed mouse-like technique by comparing a tablet-like one. We studied eight subjects, and found that the mouse-like technique had reduced pointing times and obtained more stable operations. Also, the inquiries after the experiments indicated that the mouse-like technique was easier to use and caused less fatigue.

Our future work includes improving the recognition of hand gestures. There are still many hand gestures that cannot be precisely recognized. To enhance the usefulness of hands-free gesture pointing techniques, we need more precise recognition of hand gestures. Other future work is to devise a better method for evaluating gesture pointing techniques since the experiments that we performed were originally designed for mouse-based pointing techniques.

Acknowledgement. This work was supported by JSPS KAKENHI Grant Number 25540029.

References

1. Adjusting the acceleration of a mouse pointer on Windows XP. http://07.net/mouse/
2. Asano, T., Sharlin, E., Kitamura, Y., Takashima, K., Kishino, F.: Predictive interaction using the delphian desktop. In: Proceedings of the ACM UIST. pp. 133–141 (2005)
3. Averkiou, M., Dodgson, N.A.: Comparison of relative (mouse-like) and absolute (tablet-like) interaction with a large stereoscopic workspace. In: SD&A. Proceedings of the SPIE, vol. 7863, p. 41 (2011)
4. Plemmons, D., Mandel, P.: Introduction to motion control (2014). https://developer.leapmotion.com/articles/intro-to-motion-control
5. Vogel, D., Balakrishnan, R.: Distant freehand pointing and clicking on very large, high resolution displays. In: Proceedings of the ACM UIST. pp. 33–42 (2005)

Reasoning, Optimisation and Machine Learning for HCI

Recent Harmony Search Algorithms for 0–1 Optimization Problems

Broderick Crawford[1,2,3]([✉]), Ricardo Soto[1,4,5], Néstor Guzmán[1],
Franklin Johnson[1,6], and Fernando Paredes[7]

[1] Pontificia Universidad Católica de Valparaíso, Valparaiso, Chile
{broderick.crawford,ricardo.soto}@ucv.cl, nestor.guzman@live.cl
[2] Universidad Central de Chile, Santiago, Chile
[3] Universidad San Sebastián, Santiago, Chile
[4] Universidad Autónoma de Chile, Santiago, Chile
[5] Universidad Cientifica del Sur, Lima, Peru
[6] Universidad de Playa Ancha, Valparaiso, Chile
franklin.johnson@upla.cl
[7] Escuela de Ingeniería Industrial, Universidad Diego Portales, Santiago, Chile
fernando.paredes@udp.cl

Abstract. The Set Covering Problem (SCP) has long been concentrating the interest of many researchers in the field of Combinatorial Optimization. SCP is a 0–1 integer programming problem that consists in finding a set of solutions which allow to cover a set of needs at the lowest cost possible. There are many applications of these kind of problems, the main ones are: location of services, files selection in a data bank, simplification of boolean expressions, balancing production lines, among others. Different metaheuristics have been proposed to solve it. Here, we present the possibilities to solve Set Covering Problems with Harmony Search.

Keywords: Set covering problem · Metaheuristics · Harmony search algorithm

1 Introduction

The Set Covering Problem (SCP) [9,10,19] is a classic problem that consists in finding a set of solutions which allow to cover a set of needs at the lowest cost possible. There are many applications of these kind of problems, the main ones are: location of services, files selection in a data bank, simplification of boolean expressions, balancing production lines, among others.

In the field of Metaheuristics, many algorithms have been developed to solve the SCP. Examples of these optimization algorithms include: Genetic Algorithm (GA) [22,26], Ant Colony Optimization (ACO) [23], Particle Swarm Optimization (PSO) [2,11], Artificial Bee Colony (ABC) [8,9,13], Cultural Algorithms [10] and 2-level Metaheuristics [12,27].

© Springer International Publishing Switzerland 2015
C. Stephanidis (Ed.): HCII 2015 Posters, Part I, CCIS 528, pp. 567–572, 2015.
DOI: 10.1007/978-3-319-21380-4_96

Here, we present the possibilities to solve Set Covering Problems with Harmony Search (HS). The HS algorithm is a relatively new population-based metaheuristic optimization algorithm. It imitates the music improvisation process where musicians improvise toning their instruments by searching for a perfect harmony. Since the emergence of this algorithm in 2001, it attracted many researchers from various fields especially those working on solving hard optimization problems.

More specifically, our interest is to solve the column-based representation of the SCP (its binary representation) and to solve binary optimization problems, several instances of Harmony Search have been developed recently [21, 29–31].

2   The Set Covering Problem

The SCP [6] can be formally defined as follows. Let $A = (a_{ij})$ be an m-row, n-column, zero-one matrix. We say that a column j can cover a row if $a_{ij} = 1$. Each column j is associated with a nonnegative real cost c_j. Let $I=\{1,...,m\}$ and $J=\{1,...,n\}$ be the row set and column set, respectively. The SCP calls for a minimum cost subset $S \subseteq J$, such that each row $i \in I$ is covered by at least one column $j \in S$. A mathematical model for the SCP is

$$v(\text{SCP})= \min \sum_{j \in J} c_j x_j \tag{1}$$

subject to

$$\sum_{j \in J} a_{ij} x_j \geq 1, \quad \forall\, i \in I, \tag{2}$$

$$x_j \in \{0, 1\}, \forall\, j \in J \tag{3}$$

The objective is to minimize the sum of the costs of the selected columns, where $x_j = 1$ if column j is in the solution, 0 otherwise. The restrictions ensure that each row i is covered by at least one column.

The SCP has been applied to many real world problems such as crew scheduling [1], location of emergency facilities [24], production planning in industry [28], vehicle routing [3], ship scheduling [15], network attack or defence [4], assembly line balancing [16], traffic assignment in satellite communication systems [25], simplifying boolean expressions [5], the calculation of bounds in integer programs [7], information retrieval [14], political districting [17], stock cutting, crew scheduling problems in airlines [20] and other important real life situations.

3   The Harmony Search algorithm

Harmony search [18] is a relatively new population-based metaheuristic optimization algorithm, that imitates the music improvisation process where the musicians improvise toning their instruments by searching for a perfect state of harmony. It was able to attract many researchers to develop HS-based solutions for many optimization problems. HS imitates the behavior of musicians when they cooperate the pitches of their instruments together to obtain a fantastic harmony as measured by aesthetic standards.

HS is a very successful metaheuristic algorithm that can explore the solutions of a given problem, where each solution (harmony) is generated exploring and exploiting intelligently the search space. HS performs optimization analogizing the improvisation process of musicians:

- Each musician corresponds to each decision variable.
- Musical instruments pitch range corresponds to the decision variables value range.
- Musical harmony at a certain time corresponds to a solution at a certain iteration.
- Audiences aesthetics corresponds to the objective function.

HS possesses several advantageous characteristics:

- The generation of a new solution after considering all the existing solutions, rather than considering only some solutions as in other metaheuristics.
- The independent consideration of each decision variable in a solution.
- It does not require any starting values of the decision variables nor does it require complex derivatives as in gradient-based methods.

Other important strengths of HS are their improvisation operators, memory consideration, pitch adjustment and random consideration. All above achieving the desired balance between the two major forces for any metaheuristic: exploitation and exploration.

Besides the good features offered by the original HS algorithm, recently have emerged new HS variants of our special interest to address binary problems [21, 29–31]. Following we describe briefly the Novel Global Harmony Search [31] in our attempt to find new ways of solving the SCP.

3.1   A Novel Global Harmony Search

Inspired by the swarm intelligence of particle swarm, in [31] a Novel Global Harmony Search algorithm (NGHS) is proposed to solve 0–1 knapsack problems. It is unsurprising that the HS algorithms can be used to solve 0–1 problems. However, the HS needs be modified for solving some difficulty binary problems. We intend to rescue these new capabilities to attack the column-based SCP.

The NGHS and the HS are different in the following:

- HS parameters Harmony Memory Considering Rate (HMCR) and Pitch Adjusting Rate (PAR) are excluded from the NGHS, and genetic mutation probability P_m is included in the NGHS.

– The NGHS modifies the Improvisation Step of the HS as follows:

Algorithm 1. $NGHS()$

1: **for** $(i = 1$ to $n)$ **do**
2:     $step_i = |x_i^{best} - x_i^{worst}|$ % calculation of the adaptive step
3:     $x_i^{new} = x_i^{best} \pm \bigcup(0,1) \, step_i$ % position updating
4:     **if** ($\bigcup(0,1) \leq P_m$) **then**
5:         $x_i^{new} = x_{iL} + \bigcup(0,1) \, (x_{iU} - x_{iL})$ % genetic mutation
6:     **end if**
7: **end for**

Where x_i^{best} and x_i^{worst} denote respectively the best and worst global harmony. $\bigcup(0,1)$ represents uniformly generated random numbers in $[0,1]$. Dynamically adjusted $step_i$ keeps a balance between the global search and the local search. Genetic mutation operation with a small probability is carried out for the worst harmony of harmony memory after updating position, preventing the premature convergence.

– After improvisation, the NGHS replaces the worst harmony x^{worst} in HM with the new harmony x_i^{new} even if x_i^{new} is worse than x^{worst}.

4   Conclusion

In this paper, we turn the attention in the Harmony Search algorithms, they have several characteristics that make it a good alternative to tackle the Set Covering Problem, exploring the search space in both intensification and diversification in order to provide a near-optimal solution within a reasonable time.

Some modification and improvements to HS have been implemented in various domains. In order to find satisfactory solutions for the 0–1 optimization problems, several variants of HS have been developed. One of the most promising is the Novel Global Harmony Search Algorithm [31]. Given the good capabilities of NGHS to solve binary problems, it is considered feasible and motivating to devote efforts in its implementation to solve SCP problems.

Acknowledgments. Broderick Crawford is supported by Grant CONICYT / FONDECYT / REGULAR / 1140897. Ricardo Soto is supported by Grant CONICYT / FONDECYT / INICIACION / 11130459.

References

1. Ali, A.I., Thiagarajan, H.: A network relaxation based enumeration algorithm for set partitioning. Eur. J. Oper. Res. **38**(1), 76–85 (1989)
2. Porto, V.W., Waagen, D. (eds.): EP 1998. LNCS, vol. 1447. Springer, Heidelberg (1998)
3. Balinski, M.L., Quandt, R.E.: On an integer program for a delivery problem. Oper. Res. **12**(2), 300–304 (1964)

4. Bellmore, M., Ratliff, H.D.: Optimal defense of multi-commodity networks. Manag. Sci. **18**(4–part-i), B174–B185 (1971)
5. Breuer, M.A.: Simplification of the covering problem with application to boolean expressions. J. ACM **17**(1), 166–181 (1970)
6. Caprara, A., Fischetti, M., Toth, P.: Algorithms for the set covering problem. Ann. Oper. Res. **98**, 353–371 (2000)
7. Christofides, N.: Zero-one programming using non-binary tree-search. Comput. J. **14**(4), 418–421 (1971)
8. Crawford, B., Soto, R., Cuesta, R., Paredes, F.: Using the bee colony optimization method to solve the weighted set covering problem. In: Stephanidis, C. (ed.) HCI 2014, Part I. CCIS, vol. 434, pp. 493–497. Springer, Heidelberg (2014)
9. Crawford, B., Soto, R., Cuesta, R., Paredes, F.: Application of the artificial bee colony algorithm for solving the set covering problem. Sci. World J. **2014**(189164), 1–8 (2014)
10. Crawford, B., Soto, R., Monfroy, E.: Cultural algorithms for the set covering problem. In: Tan, Y., Shi, Y., Mo, H. (eds.) ICSI 2013, Part II. LNCS, vol. 7929, pp. 27–34. Springer, Heidelberg (2013)
11. Crawford, B., Soto, R., Monfroy, E., Palma, W., Castro, C., Paredes, F.: Parameter tuning of a choice-a function based hyperheuristic using particle swarm optimization. Expert Syst. Appl. **40**, 1690–1695 (2013)
12. Crawford, B., Soto, R., Palma, W., Johnson, F., Paredes, F., Olguín, E.: A 2-level approach for the set covering problem: parameter tuning of artificial bee colony algorithm by using genetic algorithm. In: Tan, Y., Shi, Y., Coello, C.A.C. (eds.) ICSI 2014, Part I. LNCS, vol. 8794, pp. 189–196. Springer, Heidelberg (2014)
13. Cuesta, R., Crawford, B., Soto, R., Paredes, F.: An artificial bee colony algorithm for the set covering problem. In: Silhavy, R., Senkerik, R., Oplatkova, Z.K., Silhavy, P., Prokopova, Z. (eds.) Modern Trends and Techniques in Computer Science. Advances in Intelligent Systems and Computing, vol. 285, pp. 53–63. Springer, Heidelberg (2014)
14. Day, R.H.: Letter to the editoron optimal extracting from a multiple file data storage system: an application of integer programming. Oper. Res. **13**(3), 482–494 (1965)
15. Fisher, M.L., Rosenwein, M.B.: An interactive optimization system for bulk-cargo ship scheduling. Naval Res. Logistics (NRL) **36**(1), 27–42 (1989)
16. Freeman, B.A., Jucker, J.V.: The line balancing problem. J. Ind. Eng. **18**, 361–364 (1967)
17. Garfinkel, R.S., Nemhauser, G.L.: Optimal political districting by implicit enumeration techniques. Manage. Sci. **16**(8), B495–B508 (1970)
18. Geem, Z.W., Kim, J.H., Loganathan, G.V.: A new heuristic optimization algorithm: harmony search. Simulation **76**(2), 60–68 (2001)
19. Gouwanda, D., Ponnambalam, S.: Evolutionary search techniques to solve set covering problems. World Acad. Sci. Eng. Tech. **39**, 20–25 (2008)
20. Housos, E., Elmroth, T.: Automatic optimization of subproblems in scheduling airline crews. Interfaces **27**(5), 68–77 (1997)
21. Kong, X., Gao, L., Ouyang, H., Li, S.: A simplified binary harmony search algorithm for large scale 0–1 knapsack problems. Expert Syst. Appl. **42**, 5337–5355 (2015)
22. Michalewicz, Z.: Genetic Algorithms + Data Structures = Evolution Programs, 3rd edn. Springer-Verlag, Heidelberg (1996)
23. Ren, Z., Feng, Z., Ke, L., Zhang, Z.: New ideas for applying ant colony optimization to the set covering problem. Comput. & Ind. Eng. **58**(4), 774–784 (2010)

24. Revelle, C., Marks, D., Liebman, J.C.: An analysis of private and public sector location models. Manag. Sci. **16**(11), 692–707 (1970)
25. Ribeiro, C.C., Minoux, M., Penna, M.C.: An optimal column-generation-with-ranking algorithm for very large scale set partitioning problems in traffic assignment. Eur. J. Oper. Res. **41**(2), 232–239 (1989)
26. Aickelin, U.: An indirect genetic algorithm for set covering problems. J. Oper. Res. Soc. **53**(10), 1118–1126 (2002)
27. Valenzuela, C., Crawford, B., Monfroy, E., Soto, R., Paredes, F.: A 2-level meta-heuristic for the set covering problem. Int. J. Comput. Commun. Control **7**(2), 377–387 (2012)
28. Vasko, F.J., Wolf, F.E., Stott, K.L.: Optimal selection of ingot sizes via set covering. Oper. Res. **35**(3), 346–353 (1987)
29. Wang, L., Xu, Y., Mao, Y., Fei, M.: A discrete harmony search algorithm. In: Li, K., Li, X., Ma, S., Irwin, G.W. (eds.) LSMS 2010. CCIS, vol. 98, pp. 37–43. Springer, Heidelberg (2010)
30. Wang, L., Yang, R., Xu, Y., Niu, Q., Pardalos, P.M., Fei, M.: An improved adaptive binary harmony search algorithm. Inf. Sci. **232**, 58–87 (2013)
31. Zou, D., Gao, L., Li, S., Wu, J.: Solving 0–1 knapsack problem by a novel global harmony search algorithm. Appl. Soft Comput. **11**(2), 1556–1564 (2011)

Experiential Solving: Towards a Unified Autonomous Search Constraint Solving Approach

Broderick Crawford[1,2,3]([✉]), Ricardo Soto[1,4,5], Kathleen Crawford[1], Franklin Johnson[1,6], Claudio León de la Barra[1], and Sergio Galdames[1]

[1] Pontificia Universidad Católica de Valparaíso, Valparaiso, Chile
{broderick.crawford,ricardo.soto,claudio.leondelabarra}@ucv.cl
kathleen.crawford.a@mail.pucv.cl,
sergiogaldames@gmail.com
[2] Universidad Central de Chile, Santiago, Chile
[3] Universidad San Sebastián, Santiago, Chile
[4] Universidad Autónoma de Chile, Santiago, Chile
[5] Universidad Científica del Sur, Lima, Peru
[6] Universidad de Playa Ancha, Valparaiso, Chile
franklin.johnson@upla.cl

Abstract. To solve many problems modeled as Constraint Satisfaction Problems there are no known efficient algorithms. The specialized literature offers a variety of solvers, which have shown good performance. Nevertheless, despite the efforts of the scientific community in developing new strategies, there is no algorithm that is the best for all possible situations. This paper analyses recent developments of Autonomous Search Constraint Solving Systems. Showing that the design of the most efficient and recent solvers is very close to the Experiential Learning Cycle from organizational psychology.

Keywords: Experiential learning · Problem solving · Metaheuristics · Autonomous search

1 Introduction

In constraint solvers development projects a better understanding of the human learning phenomenon offers important insights in order to obtain more efficient algorithms and therefore better problem solutions. By constraint solver, we mean the computer implementation of an algorithm for solving Constraint Satisfaction (and optimization) Problems (CSPs) [9]. A variety of approaches can be used to tackle CSPs. Integer programming techniques and constraint programming can be applied to find exact solutions. On the other hand, there are various approaches that provide an approximate solution, including metaheuristics and neural networks [2].

© Springer International Publishing Switzerland 2015
C. Stephanidis (Ed.): HCII 2015 Posters, Part I, CCIS 528, pp. 573–577, 2015.
DOI: 10.1007/978-3-319-21380-4_97

Since the functioning of modern constraint solvers is a learning intensive activity, an understanding of its operation from a learning phenomenon perspective can provide a valuable contribution for designing and implementing optimization algorithms in general and metaheuristics in particular. In this paper we present some basal ideas and concepts about learning and intelligence related with our work of structuring novelty solvers.

2   Explaining Learning: The Learning Cycle of Kolb

Kolb [6,7] developed a theory of experiential learning that can give us a useful model by which to develop better constraint solvers. The Learning Cycle or The Experiential Learning Cycle, as shown in Algorithm 1, comprises four different stages of learning from experience.

Algorithm 1. The Experiential Learning Cycle

1: **while** stop criteria is not satisfied **do**
2:     concrete experience (DOING)
3:     reflective observation (REVIEWING)
4:     abstract conceptualization (CONCLUDING)
5:     active experimentation (PLANNING)
6: **end while**

- Concrete Experience: doing/having an experience. A new experience of situation is encountered, or a reinterpretation of existing experience.
- Reflective Observation: reviewing/reflecting on the experience. Of particular importance are any inconsistencies between experience and understanding.
- Abstract Conceptualisation: concluding/learning from the experience. Reflection gives rise to a new idea, or a modification of an existing concept.
- Active Experimentation: planning/trying out what you have learned. The learner applies them to the world around them to see what results.

The Learning Cycle suggests that it is not sufficient to have an experience in order to learn. It is necessary to reflect on the experience to make generalisations and formulate concepts which can then be applied to new situations. This learning must then be tested out in new situations.

2.1   Linking Experiential Learning and Metaheuristics

As shown in Algorithm 2, the problem solving method used by metaheuristics presents a similar structure and operation to the cycle of Kolb. Subsequently, we are conducting study and research to discover the opportunities to improve our solvers through a better understanding of the learning phenomenon described by Kolb and others authors.

Algorithm 2. The Problem Solving Method of Metaheuristics

1: construct initial solutions ($\simeq$ DOING)
2: evaluate solutions ($\simeq$ REVIEWING)
3: rank solutions ($\simeq$ CONCLUDING)
4: select best solutions ($\simeq$ PLANNING)
5: **while** stop criteria is not satisfied **do**
6:    apply the metaheuristics operators to produce new solutions ($\simeq$ DOING)
7:    evaluate solutions ($\simeq$ REVIEWING)
8:    rank solutions ($\simeq$ CONCLUDING)
9:    select best solutions ($\simeq$ PLANNING)
10: **end while**

---

3 Explaining Intelligence: The Triarchic Theory of Sternberg

According to Sternberg [11], a complete explanation of intelligence entails the interaction of three subtheories:

- Componential subtheory which outlines the structures and mechanisms that underlie intelligent behavior categorized as metacognitive, performance, or knowlege acquistion components.
- Experiential subtheory that proposes intelligent behavior be interpreted along a continuum of experience from novel to highly familar tasks/situations.
- Contextual subtheory which specifies that intelligent behavior is defined by the sociocultural context in which it takes place and involves adaptation to the environment, selection of better environments, and shaping of the present environment.

In relation with the contextual subtheory, also called practical intelligence, it can be seen as an important referent to model adaptive constraint solvers. Following the principles underlying this subtheory recently it was introduced a new category of systems: Autonomous Search (AS) Systems [4,5].

3.1 Autonomous Search Systems

An autonomous search system should provide the ability to modify its internal components (heuristics, inference mechanisms, operators, movements, value parameters ...) when exposed to changing external forces and opportunities. As corresponds to an instance of adaptive systems with the objective of improving its problem solving performance by adapting its search strategy to the problem at hand. Autonomous search is particularly relevant to the constraint solving community, where much work has been conducted to improve the efficiency of constraint solvers. AS provides to a system the ability to change its components in order to improve its problem solving performance. AS can be defined as search processes that integrate control in their solving process either by self adaptation or by supervised adaptation. This control allows an AS system to improve its solving performance by modifying and adjusting itself to the problem at hand. The notion of control is present when the parameters or heuristics are adjusted online, i.e., when the constraint solver is running. Different methods such as control encoding, control variable and value selection, and evolving heuristics have been proposed to provide control during solving.

Concerning the control, in self adaptation, techniques are tightly integrated with the search process and usually require some overhead. The algorithm is observing its own behavior in an online fashion, modifying its parameters accordingly. This information can be either directly collected on the problem or indirectly computed through the perceived efficiency of individual components. Because the adaptation is done online, there is an important trade-off between the time spent computing process information and the gains that are to be expected from this information.

The pioneer framework for AS in Constraint Programming was proposed in [1]. This approach was explainded in more details in [8] and it was applied successfully in [3,9]. The framework for AS can be seen as a 4-component architecture (see Algorithm 3): solve, observation, analysis and update.

- The *solve* component carries out the CSP resolution. The strategies employed in the process are selected from a ranked porfolio.
- *Observation* is responsible for taking and recording snapshots, which correspond to relevant information of the solving process.
- *Analysis* process the snapshots captured by *observation*. These snapshots are used to evaluate the strategies, which are stored in a database to be then gathered by *update*.
- *Update* is responsible for organizing the strategy rank.

Algorithm 3. Autonomous Search General Framework

1: **while** stop criteria is not satisfied **do**
2:     solve ($\simeq$ DOING)
3:     observation ($\simeq$ REVIEWING)
4:     analysis ($\simeq$ CONCLUDING)
5:     update ($\simeq$ PLANNING)
6: **end while**

Here, we can see the presence of the same operating structure proposed again in the cycle of Kolb.

4   Conclusions

Since the functioning of constraint solvers is a learning intensive activity, an understanding of its operation from a learning phenomenon perspective offers important insights for designing and implementing better optimization algorithms and metaheuristics. In this paper we presented some ideas, concepts and experiences related with our work of structuring constraint solvers from a novelty point of view. It is clear that formalization of these influences is an area of research that is currently under-explored.

Acknowledgments. Broderick Crawford is supported by Grant CONICYT / FONDECYT / REGULAR / 1140897. Ricardo Soto is supported by Grant CONICYT / FONDECYT / INICIACION / 11130459.

References

1. Castro, C., Monfroy, E., Figueroa, C., Meneses, R.: An approach for dynamic split strategies in constraint solving. In: Gelbukh, A., de Albornoz, A., Terashima-Marín, H. (eds.) MICAI 2005. LNCS (LNAI), vol. 3789, pp. 162–174. Springer, Heidelberg (2005)
2. Crawford, B., Soto, R., de la Barra, C.L., Crawford, K., Paredes, F., Johnson, F.: A better understanding of the behaviour of metaheuristics: a psychological view. In: Stephanidis [10], pp. 515–518
3. Crawford, B., Soto, R., Monfroy, E., Palma, W., Castro, C., Paredes, F.: Parameter tuning of a choice-function based hyperheuristic using particle swarm optimization. Expert Syst. Appl. **40**(5), 1690–1695 (2013)
4. Crawford, B., Soto, R., Olivares, R., Herrera, R., Monfroy, E., Paredes, F.: Autonomous search: towards the easy tuning of constraint programming solvers. In: Stephanidis [10], pp. 165–168
5. Hamadi, Y., Monfroy, E., Saubion, F.: Autonomous Search. Springer, Heidelberg (2012)
6. Kolb, D.: Chapter 15 - the process of experiential learning. In: Cross, R.L., Israelit, S.B. (eds.) Strategic Learning in a Knowledge Economy, pp. 313–331. Butterworth-Heinemann, Boston (2000)
7. Kolb, D.A.: Experiential Learning: Experience as the Source of Learning and Development. Prentice-Hall P T R, Englewood Cliffs (1984)
8. Monfroy, E., Castro, C., Crawford, B., Soto, R., Paredes, F., Figueroa, C.: A reactive and hybrid constraint solver. J. Exp. Theor. Artif. Intell. **25**(1), 1–22 (2013)
9. Soto, R., Crawford, B., Palma, W., Galleguillos, K., Castro, C., Monfroy, E., Johnson, F., Paredes, F.: Boosting autonomous search for CSPs via skylines. Inf. Sci. **308**, 38–48 (2015)
10. Stephanidis, C. (ed.): HCI 2014, Part I. CCIS, vol. 434. Springer, Heidelberg (2014)
11. Robert, J.: Sternberg. A triarchic approach to the understanding and assessment of intelligence in multicultural populations. J. Sch. Psychol. **37**(2), 145–159 (1999)

Towards a Framework for Adaptive Constraint Propagation

Broderick Crawford[1,2,3], Ricardo Soto[1,4,5], Franklin Johnson[1,6(✉)],
Eric Monfroy[7], Enrique Norero[8], and Eduardo Olguín[3]

[1] Pontificia Universidad Católica de Valparaíso, Valparaiso, Chile
{broderick.crawford,ricardo.soto}@ucv.cl
[2] Universidad Central de Chile, Santiago, Chile
[3] Universidad San Sebastián, Santiago, Chile
eduardo.olguin@uss.cl
[4] Universidad Autónoma de Chile, Santiago, Chile
[5] Universidad Científica del Sur, Lima, Perú
[6] Universidad de Playa Ancha, Valparaiso, Chile
franklin.johnson@upla.cl
[7] CNRS, LINA, University of Nantes, Nantes, France
[8] Facultad de Ingeniería, Universidad Santo Tomás, Viña El Mar, Chile
enorero@santotomas.cl

Abstract. In this paper we address a recent situation created by the explosive growth of web systems. For these reason we propose a framework to support adaptive elements in Web pages. Web pages can be accessed by different platforms with different browsers and through different devices such as laptops, tablets or cellphones. In particular we focus on adaptive menus for this different kind of devices or browsers to optimize the selection patterns and their implementations. We propose a framework using an Adaptive Constraint Programming technique to optimize the decision of developers. Constraint Programming is a programming paradigm able to find efficient resolution in optimization problems. In Constraint Programming a problem is defined in term of variables and constraints. The variables hold a domain and represent the unknowns of the problem, while the relations among them are modeled as constraints.

Keywords: Autonomous search · Constraint programming · Web system

1 Introduction

In this paper we address a recent situation created by the explosive growth of web systems, which can be accessed from different devices. For these reasons we have developed a framework to support adaptive elements in Web pages. Web pages can be accessed by different platforms with different browsers and through different devices such as laptops, tablets or cellphones. In particular we focus on adaptive

© Springer International Publishing Switzerland 2015
C. Stephanidis (Ed.): HCII 2015 Posters, Part I, CCIS 528, pp. 578–581, 2015.
DOI: 10.1007/978-3-319-21380-4_98

menus. The idea is to create a mechanism able to adapt the menus according different devices or browsers to optimize the selection patterns and their implementations. Developers are able to define rules for menu adaptation according to the features of the device and browser in use. We propose a framework using an Adaptive Constraint Programming technique to optimize the decision of developers. Constraint Programming (CP) is a programming paradigm able to find efficient resolution in optimization problems. In Constraint Programming a problem is defined in term of variables and constraints. The variables hold a domain and represent the unknowns of the problem, while the relations among them are modeled as constraints. We formulate an adaptive system for constraint propagation which aims at reducing domains by eliminating those values that do not lead to any solution. This is carried out by a enforcing a local consistency to the problem. The idea is to create a system capable of selecting the best propagator from a portfolio of propagators to solve our specific problem. This paper briefly describes the selected adaptation patterns and their implementation.

2 Constraint Programming

The pioneering works on constraints were motivated mainly by problems arising in the field of picture processing [4]. Artificial Intelligent research, concentrated on difficult combinatorial problems, it has contributed to considerable progress in constraint-based reasoning. Many powerful algorithms were designed that became a basis of current constraint satisfaction algorithms [1].

In computer science, constraint programming is a programming paradigm where in relations between variables are stated in the form of constraints. Constraints differ from the common primitives of imperative programming languages in that they do not specify a step or sequence of steps to execute, but rather the properties of a solution to be found [5]. This makes constraint programming a form of declarative programming. The constraints used in constraint programming are of various kinds: those used in constraint satisfaction problems [8], those solved by the simplex algorithm, and others strategies. Constraints are usually embedded within a programming language or provided via separate software libraries [2,7]. Constraint programming can be expressed in the form of constraint logic programming [3], which embeds constraints into a logic program. Whatever the language in which it is implemented, the problems should be modeled as a constraint satisfaction problem (SCP).

2.1 Constraint Satisfaction Problems

A CSP is a formal representation of unknowns variables , and the relations among them is defined as constraints. Formally, a CSP $\mathcal{P}$ is defined by a triple $P = \langle \mathcal{X}, D, C \rangle$ where:

- $\mathcal{X}$ is a set of variables $\mathcal{X} = (x_1, x_2, \ldots, x_n)$.
- $\mathcal{D}$ is a set of corresponding domains $\mathcal{D} = (d_1, d_2, \ldots, d_n)$ such that $x_i \in d_i$, and d_i is a set of possibles values for x_i.

– $\mathcal{C}$ is a set of constraints $\mathcal{C} = (c_1, c_2, \ldots, c_m)$, and a constraint c_j is defined as a subset of the Cartesian product of domains $d_{j_1} \times \cdots \times d_{j_{n_j}}$, for $j = \{1, \ldots, m\}$.

Then a solution to a CSP is an assignment $x_i \rightarrow a_i$ such that $a_i \in d_i$ for $i = \{1, \ldots, n\}$ and any constraint c_j is violated, for $j = \{1, \ldots, m\}$.

3 Framework for Adaptive Web Systems

The diversity of devices available has changed the way we access to web systems. At the same time, it has created a number of challenges for application developers. It has become more and more important to offer solid user experiences to an increasing number of contexts. The developers can create different copies of the same system to work with the different devices or we can create a mechanism to adapt a web system to different devices on real time. To adapt the characteristics of the browsers or devices exists a single code that is able to provide users with increasingly rich user interfaces, based on the characteristics of the platform, but also change the structure of the user interface to adapt to different form factors, in response to different platforms.

The first step is detecting the context of execution. This can be done, either on the server, or directly in the browser. Server side detection explores the user agent string sent by the browser in the HTTP requests. This supports obtaining detailed information about the browser and the device being used.

Client side detection is performed directly in the browser, and a number of JavaScript libraries are available to support it. With these libraries we can get features, such as support for HTML5 or CSS3 in the browser, touch or georeferencing capabilities in the device [6].

We propose a framework using an Adaptive Constraint Programming technique to optimize the pattern selection for an adaptive menu in a web system.

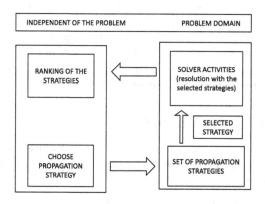

Fig. 1. Adaptive constraint propagation.

The first step is to model de pattern selection as a CSP problem, for this we propose define the variables of the problem as X=set of characteristics, the domain of the variables determines the possible patterns suitable for each characteristic. The constraints determines de possible combination of characteristics to adequate the system to the different browsers or devices.

The proposed framework implements an autonomous technique to allow the CP solver to adapt its own parameters, to selects the best propagation strategies. That is presented in Fig. 1, where the framework uses a strategy independent of the problem domain, that operates at a higher level of abstraction than the solver. It decides which strategy is applied next during the search. This decision is guided by the ranking generator which evaluates the performance of strategies. The ranking generator can be implemented using a genetic algorithm.

4 Conclusion

In conclusion we have proposed a framework able to select the suitable pattern to support adaptive elements in Web pages. The proposed framework uses an Adaptive Constraint Propagation techniques. We propose an adecuate model to adpat the pattern selction to a CSP. Also we present the scheme to representa the Adaptive Constraint Propagation framework.

Acknowledgments. Broderick Crawford is supported by Grant CONICYT/ FONDECYT/REGULAR/1140897, Ricardo Soto is supported by Grant CONICYT/FONDECYT/INICIACION/11130459, Franklin Johnson is supported by Postgraduate Grant PUCV 2014.

References

1. Apt, K.: Principles of Constraint Programming. Cambridge University Press, New York (2003)
2. de la Barra, C.L., Soto, R., Crawford, B., Allendes, C., Berendsen, H., Monfroy, E.: Modeling the portfolio selection problem with constraint programming. In: Stephanidis, C. (ed.) HCII 2013, Part I. CCIS, vol. 373, pp. 645–649. Springer, Heidelberg (2013)
3. Hentenryck, P.V.: Constraint Satisfaction in Logic programming. MIT Press, Cambridge (1989)
4. Montanari, U.: Networks of constraints: fundamental properties and applications to picture processing. Inf. Sci. **7**, 95–132 (1974)
5. Oliveira, C.: Review of essentials of constraint programming by T. Fruhwirth and S. Abdennadher. SIGACT News **35**(3), 17–20 (2004). Springer-verlag
6. Perkowitz, M., Etzioni, O.: Towards adaptive web sites: conceptual framework and case study. Artif. Intell. **118**(1–2), 245–275 (2000)
7. Soto, R., Crawford, B., Monfroy, E., Paredes, F.: Syntax extensions for a constrained-object language via dynamic parser cooperation. Stud. Inform. Control **41**(1), 41–48 (2012)
8. Soto, R., Kjellerstrand, H., Duran, O., Crawford, B., Monfroy, E., Paredes, F.: Cell formation in group technology using constraint programming and boolean satisfiability. Expert Syst. Appl. **39**(13), 11423–11427 (2012)

An Artificial Bee Colony Algorithm for the Resource Contrained Project Scheduling Problem

Broderick Crawford[1,2,3], Ricardo Soto[1,4,5], Franklin Johnson[1,6(✉)],
Enrique Norero[7], and Eduardo Olguín[3]

[1] Pontificia Universidad Católica de Valparaíso, Valparaíso, Chile
{broderick.crawford,ricardo.soto}@ucv.cl
[2] Universidad Central de Chile, Santiago, Chile
[3] Universidad San Sebastián, Santiago, Chile
eduardo.olguin@uss.cl
[4] Universidad Autónoma de Chile, Santiago, Chile
[5] Universidad Científica del Sur, Lima, Perú
[6] Universidad de Playa Ancha, Valparaíso, Chile
franklin.johnson@upla.cl
[7] Facultad de Ingeniería, Universidad Santo Tomás, Viña del Mar, Chile
enorero@santotomas.cl

Abstract. We present an approach to solve the Resource Constrained Project Scheduling Problem. This problem consists on executing a group of activities limited by constraints. Precedence relationships force to some activities to begin after the finalization of others. In addition, processing every activity requires a predefined amount of limited resources. The target of this problem is to minimize the duration of whole project. In this paper, an approach based on Artificial Bee Colony algorithm for the Resource Constrained Project Scheduling Problem is presented. That algorithm is one of the most recent algorithms in the domain of the collective intelligence who was motivated by the intelligent behavior observed in the domestic bees to take the process of forage. Thus, ABC combines methods of local search and global search, trying to balance the process of the exploration and exploitation of the space of search.

Keywords: Artificial bee colony · Metaheuristic · Project scheduling

1 Introduction

The Resource Constrained Project Scheduling Problem (RCPS) can be understood as the scheduling of project activities, so that neither resource constraints nor the precedence constraints are violated, with the aim of minimizing the completion time of the last activity, i.e., the project makespan. Therefore scarce resources are allocated to competing activities over a given time horizon for the best possible performance [7]. RCPSP is considered a NP-hard [3] problem, i.e.

© Springer International Publishing Switzerland 2015
C. Stephanidis (Ed.): HCII 2015 Posters, Part I, CCIS 528, pp. 582–586, 2015.
DOI: 10.1007/978-3-319-21380-4_99

it is a complex and difficult combinatorial problem whereby the exact methods have difficulties in solving RCPSP large, therefore other alternatives are needed to solve them. An alternative are the metaheuristics, which have the capacity to get to a near optimal solution even in large problems, minimizing the use of resources. Some approaches used to solve this problem are Genetic Algorithms (GA) [4,10], Tabu Search (TS) [8], Simulated Annealing (SA) [1], Ant Colony Optimization (ACO) [2,5], Adaptive search method (AS) [9] and Particle Swarm Optimization (PSO) [2,12].

In this paper a mathematical model of RCPSP solved with ABC algorithm is presented. We believe that ABC is a metaheuristic able to solve efficiently RCPSP capable of competing with other solutions generated by complete and incomplete techniques.

This paper is organized as follows. In Sect. 2, we describe the RCPSP. Section 3 presents the ABC metaheuristics and the model of the ABC algorithm to RCPSP. Finally, the conclusions are presented in Sect. 4.

2   Resource Constrained Project Scheduling Problem

RCPSP can be defined as projects with limited resources in an environment which must process a set of activities subject to precedence constraints and resources, the latter being shared by several activities. Thus the problem is to perform such allocation optimizing some objective function.

A project consists of a set of activities to complete the project successfully, each activity can be processed in one of several possible modes. Mode determines the duration of the activity, the requirements of different types of resources, possible flows (positive or negative) of money and other characteristics associated with the activity. Among the project activities precedence relations are defined when the order to be executed is determined, these relationships are for technological or process design reasons, for which the project is represented as a directed graph where activities are represented in a node and the precedence relationships between activities are in the arc.

Programming projects may have different objectives. In this kind of problem we have to minimize the proyect duration (makespan) and the resourses utilized are renewable. The results that may be obtained help managers decide how many resources can be used for processing an activity and minimize the time of completion of a project.

The scheduling problem with limited resources has the main components: a set of activities defined as $A = \{a_0, a_1, a_2, ..., a_n, a_{n+1}\}$, a set of renewable resources limited defined as $R = \{r_1, r_2, ..., r_m\}$, the first activity a_0 and the last activity a_{n+1} consume zero units of time and do not consume any resources, the duration for each activity is represented by $d_i \geq 0$ with $i = \{1, .., n\}$, the amount of resources consumed $q_{ij} \geq 0$, the maximum availability $Q_j \geq 0$ of each resource $r_j \in R$ at each instant of time, the precedence constraints $P_a \in A = \{a_1, ..., a_{n+1}\}$, each activity a_i can not be initiated while predecessor activities P_i have not been finalized. The set of successor activities S_i for a_i activities being

$i = \{1, ..., n+1\}$, the set of start times for each activity $T = \{t_0, ..., t_{n+1}\}$, and the Directed acyclic graph $G = \{A, E\}$ where $E = \{(a_i, a_j)/a_i \in P_a; a \in A\}$. RCPSP is represented by the following mathematical model containing the minimization of makespan and the constraints of time and resources.

$$Min \; F_{n+1} \tag{1}$$

$$F_h \leq F_j - p_j \tag{2}$$

$$\sum_{j \in A(t)} r_{j,k} \tag{3}$$

$$k \in K; t \geq 0 \tag{4}$$

$$F_j \geq 0 \tag{5}$$

$$where \; j = \{1, ..., n+1\} \; and \; h \in P_j$$

Defined F_j as the completion of the activity j therefore in the mathematical formulation should be minimized F_{n+1} since $n+1$ It is the last activity. This is represented in the objective function presented in Eq. 1, used to define the quality of a solution (Fitness). The Eq. 2 does satisfy the precedence constraint between activities since it shows that the completion of an activity h must be greater or equal to the completion of the activity j unless the predecessor activity. The Eqs. 3 and 4 show the limits for each type of resource k and each time instant t, thus not allowing the demand for activities occurring at present does not exceed its capacity. Finally the Eq. 5 defines the decision variables.

3   Artificial Bee Colony for RCPSP

The ABC algorithm is inspired by the behavior of intelligent power of a colony of bees, this is an optimization algorithm based on population introduced by Karaboga [6]. This algorithm is motivated by the intelligent behavior of honey bees, using common parameters such control as a colony size and the maximum number of cycles.

In the ABC system artificial bees fly around in a multidimensional space search and some bees that can be used or spectators choose food sources based on their own experience and their nest mates, and then adjust their positions. Some scout bees fly and food sources chosen randomly and without the use of experience, if the amount of nectar from a new source is greater than the previous one in his memory, memorize the new position and forget the above.

Therefore, the ABC system combines local search methods, carried out by bees employed and spectators, with global search methods, managed by spectators and explorers, trying to balance the exploration and exploitation process.

This algorithm comes from the intelligence swarm and is based on the behavior of natural honey bees to find their food is so in the following points is passed on to detail each of these concepts and computational bees are also analyzed.

Initialization phase. In the initialization phase all parameters are set mainly by the population size m, number of iterations of the algorithm, and the initial values of the solution, which is defined as a vector x with a dimension between 1 and n, where n is the nth dimension of the solution. The initial solution may be random or guided.

$$x_i = l_i + rand(0,1) * (u_i - l_i) \qquad (6)$$

The Eq. 6 determined as randomly initialize the dimension i of the solution x. l_i and u_i are the minimum and maximum values for x_i.

Phase Employed bees: The bees take a new neighbor solution to the current solution v, this solution is obtained by applying an operator to change random to one or more of the dimensions of the initial solution x. The fitness of v and x is then calculated, selecting the best.

Bees phase spectators: The spectators bees take your probabilistically decision based on the information provided by the Employed bees. Taking the best solution according to the highest probability calculated according to Equation.

$$p_i = \frac{fit(x_i)}{\sum_{j=1}^{m} fit(x_j)} \qquad (7)$$

After selecting the best solution x as probability. New neighbor solution v is calculated and the best solution between the two is chosen.

Phase Scout bees: Bees are choosing randomly solution. The worker bees that your solution does not improve over a period of time become explorer may use the above equation to define a new random solution.

3.1   Representation of the Solution

The solution is represented as follows, if the problem is composed of RCPSP n activities, then the bees will move in solution space n dimensions. Ie a solution is a vector x_i, where i $in1, ..., n$, the possible values for each dimension are between 0 and 1. Where each bee represents a solution in the solution space. The order of each element of the solution, represents the order in which to perform the activities. This representation is based on a priority represented by Zhang 2006 [11].

We use a change operator based in simple swap. The different types of swap are Type N, NS, NSC. Type N: such is the nearest neighbor and is choosing a random value as the image you choose Activity 3 and exchanged for activity 4.

Type NS: this rate is to choose a random number as in the picture you can see activity 4 is selected and then has 4 spaces to the right and make the change, then exchanged the 4 activity 8.

Type NSC: in such an activity and randomly select the image that activity 7 is selected and then count backwards 4 spaces for putting this activity in the position being located activity in the rest position and ran forward.

4 Conclusion

In conclusion we have proposed a bio-inspired metaheuristic able to find solutions to RCPSP using the behavior of natural bee colonies. The mathematical model of the problem is clearly presented and it is delivered a clear description of the behavior of ABC. Also we present the model that solves the problem using ABC. Through this algorithm we believe that it is possible generate competitive solutions. As future work is expected develop this proposal and compare with other techniques.

Acknowledgments. Broderick Crawford is supported by Grant CONICYT/FONDECYT/REGULAR/1140897, Ricardo Soto is supported by Grant CONICYT/FONDECYT/INICIACION/11130459, Franklin Johnson is supported by Postgraduate Grant PUCV 2014.

References

1. Bouleimen, K., Lecocq, H.: A new efficient simulated annealing algorithm for the resource-constrained project scheduling problem and its multiple mode version. Eur. J. Oper. Res. **149**(2), 268–281 (2003)
2. Chen, R.-M., Wu, C.-L., Wang, C.-M., Lo, S.-T.: Using novel particle swarm optimization scheme to solve resource-constrained scheduling problem in psplib. Expert Syst. Appl. **37**(3), 1899–1910 (2010)
3. Chiarandini, M., Di Gaspero, L., Gualandi, S., Schaerf, A.: The balanced academic curriculum problem revisited. J. Heuristics **18**(1), 119–148 (2012)
4. Hartmann, S.: A competitive genetic algorithm for resource-constrained project scheduling. Naval Res. Logistics (NRL) **45**(7), 733–750 (1998)
5. Herbots, J., Herroelen, W., Leus, R.: Experimental investigation of the applicability of ant colony optimization algorithms for project scheduling. DTEW Res. Rep. **0459**, 1–25 (2004)
6. Karaboga, D.: An idea based on honey bee swarm for numerical optimization. Technical report, Technical report-tr06, Erciyes university, Engineering Faculty, Computer Engineering Department (2005)
7. Kempf, K., Uzsoy, R., Smith, S., Gary, K.: Evaluation and comparison of production schedules. Comput. Ind. **42**(2), 203–220 (2000)
8. Nonobe, K., Ibaraki, T.: Formulation and Tabu search algorithm for the resource constrained project scheduling problem. In: Ribeiro, C.C., Hansen, P. (eds.) Essays and Surveys in Metaheuristics, pp. 557–588. Springer, London (2002)
9. Schirmer, A.: Case-based reasoning and improved adaptive search for project scheduling. Naval Res. Logistics (NRL) **47**(3), 201–222 (2000)
10. Valls, V., Ballestín, F., Quintanilla, S.: Justification and RCPSP: a technique that pays. Eur. J. Oper. Res. **165**(2), 375–386 (2005)
11. Zhang, H., Li, H., Tam, C.: Particle swarm optimization for resource-constrained project scheduling. Int. J. Project Manag. **24**(1), 83–92 (2006)
12. Zhang, H., Li, X., Li, H., Huang, F.: Particle swarm optimization-based schemes for resource-constrained project scheduling. Autom. Constr. **14**(3), 393–404 (2005)

A Semi-Automatic Word-Level Annotation and Transcription Tool for Spelling Error Categories

L. Linhuber[1], S. Stüker[1(✉)], R. Lavalley[2], and K. Berkling[2]

[1] Institute for Anthropomatics and Robotics, Karlsruhe Institute of Technology,
Karlsruhe, Germany
sebastian.stueker@kit.edu
[2] Department of Computer Science, Cooperative State University,
Karlsruhe, Germany
berkling@dhbw-karlsruhe.de

Abstract. In order to train and evaluate tools for the automatic transcription of misspelled texts and automatic annotation of over 20 spelling error categories, it is important to create training data. A very large database of children's freely written text was collected in the past and in this paper we describe the tool that we have developed in order to manually transcribe and annotate the data. The manual transcription comprises the reconstruction of the orthographically correct word sequence. Annotation is performed on a per-word basis with respect to committed (child spelling) and potential (correct word) spelling error categories. The tool supports human transcribers by suggesting automatically generated annotations. Consistent annotations are propagated and data is presented to the user in a sorted manner to minimize human effort. The tool has been implemented as a web application that makes use of PHP on the server side and a lightweight Java GUI on the client side. The annotated data is stored in a custom made XML schema.

Keywords: Annotation · Transcription · Applications for education · Language resources · Orthography

1 Introduction

Proficient reading and writing skills are a prerequisites for successful citizens in today's society. Comparative studies in Germany, such as the *Program for International Student Assessment* (PISA) and the *Progress in International Reading Literacy Study* (PIRLS) [3], have shown that around 25 % of German school children do not reach the minimal competence level necessary to function effectively in society by the age of 15. Diagnostic tools on the market today offer pricey one-time spelling diagnosis on a fixed test set with high-density error-prone and unnatural text and pre-specified word field analysis. Research by Fay [4] has shown that this sort of error analysis deviates, at least in parts, significantly from the error profile

C. Stephanidis (Ed.): HCII 2015 Posters, Part I, CCIS 528, pp. 587–592, 2015.
DOI: 10.1007/978-3-319-21380-4_100

derived from a child's freely written text. Thus an analysis of freely written text gives a more natural picture of the child's competence level.

The goal of this work is to support or replace manual expert effort with automated transcription of child text (achieved) into correctly written text (target) followed by automated annotation of error categories.

2   Previous Work

In [2,5,6] we have demonstrated on a small available data set the feasibility of creating a system for automatic error category analysis.

In order to obtain the data necessary for training, development and evaluation of our automatic tool we have collected a large amount of data at German schools [1]. The collected data contains 14,563 sentences which then needed to be transcribed and annotated.

The transcription part of this task consists of reconstructing the orthographically correct version (*target text*) of what the child has written (*achieved text*). A significant part of the work consists of creating an accurate word-level alignment from the text. This task poses some difficulty when the child's spelling errors are committed at the supra word level, adding superflous words ("Ich gehe in zu die Stadt"), splitting or connecting words ("Haustier"vs."Haus Tier"), wrong grammatical forms ("auf den Baum"instead of"auf der Baum") or word choice ("Ich gehe in die Stadt"vs."Ich gehe zu die Stadt"). The alignment is therefore not injective. Since we do not deal with grammatical errors, including supra word level problems listed above, the alignment is always surjective.

The purpose of this paper is to present the unified transcription/annotation tool that supports the human annotation task in several ways.

- It propagates annotations so that annotators see each error category only twice.
- It determines the order in which to annotate the data as to reduce human effort.

The tool stores the annotated data in XML-format using a custom made schema which is well suited for the processing necessary for training and evaluating our automatic spelling error categorization tools. The details of this format can be found in [1] and are beyond the scope of this paper.

3   System Overview

Our tool has a client server architecture as depicted in Fig. 1. The server contains the main functionality and is programmed in PHP. A lightweight client is written in Java. The server works with the outputs of either Module 1 or Module 2. After converting the output to XML-format, these are then sorted and serve as the basis from which the GUI will select the top X files presented to the human. Not all are presented due to performance reasons. The sorting algorithm is modular

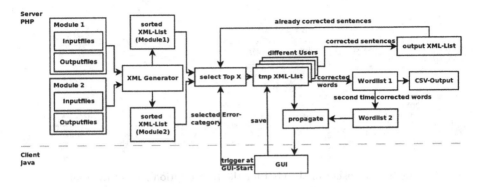

Fig. 1. System architecture of the annotation tool

and can be exchanged as necessary based on the task. The client gives the user the option of choosing module and error category to edit, thereby triggering the server to present the relevant selected top sentences. Sentences in the list contain only those which have not been finished yet, containing at least one word that was not yet propagated or labeled for the chosen error category. The selected sentences are then written to a temporary file. A new temporary list is generated when the old list is finished or when another client triggers the process. Sentences from the client are saved into the *Temporary XML-List* as the user browses through the sentences with "next" or "prev". Saving a sentence results in removing it from *Temporary XML-List* of files and storing the completed sentence in the *Output XML-List*.

In addition, all corrected words occurring in processed sentences (after saved and moved to *Output XML-List*) are saved in *Wordlist 1*. All words in *Wordlist 1* that contain the error category that is presently annotated, are also saved in *Wordlist 2* unless they already exist in *Wordlist 2*. If there are discrepancies between the two lists regarding the annotation, an error message is sent to the user and the user has the opportunity to correct the mistake. If the user consistently annotates the word with the same error given "target" and "achieved" word annotations, this is noted by comparing *Wordlist 1* and *Wordlist 2*. As a result, the annotation is then propagated. Propagation of previous annotations is done in a modular way. The data to be worked on is not altered. Instead the alteration is done when displaying new data in the GUI. In this way, the propagation hold for all new data sets. The annotation is saved as the user moves through the sentences and saves them into *Output XML-List*.

4   Graphical User Interface

This section describes the GUI in more detail. On the start-up screen, the user chooses from Module 1 (correcting word alignment and transcription) or Module 2 (annotation of spelling errors). The error category to be worked can be chosen. (It's easier and faster to correct only one error category at a time instead of all error categories at the same time.)

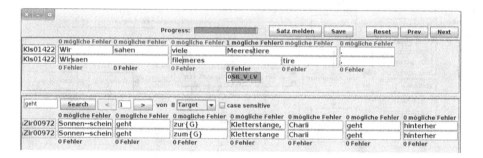

Fig. 2. Screenshot of the GUI for the transcription part of the tool

4.1   Transcription

After choosing module and error category to label, various pieces of information about the sentence are presented to the human transcriber. The upper part of the GUI shows the current target- and achieved-sentence with the word alignment and the spelling error categories. A word can consist of one or several different word-parts. A word or word-part in the target-sentence is always connected to exactly one word or word-part in the achieved-sentence and vice-versa. If a child for example wrote two words mistakenly as one (As in "Wirsahen" in Fig. 2) the achieved-sentence will contain one word with two word-parts (namely "Wir", "sahen" connected to the words "Wir" und "sahen" on the Target side). Word-parts are separated by a red line. The human annotator can change the word alignment and the word-text by splitting, merging, deleting or inserting words or word-parts.

4.2   Navigation

The following buttons provide further functionality: Navigation with the buttons 'next' and 'prev'; by clicking on 'save' the word disappears and is saved on the server; The button 'reset' undoes the last operation; The button 'Satz melden' marks and removes sentences with an unexpected or unusual error. In the lower part of the GUI the user can search for a word in all already corrected sentences.

4.3   Annotation and Propagation

Error annotation is done by using the pop-up window that is presented at word level, either achieved or target word. The user then specifies the number of potential errors for target words and the number of committed errors for achieved words. As explained in the previous section the GUI has the ability to propagate error annotations. Therefore, the user has to correct the same word only twice. Propagated words are marked in red for the user. The error category occurrence of potential errors with respect to the target word are independent of the errors committed in the achieved word. Target words can then be propagated without relation to achieved words. In contrast the error rate of an achieved word depends on the target word. E.g., the achieved word 'im' can be a misspelling of the target word 'ihm' or can be correctly spelled if the target word is im'. Achieved words are therefore propagated only in combination with their corresponding target word. An already propagated word cannot be changed or overwritten. To avoid the propagation of a wrongly annotated word, the system checks for annotator consistency. At the moment, a word has to be annotated twice in the same manner before propagation. If a second annotation of a word differs from the first annotation of the word, a message window is displayed. The user can then decide to overwrite the already saved value or to change the current annotation before the result is then propagated.

5   Preliminary User Tests

After determining the best order in which to present sentences in a simulation we have used the system for a first round of annotations. Two annotators have worked on a subset of 1,000 sentences for two different error categories. Namely, SIL_V_LV[1] (e.g., 'nehmen') and SIL_V_KV (e.g., 'nennen'). For error category SIL_V_LV Fig. 3 plots preliminary results for the propagated word rate over the 1,000 sentences, indicating a significant reduction in labor.

The word rate is calculated as the number of not yet propagated words divided by the number of all words. As it can be seen the word rate decreased from 1 (100 % of the words still need to be propagated) in the beginning to about 25 % after only 1,000 sentences. This means that 25 % of words have not been seen twice in these 1,000 sentences. Thus the reduction in the amount of work due to propagation is about 75 %. It took two hours and 53 min to annotate the 1,000 sentences with an average sentence annotation time of about 10.4 seconds. For these sentences of average length of 9.0 words, annotators were able to annotate 104 words per minute and 30.0 unique words per minute.

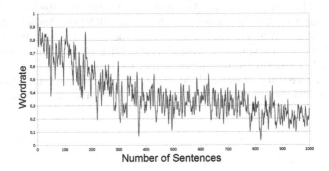

Fig. 3. Propagated word rate over 1000 sentences

---

[1] LV (length vowel) denotes the notation of length for vowels through the use of the letter <h>, preceding a consonant.

6   Conclusion

In this paper it has been shown through preliminary usage of a newly built GUI for data annotation that annotation of word-level tags can be achieved in a robust and time-saving manner. While there are other tools in the market that work with time-aligned data, our hope is that in future work, we will be able to integrate the XML output with these tools to support reuse of data annotation tools. Furthermore, the system is built in such a way that it can support user-specific annotation schemes. The tool is therefore not hard-coded for our presently used error categories. Any word-level tag can be integrated into the GUI simply by changing the tags of the input CSV-formatted files.

Acknowledgements. The work leading to these results was in part funded by a research grant from the German Research Foundation (DFG).

References

1. Berkling, K., Fay, J., Ghayoomi, M., Hein, K., Lavalley, R., Linhuber, L., Stüker, S.: A database of freely written texts of german school students for the purpose of automatic spelling error classification. In: The 9th Edition of the Language Resources and Evaluation Conference (LREC 2014), Reykjavik, 26–31 May 2014
2. Berkling, K., Fay, J., Stüker, S.: Speech technology-based framework for quantitative analysis of german spelling errors in freely composed childrens texts. In: The 2011 Workshop of the ISCA Special Interest Group on Speech and Language Technology in Education (SLaTE 2011), Venice, August 2011
3. Bos, W.: IGLU: Einige Länger der BRD im Nationalen und Internationalen Vergleich. Waxmann Verlag, Münster (2004)
4. Fay, J.: Kompetenzfacetten in der Rechtschreibdiagnostik. Rechtschreibleistung im Test und im freien Text. In: Bermerich-Vos, A. (ed.) Didaktik Deutsch: Symposium Deutschdidaktik, vol. 29, pp. 15–36. Schneider Verlag, Germany (2010)
5. Fay, J., Berkling, K., Stüker, S.: Automatische Analyse von Rechtschreibfähigkeit auf Basis von Speech-Processing-Technologien. In: Didaktik Deutsch, Halbjahresschrift für die Didaktik der deutschen Sprache und Literatur, vol. 19(33) (2012)
6. Stüker, S., Fay, J., Berkling, K.: Towards context-dependent phonetic spelling error correction in childrens freely composed text for diagnostic and pedagogical purposes. In: Proceedings of the 12th Annual Conference of the International Speech Communication Association (INTERSPEECH 2011), Florence, August 2011

The Complexity of Designing and Implementing Metaheuristics

Ricardo Soto[1,2,3](✉), Broderick Crawford[1,4,5], Rodrigo Olivares[1],
Cristian Galleguillos[1], Kathleen Crawford[1], Franklin Johnson[6],
and Fernando Paredes[7]

[1] Pontificia Universidad Católica de Valparaíso, Valparaíso, Chile
{ricardo.soto,broderick.crawford}@ucv.cl, rodrigo.olivares@uv.cl,
cgalleguillosm@ieee.org, kathleen.crawford.a@mail.ucv.cl
[2] Universidad Autónoma de Chile, Santiago, Chile
[3] Universidad Científica del Sur, Lima, Peru
[4] Universidad Central de Chile, Santiago, Chile
[5] Universidad San Sebastián, Santiago, Chile
[6] Universidad de Playa Ancha, Valparaíso, Chile
franklin.johnson@upla.cl
[7] Escuela de Ingeniería Industrial, Universidad Diego Portales, Santiago, Chile
fernando.paredes@udp.cl

Abstract. Optimization problems can be found in several real application domains such as engineering, medicine, mathematics, mechanics,
physics, mining, games, design, and biology, among others. There exist
several techniques to the efficient solving of these problems, which can be
organized in two groups: exact and approximate methods. Metaheuristics are one of the most famous and widely used approximate methods
for solving optimization problems. Most of them are known for being
inspired on interesting behaviors that can be found on the nature, such
as the way in which ants, bees and fishes found food, or the way in
which fireflies and bats move on the environment. However, solving optimization problems via metaheuristics is not always a simple trip. In this
paper, we analyze and discuss from an usability standpoint how the effort
needed to design and implement efficient and robust metaheuristics can
be conveniently managed and reduced.

Keywords: Optimization problems · Metaheuristics · Local solution ·
Optimal solution

1 Introduction

Optimization problems can be found in several real application domains such as
engineering, medicine, mathematics, mechanics, physics, mining, games, design,
and biology, among others. There exist several techniques to the efficient solving
of these problems. On one hand, we found the exact methods, which aim at
providing the global optimum of the given problem by exploring the complete

© Springer International Publishing Switzerland 2015
C. Stephanidis (Ed.): HCII 2015 Posters, Part I, CCIS 528, pp. 593–597, 2015.
DOI: 10.1007/978-3-319-21380-4_101

search space of potential solutions. A main problem of these techniques is that for several optimization problems, the search space cannot be completely explored in a reasonable amount of time. The approximate methods tackle this concern, which on the contrary, explore only promising regions of the search space in order to provide a good enough local optimum in a limited amount of time. However, they are unable to always guarantee the global optimum.

Metaheuristics are one of the most famous and widely used approximate methods for solving optimization problems [1,10]. Most of them are known for being inspired on interesting behaviors that can be found on the nature, such as the way in which ants, bees and fishes found food, or the way in which fireflies and bats move on the environment. However, solving optimization problems via metaheuristics is not always a simple trip, mainly because metaheuristics are not black boxes ready to be used to solve any optimization problem and there are different topics that must be handled before designing and implementing a metaheuristic: iterations, exploration, exploitation, move operators, and representation of solutions, among others. They must be smartly adapted to the nature of the problem and most of them must be efficiently tuned to reach good results in a reasonable amount of time. This commonly demands specific and advanced knowledge from the user. In this paper, we analyze and discuss a method in order to reduce the effort for designing and implementing metaheuristics.

2   Discussion

In general, when trying to solve optimization problems, we consider different solution techniques. The metaheuristics are one of these techniques, but succeed in correctly using them depends on the maturity of certain implementation and design knowledge. The task is not trivial, as each metaheuristic has its own behavior and characteristics, so you cannot consider it as a black box. Firstly, we need to select among single solution or population-based metaheuristics. Secondly, the representation of the solution must be established. After that, we need to identify the move operators that allow to find or to generate potential solutions. Then, the treatment of unfeasible must be handled, from which we can use three classic methods: penalization, discarding, or repairing. Finally, it will be useful to design a sampling process for the initial configuration of the metaheuristic. Details about those instructions are given in the following.

- The *selection* of the metaheuristic is the first step to determine which algorithm will attempt to solve the optimization problem. As mentioned earlier, there is a strong link between the implementation of the metaheuristic and the problem.
- The *representation of the solutions* is a key process to design and implement a metaheuristic. This process is responsible for defining the data structure to model the solution. This structure is independent from the problem domain, but is bounded by the dimension of the problem.

- The *variable domains* of the problem are the set of values that can take a solution and it is defined by the mathematical model of the optimization problem. This is strongly linked to the representation of the solution.
- The *move operators* generate a new solution, generally from an existing one. They are usually mathematical functions that define the behavior of the metaheuristic.
- The *unfeasible solutions* must be treated in different ways. When move operators generate solutions that are not in the problem domain, you must consider three classic alternatives: discard the solution, penalize, or repair it. These three alternatives are commonly part of the metaheuristic implementations.
- The *sampling process* is an important part of the process. Each metaheuristic has its own configuration so it is necessary to develop an a priori sampling and to define values for each parameter. This process is iterative and depends on the robustness of the implementation of the metaheuristic.
- The *sampling process* aims at defining proper values for each metaheuristic parameter. This process may be useful for the robustness of the metaheuristic.
- At the end, it is crucial to evaluate the performance of the implemented metaheuristic. To this end, the *trial and error process* is key in demonstrating the robustness of the metaheuristic.

This method can be seen as a knowledge discovery process that solves optimization problems using metaheuristics as solving technique. This method has been repeatedly applied by computer science students from the Pontificia Universidad Católica de Valparaíso, Chile. This method has been conducted over a period of five months, corresponding to one semester of study. Students must solve the set covering problem applying metaheuristics and compare their results with 65 reported instances. In Table 1 we illustrate the progress of three iterations of the metaheuristic implementation. In the first iteration, is hard to achieve optimal values, however several values can be close to the optimal one. At the second, and third iteration the number of optimal values improve. Finally, incorporating tuning and efficient repairing, several optimal values can be found. Indeed, several articles have been published based on the student results reached by using this method [2–9].

Table 1. A performance example of three students.

Student	Iteration #1 optimal reached (%)	Iteration #2 optimal reached (%)	Iteration #3 optimal reached (%)
A	0	≤ 2	≤ 21
B	0	≤ 1	≤ 15
C	0	≤ 1	≤ 19

3   Conclusion

In this paper, we have illustrated a method for designing and implementing metaheuristics for solving optimization problems. This method depends on the maturity of certain basic concepts for all metaheuristic. The aim is to identify and define each of these step according to the given problem and metaheuristic. This method can be seen as a process of knowledge discovery, which has phases that must be resolved for success in the design and implementation of metaheuristic. To date, this method has been used by computer science students with very promising results. We expect to continue improving this method, detailing each of the stages.

Acknowledgments. Ricardo Soto is supported by Grant CONICYT / FONDECYT / INICIACION / 11130459, Broderick Crawford is supported by Grant CONICYT / FONDECYT / REGULAR/1140897, Fernando Paredes is supported by Grant CONICYT / FONDECYT/REGULAR/1130455 and Rodrigo Olivares & Cristian Galleguillos are supported by Postgraduate Grant Pontificia Universidad Católica de Valparaíso 2015.

References

1. Blum, C., Roli, A.: Metaheuristics in combinatorial optimization: overview and conceptual comparison. ACM Comput. Surv. **35**(3), 268–308 (2003)
2. Crawford, B., Soto, R., Cuesta, R., Olivares-Suárez, M., Johnson, F., Olguín, E.: Two swarm intelligence algorithms for the set covering problem. In ICSOFT-EA 2014 - Proceedings of the 9th International Conference on Software Engineering and Applications, 29–31 August, 2014, Vienna, Austria, pp. 60–69 (2014)
3. Crawford, B., Soto, R., Cuesta, R., Paredes, F.: Application of the artificial bee colony algorithm for solving the set covering problem. Sci. World J. **2014**, 8 (2014)
4. Crawford, B., Soto, R., Cuesta, R., Paredes, F.: Using the bee colony optimization method to solve the weighted set covering problem. In: Stephanidis, C. (ed.) HCI 2014, Part I. CCIS, vol. 434, pp. 493–497. Springer, Heidelberg (2014)
5. Crawford, B., Soto, R., Olivares-Suárez, M., Paredes, F.: A binary firefly algorithm for the set covering problem. In: Silhavy, R., Senkerik, R., Oplatkova, Z.K., Silhavy, P., Prokopova, Z. (eds.) Modern Trends and Techniques in Computer Science. Advances in Intelligent Systems and Computing, vol. 285, pp. 65–73. Springer International Publishing, Switzerland (2014)
6. Crawford, B., Soto, R., Olivares-Suárez, M., Paredes, F.: Using the firefly optimization method to solve the weighted set covering problem. In: Stephanidis, C. (ed.) HCI 2014, Part I. CCIS, vol. 434, pp. 509–514. Springer, Heidelberg (2014)
7. Crawford, B., Soto, R., Olivares-Suárez, M., Paredes, F., Johnson, F.: Binary firefly algorithm for the set covering problem. In: 2014 9th Iberian Conference on Information Systems and Technologies (CISTI), pp. 1–5, June 2014
8. Crawford, B., Soto, R., Palma, W., Johnson, F., Paredes, F., Olguín, E.: A 2-level approach for the set covering problem: parameter tuning of artificial bee colony algorithm by using genetic algorithm. In: Tan, Y., Shi, Y., Coello, C.A.C. (eds.) ICSI 2014, Part I. LNCS, vol. 8794, pp. 189–196. Springer, Heidelberg (2014)

9. Cuesta, R., Crawford, B., Soto, R., Paredes, F.: An artificial bee colony algorithm for the set covering problem. In: Silhavy, R., Senkerik, R., Oplatkova, Z.K., Silhavy, P., Prokopova, Z. (eds.) Modern Trends and Techniques in Computer Science. Advances in Intelligent Systems and Computing, vol. 285, pp. 53–63. Springer International Publishing, Switzerland (2014)
10. Glover, F., Kochengerger, G.: A Handbook of Metaheuristics. Kluwer Academic Publishers, Boston (2003)

A Filtering Technique for Helping to Solve Sudoku Problems

Ricardo Soto[1,2,3], Broderick Crawford[1,4,5], Cristian Galleguillos[1(✉)],
Kathleen Crawford[1], and Fernando Paredes[6]

[1] Pontificia Universidad Católica de Valparaíso, Valparaíso, Chile
{ricardo.soto,broderick.crawford}@ucv.cl
{cristian.galleguillos.m,kathleen.crawford.a}@mail.ucv.cl
[2] Universidad Autónoma de Chile, Santiago, Chile
[3] Universidad Científica del Sur, Lima, Peru
[4] Universidad Central de Chile, Santiago, Chile
[5] Universidad San Sebastián, Santiago, Chile
[6] Escuela de Ingeniería Industrial, Universidad Diego Portales, Santiago, Chile
fernando.paredes@udp.cl

Abstract. This paper highlights the current usability issues when solving Sudoku problems. This problem is a well-known puzzle game which consists in assigning numbers in a game board, commonly of 9 × 9 size. The board of the game is composed of 9 columns, 9 rows and 9 3 × 3 sub-grids; each one containing 9 cells with distinct integers from 1 to 9. A game is completed when all cells have a value assigned, and the previous constraints are satisfied. Some instances are very difficult to solve, to tackle this issue, we have used a filtering technique named Arc Consistency 3 (AC3) from the Constraint Programming domain. This algorithm has revealed which is much related to the strategies employed by users in order to solve the Sudoku instances, but in contrast, this technique is executed in a short time, offering a good resolution guide to the users. In general, filtering techniques make easier solving Sudoku puzzles, providing good information to users for this.

Keywords: Sudoku · Constraint programming · Arc consistency

1 Introduction

Sudoku is a mathematician game, widely known for being a very entertaining pastime, which consists in assigning numbers in a game board. Traditionally this board is a grid of 9 × 9 size, then there exists 81 positions which are called cells. The grid is composed of 9 columns, 9 rows and 9 3 × 3 sub-grids; each of these structures containing 9 cells. The game begins with distinct integers from 1 to 9 sparsely assigned in the grid, these are called "givens". The givens must be at least 17 digits to ensure that the game will have a unique solution [7].

An instance of the game is completed, when all cells have a assigned value, but it is not so easy, the digit assignments must comply the problem constraints.

© Springer International Publishing Switzerland 2015
C. Stephanidis (Ed.): HCII 2015 Posters, Part I, CCIS 528, pp. 598–603, 2015.
DOI: 10.1007/978-3-319-21380-4_102

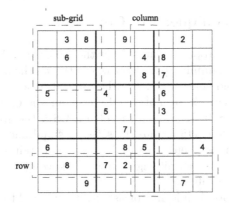

Fig. 1. Example of a Sudoku instance with 24 givens.

The constraints can be reduced to a single statement which says, every cell must have a number, it must be unique in the row, column and sub-grid which it belongs to. Then, if the statement is separated in single constraints, we have 3 constraints for every cell making this game very difficult to solve (Fig. 1).

Such a puzzle belongs to the NP-complete collection of problems [14], this problem has widely been studied, proposing several approaches during the last years to solve it, from complete search methods such as constraint programming [10,11] and boolean satisfiability [3] to incomplete search methods such as genetic programming [5], metaheuristics in general [1,2,6,8,9], and hybrid algorithms [12,13]. The main interest of the Sudoku problem is due to some instances are very difficult to solve.

To tackle this issue, we have used a filtering technique in order to validate the assignation from users, moreover to meet the possible value assignation to facilitate the Sudoku resolution and determining whether or not is a solution in an earlier stage of the resolution process by users, in relation to assigned and given values. The filtering technique chosen is named Arc Consistency 3 (AC3) from the Constraint Programming domain, which is an algorithm that enforces the arc consistency property on a constraint network. After reviewing its resolution process, we have realized that the resolution phase is much related to the strategies employed by users in order to solve the instances, but in contrast, this technique is executed in a short time, offering a good resolution guide to the users.

The effectiveness of filtering techniques was addressed performing an evaluation; it was realized in order to identify the quality of filtering over the different difficulties of the Sudoku puzzle. In general, filtering techniques make easier solving Sudoku puzzles, providing good information to users for this.

This paper is organized as follows. In Sect. 2, the employed filtering technique is explained. We describe the game prototype in Sect. 3, and the corresponding discussions. Finally, our conclusions are presented.

2   Filtering Technique: Arc Consistency

The Arc Consistency property comes from the Constraint Programming (CP) domain. CP is a programming paradigm where the mathematical problems are stated as variables and constraints, and then solved by a CP solver. A problem which is stated in terms of variables and constraints is called Constraint Satisfaction Problem (CSP). In order to resolve a CSP, the state of the variable are searched and the restrictions must be satisfied simultaneously. This property establishes a relation between two variables and maintain only feasible values in each variable domains, permitting to reduce the combinatorial search space, deleting the unfeasible values.

To ensure that a problem is arc consistent, it is needed to apply a filter technique, existing different algorithms to ensure the property, the algorithm used in this research was Arc Consistency Algorithm #3, defined by Alan Mackworth [4].

To apply the mentioned algorithm, the problem must be stated as a CSP, then a 9×9 Sudoku can be modeled as:

- $X = (x_{11}, \ldots, x_{99})$ is the sequence of variables, and $x_{ij} \in X$ identifies the cell placed in the ith row and j^{th} column of the Sudoku matrix, for $i = 1, \ldots, 9$ and $i = 1, \ldots, 9$.
- D is the corresponding set of domains, where $D(x_{ij}) \in D$ is the domain of the variable x_{ij};
- C is the set of constraints defined as follows:
  - To ensure that values are different in rows and columns:
    $x_{k,i} \neq x_{k,j} \wedge x_{i,k} \neq x_{j,k}, \forall (k \in [1,9], i \in [1,9], j \in [i+1,9])$
  - To ensure that values are different in sub-squares:
    $x_{(k1-1)*3+k2,(j1-1)*3+j2} \neq x_{(k1-1)*3+k3,(j1-1)*3+j3}, \forall (k1, j1, k2, j2, k3, j3 \in [1,3] | k2 \neq k3 \wedge j2 \neq j3)$

Algorithm 1. Revise3

Input: x_i, c
Output: $CHANGE$

```
1    CHANGE ← false
2    Foreach vi ∈ D(xi) do
3      If ∄τ ∈ c ∩ πX(c)(D) with τ[xi] = vi do
4        remove vi from D(xi)
5        CHANGE ← true
6      End If
7    End Foreach
8    Return CHANGE
```

The AC-3 algorithm if composed from the Algorithm 1 and 2. The main idea of these algorithms are the examination of value pairs and remove every value in $D(X_i)$ that is inconsistent with the problem constraints, this is performed by the function **Revise3**. If the pair of the value v_i is eliminated from $D(x_i)$, then it is necessary to verify the arc from the other direction. Every domain must be consistent, doing a detailed revision of all the domains. This is done by using a loop that verifies arcs until no change happens. The algorithm ends when all arcs are revised and no more changes exists (Q is empty), and it returns true when all arcs have been verified and remaining values of domains are arc consistent for all the problem constraints.

Algorithm 2. AC3/GAC3

Input: X, D, C
Output: Boolean
1    $Q \leftarrow (x_i, c) | c \in C, x_i \in X(c)$
2   **while** $Q \neq \emptyset$ **do**
3   select and remove (x_i, c) from Q
4   **If** Revise3(x_i, c) **then**
5   **If** $D(x_i) = \emptyset$ **then**
6   **return false**
7   **Else**
8            $Q \leftarrow Q \cup \{(x_j, c') | c' \in C \wedge c' \neq c \wedge x_i, x_j \in X(c') \wedge j \neq i \}$
9   **End If**
10   **End If**
11   **End While**
12   **Return** true

3   Experiments and Discussions

In Fig. 2, it is possible to see the gameboard with a Sudoku instance at the left. When a user selects a cell, if the checkbox "Help" is checked on the right side, an assistance for solving is given. Before and after typing an digit on the board, the AC3 algorithm is executed and the constraints are checked, delivering the possible assignations. It is possible to recognize that the algorithm is very effective for helping to solve, because a guidance through all the resolution process is given, making more easy to solve the game instances.

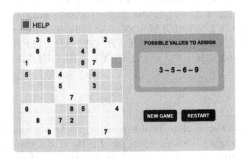

Fig. 2. Showing help solving an instance to a user.

If a wrong digit is entered, the prototype will show an error message on top, and the possible assignations will be shown, as appear in Fig. 3. If there are not possible assignations, clearly the arc consistency has detected an unfeasible assignation, and the previously entered digits were wrongly entered to the gameboard.

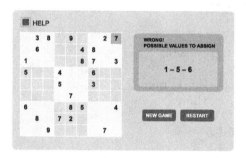

Fig. 3. Correcting an error, in order to help solving an instance to a user.

4   Conclusions

In this paper, we have presented a very useful technique in order to facilitate the resolution process of the Sudoku game. This game is known to be a NP-Complete problem, being a popular game in research fields like Constraint Programming and Metaheuristics, involving instances very difficult to solve. We have used the AC3 algorithm in order to offer a resolution guide to the users. This technique is similar to the strategies employed by users at the resolution process, but this technique is executed in a short time, making more easier and faster the solving process of the Sudoku puzzles.

Acknowledgments. Cristian Galleguillos is supported by Postgraduate Grant Pontificia Universidad Católica de Valparaíso 2015. Ricardo Soto is supported by Grant CONICYT / FONDECYT / INICIACION / 11130459. Broderick Crawford is supported by Grant CONICYT / FONDECYT / REGULAR / 1140897. Fernando Paredes is supported by Grant CONICYT / FONDECYT / REGULAR / 1130455.

References

1. Asif, M.: Solving NP-complete problem using ACO algorithm. In: International Conference on Emerging Technologies, pp. 13–16. IEEE Computer Society (2009)
2. Lewis, R.: Metaheuristics can solve sudoku puzzles. J. Heuristics **13**(4), 387–401 (2007)
3. Lynce, I., Ouaknine, J.: Sudoku as a sat problem. In: International Symposium on Artificial Intelligence and Mathematics (ISAIM) (2006)

4. Mackworth, A.: Consistency in networks of relations. Artif. Intell. **8**(1), 99–118 (1977)
5. Mantere, T., Koljonen, J.: Solving, rating and generating sudoku puzzles with ga. In: IEEE Congress on Evolutionary Computation, pp. 1382–1389. IEEE (2007)
6. Mantere, T., Koljonen, J.: Solving and analyzing sudokus with cultural algorithms. In: 2008 IEEE Congress on Evolutionary Computation. CEC 2008. (IEEE World Congress on Computational Intelligence), pp. 4053–4060, June 2008
7. McGuire, G., Tugemann, B., Civario, G.: There is no 16-clue sudoku: Solving the sudoku minimum number of clues problem. CoRR, abs/1201.0749 (2012)
8. Moraglio, A., Togelius, J.: Geometric particle swarm optimization for the sudoku puzzle. In: Proceedings of the 9th Annual Conference on Genetic and Evolutionary Computation, GECCO 2007, pp. 118–125. ACM, New York, NY, USA (2007)
9. Moraglio, A., Togelius, J., Lucas, S.: Product geometric crossover for the sudoku puzzle. In: IEEE Congress on Evolutionary Computation, pp. 470–476. IEEE Computer Society (2006)
10. Rossi, F., van Beek, P., Walsh, T.: Handbook of Constraint Programming. Elsevier, New York (2006)
11. Simonis, H.: Sudoku as a Constraint Problem. In: Hnich, B., Prosser, P., Smith, B. (eds.) Proceedings 4th International Workshop on Modelling and Reformulating Constraint Satisfaction Problems, pp. 13–27 (2005)
12. Soto, R., Crawford, B., Galleguillos, C., Monfroy, E., Paredes, F.: A hybrid ac3-tabu search algorithm for solving sudoku puzzles. Expert Syst. Appl. **40**(15), 5817–5821 (2013)
13. Soto, R., Crawford, B., Galleguillos, C., Monfroy, E., Paredes, F.: A prefiltered cuckoo search algorithm with geometric operators for solving sudoku problems. Sci. World J. **2014**, 12 (2014). cited By (since 1996)2
14. Yato, T., Seta, T.: Complexity and completeness of finding another solution and its application to puzzles. IEICE Trans. **E86–A**(5), 1052–1060 (2003)

Local Learning Multiple Probabilistic Linear Discriminant Analysis

Yi Yang[⊠] and Jiasong Sun

Tsinghua National Laboratory for Information Science and Technology, Department of Electronic Engineering, Tsinghua University, Beijing, China
{Yangyy, sunjiasong}@tsinghua.edu.cn

Abstract. Probabilistic Linear Discriminant Analysis (PLDA) has delivered impressive results in some challenging tasks, e.g. face recognition and speaker recognition. Similar with the most state-of-the-art machine learning techniques, PLDA tries to globally learn the model parameters over the whole training set. However, those globally-learnt PLDA parameters can hardly characterize all relevant information, especially for those data sets whose underlying feature-spaces are heterogeneous and abound in complex manifolds. PLDA has the data homogeneous assumption which could be interpreted by involved parameters estimated through the entire training dataset. Such a global learning idea has been proven ineffective in the case of the heterogeneous data. In this paper, we alleviate this assumption by separating the feature space and locally learning multiple PLDA models of each space. Various standard datasets are performed and the superiority of the proposed method over the original PLDA could be found. We complete this work by assigning a probability to measure which models the test individual data match. This probabilistic scoring approach could further integrate different recognition technologies including other kinds of biological characteristics recognition. We propose the novel log likelihood score in recognition part includes three steps to complete.

Keywords: Local learning · Probabilistic linear discriminant analysis · Clustering · Bayesian method · Fusion

1 Introduction

Probabilistic Linear Discriminant Analysis (PLDA) [1], as a probabilistic extension of LDA [2], has been demonstrated as an effective approach to learn the low-dimensional representation of feature by its excellent performance on both face recognition [1] and speaker recognition [3]. A generative model is adopted which incorporates both within-individual and between-individual variation. In the recognition stage, PLDA calculates the likelihood that the differences between face images are entirely due to within-individual variability.

Similar with the most state-of-the-art machine learning techniques, PLDA tries to globally learn the model parameters over the whole training set. Nevertheless, those globally-learnt PLDA parameters can hardly characterize all relevant information,

© Springer International Publishing Switzerland 2015
C. Stephanidis (Ed.): HCII 2015 Posters, Part I, CCIS 528, pp. 604–610, 2015.
DOI: 10.1007/978-3-319-21380-4_103

especially for those datasets whose underlying feature spaces are heterogeneous [4] and abound in complex manifolds [5]. Plenty of recent works have been presented to train the models locally rather than globally [6–8]. Observing these facts, we propose a novel approach to consider heterogeneous subtle data structures by locally learning the PLDA model parameters.

The rest of this paper is organized as follows. Some related work is briefly reviewed in Sect. 2. In Sect. 3, we simply review the PLDA algorithm. In Sect. 4, we propose a novel robust locally learning multiple PLDA method to overcome the non-linear subspace problem and extend this method by introducing individual clustering to deal with the trouble caused by noise distribution, and we give the log likelihood method to score this model. Experimental results on face recognition data as well as speaker recognition data are presented in Sect. 5, respectively, comparing our method with other methods, which is followed by the conclusions and future works of this paper.

2 Locally Learning Multiple PLDA Models with Clustering

Linear Discriminant Analysis (LDA) [6] is a powerful method for face recognition, yielding a linear transformation matrix on the original data space and subsequently projecting it into a low-dimensional feature space. The well-known Fisher criterion [2, 10] is adopted, meaning that the centroid of different classes is pushed away and the data from the same class are pulled closely to the great extent. This can be realized by maximizing between-class variation and minimizing the within-class variation. LDA has the small-sample problem and other improvements of LDA could not handle the situation on the large changes of light and posture which always are regarded as interference.

The details of this are rather involved and are presented in [1].

2.1 Locally Learning Multiple PLDA

Locally learning algorithm always attempts to find a locally mapping which projects individual features to an explicit point in each subspace. The capacity of a locally learning algorithm is decided by its optimal parameters. In this section we adopt nonlinear locally learning method to reduce the problem caused by dimension mismatch. Matching between the two individual features is based on the distance between the two mapped individual features. Assuming that the observed features were generated as follows:

$$y_i, c = w_c x_{i,c} + m_c \tag{1}$$

Where $y_{i,c}$ is the feature vector of the i-th person in the c-th PLDA models. w_c denotes the subspace projection mapping matrix in the c-th PLDA models. m_c is the bias vector in the c-th PLDA models.

The minimum mean-square error compression of data is the formulation for PCA that can be generalized to the case with missing values in a very straightforward manner [9]. By this method, the weighted cost function of Eq. 1 is:

$$\hat{y}_i, c = \arg\min_{w \in W}(w_c^T x_{i,j,c} + m_c) = \arg\min_{w \in W}(\Sigma_{k=1}^K w_{ck} x_{ck} + m_c) \tag{2}$$

Where W is defined as the subsets of weighted space. $\hat{y}_{i,c}$ is the least squares estimated value of $y_{i,c}$. And

$$K = \Sigma_{i \in O}(y_{i,c} - \hat{y}_{i,c})^2 \tag{3}$$

Where O is defined as the individual feature value space. This method is trying to find a constant approximation of $y_{i,c}$ as the desired output in each subspace. We have the same nonlinear locally learning weight in training part and recognition part.

2.2   Novel Log Likelihood Score

First, the probability of test individual data belonging to one of multiple separating space is defined as:

$$P(t = k) = \frac{\Sigma_{k=0}^K P(c = k)P(t = k|c = k)}{\Sigma_{k=0}^K P(t = k|c = k)} \tag{4}$$

Where $P(t = k)$ is probabilities of test individual data belongs to the k th space. $P(c = k)$ is probabilities of train individual data c belongs to the k th space. $P(t = k|c = k)$ is the conditional probability of above. $k = 0, \ldots, K$ and K is the total number of space. And the classified test individual data is projected to same subspace as in training part:

$$\hat{y}_{i,c} = w_c^T x_{i,j,c} + m_c \tag{5}$$

Second, the novel log likelihood score is computed by the probability of classified test individual data which generated from certain c-th PLDA models is the summing of all variables:

$$P(\hat{y}_c|\theta_c) = \Sigma_{c=1}^K \int \int P(\hat{y}_c, h_{i,c}, w_{i,j,c}, c) dh_{i,c} dw_{i,j,c} \tag{6}$$

Finally, the decision fusion is to combine multiple PLDAs θ_c by Bayes criterion into one PLDA model whose matching likelihood of $\hat{y}_i$ and $\hat{y}_j$ is:

$$P(\hat{y}_i, \hat{y}_j|\theta_c) = \prod_{c=1}^K P(\hat{y}_{i,c}, \hat{y}_{j,c}|\theta_c) \tag{7}$$

And the log likelihood score is defined as:

$$L_\theta = \frac{\Sigma_{c=1}^{K}[P(t=c)P(\hat{y}_i, \hat{y}_j | \theta_c)]}{log \Sigma_{c=1}^{K}[P(t=c)(1 - P(\hat{y}_i, \hat{y}_j) | \theta_c)]} \tag{8}$$

Where L_θ calculate the ratio of log likelihood with the one PLDA model that two individual test data match to that of two individual test data do not match. i and j separately represents the i-th individual and the j-th individual of test data. $\Sigma_{c=1}^{K}[P(t=c)P(\hat{y}_i, \hat{y}_j | \theta_c)]$ and $\Sigma_{c=1}^{K}[P(t=c)(1 - P(\hat{y}_i, \hat{y}_j) | \theta_c)]$ separately represents the matching likelihood and the not matching likelihood with the c-th PLDA model.

3 Experimental Results

3.1 Data Preprocessing and Experimental Setup

We performed experiments on three standard corpora: TIMIT and PIE. In TIMIT there are 48 possible phonetic classes for the training, which are later merged into 39 classes for the performance evaluation. The sizes of the training, testing, and development (for parameter tuning) sets are around 140, 7, and 15 thousand, which are the common practices in the speech society [9], based on which we also generate acoustic feature vectors. Since PLDA is a classification algorithm, the PIE dataset, as a face dataset, is used, which consists of more than 40,000 of faces and authors in [5] suggested a representative portion of this corpus. We choose to use 30 samples to train the models and the remainders to test. Commonly, the experiments on PIE were repeated 10 times of random data splitting and the average results are to be reported.

3.2 Results

Figures 1 and 2 shows the individual verification results by four methods on TIMIT and PIE datasets. Table 1. In Fig. 1(a) the PLDA (C = 1, S = 60) method received the highest score and PLDA (C = 1, S = 50) has the second score which indicates that separating space improving the original PLDA under different PLDA subspace projection dimension. Also we can know the nonlinear locally learning will promote the performance under three conditions (C = 1, 2, 3). But with the reduced dimension of nonlinear locally learning, the correct rate has a significant decline under all the PLDA subspace projection dimension. In Figs. 2(b) and 2(c) the PLDA (S = 60) also has the highest score but PLDA (S = 50) has the second score. At the same time we can observe the better results on each nonlinear locally learning method being used. Compared with TIMIT data, Fig. 2 shows the face recognition corpus PIE result with seven methods. Same as TIMIT, The PLDA (S = 120) has the highest score and PLDA (S = 100) has the second score. And it presents the reduced dimension of nonlinear locally learning does make worse influence on PIE data.

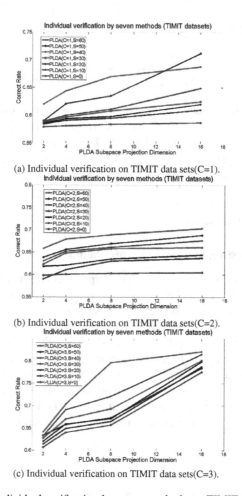

(a) Individual verification on TIMIT data sets(C=1).

(b) Individual verification on TIMIT data sets(C=2).

(c) Individual verification on TIMIT data sets(C=3).

Fig. 1. Individual verification by seven methods on TIMIT data sets.

Table 1. Conditions with their parameters for example

Methods	Separating	Subspace dimension
PLDA(C = 1,S = 0)	1	NONE
PLDA(C = 1,S = 60)	1	60
PLDA(C = 2,S = 0)	2	NONE
PLDA(C = 2,S = 120)	2	120
PLDA(C = 3,S = 0)	3	NONE
PLDA(C = 3,S = 60)	3	60
PLDA(C = 3,S = 0)	3	NONE
PLDA(C = 3,S = 120)	3	120

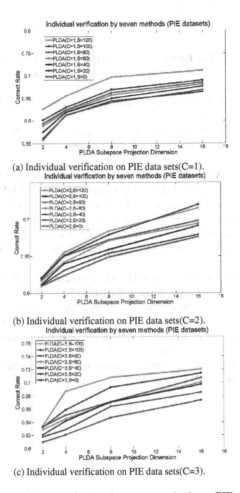

(a) Individual verification on PIE data sets(C=1).

(b) Individual verification on PIE data sets(C=2).

(c) Individual verification on PIE data sets(C=3).

Fig. 2. Individual verification by seven methods on PIE data sets.

4 Conclusions

In this paper, we have presented one approach to generate multiple PLDA models based on feature space separating which enables us to obtain better results than original single PLDA model. We have also shown that our approach is robust both on speaker recognition and on face recognition standard corpus without other prior information. And a new probabilistic scoring approach is proposed to achieve soft decision based on feature space separating and locally learning multiple PLDA models. Combining other biometric individual components with our model is a promising approach to many recognition tasks.

Acknowledgement. Thanks to NSFC (61105017) agency for funding.

References

1. Prince, S.J.D., Elder, J.H.: Probabilistic linear discriminant analysis for inferences about identity. In: 11th International Conference on Computer Vision 2007, ICCV 2007, pp. 1–8. IEEE, 14–21 October 2007
2. Fisher, R.A.: The use of multiple measurements in taxonomic problems. Ann. Eugen. **7**, 179–188 (1936)
3. Senoussaoui, M., Kenny, P., Brummer, N., Dumouchel, E.d.V.P.: Mixture of plda models in i-vector space for gender independent speaker recognition. In: Interspeech 2011, pp. 1–19. IEEE (2011)
4. Kumar, N., Andreou, A.G.: Heteroscedastic discriminant analysis and reduced rank HMMs for improved speech recognition. Speech Commun. **26**, 283–297 (1998)
5. He, X., Niyogi, P.: Locality preserving projections. In: Proceedings of Neural Information Processing Systems, vol. 16, Vancouver, British Columbia (2003)
6. Kim, T., Kittler, J.: Locally linear discriminant analysis for multimodally distributed classes for face recognition with a single model image. IEEE Trans. Pattern Anal. Mach. Intell. **27**, 318–327 (2005)
7. Liu, Y., Liu, Y., Chan, K.: Tensor-based locally maximum margin classifier for image and video classification. Comput. Vis. Image Underst. **115**(3), 300–309 (2011)
8. Mahanta, M., Aghaei, A., Plataniotis, K., Pasupathy, S.: Heteroscedastic linear feature extraction based on sufficiency conditions. Pattern Recognit. **45**, 821–830 (2012)
9. Ilin, A., Raiko, T.: Practical approaches to principal component analysis in the presence of missing values. J. Mach. Learn. Res. **11**, 1957–2000 (2011)
10. Halberstadt, A.: Heterogeneous acoustic measurements and multiple classifiers for speech recognition, Ph.D. thesis, MIT (1998)

Information Processing and Extraction for HCI

Predicting and Visualizing Wine Characteristics Through Analysis of Tasting Notes from Viewpoints

Brendan Flanagan[1(✉)], Nao Wariishi[2], Takahiko Suzuki[3], and Sachio Hirokawa[3]

[1] Graduate School of Information Science and Electrical Engineering, Kyushu University, Fukuoka, Japan
b.flanagan.885@s.kyushu-u.ac.jp
[2] Department of Electrical Engineering and Computer Science, Kyushu University, Fukuoka, Japan
wariishi.nao.141@s.kyushu-u.ac.jp
[3] Research Institute for Information Technology, Kyushu University, Fukuoka, Japan
{suzuki,hirokawa}@cc.kyushu-u.ac.jp

Abstract. When describing complex characteristics of a specific genre, specialist expressions are often used. This can become quite a problematic situation for an inexperienced person, as expressions not used in everyday language are difficult to understand. This is particularly apparent when trying to describe wines, known as winespeak, as a range of specialist expressions are used in a subjective manner. In this paper, we propose that the descriptions of wines can be analyzed from various points of view to automatically predict and visualize the sensory sentiment characteristics described within the expressions as a radar chart. This would enable those not knowledgeable in winespeak to visualize and compare the complex descriptions often found in expert tasting notes.

1 Introduction

Areas of specialty often require a set of expressions that are tailored to meet the need of a specific genre. As these expressions are not used commonly in everyday communication, for people that are not familiar with the specialty terminology or expressions it can be quite baffling and difficult to understand. An area of particular interest to the authors is the language that is used to describe and express complex emotions and senses. A good example of this can be seen in the description of food and beverages that consist of complex aromas, flavors, and many other characteristics as they usually are expressed using specialist terminology used in a subjective manner. Within this area, the descriptions of wine are notorious for the use of specialist terminology and the expression of commonly used words in an uncommon manner. This is formally known as winespeak, and is used by wine reviews/tasters and also in the descriptions on the back label of wine bottles. To the uninitiated, it might be difficult to understand what a wine with "slightly pungent notes of green tomato or crushed tomato leaf" might be like, as used by Joe Czerwinski in his review of a Villa Maria 2009 Sauvignon Blanc [2].

© Springer International Publishing Switzerland 2015
C. Stephanidis (Ed.): HCII 2015 Posters, Part I, CCIS 528, pp. 613–619, 2015.
DOI: 10.1007/978-3-319-21380-4_104

In this paper, we propose a method for the automatic visualization of wine characteristics form viewpoints based on the sense sentiment analysis of a corpus of wine tasting notes. A subset corpus consisting of wine tasting notes that have been manually classified into four sense sentiment viewpoints will be analyzed to train and evaluate Support Vector Machine (SVM) classifiers for sentiment analysis. By analyzing target wine tasting notes with these classifiers, a score will be predicted from each of the sense sentiment viewpoints. These predicted scores will then be visualized in the form of Radar Charts so that the characteristics of wines may be compared.

2 Related Work

There are many papers on research into the language that is used to describe wines, called winespeak. Some of this research is dedicated to analyzing wine tasting notes from different points of view. Paradis and Eeg-Olofsson [5] examined tasting notes to identify expressions and words that are related to the viewpoints of vision, smell, taste, and touch. 39 typical phrases of these sensory expressions were identified. Caballero [1] focused on how manner-of-motion verbs are used from the point of view of describing a wine's intensity and persistence, and collected 56 typical sentences that contain such verbs. In this paper, wine sentiment analysis is conducted using the four sensory viewpoints defined by Paradis and Eeg-Olofsson [5]. There is also related research into the visualization of wine tasting notes for linguistic analysis. Kerren et al. [4] visualized wine tasting notes using word trees generated from parts of speech and words. Their system enables the analysis of linguistic patterns within single wine reviews or based on regions and varieties. However the system is highly specialized and not intended for general use. In previous research, we examined the relations of Winespeak expressions and visualized these as mindmaps [3]. In this paper, the language used in tasting notes is automatically analyzed from different sensory viewpoints. The results are then visualized as radar charts so that the sensory sentiment content of the wine tasting note can be conveyed without having an understanding of winespeak.

3 Data Collection

In this paper, we propose that tasting notes can be analyzed to predict the classification of wines from various points of view. The target data for analysis is a corpus that consists of 91,010 wine tasting notes, or 255, 966 sentences, that were collected from the Wine Enthusiast website.[1] The attributes of each wine, such as: winery, region, and grape variety were collected along with the text of the wine tasting notes. This data was then indexed to construct a special use search engine using GETA.[2] A subset of the data consisting of 992 sentences from wine tasting notes was randomly selected for use

---

[1] http://buyingguide.winemag.com/.

[2] http://geta.ex.nii.ac.jp/.

in the training, testing and evaluation of sentiment models. This data subset was manually classified by hand into four different sensory category viewpoints, as defined by Paradis and Eeg-Olofsson [5].

4   Sensory Viewpoint Analysis and Prediction

An overview of the analysis in this paper, which involves training SVM models to predict four sense sentiments for visualization as radar charts, is shown on the left in Fig. 1. Firstly, a data subset of 992 manually classified sentences was vectorized, with each feature vector consisting of the words contained within a wine tasting note. The feature weights were normalized at the feature vector for each sentence to ensure that the number of features does not have an influence on model training. An SVM classifier for each sense was initially trained using all the data in the subset. The weights from these models was then extracted and used to score feature words for feature selection. An example of the top 10 positive and negative score feature words for the sense smell are shown in Table 1.

The words are ranked by the absolute value of the weight score, with the top N ranked words selected for training and testing. For each set of N top words, 5 SVM classifiers were trained and tested using 5-fold cross validation with a training/test data ratio of 4:1. Evaluation of the prediction performance for increasingly larger N was calculated, which can be seen on the right in Fig. 1 for the smell sense. The N with the greatest average prediction performance from the 5 SVM models by F-measure is selected as the optimum model. For the smell sense, the baseline prediction performance is an F-measure of 0.59 for a model created by analyzing all feature words. Prediction performance peeked at an F-measure of 0.63 for a model created by analyzing 500 of the top ranking words. This indicates that the top 500 words are representative features for the smell viewpoint.

The feature selection process was applied to all four sense sentiment models. The optimal N for each of the sensory viewpoint model, the evaluation of the model, and the baseline F-measure are shown in Table 2. Models trained on optimal feature selection are used to predict the sense sentiment of wine tasting note visualization.

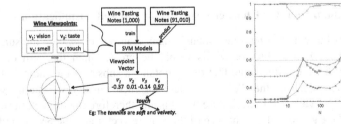

Fig. 1. Left: an overview of the automatic prediction and visualization of wines from multiple viewpoints; right: prediction performance of feature selection using the top N absolute value score words for the touch sense.

Table 1. Top 10 positive and negative score words for the smell sense

Positive		Negative	
Score	word	Score	word
1.2935	aroma	-0.4143	flavor
1.1981	note	-0.3202	juice
0.9632	nose	-0.3189	tannic
0.6752	smell	-0.2660	finish
0.5676	accent	-0.2503	chewy
0.4608	oak	-0.2359	bitter
0.4601	scent	-0.2298	card
0.4450	smoky	-0.2235	richness
0.4381	spice	-0.2218	sweet
0.4011	perfume	-0.2166	acidity

Table 2. Feature selection: optimal N and evaluation for each of the sensory viewpoints

Sense	Optimal N	Precision	Recall	F	Baseline	Accuracy
Smell	500	0.4726	0.9788	0.6356	0.5960	0.6438
Taste	600	0.6503	0.9889	0.7839	0.7397	0.7071
Touch	200	0.4754	0.9728	0.6370	0.5646	0.6426
Vision	700	0.2488	0.8942	0.3872	0.2986	0.5755

5 Visualization of Sensory Sentiment as Radar Charts

By reading the descriptions on a wine bottle, or a tasting note for a single wine, we might be able to roughly understand some of the wines characteristics without having a mastery of winespeak. However, it is much harder to grasp the characteristics of a wine region without reading about all the different wines produced. Sensory sentiment analysis from different viewpoints can provide an overview of the characteristics of a wine region, and then be plotted as a Radar Chart for easy comparison with other regions.

5.1 Model Normalization for Characteristic Prediction and Visualization

If a feature vector of a wine tasting note contains many feature words, then the sum of the predicted scores of these feature words would be greater than the sum of the predicted scores of a wine tasting note that only contains a subset of the same feature words. Also, because each of the SVM classifiers for each sensory viewpoint were trained by 5-fold cross validation, the feature weights and therefore the prediction score range is different for each model. As the size of the feature vector and the SVM models that classify the sensory sentiments of wine tasting notes can influence the final score given, both the feature vector and SVM model prediction scores need to be normalized before visualization of the results.

When vectorizing the tasting notes of a region, the weight of each word in the feature vector was determined by Eq. 2,

$$weight(w_i) = \frac{DF(w_i)}{\sqrt{\sum_{w_j \in W} DF(w_j)^2}} \tag{1}$$

where $DF(w_i)$ is the document frequency of the word w_i from the search query. This normalization ensures that a feature vector with many terms is not of greater weight that a feature vector that contains only a few terms. Thus, the number of terms does not influence the analysis of the characteristic features.

Also the prediction score from each SVM classifier can be over a different range, and therefore the prediction score needs to be normalized so that a fare comparison can be made. Equation 2 was used to normalize the prediction scores for each feature vector from each SVM model,

$$norm(v_i, m_j) = \frac{score(v_i, m_j) - min(m_j)}{max(m_j) - min(m_j)} \tag{2}$$

where $score(v_i, m_j)$ is the predicted score for the feature vector v_i from the SVM model m_j, and the maximum and minimum model feature weights are represented by $max(m_j)$ and $min(m_j)$ for the model m_j.

5.2   Visualization of Sensory Sentiment by Region

In the data that was collected for analysis there are 4,675 regions, including major and sub-region combinations. The characteristics were calculated based on the wine tasting notes for each region as an example of sensory sentiment analysis. The chart with the largest summed score was from the Pelješac region in Croatia, as seen in Fig. 2 on the left.

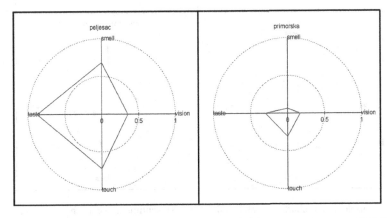

Fig. 2. Example radar charts: regions with the smallest and largest graph area are Pelješac (left) and Primorska (right) respectively.

The chart shows three large positive scores, with the vision sense not scoring highly. The region with the smallest summed score was from the Primorska region in Slovenia. The chart for this region shows that few sense descriptive feature words were used in the wine tasting notes, with only a slight emphasis on the taste and touch senses.

Extreme sense sentiments can be seen in the charts of Fig. 3. These charts represent the highest score values for each of the four sense sentiment viewpoints. The chart for the Sonoma County, Santa Barbara County region in the USA shows a large number of features representing taste were used to describe the wines. This could suggest that the wines from that region have more taste qualities than smell, vision, and touch. In the chart for Alto Adige Valle Isarco region in Italy is the highest scoring region for the vision sense, but it would seem that negative scoring features for the vision sense are also prominent in the wine tasting notes. This would explain why the score is less than seen in other charts. The chart for the Ioannina in Greece scores highly on the smell sense viewpoint. This suggests that aromas play an important point in the description of the wines from that region. Lastly the chart for the Barossa Valley, Clare Valley region in Australia scores highly in sense sentiment for touch, suggesting feature words to do with the texture of the wine are often used.

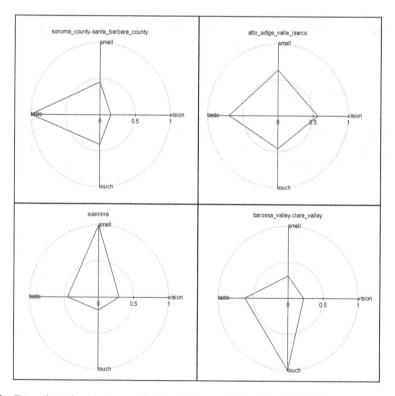

Fig. 3. Example radar charts: graphs with strongest sentiment for each sense are Sonoma county, Santa Barbara county for taste (top right), Alto Adige valley Isarco for vision (top right), Ioannina for smell (bottom left), and Barossa valley, Clare valley for touch (bottom right).

6   Conclusion and Future Work

In this paper, we analyzed 992 manually classified sentences of wine tasting notes to create SVM models from four sense sentiment viewpoints: vision, smell, taste, and touch. The models were evaluated and a search was performed to find the optimal feature selection for each model. The optimal models were then used to analyze the four sense sentiment viewpoints of 4,675 regions in a corpus consisting of 91,010 wine tasting notes. The results of the analysis were then normalized for fare comparison between models and sense sentiment viewpoints. Six examples of visualizations by Radar Chart were given representing the largest, smallest, and strongest sentiment for all four of the sense viewpoints.

In future work, we plan to investigate what viewpoints are suitable for understanding and comparing the characteristics of wines from tasting notes. Also, we plan to undertake a formal evaluation of the effectiveness of the visualization.

Acknowledgment. This work was partially supported by JSPS KAKENHI Grant Number 24500176.

References

1. Caballero, R.: Manner-of-motion verbs in wine description. J. Pragmat. **39**(12), 2095–2114 (2007)
2. Czerwinski, J.: Villa Maria 2009 Taylors Pass Vineyard Sauvignon Blanc (Marlborough) Wine Tasting Note (2010). http://buyingguide.winemag.com/catalog/villa-maria-2009-taylors-pass-vineyard-sauvignon-blanc-marlborough. Accessed 11 November 2014
3. Hirokawa, S., Flanagan, B., Suzuki, T., Yin, C.: Learning winespeak from mind map of wine blogs. In: Yamamoto, S. (ed.) HCI 2014, Part II. LNCS, vol. 8522, pp. 383–393. Springer, Heidelberg (2014)
4. Kerren, A., Prangova, M., Paradis, C.: Visualization of sensory perception descriptions. In: Proceedings of the International Conference on Information Visualization, pp. 135–144 (2011)
5. Paradis, C., Eeg-Olofsson, M.: Describing sensory experience: the genre of wine reviews. Metaphor Symbol **28**(1), 22–40 (2013)

Extraction of Key Segments from Day-Long Sound Data

Akinori Kasai, Sunao Hara, and Masanobu Abe[(✉)]

Graduate School of Natural Science and Technology,
Okayama University, Okayama, Japan
{kasai,hara,abe}@a.cs.okayama-u.ac.jp

Abstract. We propose a method to extract particular sound segments from the sound recorded during the course of a day in order to provide sound segments that can be used to facilitate memory. To extract important parts of the sound data, the proposed method utilizes human behavior based on a multisensing approach. To evaluate the performance of the proposed method, we conducted experiments using sound, acceleration, and global positioning system data collected by five participants for approximately two weeks. The experimental results are summarized as follows: (1) various sounds can be extracted by dividing a day into scenes using the acceleration data; (2) sound recorded in unusual places is preferable to sound recorded in usual places; and (3) speech is preferable to nonspeech sound.

Keywords: Life-log · Multisensing · Sound · Acceleration · GPS · Syllable count

1 Introduction

The activities of our daily lives are frequently recorded electronically from various information sources. This is referred to as a life log, which is a massive electronic database of every activity, including cyberspace activities (e.g., web sites visited, keywords for searching, and e-mail content) and real-world activities (e.g., photos, videos, physical locations recorded via wearable global positioning systems (GPSs), and body movements captured by acceleration sensors). Extensive research into life logs has been conducted [1–4], and a promising application area is tools that facilitate remembering personal memories. It has been reported that logging more data increases the chance that the "memory hook," which helps users find what they seek, will be stored. It has also been reported that users rarely regret capturing material; however, they often regret not capturing more material. In this context, in terms of a new life log information source, we introduce sound to recall the atmosphere of places, excitement of events, and emotions in conversations. We believe that recorded sound has several benefits. First, sound is a nondirectional information source; therefore, we can be aware of events that occur all around us. Sound helps us remember memories and occasionally allows us to recall an event that has not been remembered consciously when we hear a recorded sound that is associated with the given event. Second, recorded sound helps us confirm what is said in conversations. Third, sound data consumes less

© Springer International Publishing Switzerland 2015
C. Stephanidis (Ed.): HCII 2015 Posters, Part I, CCIS 528, pp. 620–626, 2015.
DOI: 10.1007/978-3-319-21380-4_105

storage space than video data. Although sound contained in video can provide the two abovementioned features, the smaller storage requirements of sound data is a significant advantage. Moreover, owing to recent device technologies, many recording devices are available at low cost.

In this study, we propose a method to extract key sound segments from day-long sound data. Recording sound for an entire day is especially important for recalling events that have not been consciously remembered. Because day-long sound contains a significant amount of unnecessary sound, such sound must be discarded. To solve this problem, the proposed method utilizes human behavior based on a multisensing approach.

The remainder of this paper is organized as follows. In Sect. 2, we describe the proposed method, and in Sect. 3, we discuss evaluation experiments.

2 Proposed Method for Extracting Key Sound Segments

Figure 1 shows an outline of the proposed method. To facilitate a multisensing approach, location information obtained by GPS and acceleration data are used. The details are explained in the following figure.

2.1 Scene Segmentation by Activity Modes

To remember a past event, it is not necessary to listen to all sounds related to the event. It is sufficient to listen to only a part of the sound data. This is beneficial from a time efficiency perspective because it is time consuming to listen to all sound data. In addition, in terms of remembering, it is important to select sounds from as many various situations as possible because extracting a very long sound segment from a single event is less effective than extracting sound segments from several events during the course of a day. For these reasons, the proposed method divides a day into scenes and extracts parts of the sound data from each scene.

Scene segmentation is performed based on the activity modes in block (a) shown in Fig. 1. The activity modes include staying and moving modes, which are determined by the acceleration data. Note that scenes are at least changed when the activity mode changes. The activity mode is determined as follows. Triaxial acceleration data are obtained every 0.05 s (sampled at 20 Hz). After extracting the acceleration data with a 1-s window for each axis, three variances are calculated for each axis. If the average of the three variances is less than $0.1G^2$, the activity mode is staying, otherwise it is moving.

In block (b), a scene is constructed by checking the duration of the activity mode. If the staying mode continues for more than 60 s, the period is set to one scene. In the same manner, if the moving mode continues for more than 10 s, the period is set to one scene. According to our preliminary experiments, a day is typically divided into 10 to 50 scenes.

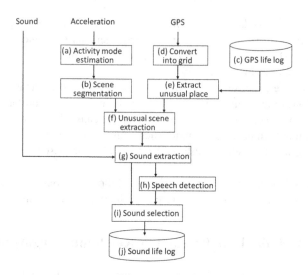

Fig. 1. Outline of the proposed algorithm

2.2   Estimation of Unusual Places with GPS Data

The rarer a situation is, the more people might have what they want to remember. To consider this factor, the proposed method controls rare situation using the places visited as follows. Each person collects GPS data every 30 s. To ignore small differences in longitude and latitude in the location data, all GPS data are converted to grids of side about 125 m (at latitude 35 degree) with unique IDs. Then, a counter for each grid ID is incremented when the person enters that grid; however, the increment is only allowed once per day for each grid ID. These procedures are performed on a daily basis for the collected GPS data for a certain time period. Then, the counted numbers of all grid IDs are stored as a GPS life log ((c) in Fig. 1). The GPS life log contains how many days the person visited places that correspond to the grid IDs. In block (d), the GPS data collected by each person are converted to grid IDs. In block (e), the counted numbers of grid IDs are taken from the GPS life log, and locations with low count numbers are selected as unusual places.

Finally, in block (f), segmented scenes that occur in the unusual places are selected as unusual scenes.

2.3   Extracting Key Sound Segments

There are at least two types of sound data, i.e., speech and nonspeech. To handle speech, the proposed method uses Julius [5], which is an automatic speech recognition (ASR) system.

In block (g), sound recorded during unusual scenes is extracted from the day-long sound data. In block (h), the extracted sound is cut out with a 10-s window, which is referred to as a segment. Then, Julius is applied to the segment. Note that Julius is not used to recognize what people actually say. It is used to select only a period of speech. The proposed method determines the degree of speech likelihood using the number of syllables contained in a given segment. In addition, for the output of block (g), the sound energy is calculated every 10 s in the same manner. The proposed method determines the degree of nonsilence likelihood according to the sound energy of a segment.

3 Evaluation of the Proposed Method

Experiments were performed to evaluate the following: (1) effectiveness of scene segmentation by activity modes; (2) effectiveness of rare situation determined by the frequency of visiting locations; and (3) importance of speech to remember events.

3.1 Data for Evaluations

Five Okayama University students who live alone in Okayama city participated in the experiments. Table 1 shows the data collected by the participants. To construct the GPS life log, participants collected GPS data for 3–12 months. Participants also collected GPS, sound, and acceleration data for approximately two additional weeks using the devices shown in Table 2. They were asked to carry the devices all day. When seated, participants placed the integrated circuit (IC) recorder on a table or desk. However, when moving, the device was carried in different ways. Some participants placed the device in a breast pocket and others put it in a bag. Human Activity Sensing Consortium HASC-Logger software [6] on ASUS Nexus7 was used to collect GPS and acceleration data.

Table 1. Data collected by participants

Participant ID	Recording days	Recording duration	GPS life log (days)
M1	11	122 h 43 min	326
M2	26	237 h 56 min	317
M3	19	149 h 53 min	97
M4	14	113 h 47 min	247
M5	22	195 h 45 min	179

Table 2. Devices used to collect data

Sound recording equipment	IC-recorder OLYMPUS Voice Trek V-823
Sound sampling frequency	44,100 Hz/16 bit
Application to collect GPS and acceleration	HASC logger [6]

Table 3. Variance for users

Participants ID	Average division number (N)	Average variance
M1	26	12.32
M2	15	9.08
M3	18	6.20
M4	17	7.37
M5	17	7.05

3.2   Effectiveness of Scene Segmentation by Activity Modes

The proposed method divides a day into scenes and extracts a sound segment (10 s) from each scene, which allows extraction of sound from many situations. The effectiveness of scene segmentation is compared with a simple method. In the simple method, the sound energy is calculated every 10 s from the sound for an entire day. After sorting all segments by sound energy in descending order, the Nth-largest segments are selected. Here, N is the number of divisions in a day. Finally, the number of segments extracted from each scene generated by the proposed method is counted. Table 3 shows the variance of counts obtained from all data collected by participants. The proposed method selects a sound from a scene; therefore, the variance is always 0. In comparison, the variance obtained by the simple method is much greater than 0. Thus, it is evident that scene segmentation by activity mode is effective.

3.3   Evaluation of Rare Situation and Importance of Speech

Three sets of sound data are extracted from the sound collected by participants. Each set consists of 10 sound segments (10 s). We denote speech recorded at unusual places, speech recorded at usual places, and sound recorded at unusual places as Sp-Un, Sp-Us, and So-Un, respectively. Unusual places, usual places, speech, and sound are determined as follows. Unusual places are those whose count number (Sect. 2.2) is ranked in the bottom 30 %. Usual places are those whose count number is ranked in the top 30 %. Speech is speech that has the top 10th degree of speech likelihood (Sect. 2.3). Sound is sound that has the top 10th degree of nonsilence likelihood (Sect. 2.3).

The 30 sounds are ordered chronologically and presented to the participants. The participants are asked to listen to each sound and determine whether they want to preserve the sound using a five-point scale. When listening, the date, time, and location the sound was recorded are shown on a map displayed on a PC.

The experimental results are shown in Fig. 2. Sp-Un was assigned a rank of five four times more frequently than Sp-Us, which indicates that there is a significant amount of speech from unusual places to remember. However, sound from unusual places are an insufficient condition for remembering because Sp-Un and So-Un are both recorded in unusual places but So-Un obtains the worst scales. According to detailed analysis, this occurs because So-Un includes more loud noises than speech.

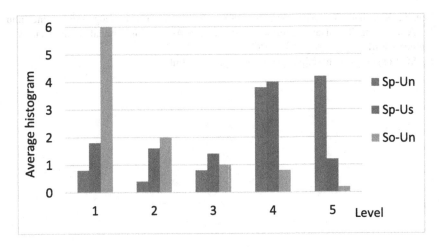

Fig. 2. Experimental results

This means that participants pay more attention to speech sounds to facilitate remembering.

4 Conclusions and Future Work

We have proposed a method to extract particular sound segments from sound recorded over the course of an entire day. In the proposed method, we used multiple sensors and an ASR system to determine important sounds. Our experimental results indicate that the proposed method can successfully extract speech recorded in an unusual location from several hundred hours of sound data. We have also confirmed that the extracted segments show much better preference scores than the sounds recorded at usual locations. In future, we would like to extract sounds other than speech, including bird songs and music. Moreover, we would also like to introduce userspecific factors, such as preferable time, days of the week, and preferable location.

References

1. Gemmell, J., Bell, G., Lueder, R.: MyLifeBits: a personal database for everything. Commun. ACM **49**, 88–95 (2006)
2. Silva, G., Yamasaki, T., Aizawa, K.: Ubiquitous home: retrieval of experiences in a home environment. IEICE Trans. Inf. Syst. **91**(2), 330–340 (2008)
3. Kern, N., Schiel, B., Schmidt, A.: Recognizing context for annotating a live life recording. Pers. Ubiquit. Comput. **11**(4), 251–263 (2007)
4. Gemmell, J., Aris, A., Lueder, R.: Telling stories with Mylifebits. In: Proceedings IEEE International Conference on Multimedia and Expo, pp. 1536–1539 (2005)

5. Lee, A., Kawahara, T.: recent development of open-source speech recognition engine Julius. In: Asia-Pacific Signal and Information Processing Association Annual Summit and Conference APSIPA ASC, pp. 131–137 (2009)
6. HASC Logger. http://hasc.jp/hc2011/hasclogger-en.html

A Model of Decision Support Based on Estimation of Group Status by Using Conversation Analysis

Susumu Kono[1]([✉]) and Kenro Aihara[1,2]

[1] The Department of Informatics, SOKENDAI (The Graduate University
for Advanced Studies), 2-1-2 Hitotsubashi, Chiyoda-ku, Tokyo 101-8430, Japan
{su-kono,kenro.aihara}@nii.ac.jp
[2] The Department of Informatics, National Institute of Informatics,
2-1-2 Hitotsubashi, Chiyoda-ku, Tokyo 101-8430, Japan

Abstract. We propose a model for a decision support of a group based on estimations of group status through utterance analysis. Based on methods used in prior studies of group dynamics and utterance analysis, we measured the utterance characteristics of group members to estimate group status; moreover, we aim to enhance the overall condition of the group by providing appropriate reference information in a timely manner through a conversational agent system.

The goal of this model is a more satisfying decision-making process. Future work will focus on manufacturing a prototype system to verify both the operations involved in the test case and the ability to estimate group classification and status according to group dynamics.

Keywords: Conversation estimation · Group status estimation · Utterance feature · Conversational agent · Intention extraction

1 Introduction

In group decision making, it is not necessarily the case that the opinions of all members will match; some members may even become frustrated with some final group decisions. In this research, therefore, we focus on estimating the group status and aim to support members in the weak position rather than those in the strong position in group. Particularly, we are motivated for this research to solve this problem by using speech recognition and the extraction of intentions.

Our objective is to clarify the effectiveness of estimating the classification and status of a group by measuring the utterance characteristics of the group members. We also aim to lead overall group to good condition by providing appropriate reference information and suggestions in a timely manner by using status estimations based on a group dynamics approach.

© Springer International Publishing Switzerland 2015
C. Stephanidis (Ed.): HCII 2015 Posters, Part I, CCIS 528, pp. 627–632, 2015.
DOI: 10.1007/978-3-319-21380-4_106

2   Background

2.1   Group Dynamics

Group dynamics refers to a system of behaviors and psychologically influential interpersonal processes [4]. Here we focus on the former aspect of group dynamics, and in particular we apply intragroup dynamics approaches to the estimation of the decision-making behavior of small groups through conversation. Previous group dynamics research has found groups to have many measurable characteristics, including relationships, homogeneity durability, permeability, common goals, common outcomes, and size [9].

In groups, the relationships between members are various and can change dynamically based on their particular classifications and current status [13]. For example, groups are affected variously based on the classifications and tasks of their individual members [8].

We define *group* as an aggregate of individuals who have frequent interaction, mutual influence, common feelings of camaraderie, and who work together to achieve a common goals. We define *member* as an individual who joins a group.

2.2   Group Decision-Making

Decision-making in group conversation is affected by the classification and status of the group. For example, it is easy to feel sympathy in groups in which there is a high degree of aggregation. Conversely, it is not only easy to feel sympathy but also contradiction in groups in which the members are able to speak straightforwardly to each other [3].

The members of a group can be easily satisfied with forming a consensus if members can argue for their opinions and some of them are adopted in the course of making a group decision through conversation [2,5,7].

2.3   Utterance Analysis

In prior studies of utterance analysis, it was shown that the utterance feature values in dialogue (e.g., tone, speed, overlapping) can be utilized for identifying various types of group status (e.g., tuning trend, familiarity, upsurge) [10–12]. Examples of utterance feature values are shown in the Table 1.

We define *utterance* as the smallest unit of speech of spoken language, that is a continuous piece of speech beginning and ending with a pause, *speech* as the vocal form of human communication, *conversation* as a form of interactive, spontaneous communication between two or more people, typically occurring in spoken communication, and *conversational agent* as a computer system intended to converse with humans.

The utterance feature values like spectrum of utterance power levels have been also used for estimation of member tension in previous research [1]. *Tension* is defined as mental appearances of physiological responses in this paper. Methods of intention extraction in spoken dialogue utterances have been established by prior research [6].

Table 1. Examples of utterance feature value for group status estimation.

Parameter	Unit	Calculation method
Length	msec	Length (time duration) of each utterance
Times	times/min	Times of occurred utterances per minute
Power level	dB	Power level (loudness) of each utterance
Tone (F0)	Hz	Fundamental frequency
Mora	mora	Unit numbers in phonology that determines syllable weight
Speed	mora/sec	Number of moras per second
Overlap	times/min	Times of overlapped utterances per minute

We define *intention in spoken dialogue* as a plan or an expectation in a speaker's mind to do something that has been mentioned in their speech, and it can be estimated by comparing the text data between speech recognition results and spontaneous dialogue corpora.

3 Models

3.1 Group Model

Based on previous group dynamics research, we defined our group model as one that discusses and decides some undecided or changeable matters through conversation; in particular, we focused on aspects of group status.

Group dynamics prior research shows that groups are classified by using the intimacy, the task and the social relationships such as *intimacy group, task group* and *social group* [4]. In this classification, the relationship between members and the structure of group are not uniformly for each classification, and it is difficult to identify the intimacy and the structure of group by this classification, particularly in the case of social group.

We aim to estimate the group status based on the group classification. Therefore, we proposed the original classification of groups in our group model. We assume that groups can be classified based on their intimacy, structure, and relationship between members, which can be estimated by using analysis of captured data of conversation. Particularly, we prepared following 3 types of classification which are supposed to be detectable.

1. groups that have high intimacy and flat relationships (e.g., friends)
2. groups that have high intimacy and hierarchy (e.g., families)
3. groups that have low intimacy and hierarchy (e.g., bosses and subordinates at work).

In group decision making, reference information is not dealt in discussion, if it is not provided appropriately [7]. Then we aim to provide the reference information by the method based on the group classification in our model of decision support shown below.

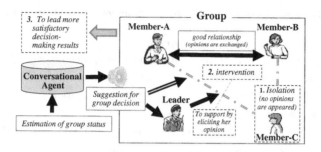

Fig. 1. Intervention to group in our proposed model

3.2   Model of Decision Support Based on Group Status

We propose a model of decision support based on group status estimation by using group dynamics approach and conversation analysis. We assumed that the conversational agent system provides reference information and suggestions that take into account the wishes of each group member, using the synthetic voice at an appropriate time based on the estimated group status, resulting in more satisfactory decision-making.

In this model, first, we investigate relationships between group members by using the result of extraction of intention and estimation of tension in each utterance during conversations occurring among the group members, which shows what and how members communicate with whom, and it also apply to estimation of intimacy and structure of whole group. Thus, we can classify the group according to the group classification above by such relationships between group members, intimacy and structure of whole of group.

Our proposed intervention examples for typical detectable classification group are as follows. The agent provides information through leader, if leader exists, or the agent provides to target member, if not so.

1. High intimacy and flat connection group
   The members of this group classification are assumed to share their opinions frankly. For example, by asking for each member's opinion, one by one through the conversational agent, and it can be determined whether the members have any specific ideas or requests. Then the agent can provide detailed information based on the situation of each member.
2. High intimacy and hierarchy group
   This group classification assumes that the older member knows the views of each member. For example, the dialogue may start by the conversational agent asking the older member which kind of information is preferred by all the members. Then the conversational agent can provide the detailed information to the members, and thus it will be easy for them to discuss or make a selection from the available options.
3. Low intimacy and hierarchy group

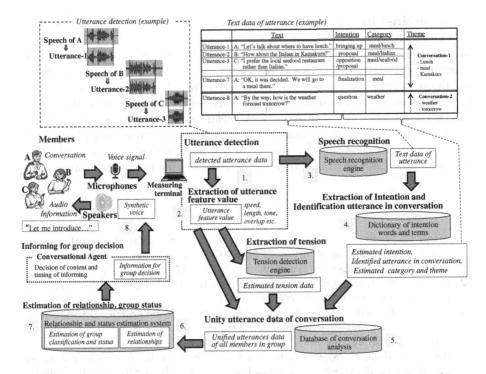

Fig. 2. Processes of group status estimation and provision of group decision-making.

This group classification assumes that an older member leads the group and that junior members may be hesitant to express their feeling directly. Then, it is started to found members in the weak position like isolation from other members, and it aims to support such members by eliciting their opinions from them with appropriate reference information or suggestions. (Fig. 1)

4 Methodology

The processes to estimate the group status by measuring utterance characteristics of group members are shown as follows, as well as in Fig. 2.

1. Voice signal monitoring and utterance detection
2. Utterance feature value extraction
3. Speech recognition and text conversion
4. Extraction of intention and identification of utterance in a single conversation
5. Unification of utterance data in a single conversation
6. Estimation of relationships among group members
7. Estimation of classification and status of the group
8. Intervention to Group in Decision-Making

5 Conclusion

In this paper, we proposed a model to estimate the group status by measuring utterance characteristics of group members, and to enhance the overall group condition through a conversational agent system based on their estimations. The proposed model can obtain all utterance feature values and combine them with the extracted intention of utterances. We can mention that the estimating of group status by measuring the utterance characteristics of users is basically possible through our basic function test. In future work, we will confirm availability of our proposed model to intervene to the group by the prototype system.

References

1. Ariga, M., Yano, Y., Doki, S., Okuma, S.: Mental tension detection in the speech based on physiological monitoring. In: 2007 IEEE International Conference on Systems, Man and Cybernetics, ISIC, pp. 2022–2027. IEEE (2007)
2. Desanctis, G., Gallupe, R.B.: A foundation for the study of group decision support systems. Manage. sci. **33**(5), 589–609 (1987)
3. Deutsch, M., Gerard, H.B.: A study of normative and informational social influences upon individual judgment. J. Abnorm. Soc. Psychol. **51**(3), 629 (1955)
4. Forsyth, D.: Group Dynamics. Cengage Learning, Belmont (2009)
5. Herrera-Viedma, E., Martinez, L., Mata, F., Chiclana, F.: A consensus support system model for group decision-making problems with multigranular linguistic preference relations. IEEE Trans. Fuzzy Syst. **13**(5), 644–658 (2005)
6. Hodjat, B., Amamiya, M.: Applying the adaptive agent oriented software architecture to the parsing of context sensitive grammars. IEICE Trans. Inf. Syst. **83**(5), 1142–1152 (2000)
7. Hogg, M.A., Tindale, S.: Blackwell Handbook of Social Psychology: Group Processes. Wiley, New York (2008)
8. Kelley, H., Thibaut, J.: Interpersonal relations: a theory of interdependence. Wiley, New York (1978)
9. Lickel, B., Hamilton, D.L., Wieczorkowska, G., Lewis, A., Sherman, S.J., Uhles, A.N.: Varieties of groups and the perception of group entitativity. J. Pers. Soc. Psychol. **78**(2), 223 (2000)
10. McCoy, W., Pelz, J.B., Alm, C.O., Shi, P., Calvelli, C., Haake, A.: Linking uncertainty in physicians' narratives to diagnostic correctness. In: Proceedings of the Workshop on Extra-Propositional Aspects of Meaning in Computational Linguistics, pp. 19–27. Association for Computational Linguistics (2012)
11. Oviatt, S., Darves, C., Coulston, R.: Toward adaptive conversational interfaces: Modeling speech convergence with animated personas. ACM Trans. Comput.-Hum. Interact. (TOCHI) **11**(3), 300–328 (2004)
12. Pon-Barry, H., Shieber, S.: The importance of sub-utterance prosody in predicting level of certainty. In: Proceedings of Human Language Technologies: 2009 Annual Conference of the North American Chapter of the Association for Computational Linguistics, pp. 105–108. Association for Computational Linguistics (2009)
13. Walster, E.: The effect of self-esteem on romantic liking. J. Exp. Soc. Psychol. **1**(2), 184–197 (1965)

Computer System for Musicians and Composers to Analyze Music Composition Process

Tetsuya Maeshiro[1,2](✉) and Midori Maeshiro[3]

[1] Faculty of Library, Information and Media Science,
University of Tsukuba, Tsukuba 305-8550, Japan
maeshiro@slis.tsukuba.ac.jp
[2] Research Center for Knowledge Communities,
University of Tsukuba, Tsukuba 305-8550, Japan
[3] School of Music, Federal University of Rio de Janeiro,
Rio de Janeiro, Brazil

Abstract. This paper presents a computer system and its interface for musicians and composers to analyze musical pieces described as a sequence of decision making process during the composition of musical pieces. Representation of musical pieces from the viewpoint of creation process is valuable for both composers and musicians. For composers, it is valuable to verify her own composition techniques and creative process. And for musicians, it offers different viewpoints to understand the musical piece that results in better execution of the musical piece.

Keywords: Music composition · Decision making

1 Introduction

This paper presents a computer system and its interface for musicians and composers to analyze musical pieces described as a sequence of decision making process during the composition of musical pieces. This is a novel system, and no conventional computer system is able to process and visualize musical pieces from the viewpoint of creation process. Such information is valuable for both composers and musicians. For composers, it is valuable to verify her own composition techniques and creative process. And for musicians, it offers different viewpoints to understand the musical piece that results in better execution of the musical piece.

With the wider use of computer scoring system, the so called digital audio workstations, to compose music, which allows annotations of musical pieces in digital format, searching similar parts or by keywords and comparison of partial pieces are becoming easier and faster on daily basis, due to the advance of computer processing speed. The main factor that influences the usefulness of the software to study musical pieces is the type and quantity of available data in the system. Many music production software exist, such as Logic[1], Cubase[2]

---

[1] https://www.apple.com/logic-pro/.
[2] http://www.steinberg.net/en/products/cubase/start.html.

© Springer International Publishing Switzerland 2015
C. Stephanidis (Ed.): HCII 2015 Posters, Part I, CCIS 528, pp. 633–638, 2015.
DOI: 10.1007/978-3-319-21380-4_107

and Performer[3]. Although these software are created to compose music, these are also useful to study musical pieces. However, data available by these software are limited to data directly represented in the musical sheet, such as pitch, duration, chord type, among others. Surely these information are essential to study, we recognize these are insufficient.

Our system displays the music sheet together with the decisions involved in composition of phrases and passages that constitute the musical piece. Users are able to change the visualization detail of the decisions and to compare selected decisions, and edit the descriptions of decisions.

2   System

The hypernetwork model is extended from the bipartite representation of the hypergraph [5]. The hypernetwork model has more representation power than conventional knowledge representation models that are based on graph [4]. The main difference is the capability to represent N-ary relationships, the property of duality, and creation of relationships among relationships. The hypernetwork model follows basic definitions of semantic networks, where a node is connected to other nodes (1) to specify the nodes or (2) when nodes are related by some relationship.

A uniqueness of the hypernetwork model is the existence of three types of description elements, equivalent to the types of nodes. Graph and hypergraph models consist of nodes and links connecting the nodes. In the basic representation of a decision, a node represents any fact or concept, and a link connects two or more concepts based on causal relationship. In a visualized diagram, a link connects two or more nodes. The generated representation is then converted automatically to bipartite representation, where links that represents relationships also become nodes, and links of a new type are inserted to connect the nodes and nodes converted from links. The bipartite representation consists of two types of nodes: (1) the vertex node that represents nodes that originally are nodes in basic representation, and (2) relation node that is converted from a link in basic representation. The vertex node serves to represent substances or phenomena or concepts, and the relation node to describe relationships among them.

Details or properties of a concept represented by a vertex node can be specified in two ways: by attachment of attribute nodes, or by relating to other vertex nodes through relation nodes. The attribute node exists to specify any of three node types. Two connections are prohibited: between vertex node and vertex node, and between relation node and relation node, constraint imposed from their role in hypergraph.

In order to represent decisions in music composition, we use the text description of decisions involved during the composition process. The text is written after each work stage defined by the composer himself, written by the composer

---

[3] http://www.motu.com/products/software/dp.

himself. The number of stages depends on the composer's work style and musical piece being composed, as some pieces take years to be accomplished. Therefore, a stage is anything with varied work amount, number of created and edited notes, and working time durations. In other words, a stage corresponds to the amount of composition work between subsequent intermissions defined by the composer.

In each intermission and after the completion of composition, the composer reviews the modifications since the previous version of the music piece, enumerating every single alterations. Then the composer writes the Decision List Report, a text explaining each modification points, describing the decision type and the details. The decision type should be chosen from (a) Theoretical, (b) Selective, and (c) Intuitive. Theoretical decisions denote decisions based on Music theory. Empirical (heuristic) foundations are excluded because they are empirical and lack theoretical bases. The second type and the third type are used when multiple options exist. It is possible that a decision is theoretical and simultaneously either selective or intuitive, when multiple options exist. The selection of a theory is chosen from multiple possibilities or intuitively. Only one type is associated with decisions, however.

In order to homogenize the granularity of decision sizes, each decision description is analyzed to subdivide into smaller decisions or to join with other decisions depending on the explanation text. Two types of decisions exist, (1) Framework decisions and (2) Component decisions, differing on the extent affected by decisions. Framework decisions are global decisions, and affect the entire musical piece, such as tempo and instruments used. Component decisions are local decisions, modifying passages or a part of musical piece. Basically a component decision consists of a single modification on a single region of an instrument part. A region may contain any number of notes, between a single note, a single chord, or dozen of notes encompassing multiple measures. It may not involve any notes.

The next step is the generation of hypernetwork representation of extracted decisions. The hypernetwork model is explained in next section. The sizes of hypernetwork representation of all decisions are uniform, because the granularity of size of decisions are standardized in the previous step.

Then decisions are interconnected based on: Type-I: decision sequence, subdivided into Type-IA: Global order and Type-IB: Order within overlapped target region; Type-II: Overlap on target region (notes, measures, phrases, among others); Type-III: Identical element node (decision component); and Type-IV: Semantic relationship among element nodes (decision components). This connection process is semiautomatic using computer program. The Type-I connections generate sequence relationships among decisions. The second type of relationships, Type-II, connects decisions affecting at least one identical musical element. It connects multiple decisions that generate N-ary relationships, which are impossible to be generated using conventional representation models. The overlapped element is described in relationship entity, which also functions as a "concept" entity when a person reads the music score. Connections based on same musical element are used to connect multiple decisions if they contain identical elements. The hierarchical level of elements may differ in each decision. For instance, the composer refers to musical elements in other region to employ a variation of these elements. In this case, the hierarchical level of referred elements in decision structure will be different. In other cases, a same thematic element may be used multiple times, and the element description appearing in relevant decisions are linked. The semantic connections, Type-IV, are based on semantic relationship among decision elements. The semantic relationship types used in our representation are: hierarchy of concept, hierarchy of target region, antonym (opposite concept), and synonym concept.

3 Discussions

The disclosure of description of intermediate composition process is useful for both composers and musicians. For composers, it is valuable to overview and clarify his own composition process to improve the composed opus, besides the benefit to reorganize his ideas. For musicians, the acquisition of background and underlying phylosophy is invaluable, because deeper understanding of musical piece is fundamental and crucial for good execution. Before the execution, every musician analyzes the musical piece he/she will perform. During the analysis, musicians investigate every note and their context, their raison d'être, and instructions on execution indicated by the composer. Our method differs from conventional works because the musical piece is represented by a temporal sequence of decisions. Such a creation history is more valuable than static structures generated by conventional methods, such as Generative Theory of Tonal Music (GTTM), due to reasons discussed before.

Musical score is the de facto representation of musical pieces. Musical score encompasses every aspect of the musical piece, and it describes what to be performed, how to be performed, and composer's intentions. Everything is in the score, as some say. John Cage once said that by looking at the music sheet, one can judge the composer's talent, but not by listening to the performance of a musical piece. Music composition process involves a wide range of fields, and the list of fields depends on the music style. Even limiting to fields directly related to music, a composer should be familiar with many disciplines of musical theory inclluding Harmony, acoustics of musical instruments, and genre-dependent articulations of each musical instrument.

Our system treats the creation process, or composition process, from a blank music sheet to the final work. This is a "creation history" of musical piece. Obviously if the data on intermediate process is absent, the representation will only be about the final status of the music. Composers input and annotate each decision making during the music composition. Each decision making is represented as causes, details of the decision, and results. For each musical phrase or passage, decision making structure that originated the relevant musical passage is visualized in our computer system.

Figures 1–3 are examples of representations of the same passage shown in the upper part of the figures. Other representations are also possible. The representation in Fig. 1 focuses in the relationships among musical elements, highly

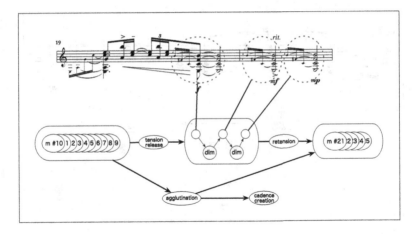

Fig. 1. Representation-1 of a passage (measures 19–20) of music β

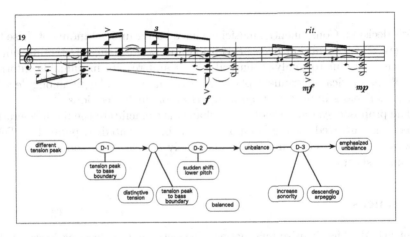

Fig. 2. Representation-2 of a passage (measures 19–20) of music β

similar to conventional representations that treat directly the musical elements. On the other hand, representations in Figs. 2 and 3 are unique to the proposed system, where the descriptions are based on the composer's decisions during composition, unavailable in conventional systems.

Obviously such information is unavailable in most musical pieces. Howerver, preliminary uses by professional composers and musical instrument players indicate that information related to composers' decisions are useful and important for the understanding of the musical piece. Once the usefulness of such information is established, composers might describe such information during their composition.

The visualization of decision making is useful for musicians and also for composers. The proposed system detects dissimilar passages but are similar in com-

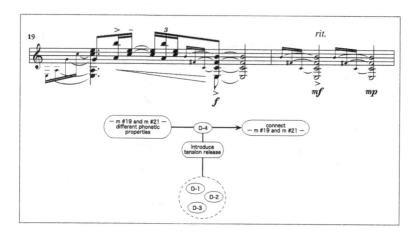

Fig. 3. Representation-3 of a passage (measures 19–20) of music β

poser's decision. Consequently, musicians have better understanding of these two passages, which results in better execution and performance. Detecting similar decisions is useful to analyze musical pieces and results in valuable information for the musical instrument players. Furthermore, similarity among decision sequences is more important than comparison of single decisions.

The proposed system also offers mechanisms to facilitate the input operation of decisions involved during composition, to be activated in parallel to DAW software for composers using DAW, and solely activated for those using pencil and music sheets.

References

1. Polanyi, M.: The Creative Imagination. Chemistry and Engineering News, pp. 85–93, 25 April 1966
2. Klein, G.: Sources of Power: How People Make Decisions. MIT Press, Cambridge (1999)
3. Lerdahl, F., Jackendoff, R.S.: A Generative Theory of Tonal Music. MIT Press, Cambridge (1996)
4. Berge, C.: The Theory of Graphs. Dover, New York (2001)
5. Berge, C.: Hypergraphs: Combinatorics of Finite Sets. North-Holland, Mathematical Library (1989)

Using Structural Topic Modeling to Detect Events and Cluster Twitter Users in the Ukrainian Crisis

Alan Mishler[✉], Erin Smith Crabb, Susannah Paletz, Brook Hefright, and Ewa Golonka

University of Maryland, College Park, MD, USA
{amishler, ecrabb, paletz, hefright, egolonka}@umd.edu

Abstract. Structural topic modeling (STM) is a recently introduced technique to model how the content of a collection of documents changes as a function of variables such as author identity or time of writing. We present two proof-of-concept applications of STM using Russian social media data. In our first study, we model how topics change over time, showing that STM can be used to detect significant events such as the downing of Malaysia Air Flight 17. In our second study, we model how topical content varies across a set of authors, showing that STM can be used to cluster Twitter users who are sympathetic to Ukraine versus Russia as well as to cluster accounts that are suspected to belong to the same individual (so-called "sockpuppets"). Structural topic modeling shows promise as a tool for analyzing social media data, a domain that has been largely ignored in the topic modeling literature.

Keywords: Structural topic modeling · Event detection · Authorship attribution · Public opinion measurement · Social media

1 Introduction

Topic modeling is a statistical and computational technique for discerning information about the contents of a large corpus of documents without reading or annotating the original texts [1]. A topic model uncovers patterns of word co-occurrence across the corpus, yielding a set of word clusters, together with associated probabilities of occurrence, which constitute the 'topics'.

Topic modeling is of interest to any user who wishes to gain insight into a collection of documents, including researchers who want to understand what is being discussed online. While the use of topic modeling is well attested with texts such as novels or news stories [2, 3], relatively little work has been done in the realm of social media. Modeling in this domain is often more challenging given character limits, which cause users to condense their messages in a variety of ways, such as by using URL shortening services when posting links [4].

The standard topic modeling technique, Latent Dirichlet Allocation (LDA), may have limited utility in the realm of social media. LDA makes a statistical assumption that all texts in the modeled corpus are generated by the same

© Springer International Publishing Switzerland 2015
C. Stephanidis (Ed.): HCII 2015 Posters, Part I, CCIS 528, pp. 639–644, 2015.
DOI: 10.1007/978-3-319-21380-4_108

underlying process [5]. Thus, it is not ideally suited to examining differences in topical content that are affected by external variables such as author identity or time of writing.

Structural topic modeling (STM) is a recently introduced variant of LDA that is designed to address precisely this limitation [6]. STM can represent the effect of external variables on both topical content and topical prevalence. Topical content refers to the probabilities associated with words in each topic, while topical prevalence refers to the proportions of different topics that occur within documents. The external variables can consist of any metadata that distinguishes one text from another, including variables relating to author identity (gender, age, political affiliation, etc.), textual genre (for example, news stories versus academic articles), and time of production.

Since STM is a relatively recent innovation, its full utility has not yet been well demonstrated. We investigated two particular applications of STM related to Russian and Ukrainian social media data. In the first study, we show that STM can be used to detect major real world events such as the downing of Malaysia Air Flight 17 (MH 17) in Ukraine. In the second study, we demonstrate that STM can be used to group and distinguish Twitter users with different political sympathies, namely, those sympathetic to Russia versus Ukraine.

2 Study 1: Event Detection

2.1 Methods

We downloaded 50,000 posts from VKontakte, a Russian-owned social media site similar to Facebook. The posts were gathered using TweetTracker, a web-based portal for collecting tweets and other social media data [7, 8]. As a filter for selection, we used the "VK:Ukraine" task, a publicly available search filter designed to gather data pertaining to Ukraine. Specifically, we harvested 25,000 posts from July 16, 2014, the day before the MH 17 crash, and 25,000 posts from July 18, 2014, the day after the crash. We gave the posts a label of "t1" (Time 1) and "t2" (Time 2), respectively. In order to ensure that the model did not simply identify clusters of words based on the source language, we collected posts in a single language, Russian, as determined by the Google Translate language code included in the TweetTracker metadata.

We constructed a 30-topic structural topic model of the data using the stm package in R [9]. Prior to modeling, strings beginning with "#", "@", and "http" were removed, as were non-UTF-8-encodable characters and function words such as "and" and "the." Words were stemmed using the *textProcessor* function in the stm package. Since the goal was to detect a change in expressed content from Time 1 to Time 2, we conditioned both topical content (the probabilities associated with words in each topic) and topical prevalence (the proportions of different topics that occur within documents) on the two-level time covariate ("t1" versus "t2").

2.2   Findings

Topical prevalence differed substantially from Time 1 to Time 2 for nearly all of the 30 topics modeled (Fig. 1). In particular, two topics, identified arbitrarily as Topic 2 and Topic 13, were significantly more common in the corpus at Time 2 than at Time 1.

An examination of prominent words within each topic (Table 1) makes it clear that these topics relate to the MH 17 crash and its purported cause – namely, the Buk missile system that is believed to have been used to shoot down the plane [10].

As predicted, the model easily detected changes in content that resulted from the MH 17 crash. A researcher with minimal training in interpreting the results of topic models and no prior knowledge of the MH 17 event would be able to readily infer from these results that a catastrophe involving a plane and a missile system occurred between

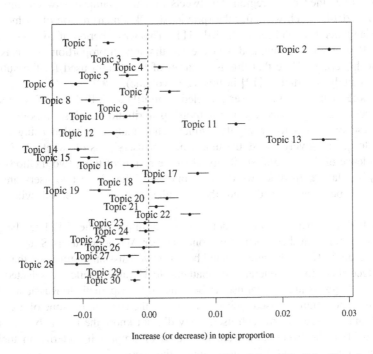

Increase (or decrease) in topic proportion

Fig. 1. Difference in topic prevalence from Time 1 to Time 2 for each of the 30 topics modeled in study 2A. A positive value indicates that the topic is more prevalent at Time 2; a negative value indicates that the topic is more prevalent at Time 1.

Table 1. Study 1: prominent words in Topic 2 and Topic 13. These two topics are significantly more prevalent in the corpus at Time 2 than at Time 1.

Topic	Prominent words
Topic 2	*самолет* 'airplane', *боинг* 'Boeing', *бук* 'Buk (missile system)'
Topic 13	*Расследован* 'investigated', *катастроф(a)* 'catastrophe', *малайзийск(ий)* 'Malaysian', *борт* 'board'

July 16 and July 18. The researcher could then examine a subset of the actual VK posts or other documents to determine the precise nature of the event.

3   Study 2: Clustering Twitter Users

3.1   Methods

The dataset for this study consisted of approximately 4,000 Russian language tweets collected via the "Crimea" TweetTracker query. The "Crimea" query returns tweets that include a key word or hashtag referencing a set of pre-defined key words pertaining to Crimea or Ukraine, come from a particular set of users related to Crimea, or are geotagged as originating from the area defined by a geographic coordinate bounding box in the Crimea region. The tweets were timestamped between June 25 and August 25, 2014, which was after the (previously Ukrainian) region of Crimea joined the Russian federation on March 18, 2014 [11]. This was a period of continued tension between Russia and Ukraine, and we expected that a high proportion of tweets would be about this crisis. (Note that this is a subset of the dataset used for the authorship attribution study reported in [12] in this same volume).

The tweets came from four users, labeled arbitrarily as S, K, L, and T. Users K and L were selected in part because the authorship attribution analysis reported in [12] found these two users to be highly similar. That analysis entailed using character bigrams to quantitatively assess the uniqueness of users' sets of tweets. If STM also finds evidence of these users' similarity, then the results of these two methods will be mutually validating. In other words, the conclusion that these two users are highly similar will be strengthened, and the confidence in each method will also be strengthened.

An additional goal with this model was to determine whether STM can be used to group and distinguish these users from one another. We added users S and T toward this end. Users S, K, and L were selected because two Russian linguists on the research team judged them to be generally sympathetic to Ukraine, while we selected user T because the linguists judged that user to be generally sympathetic to Russia and hostile to Ukraine. The linguists based their judgments on the content and tone of a sample of several hundred tweets from each user. They did not know the results of the analysis prior to reading the tweets and were instructed to simply characterize in their own words any similarities and differences among the users.

We preprocessed the data in the same manner as in Study 1 and modeled it again using the stm package in R [9]. Due to the small size of the corpus and the fact that tweets are limited to 140 characters, we modeled only five topics (as compared to 30 in Study 1). We conditioned topical prevalence on the four-level factor author identity, with each author constituting a factor level.

3.2   Findings

Plots of topic prevalence by author show that tweets from users S, L, and K are topically similar, while the content of user T's tweets is markedly different.

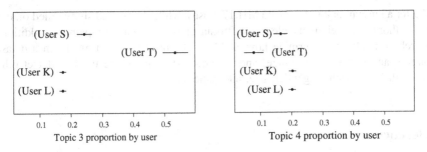

Fig. 2. Study 2: Proportion of words from Topics 3 and 4 for each user, across all of that user's tweets.

Table 2. Study 2: prominent words in Topics 3 and 4

Topic	Prominent words
Topic 3	*США* 'USA', *границ(ы)* 'borders', *Крым* 'Crimea', *Росс(ия)* 'Russia', *Путин* 'Putin'
Topic 4	*Донецк* 'Donetsk', *Луганск* 'Luhansk', *обстрел* '[arms] fire', *град* 'a multiple rocket launcher system', *погиб(ли)* 'died', *силовик* 'political actor associated with Russian special services'

In particular, user T relies substantially on Topic 3, while the other four topics are less prevalent in user T's tweets than in the other users' tweets (Fig. 2; again, the indices used to identify topics are arbitrary). Topics 1, 2, and 5 are not plotted, but they have similar distributions to that of Topic 4.

These results confirm and strengthen the conclusion from the sockpuppet detection analysis reported in [12] that users K and L are highly similar. Additionally, they reveal the expected two clusters of users: the three users sympathetic to Ukraine versus the one user sympathetic to Russia. Prominent words from Topics 3 and 4 give some indication of how the content of these users' tweets differs (Table 2). Notably, Topic 4 contains references to weaponry, death, and Russian special services, while Topic 3 appears to be primarily related to geographic locations and geopolitical actors.

A researcher or analyst with no prior knowledge of the content of these three users' tweets would easily be able to discern that users S, K, and L cluster together, while user T is distinct (Fig. 2); additionally, the researcher would be able to make some inferences about how these users differ, which could then be confirmed or further refined by inspecting a representative sample of tweets from each user.

4   Future Work

The results of these two studies serve as a proof-of-concept for two applications of STM to the analysis of social media data: (1) detecting significant events through changes in social media data over time, and (2) grouping and distinguishing authors or sources on the basis of textual content. The first study relied on data taken from before and after a known major event (the MH 17 crash), while the second study relied on data from authors with relatively clear pro-Russia or pro-Ukraine sympathies. Additional research is needed to determine how STM can be used to detect events in a dataset spanning an arbitrary time range, and to what extent it can be used to detect other author attributes such as gender, age, and nationality.

References

1. Blei, D.M.: Probabilistic topic models. Commun. ACM **55**, 77–84 (2012)
2. Mimno, D.: Computational historiography: data mining in a century of classics journals. J. Comput. Cult. Heritage (JOCCH) **5**, 1–19 (2012)
3. Yang, T.-I., Torget, A.J., Mihalcea, R. Topic modeling on historical newspapers. In: Proceedings of the 5th ACL-HLT Workshop on Language Technology for Cultural Heritage, Social Sciences, and Humanities, pp. 96-104. Association for Computational Linguistics, Portland, Oregon (2011)
4. Hong, L., Davison, B.D.: Empirical study of topic modeling in Twitter. In: Proceedings of the First Workshop on Social Media Analytics, pp. 80–88. Association for Computational Linguistics, New York (2010)
5. Blei, D.M., Ng, A.Y., Jordan, M.I.: Latent dirichlet allocation. J. Mach. Learn. Res. **3**, 993–1022 (2003)
6. Roberts, M.E., Stewart, B.M., Airoldi, E.M.: Working Paper (2014). http://scholar.harvard.edu/bstewart/publications. Accessed 24 September 2014
7. Kumar, S., Barbier, G., Abbasi, M.A., Liu, H.: TweetTracker: an analysis tool for humanitarian and disaster relief. In: Proceedings of the International Conference on Weblogs and Social Media, pp. 661–662. AAAI, California (2011)
8. Kumar, S., Morstatter, F., Liu, H.: Twitter Data Analytics. Springer, New York (2013)
9. Roberts, M.E., Stewart, B.M., Tingley, D.: stm: R Package for Structural Topic Models. Retrieved from The Comprehensive R Network (2014). http://cran.r-project.org/web/packages/stm/stm.pdf
10. New York Times. What Happened to Malaysia Airlines Flight 17. http://www.nytimes.com/interactive/2014/07/18/world/europe/malaysia-airlines-flight-mh17-q-a.html?_r=0 Accessed 23 July 2014
11. Washington Post. A year after Crimean annexation, threat of conflict remains. http://www.washingtonpost.com/world/europe/a-year-after-crimean-annexation-threat-of-conflict-remains/2015/03/18/12e252e6-cd6e-11e4-8730-4f473416e759_story.html Accessed 18 March 2015
12. Crabb, E.S., Mishler, A.M., Paletz, S.B., Hefright, B., Golonka, E.: Reading between the lines: a prototype model for detecting Twitter sockpuppet accounts using language-agnostic processes. Communications in Computer and Information Science (CCIS). Springer, New York (2015)

Improvement of Chance Index
in Consideration of Cluster Information

Ryosuke Saga$^{(\boxtimes)}$ and Yukihiro Takayama

Graduate School of Engineering, Osaka Prefecture University,
Gakuen-Cho, Naka-Ku, Sakai, Osaka, Japan
saga@cs.osakafu-u.ac.jp

Abstract. This paper describes an improved chance index for chance discovery. A chance is an important event or circumstance that can be used by analysts to make decisions. Discovery chance, i.e., chance discovery, is important for knowledge to be used effectively in understanding the background and causes hidden in a dataset. However, chance discovery depends on analyst's inference. Therefore, we propose a chance index that quantitatively evaluates chance. The method is based on betweenness centrality and the strength of co-occurrence. This study improves the accuracy of chance index by considering cluster information.

Keywords: Knowledge extraction · Co-occurrence network · Chance index · Chance discovery

1   Introduction

Chance is an important event or circumstance that can be used by analysts to make decisions [1]. Knowledge discovery in database process exists in data mining [2]. Analysts can obtain various large data and often use data mining to gain knowledge. However, the final purpose of the analyst is not knowledge discovery from data mining, but to understand the causes and background of the gained knowledge and to utilize this knowledge.

For example, by analyzing sales data, analysts can identify products that are selling well. This is knowledge discovery. Of course, obtaining this knowledge alone does not directly result in profits for the store. Analysts discover the factors affecting the high product sales and apply those factors to other products. In this example, data analysis only has meaning or value when analysts can use the obtained knowledge to increase sales. The causality associated with a product that sells well is considered chance. Thus, chance discovery is the final purpose of analysts.

Traditionally, chance discovery depends on the analyst's experience and background because chance discovery needs analyst's inference. To support chance discovery, several methods have been proposed. KeyGraph is a famous method [3] that maps the relationships of data into a co-occurrence network based on frequency, and analysts observe and infer from the network to discovery nodes

© Springer International Publishing Switzerland 2015
C. Stephanidis (Ed.): HCII 2015 Posters, Part I, CCIS 528, pp. 645–649, 2015.
DOI: 10.1007/978-3-319-21380-4_109

regarded as chances. This methodology is useful because the process promotes divergence and convergence, similar to the KJ method [4]. However, chance is often passed over or misunderstood in the chance discovery process.

To solve the problem, we have propose a *chance index* [5], which estimates whether a node is a chance in a co-occurrence network. Chance index quantitatively measures the degree of chance. However, chance index has room for improvement when used in a complex network with a high density network. Therefore, this paper describes the improvement of chance index by using the border information between clusters.

2 Chance Index and Its Improvement

Chance index is established based on the structural pattern analysis of chance discovery results. The pattern analysis revealed the following features: (i) chance nodes, which are regarded as chance in a co-occurrence network, are located in the border of clusters, and (ii) chance nodes connect to others with weak links. Based on the features, chance index of node i is formulated by the following Eq. (1):

$$CI_i = (i) + \beta f_e(i) \tag{1}$$

where CI_i is the chance index of node i. The two terms, namely, $f_v(i)$ and $f_e(i)$, show betweenness centrality, which indicates the connectivity between clusters and the strength of links. α and β are the weights for the combination between $f_v(i)$ and $f_e(i)$.

By using the chance index, we can find chance nodes from two simple co-occurrence networks without inference. However, the accuracy for a complex network is lower. Some nodes have high betweenness despite their location at the center of a cluster. In this case, the cluster information cannot be shown clearly in Eq. (1). Therefore, we add a new term to Eq. (1) to show the cluster more clearly. The amended equation is shown in Eq. (2), as follows:

$$CI_i = \alpha f_v(i) + \beta f_e(i) + \gamma f_c(i) \tag{2}$$

where $f_c(i)$ is cluster information, and γ is a parameter that is similar to α and β. To consider cluster information, we adapt two types of clustering, as follows: hard clustering and soft clustering. The former allows a node to belong to only one cluster, whereas the latter permits a node to belong to multiple clusters. Based on these types, $f_c(i)$ in the case of soft clustering is 1 when node i belongs to multiple clusters and is located on the borders between clusters; otherwise, the $f_c(i)$ is 0. In the case of hard clustering, $f_c(i)$ is set to a value where node i is located on the border between clusters. We consider the case in which the value is uniformly 1, and the case in which the value changes the number of links between clusters. Table 1 shows the value of $f_c(i)$ in examples shown in Figs. 1 and 2.

Table 1. The value of $f_c(i)$ in the cases depicted in Figs. 1 and 2

	$f_c(1)$	$f_c(2)$	$f_c(3)$	$f_c(4)$	$f_c(5)$	$f_c(6)$
Hard clustering (fix)	1	1	1	0	0	0
Hard clustering (change)	1	1	2	0	0	0
Soft clustering	0	0	1	0	0	0

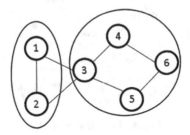

Fig. 1. Example of hard clustering

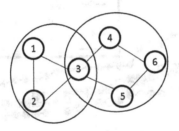

Fig. 2. Example of soft clustering

3   Experiments

3.1   Goal and Environment

We performed experiments to verify the usability of the improved chance index. We applied the proposed method to KeyGraph networks with known nodes to verify if the chance nodes can be extracted by the proposed method. In the verification experiment, we used an interview network that has been used in our previous study, as shown in Fig. 1.

We set the similarity of links for weak links (dotted line) to 0.1–0.3, medium strength links (dark dotted line) to 0.4–0.6, and strong links (solid lines) to 0.7–0.9. We use the average reciprocal of the strengths of links as $f_e(i)$. The parameters α, β, and γ are set to 1. Moreover, in these experiments, we perform clustering manually to sidestep the accuracy of automatic clustering. Soft clustering is performed by six persons, and hard clustering is performed by seven persons. Moreover, $f_v(i)$, $f_e(i)$, and

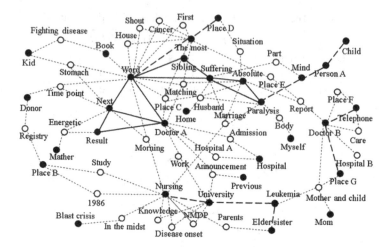

Fig. 3. Interview network

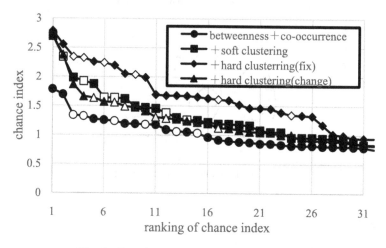

Fig. 4. Experiment result among chance indices

$f_c(i)$ have different range values. Thus, we normalize these values between 0 and 1 (Fig. 1).

3.2 Result

Results are shown in Fig. 4. In this Figure, white marks are chance nodes that are regarded as chance in the previous research. Circles are the original chance index based on Eq. (1). Squares are the chance index with cluster information based on soft clustering. Diamonds are the chance index with cluster information based on hard clustering (called fix), and triangles attach the number of links across clusters. Also,

Table 2. Statistical information of the experiment results

	Original	+soft clustering	+hard clustering (fix)	+hard clustering (change)
Average rank	8.7	**7.5**	10.5	10.0
Average in top 3	4.7	**4.0**	**4.3**	6.7
Variance	19.6	**17.9**	57.6	15.3
Best rank	3	**2**	3	5
Worst rank	15	14	24	17

Table 2 shows the average rank of all data, the average rank of top 3, the variance, the best rank, and the worst rank.

From the Figure and Table, we discover that the chance index with soft clustering works better than the original one. However, the chance index with hard clustering does not improve. In particular, in the case of the chance index with hard clustering wherein the number of links (triangle one) is considered, the worst rank of chance index is the lowest.

4 Conclusion

This paper describes an improved method for estimating whether a node is a chance in a co-occurrence network. The previous method expressed chance index by using betweenness and the strength of links. This study adds cluster information to the previously described method. In the experiment for interview network, which consists of 65 nodes and 104 links, the chance index using cluster information based on soft clustering is more useful than the previous chance index.

Acknowledgement. This research was supported by the Ministry of Education, Culture, Sports, Science, and Technology (MEXT), Japan Society for the Promotion of Science (JSPS), Grant-in-Aid for Scientific Research (A) and (C), 25240049, 25420448.

References

1. Ohsawa, Y., McBurney, P. (eds.): Chance Discovery. Springer, Berlin Heidelberg, Berlin, Heidelberg (2003)
2. Fayyad, U., Piatetsky-Shapiro, G., Smyth, P.: The KDD process for extracting useful knowledge from volumes of data. Commun. ACM **39**, 27–34 (1996)
3. Ohsawa, Y., Benson, N.E., Yachida, M.: KeyGraph: automatic indexing by co-occurrence graph based on building construction metaphor. In: Proceedings IEEE International Forum on Research and Technology Advances in Digital Libraries, 1998. ADL 1998, pp. 12–18 (1998)
4. Kawakita, J.: The Original KJ Method, (Revised edn.). Kawakita Research Institute (1991)
5. Takayama, Y., Saga, R.: Proposal of Chance Index in Co-occurrence Network, IEEJ transactions on electronics, information and systems C (2015) (printing)

Knowledge Extraction from Web Reviews Using Feature Selection Based on Onomatopoeia

Fumiaki Saitoh[⊠], Hikaru Aoki, and Shohei Ishizu

Department of Industrial and Systems Engineering, College of Science
and Engineering, Aoyama Gakuin University, 5-10-1 Fuchinobe, Chuo-Ku,
Sagamihara City, Kanagawa, Japan
saitoh@ise.aoyama.ac.jp

Abstract. In the field of Buzz marketing, it is important to extract knowledge to improve products and services from the voice of the customer represented by customer reviews. In Japanese web review sentences, words that co-occur with onomatopoeia it has been confirmed that easy to combine with use sense of product. For sensory evaluation using a products can be easily associated with the satisfaction is obvious, onomatopoeia can be expected to contribute in knowledge extraction on customer satisfaction. A knowledge model for customer satisfaction is constructed by a regression tree that co-occurrence words with onomatopoeias are used as explanatory variables. Effectiveness of the proposed method I was confirmed through the analysis for the customer review data of ramen shop in Tokyo. The knowledge model acquired by our approach contained many words associated with noodles and food, on the other hand the normal regression tree model was included many meaningless words and unrelated words.

Keywords: Text mining · Online reviews · Voices of the customer (VOC) · On-omatopoeia · Regression tree

1 Introduction

This research presents a method of extracting knowledge about customer satisfaction from customer review data. In the field of buzz marketing, it is important to extract knowledge in order to improve products and services by taking cues from the voice of the customer expressed in customer reviews. In this study, knowledge models are constructed by using the regression tree method in order to predict customer satisfaction.

However, it is difficult to understand the regression tree because certain words that have no relationship with the evaluation object are also included in the model. Prior studies on Japanese web review have confirmed that words which co-occur with onomatopoeia frequently comment on the utility of the product. For sensory evaluation, using a products can be easily associated with the satisfaction is obvious. Onomatopoeia is expected to generate evaluative feedback and support knowledge extraction on customer satisfaction.

C. Stephanidis (Ed.): HCII 2015 Posters, Part I, CCIS 528, pp. 650–655, 2015.
DOI: 10.1007/978-3-319-21380-4_110

Therefore, in this study, we focus on feature selection based on onomatopoeia for the construction of knowledge models. Co-occurrence words with onomatopoeias are used as explanatory variables in the regression tree. By using this model, factors affecting customer satisfaction (or dissatisfaction) will be determined.

Effectiveness of the proposed method was confirmed by analyzing the customer review data of a shop serving ramen (Japanese noodle soup dish) in Tokyo. We confirmed the intelligibility of knowledge acquired by using the proposed method, wherein we compared the contents of knowledge of the normal regression tree and the knowledge that was acquired through the proposed method. The knowledge model constructed through our approach contained many words associated with noodles and food. On the other hand, the normal regression tree model included many irrelevant and unrelated words. We evaluated the prediction accuracy of customer satisfaction by using cross-validation, and confirmed that the proposed method makes knowledge extraction possible without sacrificing prediction accuracy.

2 Knowledge Extraction on Customer Satisfaction

2.1 Feature Selection Based on Onomatopoeia

In this study, we focus on the onomatopoeia in feature selection of text mining. Onomatopoeia has the property that easily related to the feeling of use of the product in Japanese language (see Fig. 1). We thought words that co-occur with onomatopoeia are easy to combine with product evaluation and satisfaction. Therefore, onomatopoeias can be expected as powerful extraction toot of words that that are directly involved in product evaluation.

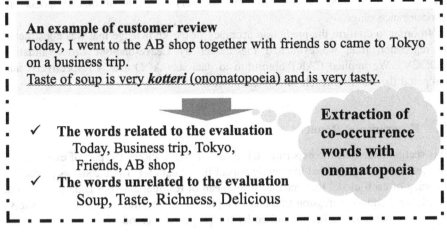

Fig. 1. Schematic diagram of the feature selection in the proposed method

2.2   Knowledge Extraction Using a Regression Tree

In our proposal, the knowledge about the factors that affect the level of satisfaction from the text data of the review sentences are extracted by the regression tree. It becomes possible to understand without reading all the review sentences by constructing a model that predicts satisfaction by the combination of conditional branches. In the prediction of satisfaction, the knowledge constructed by regression tree applied the word frequency in conditional branch, and predictive model will be available as a knowledge that can be understood.

The processing flow of the proposed method is as follows.

Step.1:	Words that co-occur with onomatopoeia are extracted, and they are treated as a word set O.
Step.2:	All the words contained in the data set to be analyzed are treated as a word set A.
Step.3:	A words set A∩O that has common elements to A and O is extracted, in this step.
Step.4:	To learn a regression tree, term frequencies of A∩O are used as explanatory variables, and customer satisfaction are used as objective variables.

3   Experimental

3.1   Experimental Settings

Effectiveness of the proposed method was confirmed through the analysis for the customer review data of ramen (Japanese noodle soup dish) shop in Tokyo. Parts of speech that used for analysis are verbs and adjectives. We adopted these frequencies as explanatory variables, and we utilized customer satisfaction, which is represented by five stars as objective variable. Before (or after) 5 words of onomatopoeia are co-occurrence range.

In order to confirm the prediction accuracy of the knowledge that was constructed by regression tree, we evaluated the model by Leave-one-out Cross-validation (LOOCV). We applied CART algorithm to data sets A∩O and A respectively, and compared the learning result of regression tree.

3.2   Experimental Results

This section describes the experimental results. Table 1 shows the part of examples of Japanese onomatopoeia that frequently appear in our data set. Table 2 shows prediction accuracy of each model that calculated by mean of residual and its standard deviation.

Figure 2 shows regression tree that is applied to the normal data and Fig. 3 shows regression tree that has been acquired by the proposed method.

Table 1. Examples of Japanese onomatopoeia

Japanese onomatopoeia	Alphabetical notation	Meanings in English
あっさり	assari	*ASSARI* describes (1) a light, plain, simple flavor, (2) To appear simple, plain, or light yet delicate.
こってり	kotteri	*KOTTERI* describes rich or heavy taste of a food.
べたべた	beta-beta	*BETA-BETA* describes (1) something sticky (2) someone clinging to another.
つるつる	tsuru-tsuru	*TSURU-TSURU* describes (1) slipping on a smooth surface (2) the sound made by someone slurping noodles.
がつがつ	gatsu-gatsu	*GATSU-GATSU* describes someone eating greedily.

Table 2. prediction accuracy

Prediction Accuracy	Word set A	Word set A∩O
Mean	0.575	0.598
SD	0.554	0.483

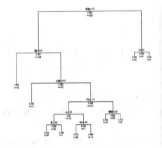

The words used for conditional branches

Shopkeeper, Soy, Mr., 8, man, time
RYU (It is representing the Dragon in Japanese),
etc.

Fig. 2. A knowledge model acquired by the proposed method

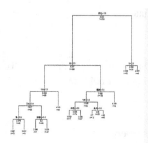

The words used for conditional branches

Shopkeeper, Minute,
Dipping noodle, Soy sauce,
Seafood (Soup stock), Woman customer
etc.

Fig. 3. A knowledge model acquired by regression tree using a normal data

3.3 Discussion

In the comparison of two models, a clear difference in the prediction accuracy was not observed (see Table 2). On the other hand, clear difference between these models appeared on the readability and understanding. The proposed method has been included words related to evaluation objects more than the conventional method. From the above, it can be said that understandable knowledge is acquired without compromising of the prediction accuracy of satisfaction by the proposed method.

4   Conclusion

In this study, we improved the quality of the knowledge of customer satisfaction extracted from web review sentences, through feature selection based on co-occurrence of onomatopoeia. By focusing on onomatopoeia, we achieved an easy extraction of word sets tend to be associated with the evaluation. Furthermore, intelligibility and readability of the acquired regression tree (knowledge) were improved. We have confirmed the effectiveness of the proposed method through the analysis of Web Review for Tokyo ramen shop.

References

1. Sakamoto, M., Ueda, Y., Doizaki, R., Shimizu, Y.: Communication Support System Between Japanese Patients and Foreign Doctors Using Onomatopoeia to Express Pain Symptoms. J. Adv. Comput. Intell. Intell. Inf. **18**(6), 1020–1025 (2014)
2. Komatsu, T.: Choreographing Robot Behaviors by Means of Japanese Onomatopoeias. In: Proceedings of the Tenth Annual ACM/IEEE International Conference on Human-Robot Interaction, pp.23–24 (2015)
3. Lertsumruaypun, K., Watanabe, C., Nakamura, S.: Onomatoperori: Recipe Recommendation System Using Onomatopeic Words, IPSJ SIG Technical report vol.73, no.6, pp.1–7 (2009) (in Japanese)
4. Fukushima, H., Araki, K., Uchida, Y.: Disambiguation of Japanese Onomatopoeias using Nouns and Verbs. In: Proceedings of 17th International Conference Text, Speech and Dialogue, pp.141–149 (2014)

5. Kato, A., Fukazawa, Y., Sanada, H., Mori, T.: Extraction of food-related onomatopoeia from food reviews and its application to restaurant search. J. Adv. Comput. Intell. Intell. Inf. **18**(3), 418–428 (2014)
6. "The JADED NETWORK," http://thejadednetwork.com/sfx/ (Accessed on 18 March 2015)

Reading Between the Lines: A Prototype Model for Detecting Twitter Sockpuppet Accounts Using Language-Agnostic Processes

Erin Smith Crabb[(⊠)], Alan Mishler, Susannah Paletz,
Brook Hefright, and Ewa Golonka

University of Maryland, College Park, MD, USA
{ecrabb, amishler, paletz, hefright, egolonka}@umd.edu

Abstract. Sockpuppets are online identities controlled by a user or group of users to manipulate the dissemination of information in digital environments. This manipulation can distort computational assessments of public opinion in social media. Using Russian-language Twitter data from the Ukrainian crisis in 2014, we present a proof-of-concept model employing character n-gram methods to detect sockpuppets. Previous research has demonstrated that n-gram authorship attribution methods can capture lexical preferences, including grammatical and orthographic preferences, while also being less computationally intensive than grammatical or compression language models. Additionally, they can be applied to any language data irrespective of orthography. In this study, a Naïve Bayes classifier was constructed using normalized frequencies of parsed character bigrams to contrast author bigram use. The created model illustrated that suspected sockpuppet accounts were less likely to be correctly classified, showing lower precision, recall, and f-measure rates than other accounts, as predicted.

Keywords: Sockpuppetry · Authorship attribution · Character n-grams · Public opinion measurement · Social media

1 Introduction

Sockpuppets are, "fake identities through which members of the Internet community praise or create the illusion of support for the product of one's work, pretending to be a different person," [1]. Although they are not always used to show support, these identities can have profound effects on the information observed and measured in social media, creating the illusion that many more people share or disagree with a viewpoint than actually do. Researchers have previously used authorship attribution methods to try to detect sockpuppet accounts. These methods, including n-gram, grammatical tag, and compression modeling techniques, attempt to identify sockpuppets based on the features of the texts they produce in order to correctly account for their presence in social media analysis.

C. Stephanidis (Ed.): HCII 2015 Posters, Part I, CCIS 528, pp. 656–661, 2015.
DOI: 10.1007/978-3-319-21380-4_111

This preliminary study investigates the sockpuppetry phenomenon, using character n-gram methods to illustrate that a quantitative difference can be observed when comparing genuine authors and suspected sockpuppet accounts. Section 2 contains a brief review of sockpuppetry as a form of persuasion and character n-grams as a method for sockpuppet detection. Section 3 details the methods and dataset we created for this study, and Sect. 4 summarizes our findings. Finally, Sect. 5 offers some suggestions for this research going forward.

2 Sockpuppetry as Persuasion

In psychological theory, persuasion can act either via effortful thinking or via a "peripheral" route, where the persuader and the person persuaded rely on simple, low-effort strategies and heuristics [10, 11]. These heuristics can include repetition of the same argument, source attractiveness (for example, perceived expertise of the source or trust in the source), and emotional manipulation, which may or may not be relevant to the topic being argued. Even before an explicit persuasive appeal is made, the proponent can set the stage by using the pre-persuasion techniques of biased language, framing, and creating or applying norms [12]. The use of sockpuppets draws on pre-persuasion techniques of establishing an anchor for social comparison and presenting a norm. These accounts also rely on repetition, a peripheral persuasion technique, to create the false perception of different sources saying and believing the same thing.

In order to identify sockpuppet accounts, a variety of authorship attribution methods, including n-gram, grammatical, topic modeling, and compression methods, have been applied to computationally contrast authors' texts [1, 3]. Some studies have further complemented these by using non-linguistic features, such as time stamps and profile information [14]. Character n-gram methods involve comparing the frequencies of sequences of n numbers of contiguous characters in documents [2]. (For example, the word Ukraine would include the bigrams ($n = 2$) of Uk, kr, ra, ai, in, and ne.) N-gram methods can be particularly useful for capturing lexical preferences, including grammatical and orthographic preferences [5]. Additionally, unlike grammatical features and function word analysis, character n-grams can be calculated without deep linguistic knowledge of the language being studied, making application of this method much more straightforward and less computationally intensive than methods requiring language-specific knowledge and resources [5].

Luyckx and Daelemans [9] explore the application of character n-gram authorship attribution models to Twitter data, concluding that of all the methods they tried, character n-grams were the most successful at predicting authorship. Kukushkina, Polikarpov, and Khmelev [6], the only study we are aware of which addresses authorship attribution of Russian data, find that character bigrams are the most reliable and accurate features for predicting authorship of Russian-language documents, scoring higher than the frequency of word n-grams, single grammatical classes, and grammatical class bigrams. Because of the ease of application and the previous success of this method with Russian, we utilize the character bigram model to compare authors quantitatively in order to identify sockpuppets.

3　Methods

The dataset for this study was comprised of Twitter messages, or "tweets," obtained in JSON format from TweetTracker, a web-based portal for collecting tweets and other social media [7, 8]. We identified the harvested tweets via the "Crimea" TweetTracker query covering a two-month period from June 25 to August 25, 2014. Utilizing this query to collect tweets ensures that they either include a key word or hashtag referencing a set of pre-defined key words pertaining to Crimea or Ukraine, are a particular user, or are geotagged as originating from the area defined by a geographic coordinate bounding box. Prior to identifying authors for this study, we selected Russian in TweetTracker as the preferred language of returned tweets [7].

From this set of possible tweets, we chose 23 authors who had posted more than one hundred tweets between June 25, 2014 and August 25, 2014, and exported their data. Based on our reading of a sample of the tweets, we suspected that three of the 23 authors were sockpuppets (accounts K, L, and Q: see Table 1); these accounts seemed dedicated to tweeting news headlines, and spot-checking identified some very similar

Table 1. Precision, recall and f-measure scores for each author, followed by weighted averages

Accounts	Precision	Recall	F-measure
A	0.214	0.18	0.196
B	0.747	0.59	0.659
C	0.898	0.97	0.933
D	0.182	0.18	0.181
E	0.374	0.43	0.4
F	0.511	0.7	0.591
G	0.169	0.14	0.153
H	0.234	0.18	0.203
I	0.306	0.26	0.281
J	0.282	0.2	0.234
K	**0.192**	**0.23**	**0.209**
L	**0.089**	**0.11**	**0.099**
M	0.292	0.21	0.244
N	0.145	0.16	0.152
O	0.273	0.41	0.328
P	0.156	0.17	0.163
Q	**0.04**	**0.05**	**0.045**
R	0.189	0.14	0.161
S	0.541	0.4	0.46
T	0.635	0.73	0.679
U	0.237	0.18	0.205
V	0.261	0.35	0.299
W	0.21	0.17	0.188
Weighted Average:	*0.312*	*0.31*	*0.307*

tweets. For each account, we selected the first one hundred tweets and used them to create the n-gram models discussed below. We chose this number of tweets because Luyckx and Daelemans [9] state that their models have had success attributing texts to authors for whom they only have a minimum of 1,400 words, although providing more data could increase the model's accuracy [5, 9]. Thus, by providing one hundred tweets, our models should have far more data than this minimum to work with.

Prior to the analysis, we conducted several pre-processing steps on the 23-author dataset to ensure that the tweets contained only the authors' actual text. First, we used a computational algorithm to delete non-UTF-8 characters, such as the "thumbs-up" and "house" symbols. We then removed hyperlinks, user mentions, and hashtags. These have a high probability of producing uninformative features because of their purely lexical value: because they are so rare, they can result in overfitting for particular authors. Additionally, they may not be the author's own words. Finally, we removed labeled retweets from each author's data.

We then extracted n-gram features from the cleaned tweets, decomposing them into their component character bigrams and calculating the frequency of each bigram at the tweet level to normalize the values. The resulting output was a feature matrix displaying the frequencies of each bigram normalized by the total number of bigrams per tweet.

We used WEKA [4], a tool implementing a variety of classification and clustering algorithms, to analyze the resulting feature matrix. We tried several classifiers, using ten cross-fold validation to test their performance, and obtained the most compelling results with WEKA's implementation of a general Naïve Bayes classifier [4]. In addition to scoring the classifiers, WEKA provided a confusion matrix displaying how each author's tweets were assigned, which we discuss further below [4].

4 Findings

Under the assumption that all 23 authors were distinct, the classifier had a weighted average precision score of 0.312 and a recall score of 0.31, for an f-measure of 0.307. As seen in Table 1, some authors had much higher individual f-measures (as high as f = 0.933) and others had much lower measures (f = 0.045). Low precision and recall rates are expected for authors with very similar or identical content. Thus, rather than interpreting the overall f-measure, precision score, or recall score as an absolute ideal number, the utility of this method is to identify specific authors and examine the hypothesis that the authors with low scores are not all distinct (i.e., are potential sockpuppets).

Notably, two of the lowest score sets belong to accounts L and Q, which were two of the suspected sockpuppet accounts. The third suspected sockpuppet account, K, achieved a higher f-measure, but it was still in the lower half of scores. When we re-ran the classifier without the three suspected sockpuppets, the average f-measure increased to 0.35. Together, these findings indicate that these accounts may very well be sockpuppets, as their tweets were highly confusable with those belonging to other authors.

We obtained additional results from the classifier's confusion matrix, an abbreviated section of which can be seen in Table 2. For 20 of the 23 authors, the largest

Table 2. Abbreviated classifier confusion matrix for B, C, K, L, and Q

	B	C	K	L	Q
B	59	2	6	2	3
C	0	97	0	3	0
K	0	3	23	25	31
L	4	2	24	11	51
Q	0	1	32	56	5

number of tweets assigned to any of the 23 was identified as belonging to the correct author – that is, for those accounts not initially suspected of being sockpuppets, the largest number of tweets classified as belonging to any given author was correctly associated with that author. In Table 2 below, this can be seen as the 59 and 97 tweets which were accurately assigned to authors B and C respectively, whereas the possible sockpuppets, K, L, and Q were highly confusable with one another. The algorithm categorized the largest subsets of K and L as belonging to Q, while 56 of author Q's tweets were identified as author L's, indicating that these authors have so much similar or identical content as to be confusable.

Overall, this study shows that using character bigrams is a promising potential technique for identifying sockpuppets. As predicted, certain users previously considered to be sockpuppets because of their content showed dramatically low recall and precision scores, and were highly confusable with one another.

5   Future Work

There are several steps to take with this research going forward. It will be important to conduct reliability testing of this method with a ground-truth dataset. To do so, we will use the corpus documented by [13], which has established sockpuppets and genuine users. As Twitter data are stylistically different from forum postings, we will investigate whether or not a synthetic sockpuppet dataset can serve as a viable alternative to a ground-truth dataset by randomly dividing a subset of single-author accounts into multiple "authors," running the classifier, and examining precision and recall values along with confusion matrix results. These findings will be compared with the results obtained from running the algorithm against [13]. Combined, we hope these results will provide an accuracy baseline that would enable us to measure improved techniques for sockpuppet detection. We will also test how increasing authors and linguistic diversity within the data may affect the accuracy results for sockpuppet detection.

References

1. Bu, Z., Xia, Z., Wang, J.: A sockpuppet detection algorithm on virtual spaces. Knowl.-Based Syst. **37**, 366–377 (2013)

2. Cavnar, W., Trenkle, J.: N-gram-based text categorization. In: Proceedings of SDAIR-1994, 3rd Annual Symposium on Document Analysis and Information Retrieval, pp. 161–175. Information Science Research Institute, Las Vegas (1994)

3. Fornaciari, T., Poesio, M.: Identifying fake Amazon reviews as learning from crowds. In: Proceedings of the 14th Conference of the European Chapter of the Association for Computational Linguistics, pp. 279–287. Association for Computational Linguistics (2014)

4. Hall, M., Frank, E., Holmes, G., Pfahringer, B., Reutemann, P., Witten, I.: The WEKA data mining software: An update. SIGKDD Explorations 11(1), 10–18 (2009)

5. Koppel, M., Schler, J., Argamon, S.: Computational methods in authorship attribution. J. Am. Soc. Inform. Sci. Technol. 60(1), 9–26 (2009)

6. Kukushkina, O., Polikarpov, A., Khmelev, D.: Using literal and grammatical statistics for authorship attribution. Probl. Inf. Transm. 37(2), 172–184 (2001)

7. Kumar, S., Barbier, G., Abbasi, M., Liu, H.: TweetTracker: An analysis tool for humanitarian and disaster relief. In: Proceedings of the International Conference on Weblogs and Social Media, pp. 661–662. The AAAI Press, Palo Alto (2011)

8. Kumar, S., Morstatter, F., Liu, H.: Twitter Data Analytics. Springer, New York (2013)

9. Luyckx, K., Daelemans, W.: The effect of author set size and data size in authorship attribution. Literary and Linguistic Computing 26(1), 35–55 (2011)

10. Petty, R., Cacioppo, J.: The elaboration likelihood model of persuasion. Adv. Soc. Psychol. 19, 123–205 (1986)

11. Petty, R., Cacioppo, J., Strathman, A., Priester, J.: To think or not to think: Exploring two routes to persuasion. In: Brook, T.C., Green, M.C. (eds.) Persuasion: Psychological Insights and Perspectives, pp. 81–116. Sage, Thousand Oaks (2005)

12. Pratkanis, A., Aronson, E.: Age of Propaganda: The Everyday Use and Abuse of Persuasion. W. H. Freeman, New York (2001)

13. Solorio, T., Ragib, H., Mizan, M.: Sockpuppet detection in Wikipedia: A corpus of real-world deceptive writing for linking identities. Computing Research Repository (2013). arXIV: 1310.6772 [cs.CL]

14. Tsikerdekis, M., Zeadally, S.: Multiple account identity deception detection in social media using nonverbal behavior. Library and Information Science Faculty Publications, Paper 13 (2014)

Processing Specialized Terminology in Multilingual Applications: An Interactive Approach

Christina Valavani, Christina Alexandris[✉], Stefanos Tassis,
and Antonios Iliakis

National University of Athens, Athens, Greece
cvalavani@hotmail.com, calexandris@gs.uoa.gr,
{stassel,antiliak}@di.uoa.gr

Abstract. A Controlled-Language like approach with the integration of expert knowledge is applied to the pre-editing or post-editing of specialized terminology from international texts processed by the UNL System developed by Institute of Advanced Studies of United Nations University (UNU) in Tokyo, Japan. We provide an all-purpose interactive framework focusing on the automatic analysis, ambiguity resolution and editing of German financial terms and English military terms in respect to the Greek language.

Keywords: Sublanguages · Multiword terms · Universal Words · "Safety Mode" Interactive Analysis

1 Introduction

The present approach concerns the design of an interactive editor for managing terminology processed by multilingual Machine Translation Systems, Wordnets or other types of multilingual Natural Language Processing Systems, including the Universal Natural Language (UNL) System concerning the use of Universal Words [7, 8, 11]. A Controlled-Language like approach with the integration of expert knowledge is applied to the pre-editing or post-editing of terminology from international texts, in this case, texts processed by the UNL System developed by the Institute of Advanced Studies of United Nations University (UNU) in Tokyo, Japan. Here, we provide an all-purpose interactive framework focusing on the automatic analysis, ambiguity resolution and editing of two different cases of specialized terminology and language pairs, in particular, German financial terms and English military terms in respect to the Greek language.

Most types of problems encountered and classified concern the morpho-syntactic and the lexical-semantic level of linguistic analysis. Problems related to the latter level observed are mostly affiliated to inherent ambiguities in the sublanguages of financial terms and military terms, often related to different domains such as politics, Information Technology (IT), the law and the natural sciences. Furthermore, since the UNL System processes languages as diverse as Chinese, Japanese, Hindi, Russian, Portuguese and English, un-aided automatic ambiguity resolution based on morphological elements such as case or prepositions may be problematic.

© Springer International Publishing Switzerland 2015
C. Stephanidis (Ed.): HCII 2015 Posters, Part I, CCIS 528, pp. 662–668, 2015.
DOI: 10.1007/978-3-319-21380-4_112

The proposed editing and ambiguity resolution concerns the (1) interactive morphological analysis, especially of compound words and multiword terms, as well as (2) the signalization of predicted sublanguage types and possible differences in semantic content presented to the User. It should additionally be noted that the tool provides the option of registering the statistics of Users choices. The registered choices of the User are assigned a respective probability, allowing the tool to adapt to the type of specialized texts processed.

2 Interface Design

Apart from highly specialized contexts, financial terms and military terms occur in texts intended to non-specialist professionals and/or decision-makers, such as journalists, politicians and managers. These texts often contain terminology from more than one specialized domain, often resulting to ambiguities and other complications in translation or processing due to an overlap in the related fields of specialized terms. The degree of complexity in processing such text types increases when multilingual texts and an international public are involved [1]. In this case processing must be characterized by the possibility to manage terminology from multiple domains (1) with precision and correctness (2), speed and efficiency (3).

To meet the above-presented needs, the proposed design is characterized by three features, namely (1) processing in blocks, allowing (2) a language-independent and Controlled –Language like presentation of analysis, ambiguity resolution and identification of terms with implied or "hidden" components, (3) with a "fast-tack" option and a "safety-mode" option.

The first feature is the analysis of the incoming text in separate blocks, corresponding to the existing paragraphs, since in these types of texts (financial or military domain) a different type of information and sublanguage may be predominant in different paragraphs. The type of sublanguage is identified in each block, allowing the identification of multiple sublanguages and their separate treatment and processing. Text is analyzed in blocks for identifying the sublanguage which is, subsequently, linked to the User's choice to activate the option of "fast-track" or "safety-mode", namely a partially interactive or a fully interactive mode.

The "fast-track" or "safety-mode" option constitutes the second feature of the proposed design. The "fast-track" option is a partially interactive mode to be chosen by Users with expert knowledge of the predominant sublanguage type identified and/or whose native language shares many common features with the language of the text processed, for example, English and Dutch. The "safety-mode" option is a fully interactive mode to be chosen by Users with a general knowledge but no expertise in the predominant sublanguage type concerned and/or whose native language shares few common features with the language of the text concerned, for example Greek, and Chinese. The "fast-track" option can be activated according to User's choice, allowing the adaption of the present interface to various levels of expertise.

As a first step in the interaction, the User inserts the text in the respective field of the designed editor. The module signalizes the sublanguage type with the largest percentage of terms, indicating candidate sublanguage types.

In the second step of the interaction, the User chooses the sublanguage type and then either activates automatic processes related to the chosen sublanguage or selects any problematic words constituting specialized terminology. In this case, the module activates a "stepping stone" or "safety net" mode, similar to strategies employed in Speech User Interfaces (SUIs) [4].

Step in Interaction	Function	
"Insert text"	Options:	
"Choose sublanguage type" [Show Sublanguage tags] (SUBLANG-TYPE)	SAFETY-MODE Interactive Analysis (SMI-ANALYSIS)	FAST-TRACK Automatic
"Present statistics" (optional)		

Fig. 1. "Fast-track" or "Safety-mode" Options in Interaction

In the "stepping stone" or "safety net" mode, problematic words are signalized according to ambiguity type, either in respect to a sublanguage or concerning the semantic and morphological analysis, especially in the case of compound words or multiword terms ("Safety Mode" Interactive Analysis –SMI Analysis). In the latter case, the User choses the appropriate type of analysis presenting relations between words and respective readings.

The chosen relation between words and respective reading by the "Safety Mode" Interactive Analysis (SMI Analysis) may be converted in a phrase or sentence that can be easily processed by the Universal Natural Language (UNL) System or any multilingual Machine Translation or Natural Language Processing System, enabling an easier processing of different languages and language families. The User can exit the "stepping stone" or "safety net" mode and return to the automatic processing of the sublanguage and terminology.

The presentation of the statistics of the Users choices registered by the module, assisting the interactive process for future use, is an optional step in the interaction. Thus, the designed editor may be adapted to User behavior and needs and customized to User requirements [3, 9] (Fig. 1).

3 Signalizing Sublanguage Type

The identification of sublanguage type in each block (Sublang-Type) allows the separate treatment and processing of multiple sublanguages, as well as sublanguage-related error prediction and ambiguity resolution. The language-independent SMI Analysis, based on analytical forms employed in Controlled –Languages, includes the identification of "hidden" compound or multiword terms with the signalization of the chosen sublanguage. "Hidden" compound or multiword terms can be subjected to interactive analytical processing, if requested by the User. Thus, ambiguities may be resolved, both across sublanguages and within the same sublanguage. For selected sets of words, including multiword terms, a list of candidate sublanguages is signalized with the respective tag. This is of special importance in specialized terminology appearing in texts such as political and journalistic texts. The User decides the type of sublanguage activated, if multiple sublanguages are concerned.

In particular, the signalization of the sublanguage type helps resolve ambiguities, for instance, in the case of terms such as "unit", which corresponds to different concepts in the sublanguages of Finance-Economy, Computer Science – IT and the Military. Different domains corresponding to different sublanguages are already indicated in the structure of the Universal Words within the UNL framework [7, 8], as well as in systems such as OWL [5] or in other applications and language resources. Especially in languages highly productive in compound words, such as German, sublanguage type signalization helps identify and separate fixed expressions and specialist terminology from other types of compound words and multiword expressions (such as "ad hoc" compounds in German [2]), the latter often requiring a morphological analysis for the convenience of international Users.

Furthermore, the signalization of the sublanguage type helps identify the identification of "hidden" compound/ multiword terms. For example, in the case of the multiword term "Unions-Wirtschaftsfluegel" in German (retrieved from financial texts), the implied or "hidden" component is the word "Partei" – "political party", the word "Union" corresponding to different semantics according to sublanguage and context. The multiword term "Unions-Wirtschaftsfluegel" (literally "business wing of the Union party") requires expert knowledge for further processing and/or translation in the target language. Another example is the military term "patrol", where the "hidden" component is the word "unit", as a part of the compound term "patrol unit". In addition, the term "patrol (unit)" is differentiated from the verb "(to) patrol [10].

The identification of a chosen sublanguage type allows the automatic processing of a specific sublanguage to be activated, if applicable. If a sublanguage is chosen and activated, the module may function as a "stepping stone" or "safety net" [4], if problematic cases are encountered. If ambiguities occur within the same sublanguage, differences in semantic content and possible readings are presented to the User. This is the most usual case with compound words and multiword terms.

4 Morphological Analysis and the UNL Framework

Morphological analysis of compound words or multiword terms, including "hidden" compound or multiword terms (SMI Analysis) takes place in the "safety-mode" option of the interaction. The proposed editor is activated with the identification of words constituting specialized terminology identified by the User.

In order to ensure a simplified form of an independent analysis across languages and language families, the presented analyses are neither identical nor similar to but compatible with the presentations of logical relations with the Universal Word –UNL framework [7, 8, 11]. Compound words or multiword terms are analyzed according to the parameters of the natural language concerned. For example, in German compound terms, and multiword terms, the component constituting the "head" of the term [6] is identified and a set of possible relations between the components is shown, with the indication of the most probable reading. This feature is of special importance in cases where neologisms are concerned or in very productive languages such as German, where there is a continuous formation of new ("ad hoc") compound words.

GERMAN-INPUT (TEXT):	SMI-ANALYSIS:	ENG- TERM:
Preisschlacht [^{M}der Preis+ ^{F}die Schlacht-HEAD] GR-ANALYSIS: Μάχη των τιμών [^{F}η μάχη (the battle)+ ^{F}η τιμή (the price)]	[war/battle OF prices] [war BETWEEN /ABOUT prices]	price war
Umsatzrückgang [^{M}der Umsatz^π + ^{M}der Rückgang-HEAD] GR-ANALYSIS: Πτώση των πωλήσεων [^{F}η πτώση (the fall)+ ^{F}η πώληση (the sale)]	[decline/fall OF sales] [sales SUBJECT decline VERB] [lowered sales]	decline in sales (or:) sales decline

Fig. 2. SMI Analysis of German Financial Terms

The types of analyses depend on the types of natural languages concerned. In the case of German, multiword compound words are identifiable, as most components occur as a single string, in some cases separated by a dash. By applying morphological parameters, the head of German compound words and multiword terminology is identified to the right [6]. We note that English and Greek expressions constituting multiword terms do not occur as a single string and are not always easily identified, even by human editors or translators (Fig. 2).

Alternative analyses are presented in the interface, depending on what components in the multiword terms are chosen to have a closer relation each other. Presented SMI analyses are a simplified form of logical relations between components, for example, "BELONGS-TO", and "OBJECT-OF-ACTION". Furthermore, as in analytical forms of Controlled –Languages [10], multiword terms can be converted into sentences.

The statistics of Users choices for the possible analyses presented are registered and assigned a respective probability, as a stated above (Fig. 3).

UW GENERATED TERM:	SMI-ANALYSIS:	GR - TERM:
[Στρατιωτικών Πληροφοριών] "Military Intelligence"	[Service FOR Military Intelligence] => (Identified by SUBLANG-TYPE)	[Υπηρεσία Πληροφοριών Στρατού] "Military Intelligence"
[Στρατός Assault Team] "Army Assault Team"	[Team FOR Assault OF Army] [Team SUBJECT-OF-ACTION Assault] [Team BELONGS-TO Army]	[Ομάδα Κρούσης Στρατού] "Army Assault Team"
[άμεση μονάδα υποστήριξης] "direct support unit"	[unit FOR direct support] [unit OBJECT-OF-ACTION direct support]	[μονάδα άμεσης υποστήριξης] "direct support unit"

Fig. 3. SMI Analysis of English Military Terms

5   Conclusions and Further Research

Un-aided automatic ambiguity resolution may be problematic for Systems processing diverse languages and language families, especially when remarkable differences in fundamental elements expressing logical relations and grammatical information are concerned. The designed module combines automatic and interactive processing, integrating expert knowledge and Controlled-Language practices, allowing the User to proceed with fast-track editing of the texts with specialized terminology or to activate a "stepping stone" or "safety mode", as applied in SUI Systems. A full implementation allowing a contrastive evaluation in regard to both languages and sublanguages concerned is targeted to contribute to the further development of the approach and interface designed. Further research includes an extension and enrichment of the existing identified tag types and the improvement and fine-tuning of the interactive SMI Analysis.

References

1. Alexandris, C.: Managing Implied Information and Connotative Features in Multilingual Human-Computer Interaction. Nova Science Publishers, Hauppauge (2013)
2. Busch, A., Stenschke, O.: Germanistische Linguistik, Eine Einfuehrung, 2nd edn. Gunter Narr, Tuebingen, Germany (2008)

3. Jurafsky, D., Martin, J.: Speech and Language Processing, an Introduction to Natural Language Processing, Computational Linguistics and Speech Recognition, 2nd edn. Prentice Hall Series in Artificial Intelligence. Pearson Education, Upper Saddle River (2008)
4. Lewis, J.R.: Introduction to Practical Speech User Interface Design for Interactive Voice Response Applications, IBM Software Group, USA. Tutorial T09 presented at HCII 2009 San Diego, CA (2009)
5. Loaiza, F., Wartik, S., Thompson, J., Visser, D., Kenschaft, E.: The Best of All Possible Worlds: Applying the Model Driven Architecture Approach to a JC3IEDM OWL Ontology Modeled in UML. In: Proceedings of the 19th International Command and Control Research and Technology Symposium, 19th ICCRTS, Alexandria, VA 16–19 June 2014
6. Sternefeld, W.: Syntax, Eine morphologisch motivierte generative Beschreibung des Deutschen, vol. 1. Stauffenburg, Tuebingen, Germany (2006)
7. Uchida, H., Zhu, M., Della Senta, T.: Universal Networking Language. The UNDL Foundation, Tokyo, Japan (2005)
8. Uchida, H., Zhu, M., Della Senta, T.: The UNL, A Gift for Millennium. The United Nations University, Institute of Advanced Studies UNU/IAS, Tokyo, Japan (1999)
9. Wiegers, K.E.: Software Requirements. Microsoft Press, Redmond, WA (2005)
10. Xue, P., Poteet, S; Kao, A., Mott, D., Braines, D., Giammanco, C., Pham, T.: Information Extraction Using Controlled English to Support Knowledge-Sharing and Decision-Making. In: Proceedings of the 17th International Command and Control Research and Technology Symposium, 17th ICCRTS, Fairfax, VA, USA, 19–21 June 2012
11. The Universal Networking Language http://www.undl.org

Image and Video Processing for HCI

Texture Image Segmentation Using Spectral Clustering

Hui Du[1,2], Yuping Wang[1(✉)], Xiaopan Dong[1],
and Yiu-ming Cheung[3]

[1] School of Computer Science and Technology, Xidian University,
Xi'an 710071, China
duhuiywy@hotmail.com, ywang@xidian.edu.cn
[2] College of Computer Science and Engineering,
Northwest Normal University, Gansu, China
[3] Department of Computer Science, Hong Kong Baptist University,
Kowloon Tong, Hong Kong
ymc@comp.hkbu.edu.hk

Abstract. Clustering is a popular and effective method for texture image segmentation. However, most cluster methods often suffer the following problems: need a huge space and a lot of computation when the input data is large. To save the space and computation, we construct a novel algorithm for image segmentation. It consists of two phases: Sampling and clustering. First, we put some detectors into the data space uniformly using orthogonal design method. These detectors can move and merge according to the law of universal gravitation. When the detectors are in a stable status (i.e., do not move), these detectors are used as the representative samples to the next step. Second, to further improve the efficiency and avoid dependence on parameters, the Self-tuning Spectral Clustering (SSC) is used to the representative samples to do the clustering. As a result, the proposed algorithm can quickly and precisely realize the clustering for texture image segmentation.

Keywords: Texture image segmentation · Feature extraction · Gray level histogram · Sampling · Spectral clustering

1 Introduction

Image segmentation is an important component in image processing. It divides the image into several mutually disjoint sub regions, where the values of pixels in each sub-region have a higher similarity, while the values among different sub-regions have a lower one. Due to their simplicity and efficiency, clustering approaches were one of the best techniques used for the texture image segmentation. Texture indicates contextual information of image pixels [1], and it has been used in image segmentation. Because segmentation of texture images depends on pixel feature that are difficult to define and capture, it is more challenging than segmentation only using intensity of pixel. There have been many different approaches for segmentation based on different pixel feature extraction methods (e.g. [2, 3]).

© Springer International Publishing Switzerland 2015
C. Stephanidis (Ed.): HCII 2015 Posters, Part I, CCIS 528, pp. 671–676, 2015.
DOI: 10.1007/978-3-319-21380-4_113

Fuzzy c-means is one of the most popular methods for image segmentation because it doesn't need to construct the similarity matrix, is easy to implement and can achieve reasonable results at some cases. But this algorithm has the following shortcomings: it does not consider any spatial information and is easy to converge to a local optimal solution. Max Mignotte [4] proposed an original and simple segmentation strategy based on the K-means algorithm that considered spatial constraints and overcame the problem of the local convergence. D. Yang et al. [5] presented a novel clustering index in Gaussian kernel in search process, which is helpful to find the partitions for the highly overlapping and contaminating samples. And in order to improve the speed, they employed the histogram statistics to implement the pixels partition. Spectral clustering is a kind of effective clustering algorithms, and it has been proven to be powerful to image segmentation [6], applicable to different type of data sets, effective with high dimensional data, convergent to global optimal solutions. Among spectral clustering algorithms, self-tuning spectral clustering (SSC) [7] is one of the most effective ones. Since image segmentation needs to process a large amount of data, directly using SSC algorithm in image processing will get a huge similarity matrix that is far beyond the processing ability for an ordinary computer. To overcome this difficulty, we propose a novel algorithm that uses the law of universal gravitation to sample data firstly and then use SSC algorithm to cluster the resulted data (the representative samples gotten in the first phase) exactly.

The remainder of this paper is organized as follows: Sect. 2 presents the related knowledge. The proposed algorithm is presented in Sect. 3. Section 4 demonstrates the experimental results.

2   Related Knowledge

2.1   The Law of Universal Gravitation

The law of universal gravitation states that any two objects exert a gravitational force of attraction on each other. The magnitude of the force is proportional to the product of the gravitational masses of the objects, and inversely proportional to the square of the distance between them, i.e.,

$$F(t) = \frac{Gm_x m_y}{d(x(t), y(t))^2} \tag{1}$$

where t means time, and G is the acceleration of gravity.

2.2   Orthogonal Design

Orthogonal design can sample a set of representative data from a large set of data using an orthogonal matrix $L_M(Q^N)$ [8], where M refers to the number of data samples, N is the dimension of the data, Q is the number of possible values of data in each dimension called level with Q being odd generally, and M, Q N and J satisfy $M = Q^J$ and $N \leq \frac{Q^J - 1}{Q - 1}$ with J being the smallest positive integer.

3 The Proposed Algorithm

To do the image segmentation, we have to first select and extract the texture features of every pixel. Then, select the representative data (samples) from the texture features of pixels, and we call this step as "sampling". Finally, cluster these representative samples.

3.1 Feature Extraction

Feature extraction for each pixel is one of the major issues for image segmentation. If the extracted features can be representative, then the image segmentation results will be better. We selected two kinds of representative features in our feature extraction stage. One is the gray level co-occurrence matrix, and the other is the gray histogram [9, 10, 11].

3.2 Sampling

To save the space and computation, we performed sampling on the data set firstly. We use orthogonal design to put some detectors in the data space, and these detectors move based on the law of universal gravitation, small mass detectors are attracted by larger ones and may move very near to larger ones. When the distance of two detectors is smaller than a given threshold value, they will be merged into one. When all detectors do not move and cannot be merged, they are called in a stable state and are seen them as the representative samples. The detail is as follows.

1. Put detectors and classify all data. Use the orthogonal design proposed in [8] to put detectors in the data space, e.g., yellow dots in Fig. 1(a). Then each detector x defines a set $C(x)$ of data in the data space. Data z is in $C(x)$ if and only if the

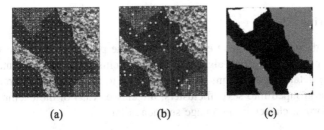

(a)   (b)   (c)

Fig. 1. (a) Put the detectors on the image (yellow points represent detectors) (b) Detectors after moving and emerging (c) Result of segmentation by proposed method (each of different gray colors represents one cluster) (Colour figure online).

degree of membership between data z and detector x is smaller than that between data z and any other detector. We call set $C(x)$ the class set of detector x.

2. Move and merge. The mass of each detector is defined as the number of data points contained in the circle of radius E with itself as the center. Thus the mass of any detector cannot be smaller than 1. Detectors move based on the law of universal gravitation as follows.

(I) Compute the radius E using Eq.(2),

$$E = pS/(2Q - 1) \tag{2}$$

where S is the largest distance between two data points in data sets, Q is defined in Sect. 2.2, p is a parameter to control the size of radius E. Based on experiments, it is better to take the value of p between 0.8 and 1.2.

(II) Compute gravity between two detectors using Eq. (1) with $G = 1$.

(III) For each detector x, find out a detector y in its neighborhood which has the largest gravity to x in the neighborhood, where the smaller mass detector will move to the larger mass one. Without loss of generality, suppose that the mass of y is smaller, then y will move to x by formula (3) iteratively.

$$y(t + 1) = (1 - \lambda)y(t) + \lambda x(t), \quad 0 < \lambda < 1 \tag{3}$$

where t is time, λ represents the step size. We take $\lambda = 1/3$ in our experiments.

(IV) If the distance between two detectors x and y is shorter than αE, merge them and keep the larger mass detector, say x. Then, put data in $C(y)$ into $C(x)$ and delete $C(y)$ and y. The parameter α is used to control the speed of the merge. In experiments, we set $\alpha = 0.25$.

(V) Repeat step (II) to (IV) until all detectors no longer move and merge, these detectors are representative samples. For example, the representative samples of detectors in Fig. 1(a) are shown in Fig. 1(b). If E is too small, the detectors may not move and merge. If E is too large, it will cause a lot of computation. Through the experiments we found that E is better to take the value between 0.8 and 1.2

3. These detectors are representative exemplars when they are in a stable state.

3.3   Clustering

After we get these representative exemplars from the previous phase, we will use the Self-tuning Spectral Clustering algorithm (SSC) to cluster these representative exemplars. For the details of algorithm SSC please refer to [7]. When these representative exemplars are grouped into several clusters, the classes $C(x)$ of the exemplars of each cluster will form a cluster in the image segmentation.

4   Experimental Results

4.1   Dataset

In the experiments for image segmentation, we use one natural image from Berkeley segmentation dataset [12] and constructed two synthetic images by selecting several images from Brodatz database [13].

4.2   Results and Comparisons

Figure 2 shows the experimental results of the four compared algorithms (SOM [14], FCM [15], K-means and our proposed method) on two synthetic images (the first two images in Fig. 2) and one natural image (the third image in Fig. 2). Table 1 shows the comparison results of the accuracy on these three images. The accuracy is computed by Eq. (4), where the number of pixels correctly classified was computed by comparing the results obtained by the corresponding method with the manual segmentation results.

$$Accuracy = \frac{the\ number\ of\ pixels\ correctly\ classified}{the\ total\ number\ of\ pixels} \tag{4}$$

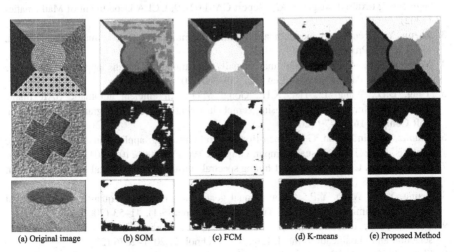

(a) Original image   (b) SOM   (c) FCM   (d) K-means   (e) Proposed Method

Fig. 2. Experimental results on the synthetic and natural images

Table 1. Comparison of Accuracy

Image	Size	SOM	FCM	K-means	Proposed Method
1	[153 × 55]	0.5997	0.9157	0.7300	**0.9201**
2	[150 × 150]	0.9362	0.9502	0.9430	**0.9589**
3	[100 × 150]	0.8371	0.9256	0.9377	**0.9382**

5 Conclusion

We propose a novel segmentation method for texture image. This method includes two phases, namely sampling and clustering. We design a new method for sampling based on the law of gravity, and then use the Self-tuning Spectral Clustering (SSC) to cluster the sampling results. The experiment results on synthetic and natural images indicate the proposed algorithm can achieve the higher segmentation accuracy compared to other three methods.

Acknowledgment. This work is supported by the National Natural Science Foundation of China (No.61472297) and supported by the Fundamental Research Funds for the Central Universities (No.BDZ021430)

References

1. Zheng, Y., Kwong, M.T., MacCormick, I.J.C., Beare, N.A.V., Harding, S.P.: A Comprehensive Texture Segmentation Framework for Segmentation of Capillary Non-Perfusion Regions in Fundus Fluorescein Angiograms. PloS one, 9(4) (2014)
2. Sandberg, B., Chan, T., Vese, L.: A level-set and Gabor-based active contour algorithm for segmenting textured images. CAM Report CAM 02-39, UCLA Department of Mathematics (2002)
3. Zheng, Y., Chen, K.: A hierarchical algorithm for multiphase texture image segmentation. ISRN Signal Process, pp. 1–11 (2012)
4. Mignotte, M.: A de-texturing and spatially constrained K-means approach for image segmentation. Pattern Recogn. Lett. **32**, 359–367 (2011)
5. Yang, D.D., Wang, L., Hei, X.H., Gong, M.G.: An efficient automatic SAR image segmentation framework in AIS using kernel clustering index and histogram statistics. Appl. Soft Comput. **16**, 63–79 (2014)
6. Schultz, T., Kindlmann, G.L.: Open-Box spectral clustering: applications to medical image analysis. IEEE Trans. Visual Comput. Graphics **19**(12), 2100–2108 (2013)
7. Zelnik-Manor, L., Perona, P.: Self-tuning spectral clustering. Adv. Neural Inf. Process. Syst. **17**, 1601–1608 (2005)
8. Leung, Y.W., Wang, Y.P.: An orthogonal genetic algorithm with quantization for global numerical optimization [J]. IEEE Trans. Evol. Comput. **5**(1), 41–53 (2001)
9. Vasantha, M., Bharathi, D.V.S, Dhamodharan, R.: Medical image feature, extraction, selection and classification. Int. J. Eng. Sci. Technol. **2**, 2071–2076 (2010)
10. Sheshadri, H.S., Kandaswamy, A.: Experimental investigation on breast tissue classification based on statistical feature extraction of mammograms. Comput. Med. Imaging Graph. **31**, 46–48 (2007)
11. Hassan, M., Chaudhry, A., Khan, A., Kim, J.Y.: Carotid artery image segmentation using modified spatial fuzzy c-means and ensemble clustering. Comput. Methods Programs Biomed. **108**, 1261–1276 (2012)
12. http://www.eecs.berkeley.edu/Research/Projects/CS/vision/bsds/
13. http://www.ux.uis.no/~tranden/brodatz.html
14. Kohonen, T.: The Self-organizing Maps. Proc. IEEE **78**(9), 1464–1480 (1990)
15. Bezdek, J.C., Ehrlich, R., Full, W.: FCM: The Fuzzy C-means clustering algorithm. Comput. Geosci. **10**, 2–3 (1984)

An Adaptive Particle Filtering for Solving Occlusion Problems of Video Tracking

Lan-Rong Dung[1(✉)], Yu-Chi Huang[1], Ren-Yu Huang[1],
and Yin-Yi Wu[2]

[1] National Chiao Tung University, Hsinchu 30010, Taiwan
lennon@faculty.nctu.edu.tw
[2] National Chung-Shan Institute of Science and Technology, Taoyuan, Taiwan

Abstract. In recent years, the visual object tracking has drawn increasing interests. There are many applications, e.g., video surveillance in airports, schools, hospitals and traffic. The object surveillance may provide crucial information about the behavior, interaction, and relationship between objects of interest. This paper addresses issues in object tracking where videos contain complex scenarios. We propose an adaptive particle filters tracking scheme with exquisite resampling (AERPF), which improves prediction, importance sampling and resampling. In prediction step, an adaptive strategy for search region and particle number is addressed for object disappearing or obstacle disturbance, which can obtain results more effectively. In addition, in importance sampling, we use optical flow to refine the particle weights using the dynamical object motion information, which results the better accuracy of object location updating. Moreover, exquisite resampling (ER) algorithm can be applied for reflecting more the posterior probability density function of true state. The proposed method can be applied for object tracking both on fixed and active camera, handling partial occlusion and full occlusion problem properly. As a result, it outperforms other existing methods.

Keywords: Object tracking · Particle filter · Occlusion problem

1 Introduction

Video object tracking is an important topic within the field of computer vision. It has a wide range of applications such as human-vehicle navigation, computer interaction, etc. Various approaches for object tracking have been proposed. Reference [1] proposed a tracking method based on mean shift. It maximizes the similarity iteratively by comparing the color histogram of the object. The advantage is the elimination of a brute force search and low computation. Reference [2] extended to 3D domain, combines color and spatial information to solve the problems of orientation changing and small scale changing. Reference [3] used stochastic meta-descent optimization method. It can track fast moving objects with significant scale change in a low-frame-rate video.

Template matching is a common and direct tracking method. It finds the position of object by minimize the error with a predefined object template. [4] used previous frame to adapt the object template, which solves the problems of appearance changing during

© Springer International Publishing Switzerland 2015
C. Stephanidis (Ed.): HCII 2015 Posters, Part I, CCIS 528, pp. 677–682, 2015.
DOI: 10.1007/978-3-319-21380-4_114

the movement. Reference [5] proposed a template updating algorithm that avoids the drifting inherent in the naive algorithm.

Particle filter is based on Monte Carlo theorem. It estimates state by posterior probability, commonly used in pattern recognition and object tracking, such as [6]. Improved from [7], this paper proposed an adaptive particle filters tracking algorithm scheme with exquisite resampling (AERPF). We will introduce it in the following section.

2 Adaptive Exquisitie Resampling Particle Filter

In this section, we will illustrate the proposed algorithm in detail. Figure 1 is the flow chart of AERPF with the basic three stages: prediction, importance sampling and resampling.

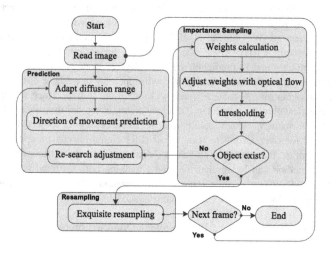

Fig. 1. The flow chart of AERPF algorithm

2.1 Particle Filter

Extended from Kalman filter, particle filter can be applied in both linear and non-linear problems. Suppose we have a system described by the equations:

$$x_t = f_t(x_{t-1}, w_t) \tag{1}$$

$$y_t = h_t(x_t, v_t) \tag{2}$$

The location of object being tracked is a state vector × which cannot be observed directly. We use a dynamic model of the state to predict how it evolves over time. Vector y represent the feature observed from location ×. We can use the observation to correct the estimate of the state.

2.2 Prediction

The first stage of particle filter is prediction stage. When object disappears, instead of randomly spreading particles, we radially spread particles from where object disappeared because of the assumption that the object will not move faraway immediately. If the object is temporarily occluded, the way we spread particles research the target more efficiently than searching globally. While in long-term occlusion, we have already spread particles globally and this can avoid missing the object.

Then, use the motion vector obtained from optical flow to adjust the diffusion range. A high standard deviation of the motion vector indicates the object moves drastically, hence we need to enlarge the diffusion range as Fig. 2(a). A low standard deviation indicates moving consistency, so the diffusion range could be shrunk, as Fig. 2(b).

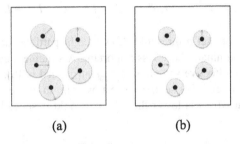

(a)   (b)

Fig. 2. (a) Diffusion ranges for high standard deviation of the motion vector; (b) Diffusion ranges for low standard deviation of the motion vector.

In addition to diffusion range, we can also predict the moving direction by motion vector. It is reasonable that the object moves toward the same direction according to the last few seconds, as a result, we spread the particles toward the same direction if moving direction has consistency.

2.3 Importance Sampling

The Second stage of particle filter is importance sampling. At this stage, the objective is to give each particle a weight, preserve the more important and eliminate the less important particles according to their weights.

Color histogram of the target model is used as feature to determine the weights. The histograms are calculated in the RGB space using $8 \times 8 \times 8$ bins. We established a target model $q = \{q^{(u)}\}$ with $\sum_{u=1}^{N} q^{(u)} = 1$ and $p(x) = \{p^{(u)}(x)\}$ with $\sum_{u=1}^{N} p^{(u)} = 1$ for the candidate. Because boundary pixels might belong to the background or get occluded easily, the center of the object is considered more important than the boundary. Hence the kernel function is used to assign small weights to the pixels further away from the region center:

$$K_E(x) = \begin{cases} c(1 - \|x\|^2) & \|x\| \leq 1 \\ 0 & otherwise \end{cases} \tag{3}$$

where x is the distance of the pixel locations from the center.

After obtaining the original weights by calculating their Bhattacharyya coefficients, we take two steps to refine them. Optical flow [8] is the apparent motion of brightness patterns in the image. Ideally, it would be the same as the motion field. Calculating the average of motion vector (4) obtained from optical flow, we can predict a new center from the last center. Promoting the weights of particles around the center which optical predicts is the first step.

$$\begin{cases} u^n = \bar{u}^n - I_x(I_x\bar{u}^n + I_y\bar{v}^n + I_t)/(\alpha^2 + I_x^2 + I_y^2) \\ v^n = \bar{v}^n - I_y(I_x\bar{u}^n + I_y\bar{v}^n + I_t)/(\alpha^2 + I_x^2 + I_y^2) \end{cases} \tag{4}$$

The second step is to set a threshold. Low-weight particles decrease accuracy, to avoid it, we hope to eliminate those less important. A suitable measure of degeneracy of the algorithm is the effective sample size N_{eff} introduced in [6]. Using (5) to obtain the the effective samples, choose the lowest weight in those samples to set the threshold. The weight which is lower than the threshold is set to be zero (6).

$$N_{eff} = \frac{1}{\sum_{i=1}^{N} (w_t^i)^2} \tag{5}$$

$$\widehat{w_t^i} = \begin{cases} 0, & if \ w_t^i < T \\ w_t^i, & if \ w_t^i \geq T \end{cases} \tag{6}$$

When all the weights are small and set to zeros, means all the particles in the whole frame are not similar to the target, in other words, there exists no object.

2.4   Resampling

The goal in this stage is to eliminate particles with small weights, concentrate on particles with large weights for the prediction stage for next time. But the original resampling algorithm causes some defects. We use Fig. 3 to illustrate the condition.

N is the total number of particles. $\{C_i\}_{i=1}^N$ represents the cumulative sum of weights. $\{U_i\}_{i=1}^N$ is a sequence of random variable which is uniformly distributed in the interval [0,1].We view U_i as a threshold, the CDF crossing over it is considered the more important one. As shown in Fig. 1, Because C_2, C_4 and C_5 cross the threshold U_2, U_4 and U_5, they are reserved for the next stage of prediction. But, we can clearly see that actually the weight of particle 2 is smaller than particle 1, and the weight of particle 4 is smaller than particle 3.This defect will lead to decreasing of estimation accuracy.

We adopt exquisite resampling [9] to overcome this defect. First, implement the same procedure mentioned above until particle 2 pierces the threshold. Then go back to

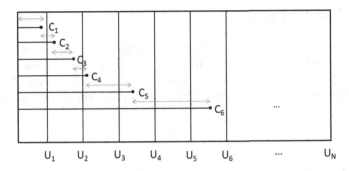

Fig. 3. A demonstration of resampling algorithm

check all the particles in this interval, and preserve the one with highest weight. So C_1, C_3 will be preserved instead. By this the true state of the pdf can be more accurately reflected.

To prove the improvement, we use the following nonlinear model as an example. The dynamic state space models are given by the following equations:

$$x_{k+1} = \alpha x_k + \beta \frac{x_k}{1 + x_k^2} + \gamma \cos(1.2k) + v_k \tag{7}$$

$$y_k = \frac{x_k^2}{20} + w_k, \quad k = 1, 2, \ldots, tf \tag{8}$$

where v_k and w_k are nonzero mean Gaussian random variables, $x_0 = 1$, $\alpha = 0.5$, $\beta = 25$, $\gamma = 8$, sample numbers = 100, Time step = 50 s.

Table 1. Comparison of AERPF with original PF

Seq.		accuracy	F-score	Mean error
Exp1	PF	96.07%	98%	30.89
	AERPF	97.38%	98.65%	19.97
Exp2	PF	42.6%	59.75%	47.54
	AERPF	96.69%	97.56%	24.71
Exp3	PF	67.47%	80.58%	55.99
	AERPF	99.83%	99.91%	38.40
Exp4	PF	52.11%	60.47%	54.14
	AERPF	99.11%	99.67%	23.37
Exp5	PF	69.64%	82.1%	19.56
	AERPF	95.49%	97.34%	4.68
Exp6	PF	81.85%	90.02%	19.84
	AERPF	92.15%	95.81%	12.01

3   Experimental Results

Table 1 shows the comparison of AERPF with original PF. Experiment 1 ~ 3 are sequence by fixed camera, and experiment 4 ~ 6 are by active camera. From the tracking results, we can see the promotion of the accuracy and F-score. At the same time, AERPF decrease the mean error, which means it can enhance the recognition of target object.

References

1. Comaniciu, D., Ramesh, V., Meer, P.: Kernel-based object tracking. IEEE Trans. Pattern Anal. Mach. Intell. **25**(5), 564–577 (2003)
2. Zhao, Q., Hai, T.: Object tracking using color correlogram. In: The 2nd Joint IEEE International Workshop on Visual Surveillance and Performance Evaluation of Tracking and Surveillance (2005)
3. Li, Z., Chen, J., Schraudolph, N.N.: An improved mean-shift tracker with kernel prediction and scale optimisation targeting for low-frame-rate video tracking. In: The 19th International Conference on Pattern Recognition, pp. 1–4 (2008)
4. Lucas, B.D., Kanade, T.: An iterative image registration technique with an application to stereo vision. In: The 7th International Joint Conference on Artificial Intelligence, vol. 81, pp. 674–679 (1981)
5. Matthews, I., Ishikawa, T., Baker, S.: The template update problem. IEEE Trans. Pattern Anal. Mach. Intell. **26**(6), 810–815 (2004)
6. Arulampalam, M.S.: A tutorial on particle filters for online nonlinear/non-gaussian bayesian tracking. IEEE Trans. Signal Process. **50**(2), 174–188 (2002)
7. Vermaak, J., Godsill, S.J., Perez, P.: Monte carlo filtering for multi target tracking and data association. IEEE Trans. Aerosp. Electron. Syst. **41**(1), 309–332 (2005)
8. Horn, K., Schunck, B.G.: Determining optical flow. Artif. Intell. **17**(1), 185–203 (1981)
9. Fu, X., Jia, Y.: An improvement on resampling algorithm of particle filters. IEEE Trans. Signal Process. **58**(10), 5414–5420 (2010)

Construction of 3-Dimensional Virtual Environment Based on Photographed Image (the Acquisition and Processing of the Photographed Image)

Tetsuya Haneta[✉], Hiroyo Ohishi, Tadasuke Furuya,
and Takahiro Takemoto

Tokyo University of Marine Science and Technology, Minato, Japan
t111044@kaiyodai.ac.jp

Abstract. In this study, we propose to construction of 3-dimensional virtual environment in the bay. To support construction of structure on the route of ship and a large ship's position for arrival at the pier, it is suitable for utilizing real images. When we construct places to put ships, for example container yards, we need to think an influence toward a route of ships and surrounding environments. There are many things we cannot understand only by design drawings. Therefore, we need to watch real environments to understand the present situation more clearly. A captain probably hopes to simulate on basis of real images before arriving in a port. Then, we consider a method of virtual environmental construction.

Keywords: Virtual environment · Image-Based rendering · Tour into the picture · Panoramic image

1 Background and Purpose of the Study

In late years studies that construction of 3-dimensional virtual environment is conducted flourishingly in fields such as Virtual Reality (VR) or the Computer Graphics (CG). Wide area and complicated space data are taken by a computer, rebuilt it in a computer and visualized it. With the operation performance gain of the computer, construction of large-scale 3-dimensional virtual environment of close reality is realized. The method of construction of 3-dimensional virtual environment is classified roughly into model-base method and image-base method.

Model-base method means that we reproduce the object using 3-dimensional geometry shape and constructed 3-dimensional virtual environment.

Image-base method means that we construct 3-dimensional virtual environment using photographed image. Using a lot of photographed image such as cityscape, it enables the rendering from any place other than the photography position [1].

Studies of related to construction of 3-dimensional virtual environment such as the cityscape have been already suggested. However, there are few studies on 3-dimensional virtual environment of congestion at sea area and narrow aqueduct. We think that it supports officer's watch if we can construct 3-dimensional virtual

© Springer International Publishing Switzerland 2015
C. Stephanidis (Ed.): HCII 2015 Posters, Part I, CCIS 528, pp. 683–689, 2015.
DOI: 10.1007/978-3-319-21380-4_115

environment of a route. In addition, we can provide the foreknowledge of some routes by showing it for a navigation office who enters the first route beforehand. As a result, we think it prevents sea disaster accident.

Therefore, in this paper, we effectively acquire photographed image of the cityscape of route from the training ship "Shioji-maru" that school owns, use image-based method based on this photographed image and suggest construction method of "*the marine virtual environment*" that we reproduce route in 3-dimensional virtual environment. At the time, it enables us to walk through in the marine virtual environment. Furthermore, corresponding to the change of the position of the virtual viewpoint, we aim at the construction of the marine virtual environment where the context of the structure is maintained.

2   For Marine Virtual Environmental Construction

2.1   Overall Flow

At first, we produce panoramic images Fig. 1-(a),(b). We separate foreground and background images from those images Fig. 1-(c). The foreground images are buildings constructed along routes. When we separated to images of Fig. 1-(c), extra domains exist. Therefore we permeabilize extra domains using alpha value Fig. 1-(d). We make permeabilized foreground images billboards Fig. 1-(e). Finally we construct marine virtual environment Fig. 1-(f).

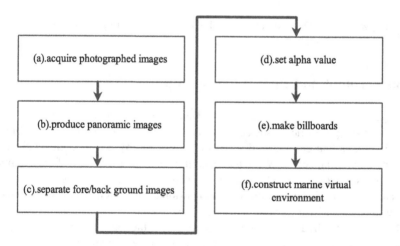

Fig. 1. Overall flow

2.2   Preparation

At first, we acquire photographed images to use for the marine virtual environment.

We captured them on the route around Hinode-Takeshiba Wharf from 13:30 to 13:40 on October 17.

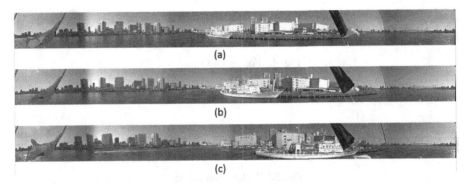

Fig. 2. Panoramic image in each time, (a) is panoramic image in time t, (b) is in time t + 30(sec), (c) is in time t + 60(sec)

We acquire a photographed images from videos which we photographed. Capture interval is 30 s. The size of captured images is 1,920*1,080. We produce panoramic image from captured images. The size of panoramic image is 10,737*847. Figure 2.

2.3   Base of Marine Virtual Environmental Construction

The marine virtual environment is constructed by the method called "Tour Into the Picture [2] (TIP)". TIP is a method to construct virtual environment from a single image. We divide a single image into five rectangles (Front wall, Ceiling, Floor, Right wall and Left wall) based on a vanishing point and map textures in virtual environment. However, the back that a certain front wall makes a pair behind a photographer is the blank in TIP. As a result, a sense of presence and a higher immersion feeling for user decrease.

Therefore, in study of Kang and others [3], they use panoramic images for an input image of TIP. On the basis of a vanishing line, they construct 3-dimensional virtual environment by mapping it onto a column. The visibility is good when we watched around in a virtual viewpoint, but it follows that a feeling of depth is spoiled in comparison with original TIP, and, as for the contextual maintenance of the structure, it is difficult.

We create the back by using panoramic images for an input image in TIP and construct the virtual environment of the hexahedron. Each rectangle with panoramic images performs a classification to be like Fig. 3.

Fig. 3. Each rectangular classification in panoramic image

Fig. 4. Foreground image

Fig. 5. Background image

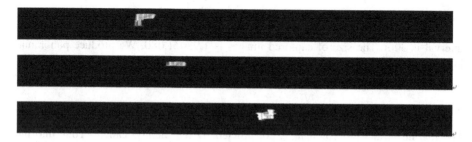

Fig. 6. Extract every structure

2.4   Separation Foreground and Background Image

As for the structure built on the both sides of the route, the context of the depth direction does not change by the change of the viewpoint position. However, we cannot express a feeling of depth with the 2- dimensional image. By separating foreground/background structure from right/left wall images and locating these in the virtual environment to keep a feeling of depth, the context of the structure can maintain.

For maintain the context of structures, we extract these from the image of right/left wall images. We use "GrowCut" which is one of the method of the image-segmentation for the extraction of this structure.

We show the result image which extracted a foreground/background images. Figures 4, 5.

Furthermore, we extract every structure from the background image. Figure 6

2.5   The Billboard of the Structures

The billboard is the plane surface which rotates while corresponding to the position of the virtual camera. This plane surface always moves so as to confront the camera. Due to maintaining context foreground/background structures, we convert structures into billboards and locate them in the marine virtual environment.

2.6   Constructing of the Marine Virtual Environment

We show the result of constructing of the marine virtual environmental. Figures 7, 8.

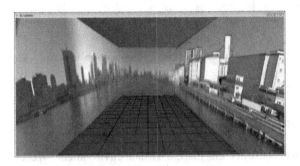

Fig. 7. Front wall

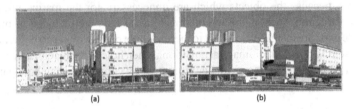

(a)   (b)

Fig. 8. Right wall, (a) is right wall from left view, (b) is from right view

The virtual environment of the hexahedron was constructed. We can watch around with the virtual viewpoint and can grasp the scene of the route easily. In addition, the structures that are equal to the background are made by billboards.

Therefore, in the right and left wall, we can reproduce a scene with a feeling of depth.

However, the height of the horizontal ground of the wall of right and left is different depend on the photography environment.

2.7   Expand the Marine Virtual Environment

In TIP, the texture is produced by projection conversion. These have blurred area. To reduce blurred area and expand the scale, we connect the virtual environments of the hexahedron. Figure 9.

In the overlapping areas, we should produce panoramic images overlapping scene of the real world.

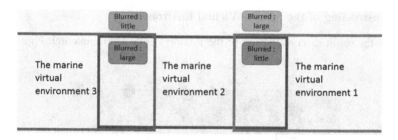

Fig. 9. Method of expanding

3   Conclusions

In this paper, we construct the marine virtual environment. We can watch around virtual viewpoint, and can walk through in the marine virtual environment. In accordance with changing position of the virtual viewpoint, we consider the contextual maintenance of the structure.

However, because the objects which are unnecessary for the marine virtual environment construction, such as the international signal flag, are included in panoramic images, hole parts are increase. So as not to increase hole parts, we have to be careful about the camera setting position for image acquisition. When hole parts increase, we are able to construct more realistic marine virtual environment by complementing hole parts [4].

4   Future Works

We can contribute to more grasp positional relation of the whole route by placing the buoys which there is in the route as a billboard in marine virtual environment.

In addition, the marine virtual environment of this paper reproduced the space with the source of light in the daytime, but it is necessary to assume it in the case of the night navigation. We aim at the marine virtual environmental construction using the virtual source of light to reproduce the scene of the route in the night.

Furthermore, with Point Cloud Library [5] (PCL), we reproduce ships in marine virtual environment and aim at the construction of higher realistic marine virtual environment.

References

1. Devebec, P.E., Taylor, C.A., Malik, J.: Modeling and rendering architecture from photographs: a hybrid geometry- and image- based approach. In: Proceedings SIGGRAPH 1996, In Computer Graphics Proceedings. ACM SIGGRAPH, Annual Conference Series, New Orleans, Louisiana, pp. 11–20, August 4–9, 1996
2. Horry, Y., Anjyo, Y., Arai, K.: Tour into the picture:using spidery mesh interface to make animation from a single image. In: ACM SIGGRAPH 1997, pp. 225–232 (1997)

3. Kang, W.H., Pyo, H.S., Anjyo, K., Shin, Y.S.: Tour into the picture using a vanishing line and its extension to panoramic images. In: Proceedings Eurographics, pp. 132–141 (2001)
4. Wexler, Y., Shechtman, E., Irani, M.: Space-Time video completion. In: Proceedings of the 2004 IEEE Computer Society Conference on Computer Vision and Pattern Recognition, CVPR 2004, vol. 1, pp. I-120–I-127 (2004)
5. Point Cloud Library. http://pointclouds.org/

A Method of Automatic Cage Generation
for Shape Deformation
by Using Elastic Models

Takayuki Kanaya[1(✉)], Yuta Muraki[2], Koji Nishio[2],
and Kenichi Kobori[2]

[1] Hiroshima International University, Hiroshima, Japan
t-kanaya@hw.hirokoku-u.ac.jp
[2] Osaka Institute of Technology, Osaka, Japan
muraki@is.oit.ac.jp,
{koji.a.nishio,kenichi.kobori}@oit.ac.jp

Abstract. Laplacian-based mesh processing technique is a kind of shape deformation in Computer Graphics modeling. It is hard to deform shapes which constructed by a lot of vertices in real time, because computational cost is high. A cages-based mesh deformation method is used in order to control the computational cost. A cage is a polyhedron which envelops an original dense model and is constructed by few meshes. The main advantages of using cages in shape deformations are controlling high speed computation. Currently, the coarse cage is constructed mainly by hand, and the construction usually takes several hours, even longer. Furthermore, when the shape of the model to be deformed is complex, it is very hard to construct its coarse cage by hand. Therefore it is important to develop a convenient method to generate the coarse cage enveloping a model. In this paper, we propose a method of automatic cage generation.

Keywords: Cage generation · Shape deformation · Computer graphics

1 Introduction

Mesh deformation is a common process in geometry modeling and computer animation. Geometry modeling techniques have become an important key technology in the industrial design and development process. Similarly, in computer animation we may want a realistic behavior, simulating physics. Therefore, we need flexible tools for mesh deformation to achieve the desired results easily. In the past years there have been many methods, such as Free-form deformation (FFD) [1], Radial Basis Functions (RBF) [2], curve based deformation [3], skeletons [4, 5] and physics simulation [6].

Also, in recent years many discrete deformation techniques based on Laplacian mesh representation have been published [7–9]. They can support interactive work by encoding differential properties and positional constraints in a linear system. Laplacian operators are described by the uniform weighting method. This approach is numerically stable, but is not able to compute in real-time, depending on the number of constraints. Especially, modern computer graphics models are often created or acquired at a very

C. Stephanidis (Ed.): HCII 2015 Posters, Part I, CCIS 528, pp. 690–695, 2015.
DOI: 10.1007/978-3-319-21380-4_116

high resolution in order to maintain a convincing level of realism. The huge number of vertices makes direct manipulation of the models tedious and computationally expensive. We would like a deformation method able to work in real-time, for interactive applications, which limits the computation time. Also, it is desirable to have a convenient and easy to use system which makes it simple for users to get quickly familiar with it. A way to reduce computational cost is to build a similar but coarse structure with fewer vertices, and then deform the dense model through the coarser structure. This coarser structure, which envelops the original dense model, is called cage.

The first approach cage based method of Laplacian mesh deformation comes from Floater et al. [10] and Ju et al. [11]. Both studies aimed at looking for an interpolation method for surfaces. Initially, Floater presented a 2D mean value coordinates (MVC) over quasi-convex polygons, then developed a 3D version of the algorithm. Then, Ju et al. developed another solution by using the Floater's 2D approach. Next, Joshi et al. [12] developed another method to set harmonic coordinates (HC) successfully avoiding some of the MVC drawbacks. Also, Lipman et al. [13] developed a method with cage faces data in deformation operators to achieve a natural deformation with shape preserving.

In cage based methods, a coarse cage enveloping a model is required to be constructed in advance for deforming the model. Currently, the coarse cage is constructed mainly by hand [10–13], and the construction usually takes several hours, even longer. Furthermore, when the shape of the model to be deformed is complex, it is very hard to construct its coarse cage by hand. Therefore it is important to develop a convenient method to generate the coarse cage enveloping a model.

2   Cage Generation Algorithm

First, we outline our method. The main steps of our method are as follows:

1. Compute the Bounding Volume (BV) of the dense mesh, and then Construct BV Tree by partitioning the BV recursively.
2. Generate the Convex Hull of a set of vertices constructing all BVs.
3. Subdivide the triangles of Convex Hull
4. Elasticize each edge of triangular net

2.1   Bounding Volumes Tree Generation

The first step of our algorithm is to compute the bounding volume (BV) of the original dense mesh model. In general, the idea is for the BV to have cheaper overlap tests than the complex objects they bound [14]. The properties for the BV include tight fitting, using little memory, encapsulating objects, and so on.

There are many kinds of the BV, such as Sphere, AABB (Axis-Aligned Bounding Box), OBB (Oriented Bounding Box), and Convex Hull [14]. We use the AABB and the OBB, as shown in Fig. 1(b). The AABB is a rectangular six-sided box categorized by having its faces oriented in such a way that its normal are at all times parallel with the axes of the given coordinate system. The OBB is a rectangular block, like an AABB but with an arbitrary orientation. The arbitrary orientation is computed by principal component analysis, and so on.

After computing BV, we generate Bounding Volumes Tree (BVT). The BVT is a tree hierarchy which is generated by partitioning the BV recursively [14]. The original set of BV forms the leaf nodes of the tree that is this BVT. We describe the way of the BVT. (1) We compute the centroid of the original dense model. (2) We select the normal of the plane partitioning the space it is in into infinite sets of points on either side of the plane. (3) We partition the space by the plane passing through the centroid with the normal. (4) We construct 2 BVs by using the vertices in each halfspace. For example of AABB, it is possible to partition it by X-Y, Y-Z, and Z-X plane, respectively. Also, it is possible to partition it into 8 parts (Octree). A partitioned example is illustrated in Fig. 1(c).

2.2   Convex Hull Generation

The next step of our algorithm is to generate convex hull by using the vertices constructing BVT. It is so quickly and easy to generate the convex hull that the number of vertices constructing each BV is 8. We use Barber method [15] to generate the convex hull. We show an example in Fig. 1(d).

2.3   Triangles Subdivision

The convex hull, which is generated in Sect. 2.2, is consisted of triangles. We subdivide these triangles, if necessary. The midpoint is inserted into each edge constructing triangles, and then we generate triangular net by subdividing triangles in quarter. A subdivided example is illustrated in Fig. 1(e).

However, several warping triangles occur, when they are subdivided. Then we remesh the triangles, if necessary.

2.4   Elasticizing Each Edge of the Triangular Net

We regard the triangular net as the net with elastic force, contract the triangular net. A vertex of triangular net is moved to the position which the energy of elastic force minimizes. Similarly, all vertices are translated iteratively until the total energy minimizes. As a result, we generate a Cage.

2.4.1   Definition of Energy

We describe the triangular net with elastic force. All vertices are connected to each other with spring. We define the energy of each vertex as follows:

$$E(x) = \alpha \sum_{i=0}^{5} \left[\max_{v_j} \{ (p(v_j) - p(x)) \bullet e_i \} \right]^2 \qquad (1)$$

where, $p(x)$ is a candidate vertex, $p(v_j)$ is each vertex connecting $p(x)$, α is spring constant, e_i is unit vector along each positive or negative axis.

We describe the contracting procedure as follows:

1. Select a candidate vertex x among vertices constructing triangular net.
2. Determine a new position which the energy minimizes when the vertex x moves very short distance from the current position to 26-adjacency, respectively.
3. Go to the step 1, until all vertices determine their new positions.
4. Move all vertices to their new positions, respectively.
5. Repeat step 1 to 4, until the all energy drops below a threshold value.

2.4.2   Collision Detection

A vertex x happens to intersect with the original model, when the x moves to the new position decided in Sect. 2.4.1. This case violates a fundamental rule that the cage includes the original model. Therefore we have to avoid intersecting with it.

In the case of intersecting of edges constructing the triangular net with faces consisting of the original model according to moving the x to the new position, we do not allow the x to move.

3   Results

Our algorithm developed in this paper is implemented with VC ++ 2010 and OpenGL, and runs on the PC with 3.4 GHz Core i7, 4.0 GB memory, and Windows 7 Professional (32bit). A result is illustrated in Fig. 1(a)−(f). The number of faces of the original dense model, is shown in Fig. 1(a), is 11,794. In this example which is shown in Fig. 1(b), we selected the AABB as the BV. Figure 1(c) is the BVT which is partitioned the BV into 2 parts along the Y axis twice, and then along the X axis twice, recursively. A convex hull, is shown in Fig. 1(d), was generated, and was subdivided. Next, the triangular net was transformed from the convex hull. We got the Cage according to contracting the triangular net as shown in Fig. 1(f). The number of the faces of the Cage is 344.

4   Conclusions

In this paper, we propose an automatic method to generate the coarse cage for a given original dense mesh. The original mesh is first enclosed the bounding volume, and the bounding volume is partitioned into 2 parts or 8 parts, recursively. Next, convex hull is generated by using the vertices constructing the bounding volumes. The convex hull is consisted of triangles. These triangles are subdivided and remeshed, if necessary. The triangular net with elastic force is contracted by moving the vertices to their new positions until the total energy minimizes. Finally, we generate a cage.

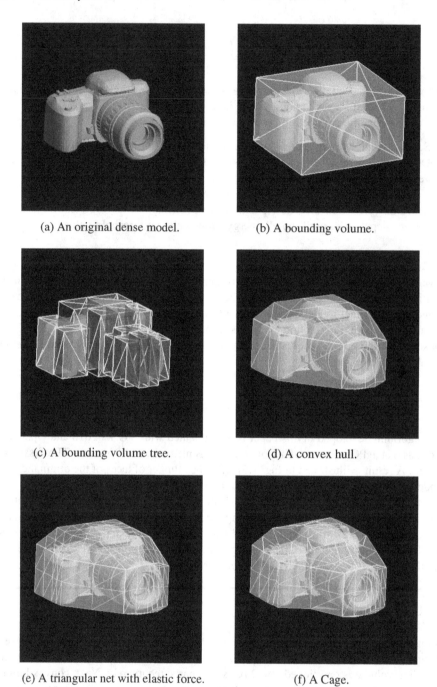

(a) An original dense model.

(b) A bounding volume.

(c) A bounding volume tree.

(d) A convex hull.

(e) A triangular net with elastic force.

(f) A Cage.

Fig. 1. An example of our method

References

1. Sederberg, T.W., Parry, S.R.: Free-form deformation of solid geometric models. SIGGRAPH Comput. Graph. **20**(4), 151–160 (1986)
2. Botsch, M., Kobbelt, L.: Real-time shape editing using radial basis functions. Comput. Graph. Forum **24**(3), 611–621 (2005)
3. Peng, Q., Jin, X., Feng, J.: Arc-length-based axial deformation and length preserved animation. In: Computer Animation 1997, pp. 86–92 (1997)
4. Yoshizawa, S., Belyaev, A.G., Seidel, H.-P.: Skeleton-based variational mesh deformations. Comput. Graph. Forum **26**(3), 255–264 (2007)
5. Yan, H.-B., Shi-Min, H., Martin, R.R., Yong-Liang, Y.: Shape Deformation Using a Skeleton to Drive Simplex Transformation. IEEE Trans. Visual. Comput. Graph. **14**(3), 693–706 (2008)
6. Terzopoulos, D., Platt, J., Barr, A., Fleischer, K.: Elastically deformable models. In: Proceedings of the 14th Annual Conference On Computer Graphics and Interactive Techniques, SIGGRAPH 1987, pp. 205–214 (1987)
7. Sorkine, O., Cohen-Or, D., Lipman, Y., Alexa, M., Rössl, C., Seidel, H.-P.: Laplacian surface editing. In: 2004 Eurographics Symposium on Geometry Processing 2004, pp.179–188 (2004)
8. Sorkine, O.: Laplacian mesh processing. In: STAR Proceedings of Eurographics 2005, pp. 53–70 (2005)
9. Nealen, A., Sorkine, O., Alexa, M., Cohen-Or, D.: A sketch-based interface for detail-preserving mesh editing. ACM Trans. Graph. **24**(3), 1142–1147 (2005)
10. Floater, M.S., K´os, G., Reimers, M.: 3D Mean value coordinates. Comput. Aided Geom. Des. **22**(7), 623–631 (2005)
11. Ju, T., Schaefer, S.,Warren, J.: Mean value coordinates for closed triangular meshes. In: ACM SIGGRAPH 2005, pp. 561–566 (2005)
12. Joshi, P., Meyer, M., DeRose, T., Green, B., Sanocki, T.: Harmonic coordinates for character articulation. ACM Trans. Graph. **26**(3), 1–9 (2007)
13. Lipman, Y., Levin, D., Cohen-Or, D.: Green coordinates. ACM Trans. Graph **27**, 78: 1–78:10 (2008)
14. Ericson, C.: Real-Time Collision Detection (The Morgan Kaufmann Series in Interactive 3-D Technology). CRC Press, Boca Raton (2004)
15. Bradford, C.B., Dobkin, D.P., Huhdanpaa, H.: The quickhull algorithm for convex hulls. ACM Trans. Graph. on Math. Softw. **22**(4), 469–483 (1996)

Employing Mobile Applications in Human-Machine Interaction in Visual Pattern Recognition Research

Amir Schur[✉] and Charles C. Tappert

Seidenberg School of CSIS, Pace University,
1 Martine Ave., White Plains, NY 10606, USA
amirschur@aol.com, ctappert@pace.edu

Abstract. This study is part of the first author's continued dissertation research in human-machine interaction in visual pattern recognition. Previous research focused on evaluating human-machine interaction using a flower recognition tool. Initial research showed that human interaction in color recognition improved accuracy significantly. We then looked more deeply into various automated color recognition algorithms and ways of combining them with human feedback. Described here is the process of upgrading the initial system into a new mobile application using Appinventor. After data collection, models were built for various color spaces. Sharing this experience may help other researchers incorporating a human-computer interaction component into their work.

Keywords: Human-computer interaction · Visual object recognition · Pattern classification · Feature extraction · Appinventor · Color space

1 Introduction

Initial research in comparing accuracy and time to accomplish visual pattern recognition tasks among humans, machines, and human-machine combinations showed favorable results for the human-machine combination. While maintaining a reasonable time to accomplish the task, human-machine interactions resulted in better accuracy compared to human activities alone or machine alone, especially when humans assisted in the color recognition process. In this flower species identification task, human activities were performed by amateurs and not experts [1]. Why human assistance is so valuable in the color recognition task is still being investigated. In addition, a different tool, or at least an upgraded one, was considered necessary in continuing this research, as well as investigating the various color spaces.

A tool upgrade to a mobile application was desired for ease-of-use and portability, as collecting flower pictures is required during data collection. The original Interactive Visual System (IVS) is a native java application running on a typical X86 machine with an option to install on a palm pilot [1].

Several development tools to accommodate mobile application development were investigated. These included NetBeans, Eclipse, and IntelliJ, as well as cross platform development tools such as Codename One where a one-time build is suitable for

© Springer International Publishing Switzerland 2015
C. Stephanidis (Ed.): HCII 2015 Posters, Part I, CCIS 528, pp. 696–699, 2015.
DOI: 10.1007/978-3-319-21380-4_117

various platforms such as Android, IOS, etc. Finally, Appinventor, created by Google, but now maintained by MIT (at appinventor.mit.edu) was investigated. This tool has gained enormous popularity in the past years, with 3 million users representing 195 countries worldwide.

Appinventor is not a typical application development tool. It has been simplified so that users do not need to master a typical programming language. It is advertised as the perfect tool for teaching basic software engineering, basic application development, and research. With the simplicity of the development process, the developer is allowed to focus more on the idea level rather than spending time developing an application, and thus not being dependent on the availability of an application developer.

As an upgrade to the original IVS, a data collection tool using Appinventor was created. The tool was utilized to perform a set of tasks and an evaluation of its performance evaluated. Due to performance issues the tool will be replaced with a web application using python with Flask framework, requiring a savvy developer to create a web application. Nevertheless, it should be mentioned that Appinventor is considered a good alternative to create a mobile application quickly.

2 Appinventor Data Collection Tool

Appinventor provides a block-based programming tool for creating an app. Users must design the screen layout with available tools/objects to display on the mobile screen. After labeling each object, activities must be defined using their building-block tool: what happens when a particular object is clicked, long clicked, etc. Users can then test the mobile application by connecting an android device to the website, or by running a simulator locally. When the user is satisfied, the application can be packaged into an android application package (apk) file and then immediately installed on the user's Android device. A simple mobile application can be built within an hour.

For human-machine interaction research, this opens a vast area of research and data collection possibilities. The mobile app can quickly collect GPS data, user activities, user behavior and responses, etc. There are various built-in sensor functionalities readily available, such as accelerometer, orientation sensor, proximity sensor, location sensor, bar code scanner and near field sensor. In this study, users chose the primary and secondary colors of petals, the primary color of the stamen, and provided a petal count.

The users took pictures of flowers via the relatively high-resolution camera built-in to mobile devices. These pictures are typically 3–4 MBs in size, compared to the lower resolution images 100–200 KBs obtained in previous data collections [1]. The Appinventor tool developed was named Interactive Visual System 2 (IVS2).

Another useful feature of Appinventor is the ability to save data in the cloud, in particular Google Drive, allowing easy access and analysis to the researcher. A native authentication method using OAuth 2.0 was implemented, allowing the team to store and view data in Google Drive.

The Appinventor mobile application tool was used to take pictures of various flower species, perform manual feature extraction, and upload the pictures and data to Google drive (Fig. 1).

Fig. 1. IVS2 data collector android app

Below are issues with the application:

- The application has too many options for the user. The application should be more streamlined during the process of using it.
- The error handling is flawed. A JSON error report is presented with a vague error code.
- The application allows a user to load the data before loading the picture. This should be restricted so that the user cannot upload data without first taking a picture or opening an existing picture in the device.
- Because the uploaded information is not cleared from the mobile device and no history of previous posts is recorded, collection of redundant data is likely. Once uploaded, the information should be cleared automatically from the mobile device, or there needs to be a way to track which pictures on your phone have already been uploaded.
- A method should also be provided to save data locally.

Although all of these problems can be easily fixed within Appinventor, these functionalities have been moved into a web application for the testing phase, which will be performed after the data modeling phase. The web application uses Python with Flask framework and is more guided in the data collection process with a changing screen after each activity is completed with automated data saving capabilities. For the web application, however, the infrastructure that can host a web application is required and this requires good programming support.

The portability and speed of a mobile application makes it a good tool for human-machine interaction data collection. Human-machine research often involves software development activities and infrastructure, which is often not readily available.

Tools such as Appinventor can be utilized by a researcher who doesn't have a software engineering background, or a software developer readily available. The researcher can quickly build a simple to moderately complex mobile application using Appinventor. The learning curve for this framework is small (days) compared to learning and becoming proficient in a computer language (months).

3 Continued Research

Once the data collection process has been established to obtain training data set, the research process will be continued. Because color perception was an issue and we were only using the RGB color space in the past [1], finding the best color space in addition to using high resolution images is expected to increase the accuracy level. For example, we expect a higher level of accuracy using CIELab color space since it is considered to be a better model for human visual perception [2]. To be complete, however, the extracted features of various color aspects of the flowers will be translated into the dominant color spaces: HSI, XYZ and CIELab.

The next step will be to build a data model using IBM SPSS Modeler. We will build separate models for each color space and then compare the accuracy results. Once we have a solid model, we can continue our testing phase. We will build the test data set and perform testing to reach our conclusions. The results will be compared with previous research to develop a better understanding of what is the best method of combination of human and machines in the visual pattern recognition process.

References

1. Schur, A., Tappert, C.: Combining human and machine capabilities for improved accuracy and speed in visual recognition tasks. In: Stephanidis, C. (ed.) HCI 2014, Part I. CCIS, vol. 434, pp. 368–372. Springer, Heidelberg (2014)
2. Ugarriza, L.G., et al.: Automatic image segmentation by dynamic region growth and multi-resolution merging. IEEE Trans. Image Process. **18**(10), 2275–2288 (2009)

How to Tune a Random Forest for Real-time Segmentation in Safe Human-Robot Collaboration?

Vivek Sharma[1,2,3]([✉]), Frank Dittrich[2], Şule Yildirim-Yayilgan[1],
Ali Shariq Imran[1], and Heinz Wörn[2]

[1] ESAT-PSI, Center for Processing Speech and Images, IMinds,
University of Leuven, Leuven, Belgium
vivek.sharma@esat.kuleuven.be
{sule.yayilgan,ali.imran}@hig.no
[2] Faculty of Computer Science and Media Technology,
Gjøvik University College, Gjøvik, Norway
{frank.dittrich,woern}@kit.edu
[3] Institute for Process Control and Robotics,
Karlsruhe Institute of Technology, Karlsruhe, Germany

Abstract. This paper is an extension of our work related to a generic classification approach for low-level human body-parts segmentation in RGB-D data. In this paper, we discuss the impact of decision tree parameters, number of training frames and pixel count per object-class during a random forests classifier training. From the evaluation, we observed that a varied non-redundant training samples makes the decision tree learn the most. Pixel count per object-class should be just adequate otherwise it may lead to under/over-fitting problem. We found a highly optimized and a most optimal parameter setup for a random forests classifier training. Our new dataset of RGB-D data of human body-parts and industrial-grade components is publicly available for lease for academic and research purposes.

Keywords: Safe human-robot interaction · Random decision forest · Parameter optimization · Image processing · Object segmentation

1 Introduction

Interest in robotics in the domain of manufacturing industry has shown an outstanding growth recently in scenarios where human beings are present too. Humans and robots often share the same workspace posing great threats to safety issues [1]. In this paper, we use a random decision forests (RDF) for pixelwise segmentation of human body-parts and industrial-grade components in RGB-D sensor data with intended use for the safe human-robot collaboration (SHRC) and interaction (SHRI) in challenging industrial environment. The major advantage of choosing an RDF approach over the classical Support Vector Machine

© Springer International Publishing Switzerland 2015
C. Stephanidis (Ed.): HCII 2015 Posters, Part I, CCIS 528, pp. 700–704, 2015.
DOI: 10.1007/978-3-319-21380-4_118

(SVM) approach and boosting is that the RDF can handle both binary and multi-class problems even with the same classification model. The goal of our work is to do high quality segmentation in real-time and this directly depends on the classifier parameters. In the experimental evaluation we discuss how to tune manually the training parameters[1] of the RDF and also investigate how they could be optimized for the real-time object-class segmentation time with high performance (mean average recall (mAR) and mean average precision (mAP)) scores in the evaluation.

2 Related Work

In [3], Shotton et al. inform that in their segmentation approch, most of the improvement in the performance is due to the pixelwise classification. In [3], the authors use boosted classifier for the segmentation task. However, we use a random forests classifier [2] for the segmentation task. The reasons for choosing to use RDF classifier rather than modeling the system with conditional random fields can be further found in [2,4,6].

Our approach is driven by three key objectives: computational efficiency, robustness and time efficiency (i.e. real-time). Our basic design of the system differs from [5] in the following aspects. In [5], all training data of human were thereby synthetically generated by applying motion capture, while we use a simple synthetic human body representation in a virtual environment using the KINECT skeleton estimations [2] which reduces the computational expense. In [5], training object samples are simple feature vectors whereas we have an optimized training strategy [2] with a reduced number of training samples while preserving the classification performance. This in turn reduces the computational expense. In [5], the authors use $F = 300\,K/tree$ with $PC = 2000$ which takes a lot of training time, has a high computational cost and has large memory consumption, while in our case $F = 1600/tree$ with $PC = 300$ is sufficient for producing almost comparable results, hence reducing computational expense and training-time. Also in [5], the authors *"fail to distinguish subtle changes in the depth image such as crossed arms"*.

3 Experimental Evaluation

Each of the parameters are tuned one by one and their effects are investigated for the evaluation of 65 real-world (Real), synthetic (Syn), and test depth frames (Data), where each frame generated from a KINECT camera was of size 640×480 pixels. A random forests classifier predicts a likelihood probability of a pixel belonging to an object-class. For showing the qualitative results, if the prediction of an object-class label assigned to a pixel is less than the probability thresholding of 0.4, then color black is shown for those pixels else object-class label is shown.

---

[1] Additive White Gaussian Noise (σ), Tree Depth (**D**), Number of Trees (**T**), Randomization Parameter (**Ro**), Number of Training Frames (**F**), Pixel Count per Object-Class (**PC**).

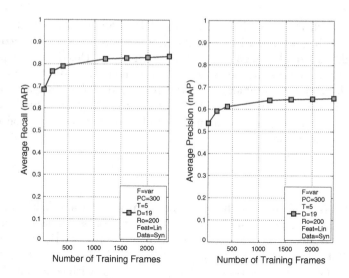

Fig. 1. Effect of the number of training frames on average recall and precision measures of pixelwise object class segmentation.

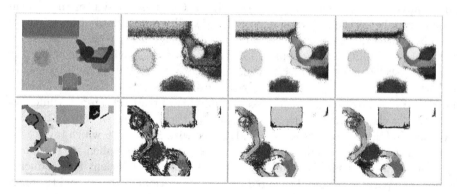

Fig. 2. Prediction results based on synthetic and real-world test depth data for number of training frames F = {40, 1600, 2400}. The first column shows the test depth data, and second, third, fourth columns show the corresponding prediction results respectively for F = {40, 1600, 2400} with probability thresholding of 0.4. Class predictions with a probability less than the thresholds are colored black in the result images.

Number of Training Frames: F = 1600 was chosen as the most optimal value for this parameter. It was found that that an the increase in number of training frames monotonically increases the testing prediction only if the training set is highly varied i.e. redundancy in training samples does not lead the decision forest to learn more, but the confidence (precision) increases at the expense of recall (see Figs. 1 and 2).

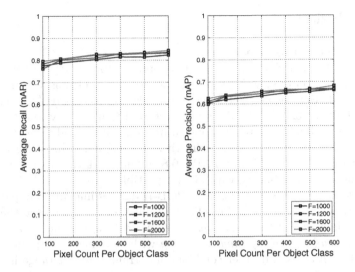

Fig. 3. Effect of the pixel count per object class on average recall and precision measures of pixelwise object class segmentation.

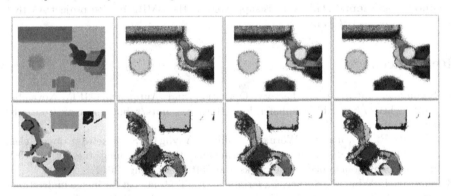

Fig. 4. Prediction results based on synthetic and real-world test depth data for pixel count per object class PC = {75, 300, 600}. The first column shows the test depth data, and second, third, fourth columns show the corresponding prediction results respectively for PC = {75, 300, 600} with probability thresholding of 0.4. Class predictions with a probability less than the thresholds are colored black in the result images.

Pixel Count per Object-Class: As the PC^2 is increased, the RDF classifier is able to use more spatial context to make decisions, nevertheless non availability of enough pixel count would ultimately risk over-fitting to this context. Though increasing pixel count adds extra run-time cost, but improves the classification results way better. In our case most of the gains happened for the case with F = 1600 and PC = 300 (see Figs. 3 and 4).

---

[2] Pixels extracted from a patch with features specific to a particular object-class.

4 Conclusion

A highly optimized fixed parameters setup (i.e. $F = 1600$, $PC = 300$, $D = 19$, $T = 5$, $Ro = 200$ and $\sigma = 15$ cm) resulted in approx. 2.076×10^6 synthetic labeled training samples per tree, with a training time of approx. 43 mins. Calculating the pixelwise predictions using the trained forest takes 34 ms on a desktop with Intel i7-2600 K CPU at 3.40 GHZ. It was demonstrated that the developed approach is robust and well adapted to the application targeted for real-time object-class segmentation in the industrial domain with humans and industrial-grade components, with $mAR = 0.891$ and $mAP = 0.809$. Our work can distinguish subtle changes such as crossed-arms, which is not possible in [5].

Besides, a new dataset of pixelwise RGB-D data of human body-parts composed of frames from *"top-view"* has been established. In the dataset, the human appearance includes: *sitting, standing, walking, working, dancing, swinging, boxing, tilting, bending, bowing, and stretching* with combinations of angled arms, single and both arms and other combinations. Human height range is between 160–190 cm.

Acknowledgements. This work is supported by the BMBF funded project AMIKA and the EU project ROVINA.

References

1. Fraunhofer Institute for Factory Operation and Automation IFF, November 2014. http://www.iff.fraunhofer.de/en/business-units/robotic-systems/research/human-robot-interaction.html
2. Dittrich, F., Sharma, V., Wörn, H., Yildirim-Yayilgan, S.: Pixelwise object class segmentation based on synthetic data using an optimized training strategy. In: IEEE International Conference on Networks and Soft Computing (2014)
3. Shotton, J., Winn, J., Rother, C., Criminisi, A.: Textonboost for image understanding: multi-class object recognition and segmentation by jointly modeling texture, layout, and context. Int. J. Comput. Vision **81**(1), 2–23 (2009)
4. Criminisi, A., Shotton, J.: Decision Forests for Computer Vision and Medical Image Analysis. Springer, London (2013)
5. Shotton, J., Girshick, R., Fitzgibbon, A., Sharp, T., Cook, M., Finocchio, M., Moore, R., Kohli, P., Criminisi, A., Kipman, A., Blake, A.: Efficient human pose estimation from single depth images. IEEE Trans. Pattern Anal. Mach. Intell. **35**(12), 2821–2840 (2013)
6. Sharma, V.: Training and Evaluation of a Framework for Pixel-Wise Object Class Segmentation based on Synthetic Depth Data. Master Thesis. Karlsruhe Institute of Technology, University of Oslo, Hospital of Oslo and Gjøvik University College (2014)

Brain and Physiological Parameters Monitoring

The Estimation of Taste Preference Based on Prefrontal Cortex Activity

Hirotoshi Asano[(⌧)]

Electronics and Information Engineering, Kagawa, Japan
asano@eng.kagawa-u.ac.jp

Abstract. The purpose of this study is to develop a method for objective evaluation about preference of taste based on brain activities. To achieve this goal, we propose a system estimated the preference from subject's brain activities by using sensitivity matrix. The system is able to estimate subject's preference by taking advantage of change of cerebral blood flow based on brain activities in the frontal lobe. The effectiveness of the system was tested through experiment. We measured the subject's brain activities during drinking a beverage by using near-infrared spectroscopy and verified the effectiveness of the system from the data. From the results, an interesting data on relationship the psychological preference and brain activities in the frontal lobe was obtained. The estimated values corresponded to subject's psychological values. The obtained data suggest that the effectiveness of the proposed approach. The finding results are a step toward identifying psychological preference of taste.

Keywords: Prefrontal cortex activity · Near-Infrared spectroscopy · Taste sensitivity matrix · Physiological and psychological measurement

1 Introduction

Taste preference is an area under active research in the food industry, and developing techniques for taste testing is a critical issue in food marketing. Sensory analysis is currently widely used as a general evaluation of taste preference. However, while sensory analysis can generate subjective evaluation of food characteristics, it is often greatly affected by individual differences and is associated with low reproducibility, urging the development of new techniques for objective evaluation of consumer preferences. Previously, we reported the possibility of performing objective evaluation of taste preferences using Near-Infrared Spectroscopy (NIRS). NIRS is a measurement method for brain activity that utilizes the high biological permeability of near-infrared light (700−900 nm wavelength), and differential optical transparency between oxygenated hemoglobin (oxyHb) and deoxygenated hemoglobin (deoxyHb) in blood. If ambiguities that arise in subjective evaluation methods can be compensated for with physiological parameters such as oxyHb values, it would be possible to corroborate results from psychological questionnaires with corresponding physiological responses. In the present study, we developed a novel technique to mechanically estimate human taste preferences from oxyHb values measured by NIRS. First, we focused on the

C. Stephanidis (Ed.): HCII 2015 Posters, Part I, CCIS 528, pp. 707–711, 2015.
DOI: 10.1007/978-3-319-21380-4_119

emotion spectrum analysis method [1]. The emotion spectrum analysis method is a technique developed by Musha to estimate human emotions using EEG, which is of interest since EEG and oxyHb are connected through neurovascular coupling. Neural activity in the brain is represented by action potentials from neurons. Upon neural activation, the peripheral vasculature expands, leading to changes in blood oxygen concentration as blood volume and blood flow are altered. Thus, since the brain blood flow response measured by NIRS is a direct secondary effect of nervous system activity, it is, in principle and technically, possible to apply this method to oxyHb levels. We focused on the emotion matrix from the emotion spectrum analysis method to consider the possibility of evaluating taste preference by combining the emotion matrix with sensory analysis. Although there are variations in values depending on the time constant, we report here the possibility of estimating taste preferences using this method, as long as the time constant is taken into consideration.

2 Experimentation

2.1 Experimental Environment

Figure 1 represents the experimental system. Room temperature is $27.0 \pm 1.0°C$ with no wind or air flow. The subject is seated with eyes closed and relaxed, as their frontal lobe is fitted with a head holder and measurement probe for the optical encephalography device (OEG-16). The device includes 16 measurement channels.

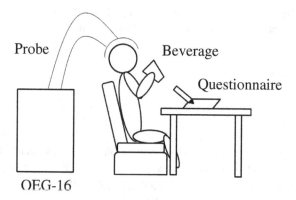

Fig. 1. Experimental system

2.2 Experiment Methodology

Each measurement time was 60 s, which consisted of: resting eyes closed for 20 s, taste test for 30 s, and resting eyes closed for 10 s. For the taste test, a sports drink was employed as the sample since it was deemed a desirable and appropriate beverage that humans would subconsciously seek under conditions of thirst. Before and after each experiment, sensory evaluation questionnaires were given to subjects, and psychological states were measured. Figure 2 represents an example of the questionnaire to measure subject's psychological state. The questionnaire included 14 evaluation points related to taste preference and condition of thirst. The experiments were performed on two different dates to compare results between conditions of thirst and full hydration. For testing under conditions of thirst, subjects were asked to refrain from drinking beverages for 2–3 h before the experiment. For testing under full hydration, subjects were hydrated just prior to the experiment.

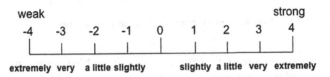

Fig. 2. An example of the questionnaire to measure subject's psychological state

3   Result and Discussion

Figure 3 shows a representative time course of oxyHb levels during a given experiment (Channel 6). From physiological evaluation, a stronger increase in oxyHb concentration was seen when the subject was in a state of thirst, compared to full hydration. The psychological evaluation showed a significant difference in results between thirst and hydration conditions with a significance level of 1 %. Figure 4 demonstrates preference relationships. We observed that taste preference was elevated when subjects were thirsty compared to when fully hydrated, suggesting that differences in physiological conditions can affect taste preference. In addition, it was confirmed that perceptions such as sweetness and flavor strengthened along with the rise of taste preference. Based on our physiological and psychological results, an emotion matrix was generated to estimate taste preferences.

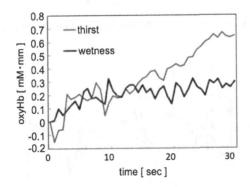

Fig. 3. Representative time course of oxyHb levels during a given experiment (Ch 6)

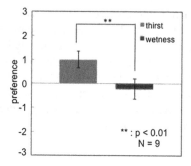

Fig. 4. Demonstrates preference relationships

Figure 5 shows estimates for each time constant in thirst conditions. At the time constant of 49, preferences 1 and 2 both showed approximately 9 % error. Figure 6 indicates estimates for each time constant in hydrated conditions. At the time constant of 46, error was approximately 1 % for preferences -1 and 0, however, 11 % error was seen for preference 1. Figures 7 and 8 represent these estimated values. These results suggest that time constants must be considered, since variations give rise to error in estimates whether in thirst or fully hydrated conditions. In addition, since the range of preferences that can be estimated are limited by the number of data points, it is critical to increase the volume of data to further improve our findings.

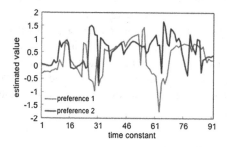

Fig. 5. Estimates for each time constant in thirst conditions

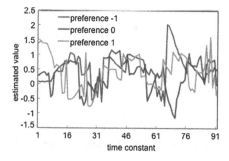

Fig. 6. Estimates for each time constant in hydrated conditions

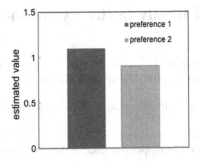

Fig. 7. Estimated values in thirst conditions

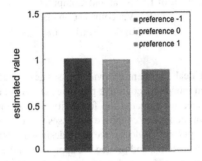

Fig. 8. Estimated values in hydrated conditions

4   Conclusion

In this study, we examined the possibility of estimating taste preference using an emotion matrix as a novel method to objectively evaluate consumer taste preferences. From our results, we observed differences in physiological and psychological states in differing thirst conditions. Moreover, in estimating taste preferences using an emotion matrix, we found that it is indeed possible to estimate taste preferences from brain activity, though margins of error vary by preference. To further understand the variations in estimation results, it is necessary to continue our studies by increasing the volume of data to gain more accurate insight into the physiology of taste preferences.

Reference

1. Musha, T., Terasaki, H., Haque, H.A., Ivanitsk, G.A.: Feature extraction from EEGs associated with emotions. Artif. Life Robot. **1**, 15–19 (1997)

Is the Mood Really in the Eye of the Beholder?

Mojgan Hashemian[1(✉)], Hadi Moradi[1], Maryam S. Mirian[1,2],
Mehdi Tehrani-Doost[3], and Rabab K. Ward[4]

[1] Advanced Robotics and Intelligent Systems Lab, University of Tehran, Tehran,
Iran
{m.hashemian,moradih,mmirian}@ut.ac.ir
[2] Department of Computer Science, UBC, Vancouver, Canada
mmirian@ut.ac.ir
[3] Tehran University of Medical Sciences, Tehran, Iran
tehranid@tums.ac.ir
[4] Department of Electrical and Computer Engineering,
UBC, Vancouver, Canada
rababw@ece.ubc.ca

Abstract. A great deal of scientific evidence suggests that there is a close relationship between mood and cognitive processes of human in everyday tasks. In this study, we have investigated the feasibility of determining mood from gaze, which is one of the human cognitive processes that can be recorded during interaction with computers. To do so, we have designed a feature vector composed of typical gaze patterns, and piloted the approach on the dataset which we gathered. It consists of 145 samples of 30 people. A supervised machine learning technique was employed for classification and recognition of mood. The results of this pilot test suggests that even during these initial steps, the approach is quite promising and opens other research paths for improvement through multi-modal recognition and information fusion. Multi-modal approach would employ the added information provided by our previously developed mood extraction approach using camera and/or the information gained by the use of EEG signals. Further analysis will be performed in feature extraction process to enhance the model accuracy by enriching the feature-set of each modality.

Keywords: Mood · Gaze · Cognition · Affective computing · Human computer interaction

1 Introduction

Mood, our background feeling which lasts for longer time in comparison to emotions, has been investigated for decades in the field of psychology [1]. In the literatures in this field, the relative importance of mood on our individual and social functions has been subject to considerable discussion. The evidence of this can be clearly seen in memory-dependent literatures [2], learning performance [3], creativity [4], etc. Another worth-mentioning role of mood is its application as a general indicator of wellness, in other words it is considered as one of the most associated evident with health and

© Springer International Publishing Switzerland 2015
C. Stephanidis (Ed.): HCII 2015 Posters, Part I, CCIS 528, pp. 712–717, 2015.
DOI: 10.1007/978-3-319-21380-4_120

illness [5]. On the other hand, the importance of this *subtle* affective state in computer user satisfaction, has aroused attention of many researchers in the field of Human-Computer-Interaction (HCI) [6]. A large and growing body of literature has investigated different approaches to provide effective and desirable HCI by designing adaptable systems based on users' affective state to make the gap between human and the machine more narrowed [7]. With this aim, the very first step would be recognition of the user's affective state in non-intrusive ways [8]. By this time, more recent attention has been focused on human behavior or his physiological conditions in this field; however, little attention has been paid to the role of cognitive dimension.

Before proceeding to examine the effect of mood on gaze, it will be necessary to review evidences and hypothesis on this context. A great deal of scientific evidence reported that our mood interacts with cognitive influences, and there is a close relationship between this affective state and cognitive processes [1, 18]. To commence, the nervous system is organized in such a way that there is a linkage between various mood states and cognitive material that has been associated with those states. As an example, a relation between mood and memory, as a cognitive function, has been examined and investigated extensively for decades [2, 9]. Furthermore, a strong relationship between mood and attention has been reported for long time [1]. In addition another factor affecting mood is the occurrence of external events, while the interpretation of such events is highly affected by cognition [5]. These three factors each of which are considered as the most important cognitive processes proved to have direct synergy with our mood. On the other hand, there are more evidences that highlight this synergistic relation which are discussed in the following.

Furthermore, it has been proven that our energetic and tension arousal are two main physiological associations affecting our moods. On the other hand, various cognitive factors interact with energy and tension both directly and indirectly [5]. Although the evidence is limited, there is a little doubt that cognitive stimuli affect energetic arousal, i.e. cognitive-affective state association relates to naturally occurring mood [10]. Therefore, observing and examining cognitive processes may give us some clues on the ongoing mood states.

On the other hand, motor behavior is another human characteristic which is proved to be affected by mood [1110, 11]. One of the evidences of human motor behavior is "Gaze" which signifies cognition. Knowing this fact that mood is affected by our cognitive processes, we can recognize it by tracking the influence of these types of processes, for example by examining eye movements. So in this paper, we are going to propose a method in order to investigate the relationship between individuals' mood and gaze.

2 Method

In recent years, there has been an increasing interest in using Gaze data as a source of information in fields such as cognitive psychology, human computer interaction (HCI), neuroscience and healthcare system. Thanks to the recent progress in technology, the recording of gaze data has been made easy and totally non-intrusive. The emergence of wearable wireless eye-trackers, [12], provides an opportunity to build body-network-areas with social purposes. This opportunity offers a great incentive for scientists in different areas of research, especially those in the field of HCI or ubiquitous computing, to use this information in isolated and social-oriented tasks.

In this paper, we propose an approach for recognizing the mood states of a user via a non-intrusive yet easy to implement method. Based on this method, the user's mood state is detected by using typical features extracted from the gaze data. In this study, we propose a statistical model, which is capable of determining the user's mood state over a short duration of time. The minimum required time is not discussed in this paper and it should be evaluated in our future work, via a different set of experiments for the specific settings discussed below.

Table 1. Gaze features extracted for mood detection

	1	2	3	4	5	6	7
Fixation Saccade	Counts	Rate in second	Mean of duration	Min of duration	Max of duration	Variance of duration	First Fixation in each Phase

In Table 1, fixation refers to the pause of the eye-movement on a specific area of the visual field while during this pause brain starts to process the visual information received from the eyes; this length varies from about 100 to 600 ms. Saccade refers to quick, simultaneous movement of both eyes between two consecutive fixations [20]. We consider 7 different categories of features, shown in Table 1. The first category, "counts", stands for the total number of fixations followed by saccades during the interaction of the subject with the system. The second category refers to the rate of occurrence of each fixation/saccade throughout this time of interaction. The next four categories refer to descriptive statistics of fixation and saccade. They describe the main features in quantitative terms. Finally, the category seven is the time taken to the first fixation. We have considered these features since we believed that each of these features might provide additional information about the pattern of gaze in different mood states. All the considered features should be normalized based on the duration of interaction.

To the best of our knowledge, no standard dataset of gaze records tagged by users' mood state has been published yet. Thus we gathered a (large) dataset which is discussed in Sect. 4 in detail. In order to develop a data-gathering setting, we have designed a web-based platform that records the mood of the subject through a questionnaire. In each setting, a set of short video clips (minimum length of 38 s, and maximum of 2 min and 12 s) are shown to the subjects so he/she can select one of them. This platform has been already used for a camera based mood extraction [13, 14].

Since gaze is highly affected by the structure of the given task environment [10], we designed a four-phase-experiment to cover these differences as much as possible, in order to prove the generality of the work. The structure of the platform and description of each phases are discussed in Sect. 4.

3   User Study

As mentioned earlier, one of the contributions of this work is that of obtaining a dataset of gaze data labeled with the ongoing mood state of subjects performing different tasks. To gather the data, we ran an experiment using the developed web-based platform. The experiment was conducted on 30 people, including 8 females and 22 males aged between 19 and 32 (mean 25 years old). A total of 145 video samples were recorded during a two-week period by an unobtrusive eye-tracker (Tobii X2-30) with an accuracy ranging from $0.4°-1°$, and a precision between $0.29°-0.80°$ [15]. Data Preparation and Processing.

As discussed in Sect. 2, the experiment is designed in four separate phases with different structures. The first phase is designed to record the normal behavior of the participants while working on a routine computer task. In this phase the participants are asked to sign in to the web-based platform and read the instruction manual.

Next, the subjects are asked to fill in a mood questionnaire. This will be considered as the ground-truth or gold standard data indicating the real mood state of the subjects. Then a list of diverse video clips is offered to the subjects. Then each person has to choose one clip to continue to the next phase. These two consecutive steps, in which participants are supposed to choose one option among different alternatives, resemble decision making tasks in cognitive science. Decision making is considered one of the basic cognitive processes of human behavior. When people are faced by a problem with multiple, and possibly conflicting, alternatives and they are supposed to choose one of them based on their preferences [16]. Thus during the phase of filling the questionnaire and choosing the clip, the gaze pattern was also recorded while the decision making was going on.

A relationship between scene viewing and cognitive behavior is reported in [11], thus the third phase is devoted to the subjects, while watching a clip selected in the previous phase. It is worth mentioning that all the video clips are displayed in a specified and a predefined size that are fixed and unchangeable. In this phase, the subjects' gaze pattern during clip-viewing is recorded.

In the last phase, a participant fills in a survey that asks him/her about his/her opinion about the clip. This phase resembles the second phase. The only difference is the influence of emotion induction, induced by the watched clip. This phase provides us the opportunity to compare the two phases result. All the provided clips were believed to be "funny" and could induce happiness emotion.

To classify the data, we composed a feature vector including the features listed in Table 1 for each phase. After labeling the data by the information obtained from the self-reports, we employed LibSVM toolbox and trained by 10-fold cross-validation using Weka [17]. The classification outcomes are one of 3 moods: good, bad and neutral mood. The system yielded a 49.3 % (±1.1) classification accuracy in discriminating between the 3 moods. This is better than the 33.3 % accuracy which a random classifier would yield in this case.

4 Conclusion and Future Works

To the best of our knowledge, this is the first attempt to recognize mood based on gaze data in a non-intrusive fashion. As pointed out in the abstract, the aim of this paper is mainly to a report on our work in progress. The results so far have showed that this approach appears to be promising in recognizing mood states in a non-intrusive way and surpasses a random classifier (which leads to 33 % accuracy as we have considered 3 types of moods).

The results could lead to higher accuracy by performing many possible improvements. The first and foremost possibility in enriching the feature-set, is by considering a broader range of general eye-tracking features (in both the time domain and the frequency domain) such as eye-movement speed, or more complex features such as relative saccade angle. A personalized analysis may lead to higher accuracy since people usually have different page navigation habits and these habits may sometimes lead to unique gaze patterns. For instance, some people use mouse-wheel to scroll, while others prefer to use the scroll bar and fixate on it for a while before scrolling. In addition, calculating the features within a specific region of interest (ROI) may lead to more accurate results. As an example, in the third phase, i.e. scene viewing, the clip constitutes a portion of the screen and the likelihood of looking at other parts of the screen is less in this phase. Considering this fact, may lead to more accurate results.

Moreover, as mentioned in the previous section, the second and fourth phases resemble decision making tasks and provide an opportunity to investigate the effects of induced emotion on gaze. It should be mentioned here that the relation between emotion and cognition has been investigated for decades and there is a large number of published studies that have investigated the relation between emotion and gaze [19]. On the other hand, in our previous study [13], we investigated the influence of mood on emotions induced by an emotion induction technique. Hence, by comparing the patterns in the second and the fourth phase of this experiment, the effect of mood on emotion could be more highlighted considering changes in gaze pattern and vice versa. These further analyses have been considered for future

Another step that is worth-performing is that of calculating the minimum required time to be able to recognize the mood states from the gaze patterns. This would make this approach usable in many applications such as in medical and health applications, especially in applications that require real-time or near real-time constraints. By taking advantage of wireless eye-tracker, our proposed approach could also be employed in mobile Health systems aimed at developing efficient disease management. Thus we plan to benefit from the use of a multi-modal approach in which several sensory information and modalities are employed to improve the mood recognition. The initial step would involve incorporating our camera-based mood detection approach [13], and the use of EEG signals as well. Finally, we would investigate frameworks that use for example the Dempster-Shafer Theory of combination for integrating the knowledge gained from the different modalities employed.

Acknowledgements. The first author would like to thank members of Advanced Robotics and Intelligent Systems lab, Social Networks lab, and Mobile Robot lab for their endless helps and participation in the experiment. This work was supported by NPRP grant 09- 310-1– 058, and grant 7-684-1-127 from the Qatar National Research Fund (a member of Qatar Foundation). The statements made herein are solely the responsibly of the authors.

References

1. Thayer, R.E.: The Biopsychology of Mood and Arousal. Oxford University Press, New York (1989)
2. Lewis, P.A., Critchley, H.D.: Mood-dependent memory. Trends Cogn. Sci. **7**(10), 431–433 (2003)
3. Bryan, T., Mathur, S., Sullivan, K.: The impact of positive mood on learning. Learn. Disabil. Q. **19**(3), 153–162 (1996)
4. Suzanne, K., Vosburg, G.K.: 'Paradoxical' mood effects on creative problem-solving. Cogn. Emot. **11**(2), 151–170 (1997)
5. Thayer, R.E.: The Origin of Everyday Moods. Oxford University Press, New York (1996)
6. Hashemian, M., Nikoukaran, A., Moradi, H., Mirian, M.S., Tehrani-doost, M.: Determining mood using emotional features. In: 2014 7th International Symposium on Telecommunications (IST), pp. 418–423. IEEE (2014)
7. Hudlicka, E.: To feel or not to feel: the role of affect in human–computer interaction. Int. J. Hum. Comput. Stud. **59**(1), 1–32 (2003)
8. Picard, R.W.: Toward computers that recognize and respond to user emotion. IBM Syst. J. **39**(3–4), 705–719 (2000)
9. Bower, G.H.: Mood and memory. Am. Psychol. **36**(2), 129 (1981)
10. Zimmermann, P., Guttormsen, S., Danuser, B., Gomez, P.: Affective computing–a rationale for measuring mood with mouse and keyboard. Int. J. Occup. Saf. Ergon. **9**(4), 539–551 (2003)
11. Henderson, J.M., Hollingworth, A.: Eye movements during scene viewing: an overview. In: Eye Guidance in Reading and Scene Perception, vol. 11, pp. 269–293 (1998)
12. http://www.tobii.com/en/eye-tracking-research/global/landingpages/tobii-glasses-2/
13. Hashemian, M., Moradi, H., Mirian, M.S., Tehrani-doost, M.: Determining mood via emotions observed in face by induction. In: 2014 Second RSI/ISM International Conference on Robotics and Mechatronics (ICRoM), pp. 717–722. IEEE (2014)
14. Hashemian, M., Moradi, H., Mirian, M.S., Tehrani-doost, M., Mahmoudyar, N.: Recognizing Mood using Facial Emotional Features. IEEE Transaction on Affective Computing (Under Review)
15. Tobii Technology AB. Accuracy and precision Test report X2-30 fw 1.0.1. 28 May 2013
16. Frederick, S.: Cognitive reflection and decision making. J. Econ. Perspect. **19**, 25–42 (2005)
17. Hall, M., Frank, E., Holmes, G., Pfahringer, B., Reutemann, P., Witten, I.H.: The WEKA data mining software: an update. ACM SIGKDD Explor. Newsl. **11**(1), 10–18 (2009)
18. Martin, E., Kerns, J.: The influence of positive mood on different aspects of cognitive control. Cogn. Emot. **25**(2), 265–279 (2011)
19. Subramanian, R., Shankar, D., Sebe, N., Melcher, D.: Emotion modulates eye movement patterns and subsequent memory for the gist and details of movie scenes. J. Vis. **14**(3), 31 (2014)
20. Tobii eye-tracking white papers. http://www.tobii.com/en/eye-tracking-research/global/library/white-papers/tobii-eye-tracking-white-paper/. Accessed 9 April 2015

Towards EMG Based Gesture Recognition for Indian Sign Language Interpretation Using Artificial Neural Networks

Abhiroop Kaginalkar$^{(\boxtimes)}$ and Anita Agrawal

Birla Institute of Technology and Science – Pilani, K.K Birla Goa Campus,
Goa, India
akaginalkar@gmail.com, aagrawal@goa.bits-pilani.ac.in

Abstract. There are several techniques of data measurement for gesture recognition, with applications ranging from prosthetic or autonomous control to human-computer interfacing. Most of the typical techniques depend on image processing, and might face portability hurdles. This paper discusses a method to classify gestures based on the surface EMG (sEMG) readings, thereby allowing user portability. These sEMG readings acquired from the upper forearm provide a direction towards gesture recognition for Indian Sign Language (ISL) interpretation. An Artificial Neural Network (ANN) based on the Scaled Conjugate Gradient (SCG) assisted learning is used to process the data and classify gestures with an accuracy of 97.5 %. The training involved 120 samples corresponding to four distinct wrist gestures. Additionally, the foundations for user-independent adaptablity have been laid in this paper.

Keywords: Human-computer interaction · Biomedical electronics · Artificial neural networks · Sign language interpretation · EMG

1 Introduction

Indian Sign Language (ISL) comprises of a common ground for a variety of different dialects specific to various regions over India. It comprises of multiple hand gestures, coupled with simple or complex motions. A single word might not necessarily be gesticulated by one distinct motion. In the light of such a complexity, it is highly imperative to develop an interpretation system that will efficiently process all the nuances in the gestures, and extract the meaning with minimal computation and inconvenience.

Most of the existing approaches to this issue are based on image processing [1] or wearable flex-sensing technologies. Rajam et al. [2] make use of an edge detection algorithm to convert the wrist images into a binary classification of finger positions by relying on Euclidian distances with respect to a fixed base-point. Adithya et al. [3] also depend on Euclidian distances and the Fourier descriptors of their projection vectors, making the system robust with respect to noise. Agrawal et al. [4] implement a feature extraction approach that uses a Support Vector Machine for classification based on the extracted data.

© Springer International Publishing Switzerland 2015
C. Stephanidis (Ed.): HCII 2015 Posters, Part I, CCIS 528, pp. 718–723, 2015.
DOI: 10.1007/978-3-319-21380-4_121

The major issue associated with an image based gesture recognition system is the portability limitation. It is very tedious and inconvenient for the user to have an image capture system aptly set in place. The relative distances between these image capturing devices and the hand performing the gestures affect the clarity and introduce inconsistencies. Most of such measurements require a good contrasting background to detect the hand and its shape, which is something that might not always hold. Approaches that depend on edge detection might face trouble when gestures consist of overlapping hand or figure scenarios. In a lab-setting, many of the mentioned approaches, quite effectively, fulfill the gesture recognition task, but fail to take into account the practicality of the usage. This paper proposes an approach keeping the usability and convenience as the primary motive. Some novel EMG based technologies have been proposed [5, 6] that attempt to bypass the above mentioned issue with existing gesture recognition solutions. Some of the approaches make use of k-NN and Bayes classifiers [7] and Statistical Feature Extraction from EMG waveforms [8]. This paper proposes a Scaled Conjugate Gradient (SCG) based approach to the EMG based gesture recognition problem specific to the ISL. The assisted learning ANN is used to distinguish among 4 distinct wrist gestures from the underlying noise. The intention of this research was to recognize an ANN based gesture recognition approach that can be applied to Indian Sign Language interpretation and in other hand-motion based control scenarios. This methodology of data acquisition and classification, coupled with sensor-based hand motion/orientation detecting algorithms, will pave the way for a practical solution to the sign language interpretation problem.

2 Methodology

2.1 Surface EMG Interfacing

The electrodes used for EMG signal acquisition were standard Ag/AgCl button electrodes connected with a multi-stranded shielded cable. A single channel was used to measure the myo-electrical activity on the surface of the upper-arm. After a couple of initial trials an electrode placement directly over the Flexor Carpi Radialis was chosen (owing to best relative voltage readings and minimal noise encountered). The distance between the two measurement electrodes was maintained at 5.5 cms. The reference electrode was placed over the elbow bone so as to provide minimum interference.

2.2 Digital Signal Conditioning

Data received (at 1 kHz) via the Arduino was processed sequentially through a scalar Kalman Filter (sKF) with Q and R values empirically tuned to 0.0001 and 0.01 respectively. An algorithm was constructed to select a temporal region of activity. This reduced the computational and storage requirements by restricting the analysis to an activity window. A particular activity threshold in the recorded voltage levels was recognized during an initial training/setup period. This threshold was used as a trigger to identify the window of activity, and subsequently, isolate it for further analysis. The window captured any voltage fluctuations associated with the motion within a time-span of 3.5 s.

3 Gesture Recognition

3.1 Artificial Neural Network

AANs mimic complex arithmetic equations, which, when fed with inputs and desired outputs (in the case of assisted learning) adjust the free parameters (weights) so as to reduce the net error. For this study an ANN based on a SCG assisted learning approach has been implemented. This type of learning is more robust and efficient when it comes to pattern recognition [9], as opposed to the standard steepest gradient and conjugate gradient methods. This particular learning technique relies on the steepest gradient along consecutively conjugate vectors, eliminating the directional redundancies and decreasing the number of iterations required to converge. The SCG approach implies an optimization problem that utilizes mutually orthogonal gradients and conjugate directions for minimizing the cost function, which is the error function. The SCG optimization algorithm works with the second order approximations and avoids the line search per learning iteration by using the Levenberg-Marquardt approach to scale the step size [9]. The ANN implemented had 350 inputs that were fed with the EMG waveform transformed to the frequency domain. The output of this ANN had 4 outputs each associated with a wrist motion – fist clench, wrist flick, double wrist clench and no operation. The output layer of the ANN was implemented with trans-sigmoid activation functions. An algorithm then selected the output with the highest confidence score (ranging from 0 to 1).

3.2 Training

In this particular experiment, we used data recorded from the right forearm measured from multiple users. Users were trained to perform specific wrist gestures in a time-dependent fashion based on the visual cues provided by the graphical user interface. The training used a semi-batch approach, wherein, the data collected during each activity window was processed and fed into the ANN for training. The training was planned in two phases:

3.2.1   Phase 1
The first where, a background noise reading was measured (each time a new user wore the electrodes) and smoothened using a cubic spline function approximation to obtain an upper threshold (Highest_Noise_Voltage) of noise. This was then used to detect the activity window in contrast to the underlying noise. The detection algorithm was heuristically programmed to detect any voltage fluctuation above 1.2 times the Highest_Noise_Voltage. The user was provided with a visual cue to maintain the forearm in a relaxed position to allow the accurate recording of the inherent noise in the

measurement setup. The noise readings were recorded over a period of 5 s before the beginning of each new trial.

3.2.2   Phase 2

The second phase involved training the ANN based on SCG supervised learning. A sample set of 120 distinct wrist motions (among the ones mentioned above) were fed into the ANN with a template of the expected outputs. After a number of trials the best performance (for 4 distinct wrist gestures) in terms of the fastest convergence was obtained for an ANN with 10 hidden layers. The training was a batch process based on pre-measured data.

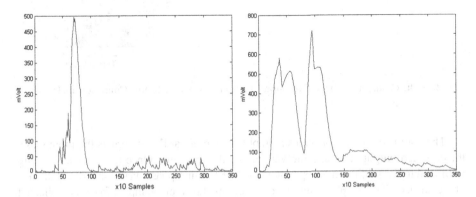

Fig. 1. The waveform on the left represents a single wrist clench and the waveform on the right represents a double wrist clench.

4   Results

4.1   sEMG Waveforms

The surface EMG waveforms obtained after being processed through the scalar Kalman filter are shown in Fig. 1. Each activity window was successfully identified and the measurement noise was successfully filtered so as to obtain visually distinct waveforms associated with each wrist motion. On the left is the resultant waveform when the user quickly clenched and released the fist of the right hand. On the right is the resultant waveform when the user repeated the clench-release cycle twice in quick succession. Visually the waveforms are distinguishable, and the ANN was programmed to recognize this difference. We have included the detection of a no-operation waveform in the ANN. The primary reason for this inclusion is to allow the ANN to effectively discern between the underlying noise readings and a no-operation period (either between two signs or when the arm is relaxed). By doing so, we have managed to reduce the effect of motion artifacts, which sometimes introduce spikes within an order of magnitude of the actual EMG voltages, by a considerable extent.

4.2 Performance Parameters

The performance was quantified based on the Confusion Matrices for each trial and test pair. The training phase was stabilized with the lowest gradient measure of 0.005316 in 61 epochs of the 120 input set (Fig. 2).

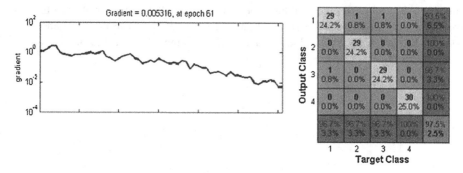

Fig. 2. Left: Gradient minimization during the training phase. Right: Confusion matrix for 4 distinct gestures.

The confusion matrix provides a graphical 'scoreboard' that depicts the input class, the expected output class and the variance in the mapping. Once the gradient reading stabilized to the minimum acceptable value, the training phase was stopped and the test phase ensued. The test phase involved presenting 120 input samples from the collected dataset in a random manner. The results were then plotted and analyzed based on the confusion matrix. The Fig. 2 depicts the performance of one of the trials conducted:

The following are the observations based on this matrix:

- The first, second and third classes correspond to the single wrist clench, double wrist clench and wrist flick actions respectively. Out of the 30 samples for each class, one of the samples led to an erroneous prediction.
- The fourth class corresponding to the no-operation input resulted in favorable results. This was expected as the no-operation waveform was significantly different from the others (more passive), leading to a better classification.
- The overall performance for 120 randomly ordered samples led to an accuracy of 97.5 %.
- The predictions can be made more accurate by increasing the complexity of the ANN, but compromising on the computation and trial time. Hence, an expected tradeoff exists between the complexity, computation time, storage and accuracy. Each of these can be adjusted depending on the application and acceptable ranges.

5 Conclusion

Through this research we have developed a fundamental base for using SCG based ANNs in gesture recognition for the interpretation of sign language. We have managed to distinguish between 4 gesture types, thereby, establishing a proof-of-concept methodology. The next step will be to establish an extensive database of ISL signs and construct a corresponding ANN for the same. This will involve scaling the existing network by increasing the layer count and input/output parameters. The data collected can be used with other motion sensors to design an integrated sign language recognition system. The ANN proposed in this paper can be replicated using a microprocessor and, thereby, be used in a portable sign language interpretation solution.

References

1. Ong, S.C.W., Ranganath, S.: Automatic sign language analysis: a survey and the future beyond lexical meaning. IEEE Trans. Pattern Anal. Mach. Intell. **27**(6), 873–891 (2005)
2. Rajam, P.S., Balakrishnan, G.: Real time indian sign language recognition system to aid deaf-dumb people. In: 2011 IEEE 13th International Conference on Communication Technology (ICCT), pp. 737–742 (2011)
3. Adithya, V., Vinod, P.R., Gopalakrishnan, U.: Artificial neural network based method for Indian sign language recognition. In: 2013 IEEE Conference on Information and Communication Technologies (ICT), vol., no., pp. 1080–1085 (2013)
4. Agrawal, S.C., Jalal, A.S., Bhatnagar, C.: Recognition of Indian Sign Language using feature fusion. In: 2012 4th International Conference on Intelligent Human Computer Interaction (IHCI), pp. 1–5 (2012)
5. Mitra, S., Acharya, T.: Gesture recognition: a survey. IEEE Trans. Syst. Man Cybern. Part C-Appl. Rev. **37**(3), 311–324 (2007)
6. Yun, L., Chen, X., et. al.: Automatic recognition of sign language subwords based on portable accelerometer and EMG sensors. In: Proceedings of the International Conf. on Multimodal Interfaces and the Workshop on Machine Learning for Multimodal Interaction, 17 (2010)
7. Kim, J., Mastnik, S., Andre, E.: EMG-based hand gesture recognition for realtime biosignal interfacing. In: Proceedings of the 13th International Conference on Intelligent User Interfaces, pp. 30–39 (2008)
8. Shroffe, E.H., Manimegalai, P.: Hand gesture recognition based on EMG signals using ANN. Int. J. Comput. Appl. **2**(3), 31–39 (2013)
9. Moller, M.F.: A scaled conjugate gradient algorithm for fast supervised learning. J. Neural Netw. **6**(4), 525–533 (1993)

A Crystal Ball for Meditators?

Can Meditation Be Measured by Wireless Devices, and in Particular by the Neurosky Mindwave Mobile?

Andrew Levine[✉]

Instructional Technology Department, San Francisco State University,
San Francisco, USA
andruoll@yahoo.com

Abstract. A popular brand of consumer EEG headbands claims to be able to detect meditation from the user's brainwave pattern, and send a signal to your cell phone with the score from 1–100. The invention described in this paper links together the headband with a wireless light bulb. The invention should show a meaningful pattern of flashes of light. Instead only random noise is detected. The author explores possible reasons why.

Keywords: EEG (electroencephalography) · Biofeedback · Meditation

1 Introduction

Several years ago I first had the idea: by combining consumer electronics, I could make a crystal ball that glows when you meditate. Hadn't the EEG headband I saw advertised say that it could detect meditation? Combined with a wireless light bulb and some iPhone coding, the crystal ball would be a reality.

Several hundred dollars and dozen man-hours later, I was left with an app on my iPhone which could, in effect, make my overhead light flicker on and off at random. It was supposed to flicker according to my meditation level, but I had neglected to test the basic validity of the eSense meditation meter before building a crystal ball that works based on its data.

The problem may be that no meditation experts have tried the machine, and this produces results in the meter that are all over the place; but I could get no valid results out of it for myself and my parents. Not only that, but the eSense attention meter was likewise all over the place, though it is the one supposed to be easiest to control.

2 Hypothesis

For those that are not familiar with the principles of EEG, the scalp has a tiny electrical current which peaks and falls between 1–100 Hz (times per second). It is relatively easy to tell if someone is awake or sleeping by the number of Hz observed at their scalp. Brain researchers invited to Tibet by the Dalai Lama have claimed to see a similar phenomenon in those who are experienced at meditating vs. unskilled

© Springer International Publishing Switzerland 2015
C. Stephanidis (Ed.): HCII 2015 Posters, Part I, CCIS 528, pp. 724–726, 2015.
DOI: 10.1007/978-3-319-21380-4_122

meditators (Davidson 2008). Among the characteristic qualities exposed by the masters were "higher-amplitude sustained gamma band oscillations"[1] and "long-distance phase synchrony" between different places on the scalp.

Is the problem that only a true master is able to command the crystal ball, and everyone else gets results that are all over the place? My hypothesis in this paper is that our lack of expertise in meditation was not the limiting factor, and that similar random readings would be seen no matter who was wearing the headband. Thus I predict that if I am able to experiment as a poster presenter at the conference, nobody will be able to control the eSense meter to give consistent, bright readings from the top of the scale that light up the crystal ball for sustained periods of time.

There are several possible explanations that show why meditation could be so clearly demarcated for researchers in Tibet, and yet so vague for EEG headband users here. One involves the superiority of using human EEG operators to identify meditation patterns in different subjects. The Neurosky chip is an automated brainwave scanner.

Also, traditional EEG uses 19 sensors to pick up readings from all over the scalp, while the headband just uses one contact point. Therefore, while it may be possible to repeat this experiment with a full EEG machine plus human operator, the derived eSense meters of the miniaturized EEG headband give equivocal results.

3 Procedure

3.1 Parts

All parts listed as e.g. are the actual model number of the part used in the experiment.

- Neurosky Mindwave Mobile, e.g. Brainwave Starter Kit ($130)
- Philips Hue Personal Wireless Lighting, e.g. Starter Pack with hub and 3 lights, #431643 ($200).
- [Two lights will be used for showing eSense attention meter and eSense meditation meter values in % of maximum brightness.]
- An internet router, e.g. Apple Time Capsule #A1355 ($50)
- A developer's subscription with Apple ($99/year)
- An iPhone

3.2 Programming

Both Phillips and Neurosky have allowed public access to their products' APIs and published sample Objective-C projects for the iPhone. The app that links the headband to the light bulb is a copy of the Philips demo project, with the following changes:

- The library file `libTGAccessory.a` was copied over from the Neurosky demo project and linked

---

[1] Gamma band is 25–100 Hz, most typically at 40.

- `PHControlLightsViewController.m` has new functions copied over from the Neurosky demo project, including `dataRecieved`, where the brightness level of the wireless light bulb is set, and `accessoryDidConnect`, where the TGAccessoryManager is set up that calls dataRecieved

A zip file of the modified Apple Xcode project is posted at http://www.picatino.com/eeg/. To make edits, you'll need a Macintosh computer with the latest OS. In addition, an Apple developer's subscription is necessary to be able to bypass the App Store and install custom apps on your iPhone.

4   Conclusions

The next step seems to be devising some scientific way to see if Neurosky's idea of meditation has anything in common with either the Dalai Lama results described above or the user's feelings.

My first impulse was to propose that test subjects push a button when they sense in themselves heightened levels of either "attention" or "meditation." If the eSense readings were positively correlated, negatively correlated, or completely uncorrelated to their perception of reality, this would yield results of some kind. This test might not be possible in people who are experiencing meditation, however, since the act of pressing the button might break the trance.

A more physiological test would be to backstop the Mindwave Mobile with perhaps a pulsemeter to count when the subject's heartbeat drops below a threshold, and if that is correlated with higher meditation readings on the EEG headset it would serve as partial proof that at least something was going on.

I would like to do a lie-detector test at the same time as getting readout for attention or meditation. That way you would get a readout of how false you felt the eSense to be, moment by moment. It would also be useful to give the Mindwave Mobile to an expert meditator and see if they can produce any change in readings.

The obvious question is now to ask if not Neurosky, can someone else make a headset that detects meditation? The answer is yes, and especially if the person who is meditating is a Buddhist master who has practiced for a long time. But a crystal ball that works for only 1 % of the population is harder to justify buying.

Reference

Davidson, R.J., Lutz, A.: Buddha's brain: neuroplasticity and meditation. IEEE Signal Process. Mag. **25**(1), 174–176 (2008). http://www.ncbi.nlm.nih.gov/pmc/articles/PMC2944261/

Development of a Glasses-Like Wearable Device to Measure Nasal Skin Temperature

Tota Mizuno[1]([✉]) and Yuichiro Kume[2]

[1] The University of Electro-Communications, 1-5-1 Chofugaoka,
Chofu, Tokyo 182-8585, Japan
mizuno@uec.ac.jp
[2] Tokyo Polytechnic University, 1583 Iiyama, Atsugi, Kanagawa 243-0297, Japan
kume@mega.t-kougei.ac.jp

Abstract. Since nasal skin temperature is said to provide a good reflection of autonomic nerve activity, nasal skin temperature measurements have been used to assess various human physiological and psychological states, such as pleasant and unpleasant emotions, alertness levels, and mental work load (MWL). In addition, nasal skin temperature has the advantage of enabling non-contact measurement, using such as thermography and radiation thermometers.However, a problem exists with approaches using these device because it is difficult to make accurate assessments if the test subject moves during measurement.

This study aims at resolving this problem via the development of a wearable device that measures nasal skin temperature with small thermopile sensors attached to spectacle frames, thus enabling temperature measurements even when the wearer moves.

Keywords: Nasal skin temperature · Autonomic nerve activity · Wearable device

1 Introduction

Since autonomic nerve activity is closely related to physical and physiological stress, its measurement or estimation using biological information can serve as the foundation for methods of objectively assessing bodily activity or physical and physiological stress in human beings.

One such method, which uses body surface temperature [1,2] is based on the knowledge that the body surface temperature of humans depends on the blood flow rate through the blood vessels below the skin. When muscle contraction and relaxation occur as a result of autonomic nerve activity, the blood flow rate through the capillaries close to the body surface changes, and large amounts of blood flow into arteriovenous anastomoses (AVAs). Since the area around the nose has a substantially higher distribution of AVAs than other parts, autonomic nerve activity changes have a particularly strong influence on the surface temperature of the nose. Specifically, it can be observed that when the activity

© Springer International Publishing Switzerland 2015
C. Stephanidis (Ed.): HCII 2015 Posters, Part I, CCIS 528, pp. 727–732, 2015.
DOI: 10.1007/978-3-319-21380-4_123

of sympathetic nervous system of the autonomic nervous system increases, the surface temperature of the nose decreases. It then follows that monitoring nasal skin temperature makes it possible to indirectly assess autonomic nerve activity.

However, nasal skin temperature is dependent on an individual's deep body temperature and the measurement environment. If the deep body temperature or measurement environment changes while nasal skin temperature is being monitored, the resulting noise and artifacts decrease the assessment accuracy. One method of countering this problem is to use the difference in body surface temperature between the nose and the forehead. Since the density of AVAs in the forehead is low, body surface temperature in this area is less susceptible to changes resulting from autonomic nerve activity. Therefore, subtracting the forehead surface temperature from the nose surface temperature reduces the influence of deep body temperature and/or measurement environment changes.

Since using the patterns of change in autonomic nerve activity obtained with this method as feedback allows for the possibility of, for example, reducing human error, adverse health effects, or stress, a wide range of studies are currently being conducted.

In an earlier study, assessments of human physiological and psychological states, such as pleasant and unpleasant emotions, degree of alertness, and mental work load (MWL) were conducted [3]. Low-restraint, non-contact measurement of nasal skin temperature can be performed using approaches such as thermography and radiation thermometers, but the measurement environment imposes limitations. For example, it is difficult to make assessments if the test subject moves during the measurement.

In an attempt to resolve this problem, we developed a glasses-like wearable device to measure nasal skin temperature that allows autonomic nerve activity to be measured or estimated even if the test subject moves. In this report, we aim to verify the reliability of measurement with this device.

2   The Developed Device

Figure 1 shows a facial thermal image of a test subject while under an MWL imposed by mentally performing arithmetic calculation tasks. As can be seen in the figure, a temperature difference between nose and forehead is evident. In an earlier study, the mean surface temperatures of the nose and forehead regions were obtained using infrared thermography, as shown in Fig. 1, and this temperature difference was used for assessment. Figures 2 and 3 show a diagram of our newly developed glasses-like wearable nasal skin temperature measurement device and a photo of its appearance when worn.

In this study, these body surface temperatures of the nose and forehead were obtained using small, high-accuracy, thermopile sensor modules (HTIA-E, Heimann Sensor GmbH, Dresden, Germany) attached to the spectacle frames. The sensors operate at a source voltage of 5 V, provide a viewing angle of 10°, have a measurable temperature range of 30° to 500° C, and a accuracy of approximately ±0.1° C.

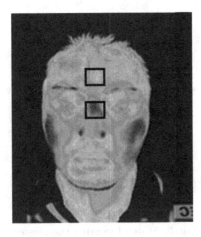

Fig. 1. A facial thermal image of a test subject while under an MWL

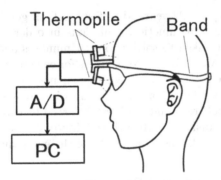

Fig. 2. Developed glasses-like wearable nasal skin temperature measurement device

Furthermore, the modules used are light, weighing 1.07 g, so wearing the device feels much like wearing ordinary glasses. Thus, the design of the device enables simultaneous low-restraint, non-contact measurement of nose and forehead surface temperatures. The thermopile outputs are received on a personal computer (PC) via an analog-to-digital (AD) converter (Turtle Industry Co. Ltd., TUSB-0216ADMZ). The sampling frequency is 250 Hz and the mean value of the body surface temperature measurements is recorded each second.

3   Verification Experiment

3.1   Aim of Experiment and Experimental Protocol

The following experiment was conducted to verify whether changes in nasal skin temperature could be assessed with the developed device when a test subject is under an MWL.

Fig. 3. State of wearing the glasses

In our experiment, five 22-year-old test subjects in good health were tasked with performing mental arithmetic calculations in order to impose an MWL. Specifically, they were asked to solve two-digit numbers addition problems displayed on a PC. They were given three seconds for each problem, after which the next problem appeared, regardless of whether or not their answer was correct. After the test subjects relaxed for a few minutes in a seated position, measurement commenced with three minutes of rest, followed by three minutes of mental arithmetic calculation tasks, and then three minutes of rest, at the end of which measurement was stopped. The total length of the experiment was 9 min.

3.2   Experiment Results and Discussion

The results are shown in Fig. 3. During the initial rest period various minor fluctuation were recorded, but a drop in temperature was noted for several test subjects during the initial calculation task period. In those cases, the temperature returned to its original value during the following rest period. These results indicate that the mental arithmetic calculation task imposed an MWL burden on those test subjects, which influenced their autonomic nerve system responses.

However, despite being tested under the same protocol, not all test subjects exhibited the above temperature change. There are several possible reasons for this, which are outlined below (Fig. 4):

1. The mental arithmetic calculation tasks did not impose a noticeable MWL burden on those test subjects, so their autonomic nerve systems were not influenced.
2. For some test subjects, differences in the distance from the thermopiles attached to the glasses and the nose or forehead caused by head or face shape variations prevented appropriate measurements.
3. There were individual differences between the locations where temperature change occurred.

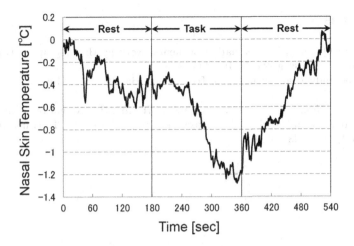

Fig. 4. Result

To investigate the first hypothesis, it will be necessary to impose a variety of tasks. The second and third hypotheses stem from the fact that the thermopiles used have a narrow viewing angle. Since the current attachment position is about 6 mm in diameter, the temperature is measured as the mean temperature of a very small area. The results of the earlier study (Fig. 1) suggest that a diameter of around 2 to 3 cm is necessary to ensure reliable mean temperature assessments. In our future studies, it will be necessary to solve this problem by adjusting the distance between the thermopiles and the nose and forehead of the test subjects.

4   Conclusion

In this study, a glasses-like wearable device that can be used to measure nasal skin temperature was developed and its reliability was assessed. The results show that the device makes it possible to estimate autonomic nerve activity. This has the potential to pave the way for everyday applications such as routine monitoring (life-log) of autonomic nerve activity.

However, autonomic nerve activity cannot be assessed in some cases due to the shape of the test subjects head or to the positioning of the device. Therefore, in our future studies it will be necessary to facilitate sensor position and angle adjustments in order to improve lightness and accuracy. It will also be necessary to utilize a structure that does not impede the view, and to conduct comparison experiments using a technique such as infrared thermography.

References

1. Iwata, H.: Quantitative Evaluation of mental work by thermography. Trans. Soc. Instrum. Control Eng. **24**(2), 107–111 (1988)
2. Advanced Industrial Science and Technology: Handbook of Human Mesurement (2003)
3. Mizuno, T., Nomura, S., Nozawa, A., Asano, H., Ide, H.: Evaluationof the effect of intermittent mental work-load by nasal skintemperature. IEICE Trans. Inf. Syst. **J93–D**(4), 535–543 (2010)

Decoding of Upper Limb Movement Using EEG and Sparse Coding

Masashi Yamashita[✉]

Toyota Technological Institute, Hisakata 2-12-1, Tempaku-ku, Nagoya, Aichi
468-8511, Japan
m-yamashita@toyota-ti.ac.jp

Abstract. In this paper, a system is proposed for decoding upper limb movement from EEG. The signal processing procedure consists of a learning phase and test phase. In the learning phase, a Kinect sensor is utilized to measure the true values for a hand's movement. Sparse coding is applied to calculate the weight of a linear decoding model. Because sparse coding can be used to derive the sparse weight, most of the elements are zero, with the remaining elements being non-zero. Thus, it is an effective method for reducing the calculation costs. Sparse coding was combined with noise reduction of the EEG signals to achieve good estimation for upper limb movements in the experimental results.

Keywords: Electroencephalogram · Sparse coding · Decoding · Rehabilitation

1 Introduction

Owing to an aging society, the recovery of stroke patients has become an important issue in recent years. The use of electroencephalogram (EEG) signals with rehabilitation robots has gained attention for the efficient treatment of paralysis. Previous research has suggested that event-related desynchronization (ERD) [1, 2] calculated from EEG signals can be used to detect motor imagery and develop references for the rehabilitation robots. However, because ERD is a binary event, it is only used as a trigger command. To produce continuous intent, decoding methods that convert an EEG signal to a body's kinematic movement (e.g., an upper limb) are preferable. Because many previous studies have used an extended Kalman filter [3] or the least squares method [4–6] for decoding, the weight representing the relationship between the EEG signal and a movement is a large matrix full of non-zero elements. Therefore, the computational costs need to be reduced for movements to be estimated in real time.

In this paper, we propose a system for decoding upper limb movement from EEG signals. The signal processing procedure consists of a learning phase and test phase. In the learning phase, a Kinect sensor is utilized to measure the true values for a hand's movement. Sparse coding is applied to calculate the weight of a linear decoding model. Because sparse coding can be used to derive the sparse weight, most of the elements are zero, with the remaining elements being non-zero. Thus, it is an effective method for reducing the calculation costs. Sparse coding was combined with noise reduction of the EEG signals to achieve good estimation for upper limb movements in the experimental results.

© Springer International Publishing Switzerland 2015
C. Stephanidis (Ed.): HCII 2015 Posters, Part I, CCIS 528, pp. 733–738, 2015.
DOI: 10.1007/978-3-319-21380-4_124

2 Related Work

Many decoding methods have been proposed in recent years. In [3], an extended Kalman filter was applied to infer the position and velocity of the hand from the neural spike activity, and the results were compared to those of a linear filtering model. In [4–6], the least squares method was used to reconstruct three-dimensional hand movements from noninvasive EEG signals. The results suggest that low-pass-filtered signals from EEG retain variable information for movement. In the present study, low-pass-filtered signals from EEG were used based on [4, 5]. As an alternative approach, sparse coding has gained attention in the image and acoustic processing fields. In [7], sparse coding was used to remove the noise from an original image using learned dictionaries. In the present study, the response matrix made from EEG signals was assumed to be a dictionary, and sparse coding was applied to select sparse weights for hand decoding.

3 Experimental Setup

Figure 1 shows the experimental setup for decoding upper limb movement from EEG signals. The EEG amplifier (g.tec) was connected to 16 active electrodes and used to measure the EEG signals, mainly over the primary motor cortex and primary somatosensory cortex. The EEG signals were filtered using an eighth-order band-pass filter at 0.1–30 Hz and notch filter at 60 Hz. The sampling frequency was 128 Hz. A Kinect sensor measured the upper limb movement. An assistive robot with two degrees of freedom was prepared to execute the tracking task in accordance with a reference marker on the monitor. Because this study was considered to be a preliminary test, the subject moved his hand for decoding while not grasping the grip of the robot. A regression-based method was used to remove artifact noise due to eye blinking and movement [8].

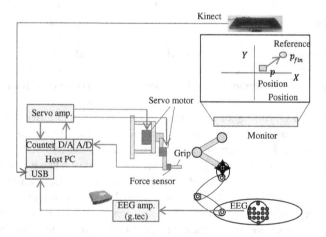

Fig. 1. Experimental setup

4 Decoding System Design

Figure 2 shows the signal processing diagram for decoding. In the learning phase, weights are calculated from both EEG signals and the true values of the movement using sparse coding. In the test phase, the movement is estimated from only EEG signals using a linear decoding model with the learned weights. As described in [4–6], a fourth-order low-pass filter with a cutoff frequency of 1 Hz is applied. The time difference between the filtered signals is calculated, and the time shift operation is executed 1 to N times. Then, the response matrix A_{meas} can be obtained as follows:

$$A_{meas} = \begin{bmatrix} 1 & d_0^1 & \cdots & d_{-N+1}^1 & \cdots & d_0^C & \cdots & d_{-N+1}^C \\ 1 & d_1^1 & \cdots & d_{-N+2}^1 & \cdots & d_1^C & \cdots & d_{-N+2}^C \\ \cdot & \cdot & & \cdot & & \cdot & & \cdot \\ 1 & d_{M-1}^1 & \cdots & d_{M-N}^1 & \cdots & d_{M-1}^C & \cdots & d_{M-N}^C \end{bmatrix} \quad (1)$$

where d is the time difference, C is the number of EEG channels, N is the maximum number of time shift operations, and M is the number of measured data points.

Using Eq. (1), the linear decoding model can be represented in matrix form:

$$y = A_{meas}\theta \quad (2)$$

where θ represents the weights of the linear decoding model and y represents the true values of the hand's movement.

In this study, the estimated weights $\hat{\theta}$ were designed using sparse coding as follows:

$$\hat{\theta} = \underset{\theta}{\mathrm{argmin}}\|\theta\|_0 \mathrm{sub.to}\ A_{meas}\theta \approx y \quad (3)$$

where $\|\theta\|_0$ is the number of non-zero elements inside the weights θ. The orthogonal matching pursuit method [9] is applied to solve Eq. (3). Note that the number of non-zero elements is only 29, even though the length of the weights θ is 99.

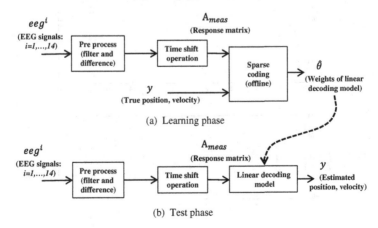

(a) Learning phase

(b) Test phase

Fig. 2. Signal processing diagram

5   Experimental Results

A healthy subject was used to evaluate the decoding system. The evaluation was intended as a preliminary test before training applications to stroke patients. Figures 3 and 4 show the experimental results for the first trial in the test data with regard to the velocity and position, respectively. In each figure, the upper and lower plots are the results in the lateral and longitudinal directions, respectively. The dashed and solid lines are the true and estimated values, respectively.

Table 1 lists the decoding performance based on correlation coefficients. In the test data, the mean values of correlations for the velocities (Vx and Vy) were 0.50 and 0.49,

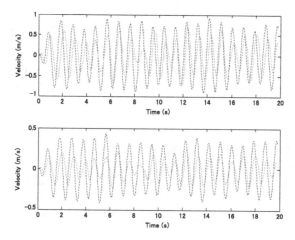

Fig. 3. Comparison between true and estimated values for velocity

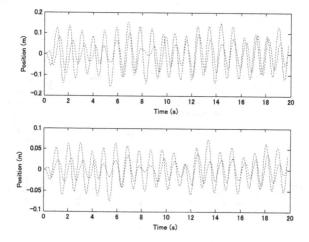

Fig. 4. Comparison between true and estimated values for position

respectively, and the mean values of correlations for the positions (X and Y) were 0.42 and 0.39. Based on these results, good estimation was achieved compared with the chance level. Thus, sparse coding can automatically select the important basis from the response matrix and reconstruct a good estimation using the basis and sparse weights.

Table 1. Decoding performance based on correlation coefficients

	Trial	Vx	Vy	X	Y
Leaning data	1st	0.8531	0.8693	0.8549	0.8452
Test data	1st	0.5717	0.6677	0.5755	0.636
	2nd	0.279	0.3953	0.304	0.3973
	3rd	0.2563	0.347	0.3035	0.3454
	4th	0.7291	0.573	0.5182	0.3432
	5th	0.6258	0.5253	0.4079	0.3168
	6th	0.5649	0.4598	0.4246	0.3101
	Mean	0.504467	0.494683	0.422283	0.391467
	Variance	0.037155	0.013982	0.012198	0.015296

6 Conclusion

In this paper, a system is proposed for decoding upper limb movement from EEG signals. Sparse coding is applied to calculate the weight of a linear decoding model. Because sparse coding can be used to derive the sparse weight, most of the elements are zero, with the remaining elements being non-zero. Thus, it is an effective method for reducing the calculation costs. Sparse coding was combined with noise reduction of the EEG signals to achieve good estimation for upper limb movements in the experimental results. Future research will involve applying the decoding results to a rehabilitation robot.

References

1. Pfurtscheller, G., Silva, F.H.L.D.: Event-related EEG/MEG synchronization and desynchronization: basic principles. Clin. Neurophysiol. **110**, 1842–1857 (1999)
2. Takahashi, M., Takeda, K., Otaka, Y., Osu, R., Hanakawa, T., Gouko, M., Ito, K.: Event related desynchronization-modulated functional electrical stimulation system for stroke rehabilitation: a feasibility study. J. Neuro Eng. Rehabil. (2012). doi:10.1186/1743-0003-9-56
3. Wu, W., Black, M.J., Gao, Y., Bienenstock, E., Serruya, M., Donoghue, J.P.: Inferring hand motion from multi-cell recordings in motor cortex using a Kalman filter. In: SAB 2002-Workshop on Motor Control in Humans and Robots, pp. 66–73 (2002)
4. Bradberry, T.J., Gentili, R.J., Contreras-Vidal, J.L.: Reconstructing three-dimensional hand movements from noninvasive electroencephalographic signals. J. Neurosci. **30**, 3432–3437 (2010)

5. Ofner, P., Muller-Putz, G.R.: Decoding of velocities and positions of 3D arm movement from EEG. In: International Conference of the IEEE EMBS, pp. 6406–6409 (2012)
6. Warland, D., Reinagel, P., Meister, M.: Decoding visual information from a population of retinal ganglion cells. J. Neurophysiol. **78**(5), 2336–2350 (1997)
7. Elad, M., Aharon, M.: Image denoising via sparse and redundant representations over learned dictionaries. IEEE Trans. Image Process. **15**, 3736–3745 (2006)
8. Schlogl, A., Keinrath, C., Zimmermann, D., Scherer, R., Leeb, R., Pfurtscheller, G.: A fully automated correction method of EOG artifacts in EEG recordings. Clin. Neurophysiol. **118**, 98–104 (2007)
9. Pati, Y.C., Rezaiifar, R., Krishnaprasad, P.S.: Orthogonal matching pursuit: recursive function approximation with applications to wavelet decomposition. In: 27th Annual Asilomar Conference on Signals, Systems, and Computers, vol. 1, pp. 40–44 (1993)

Dialogue Systems

Towards Classification of Engagement in Human Interaction with Talking Robots

Yuyun Huang$^{(\boxtimes)}$, Christy Elias, João P. Cabral, Atul Nautiyal, Christian Saam, and Nick Campbell

The School of Computer Science and Statistics,
Trinity College Dublin, Dublin, Ireland
{huangyu,eliasc,cabralj,nautiyaa,saamc,nick}@tcd.ie
http://www.tcd.ie

Abstract. In this paper we describe ongoing work to develop an engagement classifier for human-computer interaction systems. We have successfully classified group and individual engagement in a corpus of a conversation among four people called TableTalk, by using a classifier trained with the Support Vector Machine method and audio-visual features. The goal in this paper is to extend that work for the classification of engagement in videos of interaction between an human and a talking robot. For that purpose we are using a corpus of dialogues between participants and a Lego robot named Herme, which was collected during an exhibition. We describe the techniques to improve the engagement detection by taking into account the differences between the characteristics of the videos between the two datasets. Currently we are also conducting an experiment to manually annotate the Herme videos with engagement labels. These annotations will be used for evaluation and further improvements to engagement detection.

Keywords: Robot interaction · Engagement detection · Voice quality · Visual analysis

1 Introduction

Interaction with non-human interlocutors has become common in scenarios such as talking to an automated banking service over the phone, an enquiry service of a telephone company or even talking to an automated bill payment service. However, in service-oriented scenarios the social involvement in the conversation is not usually important. Our aim in this work is to measure engagement in a social interaction scenario, that is, an human-robot conversation in a public space. There have been previous attempts to model engagement in a similar context. It has been modelled in dynamic environments, where people interact with the system and with each other in a natural manner and they may leave conversations at any time [1].

Both video and audio analysis can be used to model active listening. In [2] engagement is measured in television viewers, by using head pose, five facial

© Springer International Publishing Switzerland 2015
C. Stephanidis (Ed.): HCII 2015 Posters, Part I, CCIS 528, pp. 741–746, 2015.
DOI: 10.1007/978-3-319-21380-4_125

points, head size, and head position. In terms of speech analysis, F0 and other prosodic cues are usually employed for this type of measurement. For example, several prosodic parameters including change in syllabicity, pitch slope and loudness were analysed on non-lexical response tokens in Swedish [3]. The fusion of audio-visual features have also been used in this context, such as for detecting high-interest levels in group meetings [4] and entrainment between members of a group conversation [5].

Recently we have combined visual and speech parameters for the detection of engagement of a group of people talking around a table, from the video recordings and annotations of the TableTalk corpus [6]. This work is going to appear published elsewhere. Interestingly, we have found that voice quality parameters, which are not usually used in this type of studies, obtained good results. In this paper we describe a similar engagement detection method using voice quality and visual parameters to be applied to the corpus of human-robot dialogues.

2   Classification of Engagement in TableTalk Corpus

2.1   TableTalk Corpus

TableTalk data was captured by using a fixed omnidirectional camera. The visual feature extraction process is described in [8]. Authors used the Viola-Jones face [9] detection algorithm and a colour-based tracking method to estimate the face position and size for each video frame. Face motion estimation was performed using a subpixel block matching algorithm. Body and head activity were also measured by calculating the Sum of Absolute Differences (SAD) between the current and previous frames on the body and head regions respectively.

The corpus also contains annotations of engagement ("engaged"/"non-engaged" labels) which were performed by five psychology students [6].

2.2   Engagement Detection

In our previous work of engagement classification, we trained three classifiers using the parameter data sets: audio, visual and audio-visual. After the audio and visual features were extracted they were aligned in time and combined to obtain the speech-visual feature matrix.

The features extracted from the speech signal consisted of the prosodic parameter F0, Mel-frequency cepstral coefficients (MFCCs) and glottal parameters. The glottal parameters were the open quotient (OQ), return quotient (RQ), and speech quotient (SQ). These parameters and F0 were estimated using the method described in [7], while MFCCs were calculated using the SPTK toolkit.

In addition to the visual measurements available in the corpus, we also computed the distance between the positions of the face and the variation in face size between consecutive windowed segments. In total, the number of parameters was six: face movement (distance measure), head forward/backward movement, head horizontal motion, head vertical motion, body activity, and head activity.

We used the engagement annotations and the feature matrix for the classification of engagement with the Support Vector Machine (SVM) method. For testing we used different combinations of audio-visual parameter sets and a 10-fold cross validation approach. The highest accuracy of 76.1 % was obtained for a set of visual parameters combined with the voice quality parameters (MFCCs and glottal parameters).

We also performed a similar experiment for classification of individual engagement, but using the visual parameter set only. The average accuracy rate for the four speakers was 68.7 %. In the future, this work could be extended to incorporate speech features by performing speaker segmenation of the recording and using some method to deal with segments of overlap speech (e.g. applying a source separation technique or simply discarding them). The main limitations for the segmentation are that the automatic speaker separation using signal processing may not be accurate enough and the manual annotation alternative is very time consuming.

3 Detection of Engagement in Human-Robot Dialogues

3.1 Database of Spontaneous Dialogues

A database of human-robot dialogues was collected by using a conversational robot called Herme developed at the Speech Communication Lab of Trinity College Dublin [10]. In that experiment, Herme started conversations with random visitors during an exhibition (HUMAN+ event) that took place at the Science Gallery in Dublin, in 2011 (from April 15 to June 24). In the experiment speakers could move around while interacting with Herme or leave at any point. The "Herme's database" consists of 433 recorded conversations, with clearly included consent form id-number, collected over the three months.

The conversations were recorded from multiple angles using two Sennheiser MKH60 P-48 shotgun microphones mounted at the top of a television screen, which displayed in real-time a top-down view of the interaction. Herme was used together with an auxiliary Lego robot (they looked similar), of which the Herme's webcam was intended to capture the face of the main interlocutor while the webcam on the other robot recorded a more comprehensive scene of the conversations. An i-Sight camera was also used to gather an overall view for the remote operator. Herme was equipped with software for performing face tracking and to move forward/backwards or left/right so that it could keep facing the person.

3.2 Engagement Annotation

We are conducting an experiment for annotation of engagement in the Herme data. The engagement annotation scheme we propose is based on the following four levels of engagement: *high*, *regular*, *low*, and *not-engaged*. In the first case, there is high involvement in the conversion and the person interacts actively (e.g. using body gesture, facial expression and the voice). In this case the person may talk to someone else about the reactions of the robot but they continue to talk with the robot after a few seconds. An example for the second case is when individuals may start talking with each other about a topic unrelated with the interaction with the robot or they may be doing other activities simultaneously (e.g. reading instructions, using mobile phone, etc.). In the third case, the human-robot conversation is considered to be less frequent and participants can be more attracted to the interaction with third-parties or devices than the interaction with the robot. Non-engagement would occur when individuals are not involved in the conversion with the robot at all but they are within its close range.

Five raters will take part in the annotation task and they will be provided with the videos recorded with the robot-mounted camera and the fixed camera beside the robot.

3.3   Audio-Visual Analysis

The speech parameters are the same as those analysed in the TableTalk experiment (described in Sect. 2.2). However, for analysing Herme data we use a voice activity detector because the annotation of non-speech segments is not available (unlike in the previous experiment). Currently we use the VAD of AMR Floating-point Speech Codec [11] reference implementation. This VAD is suitable for real-time applications and we have already used it for demonstrations of Herme where people can interact with the robot.

The visual analysis can be performed on the videos from the static cameras (on the TV and the auxiliary robot) or the camera mounted on top of the moving robot (Herme). We prefer to use the videos from the mounted camera because this is more similar to the type of data that needs to be processed in typical applications of a talking robot with mobility.

In the TableTalk corpus the visual analysis method assumes that changes in the scene are only possible due to the human motion. In contrast, in the Herme data captured from the moving camera changes may occur not only due to body/head movement but also due to the camera motion and other uncontrolled factors of the scene (e.g. the movement of multiple individuals captured by the camera). However, the visual analysis method used for the TableTalk corpus does not take into account the parameter variation caused by the camera motion. We have implemented a modified version of this method that uses the information of the camera motion to analyse the following face movement features: face distance measured between contiguous video segments, head forward/backward and head horizontal/vertical motions.

3.4   Classification of Engagement

In the TableTalk corpus the face detection seems to be accurate, which is expected because the scenario is fixed and the interlocutors are sitting around the table. Sometimes the faces are not detected but this happens just for a small fraction of the video. In the Herme data, face tracking is less reliable due to an higher variability of the visual parameters during short periods of the interaction and sometimes faces are not captured by the camera or just part of the face appears in the video. Also, in this experiment a person may be looking at Herme without speaking for relatively long time, while in TableTalk the silence periods during the dialogue are relatively short. In order to take into account these characteristics of Herme data, we divide the training data into four parts to build different classifiers:

- Segments with voice and face detected are used to train a classifier using audio-visual parameters.
- Segments with voice detected only are used to train a classifier using speech parameters.
- Segments with face detected only are used to train a classifier using visual parameters.
- Segments without voice and face detected are used to train a classifier for idle mode using audio parameters (no human-robot interaction).

The idea of training the last classifier for idle mode is to model the characteristics of the surrounding noise when there is no human-robot interaction. These classifiers can be used in Herme for detection of engagement. For example, Herme can take into account this information to help the decision making and generate smart feedback to the user. For that application the classifier should be selected based on the output of the VAD and face detection components.

4   Summary and Future Work

In this paper we describe ongoing work to measure the engagement of a person with a talking robot. Recently we have studied engagement detection in a corpus of free multiparty conversations among four people sitting around a table (the TableTalk corpus). Based on the findings and developments achieved in that work we propose a method to classify engagement in a database of spontaneous dialogues between people and a robot, Herme. We measure engagement using audio-visual parameters. The speech parameters are related to prosody (F0) and voice quality (mel-cepstrum and glottal parameters), while the visual parameters are related to facial movement. An experiment is being conducted for annotation of engagement in the "Herme dataset" using a new four-level scheme, in order to provide finer descriptors than the engaged/non-engaged annotations of the TableTalk corpus. In this work we also modified the visual analysis method used to extract parameters in TableTalk so that it takes into account the movement of the camera mounted on Herme.

Previously, we obtained an accuracy rate of 76 % for detection of group engagement, based on SVM method. In the Herme corpus, we plan to compare the performance of additional classification algorithms. This classification task is expected to be more difficult than in TableTalk because the first was recorded in a public space with more uncontrolled factors that may affect the audio-visual analysis and the performance of the machine learning algorithms. Also the levels of body movement are much higher in the Herme scenario. A more extensive evaluation of engagement classification using the different modalities (speech, visual, and audio-visual) needs to be carried out because it is more frequent in this scenario that only one of the two modalities is available for detection.

As future work, we plan to investigate additional audio-visual features and integrate the engagement detector into Herme.

Acknowledgments. This research is supported by the Science Foundation Ireland (Grant 12/CE/I2267) as part of CNGL (www.cngl.ie) at Trinity College Dublin.

References

1. Bohus, D., Horvitz, E.: Learning to predict engagement with a spoken dialog system in open-world settings. In: Annual Meeting of the Special Interest Group on Discourse and Dialogue (SIGDIAL), pp. 244–252. USA (2009)
2. Hernandez, J., Liu, Z., Hulten, G., DeBarr, D., Krum, K., Zhang, Z.: Measuring the engagement level of TV viewers. In: IEEE International Conference and Workshops on Automatic Face and Gesture Recognition, pp. 1–7 (2013)
3. Gustafson, J., Neiberg, D.: Prosodic cues to engagement in non-lexical response tokens in Swedish, In: DiSS-LPSS, Citeseer, pp. 63–66 (2010)
4. Gatica-Perez, D., McCowan, I. A., Zhang, D., Bengio, S.: Detecting group interest-level in meetings. In: IEEE ICASSP, pp. 489–492 (2010)
5. Campbell, N.: An audio-visual approach to measuring discourse synchrony in multimodal conversation data. In: Henrichsen, P.J. (ed.) Linguistic Theory and Raw Sound. Samfundslitteratur, Frederiksberg (2010)
6. Bonin, F., Bock, R., Campbell, N.: How do we react to context? annotation of individual and group engagement in a video corpus. In: Workshop on Context Based Affect Recognition, Held in conjunction with SocialCom, pp. 899–903 (2012)
7. Cabral, J. P., Renals, S., Richmond, K., Yamagishi, J.: Towards an improved modeling of the glottal source in statistical parametric speech synthesis. In: Workshop on Speech Synthesis, Germany (2007)
8. Douxchamps, D., Campbell, N.: Robust real time face tracking for the analysis of human behaviour. In: Popescu-Belis, A., Renals, S., Bourlard, H. (eds.) MLMI 2007. LNCS, vol. 4892, pp. 1–10. Springer, Heidelberg (2008)
9. Viola, P., Jones, M.: Robust real-time face detection. Int. J. Comput. Vis. **57**(2), 137–154 (2004)
10. Vaughan, B., Han, J.G., Gilmartin, E., Campbell, N.: Designing and implementing a platform for collecting multi-modal data of human-robot interaction. Acta Polytech. Hung. **9**(1), 7–17 (2012)
11. Mandatory speech codec speech processing functions; Adaptive Multi-Rate (AMR) speech codec; Voice Activity Detector (VAD), ETSI Standard TS 126 194 V12.0.0 (2014)
12. Hang, J.G., Gilmartin, E., De Looze, C., Vaughan, B., Campbell, N.: Speech and multimodal resources: the herme database of spontaneous multimodal human-robot dialogues. In: LREC, pp. 1328–1331. Turkey (2012)
13. Hall, M., Frank, E., Holmes, G., Pfahringer, B., Reutemann, P., Witten, I.H.: The WEKA data mining software: an update. SIGKDD Explor. Newslett. **11**, 10–18 (2009)

On Appropriateness and Estimation of the Emotion of Synthesized Response Speech in a Spoken Dialogue System

Taketo Kase, Takashi Nose, and Akinori Ito[✉]

Graduate School of Engineering, Tohoku University, Sendai, Japan
aito@spcom.ecei.tohoku.ac.jp

Abstract. Paralinguistic features such as emotion of an utterance is as important as its linguistic content for generating better response utterances in spoken dialog systems. In this research, we carried out an experiment to reveal the effect of emotional speech synthesis in a dialogue system, and investigated what method was effective for giving emotion to the synthetic speech. Firstly, we carried out an experiment where an agent with various emotional speech talked to the user, and the appropriateness of the emotion was evaluated. As expected, users had better impression on the agent when we added emotion appropriately. Next, we examined methods of automatic estimation of emotion for the system's response, and we found that the best method was to give the same emotion as the user's previous utterance regardless of the content of the system's utterance.

Keywords: Spoken dialog system · Emotional speech synthesis · Response generation

1 Introduction

Many dialogue systems for non-task-oriented dialogues have been developed so far [1,2]. Toward better interaction with a computer, there are a number of research for generating appropriate responses based on the topic [1], context of dialogue [1] and the user's emotion [3]. When generating the system's response utterance in a spoken dialog system, not only the contents of utterance but also the paralinguistic features are very important for giving a user better impression. Emotional speech synthesis [4] is a technique that adds emotional expression into a synthetic speech, and emotional speech synthesis has been used in dialogue systems [6]. However, investigation of the effect of employing emotional speech in a system seems insufficient. Acosta and Ward [5] investigated the effect of emotional speech on the impression of the system. Because the task of their system is a counseling dialogue, it is not clear that their result can be applied to the dialogue system for chat-like system. Furthermore, methodology of how to add an appropriate emotion to the system's utterances is not established.

© Springer International Publishing Switzerland 2015
C. Stephanidis (Ed.): HCII 2015 Posters, Part I, CCIS 528, pp. 747–752, 2015.
DOI: 10.1007/978-3-319-21380-4_126

In this research, we carried out an experiment to reveal the effect of emotional speech synthesis in a dialogue system, and investigated what method was effective for adding emotion to the synthetic speech.

2 Effect of Emotional Speech on the Impression of the User

We carried out an experiment where users talked with an agent with various emotional speech to investigate effect of emotional speech synthesis in a dialogue system. We prepared three styles of emotion: "neutral," "happy" and "sad." Then we compared three kinds of synthesized speech: utterances without emotion (condition *normal*), with manually-determined emotion (condition *appropriate*) and the inappropriate emotional condition where "happy" and "sad" tags were swapped (condition *inappropriate*).

2.1 Subjective Evaluation

First we wrote scenarios of the dialogues, and twelve subjects made conversations with a virtual agent, then the subjects were asked to answer a questionnaire. We made four scenarios that have about 10 turns. All the scenarios were written in Japanese. As a dialogue system, we used MMDAgent [6]. In *normal* condition, we used only the neutral style for the utterances. In *appropriate* and *inappropriate* conditions, we added the tagged emotion utterance by utterance (one utterance may contain more than one sentence).

We employed ten evaluators for manual annotation of emotion. Each evaluator read the whole scenario and gave emotion tag (neutral, happy or sad) for each utterance. We adopted the emotion tag when 7 out of 10 evaluators gave the same tag. As a result, 6 utterances were tagged "happy" and 4 utterances "sad" out of 18 system utterances.

In the dialogue experiment, a subject made dialogues with the system in a soundproof chamber. A subject sat on a chair and talked with the female agent displayed in a PC on a table. The subjects talked with the agent using all the four scenarios and all emotion conditions. Then the subjects answered a questionnaire having four questions, "richness of conversation," "human-likeliness of the agent," "pleasantness of the dialogue" and "impression of the agent." They answered the questions using five-grade Likert scale, where 1 to be "bad" and 5 to be "excellent".

2.2 Experimental Result and Discussion

Figure 1 shows the mean values of the evaluation scores. We conducted one-way layout ANOVA for each of the items, where methods of emotion labeling as a factor. Then we found significant difference at 1 % level for "richness of conversation," "human-likeliness of the agent" and "impression of the agent," and that at 5 % level for "pleasantness of the dialogue." From these results, we verified

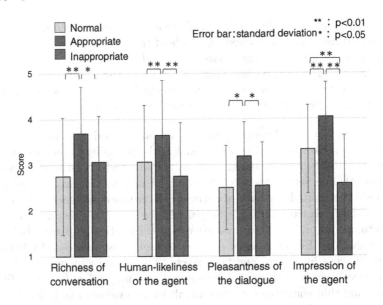

Fig. 1. Result of the subjective evaluation

that a method of emotion labeling actually changed the impression of subjects to the agent and conversation. Besides, results of multiple comparison test (t-test with Bonferroni correction) are drawn in the figure. This result showed that the *appropriate* condition gave better impression to the subjects than other two conditions. As for the "impression of the agent," score of *inappropriate* condition was significantly lower than that of *appropriate* condition. From the introspective opinions of the subjects, they felt to be teased when the agent talked with "happy" style where sad voice was appropriate.

3 Automatic Labeling of Emotion

We investigated a methods of automatic emotion labeling. We tested two methods: estimation from content of the system's current utterance (method S) and that from the user's previous utterance (method U). In both methods, we estimated the emotion from text content of the utterance [7].

Basically the estimation of emotion was based on matching between words in a sentence and a database of emotional expression. We exploited two data sources: evaluation polarity dictionary of verbs [8], and sentiment polarity dictionary of nouns [9], both were for Japanese words. The expressions and words in those dictionaries have either positive or negative polarity. Thus, if a sentence has a word or expression with positive or negative polarity, we give the sentence "happy" or "sad" emotion, respectively. If no such words are found, we give "neutral" emotion label. We employed several rules for labeling the emotion for complicated situation, as follows.

- If the emotional expression in the database is a phrase, we regard the sentence matches to the expression when all words of the phrase coincide.
- If two or more expressions are matched, we adopt the last one.
- If we find negative expression such as *nai* after the match, we reverse the polarity. (Note that the negative expressions in Japanese succeed the modified word, such as *"tanoshiku nai"* (happy not)=unhappy.)

We examined the accuracy of the estimation method described above. We used 100 sentences from the scenarios used in the previous experiment (Set A), and another 100 sentences taken randomly from ASJ-JIPDEC database [10] Vol.7 (Set B). For Set A, we used the result of manual labeling as the ground truth, and investigated the rate of correctly determined sentences. As a result, we obtained 72 % correct rate. For Set B, we first calculated results of the automatic estimation, and then we evaluated the automatically-given labels by 10 human evaluators. Each evaluator decided each of the sentence and label as one of "correct," "not incorrect" and "incorrect." The reason why we used the item "not incorrect" was that the test sentence was randomly taken from the dialogue database, and thus sometimes it was difficult for an evaluator to judge appropriateness of the emotion label without the context of the sentence. Table 1 shows the result of evaluation for Set B. As a result, more than 80 % of the sentences were judged as either "correct" or "not incorrect".

Table 1. Subjective evaluation for Set B [%]

correct	not incorrect	incorrect
64.7	21.6	13.7

4   Evaluation Experiment of Automatic Emotion Labeling

We carried out an experiment for evaluating the automatic emotion labeling methods, where users talked with an agent with various emotional speech and evaluated the dialogue. We compared four kinds of emotional labeling methods: "none" labeled all utterances to be neutral, "method S" used estimation results for the system utterance, "method U" used estimation results for the user's previous utterance, and "random" determined the emotion label randomly.

4.1   Experimental Conditions

We calculated the emotion labels using the above four methods, and conducted subjective evaluation of dialogues using the emotion labels. The experimental conditions are almost same as that of Sect. 2.1. The difference was that we employed ten subjects in this experiment.

4.2 Experimental Results

First, we observed the labeling result using "method S" and "method U." Using "method S", 7 out of 18 system utterances were labeled as "happy," and only one was labeled as "sad." When using "method U," 6 out of 18 system utterances were labeled as "happy," and 3 were as "sad." From these results, we found that "method S" cannot give an appropriate emotion label to short utterances such as answers for yes/no questions or backchannels because those utterances do not contain any expressions for determining sentiment, whereas "method U" could give labels to such short utterances. We compared the labeling results of method S and U to the manual annotation, and the consensus rate was 78 % and 72 %, respectively.

Figure 2 shows the evaluation score of dialogue and agent. Using one-way layout ANOVA for method of labeling as a factor, we observed significant difference among methods for "richness of conversation," "human-likeliness of the agent" and "impression of the agent" at 1 % significance level, and for "pleasantness of dialogue" at 5 % significance level. Results of t-test with Bonferroni correction are also shown in the figure. From this result, we can see that the results of "method U" are always better than at least one of other method.

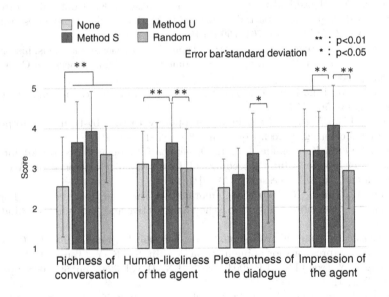

Fig. 2. Result of subjective evaluation

5 Conclusion

In this research, we carried out experiments to reveal effect of emotional speech synthesis in a dialogue system, and investigated the method of emotional labeling.

From the result of subjective evaluation, we confirmed that users had better impression on the agent when emotion labels were appropriately given to the system's utterances. Then we compared several methods for estimating emotion label, and found that the best method was to estimate the emotion label from the users previous utterance regardless of the content of the systems utterance.

Emotion estimation accuracy could be improved by combining multiple estimation results such as method S and U. Therefore we will develop such method to improve the emotion estimation accuracy. Combination of emotion estimation from audio signal is another issue. In addition, appropriateness of emotion, of course, depends on various factors such as topic of dialogue, appearance and voice quality of the agent and relation between the agent and the user. Investigation of the effect of such factors is the future work.

References

1. Higuchi, S., Rafal, R., Araki, K.: A casual conversation system using modality and word associations retrieved from the web. In: Proceedings of Conference on Empirical Methods in Natural Language Processing (EMNLP), pp. 382–390. Honolulu (2008)
2. Meguro, T., Higashinaka, R., Minami, Y., Dohsaka, K.: Controlling listening-oriented dialogue using partially observable Markov decision processes. In: Proceedings of COLING, pp. 761–769 (2010)
3. Burkhardt, F., Stegmann, J.: Emotional speech synthesis: applications, history and possible future. In: Proceedings of Electronic Speech Signal Processing Conference (ESSV) (2009)
4. Schröder, M.: Emotional speech synthesis: a review. In: Proceedings of Eurospeech, Aalborg, pp. 561–564 (2001)
5. Acosta, J.C., Ward, N.G.: Achieving rapport with turn-by-turn, user-responsive emotional coloring. Speech Commun. 53, 1137–1148 (2011)
6. Lee, A., Oura, K., Tokuda, K.: MMDAgent: a fully open-source toolkit for voice interaction systems. In: Proceedings of International Conference on Acoustics, Speech and Signal Processing (ICASSP) (2013)
7. Guinn, C., Hubal, R.: Extracting emotional information from the text of spoken dialog. In: Proceedings of 3rd Workshop on Affective and Attitude User Modeling. Pittsburg (2003)
8. Kobayashi, N., Inui, K., Matsumoto, Y., Tateishi, K., Fukushima, T.: Collecting evaluative expressions for opinion extraction. In: Su, K.-Y., Tsujii, J., Lee, J.-H., Kwong, O.Y. (eds.) IJCNLP 2004. LNCS (LNAI), vol. 3248, pp. 596–605. Springer, Heidelberg (2005)
9. Takase, S., Murakami, A., Enoki, M., Okazaki, N., Inui, K.: Detecting chronic critics based on sentiment polarity and user's behavior in social media. In: Proceedings of ACL (Student Research Workshop), pp. 110–116 (2013)
10. http://research.nii.ac.jp/src/ASJ-JIPDEC.html. Accessed 20 February 2015

Dialogue Efficiency Evaluation of Turn-Taking Phenomena in a Multi-layer Incremental Simulated Environment

Hatim Khouzaimi[1,2]($\boxtimes$), Romain Laroche[1], and Fabrice Lefèvre[2]

[1] Orange Labs, Issy-les-moulineaux, France
{hatim.khouzaimi,romain.laroche}@orange.com
[2] CERI-LI, University of Avignon, Avignon, France
fabrice.lefevre@univ-avignon.fr

Abstract. We use a simulated environment for incremental dialogue to show that incremental processing offers new possibilities to make dialogue systems more robust to noise. Traditional dialogue systems wait until the end of the user's utterance before processing it and they cannot be interrupted when taking the floor. On the contrary, incremental dialogue systems process the user's speech signal on the flow, therefore, they are able to react quickly if an error is detected. First we show that mixed initiative strategies have the advantages of both system initiative and user initiative strategies and then we show that there is still room for improvement thanks to incremental processing.

Keywords: Incremental spoken dialogue systems · User simulator

1 Introduction

In the last few years, automatic speech recognition (ASR) technology has made a lot of progress so that it is no longer a bottleneck in the development of spoken dialogue systems. Some industrial services already have a vocal interaction mode but their efficiency and their naturalness are still poor. An important aspect that still needs to be improved is floor management. Time is shared in a rigid way as the user has to wait for the system to finish its sentence before speaking and vice-versa. This is not natural, and as we show in this paper, it is not the most efficient way of interaction. In human communication, the listener understands the speaker on the flow [8]. This ability is manifested through different turn-taking phenomena and some of the most commonly studied in the field of dialogue systems have been implemented in this work.

Systems that replicate this behaviour are called incremental dialogue systems. Some sequential architectures have been published in order to design such systems [1,3,7]. In this paper we use a multi-layer architecture [5] where the turn-taking management part is handled by a *Scheduler* module that is added as an extra-layer to the traditional Dialogue Manager (DM). We show that incremental dialogue processing offers possibilities to make dialogue systems more

© Springer International Publishing Switzerland 2015
C. Stephanidis (Ed.): HCII 2015 Posters, Part I, CCIS 528, pp. 753–758, 2015.
DOI: 10.1007/978-3-319-21380-4_127

robust to noise. To demonstrate our work, a user simulator which interacts with a personal agenda assistant has been developed. Dialogue efficiency is measured through dialogue duration and task completion [2, 9]. Moreover, the turn-taking phenomena are evaluated separately in order to see which ones are critical in terms of efficiency improvement.

Section 2 introduces the simulated environment and the chosen task. Section 3 describes the experiment and the results and finally, Sect. 4 concludes and announces future work.

2   Simulated Environment

Three different modules compose the simulated environment: the user simulator, the Scheduler and the service. In order to simulate strategies that do not require incremental processing, the user simulator interacts directly with the service. On the other hand, the Scheduler is inserted as an intermediate module between the two for incremental strategies [5]. It is in charge of floor-taking decisions whereas the service handles more high-level semantic decisions (computing responses based on the user simulator's utterances).

The service is a personal agenda manager. It can accomplish three types of tasks: adding, modifying or deleting an event from the agenda. Therefore, a task is defined by four slots : the type of action (ADD, MODIFY or DELETE), the title of the event, its date and its time slot. However, overlaps between events are not tolerated. Initially, the agenda contains a few events. The user simulator is given a list of events that should be added during the dialogue. Each event has a priority and a set of alternative dates and time slots that can be used in the case of a conflict. The user simulator tries to make the maximum number of events with the highest priority fit in the agenda.

2.1   User Simulator

A simple algorithm has been implemented so that the user simulator can calculate the next action to make. When trying to add a new event, if the slot is free then it is added, otherwise it checks the alternative slots. If they are all taken, it checks whether it is possible to move a conflicting event. If it is not possible, then the priority of the event to add is compared to the less important priority among the conflicting events. If it is greater, then the conflicting event is deleted and replaced with the new event, otherwise the latter is forgotten.

After the next user act is determined, it is incrementally sent to an ASR output simulator. The increment chosen here is the word, for the sake of simplicity. Each incremental step is called a *micro-turn*. The ASR output simulator maintains an N-Best (the top recognition hypotheses with their confidence scores) corresponding to the partial utterance made so far by the user. A Word Error Rate (WER) parameter is set to control the noise level.

Real ASR modules are not monotonous: a new chunk of audio signal can modify an important part if not the whole ASR best output hypothesis. This is due to the fact that the language model suddenly recognises a pattern that is more likely to correspond to what the user just said. To simulate this phenomenon, whenever a new concept appears in a hypothesis, the corresponding confidence score is boosted (so it has a chance to be the top hypothesis). As a consequence, the last words of a partial request are more likely to change than the ones that appear earlier in the utterance and no decision should be made based on them. Thus, the Scheduler removes a few last words from the current partial utterance and makes a decision based on the remaining prefix. The latter will be called *the last stable partial utterance*. The number of words removed will be referred to as the *stability margin* (SM). In [6], if a partial utterance lasted for more that 0.6 seconds then it has more than 90 % chance of staying unchanged. In this work, we suppose that the speech rate is 200 words per seconds [10]. Hence two words are spoken in 0.6 seconds and we set SM=2.

2.2 Turn-Taking Rules

Five of the most studied turn-taking phenomena in the field of incremental dialogue have been implemented in this work. The first four require the Scheduler to make a decision and one of them depends on the user's behaviour only. At each micro-turn, the Scheduler has to decide whether it does not speak (WAIT), whether to repeat the last word of the last stable utterance (REPEAT) or whether to retrieve the last response obtained from the service (SPEAK). In the following, we explicit the rules that have been implemented in the Scheduler for each phenomenon (and in the use simulator for the last one).

FAIL_RAW: When speaking, the user has no guarantee that the system understands his message (due to noise or the use of off-domain words). Therefore, in order to prevent the user from speaking too long without being understood, if no key concept has been detected after a long enough sentence, then the Scheduler performs a SPEAK (as no key concept is present in the current partial utterance, the last service's response is *Sorry. I don't understand.*). The threshold depends on the last system act. It is set to 6 for open questions and time slot questions, to 3 for yes/no questions and 4 for dates so that the user can utter some out of domain words and the key concepts have time to stabilise.

INCOHERENCE_INTERP: Even if understood, the user's utterance can be problematic if it is incoherent with the dialogue context (trying to modify a non existing event in the agenda for example). Therefore, as soon as the service makes an incoherence alert, the Scheduler waits to get SM more words and if the partial request at time $t - SM$ is a prefix of the one at time t (no changes because of ASR instability) then it performs a SPEAK.

FEEDBACK_RAW: The last word's confidence score is estimated as the ratio between the last partial request score and the one before last. If this ratio is below a threshold, the last word is repeated (REPEAT action) SM words later if it is still present in the partial utterance.

BARGE_IN_RESP (System): When there is enough information in the partial request for the service to generate a response that improves the dialogue, the system can barge-in before the user ends his utterance. The Scheduler performs a SPEAK SM words later if the partial utterance that generates the response is a prefix of the current one (no changes because of ASR instability).

BARGE_IN_RESP (User): This phenomenon corresponds to a user's decision. We suppose that the user is familiar with the system to barge-in as soon as it has enough information without letting the system finish its utterance.

3   Experiment

Dialogue efficiency is evaluated given two criteria: the dialogue duration (given a speech rate of 200 words per minute) and the task completion. If it takes two long for the user to accomplish a task (add, modify or delete), then she hangs up. The corresponding time threshold is sampled at each new task from a distribution with a 3 min mean. The first part of the experiment is dedicated to three generic strategies used in traditional dialogue systems: system initiative (SysIni), user initiative (UsrIni) and mixed initiative (MixIni). In this work, they have been instantiated as follows: in SysIni the user is asked for the different chunks of information, one by one (action, description, date and time slot). On the contrary, in UsrIni, all the necessary information must be given in one request. Finally, MixIni behaves like UsrIni and if it fails, it switches to SysIni. In this part, the user simulator interacts directly with the service.

Next, the impact of incrementality is studied. The Scheduler, embedding the rules introduced in Sect. 2.2, is added between the user simulator and the service. In addition, the user simulator is configured to interrupt the system (BARGE_IN_RESP from the user's side). In SysIni, the utterances are short which is not adapted to incremental processing. Thus, we study incrementality in the case of UsrIni (UsrIni+Incr) and MixIni (MixIni+Incr).

To specify the task achieved during the dialogues, we define a scenario as two lists of events. The first one corresponds to the events that exist in the agenda before the dialogue whereas the second contains the events to add during the dialogue. Our experiment is based on three handcrafted scenarios (leading to dialogues with different levels of complexity because of overlaps between the two lists of events). In order to analyse the effect of noise on these strategies, we vary the WER between 0 and 0.3 with a step of 0.03. For each scenario and each WER, 1000 dialogues have been run.

For low values of WER, SysIni strategy is more tiresome and inefficient compared to UsrIni (Fig. 1). However, for high noise levels, it outperforms it showing that it is more efficient to communicate the information chunk by chunk. MixIni has the advantages of both strategies as it performs like UsrIni for low levels of WER and better than both of them in noisy situations. Incremental behaviour has been introduced to both UsrIni and MixIni (in the case of SysIni, the user's utterances are supposed to be short, so it is not relevant to add incrementality). Just like mixed initiative, incrementality is also shown to be a solution to making UsrIni more robust to noise, with even better results. Finally, we show that MixIni with incremental behaviour performs best.

In Fig. 2, the performance of each turn-taking phenomenon is represented (with MixIni as a baseline). FEEDBACK_RAW, BAGE_IN_RESP from the

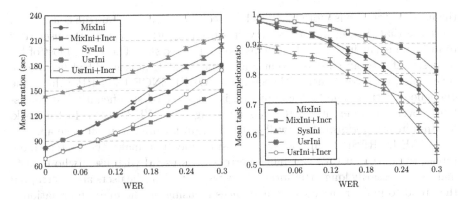

Fig. 1. Mean dialogue duration and task completion for generic strategies

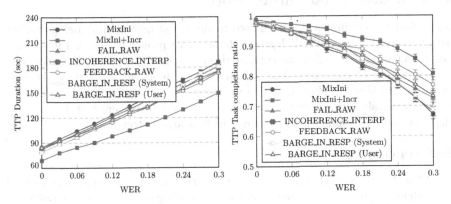

Fig. 2. Mean dialogue duration and task completion for different turn-taking phenomena

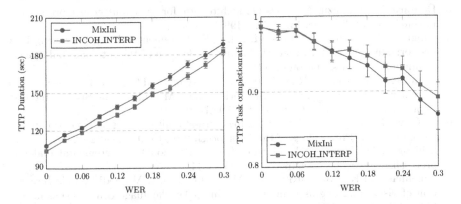

Fig. 3. INCOH_INTERP strategy in a more adapted task.

user's side and FAIL_RAW are the phenomena that have an impact on the dialogue efficiency. INCOHERENCE_INTERP is more adapted to tasks where the user's utterance is more likely to be in conflict with the dialogue context. To illustrate that, in Fig. 3, the scenario has been slightly modified: the user tries to move an event five times before discovering a free slot. Therefore, most of his requests refer to an existing event and if the event title is modified because of ASR noise, an incoherence is detected. INCOHERENCE_INTERP reduces the dialogue duration. The task completion is not reduced significantly but consistently over the different WER levels (starting from WER=0.15). In this task, MixIni already performs very well so the margin for improvement is small.

BAGE_IN_RESP from the system's side does not make the system more robust to noise as it does not handle errors. It is useful with users who tend to make unnecessarily long utterances. [4] shows that when the users are interrupted they tend to make more concise utterances focusing on the main information.

4 Conclusion and Future Work

A simulated environment has been used to show that incremental dialogue offers new possibilities to make dialogue systems more robust to noise. First, three non-incremental strategies are compared: system initiative, user initiative and a combination of the two, mixed initiative, that is shown to achieve the best performance. We then show that there is still room for improvement using incremental processing. In future work, we plan to use reinforcement learning to show that optimal turn-taking management can be learnt automatically.

References

1. Allen, J., Ferguson, G., Stent, A.: An architecture for more realistic conversational systems. In: 6th International Conference on Intelligent User Interfaces (2001)
2. Asri, L.E., Laroche, R., Pietquin, O.: Reward function learning for dialogue management. In: STAIRS (2012)
3. Dohsaka, K., Shimazu, A.: A system architecture for spoken utterance production in collaborative dialogue. In: IJCAI (1997)
4. Ghigi, F., Eskenazi, M., Torres, M.I., Lee, S.: Incremental dialog processing in a task-oriented dialog. In: Fifteenth Annual Conference of the International Speech Communication Association (2014)
5. Khouzaimi, H., Laroche, R., Lefèvre, F.: An easy method to make dialogue systems incremental. In: Proceedings of the 15th Annual Meeting of the Special Interest Group on Discourse and Dialogue (SIGDIAL) (2014)
6. McGraw, I., Gruenstein, A.: Estimating word-stability during incremental speech recognition. In: Proceedings of the Interspeech 2012 Conference (2012)
7. Schlangen, D., Skantze, G.: A general, abstract model of incremental dialogue processing. Dialogue Discourse **2**, 83–111 (2011)
8. Tanenhaus, M.K., Spivey-Knowlton, M.J., Eberhard, K.M., Sedivy, J.C.: Integration of visual and linguistic information in spoken language comprehension. Sci. **268**, 1632–1634 (1995)
9. Walker, M.A., Litman, D.J., Kamm, C.A., Abella, A.: Paradise: a framework for evaluating spoken dialogue agents. In: Proceedings of the Eighth Conference on European Chapter of the Association for Computational Linguistics (1997)
10. Yuan, J., Liberman, M., Cieri, C.: Towards an integrated understanding of speaking rate in conversation. In: Interspeech Proceedings (2006)

Comparing the Trade-off of Believability and Performance of Abstract Intelligent Agents and Humans Playing Super Mario Bros

Edward Morgan and Konstantinos Papangelis[(⊠)]

Cardiff School of Computer Science and Informatics,
Cardiff University, Cardiff, UK
{MorganEH4,papangelisk}@cardiff.ac.uk

Abstract. In this paper, we will examine how the performance and player believability aspects of abstract intelligent agents within video games interact and affect one another. We will present the study used to assess whether performance and believability do have an effect on one another and how much of an effect. Followed by the results to the study and a discussion on potential design approaches to produce more believable agents that still provide the level of effectiveness expected of them.

Keywords: Believability · Intelligent agents · Video games

1 Introduction

With games getting increasingly complex in terms of their size and capabilities comes an expanded amount of focus on artificial intelligence and the usage of abstract intelligent agents within games. The increased computing power that comes with gaming platforms now means that agents can be used more actively to boost player enjoyment and immersion within their gaming experience [1, 2].

In more complex games such as Role Playing Games (RPGs), First Person Shooters (FPS) and Massive Multiplayer Online games (MMOs), where players interact extensively with agents there is an opportunity to further the player's enjoyment and immersion by providing them with agents that are both effective and that contribute an experience that feels like you are interacting with other humans [1, 2].

The aim of this study is to explore the aforementioned and provide initial evidence on how performance of an agent affects the player believability of said agent. Player believability in this context has been defined as "Someone believes that the player controlling the character/bot is real, i.e. that a human is playing as that character instead of the character being computer-controlled" [3].

© Springer International Publishing Switzerland 2015
C. Stephanidis (Ed.): HCII 2015 Posters, Part I, CCIS 528, pp. 759–763, 2015.
DOI: 10.1007/978-3-319-21380-4_128

2 Methods of Research

The research in this study was conducted using Super Mario Bros as a benchmark for both the performance and believability aspects. Four human players and four agents were recorded playing a series of identical levels. They played three different levels of four different difficulty settings (Twelve trials in total).

The four agents use different algorithms and approaches to play the game. We will be exploring agents that use an A* search algorithm approach, a rule based approach, and two simple agents - one that attempts to always move to the right of the screen jumping whenever it detects an enemy or an obstacle within a set distance of itself, while the other one attempts to constantly move to the right, jumping at every available chance. The A* search algorithm and Rule based approach are both common methods used in game agents and are well documented. The two simple agents are likely to perform worse than the two other agents but should offer insight into whether the performance gap affects their player believability. The human player video clips are used as a control variable.

The performances of each player (both human and agent) were tracked throughout the trials to give an overall performance score. This score can then be used to compare the players. The criteria for the performance were, Level Completion, Total Kills, Mario Status, Time Left, and Mario Mode. These were recorded for each difficulty level and then a running total for the complete run (All 12 trials).

The believability portion of the research was done in two parts by using videos of each player's run through and showing them to third party observers. The first part was to show the videos to single observers, asking them after each clip whether they believed it was a human or an agent, to put how sure they were on a scale (1 being 100 % sure it was an agent, 5 being unsure and 10 being 100 % sure it was a human.), and what skill level they believed the player was (Novice, Intermediate, or Advanced). During the clips the observers would talk out loud about what they were thinking allowing for us to take notes and identify certain traits that influenced their decisions on believability. This was done for 10 interviewees.

The second part of the research was similar to the first but differed in the fact that it was done with a large group (30 observers) at once, they filled out a questionnaire as the clips were shown. As it was such a large group it was impractical for us to probe for thoughts while the video clips were being shown. Using a large group to perform research at once advanced things considerably and allowed for more statistical data to analyse.

The research participants were a mixture of males and females and were all between the ages of 18-25. The group of participants had varying degrees of video game experience.

3 Analysis

The results gained from the research discussed above can be seen in Tables 1 and 2 below. Table 1 presents the results for the agent players, and Table 2 shows the results for the human players. These tables show the number of judges that guessed whether

Table 1. Agent player result table

	1. Forward Agent	2. Rule Based Agent	3. A* Agent	4. Forward Jumping Agent
5. Performance Score	8676.36	9865.94	11675.67	9187.99
6. Human Votes	3	15	0	14
7. Agent Votes	37	25	40	26
8. Believability Score	2.4	3.9	1.2	3.8

Table 2. Human player results table

	9. Human 1	10. Human 2	11. Human 3	12. Human 4
13. Performance Score	10339.33	9113.51	11587.67	9885.19
14. Human Votes	20	21	21	37
15. Agent 16. Votes	20	19	19	3
Believability Scale	6.6	5.3	4.9	8.1

each player was human or agent and the average of the believability scale used along with their performance score.

From Tables 1 and 2 we can see that overall, the performance did have an effect on the believability scores. However this was not the sole reason for the scores as discovered from the interviewees' comments. Examples of this were the forward agent who scored a low believability score as interviewees said it was so unintelligent it was obviously an agent regardless of the performance. Similarly observers were largely unsure of human 2 as they played in a human fashion along with unintelligent behaviour displayed occasionally throughout.

The A* Agent which had the highest performance scored a 1.15 average believ-ability which implies the observers were very sure that It was an agent. While the Human 3 had only a slightly worse performance score but the observers were unsure whether or not it was an agent or a human with a score of 4.9. Comments made by the interviewees said that the speed, and the general high performance level of Human 3 led them to believe it was an agent but then at higher difficulties it was offset by the fact that there was slight mistakes, taking some non-optimal paths, and occasionally had periods of waiting (For decision making or for enemies to clear).

The only human who posted a somewhat sure 8.1 believability score was the slowest and had the third lowest performance score. This suggests that the observers were looking for anything that made them seem agent-like such as being repetitive, methodical, and fast whether it had a good or bad effect along with optimality and drew conclusions. This was because they knew the goal was to identify agents and didn't know how many of the eight players were in fact agents. However all the agents still scored lower on the scale.

Unintelligent actions were related to jumping straight into danger or holes, ducking on screen when flying enemies were present although offered no obvious danger and not going backwards to avoid enemies.

4   Discussion and Conclusion

Bearing in mind that performance has an effect on the player believability of an agent; it brings us to how an agent should be designed to provide a player believable expe-rience. The results imply that the correct level of performance has to be found to influence believability in the correct way. If the agent becomes too effective then they will come across as unhuman-like, although unintelligent decisions also suggest unhuman-likeness. This is shown from the interviewees comments made from the research.

Bungie, the developers of Halo talk about how tougher (More health points) agents leads to players believing they were smarter and more humanlike due to increased exposure and providing more of a challenge than agents who are actually more com-plex but provide less of a challenge due to being overcome quicker [5]. This of course was not their only method to provide versatile agents and has to be done in tangent with others.

While Togelius et al. [3] suggest that this should be done through a mixture of algorithm and level design optimization. This is an interesting suggestion that the level design could heavily influence the believability of agents [3]. Perhaps an agent could be designed to perform 'slower' at levels of lower difficulty opposed to performing at the highest speed capable giving a more human like feel. This change wouldn't necessarily make the agent perform worse, just at a more human manageable pace.

Using this in line with level design theory talked about by Jeremey Parish [4], could provide players with both a forgiving yet rewarding learning curve and well-rounded agents. It is conceivable that as a player progresses through a game they will become more proficient and therefore become faster at actions. Consequently as a player becomes more proficient then the agents they encounter can too become faster.

Another suggestion is to use a heavy observation learning and case-based reasoning approach to produce believable behaviour [6]. This mixed with reinforced learning to produce a high level of performance could have the potential to produce these well-rounded agents we've discussed [6].

Overall, In this study we have looked at how two important aspects of abstract intelligent agents interact and influence each other. The initial data illustrates that performance does affect the believability of an agent, and how this could possibly be addressed via both algorithm optimization as well as level design optimization.

References

1. Charles, D.: Enhancing Gameplay: Challenges for Artificial Intelligence in Digital Games. University of Utrecht, The Netherlands (2003)
2. Woyach, S.: Immersion through video games, Illumin, vol. 5, no. 4 (2004)
3. Togelius, J., Yannakakis, G.N., Karakovski, S., Shaker, N.: Assessing believability. In: Hingston, P. (ed.) Believable Bots, pp. 215–230. Springer, Berlin Hiedelberg (2012)
4. Parish, J.: 1Up, 13 August 2012. http://www.1up.com/features/learning-level-design-mario. [Accessed 31 March 2015]
5. Butcher, C., Griesemer, J.: The illusion of intelligence: the integration of AI and level design in halo. In: Game Developers Conference, San Francisco (2002)
6. Iskander, U., Mozgovoy, M., Clint Rogers, P.: Believable and effective AI agents in virtual worlds: current state and future perspectives. Int. J. Gaming Comput. Mediat. Simul. (IJGCMS) 4(2), 37–59 (2012)

Neut: "Hey, Let Her Speak"

Design of a Speech Eliciting Robot that Intervenes in Brainstorming Sessions to Ensure Collaborative Group Work

Naoki Ohshima[✉], Tatsuya Watanabe, Natsuki Saito, Riyo Fujimori, Hiroko Tokunaga, and Naoki Mukawa

School of Information Environment, Tokyo Denki University, Tokyo, Japan
sima@mail.dendai.ac.jp
http://sarl.jp/

Abstract. In this research, we developed a speech eliciting robot (Neut) that ensures a cooperative brainstorming environment. Neut creates an atmosphere that makes it easier for participants who are often overlooked to express their ideas, by promoting cooperation from the other participants. Neut moves freely on a table and approaches one or the other participant who has not yet had his/her speaking turn. After stopping in front of such a participant, it brings out a microphone and prompts the participant to speak, while looking around restlessly to suggest to others that they give the participant a chance to speak. In this paper, we will discuss the design of Neut in encouraging participants to speak out, while maintaining neutrality by not itself speaking as a participant.

Keywords: Persuasive robot · Social etiquette · Conversation analysis

1 Introduction

In recent years, interactive artifacts that facilitate human-friendly relationships, such as through sociable robots and anthropomorphic agents, has attracted considerable interest. In particular, research on the development of persuasive robots that offer useful advice to improve person's social lives is being actively promoted. Engaging and useful discussions are held each year at the ACM/IEEE International Conference on Human-Robot Interaction (HRI) and the International Conference on Social Robotics (ICSR).

An up-and-coming topic in the field of persuasive robotics research is whether a robot can remind humans of social etiquette without using words. If a robot can suggest humans without using words, interaction between robots and illiterate users (children, elderly people who may not be skilled at communication through words, as well as people with communication disabilities) can be realized.

Accordingly, our research focuses on a method of generating an effective suggestion, as in the case of a "Sociable Trash Box [2]." In general, if one wants to advise visitors to pick up garbage in a public facility, one may verbally or through non-verbal signs call attention to the appropriate disposal of garbage.

© Springer International Publishing Switzerland 2015
C. Stephanidis (Ed.): HCII 2015 Posters, Part I, CCIS 528, pp. 764–769, 2015.
DOI: 10.1007/978-3-319-21380-4_129

Fig. 1. Neut (speech eliciting robot) is encouraging a participant to speak

By contrast, the Sociable Trash Box uses a different approach. When a robot incapable of picking up garbage on its own (=Sociable Trash Box) was introduced to a public facility, visitors observing the robot began picking up garbage. In order to help this robot with its intended job — picking up garbage — the visitors ended up picking up all the garbage in the public facility. As shown by this example, even without the use of words, and by appealing to apparent inability to complete the task by itself, the robot can suggest people to appropriate disposal of garbage.

Therefore, as a method that uses a robot to remind people of social etiquette without the use of words, we focus on using a robot's inability to complete a task that it ostensibly desires to accomplish in order to motivate people in the environment to observe decorum [4]. In this study, as part of the overarching project, we held a brain-storming session where the rules stipulated that everyone could speak out, and designed a robot called "Neut" (Fig. 1) that suggested participants to the need for those who had not spoken much thus far to be given an opportunity to do so. In Sect. 2, we detail the concept underlying Neut in encouraging participants to speak out while maintaining neutrality by itself staying silent as a participant. Its application scenarios (in Sect. 3), experiment (in Sect. 4) and case study (in Sect. 5), in order to find out basic effects of Neut are mentioned in this paper. The hardware configuration and the internal processing mechanism of Neut will be discussed in a future study.

2   Neut as a Speech-Eliciting Robot

We called our robot "Neut[1]" based on the first four letters in the word "neutrality." Neut was designed based on the following five concepts:

2.1   Robot of Silence

Neut does not have a speech function in order to avoid negative influence on topics during brainstorming sessions. A robot without a speech function is quiet

---

[1] Other robots by the same name have been developed. E.g., the SWAT law-enforcement robot "Neut."

Fig. 2. Application scenario

and does not hinder human conversation but also appears a robot's inability to speak out.

2.2 Microphone and Headphone to Elicit Participant Speech

Neut has a wireless microphone in order to elicit participants' utterances, and a pair of headphones in order to appear to be listening to participants' utterances by itself staying silent.

2.3 A Big, Single Eye

A thin, plastic board modeled on a big eyeball, was attached to Neut's head. The robot looks around "restlessly" with this big eye to convince talkative participants to allow their more silent colleagues a chance to speak.

2.4 Height of a Robot

A group conversation involving more than five participants was assumed in this study. We set the height of Neut to approximately 40 cm, so that the robot's eye is level with the eyes of a human seated on a chair.

3 Application Scenario

For brainstorming to work effectively, a cooperative atmosphere is needed where all participants can exchange their ideas in a collaborative manner. In such settings, occurrences where discussion shifts from one topic to the next without verbal contribution from a limited number of participants must be avoided. In this paper, our speech-eliciting robot (Neut) that ensures a cooperative brainstorming environment. Neut promotes an atmosphere that makes it easier for participants who are often overlooked to express their ideas by eliciting cooperation from the other participants to a discussion. Neut is a small robot that moves freely on a table (S1 in Fig. 2) and approaches a participant who has not yet had his/her turn to speak (left-side person of S2 in Fig. 2), having come to a stop in front of the participant (S3 in Fig. 2), it brings out a wireless microphone and prompts the participant to speak (S4 in Fig. 2), all the while looking around restlessly to suggest to others that they give the participant a chance to speak.

4   Experiment

From the behavior of Neut (described in Sect. 3) and the interaction among participants, we observed that the robot encourages participants (1) to speak, (2) to allow others to speak, and (3) to reconstruct the Participation Framework [1]. Furthermore, the results of preliminary investigations (personality testing of the participants) and experiments conducted to ascertain the effects of Neut on participants showed that extroverts deferred to their less talkative colleagues when reminded by Neut that they were speaking out of turn, and introverts became active speakers, hence resulting in improved cooperation among participants.

4.1   Experimental Task

We built on the Desert Survival Problem [3] to create a brain-storming session. In a prototypical task, the participants were asked to imagine that they had crash landed in the middle of a desert. They had certain items, such as a torch, a jack knife, a bandage kit, a pair of sunglasses, and so on, with them. Their task was to rank these items in order of their capacity to increase their chances of survival.

4.2   Experimental Procedure

Participants were first given a brief description of the purpose and procedure of the experiment. They were asked to review and sign a consent form after a brief introduction. Following this, they filled out a preliminary questionnaire consisting of 60 questions (personality testing of the participants using the Big Five personality traits [5]) that measured five personality characteristics: extraversion, neuroticism, openness to experience, conscientiousness, and agreeableness. The experimenter then detailed the experimental task for the benefit of the participants. The participants were brought into an experiment room and seated at a table with the robot. The experimenter greeted a participant and prompted him/her to start the task. At the end of the task, the participants answered a post-experiment questionnaire regarding their perceptions of the robot. The task itself took an average of 15 and 20 min and the entire experiment procedure took an hour respectively.

4.3   Participants

A total of 11 participants (two groups), aged 20–23 years and with an average age of 20.9 years, participated in the study. The social relations in a group (Group 1) are shown in the left parts of Fig. 3 (we had to omit explanation of Group 2 for want of space).

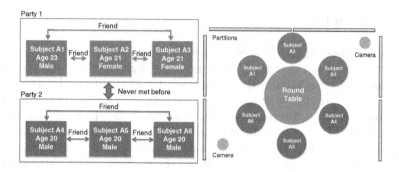

Fig. 3. Social relations between subjects (left-side) and experimental setup (right-side)

4.4   Experimental Setup

The right side of Fig. 3 describes experimental setup in Group 1. The experiment room was surrounded by white partitions. Two cameras were arranged in the room such that all subjects could be seen and the conversation could be recorded clearly. The participants were seated at a roundtable approximately two meters in diameter. The participants were free to choose their seats at the table.

5   Case Study

We hold a result of Group 1 up as an example. A result of personality testing is indicated in Table 1. According to Table 1, a value of extraversion of subject A3 indicates extremely high. Subject A3 seems the most contribute participant in this group. A value of openness of subject A5 indicates remarkably low. Subject A5 seems an less-contribute participant to express/spread his ideas.

5.1   Analysis of Video-Recorded Conversation

A minute and a half after the start of the Desert Survival Problem task, Neut suddenly approached subject A5, and subject A4 said, "This robot can move,"

Table 1. Results of personality testing (Group 1)

Subject	Extraversion	Neuroticism	Openness	Conscientiousness	Agreeableness
A1	53	54	53	42	64
A2	51	68	35	38	53
A3	<u>75</u>	44	41	30	63
A4	52	63	62	37	67
A5	37	56	<u>27</u>	40	36
A6	51	60	51	37	52

and subjects A1, A2, and A6 laughed. Two seconds after this remark by subject A4, subject A5 said, "Hi!" while bringing a hand up to the robot, and said "It is cute!" twice. Subject A5 also remarked about Neut's appearance after 8 s. Next, subject A4 said to subject A5, "You will be interviewed by the robot" to which subject A5 replied "Seriously?" and after 2 s said, "The robot does not seem to have a speak function" twice. The same subject, subject A5, said, "Leave the robot alone" after 6 s, which was followed by the laughter of all participants. Then, the Desert Survival Problem task resumed with focus on subject A3.

We summarize the above conversation in three points. (1) The robot (Neut) encouraged a participant (i.e., subject A5, whose expected openness was remarkably low, as indicated in Table 1) to speak. (2) It promoted to allowing others to speak, e.g., subject A4 persuaded subject A5 to speak by saying "You will be interviewed by the robot." (3) In Group 1, subject A3, who was expected to contribute the most to a conversation as indicated in Table 1, led the Desert Survival Problem task. However, when subject A4 and subject A5 started a topic related to the robot, subject A3 remained silent and observed their interactions. When the topic related to the robot ended, the Desert Survival Problem task resumed, with the focus back on subject A3. Thus, the robot enabled the reconstruction of the Participation Framework [1].

6   Conclusion and Future Work

In this paper, we designed and implemented a persuasive robot (Neut) that intervenes during a brain-storming session to encourage participants to speak out while maintaining neutrality by remaining silent itself. Basic effect of the ice breaker that eases the tension between the first met participants was founded. In future research, we plan to further analyze the interaction between conversational participants and Neut.

Acknowledgement. This research was partially supported by the Ministry of Education, Culture, Sports, Science and Technology (Grant-in-Aid for Scientific Research [C] 23500158, 2011–2013, [C] 26330233, 2014), and Research Institute for Science and Technology of Tokyo Denki University Grant Number Q13J-01/Japan.

References

1. Goffman, E.: Forms of Talk. University of Pennsylvania Press, Philadelphia (1981)
2. Khaoula, Y., Ohshima, N., De Silva, P.R.S., Okada, M.: Concepts and applications of human-dependent robots. In: Yamamoto, S. (ed.) HCI 2014, Part II. LNCS, vol. 8522, pp. 435–444. Springer, Heidelberg (2014)
3. Lafferty, J., Eady, P., Elmers, J.: The Desert Survival Problem. Experimental Learning Methods, Plymouth (1974)
4. Tomasello, M.: Why We Cooperate. MIT Press, Cambridge (2009)
5. Wada, S.: Construction of the big five scales of personality trait terms and concurrent validity with NPI. Jpn. J. Psychol. **67**(1), 61–67 (1996)

Author Index

Printed in the United States
By Bookmasters